The Solvency II Handbook

The Solvency II Handbook
Developing ERM Frameworks in Insurance and Reinsurance Companies

---

Edited by Marcelo Cruz

Published by Risk Books, a Division of Incisive Financial Publishing Ltd

Haymarket House
28–29 Haymarket
London SW1Y 4RX
Tel: +44 (0)20 7484 9700
Fax: +44 (0)20 7484 9800
E-mail: books@incisivemedia.com
Sites: www.riskbooks.com
       www.incisivemedia.com

Every effort has been made to secure the permission of individual copyright holders for inclusion.

© 2009 Incisive Media

ISBN 978-1-906348-19-9

British Library Cataloguing in Publication Data
A catalogue record for this book is available from the British Library

Publisher: Nick Carver
Commissioning Editor: Lucie Carter
Managing Editor: Jennifer Gibb
Designer: Lisa Ling

Typeset by Sunrise Setting Ltd, Torquay, UK

Printed and bound in the UK by Printondemand-Worldwide

Contents

List of Figures

List of Tables

About the Editor

Marcelo Cruz is an adjunct professor at New York University and a senior risk consultant. Formerly he was the group chief risk officer of Aviva, the UK's largest insurer and asset manager. Previously Marcelo was global head of operational risk analytics and quantitative risk analytics at Lehman Brothers and was the managing director and founder of RiskMaths, a boutique consultancy focused on risk management and more specifically operational risk. He also worked at UBS AG for three years as head of operational risk. Before UBS, Marcelo worked as a chief economist/strategist for an investment bank and as a derivatives trader (fixed income) for JP Morgan, where he was involved in structuring, managing and trading fixed income derivatives. Marcelo wrote one of the best-selling books in risk management (*Modeling, Measuring and Hedging Operational Risk*, Wiley 2002), and has written and edited other books in risk management. He is the founder editor-in-chief of *The Journal of Operational Risk* and sits on the board of other publications. Marcelo was also part of the GARP Board of Trustees. He holds a PhD in mathematics from Imperial College in London, an MSc in financial mathematics, an MBA and a BSc in economics.

About the Authors

Ioannis Akkizidis received his PhD from the University of Wales, UK. He is a senior financial risk analyst, working for FRSGlobal Switzerland, in Zürich. Ioannis turns the theory of financial analysis and risk management to practical implementation. He is also a visiting lecturer at the Universität Zürich, bringing financial systems analysis and applications to academia. Ioannis has authored various best-selling books: *Integrating Market, Credit and Operational Risk: A Complete Guide for Bankers and Risk Professionals* (2006), *A Guide to Optimal Operational Risk & Basel II* (2006), *Financial Risk Management for Islamic Banking and Finance* (2008) and the recently published *Unified Financial Analysis, the Missing Links of Finance* (2009).

Idriss Amor works in the FX Structuring team at the Bank of America as an analyst. He has a Masters Degree in applied mathematics and mechanical engineering from the Institut National des Sciences Appliquées de Lyon and a Masters Degree in financial engineering from HEC Paris. Idriss has worked in the financial industry for two years.

Michele Bourdeau worked for eight years at Lehman Brothers in the Risk Management Department before joining the Federal Reserve Bank of New York in 2009. Her last position at Lehman Brothers was as co-global head of model validation. She holds a PhD in theoretical physics.

Paolo Cadoni joined the Financial Services Authority (FSA) in 2004 where he has held a succession of posts in both banking and insurance. He is currently a technical specialist in the Solvency II Project Office where he has a leading role in the FSA's input into the Committee of European Insurance and Occupational Pensions Supervisors' (CEIOPS) Internal Models Working Group. Prior to becoming a regulator Paolo worked as a financial modeller in the oil and power sector. He holds a PhD in finance from the ICMA Centre and an MSc in econometrics from Southampton University.

René Doff has been a risk manager in banking and insurance since 2000. Within Rabobank, the largest wholesale bank in the Netherlands, he was involved in the Basel II and economic capital implementations. Since late 2005, René has been predominately working in insurance, especially within the Eureko Group, the largest insurance company within the Netherlands. Here, he has been involved in risk management implementation and Solvency II. In this position, René has set up the Dutch Solvency II working group and acted as a chairman. In 2006 and 2007, he worked on Solvency II for the European Insurance Federation (CEA). René has a background in finance, business administration and mathematics. In 2006, he received his PhD in risk management for insurers. He has published several articles in academic and practitioners' journals and three books. His latest book is *Risk Management for Insurers: Risk Control, Economic Capital and Solvency II* (2007).

Kathleen Ehrlich graduated in financial and economic mathematics at the Technical University of Munich in 2002. Currently she is a consultant in an insurance company and a PhD student at the University of Cologne in Germany. Kathleen is currently involved in many initiatives relating to Solvency II and risk management. She actively participates in solvency issues at both national and international levels. During her career Kathleen has gained sound and ample knowledge in many insurance disciplines. Her actual research work at the University of Cologne focuses on value-based management for insurance companies. Kathleen is a member of the German Actuarial Association (DAV) and has published several papers in relevant insurance journals.

Stephan Erasmus is a qualified actuary and member of Watson Wyatt's specialist Risk and Value Modelling team. He has been involved in the development of actuarial models for a wide range of projects, including market consistent embedded value calculations (MCEV), merger and acquisition pricing and rating agency capital projections. Stephan has assisted a large domestic insurer with the QIS4 exercise and is currently supporting a multi-national insurer performing an internal model dry run with the view to Solvency II approval. He is a trainer in Watson Wyatt's leading actuarial modelling system VIP*itech* and has assisted in the development of asset pricing and variance reduction techniques in this system.

Kamran Foroughi is a senior consultant with Towers Perrin and has been with the firm since 1998. He leads Towers Perrin's MCEV Initiative and has held this position since 2005. Kamran's responsibilities have included developing MCEV thought leadership papers, monitoring global MCEV publications, ensuring consistent application of MCEV throughout the firm and monitoring how key market-consistent valuation elements are applied across MCEV, IFRS and Solvency II. He has worked with many insurance companies in implementing the MCEV Principles and developing approaches in light of the global financial crisis, including helping them understand the implications for their business strategies. Kamran has published many papers on the subject of market-consistent valuations and embedded values and is a regular speaker at professional and industry seminars. He is a fellow of the Institute of Actuaries and holds a BA in mathematics from Oxford University.

Nadine Gatzert holds the chair of insurance management at the University of Erlangen-Nuremberg, Germany. She studied mathematics and economics at the University of Ulm, Germany and at the University of Southern California in Los Angeles, US, majoring in mathematical finance and actuarial science. Nadine worked as a senior research fellow and project manager at the Institute of Insurance Economics of the University of St Gallen, Switzerland, where she received her doctoral degree and her postdoctoral qualification. Nadine's research interests include enterprise risk management, alternative risk transfer, solvency regulation and embedded options in life insurance contracts. She has published numerous articles in these fields in peer-reviewed journals.

Werner Hürlimann, born 1953, has studied mathematics and physics at ETH Zürich, where he obtained his PhD in 1980 with a thesis in higher algebra. After postdoctoral fellowships at Yale University and at the Max Planck Institute in Bonn, he became an actuary in 1984 at Winterthur Life and Pensions. Werner has been working as a senior actuary for Aon Re and IRMG Switzerland 2003–06, senior consultant at IRIS in Zürich 2006–2008, and is currently employed as a business expert at FRSGlobal Switzerland. He was the visiting associate professor in actuarial science at the University of Toronto during the academic year 1988–89. Werner has written more than a hundred papers, published in refereed journals or presented at International Colloquia. His interests in actuarial science and finance encompass theory and applications of risk management, Solvency II and the Swiss Solvency Test (SST), the Libor market model, claims reserving, portfolio management, immunisation, pricing principles, ordering of risks, computational statistics and data analysis, etc.

Rahul Karkun works in the Interest Rates Structuring Team at the Bank of America as a vice president. He has an undergraduate degree in electrical engineering from the Indian Institute of Technology, Delhi and an MBA from the Indian Institute of Management, Calcutta. Rahul has worked in the financial industry for five years.

Stefan Kassberger is head of analytics in the structured credit division at DekaBank and lecturer in financial mathematics at Ulm University and the Frankfurt School of Finance and Management. He studied business mathematics and economics at Ulm University and the University of St Gallen. After having obtained a PhD in financial mathematics from the London School of Economics, Stefan was a visiting scholar at the Wharton School of the University of Pennsylvania.

Philipp Keller is a partner in Ernst & Young's Swiss practice and a managing partner of the Ernst & Young Solvency II Task Force project office. He rejoined Ernst & Young from FOPI, the Swiss Private Insurance Regulator, where he was the leader of the SST project and member of the board. In this role Philipp developed the SST model design, and also managed the day-to-day implementation process. Prior to joining FOPI in 2003, he was Manager at Andersen and, after the merger, at Ernst & Young in Zurich. During this time Philipp focused on the design and implementation of economic capital models for banks and insurance firms, a position he assumed after spending a number of years as a marketing actuary for Swiss Re Italy. Philipp is a qualified actuary and holds a PhD in mathematics.

Juliana Kim Moustakas works in the Derivative Sales Team at the Bank of America as a managing director. She has an undergraduate degree in economics from Brown University, a Masters in public policy from Harvard University and an MBA from INSEAD. Juliana has worked in the financial industry for over 12 years.

Roy Kouwenberg is chair of the PhD programme and assistant professor at Mahidol University, College of Management, in Bangkok, Thailand, and visiting assistant professor at Erasmus University Rotterdam, The Netherlands. He received a PhD in finance from Erasmus University in 2001 and is a CFA charterholder. Roy has previous working experience as a postdoctoral fellow at the University of British Columbia in Vancouver, Canada and as a quantitative analyst at the equity department of AEGON Asset Management in The Hague, The Netherlands. His research reflects his interest in investment, asset–liability management, optimisation and empirical finance. Roy's work has appeared in various academic journals, including the *Review of Economics & Statistics, Journal of Banking and Finance, Journal of International Money and Finance, Journal of Economic Dynamics & Control* and *Operations Research*.

Andreas Kull is AXA-Winterthur's chief risk officer and head of the Risk Management and Actuarial department. Prior to joining AXA-Winterthur, he was an executive director at Ernst & Young's Global Financial Services Risk Management practice focusing on the development and validation of internal capital models and related regulatory issues in the context of Solvency II and the SST. Other work experience includes various actuarial and risk management positions at Converium (now SCOR) and Zurich Financial Services. Andreas is a qualified actuary and holds a diploma in physics from the University of Berne and a PhD from Ludwig-Maximilans-Universität in Munich.

Gaurav Kwatra is currently a member of Watson Wyatt's Investment Consulting service. Prior to joining the Investment Consulting team, he was a member of Watson Wyatt's Insurance and Financial Services Practice, working for the Risk and Value Modelling Team where he specialised in advising insurance companies on quantitative risk modelling, hedging solutions, model selection and review, stochastic asset modelling, derivative pricing and econometric models. Gaurav joined Watson Wyatt in October 2004 after completing his MSc in finance at the University of London and is currently studying for the Chartered Financial Analyst exams.

Kris Luyten studied engineering and business economics at the University of Leuven, Belgium. He is a senior consultant at riskVentures. Kris worked in partnership with IRIS integrated risk management (newly FRSGlobal) in Zürich and was responsible for the development of the credit risk and Basel II modules of the riskPro product. In addition to this, he executed numerous customer projects, also in the areas of liquidity risk, market risk and asset–liability management. After that Kris became responsible for marketing in Northern Europe. Prior to working at IRIS, he was with KBC Bankassurance in Brussels, first as a business analyst and later he was responsible for the combined risk management systems. Before turning to finance and risk management, Kris gathered experience in academia and in the shipping and packaging industries.

Tamas Mayer is working as a senior consultant at Ernst & Young's Financial Services Risk Management practice. His areas of interest include market and credit risk as well as insurance modeling. Tamas studied physics at the University of Zürich, where he received his PhD in 2005. He also holds an advanced degree in mathematical finance (master of advanced studies in finance UZH/ETH Zürich).

Francesco Menoncin is associate professor of economics at Brescia University where he teaches "Market Risks" and "Derivatives and Financial Hedging". He has worked on optimal asset allocation for institutional investors and, mainly, for pension funds. Most of Francesco's articles have been published in *Annals of Operations Research, Insurance Mathematics and Economics, European Journal of Finance* and *Managerial Finance*. Finally, Francesco has written some Italian textbooks in finance.

Albert Mentink is currently an operational manager at the Asset & Liability Management department of AEGON Netherlands. He received his PhD degree in finance from the Erasmus University Rotterdam in 2005. Albert's work has been published in chapters in books and journal articles (*Journal of Banking and Finance* and the *Journal of Derivatives*). His research interests are in the fields of interest rate, credit and liquidity risk of corporate bonds.

Francesco Nagari is a partner at Deloitte LLP, based in London, where he joined to take the position of global IFRS insurance leader from October 2008. He is a member of the Insurance Accounting Working Group of the European Financial Reporting Advisory Group (EFRAG), which will support EFRAG, influencing the development of IFRS and IFRIC interpretations on insurance specific matters and their application within Europe. Since IFRS became the financial reporting reference for European insurers Francesco has concentrated his work on advising most of the large insurance and banking groups in the world to develop solutions for their IFRS issues around insurance reporting. He is the author of several articles and publications on the subject of reporting in the insurance sector and regularly speaks at conferences on insurance IFRS accounting issues. Francesco holds a Laurea in economia e commercio from the University of Pavia in Italy, where he also qualified as Dottore Commercialista (1991) and Revisore Contabile (1995).

Annamaria Olivieri is professor of mathematical methods for economics, actuarial science and finance at the Faculty of Economics, University of Parma and is also an actuary. She is involved in Continuous Professional Development courses, for both actuaries and non-actuaries on the following subjects: valuation of the life insurance business; mortality projections and management of mortality risks; health insurance and long term care insurance; plus life contingencies. Annamaria's main research areas are: the valuation of the life insurance business; risk management for life insurance and pension funds (in particular, with reference to longevity risk); solvency for life portfolios and pension funds; actuarial perspectives of annuitisation and post-retirement choices in pension products; multi-state models for the insurances of the person; pricing and reserving for life insurance products; and pricing and reserving for health insurance products.

Thorsten Pfeiffer is currently working as head of the Actuarial Office at the Swiss Financial Market Supervisory Authority FINMA. He joined the Swiss regulator in 2006 as a scientific advisor. In addition to other actuarial work, Thorsten develops, improves and implements the SST, including internal model approval, and assesses the results. He holds a PhD in mathematics, is a member of the German Actuarial Association (DAV) and a regular speaker on quantitative and risk based topics at conferences. In previous roles Thorsten worked as a pricing, reserving and marketing actuary for various companies in the primary and reinsurance industry.

Ermanno Pitacco is professor of actuarial mathematics at the Faculty of Economics, University of Trieste, the academic director of the MIRM (Master Insurance and Risk Management) at the MIB School of Management, Trieste and an actuary. He is involved in Continuous Professional Development courses, for both actuaries and non-actuaries on the following subjects: valuation of the life insurance business; mortality projections and management of mortality risks; health insurance and long term care insurance; plus life contingencies. Ermanno is an associate editor of the international journals *Insurance: Mathematics & Economics* and *Decisions in Economics and Finance*. He is a member of the Groupe Consultatif Actuariel Européen; member of the Education Committee of the Groupe Consultatif Actuariel Européen; member of the Education Committee of the International Actuarial Association; member of the Health Section Committee of the International Actuarial Association; member of the National Council of Ordine Nazionale degli Attuari; and member of the Council of Istituto Italiano degli Attuari. Ermanno's main research areas include: multi-state models for the insurances of the person (life insurance, disability insurance and LTC insurance); valuation of the life insurance business; models for longevity risk; solvency for life portfolios and pension funds; actuarial perspectives of annuitisation and post-retirement choices in pension products; pricing and reserving for life insurance products; and pricing and reserving for health insurance products. He won the INA Award for Actuarial Mathematics from the Accademia Nazionale dei Lincei (1996).

Helga Portmann heads the social insurance supervision division of the Swiss Federal Office of Public Health (FOPH). She joined the FOPH after working for Ernst & Young in the Financial Services Risk Management team. Before that Helga headed the Group and Conglomerate Supervision at the Swiss Federal Office of Private Insurance (FOPI). She holds a Master in mathematics and statistics.

Rainer Sachs heads the Emerging Risk Management and Accumulation Control team at Munich Re's Integrated Risk Management division, developing risk identification and quantification tools for Munich Re's global business operations. Before joining Munich Re, he worked in the Credit Risk Management division at HypoVereins bank. During Rainer's 10-year career in risk management, he has held various positions in financial and insurance risk management, both in Germany and Australia. His current research interests focus on modelling system revolutions, behavioural economics and the human factor in risk management. Rainer holds a PhD in theoretical physics (complex systems theory) from the University of Munich and a Master in cosmology from University of Pune (India).

Mark Schouten holds two MSc degrees in econometrics (specialising in operations research) and economics (specialising in the finance of ageing) from Tilburg University. Currently he works at the asset and liability management department of AEGON Netherlands as a junior analyst. Mark's research interests cover hedging financial risks and asset allocation in the presence of liabilities.

Heinrich R. Schradin holds the chair of general business administration, risk management and insurance apprenticeship at the University of Cologne, Germany. Since 1999 he has been the managing director of the Institute of Insurance Sciences at the University of Cologne. After Heinrich's apprenticeship in a banking corporation (1982–1984) he graduated in business administration from the University of Mannheim, Germany in 1989. In 1993 he reached his Doctorate also at the University of Mannheim, Germany. In 2001 Heinrich became vice president of the University of Cologne (until 2005) and from 2005–2007 he was senator of the faculty of management, economics and social sciences at the University of Cologne. His actual research work focuses on risk management and accounting for insurance companies. Heinrich previously worked as a lecturer at the University of Economics and Finance, St Petersburg, Russia (1994–1998). He was a guest professor at Vienna University of Economics and Business Administration, Institute of Risk Management and Insurance (2005) and at the University of Salzburg, Salzburg Institute of Actuarial Studies (2006, 2008). He is a member of the board of directors of the German Association for Insurance Sciences, a member of the German Society for Financial and Insurance Mathematics and a member of the German Academic Association for Business Research.

Andrew D. Smith is a partner at Deloitte with more then 20 years experience in the insurance industry. His projects have included: the use of modern financial techniques to value assets and liabilities consistently with market prices. In the late 1990s, Andrew published some of the earliest methodologies for market consistent liabilities and market consistent embedded value. His seminal 2004 paper (co-authored with Tim Sheldon) has become the authoritative reference on the subject in a life insurance context. Andrew has played a leading role in the reform of financial reporting for defined benefit pension schemes. He was a co-author, with Jon Exley and Shyam Mehta, of the definitive (but then deeply unpopular) 1997 paper "The Financial Theory of Defined Benefit Pension Schemes", which, as reported in the *Economist* in 2006, "laid the foundations for a completely new actuarial school". Andrew has worked with many insurers and reinsurers on economic product pricing and shareholder value measurement. He has specialised in the use of economic theory to understand market consistent liability valuation, the pricing of capital usage and the setting of profit targets. Andrew's paper "The Cost of Capital for Financial Firms" (with Jon Exley, 2006) is the authoritative reference on this subject. In 2008 the Institute of Actuaries awarded Andrew a Finlaison Model for his contribution to Actuarial Science.

Elliot Varnell is a fellow of the Institute of Actuaries in the UK working as a principal advisor within the Risk, Actuarial and Regulatory practice of KPMG in London, where he specialises in economic capital modelling, enterprise risk management and Solvency II. He leads on economic scenario generator (ESG) related services across Europe for KPMG. Elliot is a member of the ERM Research Committee and Extreme Events Working Party of the Institute of Actuaries in the UK, a member of the Groupe Consultatif Solvency II Working Group for Internal Governance, Supervisory Review and Reporting. He is also a regular speaker at conferences across Europe. In previous roles Elliot was head of European Insurance for the financial consultancy and ESG software provider, Barrie & Hibbert. Before this he was a senior consultant at Deloitte developing and advising on risk management and ESG models.

Russell Ward is a fellow of the Institute of Actuaries in the UK and has 20 years experience in the life insurance industry. He joined Ernst & Young in 1999 focusing on stochastic asset liability modelling and economic capital. During 2005, Russell was seconded to the FSA to help develop and implement the actuarial review of insurers' Individual Capital Assessments. He now leads the development of Ernst & Young's life actuarial modelling and ESG related services across Europe. Russell started his career with Albany Life before moving to a small consultancy, Jardine Arber, specialising in the provision of actuarial analysis and support for the retail distribution of life insurance products.

Susan Witcraft is a managing director with Guy Carpenter & Company, LLC and has been with the firm since 2002. She leads Guy Carpenter's

Financial Intelligence Team, a group focused on research, development and education in the areas of rating agencies, capital evaluation and enterprise risk management. Susan's responsibilities include analysis of reinsurance structures and broader capital issues using Guy Carpenter's economic capital model, MetaRisk. She is also responsible for overseeing the development of the financial, rating agency and solvency measurement aspects of MetaRisk. Prior to joining Guy Carpenter, Susan was chief actuary at a small worker's compensation insurer and spent nearly 20 years as an actuarial consultant for Milliman where she led initiatives for developing dynamic financial modelling capabilities. She is a frequent author and speaker on actuarial and financial analysis topics. Susan is a fellow of the Casualty Actuarial Society and holds a BS in statistics from Stanford University.

Foreword

Bisogna cambiare tutto per non cambiare nulla (G. Lampedussa)

When asked about providing a foreword for a book on Solvency II, two things came to my mind. The first one could be summarised in two words: "at last" and, of course, I was not thinking about myself, but about the Solvency II project – its relevance and its implications. The second one goes back to the summer of 2001, when, during my vacation I was reading an excellent biography, *The Last Leopard: A Life of Giuseppe di Lampedussa* by David Gilmour, and, at the same time, the so-called KPMG report on Solvency II. Both were linked by the quotation with which I have started this foreword: "we need to change all (the Solvency rules for insurance companies) to ensure that nothing changes" (ie, that insurers remain sound). Solvency I has worked well, but we need to change and improve it when it is still a valid framework, rather than waiting until it proves to be no longer fit for the purpose. Isn't this, by the way, what responsible risk management is about? Improving things that still work rather than fixing things that no longer do.

The fact that I am looking back almost ten years shows that the project has been in development for a number of years. But how well prepared are we for Solvency II? The insurance industry needs to meet a number of challenges arising from such an ambitious project. Preparedness is the key for both the industry and the supervisory authorities, and this is something that we cannot postpone. A book that covers the different areas of the project, with a particular focus on risks, will be a useful tool in deepening the level of preparedness for the challenging, yet promising in terms of opportunities, new landscape.

The ambition behind Solvency II is to become the reference point when it comes to risk-based supervision, not only within the insurance sector, but globally as well. To help you understand why this is the case, the book in your hand does not limit itself to technical argument alone. It also, and more importantly, provides a number of different points of view through expert contributions to the book. Solvency II has, among its other virtues, brought together a number of different supervisory cultures, taking the best out of each of them and creating a consistent and convergent framework in the process.

A lot has been said about Solvency II, but not much written, with the exception of the technical advice provided by CEIOPS, the Committee of European Insurance and Occupational Pensions Supervisors. What has been long overdue is a comprehensive, yet interesting, approach to the subject in the form of a book like this one. May I invite you to start reading and welcome you to the world of Solvency II.

Carlos Montalvo Rebuelta
Secretary General
CEIOPS

Introduction: A Journey to Solvency II

Marcelo Cruz

New York University

The process towards Solvency II implementation makes up the insurance leg of a much broader framework from the European Union (EU) for market integration. The Solvency II framework aims to facilitate the development of a single market for insurance in the EU, while at the same time developing a stronger level of insurance consumer protection. Many of the Member States have concluded that the current EU minimum requirements are not sufficient and have implemented their own reforms, thus leading to a situation where there is a patchwork of regulatory requirements across the EU. All these are barriers to the development of a single European market.

Due to this seed for European integration, Solvency II is, so far, exclusive to Europe and, therefore, mandatory only for European insurance firms (or firms operating in Europe). The process has been based on the Basel II rules that govern capital adequacy for banking institutions worldwide. However, even before it becomes the standard used by European insurers, Solvency II is becoming a desired standard for insurers and reinsurers worldwide; many firms in the US, Latin America and Asia have stated in their annual reports the desire to pursue Solvency II standards for capital adequacy.

In historical terms, the solvency margin is the amount of regulatory capital an insurance firm needs to hold against unforeseen events (risks). Solvency margin requirements have been in place since the 1970s; it was acknowledged in the third-generation Insurance Directives (adopted in the 1990s) that the EU solvency rules should be reviewed. These directives established an "EU passport" (single license) for insurers based on the concept of minimum harmonisation and mutual recognition. The directives required the EU to conduct a review of solvency requirements; following this review, a limited reform was agreed by the European Parliament and then the Council, in 2002. This reform is known as Solvency I.

The European Parliament approved the Solvency II framework directive on 22 April 2009; it is now scheduled to come into force on 31 October 2012. Although the details of the new requirements will have to wait until the European Commission finalises the extensive measures that will be implemented by June 2011, the insurance industry in the EU can use the Framework Directive to begin its preparation for the new regime with certainty at least on timeframes. Solvency II aims to implement solvency requirements that better reflect the risks that companies face and deliver a supervisory system that is consistent across all Member States. The new regulations are being developed using a three-pillar approach to the solvency position of insurance companies, with each pillar governing a different aspect of the solvency position. As well as being required to disclose their capital and risk frameworks, firms must also demonstrate how and where they are embedded in their wider activities.

Solvency II will be based on economic principles for the measurement of assets and liabilities. It will also be a risk-based system, in that solvency capital requirements will depend directly on risk, which will be measured on consistent principles. While the Solvency I directive was aimed at revising and updating the current EU solvency regime, Solvency II takes a much wider scope. As under Basel II, insurers will be able under Solvency II to use their own internally developed models to calculate the economic capital against their risks. In a process similar to that required of banks, insurers will have to calculate capital for three purposes: economic (internal), regulatory and rating agency (external). It is important to note that the objective of Solvency II is not to complicate the capital framework but to offer capital-reduction incentives to insurers that invest in developing best practices in risk management and control. Table 1 describes the different types of capital that needs to be calculated by insurers.

The financial and economic crisis that arose in 2007 and is still ongoing made insurers around the world face tremendous challenges as most of them had liquidity and capital issues. This crisis, which began in the midst of the final discussions of the Solvency II

Table 1 Types of capital that insurers need to calculate

Type	Economic capital	Regulatory capital	Rating capital
Main stakeholder	Internal (management)	External (regulator)	External (rating agencies)
Solvency II impact	Pushing insurers to develop/improve economic capital models	Push regulatory capital to be closer to economic capital	Rating agencies models will tend to converge to economic capitals
Impact of capital issues	Not significant, if limits are exceeded	Very high, might end up in regulatory intervention	Downgrade, increase cost of funds and investor confidence
Main objectives	Optimal risk–return allocation, efficient operations	Protect the customer by maintaining minimum capital to sustain business	Verify financial strength

process, showed insurers how they would benefit from a more robust framework.

Our objective with this book is to consolidate in one compendium the best articles and discussions around the Solvency II process, the changes it will bring to insurers and reinsurers and what these should do to comply with this new framework. The book is divided into five sections. Section 1 works as an introduction to Solvency II and how concurrent initiatives, such as IFRS 4 and MCEV, fit into the overall framework. Section 2 is about financial risk, an area that will face significant changes due to Solvency II; we include excellent chapters on how insurers should tackle some aspects of market and credit risk measurement and asset–liability management. In Section 3 we present chapters on life and non-life risks and what will change, given that risk managers (and not just actuaries) will have to be involved in the measurement and management of these risks. Section 4 deals with operational risk, a very new issue for insurers – one so new that the section consists of a single chapter, which I have crafted myself, drawing on my lengthy experience in the area. In the last section we show a more general view of economic capital under Solvency II, with articles on risk sharing, hedging and measuring correlations using copulas.

This book acts as an important contribution to the improvement of enterprise risk management in the insurance industry and to the disclosure of information on Solvency II. The changes brought by Solvency II will revolutionise risk management in insurance companies and bring a long overdue upgrade to the risk framework in these companies. We hope this book will provide some help and guidance as to these new developments.

Section I

Introduction to the Solvency II Regime

Introduction

Marcelo Cruz

New York University

This section is organised to provide an overview of the current status of enterprise risk management and how Solvency II will impact on the insurance industry in the next few years. In the first chapter René Doff provides an excellent overview on how risk management is structured in European insurers. As readers will observe, most chief risk officers (CRO) still sit on the second layer of insurance companies, usually reporting to the chief financial officer (CFO). This is certainly bound to change, given that in Pillar II of Solvency II, there is the expectation that risk management will become fully a part of the decision-making process; we should see more and more CROs reporting directly to the chief executive officers and boards of directors.

In Chapter 2, Francesco Nagari provides a great view on whether there is a confluence of ideas and methods between Phase II IFRS 4 and Solvency II. This is an important discussion that has been a key topic at many industry seminars. In Chapter 3, Stephan Erasmus and Gaurav Kwatra show us what is needed to build internal models to measure risk in insurance companies and to generate reports that will allow these companies to manage risk.

In Chapter 4, we are blessed to hear about the new regulations from the "horse's mouth". Paolo Cadoni, from the Financial Services Authority in London, explains what the requirements are to use internal models in Solvency II. This is mandatory reading – a very up-to-date chapter summarising all the new legislation.

The last chapter of this section deals with the convergence of market-consistent embedded value (MCEV) and Solvency II. This is a very good chapter, contributed by Kamram Foroughi, which provides us a clear view both of what converges and of what the key differences are and how to tackle these.

1

Risk Management Implementation in the Insurance Industry

René Doff

Eureko/Achmea, Universiteit van Amsterdam

Solvency II is a fundamental review of financial regulation of (re)insurance companies operating in the European Union. Currently, insurance companies across Europe are preparing for Solvency II implementation in their businesses. Estimates as to the effort required vary but it is clear from the QIS4 report of the Committee of European Insurance and Occupational Pensions Supervisors (CEIOPS) that in general companies are not compliant yet. This chapter does not attempt to address the policy issues that still exist, but rather it aims to assess how companies are progressing with their implementation of the Solvency II framework. The analysis is based on publicly available information, such as existing surveys and annual reports.

The remainder of this chapter is organised as follows. The next section highlights the most important organisational requirements for Solvency II and discusses a number of observations from the relevant literature. The section "Review of public surveys" analyses existing surveys on risk management and Solvency II that are already available. We will see that a number of general areas for further work arises from these surveys. In the section "European best-practice: CRO Forum companies" we analyse the annual reports and other risk management disclosures from a number of chief risk officer (CRO) Forum companies. These serve as best practice examples although work remains to be done here as well. The section "Challenges lying ahead. . ." summarises and concludes.

A GENERAL DEVELOPMENT PATH

Solvency II has been developed since the early 2000s with the first Call for Advice from the European Commission in 2004. The development of Basel II in the banking industry has basically caused an evolution of the risk management profession within the financial industry as a whole. Most of the lessons learnt from the Basel II process have been beneficial to the development of Solvency II. This has resulted in a higher level of risk management knowledge as a basis for the Solvency II process. This is true particularly for the area of risk measurement and economic capital applications, but also in relation to the structure of financial regulation. Much of the Solvency II framework has been borrowed from the banking industry and Basel II (Doff 2007). Examples of this are the three-pillar framework, the risk-oriented approach, allowance for internal models and the value-at-risk (VaR) measure. At the same time, however, the Solvency II framework is sufficiently adapted to the insurance industry to incorporate the specific necessities of the insurance business. The most dominant element is the valuation of insurance liabilities. The debates around Solvency II have resulted in a relatively well-accepted methodology for the market-consistent valuation of insurance liabilities.

In this chapter, we assume that the reader is familiar with Solvency II.[1] The policy papers on Solvency II are quite elaborate, for example the Solvency II proposal by the European Commission, the various consultative papers by CEIOPS and the position papers by the European Insurance and Occupational Pensions Committee (EIOPC). However, in short, we believe that to comply with Solvency II an insurance company should at least address the following crucial challenges as organisational requirements (this list highlights the most important elements):

1. (a) An insurer should be able to determine best-estimate technical provisions based on cashflow patterns, including the value of embedded options and profit sharing in insurance products (CEIOPS 2007, Article 76–85).
    (b) Furthermore, an insurer should be able to derive the market value of assets, including those assets that are not traded in a deep liquid market (CEIOPS 2007, Article 74).

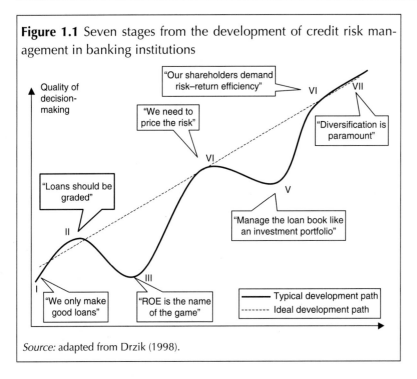

Figure 1.1 Seven stages from the development of credit risk management in banking institutions

Source: adapted from Drzik (1998).

2. An insurer should be able to calculate the solvency capital requirement (SCR) (CEIOPS 2007, Article 104–108). As the SCR modules are likely to be based on factors and scenarios, an important requirement is that insurers should be able to perform scenario analysis on the assets and liabilities.

3. An insurer should have a governance structure in place to address risk throughout the organisation (CEIOPS 2007, Article 41).

Drzik (1998) describes the evolution of how credit risk management has developed in banking institutions through seven stages. Although Drzik's evolution is designed for credit risk management in banks, it gives us some insight into the steps that are required for insurance companies in the process of implementing risk management (and Solvency II). Figure 1.1 shows the seven stages. In phase I all key decisions in the production process are decentralised and judgemental. In phase II, the evaluation of the relative risk of different products is integrated into the decision-making process by introducing risk grades. However, most loans appear to fall into one risk grade. Phase III characterises itself by initial risk–return trade-offs and by focusing on return on capital (non risk-adjusted). In phase IV, a company expands its risk-grading system and introduces a system in which risk is adequately priced for. This is typically the phase in which economic capital models are built, ie, risk is more adequately quantified/measured. In phase V a portfolio of individual products begins to be managed like an investment portfolio. Due to the insufficient quality of the risk models and input data, results are dissatisfying. The key to overcome this phase is not to stop modelling, but to improve company-wide data processes and model qualities. In phase VI, a company is able to measure risk on a company-wide basis and to start setting risk limits on client sectors and other portfolio segmentations. A company is required to significantly invest in IT solutions to generate the management information that is necessary for these portfolio decision-making processes. In phase VII, diversification is the key management variable to achieve risk–return efficiency and attain added value.

Although these stages were developed in a period when statistical risk measurement was still in its infancy (1998), this evolutionary path provides us with some insight into the implementation status of risk management in the insurance industry a decade later (ie, 2009). For example, risk grading for individual products (phase II) during the underwriting process is hardly implemented in the insurance industry, where products are managed as a portfolio and the lowest level of risk measurement is the entire portfolio rather than the individual product. Also, gathering data for risk models (phase V) is often challenging for companies. Finally, measuring correlations, which is so crucial to phase V, is extremely problematic in the insurance industry of 2009. A similar framework is described by Van den Tillaart (2003), although this framework emphasises the fact that model failure is required for substantial improvements. Also, this framework is applicable to risk management in general, whereas the model of Drzik (1998) focuses on credit risk in the banking industry.

Santomero and Babbel (1997) describe the elements in the risk management process specifically for insurance companies. Their main focus is on (1) standards and reports; (2) underwriting authority and limits; (3) investment guidelines and strategies; and

(4) incentive contracts and compensation. For the underwriting risks, the first concern of these authors in 1997 was the management and measurement of embedded options in life contracts. As of 2009, embedded options granted in the past are still a topic of discussion in the insurance industry. Secondly, the implementation of software tools to support risk management decision making caused concern. Even though insurance companies at that time (1997) started to implement specific software tools to measure the risks and value of an insurance portfolio, the data requirements of the tools were rarely met, even by companies that had data available. Also, staff were unable to interpret the output of the software tools. Surprisingly, Santomero and Babbel (1997) found an increasing interest in market risk measurement and asset–liability management (ALM). They reported that most insurers run software systems that supported scenario modelling of interest-rate risk, including convexity. However, this research was executed specifically for the insurance industry in the US, where market risk and credit risk have been included in the capital adequacy rules of the national association insurance commissioners since 1994. One of the most striking recommendations in the research of Santomero and Babbel (1997) is the aggregation of risks: an area where differences existed in the measurement (quantitative/qualitative) and reporting. The authors expressed their concern about the firm-wide risk frameworks for the firms researched. At the time of the research, the approaches differed within a company for the various risk types and between companies for the level of sophistication of the risk measurement.

Preliminary conclusions

The evolutionary process of risk management within insurance companies includes phases where data gathering and the application of software tools is crucial for a next step in the process. This often goes hand in hand with substantial modelling improvements. We expect that market risk management will develop well, consistently, in line with the situation in the US. Later in this chapter we will investigate where insurers are in the process of Solvency II implementation. We focus on the general Solvency II requirements described at the start of the chapter. We assess whether insurers face similar problems to the ones described by

Table 1.1 Existing surveys used as a data source

Survey name	Participation	Scope	Survey period
Capgemini	63	Mix of larger and smaller companies	2006
Ernst & Young	54	European top 100 players	February–July 2006
CEA	442	European market	June–September 2006
Towers Perrin	359	Insurers globally	May–June 2008
CEIOPS QISs	Varies	European market	Multiple

Drzik (1998). Based on the findings of Santomero and Babbel (1997) we are interested to see whether the risk measurement issues still exist.

REVIEW OF PUBLIC SURVEYS

Over time a number of surveys have investigated the status of enterprise risk management (ERM) in the insurance industry and how prepared the industry is for Solvency II. Most of these surveys not only investigate risk measurement capabilities but also aspects of risk governance in insurance companies. The conclusions from these surveys give us an insight into where European insurers stand with regard to Solvency II. Table 1.1 highlights four surveys and the quantitative impact studies (QISs) that we have included in the analysis. Although the surveys give us a number of interesting insights, we have to interpret the outcomes with care. Often, the companies that participate in surveys are relatively more advanced. Dowd *et al* (2008) state that ". . . there is a significant 'tail' of firms that are not practising any serious risk management at all".

To date CEIOPS has organised four QISs to test the suitability of methodologies proposed under Solvency II and to test the impact of Solvency II proposals on insurance companies' balance sheets. The increasing participation (see Table 1.2) of insurance companies in the QISs is an indication of the growing involvement in Solvency II. Moreover, it is an indication of the increasing capabilities of European insurers to perform the calculations required under Solvency II. From the QIS reports we can also conclude that over time the quality of the submissions also increases.

Table 1.2 Overview of CEIOPS' QISs

	QIS objective	Participation rate	Market share (%)
QIS1	Testing level of prudence within liabilities; testing a method of market value margin	272	5
QIS2	Testing liabilities and SCR methodologies	514	10
QIS3	Test entire framework, suitability of calculations, impact on balance sheets	1,027	19
QIS4	Test impact of proposals on balance sheets	1,412	27
	Total European market[a]	5,275	100

[a] *Source:* CEA (2007a).

It was concluded by CEIOPS (2008) that the proposed QIS4 valuation methodology did not create any major difficulties for most participants in countries that already apply the accounting principles of international financial reporting standards (IFRS). However in QIS4, a lack of data and the data segmentation caused problems for smaller and medium-sized insurers. Also, calculating the effect of profit sharing was problematic and burdensome for some insurers. The majority of the QIS4 participants consider a partial or full internal model. This is an indication that insurers expect to be capable of calculating the SCR as well. Since the risk governance structure has, to date, been beyond the scope of the QISs, we cannot draw any conclusions on this issue.

The Capgemini survey covered companies in eight European countries. The topics of the survey covered risk areas, risk management organisation, internal risk reporting, legal framework and the available risk management methods. The survey report presents the outcomes in two segments: (1) large versus small insurers with the threshold for large companies being €1.5 billion premium; and (2) per insurance type: life versus non-life versus combined companies. The Ernst & Young survey was a European follow-up of a French survey in 2005. The focus was on the extent to which insurers are ready for Solvency II and the gap between Solvency II and companies' current practices. Participants were companies from

15 European countries and had an average asset size of €110 billion. The report interestingly also discusses the lessons learnt from Basel II in the banking industry. The European Insurance Federation (CEA) survey was executed on behalf of the European Commission to assess the impact of the foreseen Solvency II framework.[2] The 442 respondents were from 27 European countries so the outcomes were considered representative of the European insurance market. The focus of the CEA survey is the additional impact of Solvency II given the fact that companies are already developing risk-based economic approaches for their internal (ie, non-regulatory driven) purposes. The Towers Perrin survey involved 359 large insurance companies around the globe. European participants represented 31% of the respondents. The focus of the report was the status of ERM.

As we focus on whether insurance companies are ready for Solvency II, we would like to highlight four main areas, with reference to the Solvency II requirements summarised in the section "A general development path":

1. What is the status of the market-consistent valuation of the balance sheet? Are insurers able to calculate the market value of the technical provisions? Are insurers able to value embedded optionalities in their products?
2. What is the status of the risk models? Are insurers able to calculate the SCR?
3. Do insurers have a risk governance structure in place?
4. Other interesting observations from the surveys.

Economic valuation and embedded options

We have to admit that the information in the surveys is relatively scarce on the economic valuation of assets and liabilities. We have the impression that the surveys assume that companies are able to determine the market-consistent value of assets and liabilities, including the embedded options. After all, market-consistent valuation is basically a prerequisite for economic capital modelling because stochastic scenarios are applied to the market values of assets and liabilities. We believe, however, that the data issues and the modelling quality issues that are mentioned in the survey reports (discussed later in more detail) apply equally well to the models that determine the market-consistent value of non-traded assets and liabilities as to the risk models that determine the economic capital/SCR. The CEA report indicates that 59% of the participating companies consider the Solvency II approach similar or identical to their internal approach for economic valuation of assets and liabilities. Only 7% of the respondents consider the approach "very different". The differences between countries or company types are not reported. The Towers Perrin survey reports that globally only half of the respondents use market-consistent balance sheets as a basis for economic capital calculations. For multi-line and life insurers this approach is more common (85% and 67% respectively). Non-life companies often use generally accepted accounting principles/IFRS (35%) or regulatory (24%) balance sheets. Elsewhere in the Towers Perrin report, it is indicated that European insurers are more advanced when it comes to economic capital calculations, so it might be true that within Europe more insurers are able to determine the market-consistent value than indicated in the Towers Perrin report.

Risk measurement and models
Generally, the CEA report indicates that 62% of the participating companies are implementing or improving their risk framework in line with Solvency II. For larger companies, the figure is 80%, and for smaller companies it is 56%. The UK (86%) is above the average, partly because of the individual capital assessment (ICA) framework that is already in place. Eastern European companies are lagging behind with 27%. The CEA survey concludes that companies are well underway in their Solvency II preparation when it comes to risk measurement. The Capgemini survey investigates four risk measurement methods: stress testing, scenario analysis, simulation and actuarial methods. The report shows that actuarial models are mostly used for underwriting risks, whereas stress testing and scenario analyses are the preferred methods for market risk and ALM. It is not too clear from the survey exactly what the actuarial methods are, they can be both stochastic and deterministic and both can be used for calculating technical provisions (such as claim ladders). Furthermore, risk measurement methods are more or less equally used across risk types. According to the Ernst & Young survey, market risk measurement is most advanced, followed by

credit risk measurement. However, this contradicts the outcome of Dowd *et al* (2008) who conclude that within the UK market credit risk is one of the most serious concerns. Areas for improvement are appropriate management information and separation of duties in credit analyses. This is, however, in contradiction to the Financial Services Authority (FSA) (2005), which concludes that most firms are using sophisticated tools and have an in-depth understanding of risk profiles.

The CEA report indicates that the majority of the respondents (57%) consider the VaR approach of Solvency II identical or similar to their internal models. Only 9% consider the Solvency II approach very different, which indicates that companies are well on track with regard to risk measurement. The Towers Perrin survey is somewhat less optimistic, by stating that only 10% of the respondents were well able to calculate economic capital (ie, SCR) in an appropriate manner. The improvements that companies were planning were in the area of (1) modelling methodologies; (2) data quality; and (3) extending the risks covered. All three aspects were reported by over 40% of the respondents. This implies that companies in the Towers Perrin survey were still focused on getting the basics right rather than fine-tuning the calculations. Of the European participants of the Towers Perrin survey, 63% of the respondents indicated that internal model approval for Solvency II purposes would be one of the greatest challenges lying ahead. This is in line with the conclusions of Dowd *et al* (2008) reporting four key concerns about risk measurement in the UK market: (1) choice for correlation assumptions; (2) absence of appropriate testing and validation of models; (3) documentation and sensitivity analysis of key assumptions; and (4) choice for risk measure, such as VaR versus tail-VaR.

Risk governance

Risk governance has not yet been debated as heavily as risk measurement in the Solvency II preparations within the industry. The surveys indicate, however, that there are serious shortcomings in risk governance. The Capgemini survey shows that roughly 15%–20% of the respondents have no properly established risk management procedures for market and underwriting risks. For other risk categories, these estimates are even higher. The Capgemini survey indicates that procedures for managing liquidity risk are least advanced, but we expect that the situation has improved over the last two years due to the liquidity crisis in the global financial markets. Also, the Capgemini survey shows that almost 50% of respondents have not adequately assigned responsibilities for risk to departments. For companies that have assigned the responsibility for risk, dedicated risk management departments have been set up. In other companies, the controlling department has the responsibility. The other three surveys do not discuss the topic of risk governance in depth. However, Dowd *et al* (2008) focus extensively on this issue. The authors discuss four surveys that describe the situation in the UK insurance market. They conclude that firms have only fairly recently set up risk management departments (or functions) and some have appointed CROs. Dowd *et al* (2008) state that ". . . the size of these [risk management] departments are relatively small compared to banks". Also, the risk reporting cycle does not form part of the standard management information, ie, it is not (yet) integrated. The Capgemini survey shows that reports are mostly sent to the board only, with few business unit managers involved. Also, communication and cooperation between risk management departments and actuarial and financial controlling departments is generally poor.

Operational risk
Operational risk is an area with much room for improvement. That is the conclusion of all surveys. We must admit that operational risk has been relatively underexposed in the Solvency II debates that have taken place in recent years. The calculation in the standard model has been extremely simple and straightforward, but not really risk-based. Potential reasons for this are:

- conceptual progress for other risks was more urgent, such as market-consistent valuation of assets and liabilities and risk models for other risks;
- policymakers expect to be able to copy the approach taken in Basel II;
- policymakers and the industry consider this risk to be of lesser importance; or

- policymakers and the industry expect that it is too complex to adopt a generally agreed model, given the risk measurement complexities that banks have had.

The Capgemini report shows that there are some risk management procedures in place for operational risk, but the risk itself is not considered very important. Generally, it counts for 10–15% of the risk exposure. Both the Ernst & Young and Towers Perrin reports conclude that about only 10% of the companies implemented an operational risk measurement model. Achryya and Johnson (2006) report that operational risk measurement was one of the greatest challenges to the implementation of ERM. However, operational risk is not a key ERM priority. For calculating economic capital, most companies only use simple factor-based models and only 50% of the respondents of the Towers Perrin survey expect to use internal models for Solvency II. For illustration, the percentage for other risks is about 80%. Companies have problems in collecting sufficient loss data. The FSA (2005) reports that quantifying operational risk has proven to be one of the most difficult challenges. The Association of British Insurers (ABI) has launched a loss data initiative for UK insurers, similar to the commercial initiatives that already exist in banking. Companies share anonymous loss data about events submitted by participants, so that risk modelling can take place. Although this is a good first step, it is by no means a recipe for an adequate operational risk management framework. Banks have found it extremely complex to tie the model outcomes to the internal processes within the business. This is a hurdle to overcome for insurers as well. Also, it is doubtful whether this anonymous loss data is representative of other companies (Tillaart 2003).

Implementation in the business (use test)
One of the prerequisites for Solvency II is that risk management is clearly embedded in the business process of the insurer. The Solvency II requirements for using an internal model are (CEIOPS 2007, Article 118–123):

- Use test: an insurer should demonstrate that the internal model is widely used and plays an important role in the system of governance.

- Statistical quality standards: the methods used to calculate the probability distribution forecast shall be based on adequate actuarial and statistical techniques. Data used for the internal model shall be accurate, complete and appropriate.
- Calibration standards: the internal model should be calibrated identically or consistently with a 99.5% VaR with a one-year time horizon.
- Validation standards: a regular cycle should exist for validating the model.

These requirements impose, for instance, that information technology (IT) systems produce adequate information for risk models, that risk reports are part of the standard management information and that risk management is part of the decision-making process. The CEA report shows that the least effort was required to achieve senior management buy-in. Getting the right resources (67%) and administration and data systems (61%) required more effort in order to make the Solvency II project work. The Capgemini report shows that the most important driver to improve risk management is "comply with regulatory requirements". This is consistent with the findings of Acharyya and Johnson (2006). Remarkably, the Towers Perrin survey shows that only a limited number of companies use the economic capital (SCR) outcomes for performance measurement (17%) and incentive compensation (10%). The latter is confirmed by the CRO Forum (2009). It is to be expected that this will be one of the use test criteria that is present in Solvency II. Even more, only 30% of the respondents use "risk" in incentive compensation. Therefore, the Towers Perrin survey reports that improving economic capital calculations and embedding the outcomes in the decision-making process within the business is one of the greatest challenges. That is by definition not sufficient to adequately implement risk management in the business. The Ernst & Young survey highlights that larger insurers in particular are concerned that significant IT spending may be required. Respondents report that often workarounds are in place to get the necessary data for the risk reports. Workarounds are unlikely to be viable in the long run. The Towers Perrin report shows that the economic capital outcomes are most often being used for capital adequacy assessment (44% of respondents). Other decisions such as performance measurement and incentive compensation are mentioned less often. Even more, 66% of the respondents are not planning to use risk indicators in incentive information. This is a clear signal that companies are not (yet) fully incorporating risk management information in their strategies.

Preliminary conclusion

All reports emphasise that much progress has been made within the insurance industry. Companies have improved their risk management frameworks, but much remains to be done. Being optimistic, the CEA report indicates that companies generally expect to be ready for Solvency II by 2010. By the time of the survey (CEA 2007b), only 3%–4% of the companies expected that Solvency II compliance by 2010 would be an issue. This conclusion was more or less confirmed by CEIOPS (2008), stating that valuation principles did not cause any major problems for insurers and that the majority of QIS4 participants expect to develop internal models. However, at the time that these surveys were conducted, it was not clear what the exact (use test) requirements would be for Solvency II compliance. This might have influenced the survey outcomes. The analysis above indicates that the modelling basics remain a necessary focus for insurers. This holds for market-consistent valuation as well as for economic capital calculation. The Towers Perrin survey concludes that larger firms are generally more advanced and better prepared than smaller insurers. However, even larger companies are not yet ready for Solvency II. Data processes will need to be upgraded with significant IT spending involved. In addition, risk governance and operational risk are essential elements and greater steps need to be taken in order to be Solvency II compliant. Also, insurers are not yet fully embedding risk in their day-to-day businesses.

EUROPEAN BEST PRACTICE: CRO FORUM COMPANIES

In addition to the surveys discussed previously, it is interesting to look at the development of risk management by studying individual companies. Although it is possible to study a limited number of insurance companies in depth (eg, case studies), we have chosen to study insurance companies' annual reports and other public disclosures. Nowadays most insurers include a separate section on

Table 1.3 Companies included in the analysis

	Company
1	Aegon Group
2	Allianz
3	Aviva Group
4	AXA Group
5	Eureko
6	Fortis Group
7	Generali Group
8	Groupama
9	ING Group
10	Munich Re
11	Prudential
12	Swiss Re
13	Zurich

risk management published in the annual report or accounts. This section generally includes:

- a description of the risk organisation in the company, mostly of the executive committees but sometimes also the responsibilities of the central risk management department;
- a list of the major risks involved, sometimes with an explanation of the measurement method used for particular risks;
- a detailed explanation of the risk management instruments for each risk type, such as reinsurance, underwriting and investment limits;
- a series of simple stress tests per risk category; and
- the solvency position, focusing on the required capital for regulatory purposes; only an extremely limited number of companies have a track record of (internal) economic capital outcomes for their insurance operations.

We studied the annual reports from 13 companies (see Table 1.3). These companies are the largest insurance companies and all are members of the European CRO Forum. These companies are generally considered to be representative of the best practices used in the European market. The disclosure of these insurers gives us a little insight into the detailed status of Solvency II implementation in each of the companies. The reverse however does not hold: of companies that do not disclose extensive risk management information, we cannot and must not conclude that they are lagging

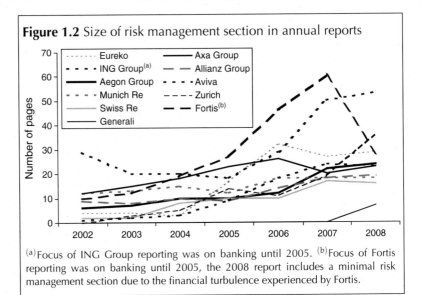

Figure 1.2 Size of risk management section in annual reports

(a)Focus of ING Group reporting was on banking until 2005. (b)Focus of Fortis reporting was on banking until 2005, the 2008 report includes a minimal risk management section due to the financial turbulence experienced by Fortis.

behind. Because companies do not disclose separate Solvency II information, we investigate the risk management issues that have been discussed in the prior section.

Firstly, we assess the development of the risk management section in annual reports. We see that for all companies in the analysis the number of pages increases over time (see Figure 1.2). Almost all risk management sections experience a significant upswing in 2005, when IFRS came into force, demanding more risk management disclosure in the annual accounts. Solvency II also became a little more concrete in 2005, with the Calls for Advice from the European Commission. Although risk management disclosures in annual accounts are intended as sensitivity analysis of the balance sheet and profit and loss statement, they give us some insight on the extent to which companies are able to perform the analysis required under Solvency II. For instance, some of the standard approach SCR modules bear similarities to the sensitivity analyses presented in the annual accounts.

Figure 1.2 highlights that in 2002, when Solvency II started as an official project, risk management disclosures were extremely limited. None of the companies published economic capital outcomes. However, we observe more elaborate risk information for instance in the Allianz Group and ING Group reports. However, the focus of the more detailed risk management sections is on the banking business, an area where (in 2002) risk management was more developed than the insurance business. For instance, for ING Group risk management disclosures for the insurance business were expanded only in 2005 while the banking risk management disclosures were already quite elaborate in 2002.

In 2002 most insurers who disclosed risk information, included at least a qualitative description of the various risks that the company was exposed to. This was typically along the lines of the economic capital components or, in terms of Solvency II, the main modules of the SCR calculation. In 2002 seven of the companies in the analysis included such a description. It is surprising that the risk types are identical to the framework of Solvency II because before the year 2002 there was a wide variety of risk classifications in the industry (European Commission 2002). Quantitative information for risk exposure is disclosed by fewer insurers. For instance Aegon and Munich Re disclose a number of stress tests whereas Eureko is the only company in 2002 disclosing economic capital outcomes for their insurance business. ING Group disclosed economic capital and risk-adjusted return on capital numbers, but focused on the banking business lines. Aegon Group and Munich Re's stress tests indicated the monetary effect of parallel interest rate shifts (typically 100 or 50 basis points) or stock market crashes (eg, 10% decrease). While such stress tests are not identically included in the Solvency II framework, they indicate how well an insurance company is able to analyse its sensitivity to market and underwriting variables. Also, parallel interest rate movements are not sufficient to get a full overview of the interest-rate risk (eg, the slope of the curve could change and even invert). From this analysis of the 2002 reports, we conclude that companies were already focusing on risk management or starting to. Some were already able to perform Solvency II-like analyses. However, the majority of the larger, advanced companies were not actively disclosing risk management analyses.

Since 2002, the number of companies disclosing stress tests has increased (see Figure 1.3). Especially since 2005 when IFRS came into force, companies have started to disclose the sensitivity of their balance sheets more often. Interestingly, ING Group and Aegon Group disclose both the sensitivity of the balance sheet (ie, equity)

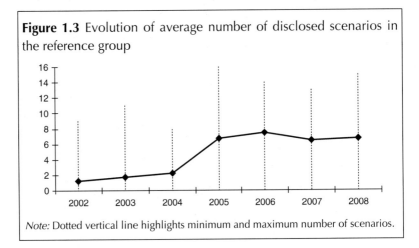

Figure 1.3 Evolution of average number of disclosed scenarios in the reference group

Note: Dotted vertical line highlights minimum and maximum number of scenarios.

and net income. Zurich even distinguishes between sensitivities of total assets, equity and income. Other insurers mainly show the sensitivity of the companies' equity (or embedded value). Although these numbers are book value rather than market value, they give a little insight into the sensitivity of the company.

In addition to separate stress tests for each risk type, some companies disclose the outcomes of the internal economic capital model. While most of the companies included in the analysis operate an internal model (CRO Forum 2009), only half of them disclose the outcome of the model in 2008, for example including analysis per risk type. These are Eureko, ING Group, Munich Re, Swiss Re and Zurich. Although others do mention the internal economic capital model, they do not disclose the outcomes. The important issue is whether these models are Solvency II compliant, whatever that might imply. We can assume that companies who disclose the outcome will at least use the models internally for steering the business. This is one important Solvency II compliance requirement, but not the only one. Other requirements are for instance the auditability of the models and data quality. The fact that some companies disclose economic capital outcomes, does not imply that these other compliance requirements are satisfied. In fact, this might still be quite challenging for each of the companies involved in the analysis.

Economic valuation and embedded options

The annual reports do not provide a sufficient overview from which to draw conclusions about the extent to which insurers in the analysis are able to determine market-consistent values of assets and liabilities. In the 2008 reports, almost all companies mention that their risk management models are based on economic calculations. Also, the valuation of embedded options and guarantees is mentioned. However, what standards are used is not always disclosed; an example is the risk-free discount rate used in the valuation. The CRO Forum (2009) states that 71% use the swap curve as a basis, but variants exist. Although we believe that most companies in the analysis are able to calculate the market-consistent value of their balance sheets, including the embedded options, the annual reports do not provide us with proof of this.

Risk measurement and models

All insurers in the analysis mention risk models in their 2008 annual reports and this has evolved over time. The companies in the analysis apply one of the following risk measures: 99.5% VaR, 99.95% VaR and 99% tail-VaR, all with a one-year time horizon. This is consistent with the CRO Forum (2009) observations that the time horizon converged. However, in 2002 only Eureko disclosed economic capital outcomes and this was for a five-year time horizon.

As indicated in the section "Review of public surveys", risk measurement involves both risk models and scenarios, as is also visible in the standard approach SCR. Given the previous discussion we can believe that most insurers are able to run scenarios – as they have done in their annual reports. Zurich also discusses in the risk management section the limitations of the scenarios performed.

The CRO Forum (2009) reports that it costs a significant amount of time to calculate economic capital, ie, to run the models. What is valid for economic capital is also most likely valid for determining the internal model SCR. Over time, the required time to run the models has not decreased, partly because the sophistication of the models has improved. Apparently, the benefit of more experience with the model and the cost of the greater sophistication of the model outweigh each other.

Aggregation of the economic capital outcomes including diversification effects is an area of much discussion. In the Solvency II framework, the SCR modules are aggregated by using correlation matrices. This is called the variance–covariance approach. The CRO Forum (2009) highlights that 60% of the companies use this approach in internal models, and hence are in line with the foreseen Solvency II framework. The level of correlation factors, however, is still difficult to determine. Often companies use expert opinion for these factors rather than statistically determined factors. However, the CRO Forum analysis shows that a limited number of companies are considering alternatives for internal model purposes, such as copulas and Monte Carlo simulation. Diversification effects are most often capitalised at the group level or the country level.

Risk governance

Although all companies in the analysis have disclosed risk management information since 2002, risk governance is still an important issue. The CRO Forum (2009) concludes that improving the risk governance framework is a particular focus for companies – as have the surveys discussed in the section "Review of public surveys".

An important element of Solvency II's pillar II emphasises that the responsibility for risk management ultimately rests with the executive board. To facilitate decision making, however, most companies in the analysis have appointed risk management departments and executive board committees. Aegon, Swiss Re and Aviva even installed a dedicated risk management committee in the (non-executive) supervisory board. The chief executive officer of Munich Re took explicit risk management responsibility by highlighting in his 2005 annual letter to shareholders how risk management and the Munich Re risk-adjusted return on capital framework would create value for shareholders. The executive board committee on risk management in most firms consists of the CRO, chief financial officer (CFO) and a number of business unit risk officers and financial officers. Often investment, ALM and reinsurance expertise is also represented in the committee. ING Group (including the banking business) set up seven risk committees, one committee for each major risk area. These are: the group credit committee – policy, group credit committee – transaction approval, group investment committee, ALCO bank, ALCO insurance, operational and residual risk committee, and finance and risk committee. Similar (although

Table 1.4 Disclosed risk governance in annual reports

Company	CRO position	Risk committee
Aegon	CRO reports to CFO	Non-executive risk committee and executive group risk and capital committee
Allianz	CRO reports to CFO	Non-executive risk committee, 2 executive committees
Aviva	Not mentioned	Group Alco and operational risk committee
Axa	Not mentioned	3 separate committees
Eureko	Not mentioned	7 separate committees
Fortis	CRO reports to CFO	Non-executive committee, executive insurance risk committee
Generali	Not mentioned	Non-executive internal control committee and executive Group risk committee
ING	CRO in board	7 separate committees
Munich Re	CRO in board	Group risk committee and global underwriting and risk committee
Prudential	CRO in board	Multiple committees
Swiss Re	CRO in board	Group risk and capital committee, group products and limits committee
Zurich	CRO in board	Non-executive risk committee, 2 executive committees

not exactly identical) structures have been set up within other companies (see Table 1.4).

Installing a CRO who has a specific delegated responsibility for risk management is another corporate governance measure. The position of the CRO in the analysis varies, both as a board member and as a direct reporter to the CFO (see Table 1.4). Although the CRO has a vital role in the risk management process (and the preparation for Solvency II), not all insurers have appointed a CRO. Liebenberg and Hoyt (2003) conclude that within their research sample of financial institutions the number of companies appointing CROs equals the number of companies that have not appointed CROs. Furthermore, they conclude that highly leveraged firms are more likely to appoint CROs. The role of the CRO in these firms is to explain to stakeholders the firm's risk profile. Generally, the presence of a CRO in the company promotes risk management implementation (Beasly *et al* 2005). Mikes (2008) characterises CROs in banking as being of four general types: modelling expert, compliance champion, strategic advisor or strategic controller. The author concludes that for retail banks, a more quantitative CRO (such as modelling champion or strategic controller) arises more often, whereas in wholesale banks the other types exist more often. A general conclusion of Mikes' (2008) research is that CROs focusing mainly on Basel II compliance often get less strategically important roles. It is likely that the same holds for the insurance industry and Solvency II. The CEA (2007b) indicates that the main driver for implementing risk management is internally driven ("shareholders requirement" and "good business practice") rather than focusing on Solvency II compliance. This should indicate that, in insurance, CROs are likely to have important roles in strategic decision making. From the analysis we notice that in the two larger reinsurance companies (Swiss Re and Munich Re), the CRO is a board member (strategic role), whereas mixed outcomes occur in primary insurers in the analysis. Primary insurance resembles retail banking more than wholesale banking and reinsurance better resembles wholesale banking.

Another corporate governance measure is the central risk management department that oversees all group risk exposures and provides aggregate risk reports to the management board. Often the risk department is headed by the CRO. Dowd *et al* (2008) concludes that the size of the risk management department in insurers is relatively small compared with banks. Unfortunately, the annual reports analysed in this chapter do not provide sufficient information to verify these results in the reference group.

Operational risk

The Solvency II requirements for operational risk are not as extensive as the Basel II requirements for banking. For instance, banks implementing the standardised approach[3] under Basel II are at least required to:

- have an operational risk function (department);
- assemble operational risk data including material losses;

- have regular operational risk reporting to the executive board; and
- validate the operational risk process by an independent review, including external auditors.

Solvency II does not (yet) include such requirements. The capital requirement (SCR) is relatively simple (Solvency II proposal, art. 106). Therefore, it can be expected that for insurers implementing operational risk, as described in Solvency II pillar I, it will not be complex. This does not, however, imply that under pillar II supervisors might pose additional requirements to insurers that face significant operational risks. It seems likely that these requirements will be in line with Basel II.

As with the Solvency II proposals, operational risk management is less advanced in the insurance industry than other risk types. While market and underwriting risks have been actively measured, at least since the 2000s, operational risk measurement started relatively recently. The approach to address operational risk varies from company to company. Some insurers such as Aviva and Eureko have installed operational risk committees since 2006 (respectively 2002). These are centralised approaches. A more decentralised approach is taken by Munich Re, which started exchanging information between business lines on operational risk in 2005. ING Group's annual report mentions a key risk indicator dashboard that was developed in 2007. An extensive operational risk framework for the insurance business is described in 2008. A similar key risk indicator dashboard was implemented by Eureko. Few insurers disclose the outcome of operational risk models. ING Group has disclosed economic capital outcomes for the insurance business since 2006, including operational risk capital. Also AXA mentions the initial developments of an operational risk model in 2006. The models are not discussed in the same level of detail as, for example, market risk.

Preliminary conclusions
Since the Solvency II project started, the larger companies have been disclosing gradually more information. For instance the number of stress tests has increased indicating a growing ability to perform the scenario analysis required under the Solvency II standard SCR

approach. While insurers have initially been reluctant to disclose economic capital outcomes, more and more insurers have started to disclose their internal model outcomes. Although we believe that the majority of companies included in the analysis are able to apply market-consistent valuation techniques to the balance sheet, publicly disclosed information cannot confirm the assumption. The time required to calculate economic capital is still significant. Also, risk aggregation is an issue for most of the companies in the analysis. Based on public information, the risk governance structure in companies is built upon risk committees and the role of the CRO and risk departments. The approaches used for risk committees differs from company to company. While some use multiple risk committees, others have installed one overarching risk committee. Some insurers even set up a risk committee in the supervisory board although this is a minority approach. From the annual reports we draw an initial conclusion that only a limited number of companies have implemented an operational risk model. Key risk indicator frameworks are used more often.

CHALLENGES LYING AHEAD...

As time passes the Solvency II implementation deadline approaches. Insurance companies in Europe have progressed with their risk management implementation. However, still much remains to be done. The analysis highlights the following observations and challenges:

- Risk aggregation, taking into account diversification, remains a challenge for companies. The correlation approach is used most often with alternatives investigated too little. Correlation factors are hard to determine and this requires much quantitative data. However, we noted in the section "A general development path" that getting correlations right is one of the key requirements of progressing to the next phase of risk management implementation (Drzik 1998; Tillaart 2003).
- In general, getting the data right is a key challenge that is crucial for risk management implementations. The public surveys as well as the CEIOPS reports highlight this as a key issue. While it is difficult to draw general conclusions on this issue, it is likely that significant IT spending will be required to get data

gathering to an adequate level in order to really benefit from the risk management efforts within the company (Drzik 1998).

- Market-consistent valuation of assets and liabilities is generally done by larger companies. Smaller companies may still face problems, especially with the embedded options and guarantees. The same holds for the scenario analyses used for calculating capital requirements. The evolutionary paradigms described in the section "A general development path" state that a serious modelling failure is a necessary step to fundamental model improvements in the market or within a particular company (Tillaart 2003). It is unclear whether the recent financial market turbulence is such a model failure and, hence, whether model improvements are likely to occur quite soon. Despite this finding CEIOPS (2008) reports that only a few companies foresee problems in this area.

- Market risk is the most well-developed risk management area. This is confirmed by both the public surveys and the annual reports of the CRO Forum companies. We note that this is consistent with the findings of Santomero and Babbel (1997) about the US.

- Operational risk remains a generally under-developed area. Given the debates in banking (Tillaart 2003), we would expect either a fundamental discussion regarding the appropriateness of operational risk measurement for insurance companies or a similar approach to Basel II. Companies are reluctant to develop operational risk models. This is a signal to supervisors that they consider operational risk modelling less appropriate than their banking counterparts. In banking the industry started modelling efforts that were later generalised into broad requirements in Basel II. Given the opposite movement in insurance, we would expect a fundamental discussion in insurance about the appropriateness of operational risk modelling.

- Governance is an area where companies could improve as well. Although the CRO Forum companies have installed risk departments and risk committees, smaller companies are not likely to have installed similar frameworks to the same level of detail, and the surveys highlight that, overall, respondents have not adequately assigned risk management responsibilities. Communication between the various departments working on risk management is especially important. For Solvency II this is a serious issue, especially in light of the foreseen pillar II framework.

- Applying the outcomes of risk models is another challenge. While this is a clear use test requirement, not all companies have implemented the necessary requirements. Despite survey conclusions that regulatory requirements are *not* the main driver for implementing risk management, companies appear not to use risk management outcomes for performance measurement and incentive compensation. Despite this, Drzik (2005) considers this one of the key lessons that insurers should learn from banking and Basel II. However, companies do not (yet) fully use risk indicators for management control purposes.

1 Interested readers may wish to consult Doff (2007, 2008), Eling *et al* (2007), and the websites of CEIOPS (www.ceiops.org), the CEA (http://www.cea.eu/index.php?page=solvency-ii) and the European Commission (http://ec.europa.eu/internal_market/insurance/solvency/index_en.htm).

2 Normally, all significant legal proposals that the European Commission submits to the European parliament should be accompanied by an impact assessment. This is to ensure that political decision-makers understand the impact of the new proposed regulation. The CEA impact assessment report was part of this total impact assessment of the European Commission with a focus on the impact of Solvency II on the insurance product and markets.

3 The standardised approach is the second-simplest approach for operational risk where the capital requirement is determined by a percentage of gross income. The percentage varies per business segment. The advanced measurement approach is based on internal models and includes even more stringent requirements, both qualitatively and quantitatively.

REFERENCES

Acharyya, M. and J. Johnson, 2006, "Investigating the Development of Enterprise Risk Management in the Insurance Industry: An Empirical Study of four Major European Insurers", *The Geneva Papers on Risk and Insurance: Issues and Practice,* Special Issue, 31, pp. 55–80.

Beasley, M. S., R. Clune and D. R. Hermanson, 2005, "Enterprise Risk Management: An Empirical Analysis of Factors Associated with the Extent of Implementation", *Journal of Accounting and Public Policy,* 24, pp. 521–531.

CEA, 2007a, "Insurance in Figures", URL: http://www.cea.eu/index.php?page=european-insurance-in-figures.

CEA, 2007b, "Results and Discussion on the Impact Assessment of the Future Solvency II Framework on Insurance Products and Markets", URL: http://www.cea.eu.

CEIOPS, 2007, "Advice to the European Commission in the Framework of the Solvency II project on Pillar I issues – further advice", March, URL: http://www.fma.gv.at/cms/solvency2//attachments/9/5/5/CH0415/CMS1175624807902/ceiops-doc-08-07adviceonpillari-issues-furtheradvice.pdf.

CEIOPS, 2008, "CEIOPS' Report on its Fourth Quantitative Impact Study (QIS4) for Solvency II", November, URL: http://www.abioric.com/media/1468/ceiops%20qis4%20report.pdf.

CRO Forum, 2009, "CRO Forum Internal Models Benchmarking Study: Summary Results", URL: http://www.croforum.org.

Doff, R. R., 2007, *Risk Management for Insurers: Risk Control, Economic Capital and Solvency II* (London: Risk Books).

Doff, R. R., 2008, "A Critical Analysis of the Solvency II Proposals", *Geneva Papers*, 33, pp. 193–206.

Dowd, K., D. L. Bartlett, M. Chaplin, P. Kelliher and C. O'Brien, 2008, "Risk Management in the U.K. Insurance Industry: The Changing State of Practice", *International Journal of Financial Services Management*, 3(1), pp. 5–23.

Drzik, J., 1998, "The Seven Stages of Risk Management", *Journal of Lending and Credit Risk Management*, February, pp. 34–39.

Drzik, J., 2005, "At the Crossroads of Change: Risk and Capital Management in the Insurance Industry", *Geneva Papers*, 30, pp. 72–87.

Eling, M., H. Schmeiser and J. T. Schmidt, 2007, "The Solvency II Process: Overview and Critical Analysis", *Risk Management and Insurance Review*, 10, pp. 69–85.

European Commission, 2002, "Study into the Methodologies to Assess the Overall Financial Position of an Insurance Undertaking from the Perspective of Prudential Supervision", May, URL: http://intranet.icea.es/solvencia/Documentos/KPMG%20solv%20final%20report-300402.pdf.

FSA, 2005, "Insurance Sector Briefing: ICAS – One Year On", November, URL: http://www.fsa.gov.uk/pubs/other/isb_icas.pdf.

Mikes, A., 2008, "Risk Management at Crunch Time: Compliance Champions or Business Partners?", *Journal of Risk Management in Financial Institutions*, 2(1), pp. 7–25.

Santomero, A. M. and D. F. Babbel, 1997, "Financial Risk Management by Insurers: An Analysis of the Process", *Journal of Risk and Insurance*, 64(2), pp. 231–270.

Tillaart, van den A., 2003, *Controlling Operational Risk: Concepts and Practices* (Amsterdam: NIBE-SVV).

2

Heading in the Same Direction: IFRS 4 Phase II and Solvency II

Francesco Nagari[1]

Deloitte LLP

BACKGROUND, OBJECTIVES AND METHODOLOGY

Solvency II has been steadily moving to the forefront of most insurers' minds in readiness for its implementation on October 31, 2012. However, the implications of Phase II of the International Accounting Standard Board (IASB) project on insurance contracts accounting (Phase II) do not seem to rank as highly on the priority lists of management, despite both proposals sharing similar timelines and issues.

Although Solvency II and Phase II have different objectives, life and general insurers will have to address similar questions and issues when dealing with their implementation.

An integrated or closely aligned approach to the implementation of the two projects is likely to minimise implementation costs and maximise benefits. But, in order to achieve this, insurers need to understand both the similarities and differences of the two regimes.

Objectives and timetable for Phase II

The goal of the IASB's Phase II project is to provide a clear and uniform system for the accounting and valuation of insurance and reinsurance contracts. The over-riding ambition is to assist investors' understanding of insurance companies' profitability and financial position. The IASB intends to achieve this objective by producing a new International Financial Reporting Standard (IFRS) with a principle-based measurement of insurance contracts that maximises the use of current market data and that aligns insurance accounting with the general principles in use for all the other IFRSs.

Phase I of the project was completed in March 2004 with the publication of IFRS 4 "Insurance Contracts". However, IFRS 4 is an interim solution that left insurance accounting in the European Union virtually unchanged from the system that existed prior to the transition to IFRS.

Phase II is where the proposals represent a fundamental change to insurance accounting under IFRS and the publication of the discussion paper "Preliminary views on insurance contracts" dealing with accounting for insurance and reinsurance contracts, issued by the IASB in May 2007, was a key step in this process.

In order to provide a more relevant method of valuing insurance contracts, the IASB (2007) proposals focused on the extensive use of market-based assessment of expected risks and rewards arising from the acceptance of insurance risks. This approach was aimed at achieving consistency of valuation not only across insurance companies but also with other financial services companies and businesses in other sectors that use fair value measurements under IFRS.

The discussion paper focused on the measurement of insurance contracts as defined in IFRS and the need for an approach that will provide more relevant and reliable financial information on the amount, timing and uncertainty of future cashflows arising from these contracts.

Subsequent to the publication of the discussion paper the IASB received and analysed extensive comments on its proposals. In late October 2008 the IASB was joined in its efforts by the American Financial Accounting Standards Board (FASB). The FASB decided to work with the IASB to develop an identical, or very similar, accounting standard that would be applied by all companies using US Generally Accepted Accounting Principles (GAAP).

In 2009 the IASB and the FASB have planned an intense season of decision making meetings that will take them to the publication of an exposure draft of the new IFRS (and new US GAAP) expected in early 2010. The finalisation of this document in the revised IFRS 4 "Insurance contracts" is expected in the first half of 2011.

At this stage, the effective date of the new accounting regime is not yet known because the IASB and the FASB wish to fully assess the complexity and the details of their own pronouncements before deciding the date on which they will have to be applied for the first time. In the author's opinion, based on the current timetable, the earliest effective date could be financial periods beginning on or after January 1, 2013.

Objectives and timetable for Solvency II

The goal of Solvency II is to ensure the protection of policyholders by giving insurers incentives for proper risk management. The European parliament approved the Solvency II Framework Directive on April 22, 2009 and it is now scheduled to come into force on October 31, 2012. Although the details of the new requirements will have to wait until the European Commission finalises the extensive "level 2" implementing measures by June 2011, the insurance industry in the European Union can use the Framework Directive to begin its preparation for the new regime with at least certainty on timeframes. Solvency II aims to implement solvency requirements that better reflect the risks that companies face and deliver a supervisory system that is consistent across all member states. The new regulations are being developed using a three-pillar approach to the solvency position of insurance companies with each pillar governing a different aspect of the solvency position of insurance companies. As well as requiring firms to disclose their capital and risk frameworks, they must also demonstrate how and where they are embedded in their wider activities.

- Pillar I considers the quantitative requirements of the system, including the calculation of market-consistent technical provisions reported with an explicit risk margin, as well as rules relating to investment management and solvency capital. It sets out a valuation standard for liabilities to policyholders and the capital requirements that firms will be required to meet. There will be two solvency requirements: the minimum capital requirement (MCR) and the solvency capital requirement (SCR). If the available capital lies in between the MCR and SCR it is an early indicator to the supervisor and the insurance company that action needs to be taken.
- Pillar II deals with the qualitative aspects of an insurance company's internal controls, risk management process and

approach to supervisory review, including that insurance companies conduct a compliant Own Risk and Solvency Assessment (ORSA). If supervisors are not satisfied with a company's assessment of its risk-based capital or the quality of the risk management arrangements, they will have the power to impose higher capital requirements.

- Pillar III is concerned with improving disclosure requirements and market discipline in order to increase transparency for all users, including customers, investors, regulators and tax authorities. Insurance companies must interpret the disclosure requirements, develop a strategy for disclosure and educate key stakeholders about the potential impact.

Methodology and sources

Comparing and contrasting the two regimes is a difficult and complicated task, since their development is not complete at the time of writing. Our sources on IFRS are "Preliminary views on insurance contracts," the discussion paper on accounting for insurance and reinsurance contracts issued by the IASB in May 2007 and also the monthly issues of "IASB Update" that contain the official reports of IASB tentative decisions. Since publication of the discussion paper, the IASB received comments on it and used them to resume its work towards the publication of an Exposure Draft of the new IFRS. At the time of writing, this is expected to be issued in early 2010 with the final standard on accounting for insurance contracts issued in the first half of 2011 for likely implementation two years later at the earliest. Following a decision made in October 2008, the FASB has joined the IASB in its work, resulting in the Exposure Draft being published also as a draft accounting principle for companies reporting under US GAAP. For all these reasons, the decisions that have been tentatively reached so far may therefore be different in the final version of the IFRS for insurance contracts.

The sources for our understanding of what Solvency II will finally look like are the European Union's Framework Directive, approved by the European Parliament in April 2009, and certain consultation papers issued by the Committee of European Insurance and Occupational Pensions Supervisors (CEIOPS). These will form CEIOPS' technical advice to the European Commission for the development of the level 2 implementing measures that will add important details to the application of the principles set out in the Framework Directive. CEIOPS will continue to issue new consultation papers on its technical advice throughout 2009 and the European Commission will only receive CEIOPS' final, technical advice during 2010. Upon receipt of the technical advice, legislative work on the development of the level 2 implementing measures will begin. These will also be subject to another round of consultation, with interested parties expected to allow the finalisation of the full set of level 2 implementing measures by June 2011. The final text of the level 2 implementing measures may be different from the draft technical advice published in the CEIOPS consultation papers and this is likely to change the way in which Solvency II and Phase II compare.

THE MEASUREMENT APPROACHES OF PHASE II AND SOLVENCY II FOR THE VALUATION OF INSURANCE CONTRACTS

According to the IASB (2007) and the following tentative decisions to date, the key features of Phase II are:

- A prospective valuation of the insurance contract based on a current estimate of the present value of all expected future contractual cashflows within the "contract boundary" as defined in the IASB Update (2009).
- The application of the Phase II measurement model to all insurance and reinsurance contracts as defined under the current text of IFRS 4.

At the time of writing, the IASB had not yet finalised its decision to select the economic context within which to develop the prospective valuation noted above.

The IASB is considering two alternative models representing the relevant economic context in which the accounting standard will be developed: a current exit price and a current fulfilment value. The former would require accounting for the residual rights and obligations of insurance contracts in force at the balance sheet date as if they were transferred to another insurer. This approach was presented by the IASB (2007) and it would look at a market-consistent form of accounting similar to fair value. The latter would require the accounting for insurance contracts to be based on the specific insurer's estimate of the current value of fulfilling the residual rights and obligations towards the policyholders. The context of this accounting model refers to the specific situation of the insurance company rather than the assessment of a hypothetical transferee.

Typically the current exit price of an insurance liability is rarely an observable price. For this reason, the IASB's (2007) proposals suggested that current exit value of insurance contracts is calculated using three building blocks.

- Block 1: estimate of future cashflows – explicit, unbiased probability-weighted, market consistent and current estimates of the contractual cashflow.
- Block 2: effect of time value of money – current market discount rates that adjust the estimated future cashflows for the time value of money.
- Block 3: margins – an explicit, market consistent and unbiased estimate of the margin to reflect the estimation uncertainty arising from block 1 (the risk margin).

The current exit price and current fulfilment value would consider block 1 differently. Under the current exit price approach, an insurer would have to make estimates consistent with market prices even when they are not observable (eg, in the estimation of the cost of settling insurance claims). To produce current fulfilment value valuations the insurer would be required instead to estimate future cashflows based on its specific situation.

Another difference exists for block 3 where the current exit price proposed in IASB (2007) required the insurer to estimate the risk margin as the "market price for risk" another insurer would have demanded to bear the uncertainty from the insurance contracts in force, in addition to the cash covering for the discounted expected value of the same in-force portfolio of contracts. The current fulfilment value model, more recently developed, would take an entity-specific "cost of risk" for the same underlying uncertainty. At the time of writing, the IASB was debating whether, in the absence of an active and liquid secondary market for insurance portfolios, the two models would produce the same result, suggesting that this component of the insurance liability could be determined only from an entity-specific perspective.

The measurement of insurance contracts under the Solvency II regime aims to produce a solvency balance sheet that can be used to determine the extent the insurance company can cover its SCR.

The valuation of insurance contracts ("technical provisions" under the Solvency II definition) will be part of the tier 1 capital of an insurance company. This is defined as

> assets that are free from any foreseeable liabilities [that] are available to absorb losses due to adverse business fluctuations, both on a going-concern basis as well as in the case of winding-up. Therefore the vast majority of the excess of assets over liabilities, as valued in accordance with the principles set out in this Directive, should be treated as high quality capital (tier 1).

The SCR is calculated as a function of the various risks faced by the insurer. In addition the Framework Directive requires that the level 2 implementing measures define the MCR as a formula-based calculation with limits calculated as a percentage of the SCR.

In this chapter we focus on the differences that would exist between the "technical provisions'" valuation under the Solvency II regime and their valuation as insurance contracts under the Phase II approach.

PHASE II AND SOLVENCY II: COMPARE AND CONTRAST
Purpose and scope

Phase II and Solvency II have fundamentally different purposes. Phase II will be one of the IFRSs, which are a system of principle-based standards designed to prepare general purpose financial statements, detailing the performance and financial position of the business of a given reporting entity.

General purpose financial statements are directed to assist economic decision making with respect to the reported business of existing and potential investors, lenders and the business' own employees.

The Solvency II Framework Directive instead states in its preamble that:

> the main objective of insurance and reinsurance regulation and supervision is the adequate protection of policyholders and beneficiaries. The term beneficiary is intended to cover any natural or legal person who is entitled to a right under an insurance contract.

One important difference between the purposes of the two systems is that Solvency II is a balance-sheet-driven regulatory regime, which focuses on the nature of the business and the existence of solvency capital to ensure that insurers can always pay their liabilities, even in turbulent and unprofitable financial markets. Reporting revenue, expenses and profits is not contemplated in the Framework Directive.

Under IFRS an insurer will prepare general purpose financial statements aimed at reporting both the financial position at the end of the financial period and the performance of the business for the same period, presenting its revenues, expenses and resulting profit or loss.

A second structural difference between Solvency II and Phase II is the definition of their respective scopes. Phase II has a transaction-based scope while Solvency II scope is a function of the entity's regulatory status as an authorised insurance or reinsurance undertaking.

The transaction-based scope of Phase II is based on defining what an insurance contract is. Any entity issuing a contract that meets this definition would be defined as an insurer under Phase II; it would apply the requirements of Phase II for its accounting irrespective of the entity's legal status (eg, it may not be a regulated entity). The requirement that the policyholder transfers significant insurance risk to the insurer is key to the Phase II definition of an insurance contract.

The scope of Solvency II covers the assets and liabilities of all the entities authorised to undertake insurance and reinsurance business within the European Union. Article 2 of the Framework Directive sets out the business activities for these entities that would fall within the scope of the new regulations.

From the perspective of comparing this approach with that of Phase II, we observe that these business activities would also include contracts that do not transfer significant insurance risk to the insurer as defined under Phase II. This is the case for a number of contracts under life insurance activities where the benefits due on death or survival are not significantly higher than the benefits payable under surrender or maturity.

Solvency II would require all contracts classified under these regulated business activities to be measured as insurance contracts on the Solvency II balance sheet, irrespective of whether they would meet the Phase II definition.

The liabilities of contracts that would not meet the definition of insurance contracts under Phase II are likely to be calculated under other IFRS. Usually the standards "Financial instruments: recognition and measurement" (IAS 39) and "Revenue" (IAS 18) would be used to account for these transactions in the IFRS general purpose financial statements.

This different approach to a subset of contracts that an insurance undertaking issues or holds creates differences that will impact the Solvency II tier 1 capital. We have set out below three examples illustrating this.

Example 1 Saving plan with an interest-rate guarantee accounted for at amortised cost under IAS 39.

This contract would pay benefits as a function of a reference variable interest rate (eg, Libor). It would offer also a minimum interest benefit, if the reference variable rate fell below a stated contractual guaranteed minimum.

This contract would not be within the scope of IFRS 4, instead it would be accounted for under IAS 39. However, if issued by an insurance undertaking, it would fall into one of the life insurance regulated activities and would be measured under the Solvency II provisions to calculate its liability for the solvency balance sheet.

The usual treatment for these contracts under IAS 39 would be to account for them at the amortised cost. In this case the treatment of the interest-rate guarantee would need to consider the embedded derivative close relationship test under IAS 39 paragraph AG33 (b):

> An embedded floor or cap on the interest rate on a debt contract or insurance contract is closely related to the host contract, provided the cap is at or above the market rate of interest and the floor is at or below the market rate of interest when the contract is issued, and the cap or floor is not leveraged in relation to the host contract.

This test would not require any additional liability if the reference interest rate puts the embedded guarantee "in-the-money" after it has been sold and at that time the guarantee was "out-of-the-money".

Under Solvency II measurement, this treatment would be different since the principles applicable to the technical provisions for liabilities would require the insurance undertaking to calculate the liability using the current transfer value approach, as described in Article 75. This would always calculate the cashflows of the guarantee embedded in the saving plan.

When the guarantee is "in-the-money" the Solvency II liability would be higher than under IAS 39.

Example 2 Single-premium unit-linked investment contract for which the insurance undertaking has incurred acquisition costs that have been capitalised as an asset under IAS 18.

This product would pay benefits based on the unit price of a specified fund owned by the issuing insurance undertaking. In the IFRS general purpose financial statements, this contract would not be accounted for under Phase II. Instead it would use the IAS 39 and IAS 18 accounting principles because the contract does not transfer significant insurance risk. The typical terms and conditions of these contracts would include a clause that would grant the policyholder a right to the payment of the account's balance on demand. There would also be a clause that would permit the insurance undertaking to periodically reduce the policyholder account's balance for asset management and other similar charges (eg, annual management fees).

The usual accounting treatment for these liabilities under IAS 39 would be at fair value, using the fair value option available under that particular IFRS. This would be subject to the "deposit floor" rule that prohibits the recognition of the fair value of a liability at an amount lower than the amount payable on demand (discounted from the first date that the amount could be required to be paid). In addition the insurance undertaking would have capitalised the commission costs paid to secure the contract with the policyholder as required under IAS 18.

The treatment of these items on the Solvency II balance sheet could be different since it would be the amount another insurance undertaking would demand to assume the liability as required under Article 75. A market-consistent transfer value of such a contract would take into account the right to receive future asset management fees and it would usually be lower than the amount payable to the policyholder at the measurement date.

In addition, the draft technical advice contained in CEIOPS (2009d, Paragraph 3.47) on the valuation of assets and "other liabilities" would suggest a nil value for the asset under IAS 18.

The insurance undertaking would recognise a reduction or an increase in its tier 1 capital, when the value of the Solvency II technical provision is respectively higher or lower than the net accounting value, calculated as the difference between the IAS 39 liability and the IAS 18 asset.

The sign and magnitude of this difference would need to be assessed on a case-by-case basis. It would be a function of the specific contractual terms and conditions and the market variables affecting the value of the linked assets at the time of the valuation under the two regimes.

Example 3 Contract with a legal form of a reinsurance contract that contains features that result in no significant insurance risk being transferred from the cedant to the reinsurer.

The accounting treatment of assets and liabilities under IFRS is independent of each other. An exception to this rule is the principle to measure the uncertainty from insurance contracts net of the protection given by purchased reinsurance contracts.

Under Phase II a purchased contract would need to pass the same classification test, focusing on the risk transfer characteristics of the contract rather than its legal characteristics of being issued or purchased by an authorised insurance undertaking.

A purchased reinsurance contract that met such a definition would have its accounting value calculated using the three building blocks (previously described). However, in relation to block 3 the value of the margin for risk would be calculated as a function of the reinsured risk, thus increasing the value of the asset when more uncertainty is reinsured under that contract.

This apparently counterintuitive result, which produces a higher asset if its cashflows are more uncertain, is indeed the logical consequence of the consideration of the insurance contract and the associated reinsurance contract as a single unit of measurement. The first two blocks of the measurement model are unaffected by this approach.

Under Phase II the reinsurance asset is then presented gross on the balance sheet of the insurance undertaking that has purchased it. An adjustment for expected credit losses is applied to fully reflect its economic recoverability.

A reinsurance asset that does not meet the IFRS definition would be accounted for individually under IAS 39 as a financial asset and it would not form a single unit of measurement with the related liabilities. Therefore any uncertainty would be reflected in the traditional way of a lower accounting value of the asset the more uncertain the future receipts under the asset are.

The valuation of insurance contracts

Both regimes use an approach of three building blocks to value insurance contracts. As mentioned previously, block 1 requires a probability-weighted, unbiased, current estimate of future cashflows, while block 2 requires cashflows to be explicitly discounted to reflect the time value of money and block 3 requires a risk margin that is a function of the underlying insurance risk's uncertainty. However, there are differences in the ways that Phase II and Solvency II approach the calculation of these three blocks.

Block 1: a different approach to future premiums
Both Phase II and Solvency II require insurers to explicitly calculate their unbiased, current estimates of probability-weighted cashflows on a prospective basis. Solvency II Article 75 requires the calculations to comply with a principle of "market consistency" that would be in line with the current exit price alternative currently considered for Phase II. However, if the IASB finally chooses to develop the Phase II valuation model using one of the current fulfilment value approaches, there would not be a requirement for market consistency in the estimation of block 1.

Based on current discussions at the IASB the only area where the two alternatives for Phase II would seem to have a potentially significant difference is the estimation of expenses related to the servicing of issued insurance contracts. The estimation on a market-consistent basis could estimate higher or lower expenses than those incurred by the insurance undertaking's specific systems and processes depending on how efficient it is compared with the rest of the market.

The assessment of whether this component for calculating block 1 is similar or not can only be done after the full detailed requirements of the two regimes are finalised.

However, a clearly different approach is taken in relation to the estimation of future premiums where the payment cannot be enforced by the insurance undertaking.

The approach under Phase II would require the consideration of future premiums and the associated benefits of an existing contract. The IASB (2009) tentatively decided in May that the measurement of block 1 for insurance contracts should include:

> the expected (ie, probability-weighted) cash flows (future premiums and other cash flows resulting from those premiums, eg, benefits and claims) resulting from those contracts, including those cash flows whose amount or timing depends on whether policyholders exercise options in the contracts.

The estimation of future premiums applies to all existing contracts at the valuation date. The IASB has enunciated a principle to define when an existing contract terminates and the accounting of a new contract begins. Another of the IASB (2009) tentative decisions that were reached was:

> to identify the boundary between existing contracts and new contracts, the starting point would be to consider whether the insurer can cancel the contract or change its pricing or other terms.

The application of these two principles is unconstrained and insurance undertakings under Phase II would have to calculate block 1 accordingly. For example the value of block 1 for an insurance contract with regular premiums could result in a positive value of the probability-weighted estimate of future premiums minus the future policy benefits.

This outcome would not be permitted under Solvency II where a constraint is imposed on the value that block 1 could have within the solvency balance sheet. CEIOPS (2009b, Paragraph 3.30(c)) introduces the following restriction to the inclusion of future premiums in the valuation of block 1:

> Future premiums and any resulting benefit payments to policyholders, expenses etc, which relate to an option or guarantee that provides rights under which the policyholder can renew the contract belong to the existing contract if, and only if, the inclusion of the renewals increase the best estimate.

Example 4 Consider a whole of life insurance contract that insures a policyholder against the risk of his death, promising to pay a fixed amount of cash in addition to any outstanding positive account balance kept in the contract in the event death occurs during the term of the policy.

To receive the death benefit the policyholder is required to maintain a sufficient account balance to fund the annual charges the insurer is entitled to deduct from such an account for mortality and other charges. Failing to maintain this amount would result in cancellation of the policy.

The insurance undertaking has determined the health conditions at the date the policy was sold and it has established the annual mortality charges for the cover. The policyholder has an option to cancel the contract on demand or simply by stopping the payment of cash until the account balance is lower than the next mortality charge. The insurance undertaking cannot cancel the contract or cannot ask the policyholder to undertake new medical tests to change the level of premium charged. The mortality charge at the point of sale is fixed for the duration of the contract.

The future stream of mortality charges and the expected additional payments in the account balance that the policyholder will make would be considered under IFRS because the insurer cannot cancel or reunderwrite and reprice the contract. Under Phase II the measurement of this renewal option is likely to result in a positive value (ie, an asset) at the point of sale of the contract.

This accounting result could be prohibited under Solvency II based on the draft technical advice in CEIOPS (2009b). The minimum liability for CEIOPS would be equal to the margin for risk on these contracts.

Under Phase II the margin for risk would reduce the assets calculated under blocks 1 and 2. However, there are currently no restrictions for the accounting value of an insurance contract to be an asset if the valuation indicates that to be the correct value.

Block 2: consideration of spreads for the insurer's own credit risk
There appears to be little difference in the methods used for selecting the discount rate that would be applied to the various scenarios considered for block 1. Both Phase II and Solvency II require insurance contracts to be explicitly discounted at a rate

that is independent of the assets held to match those liabilities. As per the fourth quantitative impact study (QIS4), completed in July 2008, insurance liabilities under Solvency II could be discounted using swap rates. Phase II proposals currently require a discount rate selected from market interest rates that match the currency, duration and the illiquidity of the contractual cashflows.

If the final choice of the Phase II measurement attribute between current exit price and current fulfilment value is for the former approach, the new IFRS is likely to require the inclusion of the risk that the insurance undertaking is unable to perform the contractual obligations (eg, the risk of the insurer's default, which is one of the most important non-performance risks). The logic of this comes from the application of the market-consistency principle, which would apply the same considerations surrounding non-performance risk to the determination of the exit price of a liability that a market participant would apply in pricing the corresponding asset.

The theory of the current exit price formulated in IASB (2007) was not prescriptive for which building block the insurance contract's default risk should be taken into account from. The addition of a credit spread to the discount rate would be a possible technique to allow for this risk. In this case, the selected discount rate under Phase II would differ from that in Solvency II when the risk of default is considered as an adjustment of the discount rate. Article 76(2) of the Framework Directive requires the use of a discount rate selected from a risk-free interest-rate curve:

> The best estimate shall correspond to the probability-weighted average of future cash-flows, taking account of the time value of money (expected present value of future cash-flows), using the relevant risk-free interest rate term structure.

An alternative measurement for non-performance risk would be to include a probability weighted scenario in block 1, where the insurance undertaking does not fulfil its contractual obligations. This, and all other scenarios, would be discounted based on the relevant market-consistent risk-free rate. Under this approach, and with all other variables being equal, the block 1 amount under Phase II would be lower than that measured under Solvency II, where the prohibition to take into account the insurance undertaking's own default is absolute.

Finally it should be noted that, in order to be in line with general IFRS fair value principles, the measurement of the insurer's own risk in a current exit price model is done with reference to the credit characteristics of the contract, rather than to the overall credit standing of the insurance undertaking. This means that the presence of implicit contractual guarantees, such as those provided in many retail insurance markets by government-sponsored policyholder protection funds, would also need to be considered in conjunction with the insurer's own capital strength. The adjustment to reflect the credit quality of policyholder protection funds could substantially reduce the credit spread adjustment to the discount rate and it could produce an alignment of the measurement of block 2 under Phase II and Solvency II, at least for all contracts where these guarantees exist.

However, if the ultimate measurement model for Phase II is the current fulfilment value it is conceivable that the selection criteria for the discount rate under the two regimes will be substantially similar in all cases. Under this alternative Phase II measurement model the asset-driven market considerations of the risk of default would not be taken into account. In this model the key economic dimension would be the current measurement of the fulfilment obligations from the perspective of the specific insurance undertaking and not from the perspective of another market participant.

Block 3: Phase II principle-based calculations and a Solvency II prescribed cost of capital method

Both the Phase II and Solvency II regimes require the valuation of insurance contracts to include a separately calculated margin that reflects the risk of the uncertainty of the estimation arising from the expected value, block 1. In both cases, the fact that the risk margin is explicitly determined prohibits any practices where the risk margins are implicitly calculated.

The main area of potential difference is that Phase II would not impose a specific calculation technique to determine the risk margin, while under Article 76(5) of the Framework Directive the risk margin will be based on a cost-of-capital approach:

> Where insurance and reinsurance undertakings value the best estimate and the risk margin separately, the risk margin shall be calculated by determining the cost of providing an amount of

eligible own funds equal to the Solvency Capital Requirement necessary to support the insurance and reinsurance obligations over the lifetime thereof.

The rate used in the determination of the cost of providing that amount of eligible own funds (Cost-of-Capital rate) shall be the same for all insurance and reinsurance undertakings and shall be reviewed periodically.

The Cost-of-Capital rate used shall be equal to the additional rate, above the relevant risk-free interest rate, that an insurance or reinsurance undertaking would incur holding an amount of eligible own funds, as set out in "Section 3" equal to the Solvency Capital Requirement necessary to support the insurance and reinsurance obligation over the lifetime of that obligation.

The detailed requirements of the Solvency II risk margin calculations are not yet determined. CEIOPS will be publishing draft technical advice for the final level 2 implementing measures on this subject in due course. However, based on the QIS4 experience a flat risk premium of 6% could be applied to future solvency capital ratios to determine the cost of capital.

The approach expected for Phase II will be different and less prescriptive because it will be based on a set of principles within which the insurance undertaking would need to develop a compliant calculation technique.

IASB (2007) has already set out some of these principles all of which would be met by the cost-of-capital technique prescribed under Solvency II:

(a) The less that is known about the current estimate and its trend, the higher the risk margin should be.
(b) Risks with low frequency and high severity will have higher risk margins than risks with high frequency and low severity.
(c) For similar risks, long-duration contracts will have higher risk margins than those of shorter duration.
(d) Risks with a wide probability distribution will have higher risk margins than those risks with a narrower distribution.
(e) To the extent that emerging experience reduces uncertainty, risk margins will decrease, and vice versa.

The application of these principles under the current exit price approach would result in determining the risk margin on a market-consistent basis, based on the reward a market participant would demand to bear the insurance risk uncertainty unexpired at the reporting date. Under the current fulfilment value, the approach to calculate the risk margin would be from the perspective of the specific insurance undertaking in relation to the cost that it would need to incur to bear the associated estimation uncertainty.

The IASB debate has not yet identified a clear difference in the calculation of a risk margin from a market-consistent basis compared with one done at the level of the specific insurance undertaking. The fact that the uncertainty that determines the risk margin is the same irrespective of the market or entity-specific perspective used, combined with the absence of an active market where risk prices could be observed, suggests that the final choice between these two models may not have significant practical implications. However, the IASB may ultimately decide on a current fulfilment value approach where there is no explicit risk margin at all. We analyse this option and its differences with the Solvency II regime in the next section of this chapter.

Another difference arising from the Phase II principle-based approach and the more prescriptive Solvency II regime is the definition of a portfolio to be used when calculating the risk margin.

Both regimes accept that the economics of insurance produces a reduction of risk that is substantially proportional to the number of similar risks an insurance undertaking decides to insure. This is one of the fundamental laws in probability mathematics and IASB (2007) refers to it as the "pooling of risks" effect. Both Phase II and Solvency II require that the "pooling of risks" is reflected in the valuation of insurance contracts via the determination of the risk margin at a portfolio level.

Phase II requires that the risk margin is calculated in aggregate for a "portfolio of contracts that are subject to broadly similar risks and managed together as a single portfolio."

Solvency II instead is more prescriptive and requires that a portfolio should be defined at a line of business level. The level 2 implementing measures will add further details to this requirement. CEIOPS (2009a) recommended that the level 2 implementing measures use the lines of business, identified for insurance business authorisation purposes, as the minimum segmentation level. CEIOPS (2009a) adds two requirements to this segmentation:

1. the insurance undertaking should "further segment prescribed lines of business into more homogenous risk groups according to the risk profile of the obligations" (Paragraph 3.23); and
2. the principle of unbundling different risks that are part of the same contract in order to calculate the relevant technical provisions (Paragraphs 3.28 to 3.33).

It is obviously conceivable that the principle-based definition of Phase II and the more prescriptive portfolio definition of Solvency II would deliver the same portfolio in practice. However, the different conceptual basis adopted calls for caution and this area should be carefully considered in the implementation of the two regimes. All other things being equal, if one of the two regimes produces a smaller portfolio, the risk margin liability for that portfolio is likely to be a higher proportion of the expected value/best estimate amount than it would be in the regime, permitting a larger portfolio of insurance contracts.

Another final and important difference between the calculation of block 3 under Phase II and Solvency II arises if the ultimate choice of Phase II is to develop an IFRS using the current exit price model.

In this case Phase II would require that block 3 includes also a separate service margin in addition to the risk margin. The logic of a separate margin is to add the market-consistent profit that an insurer would demand for any services other than bearing insurance risk that might have been sold to the policyholder and have yet to be delivered at the valuation date. Under both Solvency II and Phase II the cash outflows that the insurance undertaking would incur to render these services would already be included in block 1. However, all other variables being equal, the decision to utilise a specific prescribed calculation for the risk margin under Solvency II, which could be deemed valid under Phase II, leaves the Solvency II liability potentially lower than that under Phase II because of the absence of an equivalent service margin liability under Solvency II valuation rules.

The impact of IFRS performance reporting: residual and composite margins under Phase II current fulfilment value

As discussed previously, there is a different purpose served by IFRS and Solvency II. One of the key elements of the IFRS general purpose financial statements is the income statement or, under the new nomenclature, the statement of comprehensive income. This statement reports the performance of the insurance undertaking calculating for example the profit or loss for the year.

Solvency II does not have any specific requirements around the profitability of an insurance undertaking and if the capital resources are replenished regularly via capital injections an insurance undertaking would be able to comply with the requirements of Solvency II in spite of having reported losses under IFRS.

One particularly important dimension affecting performance reporting under Phase II is the possibility of recognising a net profit from selling an insurance contract. This accounting profit was the most important characteristic of the current exit price presented in IASB (2007).

During its most recent deliberations the IASB has abandoned this particularly innovative approach, responding to a request that came out of the comments on the 2007 discussion paper. The IASB has agreed that Phase II will prohibit the recognition of accounting profit when an insurance contract is sold. The commentators persuaded the IASB that the absence of a reliable secondary market for insurance contracts would have made the recognition of such accounting profit an equally unreliable figure.

At the time of writing, both the current exit price and the current fulfilment value models would include this key prohibition. When the three building blocks have been calculated, the resulting figure will have to be calibrated to the net transaction price the policyholder will have paid to the insurer for purchasing the insurance contract and for compensating the insurance undertaking for the acquisition costs incurred. The result from this calibration, when the three building blocks are less than the net transaction price, is an additional liability that the IASB currently defines as the residual margin.

In addition to this approach, which would make full use of the three building blocks, the IASB is also contemplating whether the most reliable form of accounting would be one that uses only the first two blocks (the expected value discounted at a market-consistent discount rate). Using this approach and calibrating the resulting calculation to the net transaction price would produce a margin that the IASB has tentatively defined as the composite margin.

In addition to the differences noted before, this model would not calculate a risk margin. Instead, the insurance undertaking would release to profit the composite margin liability calculated from the initial calibration exercise.

An important feature of the calibration exercise in both cases is the definition of the acquisition costs that will be permitted to be included in the calibration. This is another feature of Phase II that is not relevant to the implementation of Solvency II.

The IASB has tentatively decided that it would define acquisition costs for the purpose of calibrating the residual margin as those that are directly attributable to securing the contract and that are incremental, such as commissions. A cost is incremental, if the insurance undertaking would not have incurred it other than as a result of selling the insurance policy. Other costs such as overheads, for example, cannot be included.

The presence of the residual and the composite margin is possible only if the calibration exercise produces an additional liability to that determined using the calculated blocks. If the calibration indicates that there is a loss at the point of sale, the insurance undertaking would need to recognise it immediately in the income statement.

Under Solvency II, however, there is no concept of a residual margin and if Phase II is developed from a current fulfilment value model that only uses two building blocks with a composite margin the block 3 differences between the two regimes would be even greater.

OPEN ISSUES FOR PARTICIPATING BUSINESS
The accounting for contracts with participating business covers both insurance contracts and contracts that do not transfer insurance risk but reward their contract holders using a participating return, which involves management discretion on the allocation of a specified return from a pool of assets or other similar references.

Under Solvency II the requirements are already clearly set out in the Framework Directive where Article 77 states that in calculating its technical provisions an insurance undertaking should consider, among other items:

> all payments to policyholders and beneficiaries, including future discretionary bonuses, which insurance and reinsurance undertakings expect to make, whether or not these payments are contractually guaranteed, ...

Additional details on this requirement are included in CEIOPS (2009c); in this document CEIOPS advises the European Union legislator to develop level 2 implementing measures that require the estimation of discretionary management actions based on objectivity, realism and verifiability.

The debate on Phase II has not yet reached a final decision on the accounting for participating contracts. Future management discretionary actions under IFRS are not usually part of accounted liabilities until such time when management has made its decisions to transfer resources to third parties or an unconditional obligation arises to force management in that direction.

CEIOPS (2009c) explains in Paragraphs 3.3 and 3.4 that the calculation of technical provisions under Solvency II shall include management's discretionary actions such as an increase of unit-linked charge rates, change of asset allocation and changes in the level of discretionary bonuses.

In the absence of a more recent, tentative decision, we observe that the IASB (2007) included management actions only to the extent that they were "not discretionary" because of the presence of a "constructive obligation". This is a situation that, in spite of not arising from a legal contractual requirement, results in the entity being legally unable to avoid a particular transfer of resources to another party. Management actions favourable to the insurer's interests would be counted under the constructive obligation principle only to mitigate a larger obligation towards policyholders and they would never result in a net benefit to the insurer.

Finally, IASB (2007) did not include a declaration of bonuses beyond the level justified under a constructive obligation and such an approach could potentially result in a lower Phase II liability than under a Solvency II approach that assumes higher discretionary bonuses. This approach was not welcomed by commentators and will be debated by the IASB later in 2009.

Until such debate has taken place it is difficult to foresee the Phase II outcome. One possibility is the adoption of an approach like that of Solvency II, following the narrow definition of equity suggested by the American FASB. Another equally possible outcome in Phase II is to maintain the approach set out in IASB (2007) with a possible disclosure within the equity of the insurer of a surplus, which management might award to policyholders as future discretionary bonuses.

WILL THE TWO NEW REGIMES CONVERGE?

On the surface it appears that both Solvency II and Phase II will be launched around the same time: Solvency II will come into effect on October 31, 2012 and if the Phase II standard is published in July 2011, as is currently planned, it may be effective as early as the financial periods beginning on January 1, 2013. However, we observe that the progress made with Phase II appears to be lacking the necessary field testing that should precede such a significant change in financial reporting. The IASB will be discussing undertaking field testing during 2009.

Solvency II on the other hand, has gone through four QISs and companies are already looking at how they will implement the requirements set out in the Framework Directive and particularly those around internal models and the "use" test. The final vote of the European parliament that approved the Framework Directive in April 2009 has given more certainty to a number of regulators in the European Union. For example in the UK, the Financial Services Authority has continued its plan for a proactive adoption of the regime across UK insurance undertakings that has seen several UK-regulated businesses invest time and money in preparation for the implementation of Solvency II.

Regardless of the differences between the two regimes highlighted in this chapter, their similarities are even greater and there are already tangible opportunities for synergies. Companies could consider the requirements of Solvency II and Phase II in an integrated way to minimise implementation costs and maximise benefits for their business.

In particular, the common ground on the use of unbiased cash-flow estimates for block 1 and the use of observable market interest rates to calculate block 2 is a reasonably clear indicator of substantial overlaps in data and technology requirements, training and awareness programmes and when the insurer plans to design new suites of management information. Planning upfront to achieve these synergies will be essential to ensure a successful implementation of both regimes and build a stronger framework for both risk and financial reporting purposes.

CONCLUSION: ENOUGH CERTAINTY TO PREPARE FOR BOTH

Although considerable uncertainty still exists about the final outcomes of Solvency II and Phase II, we believe that insurers have enough information and indications about how they will operate to start to prepare now for the parallel introduction of the two new systems.

The calculation of the core components of an insurance liability can be carried out using similar bases and models with the possibility to develop adjustments that reflect the differences as they emerge from the parallel refinement of the detailed requirements. Such an approach should avoid the proliferation of different reporting regimes within the entity and the resulting additional costs.

For this reason, companies should consider running Phase II and Solvency II projects in parallel to ensure possible synergies between both regimes are exploited and implementation costs are minimised. This demands an implementation plan that takes into account the requirements of the aims and rules of both regimes, a mechanism to take into account the next steps in the two standard setting processes and a team that combines actuarial, finance and risk management skills.

The benefit of proactive and coordinated project management appears particularly compelling for non-life insurance companies, where liability measurements based on premium reserves and undiscounted outstanding claims reserves with implicit margins are likely to require fundamental rethinking. Systems will need considerable adaptation if insurers are to ensure that disclosure under the new regimes is at least equivalent to the level achieved under the present regimes.

Forward planning for capital adequacy and risk management will become a part of any new strategic venture but the "embedding" requirements as part of business as usual will also affect hedging and reinsurance strategies, product development and pricing, underwriting and investment management. Responding adequately to these new requirements will mean a major shift in thinking for many organisations – and a rigorous and planned approach to bridge the gap between today's standards and those required for 2012.

1 This author completed this chapter before June 15, 2009.

REFERENCES

CEIOPS, 2009a, "Draft CEIOPS' Advice for Level 2 Implementing Measures on Solvency II: Technical Provisions – Lines of Business on the basis of which (re)insurance obligations are to be segmented", Consultation Paper No. 27, March, URL: http://www.knf.gov.pl/Images/090326%20CP27%20draft%20L2%20advice%20TP%20segmentation%20(publconsult)_tcm20-10158.pdf.

CEIOPS, 2009b, "Draft CEIOPS' Advice for Level 2 Implementing Measures on Solvency II: Technical Provisions – Treatment for Future Premiums", Consultation Paper No. 30, March, URL: http://www.knf.gov.pl/Images/090326%20CP30%20draft%20L2%20advice%20TP%20future%20premiums%20(publconsult)_tcm20-10161.pdf.

CEIOPS, 2009c, "Draft CEIOPS' Advice for Level 2 Implementing Measures on Solvency II: Technical Provisions – Assumptions about Future Management Actions", Consultation Paper No. 32, March, URL: http://www.knf.gov.pl/Images/090326%20CP32%20draft%20L2%20advice%20TP%20future%20managmt%20actions%20(publconsult)_tcm20-10163.pdf.

CEIOPS, 2009d, "Draft CEIOPS' Advice for Level 2 Implementing Measures on Solvency II: Valuation of Assets and 'Other Liabilities'", Consultation Paper No. 35, March, URL: http://www.pwc.com/en_GX/gx/financial-services/pdf/ceiops-cp-35-09.pdf.

IASB, 2004, "IFRS 4 Insurance Contracts", International Accounting Standards Committee Foundation, URL: http://eifrs.iasb.org/eifrs/bnstandards/en/ifrs4.pdf.

IASB, 2007, "Preliminary Views on Insurance Contracts", Discussion Paper, URL: http://www.iasb.org/NR/rdonlyres/08C8BB09-61B7-4BE8-AA39-A1F71F665135/0/InsurancePart1.pdf.

IASB, 2009, "IASB Update", International Accounting Standards Committee Foundation, London, May, URL: http://www.iasb.org/Updates/IASB+Updates/2009/2009+IASB+Updates.htm.

3

Building Internal Models: Preparing for Solvency II

Gaurav Kwatra, Stephan Erasmus

Watson Wyatt

Developing an internal model can be a prolonged and challenging process. However, a good quality model can form an important part of a company's risk management toolkit. Not only do rating agencies scrutinise internal models when assessing a company's ability to deliver to debt holders and other stakeholders, but regulators will also soon require companies to have sufficiently detailed and well-documented internal models. Many companies will want to use internal models for calculating regulatory capital when the European solvency regime (Solvency II) comes into force and will therefore seek new model approval by these supervisors.

In this chapter we give an introduction to internal models for the purposes of calculating Solvency II regulatory capital and look at a few important considerations when building the component parts of these models. In the section "Where Internal Models Could Be Used" we consider the uses of internal models. The section following that discusses the main building blocks of internal models and focuses particularly on economic scenario generators (ESGs). The penultimate section emphasises the need for robust governance and the final section concludes. However, first we discuss what exactly an internal model is and how it can be used.

WHAT IS AN INTERNAL MODEL?
An internal model should aid a company, regulators and rating agencies by providing a representation of the company's current

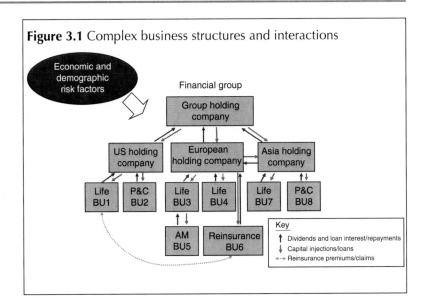

Figure 3.1 Complex business structures and interactions

and future financial position. Companies often have complex structures, consisting of many business units with various reinsurance, loan and service arrangements. A good internal model will allow for the interactions between these various elements as well as interactions with the business, economic and demographic environment (see Figure 3.1).

WHERE INTERNAL MODELS COULD BE USED

A good model should be flexible enough so that it can be applied for different purposes and easily adapted in the future (see Figure 3.2). Solvency II introduces the concept of a "use test" for companies' internal models (Council of the European Union 2009, Article 118). To obtain supervisory approval in the Solvency II regime an internal model needs to be embedded into a company's risk culture. There are a range of areas where most companies need to improve their practices to ensure that their models aid management decision making, for example the model could be used to set a quantitative risk appetite. A model should also aim to provide information sufficiently quickly and frequently to support short-term decision making. This might require more sophisticated modelling techniques such as replicating portfolios or control variates.

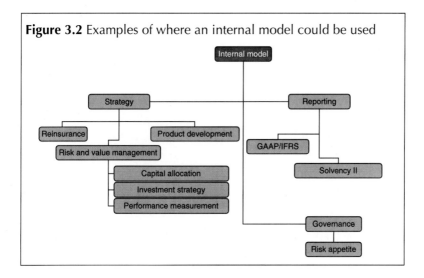

Figure 3.2 Examples of where an internal model could be used

THE BUILDING BLOCKS OF AN INTERNAL MODEL

There are three main building blocks when considering internal model development (see Figure 3.3):

- data;
- calculation; and
- reporting.

There will be a trade-off between accuracy of the model's representation of reality, which is exceedingly complex, and its practicality and transparency. We consider each of these areas in more detail.

Building blocks: data layer

Data can be seen as the cornerstone of a good internal model. Supervisors will need to be able to verify that data is accurate, complete and appropriate for the purposes of modelling following the implementation of Solvency II (CEIOPS' Internal Model Expert Group 2009). Poor quality data could seriously hamper how regular internal model results are used. A good place to start is therefore data collection, validation and, if necessary, cleansing.

Data inaccuracies may lead to significant bias in estimates. Checking procedures should therefore be established, where for example outliers, clustering or unreasonable entries are identified and analysed. Quality checks should also be performed to ensure consistency when data is being used for different purposes. In the

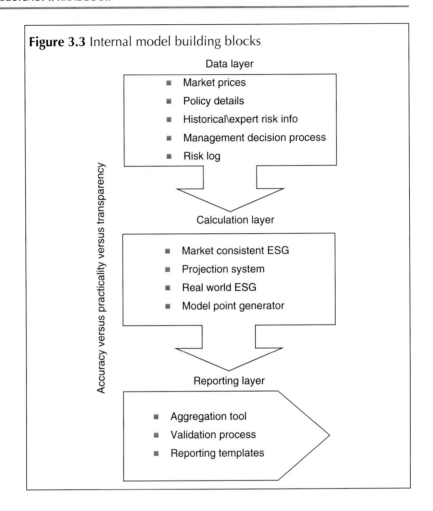

Figure 3.3 Internal model building blocks

absence of reliable information or to guarantee a more forward looking view, expert opinion may be necessary.

Data requirements can broadly be split into the following main areas.

Data layer: asset and liability information
This includes mainly policyholder data as well as information on asset holdings and market prices of assets. It is therefore essential that a company has efficient and reliable data storage systems and process controls, as well as adequate documentation of those systems and processes (Council of the European Union 2009,

Article 123). There will also be a trade-off between the granularity, availability and cost of collecting data. Data collection at a level that is too granular may introduce the risk of further data errors.

The available asset information should be compared against the modelling requirements. Up-to-date market prices will be required when calibrating models, and there may be situations where current market data has to be adjusted. For example, as will be discussed under the calculation layer, it may be necessary to adjust option prices provided by investment banks to avoid discontinuities when constructing the implied volatility surface.

Data layer: risk environment

The Solvency II Framework Directive proposed statistical quality standards for internal models (Council of the European Union 2009, Article 119) require that data sets used in the calculation of probability distribution forecasts should be updated at least once a year. Both historical risk information and expert judgement should be drawn upon when setting assumptions and modelling the risk environment. It is important that robust assumptions are built into the model, especially following the recent credit crisis, which has shaken the confidence of stakeholders in the accuracy of many crucial assumptions.

Apart from using internal data, historical data will in many cases need to be obtained from public sources or external suppliers. This data will need to go through a company's normal quality checking procedures. Where historical data is lacking, companies may have to extrapolate from the available data set or even use models to simulate data.

Table 3.1 summarises some of the main sources of risk exposure data.

Data layer: management decision making and risk logs

Effective risk information should assist the risk management function of a company to identifying, monitoring, managing and mitigating the risks to which the company is exposed. There needs to be a clear distinction between those risks relevant to the day-to-day management of a business and those risks which, if they were to materialise, would lead to significant capital requirements.

Table 3.1 Summary of the main sources of risk exposure data

Risk type	Modelling methodology	Sources of risk data
Market	Statistical model	Historical data can be used to fit probability distributions. An alternative is to use an externally supplied ESG.
Credit	Statistical model	Only limited historical data may be available to fit distributions. Bootstrapping methods can be used to extrapolate the limited available data or third-party models could also be used.
Life insurance	Expert opinion and quantitative	A combination of industry data and own experience should be used. Expert views are often used for mortality risk, since historical data may not be sufficient when, for example, estimating future mortality improvements.
Non-life insurance	Quantitative and qualitative	An analysis of own experience as well as market or industry experience could be used. However, information may not be available on new risks or new classes of business. Experience on low-frequency and high-severity risk is also often very limited. Third-party catastrophe risk models are typically used.
Operational	Scenario testing	Some companies make use of internal loss databases or risk registers. More often internal scenario analyses or operational risk factors, applied to premiums or reserves, are used. Industry-wide databases, where they exist, may also be a useful source.
Correlations	Quantitative and qualitative	Data on extreme adverse conditions is generally scarce. Quantitative data should generally be available for market risks, but correlations would usually be set largely on a qualitative basis for other risks.
Liquidity and strategic	Scenario testing	Historical scenarios, for example events where market liquidity dried up are often used.

A risk register could assist the risk management function in meeting its objectives, by giving information on, for example:

- the type of risk;
- the impact of the risk if it were to materialise (before and after mitigation);
- the likelihood of the risk materialising (before and after mitigation);
- mitigation options;
- current mitigants; and
- the owner of the risk.

Workshops could be held involving senior managers and experts from relevant departments to identify and comment on possible future risk scenarios. The scenarios for these workshops could also be used to calibrate or validate the reasonableness of the risk assumptions used in modelling.

Building blocks: calculation layer

Calculation layer: ESGs

ESGs are used in the valuation of complex financial instruments and contingent claims. This aids in the valuation of an insurance company's assets and liabilities such as in market-consistent embedded value (MCEV) and realistic balance sheet calculations, usually by simulating "market-consistent scenarios".

They are also used in the projection of assets and liabilities for capital management purposes such as individual capital assessments (ICAs) and economic capital calculations, which is achieved using "real-world scenarios".

Market-consistent scenarios are produced using ESGs the parameters of which are calibrated to the observed market prices of financial instruments such as options and bonds. Model parameters for real-world scenario models are usually calibrated by reference to the historical data.

In practice, both market-consistent and real-world ESGs suffer from limitations.

In some markets, owing to the unavailability of data (risk-free yields or implied volatilities), interpolation, extrapolation or other approximation techniques are used. For example, determining the

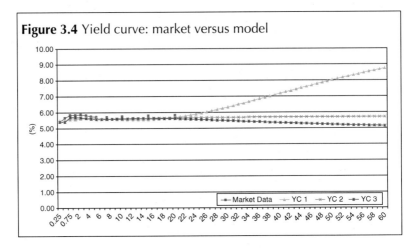

Figure 3.4 Yield curve: market versus model

shape of the risk-free yield curve after the longest maturity point is a subjective topic.

Risk-free yields: Figure 3.4 shows the smoothed yield curve for an emerging market economy. For this particular economy, extrapolating the yield curve for more than 20 years in the future (necessary to value the longest liability cashflows) will be very subjective and the yield curve can take a range of shapes. Different values for the parameters of each of the fitted yield curves result in different shapes at the long end of the yield curve, even though all three yield curves provide an equally good fit to the observed market yields.

Pitfalls for the unwary might stem from misinterpretation of the data supplied and the data required by the model. For example, is the yield curve data from a par curve, zero coupon curve or forward curve? Is it annually compounded or continually compounded? Are the yields bid, mid or ask? The Black–Karasinski model, for example, uses bond prices and the Libor market model requires one year forward rates.

Implied volatilities: implied volatility data also suffers from related issues. Extrapolation/interpolation, similarly to market yields, may be necessary where volatility for various terms is missing. In the absence of a deep and liquid market, the implied volatility data may not be appropriate or may already have been interpolated/extrapolated by the data provider. In those cases, it may be necessary to look into several other factors to come up

Figure 3.5 Equity martingale test

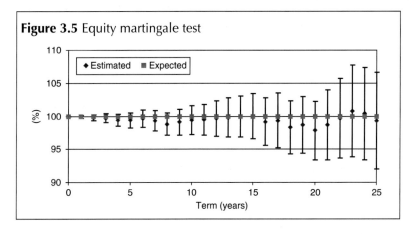

with a smoothed estimate, such as historical volatility, relevant economic factors and comparisons against countries with similar sovereign risk. Also, different investment banks might quote different figures. If there is access to more than one source, then it may be appropriate to use a mean or a median of the quoted volatilities. In addition, there might be a risk that the resulting calibration could change simply as a result of a change in the data source. Another common mistake is to use volatility derived from one index (say the FTSE 100) to model another equity index (such as FTSE All Share), or to ignore any potential adjustments when using volatilities relevant to options for the calibration of total return volatility.

For market-consistent scenarios, it may be the case that the scenarios generated do not produce a close fit to the observed market prices of particular financial instruments. One of the reasons for this inconsistency is simply due to the poor calibration to the volatility surface or the market yields, which then leads to the mispricing of those assets.

Testing the calibration: the robustness of ESGs can be tested using asset martingale tests, which validate that the return distribution of any asset has the basic properties of a risk-neutral valuation set-up, ie, the average of the discounted rolled-up asset payouts equals its current value. Figure 3.5 shows the results of an equity martingale test for a developed economy. It indicates that the expected value of the asset lies within the confidence level of the estimated martingale values. The martingale test can be considered to "fail" if a drift

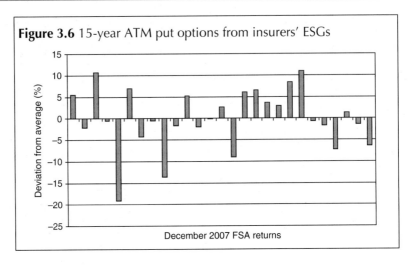

Figure 3.6 15-year ATM put options from insurers' ESGs

(upwards or downwards) is present. In that case the calibration process should be checked for obvious mistakes before signing the model as being market inconsistent. On a related issue, it is important to run the ESG for a considerable number of simulations (2,000 or more) to ensure convergence; and to run the ESG for different random seeds as some of the random seeds may fail the martingale test.

Another question that is frequently asked is how does one define market consistency? In the UK, realistic balance sheet firms have to report the modelled value of a number of benchmark assets, priced using their ESG scenario sets. Figure 3.6 shows the deviation from the average value for a number of UK realistic balance sheet insurers, when calculating the market value of a 15-year at-the-money (ATM) put option on the FTSE All Share index from their ESGs. This potentially illustrates the inconsistencies in calibrating to market data that currently exist, although some firms may technically claim that the model calibration was less good at the 15-year ATM level in order to ensure a better fit to the duration and moneyness of their liability guarantees. Solvency II may set a tougher standard.

Issues for real-world ESGs: judgement plays an important role when selecting and fitting a real-world ESG. A major issue with real-world ESGs is that of selecting appropriate initial assumptions for each asset model. Historical data may not be available for all asset classes and for all of the economies, for example, historical

UK credit spread indices date by rating is only available from the late 1990s. In cases where a long series of historical data is available, a decision needs to be made as to whether it would be more relevant only to use part of the full series of data. For example, it may be decided to only use interest rate data from the period after the Bank of England's Monetary Policy Committee gained independence (in 1997) to set interest rates.

Given the variety of models available, the question also arises as to which model is the most appropriate to use; either an unconditional or a conditional model could be chosen. This is particularly topical at the time of writing with credit spreads and equity implied volatility reaching historical highs in some markets. For interest rates, it may be appropriate to look into models that capture more than one type of movement in the full-length yield curve.

In terms of distributional assumptions, the data series (or the residuals thereof) could be tested for normality using an appropriate statistical test such as Anderson–Darling test or simply by looking at the QQ plot or the histogram. In cases where these tests indicate non-normality, different distributions should be tested and fitted.

Once the appropriate model has been selected, its parameters need to be fitted to the data. The most common estimation processes are maximum likelihood estimation or least-squares estimation. The use of goodness-of-fit tests such as Student's t test for the parameters or Akaike information criteria or Schwartz Bayesian criteria and F tests are appropriate for evaluating the overall fit of the model.

Every model and statistical method or process has advantages and drawbacks, however the aim should be to have models that are easy to fit and calibrate and, most important of all, understood by everyone using it to make decisions.

Calculation layer: modelling complex concepts
Owing to the complex nature of the environment that a model tries to capture, there will inevitably be numerous difficulties. A few of the more common complications include modelling:

- management actions;
- policyholder behaviour; and
- complex organisational structures and interactions.

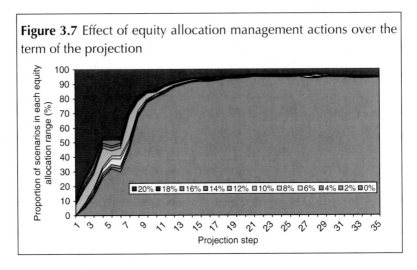

Figure 3.7 Effect of equity allocation management actions over the term of the projection

A number of simplifications will be required to allow for these complications, but care should be taken that these simplifications are suitable and the appropriate sensitivity tests should be carried out.

Management actions: modelled management actions need to be the same as the management decisions that will be implemented in practice. Figure 3.7 shows how the management action decision rules used by one insurer quickly lead to a projected 0% proportion of assets invested in equities in a high percentage of the scenarios. This was felt to be inappropriate and was adjusted accordingly.

Policyholder behaviour: models often have to allow for policyholder behaviour when evaluating product options and guarantees. Currently, this is not an area modelled in great detail by many companies recognising that there will be a trade-off between realism and materiality.

There is usually only limited data available to estimate potential policyholder behaviour, especially in extreme scenarios. Assumptions regarding policyholder behaviour will therefore need to be monitored and updated regularly. Examples of dynamic policyholder behaviour that could be modelled include lapses or guaranteed annuity option exercise. These decisions will in-turn be influenced by, for example, economic conditions or the degree of option moneyness.

Complex organisational structures and interactions: decisions will also need to be taken on the type of projection system and sophistication of modelling. Capturing the exact tax treatment will require a complicated approach, but might not add much additional benefit. In some circumstances it may therefore be more appropriate to settle for approximations when modelling tax or other complex values.

Many group companies might currently assume that there is no constraint in transferring capital from one entity to another. However, allowing for the legalities of moving capital between sub-funds or business units may have a significant impact on group risks. When modelling fungibility of capital, further consideration will also need to be given to the speed of capital transfer, frictional cost and the impact on the group's strategy and the recent financial crisis has thrown a spotlight on some of these issues (CRO Forum 2009).

The Framework Directive proposal's article on statistical quality standards implies that the modelling of dependencies between risks will be vital in receiving approval for an internal model. The "correlation matrix approach" is still the main method used by many companies to aggregate capital and allow for risk interdependencies. However, a small but increasing number of insurers go further to replace linear correlations with copulas. Scenario testing will also be an important tool to gain insight into the interaction of risks and the impact on solvency.

Calculation layer: model points
Model points can be used to represent large portfolios of business and can therefore significantly reduce run-times. When choosing model points, it is important to ensure that they are representative of the portfolio of business in a range of scenarios rather than just the best-estimate position. A common problem is that model points are often not retested following the application of an ICA or an economic capital stress scenario and may no longer be appropriate.

Building blocks: reporting layer
Solvency II is likely to have three main areas of reporting, requiring first an overview of the business and its performance, second reporting on quantitative requirements and finally reporting on

the system of governance (CEIOPS 2008). Under the quantitative requirements section a company would need to clearly state the basis, methods and assumptions used in modelling. For internal models this will tie in with the documentation standards set out in the Framework Directive proposal (Council of the European Union 2009, Article 123).

Apart from supervisory reporting, a model will also be used when reporting on an accounting basis or reporting to senior management. Ideally a company would need a single model that covers all reporting functions (for example, a model that can be used in both the MCEV and Solvency II calculations). It is therefore important that the model is transparent to supervisors, the public as well as those using the model.

Aggregation of results and non-linearity: careful consideration needs to be given to the communication of results, result validation, aggregation and any allowance for non-linearity. Many companies use the correlation matrix approach to calculate the benefits of diversification in their ICA. This involves generating a number of stresses, each at the 99.5th percentile level, and feeding the resulting capital requirements through a correlation matrix. Correlation of various risk factors can be estimated from various stress conditions as appeared in past history, which can then be used to aggregate the capital required. Alternatively, copula functions that are a much more sophisticated way of capturing increased dependence in the tails, can be used.

One drawback of this method is that, without adjustment, it fails to explore the impact of a number of risks occurring at the same time: the non-linearity effect. It assumes a linear relationship between capital and stress levels (see Figure 3.8).

Figure 3.8 shows that, for the particular with-profits policy that we have chosen, the relationship between the level of the equity stress and the resulting capital requirement is distinctly non-linear. In particular, for very large equity falls the resulting capital requirement increases quite sharply.

Non-linearity is not just a feature associated with the underlying with-profits guarantees; it can also manifest itself as a result of:

- management actions (for example making charges to asset shares in certain circumstances);

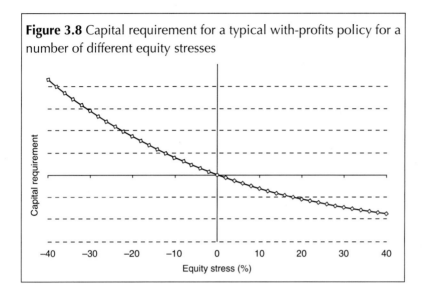

Figure 3.8 Capital requirement for a typical with-profits policy for a number of different equity stresses

- smoothing claims values (and potentially recycling past smoothing costs);
- hypothecation of assets to liabilities in each of the stresses; or
- the interaction of two or more stresses acting together.

Moreover, correlation does not change over time and works only under the assumption that the corresponding risk factors have an elliptical distribution. The results from the aggregation should therefore be validated by scenario testing, which might identify a non-linearity effect between risks. Firms then tend to apply a non-linearity scaling factor to adjust the results.

INTEGRATION WITHIN AN ORGANISATION AND GAINING MODEL APPROVAL

An internal model will need to be supported by a robust governance structure framework. This will require firms to identify and clearly allocate responsibilities like internal model development, assumption setting and approval within its organisational structure. There should also be a clear link with other functions in the organisation, like for example risk management and corporate decision making.

Companies wishing to secure internal model approval will need to begin engaging with supervisors soon, if they have not already started, building confidence in the models and supporting processes. Those companies should become familiar with the approval process and draw on the relevant guidance. With the deadline for Solvency II implementation drawing near, internal models should be at the top of many companies' agendas.

CONCLUSION

In this chapter we have highlighted the most important issues that insurance companies face in developing their internal models. Internal model development can be split into three main areas including data, calculation and reporting. Each of these areas requires detailed attention and may be subject to various pitfalls and difficulties. Economic scenario generators will play an important role when using stochastic modelling in the calculation layer. However, there are also a number of other complex modelling issues, such as management actions or policyholder behaviour that need to be considered. Care should be taken in the approach used to aggregate internal model results.

We have shown that internal models have a wide range of uses. However, to be able to gain approval for using internal models for the calculation of the solvency capital requirement under Solvency II reporting companies will need to comply with a range of standards including validation, statistical quality, calibration, documentation and the use test and demonstrate that a sound risk management process is in place. We expect internal models to develop apace.

REFERENCES

Council of the European Union, 2009, "Directive of the European Parliament and of the Council on the taking-up and pursuit of the business of Insurance and Reinsurance (Solvency II)", URL: http://register.consilium.europa.eu/pdf/en/09/st07/st07820.en09.pdf.

CEIOPS' Internal Model Expert Group, 2009, "Stock-taking report on the use of internal models in insurance", URL: http://www.ceiops.eu/media/files/publications/reports/Stock-taking-report-on-the-use-of-Internal-Models-in-Insurance.pdf.

CRO Forum, 2009, "Internal models benchmarking study", URL: http://www.croforum.org/publications/20090130_resource/File.ecr?fd=true&dn=crofintmodelbms30jan09.

CEIOPS, 2008, "Supervisory Review Process and Undertakings' Reporting Requirements", Issues Paper 18/08, URL: http://www.ceiops.eu/media/docman/public_files/consultations/CEIOPS-IGSRR-18-08%20Issues%20Paper%20on%20SRP%20and%20Reporting-final.pdf.

4

Using Internal Models to Determine the Solvency Capital Requirement: the Regulatory View

Paolo Cadoni[1]

Financial Services Authority

The past two decades witnessed remarkable advances in financial engineering and financial innovation. These innovations in financial products have also given rise to some new challenges for market participants and their supervisors.

To help fulfil their mandate to monitor and protect the safety and soundness of the financial sector, over the past decades, supervisors have focused on requiring market participants to improve their risk control frameworks. Risk-sensitive capital standards, the development of improved risk management practices and the greater role that an undertaking's own internal model (for the measurement and management of risk) are allowed to play in the definition of capital requirements, both in insurance and banking, are examples of this shift.

Solvency II is fundamentally redesigning the capital adequacy regime for European insurers and re-insurers and will be effective from October 31, 2012. The new rules continue this trend, placing demanding requirements on an undertaking's risk management. It establishes a solvency system that is better matched to the risks of each (re)insurance undertaking than the current regulations are. The new framework will be based on a three-pillar approach comprising:

- quantitative requirements for measuring capital adequacy (Pillar I);

- qualitative requirements (Pillar II); and
- increased transparency and reporting requirements (Pillar III).

This new regime uses a "total balance sheet approach", considering both assets and liabilities and aims to improve risk management and reward good practice. Solvency II establishes two levels of capital requirements:

- a lower-level minimum capital requirement (MCR), which is the threshold below which the authorisation of the (re)insurance undertaking shall be withdrawn; and
- an upper level, ie, the solvency capital requirement (SCR), which is the level below which an insurer will be subject to a much-heightened supervision.

The SCR should deliver a level of capital that enables a (re)insurance undertaking to absorb significant unforeseen losses over a specified time horizon and gives reasonable assurance to policyholders that payments will be made as they fall due. It should cover as a minimum insurance, market, credit and operational risks. It shall correspond to the value-at-risk (VaR) of the basic own funds of a (re)insurance undertaking subject to a confidence level of 99.5% over a one-year period.

Under Solvency II, undertakings will be able to calculate the SCR using a "standard formula" or their own full internal model as approved by the relevant supervisory authorities. Solvency II also allows undertakings the option of using a partial model, with some components of the standard formula (module or sub-modules/all or only major business units) replaced by results from an internal model. Compared with the banking regime (ie, the Basel II/CRD framework), Solvency II allows significant design freedom in the choice of methods, assumptions and calculation of correlations for internal models.

Although detailed requirements for the internal modelling framework have not been finalised and agreed yet,[2] the principles contained in the Solvency II directive are already clear. For further details please refer to Article 118 of the Solvency II Framework Directive.

This chapter will explore the evolution of the regulators thinking on internal models for (re)insurance undertakings. It will also provide an indication and rationale for the requirements that (re)insurance undertakings will have to satisfy to get their models approved for use to determine capital requirements under Solvency II.

WHAT IS AN INTERNAL MODEL?

When dealing with internal models, it is useful to distinguish between:

- internal models in a narrower, quantitative, statistical sense (ie, the calculation kernel); and
- internal models in a broader sense of being an integral part of a firms' enterprise risk management framework.

To this end, it is very helpful to compare and contrast the definitions provided by the International Actuarial Association (IAA, for further details please refer to IAA 2008) and the CEA-Groupe Consultatif (for further details please refer to CEA-Groupe Consultatif 2007). According to the IAA an internal model is defined as a "Mathematical model of an insurer's operations to analyse its overall risk position, to quantify risks and determine the capital to meet those risks" whereas, according to the CEA-Groupe Consultatif an internal model is defined as "A risk management system developed by an insurer to analyse the overall risk position, to quantify risks and to determine the economic capital required to meet those risks".

While these two definitions share some important characteristics (ie the analysis of the overall risk position, the quantification of risks and the determination of the capital to meet these risks) the scope, coverage and integration of these two types of models is rather different.

The narrower mathematical or actuarial view of the internal model is the system that transforms risk exposure data (how many contracts of which type are written) and risk driver data (historic information on the likelihood of certain events) to forecasts of profit and loss distributions. In practice, an undertaking may use a collection of models that make predictions for the profit and loss at different levels of aggregation, for further details please refer to CEIOPS (2006).

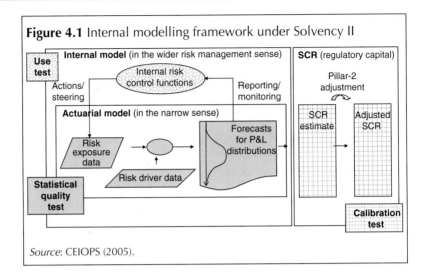

Figure 4.1 Internal modelling framework under Solvency II

Source: CEIOPS (2005).

However, this narrower view imposes some constraints. To produce a social optimum from the regulator's point of view, the interests of the market and the regulator need to be aligned. The only effective way to achieve this objective and reduce regulatory arbitrage is to align regulatory capital requirements more closely to undertakings' own assessment of economic risks by providing them with the right incentives to employ models in a prudent manner. Therefore, from a regulatory perspective, the internal model should be more than this mechanistic process and much closer to the definition of internal models in a wider risk management sense. It should also encompass the way in which the mathematical or actuarial model is integrated with the internal risk management system. Integration demonstrates that the actuarial model is genuinely relevant to the management of the business and has not been developed simply to satisfy regulatory requirements. The approval of the internal model applies in this broader context, rather than focusing solely on the mathematical and/or actuarial techniques to arrive at the forecast distributions or the single regulatory capital number (see Figure 4.1).

The Solvency II directive does not provide a definition for an internal model. It only sets the requirements that a (re)insurance undertaking has to satisfy to be able to get its internal modelling framework approved for use to determine its capital requirements. While at first sight this may be perceived as a deficiency of this new regulatory regime, this should be interpreted rather as an advantage. In line with the Solvency II philosophy, this allows for a higher degree of flexibility encouraging (re)insurance undertakings to define and tailor their internal modelling framework in accordance with their needs, risk profile and potential uses.

To this end, it becomes extremely important that (re)insurance undertakings think carefully about the scope, coverage and integration of their internal modelling framework within their risk management before submitting their application for approval to their supervisory authorities. As will be explained later, while a correct a definition of the scope and coverage of the internal modelling framework may enhance the ability of the (re)insurance undertaking to operate in the market, an incorrect one, on the other hand may impose significant constraints.

WHAT ARE THE EXPECTED BENEFITS OF AN INTERNAL MODEL UNDER SOLVENCY II?

The development of internal models can potentially deliver a wide range of benefits to supervisors, undertakings and ultimately policyholders. For example, while the Solvency II standard formula may be appropriate and easy to implement for (re)insurance undertakings without complex or highly unique risks, it cannot by definition reflect all the characteristics specific to any (re)insurance undertaking operating within the European Economic Area (EEA). Internal models can overcome some of the drawbacks related to the standard formula, but require expertise and resources for parametrisation, model building, validation, interpretation and communication. Integrating an internal capital model into key enterprise business processes can turn what is perceived to be a regulatory burden into a competitive advantage.

First of all, an internal modelling framework integrated into the risk management system and tailored to the needs, risk profile and uses of the (re)insurance undertaking allows for an improved risk sensitivity of the SCR. This leads to, amongst other things, a more adequate modelling of non-standard, especially non-linear, contracts, a better evaluation of the company's risk profile and related reinsurance and investment strategies in the context of the undertaking's risk appetite. Consequently, this would lead to an evaluation of returns on risk-adjusted capital for individual business segments, a deeper understanding of the relative contribution of the major categories of risk (non-catastrophe losses, catastrophes, reserve, credit and market) to the company's risk profile and ultimately a better allocation of capital.

Moreover, the high degree of modelling freedom allowed by Solvency II, not only strives to achieve a better alignment of regulatory capital to economic capital, reducing the regulatory burden on firms, but more importantly it also aims to encourage the innovation of risk measurement and continuous improvement of management methodologies leading again to an enhanced assessment of the (re)insurance undertaking's risk profile and capital allocation. This, in turn, is likely to translate into an improvement of policyholder protection.

The use of an internal model may also lead to a more effective Pillar II type of discussion with the supervisory authority. For example, (re)insurance undertakings that apply the standard formula are likely to follow a sequential approach. First, they would calculate the Pillar I capital requirements by applying the standard formula and only in a second time, they would proceed by accurately identifying the risks they are exposed to by preparing the Pillar II Own Risks and Solvency Assessment (ORSA). On the other hand, (re)insurance undertakings that have opted for the internal modelling route are bound to follow a different process. The design and development of an internal model requires a deeper understanding of the (re)insurance undertaking business and risk profile at inception. First of all, they would need to identify the risks they are exposed to and only subsequently, through the modelling activities, would they proceed to measure and quantify them.

Overall, this may lead to a realisation of cost efficiencies through reuse of a risk modelling infrastructure for discussion with other external parties such as supervisors, rating agencies, analysts and shareholders.

THE APPROVAL PROCESS: WHAT DOES THIS MEAN IN PRACTICE?

The approval process aims to assess if the (re)insurance undertakings' internal modelling framework can be used to calculate the SCR. This process requires undertakings to demonstrate compliance with several mandated tests and requirements. For example, amongst other things (re)insurance undertakings need to give evidence that:

- the internal model is able to calculate the SCR;
- the systems concerned for identifying, measuring, monitoring, managing and reporting risk are adequate;
- the use test, statistical quality, calibration and P&L attribution, validation, documentation, external models and data standards have been met; and
- any potential inter-relation between these requirements has been properly considered.

Moreover, if the application refers to a partial internal model the (re)insurance undertaking needs also:

- to justify the limited scope of the model (ie, provide evidence that there is no cherry picking);
- to demonstrate that the resulting SCR reflects more appropriately the risk profile of the (re)insurance undertaking; and
- to provide evidence that the partial internal model can be fully integrated into the SCR standard formula.

As undertakings' internal models may be extremely complex and varied, this would require supervisory authorities to spend a significant amount of time reviewing the internal modelling framework against the requirements before deciding on the application. However, the Solvency II directive imposes a tight timeframe of six months after receipt of a complete application, during which supervisory authorities can reach a decision on the internal model's application. To facilitate this task and to ensure that the approval process for both the undertaking and its supervisory authority is conducted in an efficient, co-ordinated and effective manner, supervisory authorities have complemented the typical approval process with the introduction of a non-mandatory pre-application stage. Therefore, under Solvency II, the process that may lead to the approval of models for use in calculating the SCR has been structured as follows:

- pre-application;
- application;
- assessment; and
- decision.

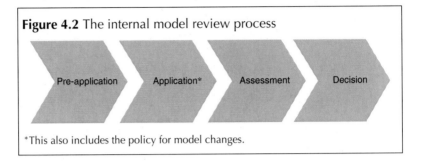

Figure 4.2 The internal model review process

Pre-application Application* Assessment Decision

*This also includes the policy for model changes.

Pre-application

This stage should precede the formal application, although it is not mandatory for a (re)insurance undertaking intending to apply for internal model approval.

The pre-application process aims to deliver a wide range of benefits both to supervisory authorities and (re)insurance undertakings. On the one hand, this would allow supervisory authorities to better plan resources for assessing the internal model, providing them with an opportunity to familiarise themselves with the undertaking's internal models over a longer time period, making the assessment stage more straightforward. On the other hand, it should enable undertakings to review and discuss with the supervisory authorities any elements of the internal model that may require further work before making a formal application. In essence, this stage may involve similar activities to those to be carried out during the application and assessment stages.

This stage should conclude with a supervisory view on how prepared the undertaking is to submit the formal application. This should also include a view on the scope of application of the internal model and a time schedule for the submission of the formal application.

Undertakings' participation in the pre-application process is particularly relevant for those firms intending to use internal models to calculate the SCR starting from October 2012.

Application and model change policy

The formal approval process begins with the (re)insurance undertaking's submission of a cover letter requesting the approval of the internal model to calculate the SCR (ie, the "application"). This letter must be supported by a set of documents (the "application pack") that should provide evidence that the internal model meets all the mandated tests and requirements. The required minimum documentation that should accompany the application is divided into:

- a cover letter requesting approval;
- the scope of application and model coverage (both for full and partial internal models);
- a description of the (re)insurance undertaking risk management process (with particular emphasis on the internal model) and risk profile;
- a self-assessment identifying the strength and limitations of the internal modelling framework and demonstrating compliance with the regulatory requirements;
- a description of the technical characteristics and structure of the internal model and its components (eg, assumptions, choice of distributions and/or dependencies);
- a description of the of external models and data used by the undertaking (eg, economic scenario generators, cat-scenarios generator), including evidence that supports the suitability of these components;
- a description of the internal model governance, system and controls, including documentation;
- a copy of the relevant organisation charts;
- a copy of an up-to-date independent review/validation report;
- the policy for changing the full and partial internal models and other policies for internal model governance;
- the plan for future model improvement; and
- an assessment of the economic capital and the SCR derived from the internal model.

The six-month period for taking a decision on the application begins on the date the relevant supervisory authorities are satisfied that they have received an application that is complete with respect to the signatory, content, minimum requirements, all the other essential aspects and it does not raise any significant doubt of non-fulfilment on this regard.

Policy for model changes
Modelling should be seen as a cycle of continuous assessment and evaluation of the soundness and fit-for-purposeness of the chosen

method. It is good practice for undertakings to update their internal models, and supervisory authorities expect them to, for example, update methodologies to reflect improved techniques. Taking into account the lessons learnt from the Basel II framework, Solvency II has introduced the requirement for undertakings' to set, *a priori*, their approach for dealing with changes to their model (ie, a policy for model changes), which is part of the undertaking's application pack. The rationale behind an approved model change policy is to facilitate the dialogue between undertakings and supervisory authority. Responsibility for creating such a policy rests with the undertaking.

There is a close link between the scope of the model change policy and the scope of application of the internal model. In fact, the scope of application of the internal model provides the boundaries for the model change policy. Undertakings should pay particular attention to this detail as an inappropriate definition of the scope and coverage of the internal modelling framework may impose significant constraints in the future. A good policy should not impede good modelling practice and reflects the need for supervisory authorities to be aware of changes and to be able to satisfy themselves that the internal model still complies with the requirements. In any case, having a policy for model changes is a good discipline and should form part of the internal model governance of the undertaking.

When developing their policy, undertakings are required to assign model changes into two categories: major and minor changes. Major changes are subject to prior supervisory approval, whereas minor changes are only subject to a reporting requirement.

Assessment

During the assessment, supervisory authorities analyse and assess the information submitted by the (re)insurance undertakings as part of the application. This may also include supplementary information provided by the (re)insurance undertaking or requested by the supervisory authorities.

The assessment is likely to be iterative with feedback to undertakings resulting in modifications to their models. Depending on the materiality of such changes and improvements, the six-month period may be either suspended or reset. For example, if minor

Figure 4.3 Policy for model changes

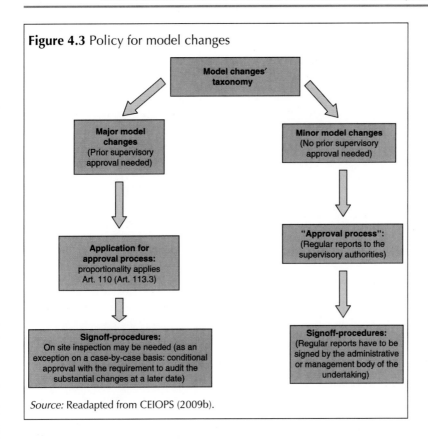

Source: Readapted from CEIOPS (2009b).

changes to the internal modelling framework are required, the six-month period may be suspended and start to run again upon receipt of the new documentation. On the other hand, if major modifications to the internal modelling framework are needed, then the six-month period may be stopped and reset. A new six-month period then restarts upon receipt of a new application.

The assessment comprises a technical review of the model (ie, its scope, design, build, integrity and applications), its coverage and ability to calculate the SCR for the undertaking, documentation, the risk management process, senior management role and their understanding of the model. The issues that supervisory authorities are expected to assess may be broken down further into the following:

- the scope and coverage of the model (both full and partial internal models);
- the methodology and documentation;

- data quality;
- quantitative procedures;
- qualitative procedures; and
- the technological environment.

What is important to note is that this process aims not only to assess how the internal model meets the Solvency II requirements in isolation, but it also considers any potential inter-relation between these requirements. The review process therefore includes the necessary steps and tools to ensure supervisory authorities are able to satisfy themselves that these requirements are met or otherwise.

The internal model assessment may include the following processes:

- Desk-based review of the information submitted by the undertaking as part of the application and any additional information provided by the undertaking or requested by the supervisory authorities.
- On-site inspection(s) of the internal model and its use, including interviews with senior management and the board.
- Requests for further information as appropriate.
- Ad hoc conversations by phone and email to clarify points.

Decision

The Solvency II internal modelling framework envisages three types of decision: approval, "limited approval" and rejection.

Approval

When the supervisory authorities have examined the application and assessed the model of the undertaking, and have considered that all requirements have been met, then supervisory authorities shall approve the use of the model for calculation of the SCR.

In this case, the undertaking shall use the internal model to calculate the SCR as soon as it is approved by the supervisory authorities, or from a later date as set out in the decision or permission document from the supervisory authorities.

In some cases, the approval may be subject to terms and conditions. For example, in line with the principle of proportionality, some model components and/or modelling approaches may be entirely adequate and appropriate to capture the risk profile of the undertaking as long as the nature, scale and complexity of the risk borne by the undertaking is limited, but not if this significantly increases. In these cases, a model may be approved, but subject to the condition that if the nature, scale and complexity of that particular risk significantly changes, a more appropriate modelling approach has to be applied.

The imposition of terms and conditions linked to the approval of an internal modelling framework is not an arbitrary decision by the supervisory authority. In fact, when determining terms and conditions supervisory authorities have to consider:

- how realistic it is for the terms and conditions to be fulfilled by the undertaking by a particular date (if any); and
- whether compliance by the undertaking with those terms and conditions can be assessed in an objective and straightforward way (by the supervisory authorities).

If the internal model approval is subject to terms and conditions, supervisory authorities may require the undertaking to submit a plan indicating the necessary steps to meet the terms and conditions.[3]

Rejection
If the assessment of the undertaking's application shows that the internal model has not met the minimum requirements, the supervisory authorities shall reject the application and the undertaking shall use the standard formula to calculate the SCR.

If supervisory authorities reject an undertaking's application for approval to use a full or partial internal model to calculate the SCR, they may enforce, on the basis of reasons communicated to the undertaking, a "waiting period" before the undertaking can submit a new application. This period is intended to provide the undertaking with time to appropriately address the shortcomings in the original application.

Limited approval
Supervisory authorities may also reject the undertaking's application for approval to use a broader scope internal model (eg, a full

internal model) and approve only those parts of the internal model that satisfy the Solvency II requirements (ie, a reduced scope approval). This third type of decision is aimed to recognise the efforts made by the undertaking in developing parts of the internal model without compromising the protection of policyholders.

In this case, the undertaking has to calculate the SCR by using the internal model only for those parts that have been approved by the supervisory authorities. For the business units and/or risk modules for which the internal model has not been approved, the standard formula has to be used to calculate the SCR.

Supervisory authorities shall only grant this "limited approval" if the parts of the model function indeed as a partial internal model, that is they comply with the specific provisions for partial internal models.

THE USE TEST

A fundamental requirement to qualify for an internal model approach to determine regulatory capital requirements is that the undertaking demonstrates to its supervisors that there is sufficient discipline in its internal model development and application such that it is "widely used and plays an important role in" the course of conducting its regular business, particularly in risk management. From a regulatory perspective, the use test philosophy boils down to the following: if an undertaking does not trust its model sufficiently to use it, why should the supervisor?

In this context, the use test (for further details please refer to Cadoni and Sharma 2008) can therefore be defined as a sort of "psychological contract" between the undertaking and its supervisor as there is a direct relationship between the degree of modelling freedom allowed by the internal model regulatory framework and the evidence the undertaking has to provide to satisfy the use test. In other words, the higher the modelling freedom, the higher the test that the undertaking has to meet to comply with this requirement. The rationale is that supervisors can take additional comfort in that an internal model is appropriate, if it is widely used and plays an important role in how the undertaking measures and manages risk in its business. In fact, if undertakings are not provided with the right incentives to employ models in a prudent manner, regulators must face the problem that undertakings have no reason to build models that measure the risks of interest to the regulator and there would be incentives to minimise capital requirements rather than produce accurate measurement of risks. Moreover, undertakings would have fewer internal incentives to keep the model and its parameters accurate and up to date. In contrast, the employment of internal models in internal decision-making creates a discipline to ensure sufficient quality and adequate robustness of the internal model and of the data fed into it, because inappropriate models would lead undertakings to poor business decisions.

The onus must be on the undertakings to document how they comply with the use test. This means providing evidence that the internal model reflects the realities of the business and the way in which the undertaking is managed. The "use test" itself must look at the processes by which the undertaking links the internal model to its business decision-making, in terms of both inputs to and output from the model. Internal use of a model, as a whole or in part, should be sufficiently material to result in continuous pressure on the quality of its components. In an undertaking that meets the use test, supervisors would, among other things, expect to see evidence of internal challenges to the accuracy, robustness and timeliness of the model resulting from any direct or indirect employment for strategy and planning processes, exposure management and reporting. Key decision-makers within the undertaking will need to be able to demonstrate their understanding of the key elements and results from the internal model. In particular, the undertaking must be able to demonstrate that they use the same engine for regulatory capital and business purposes.

INTERNAL MODEL GOVERNANCE
A robust governance framework is a prerequisite for the efficient and effective working of an organisation. According to the Solvency II Framework Directive, (re)insurance undertakings need to have an adequate and transparent organisational structure with clearly allocated responsibilities that should among other tasks, support the implementation of an effective risk management and internal control systems. This ensures that the management and control of operations are undertaken in a sound and prudent manner. These principles apply across the organisation and are

particularly relevant for internal models (for further details please refer to CEIOPS 2009c).

Internal model governance is part of the overall governance system and it is an important mitigant for model risk: the risk that the internal model does not reflect the risk profile of the business of the (re)insurance undertaking, or produces results that are misleading because of unreliable model assumptions or techniques.

While the undertaking's administrative or management body is responsible for the overall governance of the internal model, the "ownership" of the internal model rests with the risk management function. In fact, the Solvency II framework allocates to the risk management function responsibilities for:

- designing and implementing the model;
- documenting the model and any subsequent changes made to it;
- informing the administrative or management body about the performance of the model, suggesting areas needing improvement and up-dating and on the status of efforts to improve previously identified weaknesses; and
- analysing the performance of the model and producing summary reports thereon.

A feedback loop to link the high-level governance requirements with the more detailed governance requirements around the internal model is necessary. This provides the mechanism to pass the detailed information on the running of the internal model to the administrative or management body, who are responsible for high-level governance. In turn, they will make decisions about the future developments of the internal model and pass these to the risk management function for implementation.

In essence, the model governance should encourage the organisation of a dialogue between every user of the model and the risk management function about the characteristics of the internal modelling framework to increase understanding of the model and its outputs. This should lead to proposals for improvement of the model, enabling it to better reflect the risk profile of the undertaking.

STATISTICAL QUALITY STANDARDS

The statistical quality standards aim to ensure that the methodology, components and inputs underlying the model are sound. The standards apply to:

- the methodology used to select, fit and, where appropriate, combine statistical distributions (probability distribution forecasts);
- data quality;
- model dependencies and diversification effects;
- risk mitigation techniques;
- the treatment of financial guarantees and options; and
- future management actions.

Solvency II refers to a "probability distribution forecast" underlying the model and defines this as a mathematical function, which assigns to an exhaustive set of mutually exclusive events a probability of realisation. This assists in deriving the economic capital and the regulatory SCR would be a further key output of the internal model. However, although Solvency II does not prescribe methods for assessment of the probability distribution forecast, there is a requirement to use adequate actuarial and statistical techniques. By "adequate" is meant mathematically sound and reflective of the potential severity of the risks being examined. The methods used by the undertaking to calculate the probability distribution forecast must also be consistent with those used to calculate technical provisions, demonstrating the importance of linking reserving activities with the capital measurement function.

Undertakings may choose from a variety of approaches to derive the probability distribution forecast. These can range from a fully stochastic capital model (where each assumption is modelled using a simulation approach based on a statistical distribution) to a scenario-based approach (where the assessment of economic capital requirements is based on a series of extreme scenarios). Such approaches may be focused on the key drivers of the undertaking's risks, with a more simplistic approach applied for other, less complex and less risky elements, in line with the proportionality principle. In fact, an undertaking's chosen modelling approach must be considered in relation to the nature, scale and complexity of the risks it faces. This principle applies within an undertaking's internal model, such that a undertaking might model significant complex risks in more detail than smaller less complex risks.

High-quality data is essential for modelling. Solvency II puts a particular emphasis on data requirements. Undertakings seeking internal model approval need to have accurate, complete and appropriate data, as well as be able to justify any assumptions and judgement. To this end, Solvency II also requires undertakings to set out their own policy on data quality. This policy, which is subject to supervisory approval, sets out the overall data quality framework with the aim to facilitate the dialogue between undertakings and supervisory authorities with respect to the data quality assessment. Undertakings should pay particular attention to this requirement as anecdotal evidence suggests that the current quality of data in many European undertakings may fall short of Solvency II requirements (for further details please refer to CEIOPS 2009a). Moreover, as the internal model provides a projection into the future of the undertaking's finances, even an undertaking with complete historical data has to consider what adjustments may be required to reflect current and future conditions.

Undertakings using internal models have to justify the use of correlations, aggregations and dependencies, as well as any diversification benefits achieved in their assessment of capital requirements taking also account of any fungibility restrictions. Undertakings should recognise that co-dependencies between risks are not consistent throughout the distribution, in particular, co-dependency is likely to be substantially higher in the tail of the distribution (and indeed, may not exist at all at lower levels). It would be desirable if undertakings reviewed (on an ongoing basis) the most recent academic or industry developments on the subject (eg, copulas, correlation matrices and tail adjustments), in order to consider the most appropriate approach for their internal model.

Many undertakings already identify the major methods (such as reinsurance, hedging of market and credit risks, securitisation) that they use to manage and mitigate risk and the threats to the effectiveness of that risk mitigation. Undertakings should be prepared to provide evidence about the impacts of such risk mitigants on capital requirements, especially under stressed scenarios.

Solvency II also allows undertakings to include the effect of future management actions in their assessment of the internal model SCR. Where management actions have been allowed for, the undertaking should be able to quantify the impact of these management actions and demonstrate the circumstances in which they would be implemented.

CALIBRATION STANDARDS
Under Solvency II, (re)insurance undertakings using an internal model to calculate their SCR may derive the SCR using a different time period or risk measure to that set out in the directive as long as they can demonstrate to the supervisory authorities that policyholders and beneficiaries are provided with an equivalent level of protection.

The use of a different time period or risk measure does not exempt the undertaking from complying with any of the internal model requirements set out in the Solvency II framework. The choice of the time period or risk measure used for internal modelling purposes has to be both appropriate and justified. In particular, if the time period used is different from one-year, the undertaking has to:

- demonstrate that all significant risks to which it is exposed over a one-year period are properly managed;
- pay particular attention to the choice of the data used; and
- justify the choice of time horizon (if different from one year) in view of the average duration of the liabilities of the undertaking, of the business model and of the uncertainties associated with longer time horizons.

Where some reconciliation is needed between the outcomes of the internal model and the SCR, the SCR calculation has to be consistent with the methods used for internal purposes.

The undertaking has to demonstrate to the supervisory authority the equivalence set out in Article 120 of the Solvency II Framework Directive at least annually, but also when there are significant events or changes to its risk profile. On the one hand, if the reconciliation process shows that the capital held by the undertaking is lower than the SCR calculated using a VaR at 99.5% over a one-year horizon, the undertaking has to hold additional regulatory capital to make up this difference. On the other hand, if the capital held by the undertaking is greater than the SCR calculated using a VaR at 99.5% over a one-year horizon, the excess is considered free capital.

If the SCR cannot be derived directly from the probability distribution, the undertaking has to:

- explain how it rescales risks and justify that the bias introduced when doing so is immaterial; and
- explain the shortcuts used to reconcile the outputs of its internal model with the distribution of the basic own funds, if any.

Moreover, if the undertaking is using for economic capital calculations a time horizon longer than one year, it has to:

- show that any probable situation of negative net asset value happening earlier than the time horizon is properly taken into account; and
- justify the particular assumptions made to adequately take into account any temporal dependency effects.

All the other internal model requirements apply *mutatis mutandis* to the approximations used for the purposes of calibration. Undertakings have to compensate for the approximations made by additional provisions. In particular, the assumptions underlying those approximations have to be thoroughly tested against alternative assumptions in line with the validation standards.

Supervisors may require undertakings to run their internal model on relevant benchmark portfolios or using external assumptions whenever they have concerns about the calibration of the internal model and the adequacy of its specification. This may occur during the approval process or as part of the ongoing supervisory review process. In particular circumstances this request may apply to the whole market (or segments of it).

Should the test's results raise questions about the appropriateness of the calibration of the internal model and of its specifications, its consequences may encompass the rejection of the model or one of the actions set out in Article 116 (1) of the Solvency II Framework Directive.

PROFIT AND LOSS ATTRIBUTION

Solvency II requires undertakings to review the causes and sources of profit and loss for each major business unit. Undertakings must perform this analysis at least annually and show how the risk categorisation in the internal model explains the sources and causes of profit and loss. The profit and loss (P&L) attribution should make the causes and sources of profit and loss transparent. This requirement has a particular relevance for both strategic (use test) and validation reasons.

Its link with the use test is evident as the results of the P&L attribution exercise provide information that has to be used for the system of governance (including the ORSA, risk management, limit setting, allocation processes). Its link to validation (and validation tools) is related to the fact that this requirement should allow the undertaking to assess whether a model is adequately predictive in light of its experience. In fact, the P&L attribution should provide information as to whether the risks in the internal model are complete, and whether there are any material risks in the risk profile of the undertaking that are not represented in the internal model. A large part of profit and losses that is unexplained may be symptomatic of the fact that not all material risks are covered by the internal model. This, in turn, may imply that more risk factors need to be considered.

Sources and causes for the attribution process should be granular enough to allow the identification of weaknesses of the internal model. For example, any indication implying that the internal model's risk categorisation does not reflect the undertaking's risk profile has to be escalated to the administrative or management body. If further quantitative and qualitative analyses confirm these results, then the model shall be further developed accordingly.

VALIDATION STANDARDS

Internal model validation (for further details please refer to Cadoni 2009) is possibly the most important step in the model building sequence. It should be good practice for undertakings to review and validate their internal models, demonstrating that appropriate risk and capital management processes are in place. Supervisory authorities would also expect them, as part of the internal model design, to include a regular cycle of validation and necessary updates of the internal model.

However, it is perceived that quite often industry validation practices tend to be weak, particularly when the total capital adequacy of the undertaking and the overall calibration of the model is an important consideration. Once approved, improving internal models is seen by undertakings as a cost of doing business, a compliance hurdle, rather than a source of potential business benefits. It is recognised that validation is challenging when it requires evaluation at high quantiles of loss distributions combined with data scarcity and complex dependencies between distributions. Nevertheless, from a regulatory perspective, weaknesses in validation practices might result in undertakings operating with inappropriately calibrated models. Similarly, inadequately implemented validation should be of some concern to investors (and rating agencies).

Validation is important as it provides evidence that an internal model works as planned, ie, it meets its intended requirements in terms of methods employed and results obtained, addresses the right problem and provides better information about the system being modelled. Validation is concerned with the predictive properties of internal models. These models embody forward-looking estimates of risk and their validation is intimately bound up with assessing those estimates. For an internal model to be accepted and used by management to inform its decision-making, it must first be understood to be a robust representation of prospective risk, not just at an undertaking's level but at a component and sub-component level. To this end, validation should enable the undertaking to better understand the internal model's capabilities and limitations, and that the internal model and the processes supporting it are adequate and appropriate for the purpose.

It must be emphasised that validation should be viewed as an iterative process, not a one-off event, by which an undertaking using an internal model periodically refines validation tools in response to changing market and operating conditions. Similarly, it is important to recognise that there is no single method, and the structure of the validation approach naturally depends on the purpose of the internal model and its intended use. Typically the validation process amounts to a series of attempts to invalidate the internal model. The end result of this process is not a validated model, but rather an internal model that has passed all the validation tests.

Appropriate validation should allow the undertaking to quickly identify problems in the model and help the undertaking to fine-tune the internal model for optimal performance. For example, an internal model may embody assumptions about relationships between variables or about their behaviour under periods of stress. Validation strives to assess with a certain degree of confidence that the assumptions are appropriate. Securing this outcome is likely to involve a range of people within an undertaking, including some not traditionally involved in capital management and modelling activities.

Validation should encompass both quantitative and qualitative elements. While it might be possible to think of validation as a purely technical/mathematical exercise in which outcomes are compared with estimates using statistical techniques, it will likely be insufficient to focus solely on comparing predictions to outcomes. In assessing the overall performance of an internal model, it is also important to assess its components as well as the structures and processes around it.

Finally, to achieve an effective validation, objective challenge is essential. Independent model validation can help financial institutions evaluate and verify the overall performance of internal models. Proper independence of the validation function will therefore be important, whether internal or external. Individuals performing the validation must possess the necessary skills, knowledge, expertise and experience. For some undertakings, use of external validation, at least in part, may be a suitable approach. In this case, undertakings should demand that these external validators help their staff build validation expertise, so that the undertaking can run the validation process itself in the future. Regardless of the undertaking's control structure, internal audit should have an oversight responsibility to ensure that validation processes are implemented as designed and are effective.

There is a wide range of tests/tools that may be used to validate an internal model. As a rule of thumb, the more tests that are performed, the more comfort that validation is able to provide in terms of sufficient evidence for or against the appropriateness of the model. Conversely, where fewer tests of validation are used, the level of comfort diminishes. This is because each validation

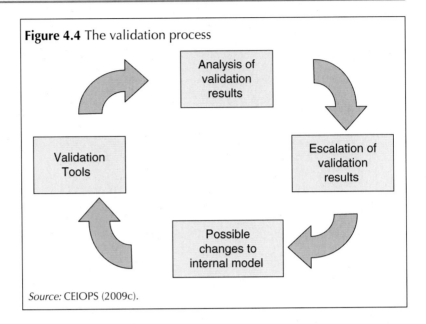

Figure 4.4 The validation process

Analysis of validation results

Escalation of validation results

Possible changes to internal model

Validation Tools

Source: CEIOPS (2009c).

test provides evidence for (or against) only some of the desirable properties of a model.

While some validation tools may prove especially useful and appropriate, it is recognised that there is no panacea of a test that would be the universal tool that can be used for all risks, portfolios and lines of business of all firms. Regulatory guidance (for further details please refer to BCBS 2008 and CEBS 2005) thus far has stressed the importance of a comprehensive effort, encompassing both quantification and management. The inference is that a firm's validation should seek to go beyond a simple regulatory "box-ticking" exercise, reflecting internal management priorities and covering all material aspects of the internal model environment. For example, validation should at least include the following.

1. An evaluation of the internal model role, structure, implementation and design.

    *   Use test: what role does the model play within the firm? Does the firm trust its model sufficiently to use it to inform its decision-making? If not, why should the supervisor?
    *   Systems implementation: has the model been implemented with integrity? Have production-level risk measurement

systems been through extensive testing prior to implementation (eg, user acceptance testing, checking of model code etc)? Is there an appropriate model version control system in place?

- Verification of the effectiveness of the model operations with the establishment of key performance indicators.

2. A review of conceptual and theoretical soundness of model assumptions, inputs (including data and expert judgment), outputs, functions and overall methodology.

- Qualitative review: does the model work in theory? Does it incorporate the appropriate risk drivers? Is the theory underpinning it conceptually well founded? Is the mathematics of the model robust?
- Validation of inputs and parameters.
- Data quality checks: what processes are in place to strive to ensure that the data used to develop, validate and operate the model is complete, accurate and appropriate (eg, data collection, storage and cleaning processes, reviews of the extent of proxy data, scaling processes, verification of transaction data)?

3. An identification of critical elements of the firm's methodologies, processes, procedures, controls and quantitative systems.

- Assessment of gaps with respect to internal standards, best industry practices and/or regulatory standards.
- Examination of assumptions – sensitivity testing: to what extent is the model sensitive to the underlying statistical assumptions (eg, specific distribution(s), dependency structure(s)), structure and formulation?
- Model replication: to what extent can the outputs be replicated by running the model with a different set of random numbers (or an independently developed algorithm)? How different are the results obtained?
- Stress and scenario testing: to what extent is the model sensitive to a specific event and/or a movement in a set of financial variables? What is the most likely event that will lead to the firm not having sufficient funds available (reverse stress testing or probability of ruin)?
- Assessment of how the model captures business environment changes (eg, acquisitions, new product platforms).

4. A review of the internal model's historical and relative performance.

- Backtesting: how well does the model forecast the distribution of outcomes?
- Benchmarking and hypothetical portfolio testing: for example, are the model results for a portfolio comparable with those of a similar portfolio, or those of publicly available data (eg, rating agency model, industry-wide models, consultancy firms, academic papers and regulatory capital models)?
- P&L attribution: how do the causes of actual profit and loss compare with the risk drivers in the model?
- A comparison of the actual results against the firm's risk tolerance.

5. An evaluation of the governance structure and current validation activities.

- Management oversight: has senior management been involved in the validation process? Did they review the outputs from the model? Do they use the internal model results in business decisions? What are the roles of the key stakeholders responsible for ensuring the ongoing performance of the internal model?
- Policies for model governance: has the firm put in place the policy document or documents that set out principles and standards for the mitigation of internal model risk. The document(s) typically describe the procedures that the institution requires to be followed for developing, maintaining and using the internal models (eg, policy for model changes, validation policy, data policy).[4]
- A review of the ongoing monitoring of internal model and surrounding processes.

6. A review of the documentation.

Finally, a comprehensive validation report should outline the gaps in the firm's existing validation activities and provide recommendations for improvement in terms of methodology, system development, control processes and data-related procedures, etc.

In the context of Solvency II, there are a number of different components to validation that undertakings should take into account in developing and implementing an internal model. More specifically, there should be a regular cycle of model validation and necessary updates to the model, which includes:

- monitoring the performance of the internal model;
- reviewing the ongoing appropriateness of its specification;
- testing its results against experience;
- an analysis of the model stability;
- testing the sensitivity of the results to changes in key underlying assumptions;
- an assessment of the accuracy, completeness and appropriateness of data used by the internal model; and
- a process to evidence that the resulting capital requirements are appropriate.

The validation standard links to the use test, and in particular to the requirement for the undertaking's senior management to be responsible for the continued appropriateness of the model. The validation standard also links to the responsibilities of the undertaking's senior management with respect to having in place systems that ensure the model operates properly on a continuous basis.

Responsibility for the design and continued adequate operation of the internal model is the responsibility of the board and is linked to the risk management function. In practice, it is a key challenge for the board to consider the nature of the validation process adopted and how their responsibilities might be delegated and reported back. This includes the responsibility for the validation process and regular management information on the validation of the internal model being presented to the board and challenged by it, as well as to satisfy themselves that model documentation is adequate enough to allow independent validation of the internal model.

To this end and to also take into account the lessons learned from the recent financial turmoil, Solvency II puts particular emphasis on strengthening firms' stress testing and validation governance frameworks. The concept of "reverse stress testing", ie, of the event or scenario most likely to cause their current business model to become unviable, is considered essential by regulators. The aim is to ensure that firms more fully explore "tail risks", which, if they were to crystallise, would cause counterparties and investors to lose confidence in them. A firm needs to be more aware of its business model vulnerabilities when making strategic business decisions, when contingency planning and when considering its risk management arrangements.

Solvency II also introduces the requirement of an internal model validation policy subject to approval of the supervisory authorities. This aims to reinforce the link between validation and internal model governance. This should describe the procedures, including allocation of responsibilities, sign-offs and escalation paths, which the institution is required to follow for the ongoing validation of the internal model.

DOCUMENTATION STANDARDS

Documentation is a crucial tool for undertakings to demonstrate to their supervisory authorities that they understand and have mastered the internal model and its use. This represents a key assessment element in the supervisory approval process.

Under Solvency II, undertakings are required to set out a detailed account of the theory, assumptions and the mathematical and empirical basis underlying the internal model. However, the Solvency II framework does not prescribe the media to be used for documentation. Therefore, (re)insurance undertakings might consider innovative ways of documenting, using electronic media in addition to paper-based documentation (for further details please refer to CEIOPS 2008).

Documentation of internal models should be thorough, sufficiently detailed and complete enough to allow an independent knowledgeable third party to understand the design and operational details of the internal model, to assess the reliability of the model and its compliance with the regulatory requirements.

It is important to stress that, as often happens, documentation should not be left to the final part of the internal model development process. It would be desirable if undertakings addressed any documentation gaps as part of their design and development of the internal model. The rationale beyond this common sense suggestion is clear. One of the main risks that an undertaking using its own internal model faces is that key persons might leave. It would clearly be a serious setback for an undertaking to lose the persons who designed, implemented, used and updated its internal model. Undertakings where these functions are performed by a small number of staff are more vulnerable to this risk. Particularly in these situations, the depth and thoroughness of the model documentation (eg, the historical development of the model and references to papers and other research that have informed the model design) is critical.

Proportionality does not exempt undertakings from adequately documenting their internal models. For simpler models, this might result in a smaller amount of documentation. However, this should be a consequence of the level of complexity of the model, and not of the thoroughness of the documentation.

The documentation has to demonstrate that all levels of management understand the relevant aspects of the internal model. To this end, the granularity of the documentation has to take into account the level at which it is intended to be used (eg, board-level information might differ from the more detailed, technical documentation needed by the actual model builders).

Undertakings are required to document where the model does not work effectively. This will show that the undertaking really understands the limitations of its model; there may be circumstances that the model cannot reflect, for example, extreme market circumstances beyond quantifiable levels or future (unknown) changes in legislation affecting claims payments.

The documentation of the design and operational details of the internal model has to be timely and up to date.

(Re)Insurance undertakings need to have documented policies, controls and procedures in place for the management of the operational details of the internal model, including written responsibilities and accountabilities. These have to be clearly understood by all incumbents. The documentation has also to include a list of all documents held that the (re)insurance undertaking considers relevant for the internal model, as well as where and how these documents can be accessed.

The documentation has to contain explicit information about data storage. This may include a general description of the databases, clear dictionaries that provide definitions of data items, description and construction of the databases, processes used to obtain and load the data, data consistency aspects, filters used to create and debug the database and security and maintenance information.

Finally, any relevant testing and validation done in relation to model changes made has also to be documented.

EXTERNAL MODELS AND DATA

Solvency II allows (re)insurance undertakings to use "model or data obtained from a third-party". This is as acceptable as the development of in-house tools and this is recognised by the Framework Directive (see Article 124). However, the use of model components or data obtained from a third party does not exempt undertakings from complying with the internal models requirements.

Use of external model components and data underlines the importance of management, control, documentation and operational transparency – all of which can be more difficult when using external data or an external model. When external model components and/or data play a material role in deriving and validating risk estimates, it is important that undertakings clearly articulate what role these products play in the estimation process and the extent to which these products are used.

Integration of external models and/or outsourced modelling activity into the undertaking's own capital model is a key area of interest for supervisors, especially with regard to appropriateness to their business, transparency, correlation with other risks and associated sensitivity and scenario testing. To this end, undertakings should explain the rationale for choosing third-party products over internally developed model and data. They have to be able to explain the alternatives considered and the decision taken for a particular external model component or data.

(Re)Insurance undertakings have to demonstrate a thorough understanding of external models and data used in their internal model processes. This encompasses an in-depth knowledge of the methodological underpinnings and basic construction of the external model, including an understanding of the models' capabilities, limitations and appropriateness. Undertakings have also to demonstrate a full understanding of the effect and significance of the proprietary elements in the external model components.

The use of external models and data has to be appropriate to the nature and complexity of the risks incorporated within (re)insurance undertakings' own risk strategy, business objectives, modelling methodologies, availability of internal data and suitable for use within their internal model. There should be a reasonable

Figure 4.5 Information to be received by the supervisory authority

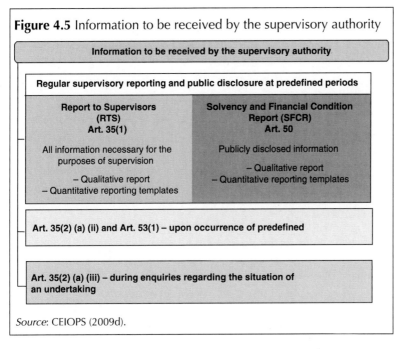

Source: CEIOPS (2009d).

degree of consistency between model inputs and the risk drivers of an undertaking's type of business, as well as a reasonable comparability between the data that was used for building the model and the undertaking's risk profile characteristics.

(Re)Insurance undertakings need to have clearly articulated strategies for validating and regularly reviewing the performance of external model results and the integrity of external data used in their internal risk quantification processes. When the developmental evidence is less than fully transparent as in the case of external model components, undertakings have to rely more heavily on alternative validation approaches. Since external model parameters are likely to have been calibrated using external data, it is critical for undertakings to test the performance of external models against internal portfolios or exposures.

Finally, (re)insurance undertakings have to recognise and document the risks arising from the use of external data and models.

SUPERVISORY REPORTING AND PUBLIC DISCLOSURES

"Pillar III" covers the supervisory reporting (RTS)[5] and public disclosure (SFCR)[6] aspects of the regime; for further details please refer to CEIOPS (2009d). This is the information undertakings are required to report to the supervisory authority and the information to be publicly disclosed to the market. Supervisory reporting requirements aim to support the risk-oriented approach to insurance supervision while, on the other hand, public disclosure requirements aim to reinforce market mechanisms and market discipline, by acting as a strong incentive to undertakings to conduct their business in a sound and efficient manner, including an incentive to maintain an adequate capital position that can act as a cushion against potential losses arising from risk exposures.

Both the RTS and the SFCR should contain a qualitative report, including quantitative data, where necessary, and quantitative reporting templates. Both reports should be designed as stand-alone documents and follow a similar structure.

Solvency II requires undertakings to submit to the supervisory authorities information:

- at predefined periods (regular basis);
- upon occurrence of predefined events; and
- during enquiries regarding the situation of the undertaking.[7]

Public disclosure and SFCR
Solvency II sets out the minimum content of information that undertakings are required to publicly disclose and establishes requirements on the updates to be provided on the disclosed information following major developments. As there are various ways an internal model can be constructed, implemented and operated, public disclosure requirements on internal models are to the extent possible based on principles having regard to harmonisation of reporting and comparability issues between undertakings.

To enable different market participants to assess the internal model and make use of the information, the level and depth of information to be publicly disclosed is based on the principle that a knowledgeable person can get a reasonably good understanding of the design and operational details of the internal model as well as to the reliability of the internal model, for example, disclosure of information related to the purpose, results, key decisions taken, etc, as a result of the use of its internal model.

Public disclosure is not required to the extent the information on internal models would prejudice to an unreasonable degree the commercial interest of the undertaking or if there are obligations to policyholders or other counterparties that bind the undertaking to secrecy or confidentiality. However, where non-disclosure of information is permitted by the supervisory authority, undertakings shall state this in the SFCR and explain the reason for this.

When an internal model is used for calculating the SCR, the information contained in the SFCR should be divided into qualitative and quantitative information, for example:

1. Qualitative information:

   - governance and risk management,
   - use,
   - scope and model coverage,
   - risk measure, confidence level, time horizon and basic own funds,
   - methodologies, including assumptions and aggregation,
   - data,
   - risk mitigation activities,
   - operational performance,
   - validation activities, and
   - documentation.

2. Quantitative information:

   - solvency capital requirement,
   - comparison and reconciliation, and
   - validation analyses.

Supervisory reporting and RTS

The RTS should contain all the information necessary for the purposes of supervision. The information should be specifically aimed at the supervisor, including all elements (although at a more granular level) set out in the SFCR. The RTS should follow a preset structure and template to facilitate its review and understanding (for further detail see the Appendix). Undertakings or groups using an approved internal model are also subject to further requirements, including amongst other things the reporting of:

- the activities performed during the year to verify the ongoing compliance with regulatory requirements for the internal model;

- analysis of the comparison and reconciliation of the last year's results, including explanations for any material changes in the SCR;
- the causes and sources of profits and losses;
- the plan for future development steps of the internal model;
- the overall solvency needs;
- the information on how capital allocation is done, both for regulatory capital and for the economic capital;
- the reconciliation between economic capital and the SCR for undertakings using different time periods or risk measures other than VaR at 99.5% over a one-year horizon; and
- the information about future management actions used in the SCR calculation.

The quantitative information covered by the RTS in addition to that required by the SFCR should at least contain:

(a) the SCR as calculated by the internal model;
(b) an estimate of the SCR according to the standard formula (if applicable);
(c) the split of undiversified capital charges and any adjustment for the loss absorbing capacity of technical provisions and deferred taxes;
(d) any capital add-on;
(e) the economic capital;
(f) the comparison and reconciliation with last year results forecasts; and
(g) the summary report of the validation results performed during the year.

The information required by points (a) and (c)–(f) has to be provided to the lowest level of granularity at which the model is used. Group internal models also have to provide this information by legal entity. In some cases, supervisory authorities may require undertakings to present the information in point (b) at a more granular level.

CONCLUSIONS

This chapter provides an insight into regulators' thinking on the Solvency II internal modelling framework and some clarification of expectations in light of the Solvency II framework for (re)insurance undertakings.

Internal models are central to regulators' thinking in terms of theoretical underpinning for a public policy approach as well as in practice. When thinking about applying for internal model approval undertakings should pay particular attention to the regulatory requirements and seek to go beyond a simple regulatory "box-ticking" exercise, reflecting internal management priorities and covering all material aspects of the internal model environment.

What is important to note is that the internal model approval process aims not only to assess how the internal model meets the Solvency II requirements in isolation, but it also considers any potential inter-relation between these requirements. The review process therefore includes the necessary steps and tools to ensure supervisory authorities are able to satisfy themselves that these requirements are met or otherwise.

It is essential that the methodologies, components and inputs used by undertakings are appropriate for the internal model and its use and enable them to identify, measure, monitor and report risks adequately.

Finally, complying with the internal models standards is not a one-off exercise. Standards have to be met on an ongoing basis and the bar should raise over time to take into account both internal and external developments. To this end, an ongoing dialogue between undertakings and regulators is essential.

APPENDIX CONTENTS OF THE REPORT TO SUPERVISORS
- Executive summary
- A.1 Business and external environment
- A.1A Objectives and strategies
- A.2 Performance from underwriting activities
- A.4 Operating/other expenses
- A.5 Any other disclosures
- B.1 General governance arrangements
- B.2 Fit and proper
- B.3 Risk management
- B.4 ORSA
- B.5 Internal control

- B.6 Internal audit
- B.7 Actuarial function
- B.8 Outsourcing
- C.1–7: Underwriting risk, market risk, credit risk (to cover both the asset and liability side), liquidity risk, operational risk, ALM risk and other material risks the undertaking may have
- C.8 Material risk exposures
- C.9 Material risk concentrations
- C.10 Risk mitigation practices
- C.11 Risk sensitivities
- C.12 Any other disclosures
- D1–3 Assets, technical provision and other liabilities
- D.4 Any other disclosures
- E.1 The structure and amount of own funds, and their quality
- E.2 Minimum capital requirement and solvency capital requirement
- E.3 The option set out in Article 305b used for the calculation of its SCR
- E.4 Differences between the standard formula and any internal models used
- E.5 Non-compliance with the minimum capital requirement and significant non-compliance with the solvency capital requirement
- E.6 Any other disclosures.

1 The views expressed in this chapter are those of the author and not necessarily those of the Financial Services Authority.

2 Publication of the Committee of European Insurance and Occupational Pensions Supervisors' (CEIOPS) advice to the European Commission on level 2 implementing measures is expected by the end of 2009.

3 Further details and guidance on the subject of terms and conditions is going to be provided by CEIOPS at level 3.

4 Such policies would typically include requirements on topics such as identification of models, categorisation of models according to business criticality and complexity, roles and responsibilities of stakeholders, including ownership and sign-offs required, version control and security, model risk, including ensuring appropriate model structure and parameter estimation, IT risk including data security and business continuity issues, documentation, model review, training, usage, etc.

5 RTS stands for report to supervisors.

6 SFCR stands for solvency and financial conditions report.

7 This may encompass any other information that supervisory authorities might deem necessary during the supervisory review process, using a wide range of methods and formats (eg, questionnaires, request for further information on a specific issue, relevant documents during on-site inspections).

REFERENCES

BCBS, 2005, "Update on Work of the Accord Implementation Group Related to Validation under the Basel II Framework", Basel Committee Newsletter No. 4, URL: http://www.bis.org/publ/bcbs_nl4.pdf?noframes=1.

BCBS, 2008, "Range of Practices and Issues in Economic Capital Modelling", Consultative Document, November, URL: http://www.bis.org/publ/bcbs143.pdf?noframes=1.

Cadoni, P. and P. Sharma, 2008, "Why do Supervisors want the "Use Test" and How to "Measure" it?", Forum Financier, Revue Bancaire et Financier, 8, pp. 454–458.

Cadoni, P., 2009, "Validating Internal Models under the Solvency II Directive", *Journal of Regulation and Risk North Asia*, I(2), pp. 59–65.

CEA-Groupe Consultatif, 2007, "Solvency II Glossary", URL: http://ec.europa.eu/internal_market/insurance/docs/solvency/impactassess/annex-co8d_en.pdf.

CEBS, 2005, "Guidelines on the Implementation, Validation and Assessment of Advanced Measurement (AMA) and Internal Ratings Based (IRB) approaches", Consultation Paper 10, URL: http://www.c-ebs.org/formupload/b1/b1460bb1-ed63-4cd1-9fc5-483b3a5eb2b8.pdf.

CEIOPS, 2005, "Draft Answers to the Second Wave of Calls for Advice in the Framework of the Solvency II Project", Consultation Paper 7, URL: http://www.ceiops.eu/media/files/consultations/consultationpaper/cp_0504.pdf.

CEIOPS, 2006, "Draft Advice to the European Commission in the Framework of the Solvency II Project on Pillar I issues – Further Advice", Consultation Paper 20, URL: http://www.ceiops.eu/media/files/consultations/consultationpaper/CP20/CP20.pdf.

CEIOPS, 2008,"Draft Advice on the Principle of Proportionality in the Solvency II Framework Directive proposal", Consultation Paper 24, URL: http://www.ceiops.eu/media/files/consultations/consultationpaper/AdviceonProportionality.pdf.

CEIOPS, 2009a, "Stock-taking Report on the Use of Internal Models in Insurance", January, URL: http://www.ceiops.eu/media/files/publications/reports/Stock-taking-report-on-the-use-of-Internal-Models-in-Insurance.pdf.

CEIOPS, 2009b, "Draft Level 2 Advice on the Procedure to be Followed for the Approval of an Internal Model", Consultation Paper 37, URL: http://www.ceiops.eu/media/files/consultations/consultationpaper/CP37/CEIOPS-CP-37-09-L2-Advice-Procedure-approval-internal-model.pdf.

CEIOPS, 2009c, "Draft Level 2 Advice on the Implementing Measures with Respect to Article 118 to 124: the Tests and Standards for Internal Model Approval", Consultation Paper 56, URL: http://www.ceiops.eu/media/files/consultations/consultationpapers/CP56/CEIOPS-CP-56-09-L2-Advice-Tests-and-Standards-for-internal-model-approval.pdf.

CEIOPS, 2009d, "Draft CEIOPS' Advice for Level 2 Implementing Measures on Solvency II: Supervisory Reporting and Public Disclosure Requirements", Consultation Paper 58, URL: http://www.ceiops.eu/media/files/consultations/consultationpapers/CP58/CEIOPS-CP-58-09-L2-Advice-Supervisory-Reporting-and-Disclosure.pdf.

Commission of the European Communities, 2008, "Amended Proposal for a Directive of the European Parliament and of the Council on the Taking-up and Pursuit of the Business of Insurance and Reinsurance (Solvency II)", February, URL: http://ec.europa.eu/internal_market/insurance/docs/solvency/proposal_en.pdf.

FSA, 2008, "Insurance Risk Management: The Path to Solvency II", Discussion Paper 08/04, URL: http://www.fsa.gov.uk/pubs/discussion/dp08_04.pdf.

IAA, 2008, "Guidance Paper on the Use of Internal Models for Risk and Capital Purposes by Insurers".

IAIS, 2008, "Guidance Paper on the Use of Internal Models for Regulatory Capital Purposes", URL: http://www.iaisweb.org/_temp/15_Guidance_paper_No_2_2_6_on_the_use_of_Internal_Models_for_regulatory_capital_purposes.pdf.

5

Market-Consistent Embedded Values Within a Solvency II Framework[1]

Kamran Foroughi[2]

Towers Perrin

Life insurance companies have been calculating and reporting embedded values for many years, with recent publications typically using the market-consistent embedded values (MCEV) approach to allow for risk. But with the adoption of market-consistent principles under Solvency II, where does this leave MCEV? In this chapter we compare and contrast the MCEV and Solvency II frameworks and consider the role for MCEV going forwards.

BACKGROUND TO EMBEDDED VALUES

Many life insurance companies regularly produce three forms of published accounts, perhaps uniquely among industries. Companies have to produce returns to regulators, designed to demonstrate the ability of companies to maintain solvency and meet policyholders' claims. Public insurance companies have to publish statutory accounts under local Generally Accepted Accounting Principles (GAAP) rules, for many countries recently under the IFRS banner. Companies also voluntarily produced embedded values (EV), which were designed to give shareholders more meaningful information than alternative approaches.

The origins of EV can be traced back to the 1959 paper by James Anderson entitled "Gross Premium Calculations and Profit Measurements for Nonparticipating Insurance", as discussed in Foroughi and True (2004) and O'Keeffe *et al* (2005). At a time when regulatory rules were based on formulaic approaches to valuation, this paper argued for a valuation and pricing method based on projecting future cashflows using best estimate assumptions and discounting the emerging surpluses using a risk discount rate reflecting the shareholders' required rate of return and the degree of risk in the business being valued. In the intervening 50 years, the key developments for EV have been:

- Wide acceptance of EV as the most realistic measure of value and profit reporting for life insurance businesses.
- The construction of complex computer models, allowing companies to value huge portfolios of business within a relatively short time frame.
- The development of analytical tools showing the drivers of the change in EV over time.
- Public reporting of EV and a gradual move towards common standards.
- The widespread use of EV by company management to measure performance and as a basis of remuneration.

MARKET-CONSISTENT EMBEDDED VALUES

In this chapter we focus on two of the three main forms of financial reporting based on a concept of "market-consistency": Solvency II and market-consistent embedded values (MCEV). Although we do not focus on primary accounting, we note some of the recent developments from the Financial Accounting Standards Board (FASB), the US accounting regulator and from the International Accounting Standards Board (IASB) – particularly the concept of "fair value" – and consider how they may influence the direction of Solvency II and MCEV going forwards.

We note that the application of MCEV predates Solvency II. The MCEV framework was described in Dullaway (2001) and Tillinghast (2003), and the first MCEVs were published in 2003. More recently, on May 5, 2004, the CFO Forum published a set of 12 principles called the "European Embedded Value" (EEV) Principles, a framework for the external reporting of embedded value. The EEV Principles led to significantly greater disclosure requirements and a requirement for a "sufficient allowance for the aggregate risks" in the business being valued. Although the

EEV Principles did not specify how to set the allowance for risk, O'Keeffe *et al* (2005) and Tillinghast (2005) described how the MCEV allowance for risk approach could be used within EEV. The strong trend from year-end 2005 onwards has been for life insurance groups to use the MCEV approach within EEV publications. Key reasons for this include:

- The allowance for risk is more objective.
- The allowance for risk is more granular, giving more meaningful information about segmental results.
- The MCEV approach enables companies to separate investment-related earnings and insurance-related earnings, giving a better insight into the sources of value creation.
- It is easier to achieve consistency between the asset and liability valuation, avoiding accounting mismatches in the profit and loss (P&L) account.

The CFO Forum published "European Insurance CFO Forum Market-Consistent Embedded Value Principles" (MCEV Principles)[3] on June 4, 2008. Upon publication, the CFO Forum pledged a compulsory adoption of the MCEV Principles from year-end 2009. However, the date for compulsory adoption was subsequently postponed from 2009 to 2011, in an announcement dated May 22, 2009. The June 2008 MCEV Principles were revised in a publication dated October 20, 2009. This was driven in particular by the financial crisis; we briefly discuss the implications on the following page.

Solvency II is the project led by the European Commission with the objective of modernising European insurance regulations, by considering a more dynamic risk-based approach to setting regulatory reserves and required capital than had been observed within existing Solvency I regulations. The "Draft Solvency II Framework Directive" was published by the European Commission on July 10, 2007. A major milestone in the process was the agreement of a revised "Framework Directive" by the European Parliament and European Council, put forth in April and May 2009, respectively. The Framework Directive is based on the market-consistent valuation of assets and liabilities.

However, most specific valuation details within this market-consistent framework will be agreed only as part of the level 2 and 3 implementing measures. Ultimately the European Commission will decide on the exact level 2 and 3 implementing measures for Solvency II. During 2009, the Committee of European Insurance and Occupational Pensions Supervisors (CEIOPS) published a series of consultation papers on various aspects of the level 2 implementing measures, although recommendations are not yet final.

COMPARISON OF SOLVENCY II AND MCEV – SUMMARY
Table 5.1 provides a summary comparison of Solvency II and MCEV, based in part on Towers Perrin Updates (2007, 2008, 2009a, 2009b). The rest of this chapter expands upon the issues raised.

IMPACT OF THE RECENT FINANCIAL CRISIS
The financial crisis has reopened the debate on a number of technical issues around the economic calibration within market-consistent valuations, including:

- the choice of calibration asset to set the risk-free rate;
- whether or not to make explicit allowance for asset illiquidity and liability predictability (referred to as liquidity premium);
- whether or not to make explicit allowance for the company's own credit risk; and
- how to calibrate stochastic models used to value embedded options and guarantees.

At the time of writing this chapter it was not clear how MCEV or Solvency II practice may evolve in this area. We briefly discuss these areas below in the section "Technical areas which remain uncertain".

AREAS OF LIKELY COMMONALITY
The following areas of commonality are likely to be observed in Solvency II and MCEV.

Concept and application of market-consistency
Within a market-consistent valuation framework, assets and liabilities are valued in line with market prices and consistently with each other. In principle, each projected cashflow is valued in line with the prices of similar cashflows that are traded on the open market. For example, the cashflows arising from an equity are valued in line with the market price of the equity, the cashflows from a bond in

Table 5.1 Comparison of Solvency II and MCEV – summary

Solvency II	MCEV
Areas of likely commonality	
Concept and application of market-consistency Market-based valuation of both assets and liabilities	
Valuation of assets Likely to follow IASB and FASB fair value proposals, using market values where markets are deep and liquid, but otherwise using mark-to-model values estimating an orderly market price	
Areas of likely differences	
Purpose of the valuation Demonstrate solvency to regulators and policyholders	Demonstrate value and sources of profit to shareholders
Published analysis of movement Developments uncertain; historically, movement of surplus analysed by types of cashflow. Internal models will require analysis of sources of surplus	Analysis of sources of surplus
Technical areas which remain uncertain	
Measurement approach In theory, transfer value, although may consider going concern value in practice	Typically fulfilment or going concern value
Risk-free rate CEIOPS proposal to use government bonds	Historical practice, government bonds or swaps; departure from this practice observed during year-end 2008
Allowance for own credit risk Framework Directive appears to rule out any allowance within policyholder and other liabilities, but open to industry feedback in level 2 consultation	Other liabilities typically valued with an implicit allowance for own credit risk
Allowance for liquidity premium To be determined in level 2 implementing measures	Limited allowance permitted for reasonably predictable liability cashflows when asset markets exhibit significant illiquidity

Table 5.1 Continued

Solvency II	MCEV
Calibrating stochastic models	
Details to be determined	Historical practice to calibrate to market prices of options; departure from this practice observed during year-end 2008 reporting
Best estimate assumptions	
Both Solvency II and MCEV use entity-specific best estimates, actively reviewed at the valuation date, aiming to achieve a probability-weighted mean. Exact details of how to interpret for extreme or asymmetric risks subject to some uncertainty	
Risk margin	
Framework Directive suggests calibration to notional transfer value using "cost of capital" approach; CEIOPS consultation paper proposes 6% "cost of capital" approach	Risk margin typically consists of tax and investment expense frictional costs plus risks not allowed for in best estimates; additional allowance for uncertainty sometimes made
Allowance for future premiums	
Some restrictions may arise	Full allowance

line with the price of that bond, and so on. Furthermore, liability cashflows (which are not usually traded) are valued in line with the traded assets they most closely resemble. A fixed liability due in 10 years would be valued in line with a 10-year zero coupon bond, and an embedded financial option in line with the market price of a similar option.

In practice, a number of short cuts and alternative approaches (eg, certainty equivalent valuation and risk-neutral stochastic valuation) are used. These make the valuation process easier while achieving the objective set out in the preceding paragraph.

Valuation of assets

A good understanding of the approach used to value assets is critical in a market-consistent valuation. This helps to ensure the objective that assets and liabilities are valued consistently.

In principle, both Solvency II and MCEV set the valuation of assets to market value for asset classes that are deep and liquid. However, the recent financial crisis has led to significantly greater illiquidity in a number of asset classes, and this has led to the question of how to set the market-consistent value of illiquid assets.

In April 2009, following feedback from the leaders of the Group of Twenty (G20), the FASB (2009) recommended updating the FAS 157 "fair value" standard to use a mark-to-model approach when markets are no longer orderly. The aim of such an approach is to estimate what the market price would be in an orderly market.

Furthermore, to address feedback from the G20, the IASB (2009a) announced in April a comprehensive and urgent review of both fair values and IAS 39, with a view to implementing amendments by the end of 2009. This led to the publication of IASB (2009b) and IASB (2009c). These contained many areas of similar guidance to FAS 157 and FAS 157-4. These recent developments by both the FASB and the IASB (yet to be finalised) help address the issue of valuing assets in illiquid markets in the "fair value" context; it appears likely that MCEV and Solvency II will follow a similar path.

AREAS OF LIKELY DIFFERENCES
Despite the numerous similarities between MCEV and Solvency II, differences are likely to arise between the two methods of reporting. In this section we explore some of the main potential differences.

Purpose of the valuation
The purposes of the Solvency II and MCEV valuations differ. Solvency II is a framework aimed at informing regulators and policyholders about the solvency of the company, whereas MCEV is intended to provide realistic value and reporting information to investors. As a result, the two frameworks can place potentially different emphasis on certain aspects of the presentation and calculation of an insurance company's results.

Published analysis of movement
One major potential area of difference between Solvency II and MCEV is the form of the P&L account, which is to say the published analysis of movement. While the form of the published analysis of movement has yet to be specified under Solvency II reporting, a best practice form in the case of MCEV was specified in Appendix A of the MCEV Principles. This is reproduced in Table 5.2.

Table 5.2 Presentation of analysis of earnings

	Earnings on MCEV analysis			
	Free surplus	Required capital	VIF	MCEV
Opening MCEV				
Opening adjustments				
Adjusted opening MCEV				
New business value				
Expected existing business contribution (reference rate)[a] [b]				
Expected existing business contribution (in excess of reference rate)[a] [c]				
Transfers from VIF and required capital to free surplus				
Experience variances				
Assumption changes				
Other operating variance				
Operating MCEV earnings				
Economic variances				
Other non-operating variance				
Total MCEV earnings				
Closing adjustments				
Closing MCEV				

[a] This represents the following two components:
- Expected earnings on "free surplus" and "required capital"; and
- Expected change in VIF.

[b] The earnings assuming assets earn the beginning of period "reference rate".

[c] The earnings is the component in excess of the reference rate reflecting the additional return consistent with the expectation of management for the business.

Source: CFO Forum (2008).

A number of features of this presentation, which provide useful information, may not be observable within the prescribed Solvency II P&L account.

- The analysis of MCEV earnings is often used as a measure of performance and remuneration; a split of this analysis into the relevant components of MCEV (free surplus, required capital and value of in force (VIF)) helps to assess any implications on the dividend-paying capacity.

- The separate identification of VNB within this analysis, including a product-level breakdown, provides useful input into decisions on new business pricing and product strategies.
- The analysis of experience variances broken down by source of risk helps to inform the process for setting the best estimate pricing and projection assumptions.

While it remains to be seen whether the Solvency II published analysis of surplus will follow a similar route, such an analysis has not been set out by the Framework Directive or any of the CEIOPS consultation papers to date. It is noted that there is some discussion in the Framework Directive about P&L attribution in internal models, where it states, "insurance and reinsurance undertakings shall review, at least annually, the causes and sources of profits and losses for each major business unit". Further advice on this is provided in CEIOPS (2009d). However, the internal model P&L attribution may not be required for publication.

TECHNICAL AREAS THAT REMAIN UNCERTAIN
Measurement approach and allowance for risk calibration
MCEV Principle 3 states:

> MCEV represents the present value of shareholders' interests in the earnings distributable from assets allocated to the covered business after sufficient allowance for the aggregate risks in the covered business. The allowance for risk should be calibrated to match the market price for risk where reliably observable.

While this does not specify the measurement approach, MCEV approaches to date have generally adopted a going concern "fulfilment" approach to calibration, where the focus is on the cost to the company of fulfilling its obligations. This can also be referred to as a settlement approach.

On the other hand, Article 75(2) of the Framework Directive states:

> the value of the technical provisions shall correspond to the current amount insurance and reinsurance undertakings would have to pay if they were to transfer their insurance and reinsurance obligations immediately to another insurance or reinsurance undertaking.

This appears to indicate a transfer notion of market-consistent valuation that focusses on the cost to the insurer of transferring its liabilities to a third party.

However, it is not clear how the Framework Directive will be interpreted. For example, the International Association of Insurance Supervisors (2007) noted its belief that "any transfer notion would be strongly influenced by the settlement obligations that the transferee would undertake".

Setting the risk-free rate used to discount insurance liabilities

The risk-free rate, referred to by the MCEV Principles as the reference rate, is effectively the yield curve used to discount projected cashflows, which are not affected by investment market movements. The June 2008 MCEV Principles set the reference rate to be "the swap yield curve appropriate to the currency of the cash flows". Most market-consistent EEV publications have tended to calibrate to swap yield curves, although a number of companies have calibrated to a government bond yield curve.

One proposal for determining an appropriate risk-free rate set out in Byrne and Dullaway (2009) and Towers Perrin Update (2009a) is to consider which are the viable calibration assets to use to set the rate, and then choose the one which is most beneficial to the insurer; this is the MCRP approach cited in Table 5.1. A similar "best use" principle can be observed in wider accounting.

The June 2008 MCEV Principles prescribed the use of swap rates, but this decision was changed in October 2009 to permit a liquidity premium adjustment (discussed further on). At the time that the CFO Forum chose to use swaps, market information suggested that this was a good proxy for the risk-free rate; indeed, it had been for a number of years. However, given that significant negative swap spreads (compared with government bonds) have been observable in many markets and durations since September 2008, swaps may be too expensive a calibration asset to use.

Given that alternative low-risk calibration assets may exist that are cheaper, the MCRP approach proposes that companies deliberately use the calibration asset that maximises the MCEV, while meeting key criteria such as being achievable in practice and a good match for the liabilities. At year-end 2008, a number of companies incorporated an upwards adjustment (from either government bond or swap yields) in setting the reference rate. A number of these companies used an MCRP philosophy to justify the adjustment.

In CEIOPS (2009b) set out a number of desirable features of choice of risk-free interest rate, including realism, reliability, high liquidity and no technical bias. Receiving particular emphasis in this consultation paper was no credit risk; this feature seemed to be a key reason behind the tentative conclusions in CEIOPS (2009b) that AAA rated government bonds were the preferred measure for the risk-free rate.

Allowance for own credit risk in the valuation of liabilities

In principle, there is nothing to stop a limited allowance for own credit risk to be made within MCEV, reflecting the limited ability of an insurance company to default on its policyholder provisions. Indeed, the calibration of the reference rate to swaps in the MCEV Principles was accompanied by a recognition that swaps contain a small level of own credit risk. However, given the protection to policyholders arising from the insurance regulatory regime, and the typical higher ranking of policyholder debt over other creditors on wind-up, it would be expected that policyholder debt generally has only a small level of implicit own credit risk.

In MCEV publications to date, companies have generally calibrated the reference rate to government bonds or swaps. It is recognised that neither measure can be considered 100% credit-risk-free, although in normal times perhaps the level of credit risk embedded in these instruments is of very small order. However, at year-end 2008 it may be considered that these instruments would have contained a higher level of embedded credit risk, although much lower than that observed in asset classes such as corporate bonds. Beyond the level implicit within calibration instruments such as government bonds or swaps, no company has disclosed an adjustment to the published MCEV in respect of own credit risk.

Under Solvency II, it appears that own credit risk cannot be allowed for in the valuation of liabilities. The Framework Directive states, in Article 74(1), "when valuing liabilities, no adjustment to take account of the own credit standing of the insurance or reinsurance undertaking shall be made". What is not clear is the interpretation of the phrase "no adjustment"; it is to be hoped that clarity will be provided as part of the level 2 implementing measures.

The Article 74(1) quote above applies not only to the insurance liabilities, but to all liabilities. This could therefore impact the allowance for own credit risk of non-insurance liabilities, such as corporate debt or pension scheme obligations. A strict interpretation of this phrase may lead to no own credit risk being allowable for such liabilities, which would lead to a very prudent regulatory balance sheet.

Market-consistent embedded value has tended to follow the primary accounts in the valuation of liabilities such as corporate debt or pension scheme obligations. Debt has typically been valued at either market value or amortised cost, depending on its classification within local GAAP rules, and pension scheme obligations have often been valued in line with local GAAP or IASB (1998). Such valuations implicitly contain some allowance for own credit risk, leading to a nil profit on day one of a debt issuance.

Allowance for liquidity premium

The June 2008 MCEV Principles did not permit the reference rate to be increased to reflect the possibility of a liquidity premium beyond that inherent in the swap yield. This strict interpretation came under pressure during 2008, as spreads on corporate bonds widened to historically high levels and swap spreads tightened significantly. In response to this, a number of companies incorporated a liquidity premium adjustment in setting the reference rate at the end of 2008.

One approach adopted by some year-end 2008 MCEV publications was an extension of the MCRP concept described earlier. A combination of a corporate bond and credit default swap (CDS) can under certain conditions be considered a viable calibration asset for certain insurance liabilities. The theory behind the use of a corporate bond yield less cost of CDS calibration in an MCEV framework is based on a number of assumptions that would limit its size and scope in practice, set out in Towers Perrin (2009a).

The October 2009 MCEV Principles amended the June 2008 version to permit a liquidity premium adjustment in the reference rate used to value liabilities with "reasonably predictable" cashflows. No guidance was provided in calibrating the liquidity premium adjustment beyond a new G14.1, which states "in evaluating the appropriateness of the inclusion of a liquidity premium ... consideration may be given to regulatory restrictions, internal constraints or investment policies which may limit the ability of a company to access the liquidity premium." The accompanying press release announced that "The CFO Forum is performing further work to develop more detailed application guidance to increase consistency going forward", but did not indicate timing of publication of further work.

The Solvency II Framework Directive does not specify whether an allowance for illiquidity in the valuation of insurance liabilities is permitted, leaving this detail to the level 2 implementing measures. CEIOPS (2009b) states:

> The great majority of CEIOPS believes that the relevant risk-free interest rate term structure should not include an illiquidity premium reflecting certain cash-flow characteristics of insurance obligations. A minority of CEIOPS members do not fully share this view and believe that this issue requires further investigation.

The outcome of this debate is far from certain.

Calibrating stochastic models used to value insurance liabilities

The level 2 implementing measures will provide the guidance under Solvency II with regards to the calibration of stochastic models, as well as the calculation of implied volatility parameters necessary for valuing many options and guarantees. However, it is expected that the underlying theme will be a calibration consistent with market-observable prices and variables.

Although MCEV Principle 15 requires the use of end-period derivative prices wherever possible, MCEV Guidance 15.3 enables "less recently observed measures and expert opinion" to be considered. A number of major companies reporting 2008 year-end MCEVs based implied volatilities on dates other than end December 2008, due to the dramatic increase in implied equity option and implied swaption volatilities during 2008. Reasons provided included a lack of deep and liquid options markets, unusual characteristics in the options markets, dislocated financial markets and a practical inability to calibrate to higher volatilities.

The direction in this regard for both MCEV and Solvency II is not clear, but perhaps asset valuation developments can be used in the context of valuing insurance option liabilities. Recent "fair value" developments propose that arguments to adjust values away from observed market prices should be based on evidence that orderly market prices would differ from observed market prices, and not on the unusual levels of observed market prices. Evidence exists to suggest that certain derivative swaptions markets continue to function well; for such markets, the case for adjusting the calibration away from market prices of options observed at the measurement date is not so clear.

Best estimate assumptions

For non-economic assumptions, the MCEV Principles glossary states that a best estimate assumption "should be equal to the mean estimate (probability weighted average) of outcomes of that risk variable". This definition is broadly aligned with that within the Solvency II Framework Directive, where Article 76(1) states that the best estimate technical provision:

> shall correspond to the probability-weighted average of future cash-flows, taking account of the time value of money (expected present value of future cash-flows) using the relevant risk-free interest rate term structure.

Both frameworks appear to leave open some of the aspects of interpretation of these definitions, in particular the extent to which extreme risks (such as operational risk) or asymmetries are allowed for.

One significant asymmetry can be found in participating business, depending on the ownership of the available capital of this business. This is not discussed further in this chapter but is discussed in Towers Perrin (2007).

Risk margin

It is debatable whether a market-consistent valuation of insurance liabilities requires a risk margin in respect of non-hedgeable risks. This is an area where practice between MCEV and Solvency II may diverge significantly.

The MCEV Principles require adjustments to be made to the value to allow for a cost of residual non-hedgeable risks (covered in Principle 9 and its related guidance). It is noted that a separate adjustment for tax and investment expense frictional costs on required capital is also required (Principle 8).

There is some consistency among MCEV publications to date in the rationale used for adjustments made for non-hedgeable risks, but a variety of approaches have been used to make the adjustments. In some part this divergence of approach is the counterweight to differences in interpreting the requirement for best estimate shareholder cashflows. For example, where companies have not made any allowance for asymmetric and/or operational risk in the assessment of cashflow themselves, they have compensated by incorporating a relatively heavy explicit allowance for non-hedgeable risks and vice versa.

This approach is encouraged by Guidance 9.1 of the MCEV Principles, which states:

> the best estimate assumptions for non-hedgeable risks . . . should reflect at least the mean expectation of outcomes of that risk variable. The total MCEV should allow for the mean impact of all non-hedgeable risks on shareholder value. The additional cost of residual non-hedgeable risks . . . should therefore take account of any additional cost that arises due to the difference between these two measures.

Absolute differences in the resultant reported MCEV from the different approaches used to calculate the risk margin may be quite small. Still, the perception of a lack of conformity may be important in its own right.

One area of potential divergence among MCEV publications is whether allowance is made for uncertainty as to the cost of residual non-hedgeable risks. Guidance 9.2 states, "an allowance for uncertainty in the best estimate of shareholder cash flows as a result of the non-hedgeable risks (both symmetric and asymmetric risks) should be considered". This is an area where differences have been observed among CFO Forum MCEV publications to date.

For Solvency II, Article 76(5) of the Framework Directive sets the broad framework for risk margins for non-hedgeable risks based on the cost of capital required to support these risks over the period to run-off of the liability. CEIOPS (2009c), on the risk margin, goes further, proposing a "cost of capital" rate set at 6% per annum in addition to the risk-free rate. There is no separate requirement for frictional costs in Solvency II and so this element can be considered implicit in the cost of capital rate.

The high level of "cost of capital" rate proposed in CEIOPS (2009c) is perhaps due to the interpretation of Article 76(3) which states "The risk margin shall be such as to ensure that the value of the technical provisions is equivalent to the amount insurance and reinsurance undertakings would be expected to require in order to take over and meet the insurance and reinsurance obligations".

The risk margin incorporated for solvency assessment under Solvency II may be acceptable for that particular purpose but may not necessarily be appropriate for general-purpose financial reporting. This approach to and calibration of risk margins appears to go beyond the level of margin required by shareholders. It is not clear whether such adjustment should be viewed as a policyholder liability or shareholder provision.

Allowance for future premiums

MCEV places no artificial restrictions on the allowance that can be made for future premiums under regular premium contracts. There may be differences in interpretation as to what constitutes a new contract, but in many cases this is not likely to give rise to a material divergence in approach.

The direction of Solvency II in this area is not clear. The Framework Directive leaves this decision to the level 2 implementing measures. CEIOPS (2009a), on treatment of future premiums in technical provisions, appears to place more restrictions than MCEV on the inclusion of future premiums in the calculation, but the guidance is somewhat ambiguous in this area.

MCEV AND SOLVENCY II GOING FORWARDS

In summary, it is clear that the adoption of Solvency II will ensure that regulatory and EV reporting will be much more aligned than has been observed in the past. However, it is clear as well that some significant presentational and technical differences are apt to remain. It is likely that MCEVs will continue to be produced by insurance companies to meet the needs of shareholders. A commercial challenge relates to how to communicate differences in results between the two approaches.

The practical challenge for insurance companies will be in integrating any remaining differences into financial reporting processes in an efficient manner. Insurance companies in their Solvency II implementation projects will have to consider how best to integrate the requirements of the Framework Directive and related legislation, with the equally important needs of the owners of their businesses. With careful planning, the needs of both shareholders and regulators can be met.

1   The contents of this chapter are copyright © Towers Perrin 2009. This chapter sets out the author's personal views, which may not necessarily correspond with those of Towers Perrin.

2   The author would like to thank Chris Daniel, James Harrison, Niamh Hensey and Michael Kluettgens for their comments on drafts of this chapter. Any remaining errors are the author's own.

3   The MCEV Principles document is copyright © Stichting CFO Forum Foundation 2008.

REFERENCES

Anderson, J. C. H., 1959, "Gross Premium Calculations and Profit Measurements for Nonparticipating Insurance", *Transactions of the Society of Actuaries*, XI, pp. 357–394.

Byrne, F. T. and D. W. Dullaway, 2009, "The market-consistent value of liabilities and the credit crunch", *Life & Pensions*, January, URL: http://www.risk.net/life-and-pensions/feature/1514987/the-market-consistent-value-liabilities-credit-crunch.

CEIOPS, 2009a, "Draft CEIOPS' Advice for Level 2 Implementing Measures on Solvency II: Technical Provisions – Treatment of Future Premiums", Consultation Paper, March, URL: http://www.knf.gov.pl/Images/090326%20CP30%20draft%20L2%20advice%20TP%20future%20premiums%20(publconsult)_tcm20-10161.pdf.

CEIOPS, 2009b, "Draft CEIOPS' Advice for Level 2 Implementing Measures on Solvency II: Technical Provisions – Article 85b – Risk-free interest rate term structure", Consultation Paper, July, URL: http://www.knf.gov.pl/Images/090702%20CP40%20L2-Advice-TP-Risk-Free-Rate_tcm20-11324.pdf.

CEIOPS, 2009c, "Draft CEIOPS' Advice for the Level 2 Implementing Measures on Solvency II: Technical Provisions – Article 85d – Calculation of the Risk Margin", Consultation Paper, July, URL: https://www.knf.gov.pl/Images/090702%20CP42%20L2-Advice-TP-Risk-Margin_tcm20-11330.pdf.

CEIOPS, 2009d, "Draft CEIOPS' Advice for the Level 2 Implementing Measures on Solvency II: Technical Provisions – Articles 118-124 – Tests and Standards for Internal Model Approval", Consultation Paper, July, URL: http://www.ceiops.eu/media/files/consultations/consultationpapers/CP56/CEIOPS-CP-56-09-L2-Advice-Tests-and-Standards-for-internal-model-approval.pdf.

CFO Forum, 2004, "European Embedded Value Principles", May, URL: http://www.cfoforum.eu/letters/eev_principles.pdf.

CFO Forum, 2008, "Market Consistent Embedded Value Principles", June.

CFO Forum, 2008, "Market Consistent Embedded Value Principles", June, URL: https://eyaprimo.ey.com/natlmktgaprimoey/Attachments/CFO_Forum_MCEV_Principles_Guidance.pdf.

CFO Forum, 2009. "Market Consistent Embedded Value Principles", October, URL: http://www.cfoforum.eu/downloads/MCEV_Principles_and_Guidance_October_2009.pdf.

Dullaway, D., 2001, "A new and improved embedded value", *Emphasis*, 2001/3, pp. 10–13, URL: http://www.towersperrin.com/rfs/2001-3_New%20Improved%20EV%20for%20MCEV%20thought%20leadership.pdf.

European Commission, 2007, "Draft Solvency II Framework Directive", July, URL: http://eur-lex.europa.eu/LexUriServ/site/en/com/2007/com2007_0361en01.pdf.

European Commission, 2009, "Solvency II Framework Directive", April.

FASB, 2009, "Determining Fair Value When the Volume and Level of Activity for the Asset or Liability Have Significantly Decreased and Identifying Transactions That Are Not Orderly", Staff Position Paper 157/4, April.

Foroughi, K. and S. C. True, 2004, "Taking Forward Embedded Values", *Emphasis*, 2004/3, pp. 10–13, URL: http://www.towersperrin.com/tp/getwebcachedoc?webc=TILL/USA/2004/ 200410/TrueForoughi.pdf.

IAIS, 2007, "The IAIS Common Structure for the Assessment of Insurer Solvency", February, URL: http://www.iaisweb.org/__temp/Common_structure_paper_for_assessment_of_insurer_solvency.pdf.

IASB, 1998, "International Accounting Standard 19 Employee Benefits" (and subsequent amendments).

IASB, 2009a, "IAS 39 Financial Instruments: Recognition and Measurement", April, URL: http://www.iasb.org/News/Press+Releases/IASB+sets+out+timetable+for+IAS+39+replacement+and+its+conclusions+on+FASB+FSPs.htm.

IASB, 2009b, "Fair Value Measurement Exposure Draft", May, URL: http://www.iasb.org/NR/rdonlyres/C4096A25-F830-401D-8E2E-9286B194798E/0/EDFairValueMeasurement_website.pdf.

IASB, 2009c, "Financial Instruments: Classification and Measurement Exposure Draft", July, URL: http://www.iasb.org/NR/rdonlyres/D1598224-3609-4F0A-82D0-6DC598C3249B/0/EDFinancialInstrumentsClassificationandMeasurement.pdf.

O'Keeffe, P. J .L., A. J. Desai, K. Foroughi, G. J. Hibbett, A. J. Maxwell, A. C. Sharp, N. H. Taverner, M. B. Ward and F. J. P. Willis, 2005, "Current Developments in Embedded Value Reporting", *British Actuarial Journal*, XI, pp. 407–496.

Tillinghast, 2003, "Market-Consistent Embedded Value: Allowing for Risk Within an Embedded Value Framework", White Paper, Towers Perrin, URL: http://www.towersperrin.com/tp/getwebcachedoc?webc=TILL/USA/2003/200310/MCEV.pdf.

Tillinghast, 2005, "Market-Consistent Embedded Value: Dispelling the Myths", White Paper, Towers Perrin, URL: http://www.towersperrin.com/tp/getwebcachedoc?webc=TILL/USA/2005/200502/MCEVll.pdf.

Towers Perrin Update, 2007, "How Consistent is Market-Consistent as a Concept?" August, URL: http://www.towersperrin.com/tp/getwebcachedoc?country=global&webc=TILL/GBR/2007/200709/Market_consistent.pdf.

Towers Perrin Update, 2008, "CFO Forum Adopts MCEV", June, URL: http://www.towersperrin.com/tp/getwebcachedoc?country=global&webc=GBR/2008/200806/MCEVupdate.pdf.

Towers Perrin Update, 2009a, "2008 EEV/MCEV: Coping with Extreme Financial Conditions", May, URL: http://www.towersperrin.com/tp/getwebcachedoc?webc=GBR/2009/200906/EEVMCEVMay2009Update.pdf.

Towers Perrin Update, 2009b, "The Solvency II Directive Agreed: Where to Now?" May, URL: http://www.towersperrin.com/tp/getwebcachedoc?webc=GBR/2009/200905/May_2009_Sol_II_Directive_agreed.pdf.

Section II

Measuring and Managing Financial Risk

Introduction

Marcelo Cruz

New York University

The area of financial risk management is one of those most affected by Solvency II. The regulators had a good reason to revamp the regulatory framework for this area. Financial risk management basically represents the management of market and credit risk, as well as asset–liability management (ALM) risks. So-called market risk amounts to more than 50% of the total risks in most insurance companies. Despite that, most insurers focus only on the ALM side, market and credit risks playing a smaller role.

Regulators want insurers to follow more of the steps that banks are using, such as more sophisticated techniques to manage market risk. The traditional duration analysis will need to be significantly extended to reach a value-at-risk (VaR) framework. Although insurers usually react to that with a cranky "we are not a bank", the reality is that large insurers are also giant financial institutions whose failure would have an impact similar to that of a bank. The case in point is AIG, lest anyone still resist the idea. After AIG, it is clear that insurers need to have a much stronger risk measurement and management framework; they are quite behind in 2009.

In this section there are five excellent chapters. In Chapter 6, we show how Solvency II has had an impact on the process of economic scenario generation, which is key for market and credit risk calculations. In Chapter 7, we translate the banking Basel II into Solvency II, giving a very good picture of what insurers should do to develop market VaR models.

There are three other chapters in this section that delve into more advanced and detailed topics. Chapter 8 provides a great view, with numerical examples, of the difficult subject of portfolio replication; this will play a great role in liability measurement. In the subsequent chapter, we delve into the subject of liquidity risk; this is a very controversial topic, even in the banking industry, as liquidity risk as a measurement is quite an elusive discipline. The authors also provide good examples, which make the chapter very interesting reading. In the last chapter of this section, we are shown how to measure reinsurance credit risk, which is something that insurers will have to do under Solvency II.

These chapters are all very interesting reading. I hope readers can appreciate the quality and readability of the texts, which is a very difficult objective to achieve many times in these very technical areas.

6

Economic Scenario Generators and Solvency II

Thorsten Pfeiffer; Elliot Varnell; Russell Ward[1]

FINMA; KPMG LLP; Ernst & Young LLP

The purpose of this chapter is to discuss the use of economic scenario generators (ESG models) in the context of Solvency II. While much has been written about Solvency II, little has been written to explain specifically how ESG models will be used under Solvency II and what issues will need to be considered.

Economic scenario generator models are a potentially very broad subject and could include many details on model design, methods for choosing economic assumptions and techniques for improving the efficiency of economic scenarios.[2] However, to keep the chapter relatively accessible to those not necessarily steeped in the underlying mathematics, we have aimed to keep the discussion at a reasonably high level.

This is an important subject; the Solvency II Framework Directive makes it clear that complex mathematics or software tools are no substitute for a genuine understanding of what drives risk within an insurance company. Senior managers and boards are going to need to understand what functions ESG models perform. However, in our experience few senior managers are currently close to this. Much material on the subject of ESG models is by necessity technical and can therefore be quite difficult to assimilate for a non-practitioner. In this chapter we have therefore steered away from the technical detail and formulas in an attempt to focus on the key issues and considerations for the effective use of ESG models in the post–Solvency II environment.

APPLICATIONS OF ESG MODELS
Solvency II

On May 5, 2009 the Economic and Financial Affairs Council, comprising of the economic and finance ministers of the European Union, agreed to adopt the Solvency II Framework Directive. In addition to its adoption in the European Union, supervisory regimes with similar features to Solvency II appear likely to be widely adopted around the globe. At the time of writing, Chile and Mexico had decided to pursue Solvency II–style insurance regulation, while Japan, Canada and Taiwan are understood to be also considering Solvency II–style proposals.

The Framework Directive mandates market-consistent valuation for all insurance business covered by the Framework Directive and gives the opportunity to use an internal risk model for the calculation of solvency capital. Economic scenario generator models are a key element of market-consistent valuation for life insurance businesses and an important tool for measuring and managing market and credit risk in an internal model.

Although the twin concepts of market-consistent valuation and internal models in Solvency II have been driving much recent interest in ESG models, we briefly mention some other drivers for their use in the insurance sector.

Rating agency criteria

Some rating agencies have introduced additional rating criteria for enterprise risk management; forthcoming criteria for economic capital management are expected. Rating agencies have considered the use of market-consistent valuation and stochastic economic scenarios for determining economic capital requirements to be good practice for demonstrating risk and capital management.

Local regulations

Even before Solvency II was agreed in Spring 2009, there were several local regulatory regimes, in Europe and elsewhere in the world, where ESG models have been a key tool for the calculation of regulatory returns and information provided to regulators.

UK

The Realistic Balance Sheet regime, where ESG models are almost always used for the valuation of participating life insurance business. Another regime is the Individual Capital Assessment (ICA) regulations, where ESG models have been used for measuring capital requirements in respect of market and credit risk.

Switzerland
Swiss Solvency Test (SST), where ESG models are used for the valuation of traditional life insurance business. They can also be used in internal models for the calculation of regulatory capital, for example in the calibration and projection of replicating portfolios.

South Africa
PGN-110, in which ESG models are used for the market-consistent valuation of with-profit business and can also be used for capital adequacy requirement risk capital calculation.

Reporting standards
CFO forum
European Embedded Value (EEV) is often calculated using real-world stochastic projections from an ESG, along with the certainty equivalent approach to capturing the approximate time value of options and guarantees. More recently, market consistent embedded value (MCEV) principles have been adopted, which usually necessitate the use of a market-consistent (risk-neutral) ESG. At the time of writing, there is some uncertainty over whether the MCEV principles will continue in their current form; implementation has been delayed until 2011.

Other uses
Early versions of ESG models were used not for prudential supervision but in the areas of asset–liability management (ALM) and life insurance product design. Economic scenario generator models are still used in these areas today and are now also being used in other areas, for example:

- The communication of the risks and rewards associated with retail insurance products.
- The dynamic hedging of individual insurance products or dynamic hedging of a book of insurance liabilities.
- The management assets backing insurance liabilities.
- The ALM of pension schemes.

THE ROLE OF ESG MODELS IN SOLVENCY II

Economic scenario generators are not required to be used for Solvency II. However, we believe that many insurers will find the requirements of Solvency II easier to meet using an ESG model. In this section we discuss the role that ESG models are likely to play within the Solvency II environment. We have organised this section into the three pillars described in the Solvency II Framework Directive:

- Pillar I
  - Market-consistent valuation
    - Assets
    - Liabilities
  - Standard model
  - Partial internal model
  - Internal model
    - Validation
    - Statistical quality
    - Documentation
    - Use test
    - Profit and loss (P&L) attribution
    - Calibration
    - External models
  - Possible approaches to solvency capital requirement (SCR) calculation methodology
- Pillar II
  - Own Risk and Solvency Assessment (ORSA)
  - Disclosure to the regulator
- Pillar III
  - Disclosure to the market.

Pillar I

Market-consistent valuation

We leave the discussion of this important topic to a dedicated section later in this chapter.

SCR: standard model

The standard model will not require the use of an ESG per se, except that in order for calculation of the SCR to be possible, the market-consistent balance sheet will need to be recalculated under each of the stresses described in the standard model. Therefore, in addition to calculating the base market-consistent value of assets and liabilities, insurers will also have to calculate the market-consistent value after separate shocks to each of the equity, property, credit and fixed nominal interest-rate markets (yield curve shifted up and yield curve shifted down). The application of these market stresses to the base balance sheet will require models to be rerun; in some cases, for example with the nominal interest-rate shocks, this will include recalibration of the ESG and regeneration of the required economic scenarios. For formal external reporting, the approach is likely to involve a full set of detailed calculations. However, for other purposes, such as the need for ongoing monitoring of the solvency position, less computationally intensive approaches are likely to be sought that will deliver results to within an acceptable level of accuracy, but faster and with reduced effort. One approach seeing increasingly widespread adoption is the use of replicating portfolios, as discussed later in this chapter.

Partial internal model

We would expect most partial internal model implementations to replace elements of the standard formula that were unsuitable for the type of business the insurer had written. This could occur at the insurer's request, where the standard formula was considered to be inappropriate. Alternatively, it could occur at the regulator's request, where the standard formula was not considered sufficiently accurate to capture the risks of the business. The expectation is that the market risk module is most likely to be replaced with an ESG-oriented partial model, where an insurer has a significant market exposure or a sophisticated asset strategy that the standard model does not credit.

Other uses for an ESG model could be to replace the default (counterparty credit exposure) module and provide a more realistic dynamic link between counterparty risk and the market risk module. Where such a partial internal model is used, the insurer will have to be satisfied that the credit model of the ESG is appropriately calibrated. For example, a model calibrated to reflect the dynamics of a diversified portfolio of credit risky assets might not be appropriate to evaluate reinsurance counterparty credit exposures.

Full internal model

There are some compelling reasons why an insurer or its regulator might believe that a full internal model using an ESG would improve the understanding of its risks and its risk-mitigation strategies. These include:

1. The ability to reflect the insurer's own views of the way economic variables might develop in the future and the statistical relationships between those economic variables.[3]

2. The calculation of 99.5% value-at-risk (VaR) based on a more sophisticated one-year stochastic projection can allow more credit to be taken for the mitigating impact of management actions as simulated economic conditions unfold during the year. This can have a material impact on the required economic capital.

3. The ability to generate full distributions of capital rather than just point estimates at given percentiles gives a deeper understanding of the market risk. For example, consistent economic capital measurements can be made at various VaR percentiles or using a tail VaR approach. In this way, different risk appetites can be tested from a single set of scenarios based on the same set of economic assumptions. While it does not mandate an approach, there are clear hints in the level 1 directive that producing a full risk capital distribution is the preferred method, where this is feasible (see European Commission 2009, Article 120 (2)).

4. The use of combined market risk scenarios generated by the ESG removes the need for external aggregation of these risks, say, via a correlation matrix or copula. Using an ESG will also pick up the impact of any non-linear interactions between the modelled risks automatically.

5. Using an ESG will not remove the need for external aggregation using correlations or copulas where market and credit risk capital need to be aggregated with other risk capital, such as insurance or operational risk. However, some insurers

intersperse risks considered to be independent of market risk (eg, mortality and NATCAT) with the scenarios from an ESG. This creates a broader set of stochastic scenarios that can be used to investigate non-linear interactions between market and some non-market risks.

Regulatory model approval
To realise the benefits of an internal model a regulator needs to be comfortable that the company's model provides enough policy-holder protection to be relied upon for prudential supervision. To acquire this degree of comfort, seven tests need to be passed before the model can be accepted into use. The tests are:

- Use test
- Validation test
- Statistical quality test
- P&L attribution
- Documentation
- Calibration
- External models.

Below we consider how an ESG would interact with each of these tests.

Use test
Where an ESG model is employed as part of an internal model it must be used to develop management information as part of the decision-making framework for the insurance company, for example, to inform the setting of the risk appetite and limits or around product design/distribution strategy, to name but a few examples. A real-world ESG is designed to directly reflect realistic views of the future behaviour of the relevant economic variables. In contrast, a market-consistent or risk-neutral ESG reflects an artificial world designed to provide a mathematically tractable approach to the pricing of derivative instruments. We feel there is likely to be increasing regulatory interest in real-world ESG models, as economic assumptions and relationships within them impact the way in which insurers view and assess market risk and they thus start to influence major decisions within insurance companies.

It appears likely that the use test will require that senior manage-ment and board members ensure the company's having a sound understanding of the features, strengths and weaknesses of the ESG, ensuring as well that an effective challenge has been provided to the methodology and parameterisation adopted. We could imagine this extending to understanding the key assumptions that drive the results and the justification for those assumptions. We could also imagine the board needing to appreciate the key risks in using the ESG model and how these risks had been mitigated. This is likely to be a significant challenge given that a typical ESG model is mathematically complex and often sourced from an external supplier.

The internal model will need to feed demonstrably into decision making around risk and capital management within the insurer. It is therefore to be expected that major decisions will necessitate a full recalculation of the internal model, which may require several recalibrations of the ESG. For example, the calculation of the SCR is likely to require several recalibrations of the market-consistent scenarios used for the valuation step. These recalibrations will need to reflect the different initial conditions required under each market stress.

The requirement to recalibrate the ESG more frequently could present major challenges if a recalibration cannot be performed easily and quickly. For example, the need to align an ESG to an arbitrary set of economic assumptions and dependencies can be particularly challenging, as the distributions of economic variables and dependencies between them in an ESG are often strongly influenced by the model design. Senior management and the board will need to ensure that a regular review of the ESG model is undertaken and reported in order to demonstrate that the models, methodology and calibration remain relevant given any changes in the economic environment or the asset classes held.

In order to use the internal model (and therefore the ESG) in major decisions, it is useful to have a common set of ESG scenarios, used throughout the enterprise, on which all decisions would be based. This can put a lot of demand on the ESG model to capture many features of the various economies relevant to an insurance company in a single calibration. The use test could require that the internal model be used for purposes such as:

- Financial reporting
- Risk management

- ALM
- Transactions (mergers and acquisitions)
- Derivatives/dynamic hedging
- Product pricing

If the ESG cannot capture enough of the features of the economy, it may be necessary to use different ESG models or different calibrations in the different business areas. This would make comparisons of economic assumptions across an insurer more difficult, and increase the risk of inconsistent decisions being taken throughout the business. Overheads are also increased if the ESG model (or calibration) in one business area needs to be reconciled to the ESG model (or calibration) used elsewhere. There will need to be a trade-off between choosing a model (and calibration) that can be used in many areas of the business and a model (and calibration) that can easily be communicated within the business and to senior management.

Validation
The output of ESG models will need to be validated against the input. This requires a demonstration that the output of the ESG is consistent with calibration parameters: means, volatilities, correlations (or other dependency measure) and higher moments (distribution asymmetry and fat tails).

Backtesting is a concept frequently discussed in the context of Solvency II model validation. The term has been borrowed from the backtesting of VaR internal models in Basel II. In that context, backtesting involves recalibrating the VaR model to historical periods of time, often at daily intervals, and measuring how many times the actual losses exceed the VaR limit. In this way the validity of the bank's internal model is tested.

The equivalent tests for an insurance internal model would be to rerun the full ALM system at past dates. The required solvency capital at each date could then be calculated. Using current ALM technology it is not practical to back-fill daily ALM results, even if an insurer had a daily history of policy, asset and expense data stretching back several years (which is unlikely to be the case).

Considering an ESG model in isolation, one approach to backtesting would be to recalibrate the ESG model to dates in the past, perhaps annually, and test how often the actual annual return exceeds the VaR percentile calculated using the ESG. Several problems arise in trying to do this.

1. For several elements of the calibration we may not have sufficient data going back historically. This makes recalibration to earlier dates challenging. Data, such as long-term equity implied volatility data, may be available only for, say, a 10-year period, and then only for short option terms. This is more of an issue for market-consistent ESG models used in the technical provision calculation, because real-world ESG projections tend to be calibrated to statistical analysis of a much longer window of time-series data.

2. This can also be an issue for real-world ESG models that are usually calibrated to historical data. We are typically interested in one-year 99.5% VaR, which means that even with 100 annual recalibrations back to the beginning of the 20th Century we would struggle to infer any meaningful statistical analysis from the results (see Frankland *et al* 2008). More frequent recalibrations could be made, but the results would suffer from statistical bias due to the overlapping time periods. Nonetheless, some additional information is captured by taking this approach. An example is where a market crashes and then recovers before the year end. In such cases using an annual projection from each month end will better capture the market crash events that have occurred.

3. From a practical perspective, many of the more complex ESG models that might be expected to pass this test (at the time of writing) have calibration procedures that involve manual intervention. Doing a Basel II–style backtest would therefore be a major undertaking.

There is likely to be a trade-off between the validation test and the use test. The validation test appears to require the demonstration of a high degree of accuracy in calculations. However, this accuracy might be difficult to achieve in a timescale that would mean the firm could use the model for decision making, and so satisfy the use test.

A key aspect of validation using ESG models will be how many scenarios are used. For example, in measuring the VaR in the tail of a distribution, we will need a lot of scenarios to improve the confidence interval around the 99.5 percentile capital estimate. This could lead to solutions where ESG scenarios are focussed on a particular area of interest, for example the tail of a distribution, using importance sampling. However, the complex nature of insurance business could reduce the effectiveness of such techniques. This is because extreme events for the solvency of an insurance company could be caused by non-extreme paths or events in the ESG. Also, understanding the behaviour of solvency under less extreme events is very useful for management understanding and decision-making purposes and this insight would be lost if attention just focussed on the distribution tails.

The validation test is important in the context of market-consistent valuation. Because market-consistent valuation is a concept that applies to all of Solvency II, not just internal models, we leave this discussion until a later section of this chapter.

Statistical quality

The main overlap between ESG models and the statistical quality standards will be evidence that the economic data used to calibrate the model was of sufficiently good quality, and was relevant to the purpose of the ESG calibration and the risk exposures of the insurer. Considerations for this test could include the treatment of outlier observations in the calibration data; if these are omitted from the data set, then justification should be provided to explain why this was done.

If the data point cannot be discounted, then the model's ability to represent such observations should be considered. If the model has limitations on reproducing extreme events, it might be appropriate to employ a more sophisticated model that better represents the data, for example by capturing skewed (distribution asymmetry) or excess kurtosis (fat tails).

For some asset classes, such as private equity, hedge fund or real estate, data is limited and can contain bias and/or significant sampling error. We expect that these limitations will need to be recorded under the Solvency II statistical quality test, and that simplifications or judgements made about the data will need to be clearly explained. Where assets such as real estate are valued using expert judgement, the prices should be checked against actual transaction prices whenever possible.

One requirement that could cause confusion is the need to show that data used in the internal model's SCR calculation is consistent with the calculation of the technical provisions. While this may be sensible for data used in risk-margin calculations, such as for mortality, expenses and lapses, it is not likely to be the case for all economic data. Some of the economic data and assumptions need to change between the ESG scenarios used to calculate the SCR, by projecting the economic balance sheet (real-world assumptions), and the ESG scenarios used for the calculation of the technical provisions (market-consistent assumptions).

Market equity implied volatilities are used in the calculation of technical provisions, for example. Market implied volatilities are usually higher than the realised standard deviations used to calibrate a real-world ESG. Using equity implied volatility for the SCR calculation may be considered penal, as insurers would import the additional margins that investment banks add to long-term trades to cover hedging costs and the banks' cost of capital.

P&L attribution

Economic scenario generator models are likely to figure in P&L attributions through the use of interim calibrations. For example, each of the differences between the market-consistent calibrations at the end of successive years could be changed in turn. This would allow the change in P&L attributable to the ESG to be broken down into elements of the calibration that had changed. The following illustrates one approach to changing the ESG parameters in an analysis of change:

1. Equity index;
2. Initial nominal yield curve;
3. Equity implied volatility; and
4. All other changes.

The impacts of each change are not independent; the breakdown of changes will depend on the order in which the changes are processed. Consequently, in order not to distort the comparability of the P&L attribution between years, the order of changes would need to remain fixed from year to year.

A pragmatic approach is needed to manage the tension between frequency/timeliness and the level of granularity and exploration of different orders of change. A reasonable approach could be to identify the ESG assumptions that the market-consistent valuation was most sensitive to and then alter the calibration, focussing on these. All other impacts could be accounted for in the final "analysis of change" step. A more granular approach could be used at the year end with a more pragmatic approach used for interim management reporting.

The most sensitive assumptions may not remain the same from year to year. Movements in the moneyness and term of options and guarantees will change the degree of sensitivity.

Documentation

The models, implementation, operation and calibration process of an ESG will all need to be fully documented. This will include a detailed explanation of the theory, the assumptions and the mathematical and empirical basis underlying the ESG model. Furthermore, the limitations of the ESG model need to be fully explained. The expectation is that it will be as important to document why decisions have been taken as it is to document the decisions themselves. Given the complexity of a typical ESG model, it will be a significant undertaking to develop a full enough understanding of the model that areas where the model does not perform well can be identified and documented.

Under Solvency II, all major changes to an internal model will need to be documented. This will extend to the ESG model so that changes to the ESG being used will need to be documented as well. This means that ESG model consumers will need to be aware when changes to the ESG model take place, and ESG model providers (internal or external) will need to provide timely updates and well-articulated descriptions of the changes that have taken place. This will include why the changes have been made and the expected impact on the model results so that insurers can report appropriately to their supervisors.

Calibration

The calibration test is concerned with the risk measure used to evaluate the SCR. The baseline risk measure is one-year VaR at the

99.5 percentile. It is possible to deviate from this risk measure for internal management processes, but it must be possible to reconcile the internal capital measure to the SCR baseline.

Value-at-risk has been criticised as a risk measure (see Artzner *et al* 1999), notably for not being a coherent risk measure and for ignoring the severity of losses beyond a particular percentile. Alternatives that have been proposed include tail VaR which addresses the limitations of VaR described before. Nevertheless, VaR has practical advantages with regard to its relative ease and speed of calculation and its broad application; it is also widely perceived as easier to communicate.

For many lines of insurance business, particularly in the long-term saving market, longer-term risk measures are more aligned with the strategic management of the business. An insurer may wish to use a long-term measure, for example, to have enough capital over 40 years to a certain percentile level. Under Solvency II, the insurer will still need to demonstrate equivalence of their long-term measure to the baseline risk measure.

How can this be achieved? The authors are not aware of a definitive way of proving this equivalence. To do so would involve proving that the amount of capital held using the insurer's measure offered equivalent policyholder protection to the baseline risk measure. The only way we could see to achieve this would be to calculate the required capital also on the one-year base measure and then reverse engineer the calibration percentile of the insurer's own risk measure to deliver at least the same level of required capital. This makes us question whether using a different risk measure adds extra insight.

Perhaps, though, supervisors will be prepared to allow periodic recalibration of the insurer's risk measure percentile to the baseline risk measure, and then permit insurers to use their own risk measure with the reverse-engineered percentile in the interim. If this were the case the calibration would just involve converting a one-year horizon return distribution into, for example, a 40-year horizon return distribution.

Economic scenario generator models offer a relatively easy way to create consistent return distributions for different time horizons that are all based on the same underlying economics and calibration parameters. For example, say we know a particular percentile value

(VaR) of an economic variable, like the 99.5% one-year return of the Consumer Price Inflation (CPI) index. This information is not enough to calculate other percentile values. In order to do this we must know the distribution of the index one year from now. We could achieve this using a directly fitted parametric distribution, an empirical distribution or a more complex distribution generated by an ESG model.

Knowing the distribution of an economic variable at a single time horizon is not sufficient for understanding how the distribution evolves at different time horizons. For example, mean reversion, heteroskedastic (stochastic volatility) behaviour or complex inter-asset dependencies will influence the future distribution.

Economic scenario generator models provide the full distribution and evolution of economic variables. Therefore they are straightforward to use for calculating economically consistent (if not necessarily equivalent) risk measures. However, there are some points to be aware of.

- The risk measures typically need to be derived empirically from the ESG, which introduces a sampling error. The sampling error is particularly strong in the extreme tails of the distribution we are concerned with.
- Any ESG distribution will depend on the model choices within the ESG and its calibration. Subject to sampling error, the risk measures will all be coherent to the ESG configuration and calibration used. If the ESG is calibrated only to a specific time horizon, then poorly calibrated risk measures may result whenever a different time horizon is used for the risk measure from the same ESG scenarios.

The authors are of the opinion that a well-designed and well-calibrated ESG represents a sound approach to aggregating a short-term distribution of economic variables to a longer-term distribution of those same economic variables.

External models
As ESG models are frequently provided to insurers by external suppliers, the provisions within the Solvency II Framework Directive about external models will often apply to the ESG.

According to the Framework Directive, all the tests for an internal model described previously will apply equally to an externally sourced component of the internal model. One specific requirement is that insurers have a good understanding of the external model. CEIOPS (2009b) sets out what would be considered necessary to show that an insurer had a good understanding of its external model:

1. in-depth knowledge of the methodological underpinnings and basic construction of external models and data, including an understanding of the models' capabilities, limitations and appropriateness for use in deriving the SCR;
2. demonstration of a full understanding of the effect and significance of the proprietary elements in the external models;
3. documentation of the rationale behind any judgment-based overrides or any other adjustments made to external data sets or external model outputs; and
4. retention of in-house expertise on the external models and data for as long as these are used to derive the SCR.

Potentially the most onerous requirement is the amount of documentation around decision making; it can often take place to tight timescales in order to meet year-end reporting deadlines. One approach could be to preagree a process that will be followed for making judgements. Then only judgements that deviate from the preagreed policy would need to be recorded. It appears likely that commercial ESG providers will need to provide a significant amount of information to insurers about the model choices that they have made and what the weaknesses of the chosen models are.

Possible approaches to SCR calculation methodology
Calculation of the SCR requires, at least, an ability to recalculate the market-consistent balance sheet under a range of stress events. However, more advanced approaches permit the generation of a full market risk distribution. In this sub-section we consider a number of these approaches, in increasing order of complexity.

The "time zero stress test" approach involves applying instant stress tests to key variables and recalculating the economic balance sheet. Changes in net assets under each stress are aggregated using a correlation matrix or hierarchy of correlation matrices or mixing

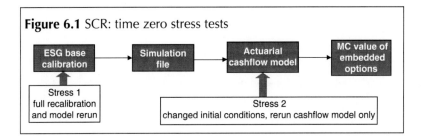

Figure 6.1 SCR: time zero stress tests

distribution functions.[4] This is an approach that can be found in the UK ICA, the SST and the standard formula model in Solvency II. Figure 6.1 illustrates this approach.

Economic scenario generator models are used to calculate the market-consistent liabilities in the base case and under stressed conditions. For some stresses, the ESG will require recalibration in order to generate an appropriate revised valuation, say, to changes in the yield curve. For other stresses, such as the equity market value shock, recalibration is not necessary and the actuarial cash-flow models are simply rerun under revised initial conditions by scaling the ESG model outputs. In some cases, a real-world ESG is also used to help estimate the economic stress tests to be applied.

The delta–gamma approach involves applying instantaneous sensitivity tests to key economic inputs and recalculating the economic balance sheet. Changes in net assets under each stress are used to calculate the way in which the overall net assets respond to changes in key economic factors. The sensitivities are then used in conjunction with a real-world ESG asset projection to infer the future distribution of net assets. Briefly, the steps involved are:

- determining the base economic balance sheet and thus the base net assets using a market-consistent ESG;
- establishing a range of sensitivities for the net assets by making small changes to key economic variables and recalculating the economic balance sheet;
- from the sensitivities determine the delta factor, gamma factor and cross for each variable and any cross-gamma factors;
- using a real-world ESG to project economic conditions for one year;
- using the delta and gamma sensitivity factors to estimate the revised net assets in each of the real-world scenarios; and

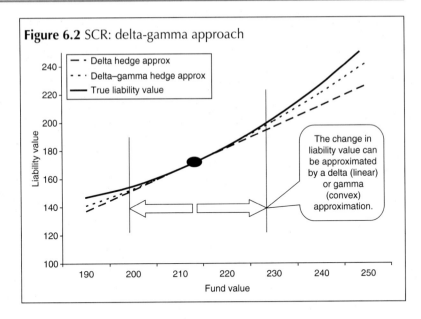

Figure 6.2 SCR: delta-gamma approach

- •	from this information the distribution of net assets one year hence can be determined and thus the 99.5 percentile of that distribution can be calculated to determine the SCR.

Difficulties may arise with this approach if the curvature captured by first and second derivatives holds close only to the current valuation and not under the large stresses or paths that lead to large losses. The delta–gamma approximation is illustrated in Figure 6.2, where (for simplicity) we have considered a portfolio of guaranteed equity bonds with a simple cap and floor on the payout. The true market-consistent value of the liability portfolio moves with the fund value but in a convex way. The delta approach uses a linear approximation to capture the movements, while the delta–gamma approach approximates the convexity as well.

In another approach a closed-form solution (eg, the Black–Scholes–Merton closed-form formula) is calibrated against the market-consistent valuation of the liability using a market-consistent ESG. This is done to determine unobservable parameters such as implied volatilities and implied correlations not traded in the market. Future market conditions are then projected using a real-world ESG, for the SCR these would be the conditions in one year's time. In each future scenario, the closed-form solutions are populated with the relevant market data and recalculated to

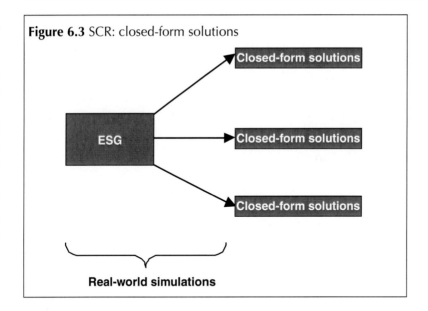

Figure 6.3 SCR: closed-form solutions

provide a revised valuation of embedded options and guarantees for inclusion on the market-consistent balance sheet. Figure 6.3 illustrates this approach.

Difficulty may arise with the projection of implied volatilities and correlations for which no historical data is likely to be available. In addition, it should be noted that not all insurance options and guarantees have closed forms.

A relatively recent alternative to the use of a closed-form solution has been the use of the replicating portfolios, which is (typically) a portfolio of simple liquidly traded instruments that approximate the cashflows of a set of insurance liabilities. Figure 6.4 illustrates this approach.

Usually a replicating portfolios is constructed using a set of candidate assets, eg, equity indexes, equity options, zero coupon bonds, swaps and swaptions. A set of economic scenarios is used to generate a set of stochastic liability cashflows. The same set of economic scenarios is used to generate cashflows from the replicating portfolios of candidate assets. Weights are then chosen for the candidate assets that minimise the difference between the true liability cashflows and the replicating portfolios cashflows.

An advantage that a replicating portfolios has compared with a closed-form solution is that the values of the candidate assets are

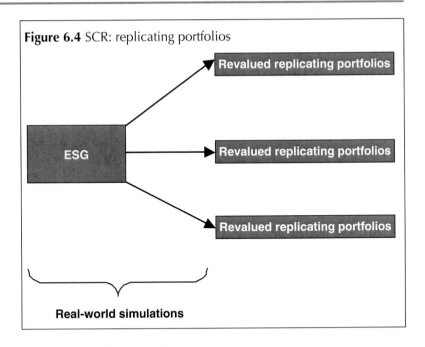

Figure 6.4 SCR: replicating portfolios

often readily available from market data sources. This means that a well-designed replicating portfolios can be revalued using market data feeds to provide real-time movements in the liability valuation. Combining a replicating portfolios with stochastic projections of the candidate assets using an ESG, some insurers have revised how they calculate their economic capital; notably they have been in Germany, Switzerland and the Netherlands.

In the nested stochastic approach (which one might call a "brute force" one), a real-world ESG is used to project economic scenarios. In each of these "outer" scenarios a new "inner" set of market-consistent economic scenarios are generated to calculate the market-consistent value of liabilities. Figure 6.5 illustrates this approach.

This is, in theory, the approach that offers the greatest flexibility to project the SCR. However, it is time- and processor-intensive, so that few firms have as yet adopted this technique. GRID and cloud computing solutions may help make this option more popular in the future.

One criticism of the nested stochastic approach is that it offers only spurious accuracy compared with using some predefined

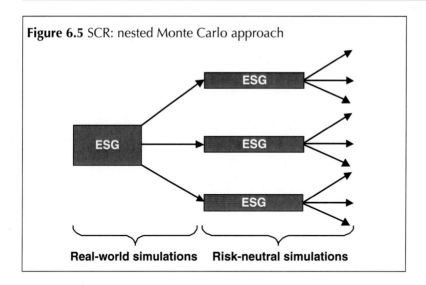

Figure 6.5 SCR: nested Monte Carlo approach

Real-world simulations   Risk-neutral simulations

stress tests. However, given the inherent non-linearity and path-dependence of insurance business, we do not believe that it is always obvious which future paths of economic variables would lead to insurer ruin. Nested stochastic scenarios have the advantage of presenting the insurer with a large selection of paths that would cause ruin. To the extent that the nested stochastic approach suggests new ruin scenarios, it provides additional insights as to the risk exposures of the insurer.

Pillar II: ORSA

At the time of writing, the latest CEIOPS (2008) chapter on ORSA included references to market risk that are generic; it is expected that further detail will emerge over the coming months, with a consultation paper on ORSA expected in autumn 2009.

The authors believe that insurers using a full internal model will use it, and the ESG component of it, in their ORSA work. Part of that work might be to investigate other risk measures or confidence levels or additional and/or emerging risks not yet captured in SCR calculations. For insurers using the standard formula, the ESG may be used to investigate additional risks in their ORSA, investigate the continued appropriateness of the standard formula for their risk profile or provide additional information for internal decision making. We believe this type of approach is consistent with CEIOPS

(2009b), which indicates that there should be a continual drive and pressure to improve the models used by insurers.

Pillar III: disclosure

At the time of writing, the disclosure requirements around Solvency II were still emerging. However, an extract from the Solvency II Framework Directive (Article 50) discusses some disclosures that could be considered relevant to ESG models.

The following extract suggests that the (market-consistent) valuation basis will need to be disclosed:

> . . . a description, separately for assets, technical provisions, and other liabilities, of the bases and methods used for their valuation, together with an explanation of any major differences in the bases and methods used for their valuation in financial statements.

Where an ESG is used for the market-consistent valuation, a full description of the economic basis would be provided in the supplying of the full set of economic scenarios. While comprehensive, this would not be practical or help understanding. A solution pioneered by the UK Financial Services Authority[5] is to request that some predefined financial instruments be valued using the same economic scenarios as the insurer has used in its regulatory submissions. An adaptation of this "option table" approach is a practical way in which the economic basis for an ESG valuation could be disclosed and the impact of differences in company practice assessed.

WHY USE AN ESG MODEL FOR VALUATION?

In this section we consider why insurers would use an ESG for the market-consistent valuation of their liabilities, then we consider some alternative approaches. Many of the uses of ESG models are in the calculation of a market-consistent value for complex life insurance policies where the assets and liabilities are not well matched. Typically these will be participating policies with management actions and policyholder actions influencing the cashflows paid.

Economic scenario generator models use a Monte Carlo technique to come up with a valuation for these policies. However, Monte Carlo valuation is not a particularly convenient method to use, as it requires many scenarios to be run. Monte Carlo valuation is also subject to sampling errors, which can be significant. Based on the UK and Swiss experience, it is typical for an insurer to use between 2,000 and 5,000 scenarios when calculating a market-consistent valuation of liabilities for a typical portfolio of participating insurance liabilities.

While this may seem like a lot of scenarios to a life insurer moving to stochastic valuation for the first time, it often seems like a low number to quantitative analysts used to running 100,000 scenarios to value exotic derivatives. In practice, life insurers have to calculate a valuation for many thousands of policies over a long time horizon. The cashflows on these policies often have complex interactions with management and policyholder behaviour. Consequently, the full policy portfolio has to be condensed to, typically, 5,000–15,000 representative contracts (model points) in order to produce valuations within reasonable timescales. New solutions based on technologies such as GRID and cloud computing are starting to emerge in the insurance industry; these should enable runtime reduction and allow more scenarios or representative contracts to be run.

Closed-form solutions

In theory it is quicker and more convenient to use a closed-form formula to calculate a market-consistent value. The most obvious example of such a formula is the "vanilla" Black–Scholes–Merton European option price formula. Generally we would not choose to value a vanilla European option using an ESG, as the formula is much more convenient and option implied volatilities are readily available from market data providers.

Many other formulas have been developed that incorporate features such as:

1. mixed underlying asset portfolios (basket options);
2. digital features such as barrier options (down and out, up and in); and
3. options on options.

There is a rich set of such options that can be considered; some authors have also developed closed-form formulas to approximate life insurance liabilities (see Sheldon and Smith 2004). Therefore, it is not obvious that an ESG is needed to value insurance policy liabilities in a market-consistent way.

In practice these formulas have not found widespread use for the calculation of market-consistent values due to several issues.

- Many insurance liabilities are options on an underlying mix of assets. Formulas for basket options would typically have a static asset allocation, whereas the actual asset allocation will be subject to dynamic changes, which will be a function not only of market returns but also of the financial health of the insurance company.

- Life insurance guarantees, often complex, may include features typically found in exotic derivatives, such as smoothing, ratchets and barriers. Even without the issues raised above, it is not obvious that formulas exist for the complexity of some of these guarantees. Neither is it obvious that new products being developed will necessarily have closed-form solutions. An insurer using closed-form solutions for valuation may find itself having to use Monte Carlo simulation on some products. This will create additional difficulties in maintaining consistency between valuations of different policies.

- Many of the closed-form formulas that are developed assume that log asset returns follow geometric Brownian motion. It is widely recognised in financial literature that this assumption is incorrect and that more complex stochastic processes are required to capture excess kurtosis and negative skewness in, say, equity returns. More sophisticated models, using features such as local volatility, stochastic volatility or jump-diffusion, have been used to capture these effects. That said, a small number of extreme scenarios tend to have less effect on the valuation of financial instruments, where we are looking across the whole of the return distribution, than they do on risk measures where the focus is on the tail. Thus, arguably, the geometric Brownian motion assumption is less of a concern for valuation purposes than for the measurement of risk.

- Fixed-interest assets require special modelling to ensure they maintain arbitrage-free dynamics. Building in the dynamics of yield curve movements further complicates the development of closed-form solutions.

- Credit exposures can have non-linear dependencies on interest rates, equity market returns or macroeconomic factors such as gross domestic product. Building in these dynamics further complicates the development of closed-form solutions.
- Exotic instruments that approximate insurance liabilities are illiquid or have poor liquidity beyond very short terms. This means that the important implied volatility or implied correlation parameters are unobservable for many derivatives with closed-form formulas. This is not always a clear argument for using ESG models; the lack of liquid markets to provide data such as market implied correlations and long-term implied volatilities also poses issues for the calibration of an ESG.
- Quantitative analysts have developed closed-form solutions for exotic options traded by wholesale banks. However, evidence from quantitative analysts[6] suggests that Monte Carlo is the most efficient calculation methodology for option pricing in situations where options are path dependent and have high dimensions (ie, are based on many underlying assets). Typical participating life insurance liabilities both are path dependent and have high dimensions; this suggests that the Monte Carlo approach is likely to be the most efficient calculation method, especially when the interaction of management and policyholder behaviour is taken into account.

These observations have resulted in insurers preferring to use an ESG to calculate the market-consistent value. Essentially an ESG defines an (arbitrage-free) economic model and calibrates it to a mixture of the following data:

- liquid market data;
- prospective economic data; and
- historical data.

If we have a complex option that can be valued using a closed-form solution, one could estimate the price by estimating the implied volatilities and implied correlations for that solution. This is difficult, though, as it is rarely obvious what the values for these parameters should be.

The alternative is to use an ESG that is calibrated to certain instruments for which the implied volatility is known, and to use economic theory (via the model structure and economic variable estimates) to supplement these values. The result is a relatively transparent valuation that can be decomposed into sources of calibration data and economic model choices.

However, in some cases there is a compelling argument for using a closed-form solution. For example, where the liability valuation has a low degree of materiality, the extra expense of doing a fully scenario-based valuation could be rejected.

In the case of a small insurance company, the use of a closed-form approximation could also be justified. For example, introducing a fully stochastic valuation could result in a disproportionate cost relative to the size of the company. Alternatively a small mutual insurer might have a very high solvency margin relative to the industry, and could argue that policyholder protection would not be compromised by a closed-form solution approximation.

Replicating portfolios as an alternative

As a means of insurance liability valuation, the replicating portfolios suffers from many of the same issues as the closed-form solution. As a result it is generally not used for primary valuation, for which an ESG is still preferred.

Summary

Economic scenario generator models have advantages in the valuation of participating life insurance liabilities. Currently, the disadvantages of sampling error and runtime are outweighed by the advantages.

THE MARKET VALUE BALANCE SHEET

Market-consistent valuation will be mandatory under Solvency II for all insurance companies, for both assets and liabilities. For most European Union countries and insurers this will represent a dramatic change in the way that their balance sheet is constructed. The last section focussed on why an ESG might be used for market-consistent valuation. This section therefore focusses on market-consistent valuation in more detail.

Assets

The market values of many assets are readily available from market data sources. Where more exotic (eg, derivative) assets are held, the insurer may rely on the issuing bank or a broker to provide a valuation. Alternatively, the insurer may choose to use an ESG to value the asset. Asset valuation using stochastic methods is a very wide subject on which much additional literature exists, so we do not explore this subject further here.

Liabilities

In this section we consider some examples of the lines of business that lend themselves to Monte Carlo valuation using an ESG. Considering the broad categories of life, non-life and health insurance, the predominant use of the ESG approach to valuation is the life sector; we therefore focus most of our attention there.

Asset–liability coherence

It is quite possible that there will be a market consistency mismatch between the assets and liabilities. For example, derivative prices in the market can reflect many implied volatility surface shapes, and bond prices can reflect many yield curve shapes. However, it is in the nature of ESG models to have constraints around the shape of yield curves and volatility surfaces that can be accommodated. This can lead to identical cashflow streams on the asset and liability sides of the balance sheet having different valuations. The insurer will need to decide whether it is better to have exact coherence in valuation between the two sides of the balance sheet or accept that there will be an accurate asset valuation but just an approximate liability valuation.

In the context of Solvency II it is proposed to use a risk-free interest-rate term structure published by a designated third party, for example the European Central Bank in the case of the euro risk-free term structure. This will cause an immediate mismatch in respect of derivative contracts that use the swap rate as the risk-free rate. This will expose insurers to an asset–liability mismatch risk by virtue of the basis risk between the swap rate and the government bond rate, even where the assets and liabilities are (apparently) cashflow matched.

Lines of business

Life insurance – traditional participation contracts

Within the life sector it is the traditional "with-profit style" participation contracts with guarantees on a policyholder fund that frequently require an ESG for market-consistent valuation. This is by virtue of the large number of risk factors affecting the underlying fund and the complexity of the guarantees that are typically offered.

Considering UK experience, there is widespread use of ESG models in the valuation of UK-style with-profit contracts where complex guarantees have been written on a fund of dynamically managed assets. Market-consistent valuations are required to produce MCEV and Financial Services Authority regulatory returns.

We also find ESG models used for the market-consistent valuation of continental-style interest-rate guarantee products that can have complex guarantees. A classical continental endowment policy is a with-profit (participating) style contract that has some management discretion. The management discretion allows for adjustment of the participation rate (sometimes within the constraints of a legal agreement), the asset allocation of the fund or recognition of investment earnings for the purpose of participation. The management and policyholder behaviour are dependent on each other and the prevailing economic conditions. This makes the modelling complex and challenging. Market-consistent valuations of these products are required for MCEV and the SST.

Life insurance: unit-linked contracts

Unit-linked lines have a large degree of market exposure by design. However, because the cashflows to policyholders and shareholders are generally linear functions of the market exposure, the market-consistent valuation is a relatively simple exercise that does not necessarily require the use of an ESG.

Even where guarantees on unit-linked contracts exist, they may be simple in structure and simple closed-form solutions may be applied. However, if policyholder behaviour (eg, lapsing, paying up) is dependent on economic conditions, the use of an ESG might be more appropriate. In this case, linkages between policyholder behaviour and economic conditions can be built into an insurer's asset–liability model to capture the required dynamics.

Some contracts have more complex guarantees. A typical continental unit-linked contract, for example, has a maturity benefit guarantee that is the bigger of the fund value and a rolled-up value at maturity. The roll-up rate is usually guaranteed by the insurer and applied to the accumulated premiums net of charges. In such cases, where future premiums impact the guarantee, valuation via an ESG is likely to be preferred.

Life insurance: variable annuities
An emerging line of business (in Europe and therefore subject to Solvency II) that requires an ESG for valuation is variable annuities. Those with benefits such as guaranteed minimum withdrawal benefit have complex embedded options on baskets of asset classes. These products lend themselves to Monte Carlo valuation. Contracts where the basket can also be amended dynamically by the policyholder lend themselves to Monte Carlo valuation even more strongly.

At the time of writing, variable annuity contracts are more common in the USA and Far East than Europe. Therefore, valuation may not be material for many European-only entities. However, where European insurers are consolidating overseas entities with significant variable annuity exposure, the market-consistent valuation of these contracts may become material.

Market-consistent valuation of variable annuity contracts is also important in the day-to-day management of a variable annuity book of business. Many variable annuity businesses dynamically hedge their variable annuity liabilities to manage the asset–liability risk. This typically requires a Monte Carlo valuation under different stress tests to determine the optimal hedge portfolio by calculating a wide range of liability sensitivities to market parameters (for example, delta and gamma factors).

Life insurance: annuity pensions
Annuity pension business that includes retail price inflation (RPI) and CPI caps and floors can also lend itself to valuation using an ESG. The case for using an ESG for valuation is less compelling in an economy with a well-developed market in inflation-hedging instruments. For example, annuity writers in the UK have been able to obtain quotes for RPI and limited price inflation[7] swap contracts.

Because they are able to construct a replicating portfolios for the financial risk in their annuity liabilities using these swaps, an ESG has not normally been required for valuation.

Economic scenario generator models lend themselves to the market-consistent valuation of Dutch-style conditional indexation pensions. Often the indexation of pensions is conditional on the solvency position of the pension company.

Non-life insurance

The life products listed before all have a significant element of market risk. For the most part non-life insurance does not have a systematic risk component (ie, one correlated with market risk), with the potential exception of inflation exposure, discussed later. Where there is no systematic risk, valuation requires only the use of a risk-free yield curve applied to the expected value of the best-estimate cashflows.

There may, however, be a case for using an ESG if there is non-linear exposure to inflation. Usually, the data used for projection of the loss triangles contains implicit historical inflation. A more market-consistent approach could be to strip out historical inflation from the data and use information on inflation from the markets instead. (Further research is needed to assess how material this is.) Another possible use of ESG models in non-life insurance might arise where claims (incidence or severity) are related to economic conditions in a non-linear way.

Health insurance

We are not aware of the use of ESG models in the market-consistent valuation of health insurance business.

Counterparty credit risk

Premium inflow from corporate partners or capital support from a parent or reinsurer can be a very large source of counterparty credit risk that credit modelling should allow for. Consider a block of in-force business between a reinsurer and a primary insurer. The premium inflows to the reinsurer have credit risk, depending on the credit standing of the primary insurer. Therefore, the different credit standings of primary insurers should lead to different values for the premium cash inflow to the reinsurer. Meanwhile the outflows from the reinsurer to the primary insurer, being policyholder benefits, should be discounted at the risk-free rate.

The issue of counterparty default can thus be expressed in terms of interest-rate term structures. One approach to market-consistent valuation would be to split cashflows into cash inflows and cash outflows. Taking the view that cash outflows are policyholder guarantees and that premium income is subject to credit risk, it could be argued that the cash outflows should be discounted at the risk-free rate and the cash inflows at a higher rate, allowing for a spread in respect of counterparty credit default risk and the credit risk premium.

Another example of counterparty credit exposure is a large derivatives position. In this case, detailed modelling of the individual counterparty exposure would be more important. In this regard, it should be noted that typical collateralisation arrangements for these contracts, while reducing counterparty risk do not eliminate it. In conditions of market stress, such as those observed in 2008, it is possible that adverse market movements result in collateral calls that the counterparty is unable to provide. Where the counterparty exposures are well diversified, common factors affecting many counterparties would be more relevant to model.

Using an ESG has the advantage that the counterparty credit exposure can be treated in the same stochastic scenarios as other financial and credit risks. However, ESG models to date have tended to have a broad-brush approach to modelling and calibrating credit risk. A proper treatment of counterparty credit risk would require detailed modelling of the credit risk for specific counterparty exposures.

ESG CALIBRATION FOR MARKET-CONSISTENT VALUATION

Many of the themes explored in internal models arise in market-consistent valuation. In this section we explore the important area of ESG calibration. We have decided to focus on the issue of calibration rather than model design, as treatment of model design would require more technical detail than we wish to present in a discussion aimed at a high-level audience.

Calibration process: market data

For a full multi-economy, multi-asset, market-consistent calibration, a great deal of data is required. For example, a typical market-consistent calibration will use at least the following information directly observable from the market: nominal risk-free curve, swaption implied volatility and equity option implied volatility.

Nominal risk-free rates

Fitting a nominal risk-free yield curve is the most fundamental task for an ESG model, as it is the function describing the time value of money. Fitting the term structure[8] is generally achieved using a time dependent function to match a (preconstructed) zero coupon bond curve. A typical approach is to use a technique such as spline interpolation or a parametric form to fit a smooth curve to a set of coupon bond prices.[9] An exact fit to all bond prices is rarely achieved; typically compromises are made such as fitting more closely but to only a subset of bonds in the market, or giving a more approximate fit to all the bonds in the market.

Swaps or government bonds

An arbitrage-free model can have only one risk-free rate term structure. If this is chosen to be the lower risk-free interest rate (eg, the government bond term structure), then a higher risk-free interest rate (eg, the swap term structure) could be modelled if it is assumed that the swap spread is purely due to credit risk. In this case, there would be some scenarios where swap cashflows would not be realised. However, if the swap curve is also assumed to be the risk-free rate, then it will not be possible to model a government bond curve too in a model used for market-consistent pricing. Such a model would contain arbitrage.

A choice therefore needs to be made regarding the definition of the risk-free rate. This choice is usually between government bond rates, swap rates or a rate between these two rates. Which is chosen can be prescribed by regulation or by financial reporting convention.

Some flexibility is occasionally allowed. For example, UK realistic balance sheet calculations assume the risk-free discount rate is the government bond rate. However, there is some flexibility to adjust this if a higher rate can be demonstrated. The convention for MCEV calculations has, by contrast, been to use the swap rate. At the time of writing, CEIOPS is consulting with stakeholders on the risk-free rate. The current position is that AAA rated central government debt instruments (which meet certain criteria to ensure they are priced in a deep, liquid and transparent market) should be used to construct the risk-free term structure.

Swap market
Nominal curves usually extend to 50-year maturities for swap markets in major developed economies. The swap rate has the advantage of being liquidly traded out to reasonably long terms, and rates are usually available at regular intervals. The rates have to follow a standard across different currencies. Such standards are not present for government bond rates. For many markets where government issuance has not been regular or where the government has not issued long-term debt, the swap market provides a richer term structure.

Swap rates usually trade as a positive spread to government bonds.[10] Arguments have been made for the swap spread being a free lunch, a spread for credit risk or a spread for liquidity risk. Many people who take the free lunch or liquidity viewpoint suggest that the swap rate is a valid risk-free rate. Others have argued that the swap spread over government bonds reflects the increased credit risk from these instruments.

At the time of writing, CEIOPS' view is that the swap spread reflects credit risk relative to government bonds; its current proposal is that swap rates should not be used as the risk-free rate, or should be adjusted to remove the credit risk if swap spreads are the closest equivalent to risk-free available.

Government bond market
Government bond term structures can be significantly shorter than swap term structures, due to a lack of long dated issuance and poor liquidity for some of the longest dated debt. Long-term debt with limited supply is often found to be held by a specific group of investors: typically, insurance companies or pension funds hedging very long-term liabilities.

In some cases, there is no liquid market in risk-free government debt beyond the medium term. This can occur in well-developed economies as well as emerging ones. For example, in some well-developed European countries, there is minimal issuance beyond 10 years. This gives insurers and pension funds particular difficulty in assessing the market-consistent value of relatively simple contracts, such as pensions in payment.

Some government bonds have a particular (downward) yield bias where they are used as benchmark bonds in market activity. CEIOPS (2009a) refer to this as a technical bias and are proposing that bond prices with technical bias are adjusted accordingly. It should be noted that where nominal yield curves are fitted to government bond rates, the resulting prices of option contracts (eg, swaptions and equity options) priced using the ESG model will be different (higher if we assume swap rates exceed government bond rates) to those observed in the market.

Nominal interest-rate volatilities

In an ESG model, nominal interest-rate volatilities are typically fitted to a swaption implied volatility surface. An alternative could be implied volatilities from interest-rate caps or floors, or options on government bonds.

While options on government bonds exist in some markets, they are typically contracted on a "cheapest to deliver basis",[11] which complicates their use for ESG calibration. Swaptions are generally preferred to caps and floors, because longer maturities are normally available and swaptions are more characteristic of some of the interest-rate guarantees found within insurance markets already using ESG models for regulatory reporting, eg, guaranteed annuity options in UK life insurance. For continental European insurance products, it is not as evident that swaptions are a better replicating asset relative to caps and floors. Nonetheless, it is still currently common practice to calibrate interest-rate volatilities to the swaption market.

For at-the-money (ATM) swaptions, implied volatility surfaces tend to be reasonably liquid in developed markets around the globe. For a major developed economy, the implied volatility surface will typically extend to 50 years (option term) into 50 year (swap term).

Typically the interest-rate models used in ESG models do not provide a perfect match to the swaption implied volatility surface.

This is especially true in extreme market conditions as witnessed at the end of 2008, when parts of the ATM swaption implied volatility surface for the US could not be well matched with widely used models. Refinements such as local volatility interest-rate models would be required to improve the fit. These more sophisticated models are not widely used at the time of writing; therefore, the current approach is to focus the interest-rate calibration in those regions of the ATM swaption surface with particular relevance to the insurer's liability profile.

The equity option implied volatility smile/skew is well documented. However, smile/skew is also present in the swaption market. Capturing swaption smile/skew is most relevant for insurance business where liabilities are strongly non-linear in nominal interest rates and where the impact of the swaption smile/skew is material. For example, many guaranteed interest-rate products in continental Europe meet these criteria. For business lines with a high degree of equity or property exposure, the higher volatility of these asset classes often dominates the pricing of embedded options and guarantees, so capturing swaption smile/skew might be considered disproportionate. Calibration to fit the swaption smile involves extending the fit beyond a two-dimensional (ATM) volatility surface to a three-dimensional volatility cube. A swaption cube contains swaption implied volatilities indexed by option term, swap term and option moneyness.

Calibration to capture smile/skew in the swaption market typically requires a local or stochastic volatility interest-rate model. In practice many ESG models do not have this added level of complexity, although some insurer in-house and commercial ESG models have done so. Not surprisingly, the development and use of interest-rate models that capture swaption smile/skew has emerged from countries with significant volumes of interest-rate guarantee products. It is worth noting that the same approach to nominal rate volatility calibration is used regardless of whether the yield curve is fitted to swap rates or government bond rates.

Real interest rates

Even in countries with a good nominal rate market, the government or swap market for real interest rates can often have poor liquidity or simply not exist. Countries with inflation-linked government bonds tend to be the exception rather than the rule. For example, index-linked issuance is currently good in the UK, the US and France. Other countries that have issued index-linked bonds are Canada, Australia (now discontinued), Greece, Italy, Japan, Sweden and Iceland. At the time of writing, issuance in these countries was low and a reliable real term structure for use in an ESG model calibration would be difficult to derive.

Equity (capital index) implied volatility

Equity implied volatility on capital return indexes can be obtained to relatively short terms (one to three years) on market data systems. Beyond these short terms, market data is less easy to source, and ESG model owners (both commercial providers and insurers) have needed to conduct private surveys of equity option implied volatility from investment banks. These surveys can typically provide data to a 10-year term. Beyond 10 years, assumptions need to be made about extrapolating the data. Extrapolation is typically driven by the model structure or by econometric analysis.

Some commercial data providers produce long-term option implied volatility data that could replace informal surveys. However, proprietary extrapolation/interpolation methods and restrictions on the dissemination of the underlying option pricing data mean this data may not be transparent or may not be available for the calibration of an ESG model.

FX implied volatility

Data is usually available similar to that for equity options. Typically, only data for ATM options is used.

Calibration process: non-market data

The areas discussed prior to this represent the best sources of market data available for ESG calibration. However, there are some obvious data sources missing. (Indeed, typically, only a minority of calibration data is derived directly from market prices.) These include but are not limited to the following.

Real estate volatility

Real estate options are very illiquid if traded at all. If these are traded the option terms are likely to be short term and therefore of limited use to insurers with long-term liabilities. The real estate assets held by insurers can vary widely and rarely correspond to an index that an option may be written on. This produces significant basis risk even if a sufficiently liquid option can be found.

Inter-asset correlation
While there are basket options written in the over-the-counter (OTC) market, these are not standardised contracts and do not trade in sufficient volume or with sufficient liquidity to be usable.

Equity total return (dividend yield)
Most life insurance contracts are exposed to total returns (including the reinvested dividends issued by companies in the index). The liquidity of total return options is poor compared to that of capital return options; therefore, total return options are rarely used in ESG model calibration. Consequently, the implied volatility for a total return options is usually constructed from a capital return volatility, dividend volatility and capital return – dividend yield correlation. The latter two components lack a market; therefore, the implied volatility on total returns from an ESG model is subject to an element of subjectivity. Typically at the 10-year horizon total return volatilities calculated using an ESG model are in the range 1%–2% lower than capital return volatilities calculated from the same ESG model. This effect is due largely to the negative correlation between dividend yields and capital returns. However, where banks quote for total return options and capital return options, the total return implied volatilities can be above, below or equal to the capital return volatilities, illustrating the poorer liquidity of the equity total return market.

Corporate bond volatility
Credit spread options could provide some useful information for short-term credit spread volatility. To the knowledge of the authors, though, they have not as yet been widely used in ESG model calibration.

Inflation volatility
Limited price inflation contracts (where they are traded) could be used to calibrate inflation volatility in ESG models, but their use has been limited in the calibration of ESG models.

Practical issues

In this subsection we discuss some practical issues around ESG calibration. The appropriateness to insurance liabilities is often cited as a constraint on ESG calibration. In practice, this means that the calibration needs to reflect the term profile and moneyness of guarantees in the underlying insurance contracts. If the ESG uses relatively simple models, then there is more need to ensure calibration points are chosen appropriately. For instance, an equity model with constant volatility would need to make some assumption about the mean duration and moneyness of the policy guarantees it was being used to value. This is not a straightforward task, given that guarantees will often be based on a basket of assets and may have very different guarantee levels, depending on when they were written.

More complex models, such as local volatility, stochastic volatility or fat-tailed models, remove some of this calibration difficulty by providing a broader fit across the market data. However, they can require substantial manual effort to calibrate and can complicate the calibration of other parameters, such as correlations. There is also the issue of the step up in mathematical complexity, which can make communication of the models' behaviour and results more difficult.

The ease and speed of calibration is an important issue to bear in mind, as it is likely that several cycles of the SCR will need to be run. Other recalibrations are likely to be required for ORSA or other management information connected with the use test. Speed of recalibration is even more important for dynamic hedging of guarantees or for managing the investment risk of variable annuity, where hedging programmes require numerous recalibrations on a daily basis so that hedging trades can be placed the same day.

PRACTICAL ISSUES IN USING ESG MODELS

In this section we address some of the practical considerations in generating outputs from ESG models, as opposed to issues related to their calibration.

Number of scenarios

How many scenarios to run, is subject to a trade-off between the runtime on the one hand and the degree of convergence needed to meet the level of materiality required for the valuation on the other. Runtime is critical because while the ESG model may be run in a relatively short space of time (say a few hours), a typical ALM system could take many times longer to run.

It is not usual to see the number of scenarios dipping below 1,000. With fewer than 1,000 scenarios, the sampling error is generally considered to be too high. However, few companies run more than 5,000 scenarios and 10,000 scenarios is generally the upper limit for life insurance portfolios. This is a low number compared with the 100,000 scenarios that might be used for a derivative valuation in a bank.

Variance-reduction techniques can be deployed to help manage the tension between sampling errors and the number of scenarios. They can be employed either to reduce sampling errors for a given number of scenarios or to reduce the number of scenarios required for a given degree of sampling errors. Some approaches known to be in use follow.

Path adjustment
This involves shifting the prices of the short rate path (or equivalently the state price deflator) such that the yield curve is reproduced precisely by the discounted cashflows. Further flat (ie, the same for all scenarios) adjustments are made to other variables that need to converge quickly. Examples include the equity total return index and property total return index.

Critics of this approach say that it produces artificially large errors in estimates of present values that have not been specifically targeted. For example, non-linear cashflows from options can experience valuation bias. Nonetheless, this method has benefits where a significant part of the cashflow being valued is linear in the underlying asset that has been "fixed".

Antithetic variates
Antithetic variates are frequently used in simulating the underlying random numbers from a symmetric distribution. Antithetic variates involve taking the negative value of a sample from a distribution as an additional observation from the same distribution. Antithetic variates do not tend to introduce bias into valuations, but they are not suitable for use with asymmetric distributions because the resulting sampled distribution will always be symmetrical.

Control variates

Control variates are used where the insurer has a reasonable proxy for the item for which a market-consistent valuation is required. For example, if a closed-form formula exists that is deemed to be a good proxy for a particular embedded insurance option, the value estimate of the embedded option might be improved, compared with the pure ESG value, using the following formula

ESG value of embedded option

+ closed form value of proxy − ESG value of proxy

Projection horizon

This is usually set by reference to the term of the policies being valued. A typical value is 40 years after which most cashflows would be run-off. Longer terms (eg, to 120 years) are sometimes used if a pensions business is being valued.

Time step

This is often annual but more sophisticated approaches might use more frequent time steps in the early years of a projection, where more detail is sought and cashflows have greater present value. Annual time steps are more typical for long-term cashflows.

The time step is normally determined as a trade-off between run-time and accuracy. Some ALM systems build a model of insurance business based on a monthly time step, which means that some approximations about what happens to non-year-end months are required when annual projection is used.

For some insurance business it could be more appropriate to model more frequently than monthly; for example, dynamically hedged variable annuity will have a cost of regular hedge rebalancing, which the insurer may need or at least want to value in a market-consistent manner.

Seed

It is usual to use a pseudo-random number generator to generate the underlying random numbers in an ESG. This is preferred to using a pure random number generator, because reproducibility of results greatly simplifies the modelling and auditing of the ESG output.

Using the same seed will not always result in the output being the same. A reordering of the variables or different selection of variables can change the way in which random numbers are used and therefore change the results. Updated versions of ESG software can also change the way random numbers are used and therefore complicate the generation of reproducible results. Therefore, some insurers find they need to retain the software version and run settings exactly as before in order to maintain a historical audit trail.

ESG outputs

The output from the ESG will need to feed into whatever ALM system is being used to project asset and liability cashflows and produce the valuation. This could be a spreadsheet or a more complex ALM system, of which several commercial varieties exist. The output from the ESG must be considered in light of the modelling requirements (and any constraints) of the ALM.

Often, in the past, asset modelling has been undertaken at a reasonably simplified level, using, say, a single market index for equities. In this case, relatively minor holdings in overseas markets and any basis risk associated with a deviation of portfolio composition away from the market index would not be reflected. Such decisions have often been made on pragmatic grounds to balance the need for detail with the modelling effort required in terms of model complexity, run times, processing capacity and output storage constraints.

For moving to Solvency II, it is likely that these decisions will need to be revisited in order to provide comfort that any shortcuts or approximations remain reasonable in light of what may be new applications of the ALM results and can be robustly justified, if challenged. If additional granularity is deemed necessary, then the results generated by the ESG model will need to be extended. In some cases, this may be a simple case of selecting extra output already generated by the ESG, eg, government bond yields for every term rather than broader term buckets. However, to address other features, such as exposure to overseas assets with its associated foreign exchange risk, the ESG model will need to be extended to enable calibration to multiple economies.

A REGULATOR AND REVIEWER PERSPECTIVE

In this section we look at ESG models from a Swiss regulatory point of view and a UK actuarial reviewer's point of view.

Regulatory point of view: the Swiss experience

Switzerland has had an internal model system under the SST for a number of years. Under this system, ESG models have had to be considered as part of an internal model acceptance criterion. With Solvency II set to follow a similar path, we believe the experience from Switzerland can be instructive.

The SST[12] (set forth in the renewed Swiss Supervisory Law) has been in force since January 1, 2006. It contains many similarities to Solvency II. For example, it requires:

- a total balance sheet approach;
- market consistency;
- the explicit valuation of embedded options and guarantees; and
- in cases where the SST standard model approach is not appropriate, the use of internal models for risk measurement and valuation.

With the SST being principle-based, the insurer has freedom to choose which methodologies to use. However, these need to be accepted by the Swiss regulator[13] (via an internal models approval process).

In the framework for a life insurance business, there are no explicit requirements for the use of an ESG model. However, an appropriate scenario-based approach for valuation and risk measurement is likely to be accepted. From 2008, the SST is mandatory for all companies; however, it is only from 2011 that the available capital has to exceed the SCR.

In a principle-based world, the insurers have to convince the supervisors that their valuation and risk measurement is fully appropriate and fully market-consistent. If a company fails to do so, the Swiss regulator has the right to reduce available capital or to increase the SCR of the insurance company. Before attempting to convince the regulator, an insurance company needs to first convince its senior management, and potentially the board, about the quality and appropriateness of its internal model and the processes around it. A regulator would typically start its analysis by considering what a well-managed company would be doing on its own.

A natural starting point for convincing regulators is a thorough documentation of the internal model, which should be read, checked and corrected by a person outside the team producing the model and model documentation. This helps develop an understanding of the internal model outside the modelling and documentation-building team (particularly, internal reviewers such as the risk team or internal regulators such as internal audit).

It is important that an insurer can explain the scope of the internal model to the regulator. For example, is the model just used for valuation, or is it also used for:

- risk measurement/management;
- reserving;
- pricing; or
- some combination of the above?

It is also important to explain what sort of insurance business is being modelled and what legal entities are covered. The documentation should explain the model choice and show a discussion of alternatives, pointing out not only the decisions made but the motivation behind them and how the company arrived at these decisions. It should also provide evidence that the conclusions have been understood within the company.

In the special case of an ESG model as part of an internal model, a typical issue is whether or not the underlying modelled economic factors are appropriate and relevant for the management rules that have been implemented and for decisions on profit sharing. The insurer should also consider if the ESG model is suitable for modelling the economics that will drive the behaviour of policyholders.

Within a total balance sheet approach, special attention should be paid to the modelling of all material parts of the balance sheet. For example, consider hybrid capital. It is important to ask if the scenarios produced by the ESG model are sufficiently extreme to model triggers in the hybrid capital and the management actions associated with these triggers. In the case of an insurance group, the insurer should also consider if the ESG model provides enough granularity to distinguish between hybrid capital triggers in different underlying legal entities. In order to do this an ESG model should be able to model different economies, and economic variables within those economies, in sufficient detail to distinguish a "solvency event"[14] in different entities across a group.

In terms of governance, it is important to check if there is awareness of, and discussion within the senior management regarding, the risks associated with the internal model. Part of this supervisory process will include checking awareness of the limitations of the ESG model. An obvious question for a regulator is "Who in senior management really understands this?" Considering the ESG model, additional questions could be but are not limited to:

- In the case of an external ESG model, how are roles and responsibilities shared within the insurer or between the insurer and the external provider? What checks and balances are in place?
- What is the scope and use of the ESG model within the company: just valuation or also risk measurement?
- What economies are covered by the ESG?
- Can the company explain why the model choice is right for them? Does the documentation show that the senior management (ie, those responsible for signing off the SST) is acting appropriately for a principle-based environment? Or does it show that management exhibit mechanical behaviour (eg, rule-based environment)?
- Are the economic factors produced by the ESG model sufficient for describing all material asset classes, combinations of asset classes, asset allocation strategies, liabilities (including hybrids), management rules and policyholder behaviour?
- How are corporate spreads modelled? This is important for the valuation of premium cash inflows from corporate partners (eg, financial reinsurance, group business). It is also important for consistency between certain asset classes without a deep and liquid market but with counterparty risk; examples include mortgages and loans (in continental Europe). In these cases the valuation results based on an ESG model should be checked against more traditional valuation techniques and potential differences explained or justified.
- The insurer should be able to explain the reason for the number of scenarios used for the ESG. For example, why is the number

used considered sufficient and what kind of test has been performed to show that it is sufficient? A regulator would want to see a description of the test and the results. It is also relevant to explain who performed the test; preferably it will be someone independent from the modelling and scenario-generating teams.

- It is important to be able to show the impact of assumptions on the result. Sensitivity tests that measure the sensitivity (or delta) with respect to input parameters are appropriate. It is of particular interest how sensitive the results are to kurtosis and tail behaviour parameters, which have a high degree of uncertainty in their estimation. A regulator would also be seeking assurance from the company that they understand the significance of underlying assumptions.

- If the ESG model is distribution based (or explicitly based on a stochastic process), a regulator could ask for samples of the underlying theoretical distribution (stochastic process) as a validation test. Any differences between the theoretical behaviour of the model and the output would need an explanation. If the ESG model is not distribution based (eg, bootstrapping), a regulator could ask to see the empirical distribution, request an interpretation of the results produced and check that the management understood the results.

- A regulator would also be interested in what financial instruments the ESG calibration has been calibrated to. For example, are the instruments traded in a deep and liquid market and are the values used as observed on the reporting date? A regulator would want to know what tests had been carried out and by whom. The regulator could ask the company to explain why it thought that their ESG model was market-consistent.

- Another area of interest is the consistency between different inflation assumptions. For example, are the ESG inflation assumptions comparable with the assumptions in the cost model and against the premium inflation (eg, group business, where future premiums depend on salaries)? The regulator might also ask if the ESG model is used for setting cost assumptions.

How can a regulator come to a decision they feel confident with? One possibility is benchmarking. Given its broad market overview and access to many different models and results, a regulator can set up a database and compare the different results to get a feeling on outliers or odd results. If there are enough companies in the market, a regulator can make the results of the individual insurers anonymous. This makes it possible to have a discussion about the position of each insurer with respect to the rest of the market. For example, a box-plot may be used to visualise the position of a single insurer in relation to the insurer's peer group. Another possibility is asking the company for peer review reports. The regulator will place more reliance on a report, the more independent the reviewing peers are.

Sometimes innovative approaches used in companies are presented and discussed in scientific journals with a good academic reputation due to their rigorous referee review process. However, many regulators would not consider this sufficient and an additional onsite inspection would be an important way of understanding how the model actually works in practice. An onsite inspection can review internal processes, communication, data handling and how the model behaves under different assumptions or for different run parameters. A regulator should also have the right to trigger an independent assessment by a third party.

The actuarial reviewer point of view: the UK experience

In the UK, the use of market-consistent ESG models is widespread in the production of a realistic balance sheet, which forms part of the assessment of Pillar I solvency capital for life offices with significant participating contracts. The use of real-world ESG models is currently less common, but with the introduction of Solvency II we expect this position to change. Below, with a focus on market-consistent ESG models, we discuss the areas that would typically form part of a UK actuarial review. These tests would be performed at initial implementation and upon subsequent changes to the model.

- Technical details of the models used within the ESG, including their theoretical basis, a demonstration of the model's arbitrage-free property, the parameters required and the process required for their calibration and the definition of the model's output generated.

- A clear rationale for the models selected in light of the risks inherent in the business being modelled: in this context, a thorough understanding of the limitations of the models and the possible consequences. For example, if the interest-rate model were not capable of reflecting the "smile" in swaption implied volatilities, then this might be addressed through analysis and careful targeting of the calibration to reflect the average moneyness of the portfolio. Alternatively, robust sensitivity testing could be used to see if changing the volatility had a material impact on the results.
- Tests to verify the correct implementation of the theoretical model. One approach would be to compare the distribution of outcomes for certain key parameters from the ESG model with those implied by the underlying theoretical model. Such comparisons are best undertaken using a large number of scenarios to reduce sampling errors; statistical tests such as the Andersen–Darling (1952) test can then be applied to check the fit.
- The standard confirmation of risk neutrality of an ESG model is that it passes the so-called "martingale" (or "1 = 1") test. The martingale test checks to see whether the following relationship holds

$$E(I(t)/C(t)) = 1$$

$I(t) =$ the index of cumulative returns to time t on the asset being considered. $C(t) =$ the accumulated return on the risk-neutral numeraire asset (often taken as the cash bank account).

- In the risk-neutral world, the expected return on every asset is the risk-free return; the martingale test aims to demonstrate consistency with this requirement. The martingale test will not be passed exactly; the greater the volatility of the underlying assets, the more likely it is to see deviations away from one. Nevertheless, the results would generally be expected to lie within a reasonable confidence interval of the expected value of one and to exhibit no pronounced trend.
- Sufficiency of scenarios – the real test of this is whether the value of the underlying insurance liabilities is stable under the number of scenarios performed. Known as "convergence testing", a typical approach would be to monitor the value

of the liabilities as the number of scenarios is increased. The value of the liabilities should clearly converge to a stable figure within the number of scenarios the insurer is using.

- To demonstrate the market consistency of the results, market prices for a selection of instruments are compared with those obtained by valuing the same instruments using ESG scenarios. This might be broken down into model fitting errors (market price versus price based on a fitted theoretical model) and simulation errors (price based on a fitted theoretical model versus price derived from simulation results). Model errors might be addressed by adjusting the calibration, say by changing the weighting applied to the various data points used or ultimately by changing the model itself. Simulation errors may be reduced through increasing the number of scenarios, though there may be runtime constraints on the downstream asset–liability cashflow model. Alternatively, variance-reduction techniques could be used, as discussed earlier. Any techniques used to reduce the number of scenarios would need to have their impact explained.

- The process and controls around the model calibration will be reviewed. In particular, the analysis performed to target the calibration to the underlying liabilities will be reviewed, as will the data sources used. If the data requires any manipulation before being used to calibrate the model, this will also need to be reviewed. Examples include fitting a yield curve to available market data points and any extrapolation beyond the last available data point. Procedures adopted for review and sign-off of the ESG scenarios would need to be shown.

- A reviewer might also look for evidence of alignment of the model with the insurer's actual investment strategy. For example, if the ESG model used a generic corporate bond index, is this consistent with the actual corporate bond portfolio?

SUMMARY

In this chapter we have tried to present the ways in which ESG models fit into Solvency II. We discussed the drivers that have led to ESG models being used within insurance companies; some of these were regulatory initiatives aimed at policyholder protection

and some were management initiatives aimed at better management of the business. We went on to explore the various pillars of
Solvency II, with particular focus on Pillar I and internal models
to see what this would mean for ESG models and how they might
be used. We outlined a number of approaches to calculate the SCR,
including the use of replicating portfolios and nested Monte Carlo
simulations.

We have considered market-consistent valuation in some detail,
asking if it is necessary to use an ESG for market-consistent valuation and comparing the ESG approach with other possibilities.
We then looked at selected aspects of the market-consistent balance
sheet, considering which lines of insurance business could be valued using an ESG model. We also reflected on the important topic of
ESG calibration and discussed which data sources had reliable data.

Then we described the perspectives of some key stakeholders
(a regulator and an actuarial reviewer) in approaching the review
of an ESG model in practice. Finally, we have collected what we
hope will be some useful extracts from regulation and accounting
standards relevant to the future regulation and accounting of the
output that ESG models produce in the following Appendix.

APPENDIX: MARKET-CONSISTENT VALUATION IN
REGULATION AND ACCOUNTING

As we have seen, there are often a number of market prices needed
for an ESG calibration where markets do not currently exist. In these
cases, we need to produce some analysis to create pseudo-prices. In
the banking world this has been known as mark-to-model. During
the recent financial crisis of 2008, these mark-to-model methods
have received some criticism as being responsible for systematic
mispricing of structured credit instruments. Where mark-to-model
is used as a measure of value, we believe, it is important that the
models and calibration methods used are well disclosed and based
on sound economic fundamentals.

In a typical ESG calibration we will have "deep and liquid"
market data for certain prices (usually to an upper time horizon).
Extrapolation will then be needed to longer terms. A key decision
is to define the boundary of the deep and liquid market.

The definition known to the authors of what constitutes a deep and liquid market comes from the Bank for International Settlements (BIS). The BIS is the architect of the Basel Capital Accord for banks, which introduced risk-based regulation to the banking sector, as well as the concept of the internal model. The definition of a deep and liquid market used throughout this chapter derives from the following:

> A liquid market is a market where participants can rapidly execute large-volume transactions with a small impact on prices.
>
> Depth denotes either the volume of trades possible without affecting prevailing market prices, or the amount of orders on the order-books of market-makers at a given time.

This definition has also been adopted by the International Association of Insurance Supervisors and has in turn been put forward by CEIOPS. While this definition is helpful, it is still subjective, with terms such as "large-volume", "small impact" and "rapidly" left undefined.

There are several places where market-consistent/fair value measures are required in accounting and regulation. These include:

- Solvency II;
- the SST (and other local European regulations); and
- fair value accounting standards (including FASB (2008) for the US).

Solvency II

Deep and liquid markets

The concept of a deep and liquid market is mentioned several times in Solvency II regulations. A recurring definition is the following, repeated in CEIOPS (2009c) and from QIS4:

- market participants can rapidly execute large-volume transactions with little impact on prices;
- current trade and quote information is readily available to the public;
- the properties [above] are expected to be permanent.

There are clear similarities between parts of this definition and parts of the one set by the BIS. The definitions are, though, still quite general.

CEIOPS (2009a), in addition to proposing that the risk-free term structure is mandated by the supervisor, has proposed a set of criteria that government bonds should pass before being admitted to the construction of the risk-free term structure. These start to provide more definition as to what would be considered a deep and liquid market in risk-free instruments under Solvency II. The criteria are as follows:

a) No credit risk
b) Realism (it should be possible to earn the risk-free rate in a risk-free manner)
c) Reliability (method should give a reliable estimate . . . especially in times of market stress)
d) High liquidity for all maturities (a reliable market value is observable from a deep and liquid market)
e) No technical biases
f) Availability for all relevant currencies
g) Proportionate availability (to all (re)insurers regardless of their size).

At present, these are being presented only as principles for a risk-free term structure, but one can see how they could be modified for other market inputs, such as equity implied volatility.

Calibration data
Solvency II has a few points to make on the calibration of market-consistent valuation, although there is still some ambiguity around the details. We start by looking at the latest Quantitative Impact Study at the time of writing (QIS4).

> QIS4 TS.I.B.2: CEIOPS proposes the following hierarchy of high level principles for valuation of assets and liabilities under QIS4:
>
> (i) Wherever possible, a firm must use mark to market in order to measure the economic value of assets and liabilities;
> (ii) Where this is not possible, mark to model procedures should be used (marking to model is any valuation which has to be benchmarked, extrapolated or otherwise calculated from a market input). When marking to model, undertakings will use as much as possible observable and market-consistent inputs.

The QIS4 guidance from CEIOPS is not particularly specific. However, the spirit is that where market data can be found it should be used and a model should be used otherwise. We see this practice by and large observed in the current calibration of ESG models.

In July CEIOPS (2009c) was released. It discusses CEIOPS' approach to mark-to-model. The tone of this approach has clearly been influenced by the global financial crisis of 2008, CEIOPS (2009c) states:

> . . . a main conclusion commonly repeated in the various reports dealing with the crisis is the necessity of limiting the scope of mark-to-model practices and non-actively traded assets, as one of the main causes of the current crisis.

It goes on to describe how cashflows that are considered non-replicable should be unbundled into a best-estimate value and a risk margin. It further says that "non-replicable" includes any cashflows:

> . . . for which there are no financial instruments for which reliable prices are observable.

This will have a potentially significant impact on ESG calibration. As we saw earlier, many of the calibration inputs to an ESG model have no reliable prices; consider, for example, all correlations and long-term equity implied volatility. The proposed advice therefore appears to require an insurer to hold a risk capital margin against all aspects of non-hedgeable inputs to the ESG calibration.

It is interesting to compare this with the Solvency II Framework Directive (2009), which states:

> The calculation of technical provisions should be consistent with the valuation of assets and other liabilities (and) market consistent . . .

> For the purpose of calculating technical provisions reasonable interpolations and extrapolations from directly observable market values may be applied.

The Solvency II Framework Directive, though not detailed, makes clear that valuation should be consistent with market values, while allowing for reasonable interpolations between market data and reasonable extrapolations from market data. This would seem to allow equity implied volatility to be extrapolated, as long as it is "reasonable" – a term not yet defined.

Therefore, at the time of writing, it is not clear how to reconcile the principle-based approach of the directive with the proposals contained in CEIOPS (2009c). One possible interpretation is that extrapolations such as equity implied volatility would be allowed in an ESG without incurring an extra risk margin, because a liquid market exists to a term of around three years and useful price data is still available to a term of 10 years. Inputs such as correlations, for which there is no reliable market, would, though, attract a risk margin. Consultation on CEIOPS (2009c) ends on September 11, 2009; CEIOPS plans to send its advice to the European Commission in the autumn of 2009.

SST[15]

Several European insurance regulators required market-consistent valuation of insurance products even prior to the introduction of Solvency II. These included the UK and Switzerland. These local regulations have been principle-based in their approach. We consider one of these jurisdictions, Switzerland, for illustration. While not part of Solvency II, the SST has many similarities to the emerging Solvency II standard. We also briefly mention some of the relevant reporting around the UK regulations.

Market-consistent valuation has existed in the SST for several years. In the SST, all assets and liabilities have to be valued on a market-consistent economic basis. The main principle of a market-consistent economic approach is that the valuation should use and not contradict information from liquid markets. The SST adds the constraint that the value of a liability towards policyholders must not reflect the insurer's own credit standing.[16]

This means, in practice, that for the purpose of constructing the economic balance sheet, if there is a market price, this has to be used for valuation. In other words "mark-to-market" is mandatory where this is possible. If it is not possible, an appropriate model has to be used: "marking-to-model".

The derivation of the market-consistent balance sheet is subject to several tests, which include a calibration test and a check as to whether the model prices would be used in an arm's length transaction and how plausible they are. If a model is applied for valuation purposes, the SST requires that it should be based on sound mathematical methods. Valuation models qualify as internal models within the SST and are subject to supervisory approval.

Fair value accounting standards

There are more precise definitions on what constitutes fair value in accounting standards. In the US, FASB (2008) has relevant material; similarly, the IASB (2009) has recently published an Exposure Draft on this subject, setting out their plans for fair value. Currently neither of these accounting boards mandates market-consistent/fair value for insurance contracts, as required in Solvency II. Nonetheless, they serve as a useful framework for approaching fair value. FASB (2009) and IASB (2009) have many similarities. For the purpose of brevity, we will just consider the former.

Deep and liquid markets

FASB (2009) refers to an active market rather than a deep and liquid market. The concept of an active market in FASB (2009) appears to include thinly traded markets. The FASB (2009) standard refers to an active market as follows:

> An active market for the asset or liability is a market in which transactions for the asset or liability occur with sufficient frequency and volume to provide pricing information on an ongoing basis.

> A quoted price in an active market provides the most reliable evidence of fair value and shall be used to measure fair value whenever available. . .

The active market definition does leave open the question of what "sufficient frequency and volume" means in practice. Various definitions could be:

- a bid-offer spread below a certain amount;
- the volume traded each day above a certain amount; or
- the number of transactions each day above a certain amount.

The FASB (2009) standard goes on to make the following comment on thinly traded markets:

> . . . quoted prices, even from thin markets, provide useful information because investors and creditors regularly rely on those prices to make their decisions.

Calibration data

FASB (2009) also makes some attempts to classify data according to how market-consistent the data is. It introduces a reasonably comprehensive description of what data can be considered for fair value calculations by introducing three data levels. These data levels can be used to label inputs to a fair value calculation (for example, the calibration of an ESG) and rank the market-consistent quality of the data inputs. Below we have some selected extracts from the standard. (We have taken extracts only; the reader is advised to read the entire standard for full details of the valuation hierarchy.)

> Level 1 inputs are quoted prices (unadjusted) in active markets for identical assets or liabilities that the reporting entity has the ability to access at the measurement date.

In the context of a market-consistent valuation, if a level 1 input is available, then it is unlikely that an ESG model is required to calculate the market-consistent valuation. The reason for this is that the value of the liability would be equal to the value of an observable market price. In practice few, if any, insurance contracts can be represented precisely by a liquidly traded financial instrument.

We now move on to level 2. To focus on the most relevant of the several level 2 definitions in FASB (2009):

> Level 2 inputs are . . .
>
> a. Quoted prices for similar assets or liabilities in active markets.

Some ESG model data inputs fall under the level 2 input definition. For example, many swaption contracts and equity option contracts are only similar to life insurance contracts. Therefore, where these contracts are used to calibrate an ESG model that will subsequently be used to value a participating life insurance contract, they can be considered level 2 input.

A swaption used to calibrate an ESG could therefore be considered a level 2 input to the calculation of a guaranteed annuity option or interest-rate guarantee. Similarly, a long-term equity option in an illiquid market could be considered a level 2 input, as it is only similar to a cash guarantee embedded in an insurance contract.

Finally, let us consider level 3, again starting with the definition of inputs at that level.

> Level 3 inputs are unobservable inputs for the asset or liability . . . the fair value measurement objective remains the same, that is, an exit price from the perspective of a market participant that holds the asset or owes the liability.

Arguably most data input to an ESG model used for the technical provision calculation will be level 3 input; that is to say, they will not be derived from market data that is observable but will instead need to be manufactured as pseudo-prices via a mark-to-model process.

While subjective, the input can still be subject to rigorous economic analysis to provide a reasonably objective view of the price that a deep and liquid market would be likely to trade at. Examples might be long-term real-estate implied volatility or implied correlation for which no market (even an illiquid one) is readily available. In such cases, analyses of historical data or economic forecasts are likely to be used to infer suitable parameter estimates.

1   All the views expressed in this chapter are those of the authors and do not represent the views of their current employers. Russell and Elliot would especially like to thank Seth Eshun of the UK Financial Services Authority for his valuable input in developing the original slides that were the forerunner to this material. Elliot would especially like to thank John Hibbert and Steffen Sorensen of Barrie & Hibbert for many useful discussions about ESG modelling. The authors would also like to thank the following people for their input to the review of this chapter: Gareth Collard (Ernst & Young LLP), Andy Cope (KPMG LLP), Andrew Hitchcox (Kiln), Søren Kruse (Aktuariebolaget), Udo Löchert (FINMA), Craig McCulloch (KPMG Actuaries Pty Ltd), Laura Santori (Standard & Poor's) and Mark Stober (FINMA). Any remaining errors are entirely the responsibility of the authors.

2   In this chapter we use the word "scenarios" to refer to stochastically generated economic simulations using a Monte Carlo–driven model. By contrast, elsewhere in risk management literature, "scenarios" can be used to mean a comparatively small number of possible future outcomes that are used as part of the risk management process.

3   To remove any doubt, this section is making reference to the real-world projection of economic variables, concerning which there could be much subjectivity, as opposed to a market-consistent projection of economic variables, concerning which more conformity would be expected.

4   Within the SST standard approach, the distribution of the so-called "analytical model" and the impact of the "scenarios" (which can be thought of as stress tests) ensure that non-normality and heavy tails are taken into account. The goal is to combine the "analytical model" and the "scenarios" into one distribution to describe the overall risk. A mix of distributions is used to calibrate the fat-tailed scenarios. For details please read the Technical Document on the SST, http://www.finma.ch/e/beaufsichtigte/versicherungen/schweizer-solvenztest/pages/default.aspx).

5   FSA Pillar 1 Peak 2 (Realistic Balance Sheet) for With-Profit Funds, Appendix 9.4A, Option Table.

6   http://www.wilmott.com/.

7   Limited price inflation contracts pay out the same cashflows as RPI contracts, except that they have an upper cap of 5% and a lower floor of 0% on the RPI inflation rate used for determining cashflows.

8 CEIOPS (2009a) has proposed that regulators should set the risk-free term structure. In particular, they propose the use of the European Central Bank interest-rate term structure for the Eurozone. The CEIOPS advice to the European Commission is expected to take place in autumn 2009.

9 CEIOPS (2009a) has proposed the use of the European Central Bank interest-rate curve, which uses the Svensson parametric model to fit a curve between three months and 40 years.

10 At the end of 2008 and up until the writing of this chapter, long-term swap spreads on some of the major economies have been negative.

11 "Cheapest to deliver" option contracts give the option writer the ability to choose to deliver a selection of similar government bonds. The cheapest bond will usually be delivered. The complication arises because the cheapest bond can change as the term structure of interest rates changes throughout the lifetime of the option contract.

12 *Verordnung über die Beaufsichtigung von privaten Versicherungsunternehmen und SST Rundschreiben, 2008/44.*

13 The Swiss insurance and banking regulator is FINMA. Their English-language website can be found at http://www.finma.ch/e/.

14 By "solvency event" we mean a set of circumstances that activates the trigger on a hybrid capital instrument.

15 http://www.finma.ch/archiv/bpv/download/e/SST_Richtlinie_InklAnhang_20081128.pdf.

16 This is a deviation from the pure market-consistent view, in that issued bonds, eg, contain a credit spread.

REFERENCES

Anderson, T. W. and D. A. Darling, 1952, "Asymptotic Theory of Certain 'Goodness-of-Fit' Criteria Based on Stochastic Processes", *Annals of Mathematical Statistics* 23(2), pp. 193–212.

Artzner, P., F. Delbean, J. M. Eber and D. Heath, 1999, "Coherent Measures of Risk", *Mathematical Finance* 9(3), pp. 203–28.

CEIOPS, 2007, "QIS4 – Technical Specifications", December, URL: http://ec.europa.eu/internal_market/insurance/docs/solvency/qis4/technical_specifications_en.pdf.

CEIOPS, 2008, "Own Risk and Solvency Assessment (ORSA)", Issues Paper, May, URL: http://www.ceiops.eu/media/docman/public_files/consultations/IssuesPaperORSA.pdf.

CEIOPS, 2009a, "Draft CEIOPS' Advice for Level 2 Implementing Measures on Solvency II: Technical Provisions – Article 85b – Risk-free interest rate term structure", Consultation Paper 40, July, URL: http://www.ceiops.eu/media/files/consultations/consultationpapers/CP40/CEIOPS-CP-40-09-L2-Advice-TP-Risk-Free-Rate.pdf.

CEIOPS, 2009b, "Draft CEIOPS' Advice for Level 2 Implementing Measures on Solvency II: Articles 118-124 – Tests and Standards for Internal Model Approval", Consultation Paper 56, July, URL: http://www.ceiops.eu/media/files/consultations/consultationpapers/CP56/CEIOPS-CP-56-09-L2-Advice-Tests-and-Standards-for-internal-model-approval.pdf.

CEIOPS, 2009c, "Draft CEIOPS' Advice for Level 2 Implementing Measures on Solvency II: Technical Provisions – Article 85c – Circumstances in which technical provisions shall be calculated as a whole", Consultation Paper 41, July, http://www.knf.gov.pl/Images/090702%20CP41%20L2-Advice-TP-Calculation-as-a-whole_tcm20-11326.pdf.

European Commission, 2009, "Solvency II Framework Directive", April.

FASB, 2008, "Statement of Financial Accounting Standards No. 157 – Fair Value Measurements", URL: http://www.fasb.org/cs/BlobServer?blobcol=urldata&blobtable=MungoBlobs&blobkey=id&blobwhere=1175818737868&blobheader=application%2Fpdf.

Frankland, R., A. D. Smith, T. Wilkins, E. Varnell, A. Holtham, E. Biffis, S. Eshun and D. Dullaway, 2008, "Modelling Extreme Market Events: A Report of the Benchmarking Stochastic Models Working Party", presented to the Institute of Actuaries, November 3. URL: http://www.actuaries.org.uk/__data/assets/pdf_file/0007/140110/sm20081103.pdf.

IASB, 2009, "Fair Value Measurement", Exposure Draft ED/2009/5, May, URL: http://www.iasb.org/NR/rdonlyres/C4096A25-F830-401D-8E2E-9286B194798E/0/EDFairValueMeasurement_website.pdf.

Sheldon, T. J. and A. D. Smith, 2004, "Market Consistent Valuation of Life Assurance Business", *British Actuarial Journal* 10(3), pp. 543–626.

7

Market Risk Measurement Under Solvency II

Michele Bourdeau[1]

Federal Reserve Bank of New York

Solvency margin requirements have been in place since the 1970s. The solvency margin is the amount of regulatory capital an insurance undertaking is obliged to hold against unforeseen events. In the 1990s, the consensus was that the European Union (EU) solvency rules needed to be reviewed. The Insurance Directives mandated the European Commission at that point to conduct a review of the solvency requirements. Following this review, a limited reform was agreed by the European Parliament and the Council in 2002. This reform is known as Solvency I. Solvency I has been implemented by national supervisors in many different ways around Europe. It became apparent during the Solvency I process that a more fundamental evaluation of the capital adequacy regime for the European insurance industry was needed. Towards this, a broader ranging review of the overall financial position of an insurance undertaking is being required; the assessment includes looking at current developments in insurance, risk management, financial techniques, international financial reporting, prudential standards and so on.

Solvency II aims to establish a set of EU-wide capital requirements and risk management standards replacing the current Solvency I requirements. The most important feature of Solvency II is its risk-based character, where the capital requirements are related to the risk profile of an insurance entity. Higher risks will lead to a higher capital requirement. A second feature is its greater focus on insurance groups (as opposed to separate legal entities). A third feature is the market-consistent valuation for assets and liabilities. Importantly, Solvency II explicitly allows for the use of models developed internally for the calculation of capital requirements.

Solvency II should help make prudential failure less likely, diminish the likelihood of consumer loss or market disruption and protect policyholders' interests more successfully. If adopted, Solvency II requirements would be uniform across the EU, making it easier for firms to do business together.

Solvency II is based on a three-pillar approach that is similar to the banking sector's Basel II but adapted for insurance (see various Solvency II websites and articles).

The first pillar contains the quantitative requirements. It sets in place the valuation standard for liabilities to policyholders and the capital requirements firms will be required to meet for insurance, credit, market and operational risk. As with Basel II, capital requirements can be calculated using a standard formula or, if the firms have received supervisory authorisation, they can use their own internally developed capital models. There are two capital requirements, the solvency capital requirement (SCR) and the minimum capital requirement (MCR), and they represent different levels of supervisory approval. The SCR is a risk-based requirement and the key solvency control level. Solvency II sets out two methods for the calculation of the SCR: the European standard formula or the firms' own internal models. The SCR covers all the quantifiable risks an insurer or reinsurer faces and takes into account any risk mitigation techniques. The MCR is a lower level requirement and its breach triggers the withdrawal of supervisory authorisation.

The second pillar contains qualitative requirements on undertakings such as risk management and supervisory activities. It consists of the supervisory review process that focuses on evaluating the adequacy of capital and risk management systems and processes. Supervisors may decide a firm should hold additional capital against any risks not adequately covered in pillar I.

The third pillar covers supervisory reporting and disclosure. Firms will need to disclose certain information publicly, such as details of their risks, capital and risk management. This will establish market discipline and help ensure the stability of insurers and reinsurers (disclosure). In addition, firms will be required to report a greater amount of information to their supervisors (supervisory reporting).

Solvency II requires firms to value their assets and liabilities on a market-consistent basis. More risk-sensitive capital requirements address asset, as well as liability, risks consistent with the domestic prudential reforms that were implemented for insurers in 2004. Solvency II also streamlines the way that insurance groups are supervised. The new regime will strengthen the powers of the group supervisor, ensuring that group-wide risks are not overlooked, and demand greater co-operation between supervisors. Groups will be able to use group-wide models and take advantage of group diversification benefits.

The new solvency regime is being developed along the lines of the Lamfalussy framework's four-level approach. It consists of:

- Level 1: primary legislation (Framework Directive) to define broad key "framework" principles of the new system.
- Level 2: the European Commission adopts detailed technical implementing measures, assisted by a regulatory committee. In addition, the Committee of European Insurance and Occupational Pensions Supervisors (CEIOPS) will give advice to the European Commission on the implementing measures.
- Level 3: co-operation among national regulators to ensure consistent interpretation of level 2 rules.
- Level 4: enforcement to ensure a consistent implementation of EU legislation.

The European Commission adopted the Solvency II proposal in July 2007. In order to take account of the adoption of further directives as regards to procedural rules and evaluation criteria for the prudential assessment of acquisitions and increase of holdings in the financial sector, as well as the upcoming adoption of the so-called Rome I Regulation on the law applicable on contractual obligations, the European Commission adopted an amended the Solvency II proposal on February 26, 2008. CEIOPS has been asked to start working on the development of further advice on future implementing measures.

The original expected timeline for this to come into force and transposition of the directive is as follows:

April–July 2008 fourth quantitative impact study (QIS4);
November 2008 QIS4 results;
2009 adoption of the directive by the European parliament and the Council;
October 2009 CEIOPS advice on implementing measures;
2010 adoption of the implementing measures;
2012 transposition of the directive.

As of March 2009, the European Commission's November 2008 target for adopting the Solvency II Framework Directive was missed. Standard & Poor's ratings service believes that the earliest implementation date is now likely to be January 1, 2013, instead of October 1, 2012 (see Jones *et al* 2009).

CAPITAL REQUIREMENTS UNDER SOLVENCY II FOR MARKET RISK MEASUREMENT

An overview of the technical aspects of Solvency II capital requirements related to market risk measurement is given below.

As part of the Solvency II project, the European Commission had requested that CEIOPS run a number of large scale field-testing exercises, called quantitative impact studies (QIS), to assess the practicability, implications and possible impact of the different alternatives considered. March 2008 saw the launch of the QIS4 on Solvency II. The exercise ran from April to July 2008.

The operational arrangements to conduct QIS4 and collate results from firms were made by national insurance supervisors separately in each member state, supplemented by a centrally-co-ordinated collation of groups' results. The results collated at a national level were then shared within CEIOPS, which produced an overall CEIOPS QIS4 report. While the results of this exercise will constitute the main quantitative input used by CEIOPS in the development of their final advice on potential level 2 implementing measures, which is due October 2009, CEIOPS final advice will not necessarily reflect the specifications laid out in QIS4. In effect, in a number of areas, a range of different options are being tested and a decision as to the best approach will only be taken after the results of QIS4 have been analysed and discussed.

As mentioned in the introduction, there are currently two capital requirements, the SCR and the MCR, which represent different levels of supervisory approval. The SCR is a risk-based requirement and the key solvency control level. The SCR covers all the quantifiable risks an insurer or reinsurer faces and takes into account any risk mitigation techniques. Solvency II sets out two methods for the calculation of SCR: the European standard formula or the firms' own internal models. The MCR is a lower requirement and its breach triggers the withdrawal of supervisory authorisation.

In the next section we review the SCR standard formula and how the market risk measure module fits in and is computed. We then describe how the SCR can be determined by using the firm's own internal models, ie, its own value-at-risk (VaR) methodology. In the process, we provide an overview of VaR and the different methodologies used to compute it. We also briefly discuss the MCR.

SCR under the standard formula

The SCR standard formula calculation is divided into modules as follows (see CEIOPS 2007, Section 3):

Overall SCR calculation: SCR has the following calculation structure. The SCR at the top of Figure 7.1 is the final SCR.

At the next-to-top level, the three building blocks' input information is required:

$\textbf{BSCR}$ = basic SCR
$\textbf{SCR}_{\textbf{op}}$ = the capital charge for operational risk
   $\textbf{Adj}$ = adjustment for the risk absorbing effect of future profit sharing and deferred taxes

These inputs give the overall SCR, the standard formula capital charge as

$$\textbf{SCR} = \textbf{BSCR} - \textbf{Adj} + \textbf{SCR}_{\textbf{op}}$$

The parameters and assumptions used for the calculation of SCR are intended to reflect a VaR measure calibrated to a confidence level of 99.5% and a time horizon of one year. This reflects the level expected of firms using their internal models to compute SCR. For an overview of VaR, see the section "What is VaR?" To ensure that the different modules of the standard formula are calibrated in a consistent manner, the calibration objectives are

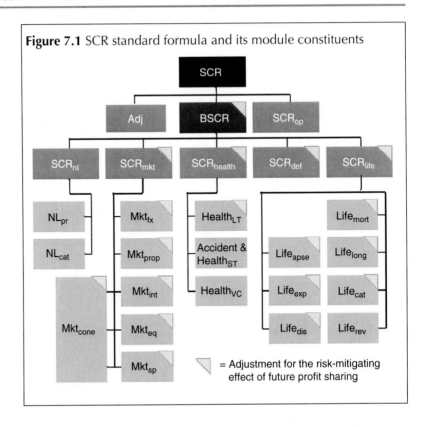

Figure 7.1 SCR standard formula and its module constituents

applied to each individual risk module. For the aggregation of the individual risk modules to an overall SCR, linear correlation techniques are applied. The setting of the correlation coefficients is intended to reflect potential dependencies found in the tail of the distributions, as well as the stability of any correlation assumptions under stressed conditions.

We now briefly describe the inputs, outputs and formulas to determine the three building blocks of SCR capital.

SCR_{op} operational risk: operational risk is the risk of loss arising from inadequate or failed internal processes, people, systems or external events. Operational risk also includes legal risks. Reputation risks and risks arising from strategic decisions do not count as operational risks. The operational risk module is designed to address operational risks to the extent that these have not been explicitly covered in other risk modules.

We will not go into detail on the calculation of the operational risk module, except to say that it includes the basic SCR described next. For further details, please consult CEIOPS (2007, Section 3).

Basic SCR: the basic SCR is computed before any adjustments and combines capital charges for five major risk categories.

The following input information is required for determining the basic SCR:

SCR_{mkt} = capital charge for market risk
$nSCR_{mkt}$ = same but including the risk absorbing effect of future profit sharing
SCR_{def} = capital charge for counterparty default risk
$nSCR_{def}$ = same but including the risk absorbing effect of future profit sharing
SCR_{life} = capital charge for life underwriting risk
$nSCR_{life}$ = same but including the risk absorbing effect of future profit sharing
SCR_{nl} = capital charge for non-life underwriting risk
SCR_{health} = capital charge for health underwriting risk
$nSCR_{health}$ = same but including the risk absorbing effect of future profit sharing
FDB = total amount in technical provisions corresponding to future discretionary benefits

The module delivers the following output:

$BSCR$ = basic SCR
Adj = adjustment for the risk absorbing effect of future profit sharing and deferred taxes
$nBSCR$ = net BSCR

The **BSCR, Adj** and **nBSCR** are determined as follows

$$BSCR = \sqrt{\sum_{rxc} CorrSCR_{r,c} \cdot SCR_r \cdot SCR_c}$$

$$Adj = Adj_{FDB} + Adj_{DT}$$

$$nBSCR = BSCR - Adj$$

where:

$CorrSCR_{r,c}$ = the cells of the correlation matrix CorrSCR

SCR_r, SCR_c = capital charges for the individual SCR risks according to the rows and columns of the correlation matrix CorrSCR

Adj_{FDB} = adjustment for the risk absorbing effect of future profit sharing

Adj_{DT} = adjustment for the risk absorbing effect of deferred taxes

The correlation matrix CorrSCR defines the correlations between the standard capital charges (SCR) SCR_{mkt}, $nSCR_{def}$, $nSCR_{life}$, SCR_{health} and SCR_{nl} defined above. Further adjustments and formulas are described in CEIOPS (2007, Section 3).

The SCR market risk module

This module corresponding to the **SCR_{mkt}** market block in Figure 7.1 is an important component in the calculation of the **BSCR** value. We describe the main features that come into the evaluation of the market risk block. For further details, please refer to CEIOPS (2007, Section 3).

According to Jorion (2006), "market risk arises from the level or volatility of market prices of financial instruments." Exposure to market risk is measured by the impact of movements in the level of financial variables, such as stock prices, interest rates, real estate prices and exchange rates.

For policies where the policyholders bear the investment risk (such as unit-linked policies), the undertaking will remain exposed to market risks where the value of the charges taken from these policies is dependent on fund performance. Exposure to interest rates will occur where fixed charges are received in the future. The value of any options and guarantees embedded within these contracts may also be exposed to market risk.

If an undertaking has purchased derivatives, provided they are in agreement with the principles of SCR risk mitigation, the risk mitigating/increasing effect should be considered within each sub-module (for example, currency forwards should be considered alongside the insurers other exposures within the currency risk sub-module).

If the financial instrument does not fall under the principles of risk mitigation, their risk mitigating effect should be excluded from the calculation of the SCR.

Risk exposures of collective investment schemes should be allocated to sub-modules on a look-through basis, if possible, and on a best-effort basis otherwise.

If a collective investment scheme is not sufficiently transparent to allow a reasonable best-effort allocation, reference should be made to the investment mandate of the scheme. It should be assumed that the scheme invests in accordance with its mandate in such a manner as to produce the maximum overall charge. For example, it should be assumed that the scheme invests in currencies other than the undertaking's reporting currency to the maximum possible extent permitted by the investment mandate. It should be assumed that the scheme invests assets in each rating category, starting at the lowest category permitted by the mandate to the maximum extent.

If a scheme invests in a range of assets exposed to the risks assessed under this module, then it should be assumed that the proportion of assets in each exposure category is such that the overall charge is maximised.

As a third choice to the look-through and mandate-based methods, participants should consider the collective investment scheme as an equity investment and apply the global equity risk charge (if the assets within the collective investment scheme are predominately listed) or other risk charge (if the assets within the collective investment scheme are predominately unlisted).

The following components are the inputs that are required to compute the market risk model:

Mkt_{int} = capital charge for interest-rate risk
$nMkt_{int}$ = same but including the risk absorbing effect of future profit sharing
Mkt_{eq} = capital charge for equity risk
$nMkt_{eq}$ = same but including the risk absorbing effect of future profit sharing
Mkt_{prop} = capital charge for property risk
$nMkt_{prop}$ = same but including the risk absorbing effect of future profit sharing
Mkt_{sp} = capital charge for spread risk
$nMkt_{sp}$ = same but including the risk absorbing effect of future profit sharing
Mkt_{conc} = capital charge for risk concentrations

$\mathbf{nMkt_{conc}}$ = same but including the risk absorbing effect of future profit sharing

$\mathbf{Mkt_{fx}}$ = capital charge for currency risk

$\mathbf{nMkt_{fx}}$ = same but including the risk absorbing effect of future profit sharing

The module delivers the following output:

$\mathbf{SCR_{mkt}}$ = capital charge for market risk

$\mathbf{nSCR_{mkt}}$ = capital charge for market risk including the risk absorbing effect of future profit sharing

The market sub-risks should be combined to an overall charge $\mathbf{SCR_{mkt}}$ for market risk using a correlation matrix as follows

$$\mathbf{SCR_{mkt}} = \sqrt{\sum_{rxc} CorrMkt_{r,c} \cdot Mkt_r \cdot Mkt_c}$$

where:

$CorrMkt_{r,c}$ = the cells of the correlation matrix CorrMkt

Mkt_r, Mkt_c = capital charges for the individual market risks according to the rows and columns of the correlation matrix CorrMkt

and the correlation matrix CorrMkt is defined as:

CorrMkt	Mkt_{int}	Mkt_{eq}	Mkt_{prop}	Mkt_{sp}	Mkt_{conc}	Mkt_{fx}
Mkt_{int}	1					
Mkt_{eq}	0	1				
Mkt_{prop}	0.5	0.75	1			
Mkt_{sp}	0.25	0.25	0.25	1		
Mkt_{conc}	0	0	0	0	1	
Mkt_{fx}	0.25	0.25	0.25	0.25	0	1

The capital charge for $\mathbf{nSCR_{mkt}}$ is determined as

$$\mathbf{nSCR_{mkt}} = \sqrt{\sum_{rxc} CorrMkt_{r,c} \cdot nMkt_r \cdot nMkt_c}$$

In the preliminary results of QIS4, it was noticed by some firms that the correlation between property risk and equity risk is too high for the SCR computation. It was also noticed that the correlation between equity risk and interest-rate risk was too low.

In order to test the impact of a different correlation situation, as has been observed during the recent and earlier periods of market turmoil, CEIOPS will carry out a sensitivity analysis by testing a new correlation factor between equity and interest-rate risk, leading to an alternative SCR value. Here, the correlation factor of 0 between Mkt_{eq} and Mkt_{int} will be replaced by a positive correlation factor of 0.25 in the scenario of a downward movement of the interest rate and by a negative correlation factor of -0.25 in the case of an upward movement of the interest rate. The results of this sensitivity analysis will be published in the final QIS4 report.

Below, we briefly gloss over the various components of the market risk module computation. We refer the interested reader to CEIOPS (2007, Section 3).

1. **Mkt_{int}**: interest-rate risk exists for all assets and liabilities of which the net asset value is sensitive to changes in the term structure of interest rates or interest-rate volatility. Assets sensitive to interest rate movements will include fixed-income investments, insurance liabilities, financing instruments (loan capital) and interest-rate derivatives. Liability cashflows received in the future will be sensitive to a change in the rate at which those cashflows are discounted.

   The value of assets and liabilities sensitive to interest rate changes can be determined using the term structure of interest rates ("zero rates"). This term structure can, of course, change over the period of a year.

   Inputs include the net value of assets minus liabilities. Outputs give the capital charge for interest-rate risk after upward shocks, after upward shock including the risk absorbing effect of future profit sharing, downward shocks, downward shock including the risk absorbing effect of future profit sharing, capital charge for interest-rate risk and for interest-rate risk including the risk absorbing effect of future profit sharing.

2. **Mkt_{eq}**: equity risk arises from the level or volatility of market prices for equities. Exposure to equity risk refers to all assets and liabilities where the value is sensitive to changes in equity prices.

   For equity risk, a distinction can be made between systematic risk and idiosyncratic risk. The latter arises out of inadequate diversification. Systematic risk refers to the sensitivity of the equity's returns to the returns of market portfolios and cannot be reduced by diversification. Therefore it is also called undiversifiable risk.

The equity risk sub-module is intended to capture systematic risk, whereas idiosyncratic equity risk is addressed in the concentration risk sub-module.

The equity risk module uses indexes as risk proxies, meaning that the volatility and correlation information is derived from these indexes. It is assumed that all equities can be allocated to an index of the provided set.

For the determination of the capital charge for equity risk, the following two indexes are considered: the equity index "Global" comprises equity listed in EEA and OECD countries, the equity index "Other" comprises equity listed only in emerging markets, non-listed equity, hedge funds and other alternative investments.

The assumed shock scenarios for the individual indexes reflect the systematic risk inherent to this market portfolio. It is assumed that the equity portfolio of the insurance companies have the same exposure to systematic risk as the index (the risk proxy) itself. It is therefore assumed that the beta is 1.

For the calculation of the risk capital charge, hedging and risk transfer mechanisms should be taken into account according to the principles of risk mitigation. However, as a general rule, hedging instruments should only be allowed with the average protection level over the next year. For example, where an equity option provides protection for the next six months, as a simplification, undertakings should assume that the option only covers half of the current exposure.

Participants should not assume to purchase additional hedging instruments (for example, as part of a rolling hedging program) beyond those in force at the balance sheet date within the standard formula SCR.

Inputs include the net value of assets minus liabilities. Outputs give the capital charge for equity risk and the capital charge for equity risk including the risk absorbing effect of future profit sharing.

3. **Mkt$_{prop}$**: property risk arises from the level or volatility of market prices of property.

Inputs include the net value of assets minus liabilities. Outputs give the capital charge for property risk and the capital charge for property risk including the risk absorbing effect of future profit sharing.

The capital charge for property risk is determined as the result of a predefined scenario where the property shock is the immediate effect on the net value of asset and liabilities expected in the event of a 20% fall in real estate benchmarks, taking account of all the participant's individual direct and indirect exposures to property prices. The property shock takes account of the specific investment policy including, say, hedging arrangements, gearing.

The scenario for property risk should be calculated under the condition that the assumptions on future bonus rates (reflected in the valuation of future discretionary benefits in technical provisions) remain unchanged before and after the shock being tested. Additionally, the result of the scenario should be determined under the condition that the participant is able to vary its assumptions in future bonus rates in response to the shock being tested. The resulting capital charge is nMkt$_{prop}$.

4. **Mkt$_{fx}$**: currency risk arises from the level or volatility of currency exchange rates.

Inputs include the net value of assets minus liabilities. Outputs give the capital charge for currency risk, the capital charge for currency risk after an upward shock, the capital charge for currency risk after a downward shock, the capital charge for currency risk including the risk absorbing effect of future profit sharing, the capital charge for currency risk after an upward shock including the risk absorbing effect of future profit sharing and the capital charge for currency risk after a downward shock including the risk absorbing effect of future profit sharing.

The capital charge for currency risk is determined as the result of two predefined scenarios: the downward and upward foreign exchange shocks, where the foreign exchange upward and downward shocks are respectively the immediate effect expected on the net value of asset and liabilities in the event of a 20% change, rise and fall, respectively, in value of all other currencies against the local currency in which the undertaking prepares its local regulatory accounts, taking account of all the participant's individual currency positions and its investment policy (eg, hedging arrangements, gearing, etc).

The scenario for currency risk should be calculated under the condition that the assumptions on future bonus rates (reflected in the valuation of future discretionary benefits in technical provisions) remain unchanged before and after the shock being tested. The size of the shock applied in the calculation for an ERM II Member State currency versus the euro should reflect the maximum fluctuations set under the general rules for ERM II (exchange rate mechanism). For the purpose of QIS4, the following shock has to be considered: 2.25% for the Danish krone and 15% for the Estonian kroon, the Latvian lats, the Lithuanian litas and the Slovakian koruna. Participants applying this provision should clearly state this in the spreadsheet.

Additionally, the result of the scenarios should be determined under the condition that the participant is able to vary its assumptions in future bonus rates in response to the shock being tested. The resulting capital charges are nMktfxUp and nMktfxDown. The capital charge for currency risk is derived from the type of shock that gives rise to the highest capital charge including the risk absorbing effect of future profit sharing:

If nMktfxUp > nMktfxDown, then Mktfx = MktfxUp and nMktfx = nMktfxUp.

If nMktfxUp ≤ nMktfxDown, then Mktfx = nMktfxDown and nMktfx = nMktfxDown.

5. **Mkt$_{sp}$**: spread risk is the part of risk originating from financial instruments that is explained by the volatility of credit spreads over the risk-free interest rate term structure. It reflects the change in value due to a move of the yield curve relative to the risk-free term structure. Assets that are allocated to policies where the policyholders bear the investment risk should be excluded from this risk module. However, as these policies may have embedded options and guarantees, an adjustment (calculated using a scenario-based approach) is added to the

formula to take into account the part of the risk that is effectively borne by the insurer.

For the purposes of determining the SCR for spread risk companies should assume the more onerous (in aggregate) of a rise or fall in credit spreads. It is not required to assume different directional movements in credit spreads when determining the different components of the spread risk sub-module. Currently, default and migration risks are not explicitly built into the spread risk module. However, the spread risk module will include parts of these risks implicitly via the movements in credit spreads. The credit indexes used for the calibration rebalance on a monthly basis and, consequently, the change of their constituents, due to downgrades or upgrades, has a monthly frequency as well. Hence, the impact of intra-month downgrades/upgrades will partly be reflected in the movements of credit spreads.

Government bonds are exempted from an application of this module. The exemption relates to borrowings by the national government, or guaranteed by the national government, of an OECD or EEA state, issued in the currency of the government.

The spread risk module is applicable to all tranches of structured credit products like asset-backed securities and collateralised debt obligations. In general, these products include transactions or schemes whereby the credit risk associated with an exposure or pool of exposures is tranched, having the following characteristics: (a) payments in the transaction or scheme are dependent upon the performance of the exposure or pool of exposures; and (b) the subordination of tranches determines the distribution of losses during the ongoing life of the transaction or scheme.

The spread risk module further covers credit derivatives, for example credit default swaps, total return swaps, credit linked notes, that are not held as part of a recognised risk mitigation policy.

Inputs include the external rating of credit risk exposure i, the modified duration of credit risk exposure i, and MVi, which is the credit risk exposure i as determined by reference to market values (exposure at default).

In cases where there is no readily-available market value of credit risk exposure i, alternative approaches consistent with relevant market information might be adopted to determine MVi.

In cases where several ratings are available for a given credit exposure, generally the second-best rating should be applied.

Outputs are the capital charge for spread risk and the capital charge for spread risk including the risk absorbing effect of future profit sharing.

6. Mkt_{conc}: market risk concentrations present an additional risk to an insurer because of:

- additional volatility that exists in concentrated asset portfolios, and
- the additional risk of partial or total permanent losses of value due to the default of an issuer.

Assets that are allocated to policies where the policyholders bear the investment risk should be excluded from this risk module. However, as these policies may have embedded options and guarantees, an adjustment (calculated using a scenario-based approach) is added to the formula to take into account the part of the risk that is effectively borne by the insurer.

For the sake of simplicity and consistency, the definition of market risk concentrations is restricted to the risk regarding the accumulation of exposures with the same counterparty. It does not include other types of concentrations (eg, geographical area, industry sector, etc).

In the case that an undertaking owns shares representing more than 20% of the capital of another insurance or financial undertaking which: (1) is not included in the scope of consolidation or supplementary supervision and (2) where the value of that participation or subsidiary exceeds 10% of the participating undertaking's own funds, these shares are exempted from the application of the concentration risk module when using a "deduction-aggregation" method for the treatment of participations. In line with this approach, when using a look-through approach for the treatment of participations, the concentration risk module should not be applied.

Government bonds are exempted from the application of this module. The exemption concerns borrowings by the national government, or guaranteed by the national government, of an OECD or EEA state, issued in the currency of the government.

Bank deposits with a term of less than three months, of up to €3 million, in a bank that has a minimum credit rating of AA are also exempted from an application of this module.

Risk exposures in assets need to be grouped according to the counterparties involved. Inputs include Ei, which is the net exposure at default to counterparty i, the amount of total assets excluding those where the policyholder bears the investment risk and the external rating of the counterparty i.

If an undertaking has more than one exposure to a counterparty, then Ei is the aggregate of those exposures at default. The rating should be a weighted rating determined as the rating corresponding to a weighted average credit quality step calculated as the *weighted average credit quality step* = round (average of the credit quality steps of the individual exposures to that counterparty, weighted by the net exposure at default in respect of that exposure to that counterparty).

All entities that belong to the same group should be considered as a single counterparty for the purposes of this sub-module. The net exposure at default to an individual counterparty i shall comprise the asset classes of equity and fixed income (including hybrid instruments, eg, junior debt, mezzanine CDO tranches and so forth).

Financial derivatives on equity and defaultable bonds should be properly attributed (via their "delta") to the net exposure, ie, an equity put option reduces the equity exposure to the underlying "name" and a single-name credit default swap ("protection bought") reduces the fixed-income exposure to the underlying "name". The exposure to the default of the counterparty of the option or the credit default swap is not treated in this module, but in the counterparty default risk module.

Also, collaterals securitising bonds should be taken into account. Similarly, a look-through approach should be applied to assets representing reinsurers' funds withheld by a counterparty.

Exposures via investment funds or such entities whose activity is mainly the holding and management of an insurer's own investment need to be considered on a look-through basis. The same holds for CDO tranches and similar investments embedded in 'structured products'.

Outputs give the capital charge for market concentration risk and the capital charge for concentration risk including the risk-absorbing effect of future profit sharing.

Solvency capital requirements using internal models

Internal models are models developed by firms that include any risk management system analysis to quantify risks and to help assess the economic capital needed to meet those risks.

Solvency II allows two methods for the computation of the capital requirements, the European standard formula or a firm's internally developed model. Firms are advised to try as much as possible to compare the results and the modelling aspects of the standard formula with those obtained from internal models.

To determine whether firms may use their own internal models for computing the SCR, firms will have to assess the quality and comparability of the data against high-level principles. Firms should be comparing results and modelling aspects of the standard formula described in the introduction with those derived from their internal models. Key areas to assess are the modelling requirements of the Framework Directive proposal and the data that firms use to calibrate their models. The differences in assumptions and definitions between existing models in firms and those expected under Solvency II are important to understand. The computations from internally developed models should be developed by keeping in mind the overall calibration objectives of the standard formula. That is, the internal models should include all the risk factors used in the standard formula (namely, for market risk, the risk factors consist of interest rates, equity, property, spread, concentration and currency) and the internal VaR model should be applied to obtain the VaR at the one-year 99.5% confidence level. Value-at-risk is a method for assessing risk by using standard statistical techniques. In broad terms, VaR measures the worst loss over a certain time horizon that will not be exceeded with a given confidence level.

Value-at-risk provides a single number summarising the total risk in a portfolio of assets and is the measure of market risk.

General criteria for using internal models
The general criteria in Solvency II for using internal models resembles the criteria used in Basel II.

Qualitatively, the insurers' undertaking must have a sound risk management system that is implemented with integrity; they must have sufficient staff skilled in the use of sophisticated models; they must have a proven track record of reasonable accuracy in measuring risk and they must conduct stress tests along the regulatory lines. In addition, the supervisory authorities have the right to insist on a period of initial monitoring and live testing of a firm's internal model before it is used for supervisory capital purposes. Moreover, the insurers' undertakings are subject to the following requirements: they should have an independent risk control unit responsible for the design and implementation of the risk management system; the risk unit should conduct regular backtesting programmes and should conduct initial and ongoing validation of the internal model. Upper management should be actively involved in the risk control process and must regard risk control as an essential aspect of the business to which significant resources need to be devoted; the internal risk measurement model must be closely integrated into the day-to-day risk management process; a routine and rigorous program of stress testing should be in place as a supplement to the risk analysis; there should be an internal routine for ensuring compliance with a documented set of internal policies, controls and procedures concerning the operation of the risk measurement system and, also, an independent review of the risk measurement system should be carried out regularly.

Quantitatively, an important part of the internal market risk measurement system, for example, is the specification of an appropriate set of market risk factors. These should be the same as the ones defined for the computation of the standard formula. These include interest-rate risk, equity risk, property risk, currency risk, concentration risk and spread risk.

The market risk measure used for internal models is computed with the general tools available for determining VaR.

What is VaR?

Value-at-risk is a method for assessing risk by using standard statistical techniques. In broad terms, VaR measures the worst loss over a certain time horizon that will not be exceeded with a given confidence level. Value-at-risk provides a single number summarising the total risk in a portfolio of financial assets and is the measure of market risk. For example, if a firm says the daily VaR of all its portfolios is US$100 million at the 99% confidence level, there will only be one chance in a 100, assuming normal market conditions, that the firm will lose an amount greater than US$100 million. This number summarises the firm's exposure to market risk, as well as the probability of an adverse move. Traditionally, VaR as a measure of risk, has been typically used by financial institutions. Value-at-risk provides an aggregate view of a portfolio's risk that accounts for leverage, correlations and current positions and can be viewed as a forward looking risk measure. The methodology applies to all financial instruments and can be extended from market risk to other types of financial risks. Regulators use VaR to help determine the capital a bank is required to keep in order to reflect the market risk it is exposed to. Traditionally, VaR has been used by corporate treasurers, fund managers and financial institutions. For a good reference on VaR, see Jorion (2006).

Consider now the probability density function of profits and losses for a particular portfolio. Either one considers the actual empirical distribution, in which case VaR is derived from the sample quantile, or one uses a parametric approximation, for example the normal distribution, in which case VaR is computed from the standard deviation.

Define now the confidence level as c, and the loss to the portfolio as *Loss*. Then VaR is the smallest loss, in absolute value, such that

$$P(Loss > VaR) \leq 1 - c$$

If we take for instance a 99.5% confidence level, $c = 0.995$, and the probability that the loss to the portfolio is greater than the VaR is less than 0.5%.

Volatility plays an important role in computing VaR. The units for measuring volatility are typically in years for pricing financial options. The volatility for an asset is quoted in days, but for VaR time is usually measured in terms of trading days (the number of trading days per year is typically taken as 252). Remembering that for independent and identically distributed returns, the variances are additive over time, the volatility grows with the square root of time. We have

$$\sigma_{day} = \frac{\sigma_{year}}{\sqrt{252}}$$

and daily volatility is defined for the purpose of VaR as the standard deviation of the asset's daily return.

There are two basic ways to derive VaR. The actual empirical distribution of the daily changes in market risk factors for the time horizon selected are considered, in which case VaR is derived from the sample quantile. The other method assumes a parametric approximation, for example a normal distribution for the risk factors. In this case VaR is computed from the standard deviation. We briefly describe how both methods work in simple cases below.

Non-parametric VaR: this method makes no assumption for the distribution of daily changes in market risk factors or variables. The method uses the daily moves (percentage changes) for all market risk factor variables over the last few years (typically four to five years). A first simulation uses the earliest date of daily moves, a second simulation uses the next to last day of daily moves and so on.

Take the simplest portfolio consisting of a single stock. We can simulate the US dollar change in the portfolio in one day for today's position S_0 by taking the vector

$$\Delta P_i = \frac{\Delta P_i}{\Delta S_i} \Delta S_i \cong S_0 \Delta x_i$$

since the delta of the option $\Delta P_i / \Delta S_i = 1$, and where $\Delta x_i = \Delta S_i / S_i$ is the percentage change in the stock price in one day (daily return for day i).

We then get a return distribution for the past four to five years of daily moves Δx_i by plotting the values of $S_0 \Delta x_i$. The VaR is then set equal to the appropriate percentile of the probability distribution of ΔP_i.

Parametric VaR: this method assumes that the daily returns follow a given distribution, usually the normal distribution. Suppose that the one-year standard deviation of returns for the asset is 20%. Over a one-day period, the volatility is then $0.2/\sqrt{252} = 1.26\%$. And the standard deviation of daily changes in the value of the portfolio is

$$\Delta P = 1.26\% \cdot S_0$$

For the 99th percentile corresponding to 2.32 standard deviations, the one-day 99% VaR is $2.32 \cdot S_0 \cdot \sigma = 2.32 \cdot S_0 \cdot 1.26\%$.

Note that it is usual to assume in VaR calculations that the expected change in the price of a market variable is zero over the short time period considered. This is a reasonable approximation, as the expected change in price of a market variable over a short period of time can be assumed small compared with the standard deviation of the change.

We now discuss methodologies based on the two methods described above that can be applied to compute VaR. The methods can be divided in two broad categories: parametric methods where the probability distribution of losses is assumed to follow a well known distribution, say, normal, and simulation methods that are used to generate a variety of different scenarios for the portfolio's value at a given date. Scenarios can be generated in a random manner (Monte Carlo simulation) or from historical data (historical simulation). The VaR is then deduced from reading off the percentile directly from the simulated distribution of losses and gains.

Methodologies for computing VaR
Parametric approach: this approach is typically called delta-normal method or variance–covariance method. The approach uses linear or delta exposures and assumes normal distribution for the market variables probability distribution. This local valuation method measures risk by valuing the portfolio once at the initial state and makes use of local derivatives to deduce possible market moves. This is in contrast to full valuation methods that measure risk by fully repricing the portfolio over a range of scenarios.

The linear or delta model can be used on a portfolio that does not contain derivatives but contains positions in stocks, bonds, foreign exchange, commodities, etc. In these cases, the changes in the value of the portfolio depend linearly on the changes in the values of the underlying market variables. Simple derivatives that can be handled by the linear model are, for example, forward contracts, which depend linearly on the underlying value. Local valuation methods then model exposures with partial derivatives.

Take a portfolio with one instrument where the value depends on a single underlying risk factor, the stock S

$$P = P(S_0)$$

The first derivative of the portfolio or instrument value with respect to the underlying stock represents the instrument's sensitivity to changes in prices evaluated at the current position. This first derivative is called the delta for a stock, or the modified duration for a fixed income instrument.

The change in value to the portfolio is then

$$\Delta P = \frac{\partial P}{\partial S}\Big|_0 \, dS = (\Delta_0 \cdot S)\frac{dS}{S}$$

with the US dollar exposure given by $(\Delta_0 \cdot S)$.

Note the linear relationship between the value of the portfolio and the underlying asset. The worst loss occurs for a very large value of S. Assuming a normal distribution the VaR is given by VaR$= |\Delta_0| \cdot \alpha \sigma S_0$, with α corresponding to the desired confidence level (eg, for a 95% level, α would be 1.645). Value-at-risk is computed through a closed-form formula by evaluating the portfolio only once at the current position.

If we have a portfolio consisting of fixed-income instruments, the methodology is similar. Simplifications are necessary in order not to define a new market variable for every single bond price or interest rate. For fixed-income instruments, the risk factor is the yield y. With the assumption that the shifts in a zero-coupon yield curve are small parallel shifts, if we take a portfolio that only depends on interest rates, the approximate price yield relationship in terms of duration is

$$\Delta P = -D \cdot P\Delta y$$

where P is the value of the portfolio, D is the modified duration of the portfolio, Δy is the size of the parallel shift in the yield curve and ΔP is the change in the portfolio value. The US dollar exposure is given by $-D \cdot P$. And the portfolio VaR is now VaR $= |D \cdot P| \cdot (\alpha \sigma)$.

Here $\sigma(dy)$ is the volatility of changes in the level of yield. Yields are assumed to be normally distributed.

When a portfolio includes options, the linear (or delta-normal) model is not adequate, as it does not take into account higher orders that come into the changes to the portfolio.

Expanding the change in portfolio value to a higher order, we have

$$\Delta P = \Delta_0 \Delta S + \frac{1}{2}\gamma_0(\Delta S)^2$$

and the VaR is given by

$$VaR = |\Delta_0| \cdot (\alpha\sigma S_0) - \frac{1}{2}\gamma_0(\alpha\sigma S_0)^2$$

Recall that Δ_0 is the rate of change of the portfolio value with respect to the underlying market variable and γ_0 is defined as the rate of change of the delta with respect to the market variable. Gamma represents the curvature of the portfolio value with respect to the underlying market variable.

For a fixed-income portfolio, the price yield relationship becomes

$$\Delta P = -D \cdot P\Delta y + \frac{1}{2}(C \cdot P)\Delta y^2$$

where C is the convexity (or gamma). The VaR is now given by

$$VaR = |D \cdot P| \cdot (\alpha\sigma) - \frac{1}{2}(C \cdot P)(\alpha\sigma)^2$$

The closed-form approximations described above apply to simple portfolios, for example those containing long and short positions in calls and puts, and any portfolio where the value is proportional to the underlying market variable. Generally this methodology cannot be applied at the highest level of aggregation for large portfolios as this would require the knowledge of all the gammas and cross-gammas of the underlying risk factors. The quadratic approximations can however be used to speed up computations of VaR with simulations (eg, Monte Carlo), where the Taylor expansion can be used to obtain, in a quick way, the simulated movements in the product value once the risk factors movements have been simulated.

Monte Carlo simulation: Monte Carlo simulations are used to generate the probability distribution for ΔP from simulating repeatedly a random variable and financial process to cover a large number of situations. The variables are drawn from predefined known probability distributions. The number of simulations is taken large enough to cover the entire distribution of portfolio values in order to read off the VaR value.

Consider now the simplest example of a portfolio consisting of one stock as discussed earlier. Here we are dealing with a single random variable. The first part of the simulation is to define a random process or stochastic model for the evolution of the stock price. The usual assumption in finance and options pricing theory is to choose a geometric Brownian motion model. This model assumes that incremental moves in the asset price are uncorrelated over time and the evolution equation for the price is given by

$$dS_t = \mu_t S_t \, dt + \sigma_t S_t \, dz \qquad (7.1)$$

Here, dz is a random variable that describes random moves of the stock price, does not depend on the past and is distributed normally with mean zero and variance dt. It is called Brownian because its variance decreases continuously with the time interval (Variance$(dz) = dt$), implying that there are no sudden jumps. Parameters μ_t and σ_t represent the instantaneous drift and volatility at time t and can evolve with time. However a common simplification is to take these parameters constant over time.

In discrete form, Equation 7.1 can be written as

$$\Delta S_t = S_{t-1}(\mu \Delta t + \sigma \varepsilon \sqrt{\Delta t})$$

where ε is a standard normal variable with mean zero and variance one. This process has a mean $E(\Delta S/S) = \mu \Delta t$ and a variance of $\sigma^2 \Delta t$. The asset price of stock S is then generated from a sequence of ε for $j = 1, 2, \ldots, n$, where $\Delta t = (T - t)/n$, with T the time horizon for computing VaR and t the present time. Thus we generate the series

$$S_{t+1} = S_t + S_t(\mu \Delta t + \sigma \varepsilon_1 \sqrt{\Delta t})$$
$$S_{t+2} = S_{t+1} + S_{t+1}(\mu \Delta t + \sigma \varepsilon_2 \sqrt{\Delta t})$$
$$\vdots$$
$$S_{t+n} = S_T$$

The choice of the number of steps depends on the VaR horizon and the accuracy desired. There is a balance to strike between reproducing the stochastic process appropriately and fastness of implementation.

We have described here a Monte Carlo simulation to simulate VaR in a simple but instructive case. We recap the steps below.

Say we want to compute the one-day VaR for a portfolio consisting of one stock. We need to simulate the values $\Delta x = \Delta S/S$ representing the daily return such that $\Delta P \cong S_0 \Delta x$:

1) take the value of the portfolio today with current values of market variables;
2) sample once from the desired probability distribution of the Δx;
3) use the value of the Δx that was sampled to determine the value of the market variable at the end of one day;
4) revalue the portfolio at end of the day;
5) subtract the value of the portfolio today from the value of the portfolio at the end of the day to determine a sample ΔP; then
6) repeat the steps many times to build up a probability distribution for ΔP.

The VaR is determined from the given percentile of the probability distribution of ΔP.

The advantages of Monte Carlo simulation are that the method is the most powerful and comprehensive method to compute VaR. It is flexible enough to include various scenarios in the daily return of market risk factors, such as fat tails or unusual scenarios.

Disadvantages include foremost that the method tends to be expensive to implement and computationally slow because the portfolio needs to be revaluated many times. For example, the use of 1,000 sample paths with a portfolio of 100 assets would amount to 100,000 revaluations. Another possibly important disadvantage derives from the assumption of the stochastic processes for the underlying risk factors. The assumptions could be wrong and should be supplemented by analysis of historical returns and sensitivity analysis.

Historical simulation: this is part of the non-parametric methods for computing VaR. It makes no assumptions about the distributions of daily changes in market variables. In practice, the distribution of daily changes often have fatter tails than the normal distribution.

As its name indicates, historical simulation uses a database of actual daily movements in market variables over the past few years (typically at last one year but up to five years).

The first simulation assumes that the percentage changes in each market variable are the same as those on the first day covered by the database (typically yesterday if VaR is revalued every day). The second simulation assumes that the percentage changes in each market variable are the same as those covered on the second day, and so on.

Take again our simple example for a portfolio consisting of one stock. We are simulating the values $\Delta x = \Delta S / S$ representing the daily return such that $\Delta P \cong S_0 \Delta x$ for each simulation. The change in the portfolio value ΔP is calculated for each simulation to obtain a probability distribution of portfolio changes. The VaR is then read off at the appropriate percentile from the probability distribution.

Advantages of the method include that it is fast, easy to implement, and accurately reflects the historical probability distribution of the market variables, if the historical data of risk factors has been stored daily. Historical simulations account for fat-tailed distributions typically found in historical data. The method makes no assumption about the distributional losses.

Disadvantages of the method include that the number of simulations are limited to the number of days of data that are available and that it is difficult to deal with market variables where limited or spotty history is available. In addition, the method assumes that the immediate future is determined by the past. Also that the window of observations may not contain important market events or the sample may contain events that will not happen again in the future. Different weighting schemes on daily data can be implemented, typically to weigh the recent past more heavily.

Stress testing and backtesting

Value-at-risk measures are based on recent historical data and can easily miss important but extreme market events, such as the stock market crash of October 19, 1987 when the S&P dropped by 20%, representing about a 20 standard deviation move.

Value-at-risk methods should be used in conjunction with regular stress-testing exercises. The purpose of these exercises is to estimate how the portfolio behaves and estimate "out-of-the-ordinary" losses under the most extreme market moves seen in the last decades. Stress testing is in fact required by the Basel committee as one of the conditions for using internally developed models in the financial world.

A tool used for stress testing involves scenario analysis, where the portfolio is evaluated under extreme but possible states of the world, typically large movements in the main market risk factors. An example would be to set the proportional changes in all market variables equal to those on October 19, 1987. Sensitivity testing consists of sequentially bumping key risk factors by an extreme amount. However correlations that account for joint movements in market variables are important and moves in correlations (as well as volatilities) need to be accessed as well.

Stress testing therefore takes into account extreme events that can and do occur occasionally even though they appear almost impossible when considering the probability distribution of losses for the financial market variables. For example, a daily move of 5 standard deviations should happen once every 7,000 years for a normal distribution, however in practice this type of move may happen once or twice every 10 years. Stress testing is increasingly used, in addition to VaR, to compute and set aside capital to absorb extreme losses and to proactively manage positions to reduce over-all exposure.

Backtesting VaR has also become an important tool in checking the VaR computations. Its purpose is to test how realistic the pro-jected VaR estimates are with respect to actual losses. For example, if we are computing one day 99% VaR, backtesting involves check-ing how often (percentage of days) the loss in a day has exceeded the one day 99% VaR. If this number is beyond a certain percentage, required capital allocation set aside should increase. Backtesting has also become an essential requirement of the Basel committee to use internally developed models for capital charges.

Principal components analysis
This methodology is used to handle risks deriving from highly correlated financial market variables. It tries to explain the historical market moves of a set of N market variables in terms of a set of N components or factors (consisting of a set of N orthogonal combination of the original market variables N) with well-defined

meanings. The transformed N variables are sorted in order of decreasing importance. The first principal component is a linear combination of the original N variables such that its variance is maximised, the second principal component is the one that has the greatest variance but is orthogonal to the first principal component vector. And this process continues for the other components. The variables then are sorted in order of decreasing importance. Economic interpretations are given to the principal components and the eigenvalues corresponding to the singular value decomposition of the original covariance matrix. Typically, if the market variables are well chosen, the eigenvalue sizes decrease quite rapidly (the smaller variances of the new variables are then considered as too small to be important), and only the first component moves need to be analysed. This implies that we can simulate movements in the original market risk factors by simulating movements in a much smaller set of relevant variables (the principal components).

Take as an example the market variables to be bond rates for different maturity dates. The new set of variables that are computed by order of importance by looking at their variances and their economic meaning are as follows. The first principal component corresponds roughly to a parallel shift in the yield curve. The second principal component consists of moves in the yield curve corresponding to twists or steepening. The third principal component corresponds to a bowing of the yield curve, that is the rates at the short and high end of the yield curve move in one direction whereas rates in the middle of the yield curve move in the opposite direction. The first three principal components are considered to represent the most important way the yield curve can move, or equivalently, most of the risks in interest rate moves can be accounted for by the first three factors. Note also that these three moves or factors are all uncorrelated with each other.

MCR

The MCR is a lower-level requirement and its breach triggers the withdrawal of supervisory authorisation.

The linear approach MCR currently under consideration requires a range of between 20% minimum and 50% maximum of the SCR. The SCR is intended to be calibrated at the 99.5% confidence level. The MCR is intended to be calibrated at around an 80–90%

confidence level, implying that the MCR should correspond to approximately 35% of the SCR. The difference between SCR and MCR provides for a window of intervention for supervisory purposes, enabling the SCR shortfall to be corrected before reaching the greater risk of the MCR breach. In general, from the preliminary results of the QIS4 exercise (QIS4 test reports) it appears that the MCR linear approach is insufficiently risk sensitive and the SCR and MCR linear approach calculations do not appear to move in a consistent way from year to year.

The MCR computation is done at a less granular level and the market risk component does not enter in it explicitly. We give below the broad inputs and outputs of the valuation, without going into further details. The interested reader should refer to CEIOPS (2007, Section 5).

The following input information is required:

MCR_{NL} = the linear MCR for non-life business (before applying any cap or floor)

MCR_{Life} = the linear MCR for life business (before applying any cap or floor)

MCR_{NL}^{*} = the linear MCR for non-life business similar to life business (before applying any cap or floor)

MCR_{Life}^{*} = the linear MCR for supplementary non-life business underwritten in addition to life insurance (before applying any cap or floor)

SCR = the SCR of the participant (where participants have provided information both on their SCR calculated using the standard formula and their SCR calculated using a full or partial internal model, the MCR should be calculated twice, first using the standard formula SCR and second using the internal model SCR

The calculation delivers the following output:

MCR_{linear} = the linear MCR, ie, the sum of the linear MCRs for each type of business undertaken by the participant, before applying any cap or floor

$MCR_{combined}$ = the combined MCR of the participant, as calculated by the combined approach, after applying the cap and the floor (50% and 20% of the SCR respectively) to the linear MCR

MCR = the final MCR of the participant, as calculated by applying the absolute minimum floor to the combined approach

Participants should first calculate the components of their linear MCR, depending on the type of business they write, namely: MCR_{NL}, MCR^*_{NL}, MCR_{Life} and MCR^*_{Life}. The instructions for the calculation of those components are further specified below.

In a second step the overall linear MCR of the participant is set equal to the sum of the components of the linear MCR:

(a) for non-life participants

$$MCR_{linear} = MCR_{NL} + MCR^*_{NL}$$

(b) for life participants

$$MCR_{linear} = MCR_{Life} + MCR^*_{Life}$$

(c) for composite participants, which conduct both life and non-life business

$$MCR_{linear} = MCR_{NL} + MCR^*_{NL} + MCR_{Life} + MCR^*_{Life}$$

In a third step, the combined MCR is calculated, by applying the cap and the floor (50% and 20% of the SCR respectively) to the linear MCR

$$MCR_{combined} = \{Min[Max(MCR_{linear}; 0.2 \cdot SCR); 0.5 \cdot SCR]\}$$

In the last step, the absolute floor referred to is applied to the combined MCR

$$MCR = Max\{MCR_{combined}, AMCR\}$$

where $AMCR$ is the absolute floor of the MCR

$AMCR$ = €1 million for non-life insurance undertakings and for reinsurance undertakings

= €2 million for life insurance undertakings

= €1 million + €2 million = €3 million for composite undertakings

Notional non-life and life linear *MCR* (for composite undertakings)

Composite participants are also requested to report the following outputs:

$NMCR_{NL}$ = the notional non-life linear MCR of the participant
$NMCR_{Life}$ = the notional life linear MCR of the participant

The notional non-life and life linear *MCR* are calculated as follows

$$NMCR_{NL} = MCR_{NL} + MCR^*_{NL}$$
$$NMCR_{Life} = MCR_{Life} + MCR^*_{Life}$$

CONCLUSION

The Financial Services Authority requires that all firms calculate the standard formula for capital requirement for the first two years under the new regime. Insurance undertakings will then have to determine whether they want to keep using the standard formula or their own internally developed VaR models to compute SCR. Internal models will most probably be considered the choice long-term solution to compute capital requirement, as they have become for Basel II for the larger financial firms. Notwithstanding the initial heavy investment in time, cost and resources around building internal models and setting up oversight and controls for their use, banking firms have discovered that in addition to having control over some aspects of the computations, the use of internal models has significantly reduced the capital requirements they have had to post. Note however that large financial firms typically are already using a VaR model to report daily market risk moves to upper management. They have only needed to modify some specifications and outputs to compute the capital requirement under Basel II.

The advantages of using the standard formula are that it is simpler to use and requires less work and expertise on the part of the users. The level of cost involved should be much less than the cost experienced in the development of internal models. The time involved to set up standard formula computations should be relatively short as well. In addition, the standard formula is by definition already approved. Firms will need to show that it has been implemented and used correctly. It is generally assumed that using the standard formula will produce significantly higher capital requirements than using internal models. However this need not always be the case, as some products, or even whole business units may require higher capital requirements with the internal models. Preliminary results from the QIS4 exercise indicate that many life insurance companies produced higher overall capital requirements under an internal model than the standard formula. However one of the aims of the QIS4 exercise was to compare results between the two approaches and the Financial Services Authority is likely to recalibrate the data used. The standard formula provides a quick way to assess the rough figure for capital requirement under Solvency II.

The main advantages of using internal models are that the models will track the risks more accurately and reduce capital requirement significantly. Less capital requirement leads to lower costs on capital and the possibility of spreading capital more adequately among the business. Internal model development will however require risk factor identification and assessment, heavy modelling, training and recruitment costs, investment in IT functions and upgrades, and time to build, test, document and create operating procedures and control frameworks and these will be quite complex. Development of internal models will help the business understanding complex risk at a more fundamental level. However there is also a risk that, given the complexity of the models, the results will be taken at face value, without critical evaluation.

In addition, in terms of regulatory approval, by June 2010, UK regulated firms that wish to implement internal models must demonstrate that they meet the "dry run" criteria, have made significant progress in meeting the model requirements, and set out their implementation plans. The FSA outlines the uses to which internal models might be applied in order to gain approval. These include reinsurance analysis and strategy, pricing, performance measurement, performance management, business strategy, communication and asset management. In conclusion, in choosing to develop internal models, a firm's image can only improve as they will have in place a sound risk management process with solid controls in place.

1 The usual disclaimer applies. The views expressed in this chapter are those of the author and do not necessarily represent those of the Federal Reserve Bank of New York or the Federal Reserve System.

REFERENCES

Various Solvency II websites and articles: http://www.fsa.gov.uk/pages/About/What/International/solvency/index.shtml; http://www.solvency-2.com/Solvency-2/Solvency%20briefings-internal%20models.pdf.
QIS4 test reports: http://www.ceiops.eu/media/files/consultations/QIS/CEIOPS-SEC-82-08%20QIS4%20Report.pdf; http://www.fsa.gov.uk/pubs/international/QIS4_report.pdf.

Jones, R., W. Rief and Y. Le Pallec, 2009, "Solvency II: Wounded, But Still Alive and Kicking". Standard & Poor's, URL: http://www2.standardandpoors.com/spf/pdf/events/INS09Article19.pdf.

CEIOPS, 2007, "QIS4 Technical Specifications". URL: http://ec.europa.eu/internal_market/insurance/docs/solvency/qis4/technical_specifications_en.pdf.

Jorion, P., 2006, *Value at Risk: The New Benchmark for Managing Financial Risk*, 3rd edn (New York: McGraw-Hill).

8

Vanilla Option Replication of ALM Shortfall Risks for Life and Pension Liabilities

Rahul Karkun, Juliana Kim Moustakas, Idriss Amor[1]

Bank of America

In the midst of ongoing risk management improvements in the life and pension sector and in preparation for the European Union Solvency II standards, hedging strategies to address asset liability management (ALM) issues have been pursued via commonly used liability-replicating techniques. This approach falls in line with the quantification of market-value or hedgable liabilities under the Solvency II principles necessary for risk capital calculations. For many of the life and pension products, precise or static hedging would require the use of exotic, bespoke and highly illiquid instruments to mimic the exact liability behaviour, making such an approach largely impractical and theoretical in nature. This concept has been tested under numerous studies and discussions about replicating techniques that involve a large number of financial instruments, as well as stochastic modelling of the underlying liability behaviour.

Here, we set forth an exploratory chapter, with the focus on generating a macro-hedge explicitly on the ALM "shortfall" or net asset value risks rather than pure liability-driven investment in order to make use of the asset pool reinvestment assumptions, which remove a large burden of replicating the compounding liability return. This technique will require eventual hedge rebalancing during the life of the liability, given that both the underlying liability as well as market conditions can change. In particular, under large market changes, vanilla replications will be more sensitive and necessitate hedge rebalancing versus a precisely tailored exotic option. However, as a benefit, this vanilla option replication may simplify the risk quantification process for a broader number of life and pension providers, as a potential first-order measure of ALM shortfall risks prescribed by Solvency II.

The aim is to provide a practical approach for risk management using a parsimonious set of market derivative instruments, if not to construct a specific hedge, then at least to be used as a risk budgeting benchmark. Stated otherwise, we simplify the true exotic risk of these liabilities into vanilla ones, using techniques employed in underwriting structured interest rate and hybrid products.

The hedge strategy is designed to fit robustly against market movements for the underlying exposures of nominal interest rates (parallel shifts and curve twists), equities and respective volatilities, as opposed to a cashflow matching exercise. The hedge is optimised for both spot and two-year forward moves to test its effectiveness over time.

DEFINING THE LIABILITY

We define the liability in a general manner, incorporating broad characteristics found in many European with-profit life and pension products. The key features in this liability include an annual minimum rate guarantee and a path-dependent participation feature, expressed as a percentage of a moving market rate or asset return.

The moving market rate serves as a proxy for a competitive return, ie, the return of an alternative investment opportunity or the return a new entrant could offer, modelled as a percentage of the prevailing euro constant maturity swap (CMS) 10-year rate. If the competitive or asset return is higher than the guaranteed rate, then this difference is treated as the "bonus" per annum. So, for example, with a competitive rate bonus, over the course of the liability's life, this compounded bonus can be expressed with the following option payout

$$\prod_{t=0}^{T-1} (1 + \text{Max}(X\% * CMS10Y_t, g)) - (1 + g)^T \times N(t)$$

where g = guarantee rate and $N(t)$ = notional at time t.

The present value of this liability with the embedded "bonus" option generates an image across interest-rate shifts akin to that of a receiver swaption or floor option.

We examine three different types of liabilities; all were priced at par as of the end of October 2008[2] with the following annual credit rate formulas

$$\text{LIABILITY 1}: \text{MAX}[3.75\%, 80\% * \text{CMS 10Y}]$$
$$\text{LIABILITY 2}: \text{MAX}[3.75\%, 35\% * \text{asset return}]$$
$$\text{LIABILITY 3}: \text{MAX}[2.00\%, 60\% * \text{asset return}]$$

All liabilities are assumed to have a cashflow profile of ten years, with net outflows modelled as a percentage of the total liabilities set at 5% of the existing balance for the first nine years and the remaining paid out in year 10. No new premium inflows are presumed.

ASSET ASSUMPTIONS

Asset backing these liabilities is modelled under three asset allocations at inception:

1. 100% in 10-year zero coupon bonds (risk-free);
2. 95% in 10-year zero coupon bonds (risk-free) and 5% in equity (mimicking the EURO STOXX 50 Index); and
3. 70% in 10-year zero coupon bonds (risk-free) and 30% in equity.

These simple asset pools are rebalanced annually to the original asset mix. We assume a correlation of zero between equities and interest rates and utilise the following modelling parameters:

- equity index volatility based on prevailing market conditions for the EURO STOXX 50;
- annual equity dividend yield of 4% paid continuously; and
- risk-free interest-rates simulation calibrated to market levels and volatility.

Given the length of the study, we have restricted the analysis to equity and interest-rate movements. To model interest rates, we use a multi-factor HJM model to capture steepening scenarios. For spot equities, we assume a lognormal process.

Asset pool B contains a small exposure to equities, which is likely to be much less than the proportion of equities typically held by European life and pensions. However, given the high level of equity volatility at the time of undertaking this study, it would not have been possible to increase the equity holding in portfolio B while keeping the liability minimum guarantee (for liability 2) and maintaining a par pricing.

Asset pool C is later reviewed in conjunction with liability 3 in order to magnify the effect of adding equity to the portfolio.

CAPTURING RISKS OF THE NET ASSET VALUE

The stylised life/pension fund balance sheet used for this ALM shortfall exercise initially holds €105 million of total assets, €100 million of liabilities[3] and €5 million of the net asset value (NAV). This fund balance sheet is stochastically modelled over the life of the liabilities, 10 years and shortfall measures to the NAV are recorded on an annual frequency and present valued to time zero. In instances where the assets backing the liabilities are not sufficient to cover the present value of the liabilities, this NAV account is then used to cover this difference.

Furthermore, should a shortfall arise such that the present value of total assets at time t (namely $ASSET(t)$) is less than the present value of liabilities at time t (namely $LIABILITY(t)$), then this negative NAV is treated as a required capital injection, such that the fund will commence the following year with a minimum NAV equal to zero. No further solvency requirements are considered, and thus as long as the NAV is not negative, the fund is presumed to continue to the next period. Therefore, the hedge costs ought to be equivalent to the reduction of the NAV shortfall measure upon hedging.

APPROACH TO HEDGING THE NAV SHORTFALL RISK

For each of the liability types, we simulate the performance of the different asset pools against these over the 10-year liability maturity period. We capture the NAV shortfall as

$$MAX[LIABILITY(t) - ASSET(t), 0]$$

This shortfall measure is taken across multiple market conditions, involving instantaneous parallel shifts and twists of the risk-free interest-rate curve, shifts in the interest-rate volatility surface, and shocks to both the level of equities and equity volatility.

The delta and vega bucket values of this NAV shortfall are mapped under these different cases.

A set of hedge instruments is selected to match these delta and vega risks for each case and then we solve the notional on the hedge instruments to minimise the NAV shortfall risks across multiple market conditions. These measures are tested on both a spot and forward (two-year) basis to assess the effectiveness of the hedge over time.

CASE 1: MAPPING OUT THE NAV SHORTFALL RISKS

In the first case, we simulate the behaviour of an asset portfolio based on 100% bonds with a constant duration of 10 years against a liability whose annual compounding rate is MAX[3.75%, 80% CMS10Y]. Much of the compounded liability growth is offset by the asset growing as a compounded 10-year zero coupon bond. However, shortfall risks do arise and we see them as follows: strongest delta risks around the five-year and 15-year buckets; largest vega risk around the five-year, seven-year and 10-year tenors on expiries of five-year, seven-year and 10-year.

Table 8.1 shows the present value of the NAV shortfall under parallel interest rate and implied volatility shifts prior to any hedging being applied.[4] As expected, we see that under falling interest rates, the NAV shortfall increases given the burden of the minimum guarantee rate of 3.75%. Moreover, as the implied volatility increases, the NAV shortfall also rises, given that the fund is short the embedded option in the liabilities.

In Table 8.2, the impact of parallel interest-rate shifts is measured alongside certain twists in the curve, which lead to steepening or flattening of the curve pivoted around the eight-year rate point. The magnitude of the twist is taken as the increase or decrease in the difference between the five-year and 15-year rate points. Therefore, a 0.10% steepening on the table indicates a steepening of the curve (with the eight-year point unchanged) so that the spread between the five-year and 15-year point goes up by 10 basis points, and all other rate points are adjusted proportionally to fit into this new curve.

Essentially, we see that the NAV shortfall sensitivity to curve steepening conditions declines as the overall rate environment falls. This is plausible given that under higher rate conditions, the

Table 8.1 Case 1: NAV shortfall sensitivities across parallel interest rate and implied volatility shifts

Volatility shifts (%)	Parallel interest-rate shifts								
	−2.0%	−1.5%	−1.0%	−0.5%	0.0%	0.5%	1.0%	1.5%	2.0%
−3.0	11.0	7.8	5.7	4.5	3.9	3.5	3.2	2.9	2.7
−2.5	11.4	8.3	6.1	4.8	4.2	3.7	3.4	3.2	2.9
−2.0	11.8	8.6	6.5	5.2	4.5	4.0	3.7	3.4	3.2
−1.5	12.1	9.0	6.8	5.5	4.8	4.3	4.0	3.7	3.4
−1.0	12.4	9.3	7.2	5.8	5.1	4.6	4.2	3.9	3.7
−0.5	12.8	9.7	7.5	6.2	5.4	4.9	4.5	4.2	3.9
0.0	13.2	10.1	7.9	6.6	5.7	5.2	4.8	4.5	4.2
0.5	13.4	10.4	8.2	6.9	6.0	5.5	5.1	4.8	4.5
1.0	13.9	10.8	8.6	7.2	6.4	5.8	5.4	5.0	4.7
1.5	14.3	11.2	9.0	7.6	6.7	6.1	5.7	5.3	5.0
2.0	14.7	11.6	9.4	8.0	7.1	6.4	6.0	5.6	5.3
2.5	15.1	12.0	9.8	8.3	7.4	6.8	6.3	5.9	5.6
3.0	15.5	12.4	10.2	8.7	7.8	7.1	6.6	6.2	5.8

Table 8.2 Case 1: NAV shortfall sensitivities across interest-rate curve twists and parallel shifts

Parallel rate shifts (%)	Interest-rate flattening/steepening										
	−0.5%	−0.4%	−0.3%	−0.2%	−0.1%	0.0%	0.1%	0.2%	0.3%	0.4%	0.5%
−2.0	13.5	13.4	13.3	13.0	12.9	12.8	12.7	12.7	12.7	12.6	12.7
−1.5	11.1	10.1	9.9	9.8	9.8	9.8	9.8	9.9	10.0	10.0	10.2
−1.0	7.8	7.7	7.7	7.7	7.7	7.8	7.9	8.0	8.1	8.3	8.4
−0.5	6.1	6.2	6.2	6.3	6.4	6.5	6.6	6.8	6.9	7.1	7.3
0.0	5.2	5.2	5.3	5.4	5.6	5.7	5.9	6.0	6.2	6.4	6.7
0.5	4.6	4.7	4.8	4.9	5.1	5.2	5.4	5.6	5.7	5.9	6.2
1.0	4.2	4.3	4.4	4.6	4.7	4.9	5.0	5.2	5.4	5.6	5.8
1.5	3.9	4.0	4.1	4.3	4.4	4.5	4.7	4.9	5.0	5.2	5.4
2.0	3.6	3.7	3.9	4.0	4.1	4.3	4.4	4.6	4.7	4.9	5.1

liability will behave more like a CMS floater rather than the fixed guaranteed rate product.

In the last set of sensitivity measures shown in Table 8.3, we map out the shortfall under cases of curve steepening versus shifts in the implied volatility surface. Here, the results show a fairly consistent pattern of higher shortfalls under steeper curves and more volatile rates. This is reasonable given that the liability bonus option is paying out a proportion of CMS10Y, which increases as curves steepen and 10-year forward rates move higher. Moreover, under our modelling assumptions, we see that the shortfall vega does not change drastically with the curve steepening.

These NAV shortfall tables were also generated for two-year forward conditions, and although not displayed here, the pattern of results was similar.

CASE 1: CHOICE OF HEDGE INSTRUMENTS

Given the prior risks observed, we select two spot starting receiver swaps for five-year and 15-year tenors. However, the impact of these swap deltas will need to be considered with respect to the delta in options utilised in the hedge as well.

In addition to the embedded liability option, we also have the NAV shortfall expressed as an option such that when we hedge vega, we must consider the effect of both of these options. We chose a 7Y × 10Y at-the-money straddle to cover some of the vega risk. While other straddles such as the 5Y × 5Y and the 10Y × 10Y could have been used, we also wanted to limit the number of hedge instruments. To cover the liability minimum rate guarantee and also address skew risk, we chose two out-of-the-money receiver swaptions struck at 3.75%, the 5Y × 5Y and 10Y × 10Y receiver swaptions. A variation of option strikes could be used to improve the hedge results, but this would add to the hedge complexity, which we aim to avoid.

All hedge instruments were measured on a stand-alone basis to identify their sensitivity. We also presumed that net hedge costs are available from resources outside the fund balance sheet, so we do not solve for zero premium hedges. Another way of interpreting this hedge cost is that it is a reflection of the expected additional solvency capital needed to mitigate the risks of liabilities for a given

Table 8.3 Case 1: NAV shortfall sensitivities across interest-rate curve twists and implied volatility shifts

Volatility shifts (%)	Interest-rate flattening/steepening										
	-0.5%	-0.4%	-0.3%	-0.2%	-0.1%	0.0%	0.1%	0.2%	0.3%	0.4%	0.5%
-3.0	3.3	3.4	3.5	3.6	3.7	3.9	4.0	4.2	4.3	4.5	4.7
-2.5	3.6	3.7	3.8	3.9	4.0	4.2	4.3	4.5	4.6	4.8	5.0
-2.0	3.9	4.0	4.1	4.2	4.3	4.5	4.6	4.6	5.0	5.1	5.4
-1.5	4.2	4.3	4.4	4.5	4.6	4.8	4.9	5.1	5.3	5.5	5.7
-1.0	4.5	4.6	4.7	4.8	4.9	5.1	5.2	5.4	5.6	5.8	6.0
-0.5	4.8	4.9	5.0	5.1	5.3	5.4	5.6	5.7	5.9	6.1	6.3
0.0	5.2	5.2	5.3	5.4	5.6	5.7	5.9	6.0	6.2	6.4	6.7
0.5	5.5	5.6	5.7	5.8	5.9	6.0	6.2	6.4	6.6	6.8	7.0
1.0	5.8	5.9	6.0	6.1	6.2	6.4	6.5	6.7	6.9	7.1	7.3
1.5	6.2	6.3	6.3	6.5	6.6	6.7	6.9	7.0	7.2	7.4	7.6
2.0	6.6	6.6	6.7	6.8	6.9	7.1	7.2	7.4	7.6	7.8	8.0
2.5	6.9	7.0	7.0	7.1	7.3	7.4	7.6	7.7	7.9	8.1	8.3
3.0	7.3	7.3	7.4	7.5	7.6	7.8	7.9	8.1	8.3	8.4	8.7

Table 8.4 Hedge notional values for case 1

Hedge instrument	Notional value
Five-year receiver swap	99.7
15-year receiver swap	−16.3
5Y × 5Y receiver swaption, $K = 3.75\%$	78.6
10Y × 10Y receiver swaption, $K = 3.75\%$	22.9
7Y × 10Y at-the-money straddle	47.1

asset selection, albeit not a complete amount of capital due to the likely further hedge rebalancing requirements.[5]

CASE 1: SOLVING FOR HEDGE NOTIONALS AND RESULTS

We solve the hedge notional values that will minimise the variation of the present value of the NAV shortfall across various market scenarios. As these are macro-hedges rather than precise cashflow matching, and hence illiquid exotic ones, hedge effectiveness is not likely to last through the life of the liability. Hence, hedge rebalancing will be required. We test the hedge process for both spot and two-year-forward conditions, and solve hedge notional values that will offer robust results across this time. We see that the hedge is most effective for small changes in delta and vega moves.

The hedge notional values in Table 8.4 were determined through an iterative process such that the residual or post-hedge NAV shortfall result would be targeted to be less than €3 million across many conditions and we limited the hedge notional on any given instrument to be less than €100 million. To keep this hedge exercise as simple as possible, we limited the number of hedge instruments. More precise hedging to reduce the post-hedge NAV shortfall can be achieved by relaxing these constraints, and, of course, the exact hedge using an exotic replication would lead to a zero shortfall condition, but with substantial bid–offer margins and highly restricted liquidity on such an instrument. We use two receiver swaps rather than one to address the cases of curve twists and because we are also examining the hedge over time (two years forward). The delta on the two swaps will vary as time passes.

From Tables 8.5 and 8.6, we see that the set of hedge instruments covers for much of the NAV shortfall risks across the different interest rate and implied volatility conditions. Overall, the central

Table 8.5 Case 1: interest-rate delta analysis across curve steepening

	Curve steepening				
	−0.50%	−0.20%	0.00%	0.20%	0.50%
Unhedged	4.14	3.78	3.52	3.32	3.00
Hedged	−1.36	−1.26	−0.76	−0.15	−0.06

Table 8.6 Case 1: interest-rate vega analysis across parallel rate shifts

	Parallel rate shifts			
	−2.0%	−1.0%	0.0%	1.0%
Unhedged	0.75	0.74	0.65	0.58
Hedged	0.34	0.31	0.29	0.30

case NAV shortfall of €5.7 million reduces to €0.9 million, implying that the cost of the hedge package is €4.8 million. The NAV shortfalls in extreme cases also decline considerably. For example, the shortfall under high volatility and low rates (3% volatility bump and −2% rate shifts) goes from €15.6 million to €0.4 million with the hedge.

CASE 2: MAPPING OUT THE NAV SHORTFALL RISKS

In the second case, we expand our study to consider an asset basket with equities, modelled on the EURO STOXX 50 Index, and alter the liability to have a bonus option dependent on the asset return performance rather than a market rate.

We simulate the behaviour of an asset portfolio based on 95% bonds with a constant duration of 10 years and 5% equities, against a liability whose annual compounding rate is MAX[3.75%, 35% * asset return].[6] Once again, part of the compounded liability growth is offset by the compounded asset growth. Note that we make the assumption in the simulations that the correlation between equity and interest rates is zero. Should this correlation assumption change, then both the NAV shortfall fair values as well as the hedges would need to be adjusted accordingly.

The steps to analyse case 2 follow that of case 1, where the NAV shortfall values are captured pre- and post-hedge. Given the addition of equities, we expand the sensitivity measures to include conditions of instantaneous equity spot level moves and equity volatility changes, as well as measuring the equity delta moves against interest-rate deltas.

The NAV shortfall value in the central case shows an expected loss of four, with increasing exposure under falling interest rates, higher volatility for both interest rates and equities, and lower instantaneous equity levels. Note though that the changes in the shortfall due to moves in equity levels or volatility are relatively small given that the proportion of equities in the asset portfolio is only 5% each year. Moreover, given that in this case 2, the liability effectively reflects 35% of the asset return (holding aside the guarantee rate), notwithstanding the small exposure to equities, the overall NAV shortfall appears to be lower than in case 1, where the "bonus" option was based on 80% ∗ CMS 10Y.

CASE 2: SELECTING AND SOLVING FOR HEDGE NOTIONALS AND RESULTS

For the interest-rate risks, we used the same hedge instruments found in case 1, and kept the same constraints with respect to maximum notional size and aim to reduce the post-hedge NAV shortfall to less than €3 million. The negative notional on the 7Y × 10Y straddle appears to balance out the vega from the two receiver swaptions.

For the equity risk exposure, we chose slightly out-of-the-money put options (strike = 2250 versus spot level of 2500) of five-year and 10-year maturities to hedge the equity downside risk and equity at-the-money straddles of five-year and 10-year tenors to cover for equity volatility.[7] The overall equity vega from the hedge instruments is positive.[8] The measure for the equity hedges is expressed as a number of contracts, whereby in each contract, a single tick move in the underlying index pays €10.

Like case 1, the hedge set in case 2 proves to be quite effective in handling NAV shortfall risks across interest-rate delta and curve steepening moves (see Table 8.7).

We illustrate here the impact of adding the small exposure to equities, and see in Table 8.8 that the level of equity shock generates a strong differentiation of pre-hedge NAV shortfall results.

We next measured the pre- and post-hedge NAV shortfall results for equity delta moves against interest-rate delta moves, and

Table 8.7 Hedge notional values for case 2

Hedge instrument	Notional value
Five-year receiver swap	75.5
15-year receiver swap	−23.9
5Y × 5Y receiver swaption, $K = 3.75\%$	100.0
10Y × 10Y receiver swaption, $K = 3.75\%$	48.1
7Y × 10Y at-the-money straddle	−14.4

Equity instruments	Contracts
Equity Put 5 Year 2250	2,348
Equity Put 10 Year 2250	−2,696
Equity Straddle 5 Year	−930
Equity Straddle 10 Year	1,215

Table 8.8 Case 2: NAV shortfalls variation with equity and interest-rate moves

Parallel rate shifts (%)	Equity level down 40%	Equity level unchanged	Equity level up 40%
−2.0	15.7	13.9	12.1
−1.5	12.0	10.3	8.8
−1.0	9.0	7.5	6.2
−0.5	6.7	5.4	4.4
0.0	5.1	4.0	3.1
0.5	3.9	3.0	2.3
1.0	3.1	2.3	1.7
1.5	2.5	1.8	1.3
2.0	2.0	1.4	1.0

observe that the hedge also works under these cases to reduce the shortfall, as shown in Table 8.9.

For case 2, the cost of this package is €4.1 million. For example, the NAV shortfall pre-hedge for −2% shift in interest rates at 3% bump in rate volatility is €15.6 million and goes to €1.9 million with the hedge. Moreover, case 2 post-hedge shortfalls are lower than that of case 1, reflecting the more benign nature of the asset return based bonus (35% ∗ asset return) versus the competitive market rate one (80% ∗ CMS10Y).

CASE 3: MAPPING OUT THE NAV SHORTFALL RISKS
In the third and last case, we address the shortcoming of the case 2 scenario for the liability and the asset pool due to the market

Table 8.9 Case 2: interest-rate delta analysis across equity spot shifts

	Change in equity spot level				
	−40%	−20%	0%	20%	40%
Unhedged	3.42	3.27	3.11	2.95	2.78
Hedged	−0.20	−0.28	−0.38	−0.45	−0.51

conditions at the time of pricing. As such, we modify the liability to have a lower guaranteed rate in return for a more realistic level of asset return participation as well as a more likely fixed income versus equity asset mix. The case 3 liability is still priced at par, and in some ways reflects how much the guaranteed rate must decline to provide more conventional levels of "bonus option" participation and asset allocation.

We simulate the behaviour of an asset portfolio based on 70% bonds with a constant duration of 10 years and 30% equities, against a liability whose annual compounding rate is $MAX[2.00\%, 60\% *$ asset return].

The NAV shortfall results show significantly higher values for the central case, and much higher variations across the same sensitivities measured for cases 1 and 2, particularly where we examine equity scenarios, where the shortfalls are quite distinctive. This suggests that equity option hedges should have larger notional values than in the previous case.

CASE 3: SELECTING AND SOLVING FOR HEDGE NOTIONALS AND RESULTS

While the set of interest-rate hedge instruments does not change for this case versus the two previous ones, we alter the choice of equity hedge instruments considerably (see Table 8.10). In this situation, we place two out-of-the-money equity puts (Strike = 2250 and 2000 versus spot level of 2500), and we also use a long-dated equity forward to hedge out any residual delta. To restrict the number of hedge instruments, we use only one straddle. Again, all of these long-dated equity hedge instruments are selected for illustrative purposes, since for more conventional purposes, shorter dated equity hedges would be rolled, leading to further rebalancing costs. All other hedge constraints remain the same as earlier.

Table 8.10 Hedge notional values for case 3

Hedge instrument	Notional value
Five-year receiver swap	38.4
15-year receiver swap	−5.1
5Y × 5Y receiver swaption, $K = 3.75\%$	100.0
10Y × 10Y receiver swaption, $K = 3.75\%$	15.9
7Y × 10Y at-the-money straddle	2.7

Equity instruments	Contracts
Equity Put 5 Year 2250	−6,580
Equity Put 10 Year 2250	9,120
Equity Straddle 10 Year	658
Equity Forward 10 Year	−536

Given the size of the equity allocation as well as the higher asset participation in the liability, we see that more contracts are required to reduce the NAV shortfall. For the two equity puts, we are short the high strike and long the low strike put with a higher notional, thereby capping the loss on the hedge. All three equity options contribute to the equity spot delta, and so to match the spot delta on the NAV shortfall, we go short a long-dated equity forward.

This seems plausible since when equity goes down, the NAV shortfall increases because of the minimum rate guarantee whereas when equity increases, the liability bonus allows for only a certain proportion of this gain to be paid out, hence reducing the shortfall. This also explains why the notional on the equity straddle is low as it is only used to handle the equity vega and is not needed to hedge out high equity performance.

Once again, as in case 2, we review the pre- and post-hedge results for the NAV shortfall for select extreme conditions across interest rate and equity level and volatility moves. The set of hedge instruments works effectively to bring down the NAV shortfall of €12.6 million (central case) to €−0.1 million, implying a hedge cost of €12.7 million. Here we see that hedging the shortfall under the equity scenarios is more difficult than in case 2, given the size of the residuals under certain extreme conditions. Nonetheless, even for these equity stresses, the largest residual we observe is €5.3 million, versus the original NAV shortfall of €41.1 million.

Table 8.11 Case 3: equity vega with equity spot variation

	Change in equity spot level				
	−40%	−20%	0%	20%	40%
Unhedged	0.56	0.59	0.60	0.58	0.55
Hedged	0.11	0.04	0.02	0.00	−0.01

Table 8.12 Case 3: interest-rate delta with equity spot variation

	Change in equity spot level				
	−40%	−20%	0%	20%	40%
Unhedged	3.96	3.61	3.22	2.89	2.61
Hedged	−0.13	0.00	0.01	−0.02	−0.01

Tables 8.11 and 8.12 illustrate the main sensitivities for equity delta against equity vega moves as well as rate delta against equity delta moves. In both circumstances, the hedge shows robust results.

CONCLUSION

In undertaking this NAV risk replication, we have considered multiple sources of market changes for the underlying assets: delta (both parallel and in twists), and vega, which in particular reinforces the point of how this risk to the NAV is a true shortfall "OPTION". This vanilla replication exercise intends to cover the risks of an exact exotic option, which could be provided to hedge out the exact shortfall risks (assuming no changes to liability and asset benchmarks) but presents practical challenges due to limited liquidity in exotic options. The vanilla replication should be considered a macro-hedge, and clearly this position will need to be adjusted over time (future mismatches will occur from the fact that the asset and liability positions decline but the hedge is not adjusted). Vanilla replications will also be more sensitive to large changes in market conditions than the precisely tailored exotic option.

1   This chapter previously appeared in an earlier version in *Life & Pensions*, March 2009.

2   Market conditions at the time of pricing: euro 10-year rate of 4.40%; euro 10Y × 10Y swaption Black–Scholes volatility of 13.5%; EURO STOXX 50 index of 2500; EURO STOXX 50 volatility index (V2X) of 60.

3   Liabilities of 100 reflect the fair market value of the discounted cashflows on a risk-free basis inclusive of the value of the bonus option.

4   All table results with NAV shortfall figures are in euro millions as per the original fund balance sheet unless otherwise stated.

5   These hedge costs are similar to the additional policyholder premium charges that have been applied under recent Norwegian regulations, whereby the NAV stakeholders quantified the risk of this liability through underwriting and explicitly charged this back to the policyholders in return for foregoing any profit-sharing agreement for the NAV stakeholder.

6   At the time of pricing the liability, high equity volatility and low rates did not allow for a higher level of asset return participation given the guaranteed rate of 3.75%, presuming par pricing. Similarly, the equity weighting in the asset basket was also low due to the high equity volatility conditions. Just six weeks prior, liabilities with an annual rate of MAX[4.0%, 55% * asset return] and an asset basket of 80% bonds and 20% equities could have been used.

7   We note that the actual liquidity in such long-dated equity hedge instruments would be quite limited, and so we use them for purely illustrative purposes. In practice, shorter dated instruments (usually one year) are rolled.

8   We have allowed for negative notional values or short equity option positions in this hedge exercise. In practice, unless considered in the context of a call spread, such short option positions may not be desirable. However, to apply a non-negative notional constraint leads to less robust hedge results.

REFERENCES

Davidson, C., 2008, "The Replication Game", *Life & Pensions*, April, URL: http://www.life-pensions.com/public/showPage.html?page=789121.

Kalberer, T., 2007, "Guaranteed Links to the Life market", *Life & Pensions*, December, pp. 39–44.

Oechslin, J., O. Aubry, M. Aellig, A. Kappeli, D. Bronnimann, A. Tandonnet and G. Valois, 2007, "Replicating Embedded Options", *Life & Pensions*, February, pp. 47–52.

Consiglio, A. and D. De Giovanni, 2006, "Evaluation of Insurance Products with Guarantee in Incomplete Markets", Working Paper 06-01, University of Palermo.

Babbel, D. F., J. Gold and C. B. Merrill, 2002, "Fair Value of Liabilities: The Financial Economics Perspective", *North American Actuarial Journal*, 6(1), pp. 12–27.

Jørgensen, P. L., 2001, "Life Insurance Contracts with Embedded Options", Working Paper Series No. 96, University of Aarhus.

9

Solvency II and Liquidity Risk in Insurance Companies

Ioannis Akkizidis; Kris Luyten[1]

FRSGlobal; riskVentures

LIQUIDITY AND ITS RISK IN INSURANCE

In general, liquidity risk arises from situations in which a party interested in trading an asset cannot do so because nobody in the market wants to trade that asset. Liquidity risk becomes particularly important to parties who are about to hold or currently hold an asset, since it affects their ability to trade. More specifically in insurance, liquidity risk refers to the inability of a company to get the expected cashflows from financial contracts needed to fulfil obligations for both assets and liabilities (ie, pay claims or costs). Liquidity is highly correlated to other types of risks and is the consequence of stressful conditions to these risks. Liquidity issues usually happen due to sudden changes in market conditions (related to market risk), counterparty downgrading (related to credit risk) or big claims, but may also stem from rumours concerning insecure market and adverse economic conditions, insolvency risk, inefficient business strategies, etc. These can affect the cash "in" and "out" flow, or liquidity, of existing and future portfolios.

In terms of liquidity analysis, an insurance institution has to identify all cashflow events circulating within the accounts and portfolios, initiated by the financial contracts.[2] An institution has to analyse and forecast all expected cashflows from existing and future investment portfolios, together with the expected premium income, potential losses and claims in terms of size and time of reporting.

But, when do liquidity problems arise in insurance companies? To answer this question we need to identify the elements and process of financial analysis, the main structure of the insurance accounts, the mechanism of exchanging cashflows derived by the financial and insurance contracts, and the two main types of financial analysis, called static and dynamic. Finally, we need to understand the market and funding liquidity risks, but more importantly, their integration for measuring, reporting and managing liquidity risk.

ACCOUNT STRUCTURES OF LIFE AND NON-LIFE INSURANCE
In a typical balance sheet, as shown in Table 9.1, of both life and non-life insurance the investment asset accounts are constructed mainly with highly rated bonds and other secured products. In principle most of the investment portfolios, in both the life and non-life insurance industries, should be supported by the receivables taken by the premiums of the policyholders. All these investments shall be used to support the expected future claims that are outstanding on the liability side.

An important difference between the life and non-life balance sheet structures is that on the latter the receivables are placed only on the asset side, whereas in the former they can be placed on either side. Finally, the equity and off-balancing structure follows a similar concept to that in banking institutions. Under normal conditions, part of the profits goes to shareholders as dividends. A reverse process of supporting claims could happen when major losses might occur. Derivatives such as swaps and money market products typically construct the off-balance sheet accounts.

The insurance liabilities are mapped by applying a replication approach, an expected cashflow delivery approach or a contract-based approach. In terms of financial analysis the last is the most effective.

FINANCIAL ANALYSIS
The elements
Financial contracts and their resultant financial events of cashflows are directly linked to and driven by:

- Market conditions, which are simply the market risk factors, ie, yield curves, commodity stock and index prices, foreign exchange rates.

Table 9.1 Typical structures of life and non-life insurance

Typical structure of life insurance	Typical structure of non-life insurance
Assets	Assets
• Receivables	• Receivables
– Policyholders	– Policyholders
– Reinsurers	– Reinsurers
• Investments	• Investments
– Highly rated bonds	– Highly rated bonds
– Stocks	– Stocks
– Securitisation products	– Securitisation products
– Time deposits, etc.	– Time deposits, etc.
Liabilities	Liabilities (for each line of business)
• Actuarial reserves	• Technical loss reserves
• Bonus fund	• Incurred but not reported
• Unearned premiums	• Unearned premiums reserves
Equity	Equity
Off-balance sheet	Off-balance sheet
• Swaps	• Swaps
• Money market	• Money market

- Credit risk defining whether counterparties are capable of fulfilling their obligations. It also defines the probability of downgrading. Finally, it is related to the ways and the size, where the credit risk exposures are covered by the counterparty or by a third entity; in insurance, the counterparty is typically the reinsurer.
- Behaviour such as prepayments, lapses, the points in time for insurance claims and the reserve development pattern in non-life insurance. In life insurance it is for instance the change of mortality estimation tables linked to longevity and invalidity.
- Insurance risk: in life insurance these are categorised as biometric types, ie, mortality, longevity and disability (morbidity and sickness) and non-biometric types, ie, lapse, expense, revision and catastrophe. In non-life insurance, occurrence claim time, unreported waiting time, severity, reserve development pattern and incurred but not reported claims are the main types of risks.

In terms of financial analysis, market, counterparty, behaviour and insurance risks are the input analysis elements, all linked to

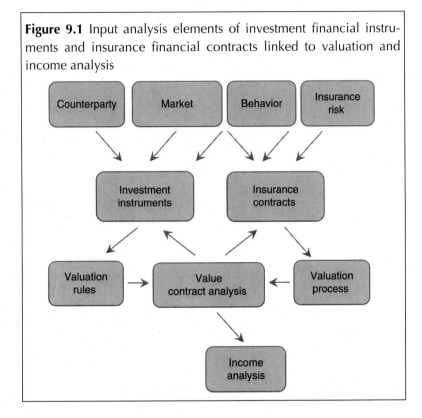

Figure 9.1 Input analysis elements of investment financial instruments and insurance financial contracts linked to valuation and income analysis

the financial contracts, as illustrated in Figure 9.1. Counterparty and insurance risks pertain only to investment instruments[3] and insurance contracts respectively, whereas market and behaviour are linked to both types.

Based on the input analysis elements, the valuation of the financial contracts can be derived. The valuation process of insurance contracts is driven mainly by insurance risk factors and in some cases by the market. Behind the value of investment instruments there are different book-keeping rules, eg, fair value, mark-to-market, historic/write-off at the end, etc, used in the discounting process and calculation of the expected cashflows of the underlying instruments. From the value we can derive the income; from the changes in the parameters of the input elements we can calculate the sensitivity, value-at-risk (VaR) and earnings-at-risk (EaR) out of the corresponding changes in value and income respectively.

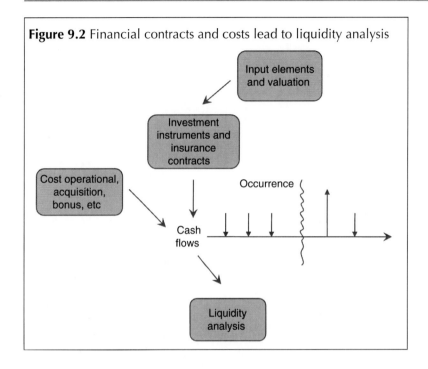

Figure 9.2 Financial contracts and costs lead to liquidity analysis

Having the input elements in place and considering the valuation rules, all financial events that lead to cashflows are available to derive liquidity analysis, as illustrated in Figure 9.2. Applying liquidity analysis, we get all expected cashflows from all financial and insurance contracts at the settlement date. Note that costs such as operational expenses, bonuses referring mainly to insurance contracts, etc, are additional input elements that are not directly linked to financial contracts but do affect the expected cashflows, and thus should also be considered in liquidity analysis.

As with VaR and EaR analysis, the calculation of liquidity-at-risk (LaR) is driven by changes to the input elements and also by the funding liquidity, as will be discussed later in this chapter.

Static and dynamic analysis

It is important also to distinguish whether the expected cashflows are derived from existing or also from future business. This makes a major difference in the liquidity, valuation, income and risk measurement analysis.

Typically, the valuation and income for financial contracts of current investment portfolios are based on assumed up-to-date but static views of market and economic conditions, the status of the counterparty and relatively known short-term expectations of behaviour. In non-life and life insurance the input risk factors, ie, distributions, tables of the biometric types of risks, etc, are derived as defined up to today.

This static view of analysis provides results of expected liquidity based on the current prices, premiums, claims and reserves, discount factors and credit spreads. Thus, in such analysis the different types of risks are stressed based on deterministic shocks of the above input analysis elements. Of course, assuming retention of only the existing financial portfolios and insurance contracts, the sizes of both assets and liabilities will roll down as the financial contracts mature.

In reality as time passes business should grow as the input factors are changing; thus dynamic analysis should be employed. This means that new economic and market conditions, counterparty status and behaviour need to be continually considered. In non-life insurance the whole range of distribution of the input risk factors, such as unreported claims and/or waiting times, and the severity within the time horizon are used in this type of analysis. In life insurance the new updated tables of biometric types of risks and the range of distributions referring to non-biometric risks need also to be considered.

As both assets and liabilities are growing by rolling over in the future, they influence liquidity heavily. New premiums of insurance contracts are applied and new investments of financial products are added to existing or newly constructed portfolios. They are driven by an institution's strategies for managing their existing and future portfolios and accounts.[4] For new financial instruments and for any repricing of the already existing financial contracts within the investment portfolios, the valuation and income parameters should be based on assumed future market and economic conditions and changes to credit spreads. Premiums are also updated based mainly on the whole range of distributions and/or updated tables of insurance risk parameters.

In the dynamic simulation type of analysis, the input elements are dynamically changing through the future time buckets driven by deterministic what-if scenarios or stochastic processes, eg, Monte Carlo approaches. The distributions of the corresponding results of value, income and liquidity are used for risk measurement.

Financial contracts

Although there is a long product catalogue of financial contracts, in principle there are few patterns that generate financial events.[5] In general, financial instruments can be classified into these basic types: fixed income maturity and non-maturity instruments, stocks, commodities and credit risk contracts. A combination of the above with some additional rules provide synthetic derivatives, eg, swaps and future/forwards, as well as options, including exotic ones. Of course there are always new products, such as securitisation, which are more advanced in structure but also more complex in terms of cashflow event patterns. The latter type contains a relatively small percentage of financial products, but in some cases these result in the largest exposures.

Typically, the expected cashflows are received from future payments, eg, interest, but also from trading the different expectations in changes to market prices. Whether an institution is receiving these cashflows at the agreed or expected points in time is fully dependent on market conditions, counterparty status and expected behaviour.

Life insurance contracts are rather simpler in structure. Most life insurance contracts are like normal savings deposits, defined as premiums, provided by the protection buyer to the protection seller. These payment instalments are usually set within long-term time buckets. The insured expects premium payments in terms of disability and coverage of mortality risk, and at survival time should receive retirement payment of a fixed sum, including bonus plus minimum interest. In some cases the contract is linked to an investment fund that pays out at survival. In most life insurance contracts an option between a final lump sum and an annuity paying until death can be exercised.

In terms of cash inflows the institution has rather steady expectations from the premiums of the long-term life insurance policies. The mortality or longevity expectations are driven by statistically based tables that provide an accurate degree of future projection. Claims and recovery parameters are mapped based on distributions.

With a non-life insurance policy, the buyer provides the premiums and expects only coverage of potential claims, if and only if an event arises. Non-life insurance contracts are renewed in a short-term cycle. In case an event occurs within the lifetime of the contract, the policyholder is eligible to request a claim within, or for some lines of business after, the maturity time of the contract. The size and the time of the claim are unknown factors and the payment pattern of coverage is planned by the institution.

As with life insurance, the expected cash inflows are steady and, in general, the patterns of claims are well defined. However, under extreme conditions the projection mapping of incurred but not reported claims may not be sufficient, as the demanding liquidity may be higher than expected.

Certain major claims on both life (eg, pandemic) and non-life (eg, natural disaster) insurance policies are covered mainly by reinsurance. The institution faces liquidity issues when the premiums from policyholders, as well as investment financial instruments, are unable to support the expected or unexpected claims.

ANALYSIS OF LIQUIDITY RISK

All financial institutions must be able to support their liquidity needs under both normal and stressed conditions within an established framework. In terms of analysis, the liquidity risk framework should contain all input elements for so-called market liquidity risk analysis, together with behaviour analysis and strategies for funding the liquidity demands under normal and stressed conditions.

Market and funding liquidity risk analysis

Asset or product liquidity risk, also known as market risk, is the risk of incurring unexpected cashflows due to any new valuation of financial contracts. Applying static analysis, the valuation of financial contracts (eg, for pricing) is determined by considering the risk factors and discounting back future cashflows. For stressing the market liquidity, deterministic shocks into the risk input analysis parameters are applied; thus, the new value of each contract and the resulting liquidity is estimated for the existent portfolios and/or accounts. In dynamic analysis, applied to both existing and future accounts, the risk factors are updated according to the future simulated conditions.[6] The valuation for each future time step bucket is driven by the corresponding conditions of risk factors.[7]

Funding liquidity risk, also known as cashflow risk, is about the action plans for fulfilling the requested demand of liquidity under normal or extreme funding obligations. In insurance, this means liquidity for supporting expected or unexpected obligations against claims from the insured.

The funding process for liquidity is based on an institution's idiosyncratic characteristics. It is modelled as the behaviour input element and reflects how the institution is managing their inflows and outflows of the existing and future financial contracts. Under normal conditions, funding liquidity is based on the expected cashflows resulting from both existing and new financial contracts, applying static and dynamic analysis respectively. In extreme stress cases where there is a high demand for cash, financial institutions may be forced to sell their liquid assets. However, under stress market conditions the liquid instruments may become illiquid[8] and also new business may be reduced.[9]

Integrating analysis of market and funding liquidity risks

In practice there is dependency between funding and market liquidity. Market effects can lead to funding idiosyncratic liquidity risk and vice versa. This integration is shown in Table 9.2.

The first row of this table is about the market liquidity risk where the market, credit and insurance risks are defined as expected. Static analysis and/or dynamic simulations can be applied, driven by the current and future expectations, providing thereby the corresponding expected cashflows. The second row refers to the market liquidity under stress conditions. Static shocks and dynamic fluctuations are applied to analyse changes to the risk parameters that are under stress to evaluate the impact of market liquidity.

- In case 1 the liquidity funding process is supporting the expected liquidity obligations. This case reflects the everyday normal market conditions, counterparty status and behaviour, and expected insurance risk; thus the liquidity should be demanded and provided without consideration of any additional discounts, spreads, risk exposures or unexpected losses.

Table 9.2 Integration of market and funding liquidity

Market liquidity	Funding liquidity	
	Expected idiosyncratic funding liquidity (normal liquidity obligations)	Contingency plan for unexpected idiosyncratic funding liquidity (extreme liquidity obligations)
Expected market and credit risk conditions	Case 1 Liquid	Case 2 Partially liquid
Stressed market and credit risk conditions	Case 3 Partially liquid	Case 4 Illiquid

- Case 2 reflects the situation of idiosyncratic stress where for instance individual external[10] or internal[11] events may arise, and thus an institution's obligations move to extreme requests for liquidity. Thus, a contingency plan has to be applied where the institution may be forced to sell additional liquid assets,[12] with expected market discount and credit spreads.

- In case 3 an institution follows the normal idiosyncratic liquidity funding process for fulfilling liquidity obligations. However, the changes in market liquidity will have a downstream effect on the expected value and liquidity. In this case the resulting cashflows will be unable to cover the liquidity needs. If no further actions are made, a financial institution may increase the risk its exposed to because of its idiosyncratic funding liquidity risk.

- Case 4 is the worst in terms of market and funding liquidity risk management. Liquidity obligations shift to an extreme degree and, thus, an institution has to apply its contingency plan for unexpected funding liquidity. The stressed market liquidity results in reduction of inflows; this means an inability to support the requested funding obligations. Under these idiosyncratic and market stress conditions, an institution may be forced to carry out some trading activities (mainly sales) of liquid assets with additional discounts; they may also request to access funding facilities and deposits, at a high cost.

Institutions should always be able to recognise which of the above cases of market and funding liquidity risk they are dealing with. More importantly, they should be able to identify when and how they may shift from one case to another and how they may control their liquidity risks accordingly. The higher the liquidity (cash), the better a financial institution is protected against unexpected situations of liquidity funding demands. But at the same time this may increase exposure due to valuation effect, and even opportunity costs: this liquidity does not bring any business or profit.

Liquidity reporting analysis and LaR

Having the expected cashflows that are generated from existing or future financial contracts, insurance institutions may define three main types of liquidity gap reports: marginal, cumulative and residual. The marginal liquidity gap shows the expected net liquidity, which is not more than the amount of future expected cash "ins" and "outs", as indicated with bar plots in Figure 9.3. Summing up the marginal cashflows for the previous time buckets, the cumulative liquidity gap is estimated and indicated as a dashed line in Figure 9.3. The cumulative report also indicates the duration of a liquidity "survivor" without external funding liquidity support. Finally, the residual liquidity gap shows the remaining cashflow position at any point in the future; in other words it shows how long or short the assets and liabilities are, in terms of expected cashflows.

The cumulative liquidity gap report, of existing financial instruments, is driven by the input analysis elements, ie, market, counterparty, behaviour and insurance risks. Thus, for measuring the LaR we need to change the parameters of these elements, based on a number of scenarios.

Applying Monte Carlo analysis, n number of market conditions can stochastically be simulated within a liquidity analysis time horizon. The resultant cashflows provide several cumulative liquidity gap reports. The LaR is defined by observing the distribution of the corresponding minimum survival periods within a set confidence level. An example is shown in Figure 9.4, where nine[13] market scenarios have been applied under normal idiosyncratic conditions for funding liquidity needs (case 3 in Table 9.2). The resulting duration of liquidity "survival" is within a range of 17 to 20 weeks, setting a confidence level of 99%, the survival period is 19 weeks.

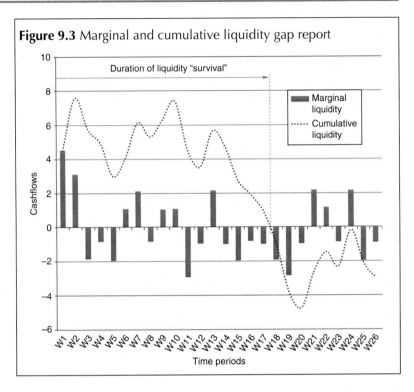

Figure 9.3 Marginal and cumulative liquidity gap report

Institutions should measure LaR under different but well-defined funding idiosyncratic liquidity status, according to what type of analysis (Table 9.2) is employed. The optimal combination of risk factors that should be employed is dependent mainly on the type of financial contracts and business, idiosyncratic characteristics and regulatory demands.

Liquidity risk in Solvency II

Solvency II focuses on liquidity risk from the perspective of risk mitigation. Indeed, principle 3 (out of 5) of risk mitigation is devoted to liquidity and definition of value. Instead of imposing limiting rules or eligibility criteria, it establishes general principles.

To be eligible for recognition, the financial risk mitigation instruments relied upon shall have a value over time sufficiently reliable to provide appropriate certainty as to the risk mitigation achieved. This presumes that the value is not negatively influenced by missing liquidity: the nearly evaporated market for AAA rated super senior tranches of CDOs comes to mind. In addition, an insurer

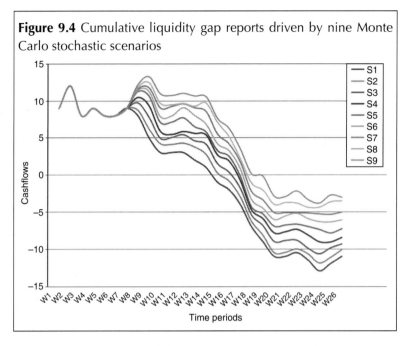

Figure 9.4 Cumulative liquidity gap reports driven by nine Monte Carlo stochastic scenarios

should have written guidance regarding liquidity requirements that financial risk mitigation instruments should meet; financial risk mitigation instruments considered to reduce the SCR have to meet these liquidity requirements.

Apart from risk mitigation, the Framework Directive recognises liquidity as one of the risks that should be covered through risk management (Pillar II), rather than through capital (Pillar I). Some market participants interpret this as such that liquidity risk should be managed in a holistic way and not be focused on specific instruments or risk mitigations. Tools commonly used by insurers are:

• liquidity planning;
• ongoing analysis; and
• liquidity scenario analysis.

Interestingly, the drafters of Solvency II do not seem to have complete trust in the risk mitigation of insurance players. The Framework Directive also states: "where the risk mitigation instrument actually increases risk, then the Solvency Capital Requirement should be increased."

In the area of valuation and discounting, further work will need to be conducted to see whether swap rates are appropriate benchmarks to determine the risk-free interest-rate term structure, taking into account liquidity considerations. A current practice for some market participants is to add an illiquidity premium to the discount rate for the valuation of annuity business.

At the supervisory level of co-operation, a decision-making process may be introduced to define financial distress situations and issue relevant guidance, with focus on retaining liquidity and the level of technical provisions (instead of the SCR).

CASE STUDIES

This chapter has treated both market and funding liquidity risk, and the interaction between both. During the financial crisis, which culminated at the end of 2008, two insurance companies were prominently in the public eye.

AIG lost its position as the largest and most diversified insurance company worldwide, to become the biggest receiver of state aid ever. Swiss Re had to accept fresh finance from one of its newer shareholders at punishing terms, which severely diluted all other existing shareholders, in order to keep its credit rating and to stay in business.

In both cases liquidity risk was to blame. More specifically, both companies found that when market liquidity hit them, funding liquidity had also dried up.

AIG

The American International Group, Inc (AIG), is a case in point of the interplay between market and funding liquidity risk, and of both hitting together once a crisis comes along. What finally ruined AIG were the collateral calls it had to make on its portfolio of written credit insurance. At the same time AIG was unable to raise money from the credit markets or from selling off subsidiaries.

AIG had to post US$20 billion collateral during the summer of 2008 for credit default swaps (CDS) it had written. And another US$32 billion was needed in the middle of September 2008 for the next 15 days. These collateral calls were triggered by the downgrade of AIG's own credit rating and by the continued fall in the value of the guaranteed securities.

At the same time, and of course related, AIG was finding it difficult to renew US$64 billion of non-government funding due

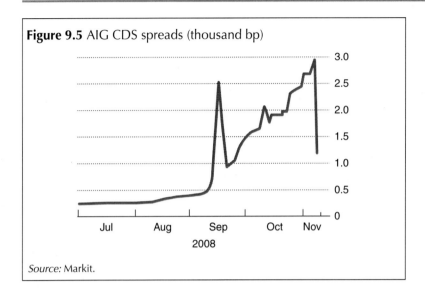

Figure 9.5 AIG CDS spreads (thousand bp)

Source: Markit.

to mature by 2011 (as of November 13, 2008). It could not sell its insurance operations to raise cash, since its competitors (the potential buyers) were also suffering from the credit crunch. Neither could it access the credit markets anymore because its credit spread suggested it was heading for default: in mid-November 2008 its credit spread was 30% (too high to be expressed in basis points), up from 2.5% only four months before (see Figure 9.5).

AIG Financial Products, a subsidiary of the AIG holding company, had built up a strong market share in super senior multi-sector CDS by offering generous terms for collateral calls (better than the monoline insurers). It had also given its counterparties rights to terminate transactions. AIG was not regulated as a bank and therefore had no requirement to hold capital against sold credit insurance. On the contrary, its bank counterparties who bought insurance could reduce their regulatory capital. European banks used AIG's credit insurance so that they did not have to hold regulatory capital against insured long-term securities. Furthermore, US investment banks took out CDS with AIG to hedge their exposure to subprime mortgage-backed securities.

AIG had an exposure of US$446 billion in sold credit derivatives (as of end of Q2 2008). Of these, US$307 billion were sold to European banks in nicely named "regulatory capital forbearance" trades. It made a loss of US$61.7 billion in Q4 2008 alone: of this amount, US$25.9 billion were "market-disruption related" losses on credit derivatives.

After receiving the exceptional amount of US$160 billion of government aid, it took the equally exceptional measure of publishing the amounts paid to counterparties and the identities of the counterparties (see Figure 9.6). The amounts paid to counterparties were (September 16 – December 31, 2008):

- US$22.4 billion collateral for CDS;
- US$12.1 billion guaranteed investment obligations for munici- palities;
- US$27.1 billion to buy securities underlying CDS to cancel them (vehicle: Maiden Lane III); and
- US$43.7 billion for AIG's securities lending operations.

Part of the direct support to AIG (US$12.5 billion) also had to be used to refund maturing debt.

AIG was a venerable 90-year-old financial institution, the largest insurance company in the world with a trillion-dollar balance sheet. It had to be saved four times between mid-September 2008 and mid-March 2009, at a total cost of US$160 billion to the US taxpayer. The government ended up owning 79.9% of the company, with preferred stakes in American International Insurance (AIG's Asian operations), American Life Insurance (active in 50 countries) and US life insurance businesses. Foreign general insurance and International Lease Finance Corporation (aircraft leasing) are expected to be sold off.

Swiss Re

Swiss Re was hit by plunging values in an illiquid portfolio, which ate into its capital and threatened its rating. At the same time, it found that funding liquidity had all but dried up and it could raise new capital only by severely diluting existing shareholders.

On February 5, 2009, Swiss Re communicated a valuation loss of Sfr6 billion in its financial markets unit. The unit had undertaken bank-like activities, particularly in the US mortgage market, including subprime loans. The loss originated from CDS, portfolio CDS and financial guarantees. Two single structured CDS concluded with an unnamed client by themselves contributed Sfr2.7 billion to the losses (incremental loss since the exposures were first revealed

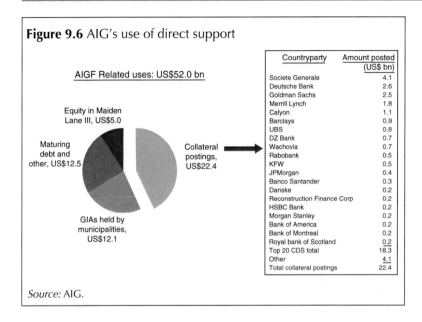

Figure 9.6 AIG's use of direct support

AIGF Related uses: US$52.0 bn

Equity in Maiden Lane III, US$5.0

Maturing debt and other, US$12.5

Collateral postings, US$22.4

GIAs held by municipalities, US$12.1

Countryparty	Amount posted (US$ bn)
Societe Generale	4.1
Deutsche Bank	2.6
Goldman Sachs	2.5
Merrill Lynch	1.8
Calyon	1.1
Barclays	0.9
UBS	0.8
DZ Bank	0.7
Wachovia	0.7
Rabobank	0.5
KFW	0.5
JPMorgan	0.4
Banco Santander	0.3
Danske	0.2
Reconstruction Finance Corp	0.2
HSBC Bank	0.2
Morgan Stanley	0.2
Bank of America	0.2
Bank of Montreal	0.2
Royal bank of Scotland	0.2
Top 20 CDS total	18.3
Other	4.1
Total collateral postings	22.4

Source: AIG.

by the end of 2007). The losses were pure valuation losses (not realised losses), but they reduced Swiss Re's capital; this in turn threatened its AA credit rating. A high quality rating is essential for a reinsurance company, not only for financing but also for business continuity.

Therefore Swiss Re had to raise new capital in the middle of the credit crunch, when investors were hard to come by. It raised Sfr3 billion from an existing shareholder, Warren Buffett's Berkshire Hathaway, at a punitive interest rate of 12% (official interest rates being close to zero). The investment was structured as a "perpetual" subordinated convertible note. The conversion rate at Sfr25 was equally favourable, given the current (depressed) share price of Sfr21.70, and would increase the stake of Berkshire Hathaway from 3% to over 20%. The execution date for conversion was set in three years' time. Swiss Re did have a buy-back right at 120%, starting from 2011. Even so, one market participant called the financial conditions "outrageously bad".

In the days prior to the communication of the loss, Swiss Re's share price had been on a roller coaster. On the day itself, February 5, 2008, it lost 28% of its value ending at a 17-year low (see Figure 9.7). In addition to the loss in the financial markets unit, there were also impairments of Sfr3 billion on the investment portfolio

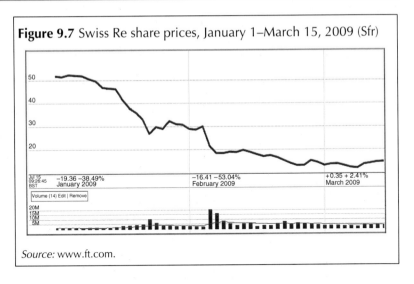

Figure 9.7 Swiss Re share prices, January 1–March 15, 2009 (Sfr)

Source: www.ft.com.

and losses of Sfr1.6 billion caused by currency movements. On the other hand, the government bond portfolio was revalued upwards by Sfr3 billion. Also, the core businesses for property-casualty and life-health remained healthy. This led to a net loss of "only" Sfr864 million for 2008.

To conserve cash, Swiss Re had cut its dividend to virtually zero and stopped its share buy-back programme. Even so, it struggled to retain its credit rating. Its capital had shrunk in the past three months by Sfr5 billion and over the year by Sfr12 billion. Consequently Standard & Poor's put its AA minus rating on negative watch. Therefore it became essential and urgent to raise new capital.

Even though all main insurers and reinsurers experienced volatile and falling asset prices in their investment portfolios, Swiss Re's venture into financial markets had led to problems on a wholly different scale. Munich Re, Swiss Re's long-standing rival, also reported strongly reduced earnings in 2008. But the group maintained its dividend and did not need new capital. It was even able to continue its share buy-back programme.

CONCLUSION

Managing liquidity risk calls for integrating market, credit and insurance risks that are applied in financial contracts to identify the corresponding expected cashflows; at the same time, it also involves structuring liquidity plans driven by the institution's idiosyncratic characteristics. Managing liquidity brings all analysis elements together in a unified financial analysis. Any individual analysis element or combination of them may cause a great loss of liquidity; thus a holistic view of financial analysis is needed for managing liquidity risk. In general we can say that liquidity management is about enterprise risk management.

Insurance institutions in particular have many complex cashflow patterns that are directly dependent on the analysis input elements; they have to be managed on a continuous basis. Any diversion from the expected pattern may result in major exposure to liquidity risk. The credit crisis starting from 2007 shows that large financial institutions can even default due to liquidity risk. As illustrated in the aforementioned case studies, the insurance industry should pay close attention to managing liquidity risk.

1 To Anne-Carole Wichoud for the valuable input of improving the contents of this text and Vivianne Bouchereau for the text review. To Katrien Marcelis for her invaluable insightful feedback.

2 Here both investment financial instruments, as in banking, and typical insurance contracts are alluded to.

3 These are typical banking financial contracts; to differentiate them from insurance contracts we call them investment instruments in this chapter.

4 Typical strategies are applied by different departments and groups that are managing the assets and investment portfolios, and/or in the liabilities are focusing on reserves, etc. For liquidity management we need to have the global view of expected cashflows from all types of accounts/portfolios.

5 The evolution of financial events from all types of contracts is described in Brammertz *et al* (2009).

6 Applying "what-if" or Monte Carlo approaches.

7 Future market fluctuations (also known as haircuts), changes to credit ratings and corresponding spreads and future fluctuations of the insurance risk parameters.

8 A financial instrument (security or asset) becomes illiquid when it cannot be traded quickly enough in the market, at a favourable price, to support liquidity demands or to prevent a loss. Unfavourable prices are considered as part of market risk, as is the risk of changing credit spreads.

9 During the recent credit crisis, institutions had to sell securitisation products, CDOs for minimising their exposure, recovering their reputation and also funding their liquidity needs. Ironically, before the crisis such products were considered highly liquid due to their high quality of senior and mezzanine tranches; but when the credit crunch stress market conditions arose, such products became rather unpopular, to the degree of being illiquid. Institutions had to apply high amounts of discounts to make them liquid, thus suffering great unexpected losses.

10 Such as major catastrophes, pandemics, etc.

11 These can include loss of reputation due to bad strategies, which have somehow been disclosed in the market.

12 From the investment portfolios.

13 In reality this number should be much greater; for demonstration purposes we only apply nine stochastic market scenarios.

REFERENCES

AIG, 2008a, "AIG reports fourth quarter and full year 2008 loss", March 2, URL: http://library.corporate-ir.net/library/76/761/76115/items/326705/87A66DC4-EE74-41DB-B73A-5FFA80472A43_4Q08_Press_Release.pdf.

AIG, 2008b, "AIG discloses counterparties to CDS, GIA and securities lending transactions", March 15, URL: http://media.corporate-ir.net/media_files/irol/76/76115/releases/031509.pdf.

Brammertz, W., I. Akkizidis, W. Breymann, R. Entin and M. Rüstmann, 2009, *Unified Financial Analysis, the Missing Links of Finance* (London/New York: John Wiley & Sons).

CEIOPS, 2008, "Report on Its Fourth Quantitative Impact Study (QIS4) for Solvency II", URL: http://www.ceiops.eu/media/files/consultations/QIS/CEIOPS-SEC-82-08%20QIS4%20Report.pdf.

European Commission, 2008, "QIS4 Technical Specifications", URL: http://ec.europa.eu/internal_market/insurance/docs/solvency/qis4/technical_specifications_2008_en.pdf.

Finance and Economics, 2008, "Cheque mate: How AIG got Uncle Sam over a barrel", *The Economist*, November 13, URL: http://www.economist.com/businessfinance/displaystory.cfm?story_id=12607251.

Finance and Economics, 2009a, "In a state: Despite another rescue for AIG, problems at the state-owned insurer weigh heavily on the markets", *The Economist*, March 2, URL: http://www.economist.com/businessfinance/displaystory.cfm?story_id=13213322.

Global Insurance, 2009b, "The next domino? Insurance firms teeter on the brink", *The Economist*, March 12, URL: http://www.economist.com/businessfinance/displaystory.cfm?story_id=13278968.

Guerrera, F., 2009, "AIG set to get new $30 bn lifeline", *Financial Times*, March 1, URL: http://www.ft.com/cms/s/0/d748d406-0688-11de-ab0f-000077b07658.html.

Insurance Industry Europe, 2008, "Black box blues: Investors still struggle to understand Europe's insurers", *The Economist*, July 24, URL: http://www.economist.com/finance/displaystory.cfm?story_id=11793057.

Johnson, M., 2009, "Swiss Re fall brings Europe down slightly", *Financial Times*, February 5, URL: http://www.ft.com/cms/s/0/6e3ccb88-f374-11dd-9c4b-0000779fd2ac.html.

Neue Zürcher Zeitung, 2009a, "Swiss Re Schockiert die Märkte mit Verlust", *Neue Zürcher Zeitung*, February 6, URL: http://www.nzz.ch/nachrichten/wirtschaft/aktuell/swiss_re_schockiert_die_maerkte_mit_verlust_1.1913307.html.

Neue Zürcher Zeitung, 2009b, "Verlorener Fokus", *Neue Zürcher Zeitung*, February 6, URL: http://www.nzz.ch/hintergrund/dossiers/boersen_und_maerkte_auf_der_achterbahn/internationale_boersen_und_maerkte_finanzkrise/verlorener_fokus_1.1913380.html.

Sender, H., 2009, "AIG saga shows dangers of credit default swaps", *Financial Times*, March 6, URL: http://cachef.ft.com/cms/s/0/aa741ba8-0a7e-11de-95ed-0000779fd2ac.html?nclick_check=1.

Simonian, H., 2009a, "Swiss Re ditches foray into financial markets", *Financial Times*, February 5, URL: http://www.ft.com/cms/s/0/fe7e3304-f3b4-11dd-9c4b-0000779fd2ac.html.

Simonian, H., 2009b, "Swiss Re taps Buffett for $2.6 bn in battle to preserve credit rating", *Financial Times*, February 6, URL: http://www.ft.com/cms/s/0/05cd3070-f3f0-11dd-9c4b-0000779fd2ac.html.

Simonian, H., 2009c, "Swiss Re turns to ex-chief amid portfolio fears", *Financial Times*, March 10, URL: http://www.ft.com/cms/s/0/7c19b834-0d13-11de-a555-0000779fd2ac.html.

Simonian, H., 2009d, "Swiss Re's new regime to focus on cutting risks", *Financial Times*, March 10, URL: http://www.ft.com/cms/s/0/4b4ea886-0d13-11de-a555-0000779fd2ac.html.

United States Securities and Exchange Commission, 2008, "Annual Report, American International Group", Form 10-K, URL: http://www.ezodproxy.com/AIG/2008/AR2007/images/AIG_10K2007.pdf.

10

Reinsurance Credit Risk

Rainer Sachs[1]

Munich Re Group

In the context of Solvency II and, in particular, in the recent discussions with regulators, eg, BaFin (Bongers and Stahl 2006), it
has become clear that the credit risk between the insurer[2] and the
reinsurer needs some clear and quantitative analysis.

The relationship between the insurer and the reinsurer is
twofold: the insurer transfers a certain amount of risk from their
business to the reinsurer. They are then entitled to relief from risk
capital, while the reinsurer has to capitalise this additional risk.
However, as real-life reinsurers are not completely free from default
risk, the insurer has to hold capital for this extra credit risk with the
reinsurer.

It is the aim of this chapter to analyse this credit risk relationship
in detail. We will identify relevant aspects of the issue that are
necessary for a quantitative assessment. Based on the findings we
propose a model framework that makes use of market best practices
for credit risk modelling in the financial industry. We also suggest a
calibration framework and choices for the relevant parameters.

WHERE IS THE RISK?

Let us start with an ideal picture of the insurance world. Taking
risks is the very basis of the insurance business, but what do we
mean by "risk?" Generically speaking, risk is intimately connected
with uncertainty and describes the possible deviation of particular
events from the expectation. To be precise on terminology here: we
talk about "risk", if we are not sure what is going to happen, but
we can at least assign probabilities and magnitudes to events. If

we do not even know probabilities and magnitudes, we talk about "uncertainty". To most people risk means negative outcomes, while chance is the positive part, ie, the upside potential.

Taking risks requires an appropriate cushion to cover unexpected future events. In the financial world this cover is called economic capital EC. Hence we define

$$EC = r(X) - E(X) \qquad (10.1)$$

where X is a stochastic process, a random quantity that describes the uncertainty of future events. $E(X)$ is the expectation value and $r(X)$ is a certain function that measures the risk.

Imagine X as the amount of claims in a portfolio of insurance policies. Economic capital EC is then the difference between the expected claims $E(X)$ and some quantification of "unexpected" or worst-case claims amount. There is clearly a range of possible choices for $r(X)$. Popular measures for $r(X)$ are variance- or quantile-based quantities, for example the standard deviation or multiples thereof, value-at-risk (VaR) or expected shortfall (ES). Among other risk factors, the value of $r(X)$ in a portfolio of insurance policies is driven by the correlation (diversification versus concentration): low diversification leads *ceteris paribus* to potentially high levels of unexpected loss.

Clearly the higher the risk of the insurance business, the more economic capital the company has to hold. Economic capital is not available for free and there are related costs. The costs of holding economic capital are important because they are drivers for the price of taking the risk in the first place.

One reason for an insurance company to transfer risk to a reinsurer is to take advantage of the higher diversification level in the reinsurance portfolio. Very broadly speaking, the reinsurer has to hold comparably less economic capital and hence can take the identical risk at lower costs. The reinsurance business model is based on the fact of higher diversification.

The total risk transfer from an insurer to a reinsurer is the net of two components that work in different directions. The transferred insurance risk has to be netted with the credit risk of the reinsurer to the insurer. In reality reinsurance companies are not free from default (insolvency) risk. By default we mean a state where the company is unable or unwilling to fulfil its financial obligations when they are due. In corporate finance these obligations are usually debt, such as bonds, while in the context of reinsurance we would mainly consider claims payments on ceded treaties as the relevant quantity. Default risk can be inferred from agency ratings or the credit risk market (credit default swap (CDS) spreads). We will propose a framework to infer default risk from the solvency position of the reinsurer later in this chapter.

Minimising the probability of default p_D can and should be part of the reinsurer's business strategy. This target can only be reached to a finite extent. The p_D will always be a positive number, albeit often a very small figure, for example, only a few basis points.[3] The p_D of the reinsurer is related directly to credit worthiness and is thus an important input to quantity credit risk.

So even if the insurer cedes parts of its business to a reinsurer, the risk is not completely mitigated as there it is offset by the credit risk of the reinsurer. In the pricing decision for the risk transfer the respective risk capital charges for both parties, which are determined by their portfolio and its diversification level, have to be taken into account as well as the capital charges for credit risk.

A CLOSER LOOK AT CREDIT RISK

Exposure

The starting point of a quantitative assessment of credit risk costs is the determination of the possible exposure, ie, maximum loss to the insurer, if the reinsurer defaults. It turns out that the exposure potentially depends on a second event: whether or not there is an insurance event and the insurer wants to claim its cover from the reinsurer.

In general this is called "wrong-way risk," which means the unfavourable dependency of exposure and default events (eg, Redon 2006). In the case presented here it is strictly speaking not the direct influence of the default event, but the insurance event driving the exposure. However, the insurance event may have some influence on the reinsurer's default risk as well, just imagine the effect of a large natural disaster on a monoline NatCat reinsurer. A large insurance event will be a capital drain and have deleterious effects on the reinsurer's capital position. This leads to an increase of credit risk.

It is beyond the scope of this chapter to accurately model wrong-way risk features in reinsurance credit risk. Instead we will look at two distinct cases. First, there is no insurance event and the reinsurer defaults (no wrong-way risk). The insurer would simply need to repurchase coverage, possibly at less favourable rates. In this case the exposure equals the cost of the reinsurance contract, ie, the commission. Second, there is an insurance event for the insurer and the reinsurer defaults, when, and possibly because, the insurer claims its losses from the reinsurer (full wrong-way risk). The exposure would then correspond to the amount of technical provisions (TP) for the ceded business, which includes outstanding claims provisions, unearned premium provisions and (possibly) other reinsurance related receivables.

The latter seems to be a reasonably conservative measure for exposure and is also a more realistic representation of an ongoing relationship between insurer and reinsurer[4]

$$\text{Exposure} = \text{Volume}_{\text{TP}} - \text{Collateral} \qquad (10.2)$$

Default probability: empirical versus economic

In this section we explain an approach to determine the default probability based on the company's capital position. Such an approach is well grounded in economic principles, the market consistent valuation of assets and liabilities and on the use of internal risk capital models to describe the dynamics of assets and liabilities.

The default probability of the reinsurer is a major input for the calculation. We would like to introduce an alternative approach to calculate the p_D, to complement the use of agency ratings and CDS market information.

We begin with a stochastic one-factor model for the market value of the assets of the company

$$X_i = \sqrt{\rho}\, Y + \sqrt{1-\rho}\, \epsilon_i \qquad (10.3)$$

The factor Y, which is common to all companies, is the systematic part and could be, say, the state of the economy. Asset values of two different companies i, j are then correlated with coefficient ρ. The factor ϵ_i is the company-specific, idiosyncratic part and describes changes to the company's asset value, which are uncorrelated to the overall economy. Naturally, there are multifactor extensions.

For the development of the argument the simple, one-factor model is sufficient.

As X is a random quantity, there is a finite probability that the asset value falls below a given threshold. There is a critical threshold, called the default point, where the company is assumed to be economically in default. It is important to realise that this economic default definition is not identical to the legal default. Industry studies, however, show high correlation of both approaches (Crosbie and Bohn 2002).

In this case the surplus, the difference between the assets and the liabilities in a market-consistent calculation, assumes a value of zero. The default point is assumed to be determined by the market-consistent value of the liabilities. In a simple setup we can assume that the market-consistent value of the liabilities is constant, hence the stochastic process for the surplus equals the stochastic process for the assets, offset by the default point. Figure 10.1 illustrates the setup and relation of assets and liabilities.

This means that from a known default probability and probability distribution for the asset value process, the distance between asset value and default point can be calculated. And vice versa: given a certain capital structure, ie, the market value of assets and liabilities, and a model for the calculation of the probability distribution for the stochastic process of Equation 10.3 a true economic probability of default can be determined. It obviously follows that a better capitalisation of the reinsurer, ie, large surplus, leads to a smaller probability of default.

The size of the surplus determines the solvency capital position of the company. Hence as surplus and default probabilities are related, default probabilities can also be related to the solvency position, for instance the solvency ratio, quantified by the excess solvency margin ASM/SCR.[5] Table 10.1 contains a numerical illustration for the relation of default probabilities to solvency ratios. Using an example for a skewed distribution similar to Figure 10.1 we first calculate the required solvency capital (SCR) to be the difference between the expected value and the 99.5% quantile. We then calibrate the ASM/SCR ratio value of 100% to an economic default probability of 50bp (between rating class "Adequate" and "Speculative") as the default probability equals one quantile. For smaller default probabilities reinsurers need to hold more capital,

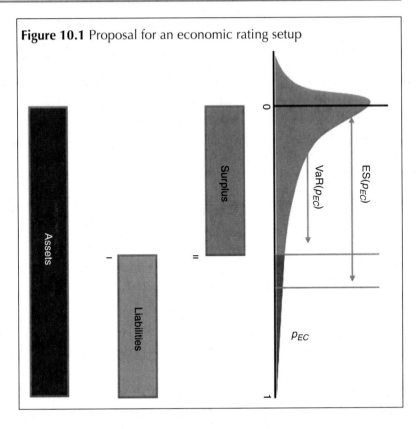

Figure 10.1 Proposal for an economic rating setup

their ASM/SCR ratio increases, for example to 165% for rating class "Very Strong".

As such a calculation would be based on the insurer's internal capital model the correct diversification in the company's portfolio would be appropriately accounted for. This would naturally lead to different results for monoline and multiline reinsurers. This is because a well-diversified reinsurance portfolio would yield lower required capital under an appropriately calibrated capital model. Better diversification leads to lower weights in the tails of the distribution and, hence, provided the surplus remains the same, to smaller default probabilities.

Next to the probability of default is the "loss given default" (LGD) another important quantity for credit risk assessment. It is the fraction of exposure that is actually lost in the event of default.[6] It can be a lot less than 100% due to third-party guarantees, cash accounts, etc. What is important in this case is the seniority of

Table 10.1 Illustration of rating categories and their corresponding default probabilities (in bp)

| Rating bucket | S&P rating | Default probability | | ASM/SCR ratio (%) |
		Empirical	Fit	
Extremely strong	AAA	0	0.4	178
Very strong	AA	0	1	165
Strong	A	4	5	142
Adequate	BBB	28	24	114
Speculative	BB	87	114	83
Very speculative	B	778	549	48
Extremely speculative	C	2,702	2,639	9

policyholders, ie, the insurer, to shareholders and holders of senior debt. In case of a default the policyholder is clearly affected the least.

The LGD depends on the capital structure of the reinsurer. Based upon the shape of the probability distribution and the value of the economic default probability p_{EC} the LGD can be calculated from two different risk measures: VaR and ES.

Obviously the following relation holds (see Figure 10.1)

$$LGD = \frac{ES(p_{EC}) - VaR(p_{EC})}{1 - VaR(p_{EC})} \qquad (10.4)$$

See the next section for definitions of these risk measures.

Providing that the internal model is built on sound economic and risk management principles and the parameters are adequately calibrated, the model could be approved by the regulator for solvency purposes. Such an approval would create sufficient trust in the various stakeholders that the proposed framework could be used to determine economic default probabilities from the solvency position of the insurer.

As such a framework is not (yet) in place, we will base the determination of default probabilities and LGD in the current proposal on empirical default and recovery rates from Standard and Poor's (2006). For ease of interpretation we will also use rating categories and label these according to the CEIOPS proposal (CEIOPS 2006). Table 10.1 contains rating categories and default rates. We have interpolated the observed default rates by an exponential function in order to generate reasonable values for p_D for all rating categories.

Guidance on the choice of LGD can be obtained from empirical bond default studies. In Standard and Poor's (2006) LGD depends on the seniority of the bond, where 40% is appropriate for senior secured bonds. Bank debt shows loss ratios of less than 25%. Policyholders are seen as even more secure than debt, so a reasonably conservative choice would be

$$LGD = 50\%$$

In Ratings (2006) Fitch comes to similar results.

Loss: expected and unexpected

The risk is the difference between the expected and unexpected events. Basically, a provision should be built in for the expected event and capitalise for the risk. Both components are relevant for regulatory purposes as well as for pricing. This distinction is important and enhances the views taken by the Gesamtverband der Deutschen Versicherungswirtschaft (2005), where the risk charge reflects only the expectation value, in particular the expected loss over a five-year horizon.

It is straightforward to quantify the loss from the expected event. This is simply the product

$$p_D \times LGD \times Exposure$$

The challenging and more interesting part is the calculation of the potential loss from the unexpected event. There are standard approaches available in the market, eg, the RiskMetrics CreditManager, the KMV PortfolioManager. These models use stochastic simulations that yield reasonably accurate results for large, diversified portfolios. In addition analytical approximations are available in these circumstances.

But the calculation is particularly tricky in a situation where the insurer cedes only to a handful of reinsurers, in some cases even to a single reinsurer only. In these situations the usual assumption of a well-diversified portfolio does not hold any more by construction. It is the main purpose of this chapter to develop a framework that can be applied to these situations. This framework is also based on standard approaches to credit risk modelling, which are well tested and understood by market practitioners. In addition parameters can be interpreted in a sensible way and calibrated to available data.

We start the development of the framework by going back to the definition of economic capital (Equation 10.1)

$$EC = r(X) - E(X)$$

A range of measures $r(X)$ can be considered to quantify the unexpected loss. Intense debates have been, and still are, going on about the appropriate choice for the "correct" risk measure. We do not want to enter this discussion, but simply give examples for different risk measures and see whether they are potentially useful for the practical problem.

The simplest approaches are typically based on standard deviation. For a single reinsurer we only have two states for the portfolio (default and non-default). The standard deviation is thus the one of the Bernoulli distribution

$$\sigma = \sqrt{p_D \times (1 - p_D)} \tag{10.5}$$

In the case of several reinsurers, this approach can be amended quite easily by using the covariance principle, where the defaults of n identical reinsurers are correlated by the default correlation coefficient ρ_D

$$\sigma = \sqrt{p_D \times (1 - p_D)(\rho_D + \frac{1}{n}(1 - \rho_D))} \tag{10.6}$$

In the standard framework, default correlation ρ_D is related to the correlation of the market consistent value of assets by

$$\rho_D = \frac{N_2(N^{-1}(p_1), N^{-1}(p_2), \rho) - p_1 p_2}{\sqrt{p_1(1 - p_1)}\sqrt{p_2(1 - p_2)}} \tag{10.7}$$

where N is the normal distribution function, N_2 is the two-dimensional distribution function. p_1 and p_2 are individual default probabilities, and ρ the correlation in the one-factor model setup (see Equation 10.3).

These approaches do not take into account the asymmetrical nature of probability distributions, in particular heavy tails in concentrated portfolios. They are hence an inappropriate measure for this purpose.

Value-at-risk is another risk measure that is commonly in use. The VaR for quantile α is defined as

$$\text{VaR}(\alpha) = \inf\{x \in \mathbf{R} \mid P(X \leq x) \geq \alpha\} \tag{10.8}$$

While VaR is widely used by practitioners, it has some conceptual disadvantages from an academic point of view (eg, Filipovic and Kupper 2006). In this case of only a few reinsurers, the VaR has a practical problem as well, as we will see in the next section. However, as VaR is the measure of choice in the Solvency II framework, we may eventually accept these shortcomings and develop pragmatic solutions.

Expected shortfall is an improvement of the VaR concept, both from a theoretical perspective, as well as for this practical application. The ES is also called tail VaR or conditional VaR in the relevant literature. It is defined as

$$\mathrm{ES}(\alpha) = \frac{1}{1 - \alpha} \int_{\alpha}^{1} \mathrm{VaR}(x) \, \underset{\sim}{x} \qquad (10.9)$$

Both VaR and ES are by construction related to specific confidence levels and capture the shape of the probability distribution, especially any asymmetries or heavy tails.

PROPOSAL

Portfolio model

For the determination of the unexpected loss we start with the portfolio approach of credit risk modelling. Despite what we have said earlier about the typical reinsurer's portfolio of an insurance company, we will assume a large and well-diversified portfolio at the beginning. We will relax this assumption in the sequel and provide an enhancement to the standard approach. The enhanced approach is capable of dealing with the "lumpiness" of portfolios. That is, the model can be used to quantify unexpected losses from a portfolio of only a few reinsurers. In the limited case of a large number of reinsurers, the enhanced model converges with the standard approach.

Standard portfolio theory assumes that risk can be separated into two components: idiosyncratic risk can be diversified, while systematic risk cannot. The latter critically depends on the correlation between the portfolio elements.

In typical credit portfolios in corporate lending businesses, the loss distributions from stochastic simulations can be approximated quite accurately by analytical solutions. For a portfolio of an infinite number of loans the loss distribution function is analytically known and it is called the Vasicek distribution function (Vasicek 1991). This approach is also used in the Basel II accord for the banking industry (Basel Committee on Banking Supervision 2006). The cumulative probability that the percentage of loss in a given portfolio does not exceed a certain maximum loss amount L is

$$\text{CDF}(L) = N\left(\frac{1}{\sqrt{\rho}} (\sqrt{1 - \rho}\, N^{-1}(L) - N^{-1}(p_D)) \right) \qquad (10.10)$$

where N is again the normal distribution function. A risk measure $r(X)$ can easily be calculated from this equation. It depends on only two parameters: the default probability p_D and the correlation coefficient ρ.

The analytical approximation is sufficiently accurate if the number of different loans in the portfolio range is in the hundreds. But several hundred reinsurers do not exist, nor is it feasible to enter into reinsurance contracts with too many different companies, if only for purely administrative reasons. We need a description for a portfolio of possibly only a small number of reinsurers. We will try to achieve this by using the correlation coefficient ρ as a measure of concentration, ie, the number of reinsurers in the portfolio.

Why do we think this is appropriate? In the case $\rho \to 1$ the analytical distribution of the homogeneous portfolio collapses to the Bernoulli distribution. This is the loss distribution for a single reinsurer: the portfolio is perfectly correlated and all (infinitely) reinsurers go into default together.

On the other hand, think of the theoretical case where an arbitrary number of reinsurance companies would be available. The model setup and the result in Equation 10.10 would be a perfect description of reality. What would be the appropriate level of correlation in this case? Let us consider this question first, before we discuss the realistic case of a limited number of reinsurers.

For well diversified loan portfolios, the Basel II accord (Basel Committee on Banking Supervision 2006) sets correlation depending on the size of the company. The maximum correlation in the portfolio is 0.24. Industry models like RiskMetrics' CreditManager (Xiao 2002) and the KMV Global Correlation Model (Crosbie and Bohn 2002) also contain a size dependency and allow for much higher correlations. However, in the KMV database only 5% of the companies exceed a correlation coefficient of 0.45. Moreover KMV also uses an upper limit of 0.65.

Given the fact that reinsurance companies tend to be quite large and also quite correlated (mostly identical, global business), we propose to use

$$\rho_\infty = 0.5$$

as the conservative lower limit in a (theoretical) portfolio of infinitely many reinsurers.

We now come to the realistic situation of a small number of reinsurers. The proposal is based on the idea that the number of reinsurers determines the level of correlation in the portfolio. The correlation should on one side approach ρ_∞ for a large number and on the other side ρ should equal 1 for the limiting case of only a single reinsurer. For the remaining realistic cases, $\mathcal{O}(100) > n > 1$, the correlation coefficient should be monotonically increasing in between.

Hence we start with

$$\rho(n) = \rho_\infty + \frac{1}{n}(1 - \rho_\infty) \tag{10.11}$$

where $\rho_\infty = 0.5$. For a single reinsurer, ρ equals 1, for two reinsurers we have $\rho(2) = 0.75$ and for $\rho(\infty) = \rho_\infty = 0.5$. This relation is an approximation, as we have assumed that all reinsurers in the portfolio take the same share of risk. These shares may well be different. It is easy to enhance Equation 10.11 by replacing the term $1/n$ with the Herfindahl index (Jaschke 2006)

$$H(n) = \frac{\sum_{i=1}^{n} w_i^2}{\left(\sum_{i=1}^{n} w_i\right)^2} \tag{10.12}$$

where w_i is the share of the reinsurer i. The Herfindahl index reflects unequal shares and for equal shares we have $H(n) = 1/n$ as before.

Thus we get

$$\rho(n) = \rho_\infty + H(n)(1 - \rho_\infty) \tag{10.13}$$

A large number of reinsurers yields lower values for ρ. As we know, ρ describes the level of systematic risk in the portfolio and therefore drives the unexpected loss and the risk in the portfolio. The lower ρ is, the lower the risk is. In other words, more reinsurers means lower risk. This means that the model allows for diversification benefits. Is it now preferable to cede business to more than a single reinsurer? The answer is yes, but, as usual, it depends.

In the following we will use the simple form (Equation 10.11) ie, all $w_i = 1/n$ and bear in mind that we will overestimate the diversification benefit, as we implicitly assume equal distribution among the different reinsurers.

Risk measure: expected shortfall

Having fixed the model and the parameters, what is the appropriate choice for $r(X)$? From the previous discussion we still have VaR and ES as potential candidates.

The homogeneous portfolio model as described with the Vasicek distribution (Equation 10.10) allows us to take a decision. In the limiting case of only a single reinsurer the correlation parameter ρ approaches 1 and the loss distribution will become similar to a Bernoulli distribution. In such a situation the quantile-based VaR leads to implausible results

$$\lim_{\rho \to 1} \text{VaR}(\alpha, p_D) = \begin{cases} 0 & \text{if } p_D < 1 - \alpha \\ 1 & \text{if } p_D > 1 - \alpha \end{cases}$$

This means that if a certain confidence level α is chosen, in the limited case of a single reinsurer, economic capital only depends on the value of the default probability relative to the level of confidence. If the p_D is larger than $1 - \alpha$ we have to keep the entire exposure as economic capital. This makes perfect sense as the probability that a loss from the relationship with the single reinsurer will be experienced is larger than the target default probability. Recall that the target default probability is given by $1 - \alpha$. The other case does not make sense at all: if the p_D is smaller than $1 - \alpha$ the required risk capital would be zero, clearly an implausible outcome.

Expected shortfall on the contrary shows much more reasonable behaviour

$$\lim_{\rho \to 1} \text{ES}(\alpha, p_D) = \begin{cases} p_D/(1 - \alpha) & \text{if } p_D < 1 - \alpha \\ 1 & \text{if } p_D > 1 - \alpha \end{cases}$$

Economic capital based on ES does increase with increasing p_D as well as the level of confidence: the better the rating, the less capital is necessary. And the higher the level of confidence, the more capital the insurer needs to hold. Both make sense.

In Figure 10.2 we illustrate the behaviour of the risk measures σ, VaR and ES as a function of p_D for a well-diversified portfolio with 10 reinsurers (top) and an extremely concentrated portfolio with only a single reinsurer (bottom). The number of reinsurers has been transformed into the correlation coefficient using Equation 10.11. The difference between VaR and ES is obvious and quite striking in the limited case $n = 1$.

Following the findings, we propose to use ES as the appropriate risk measure. The results are reasonable even in the case of very concentrated portfolios, ie, only a small number of reinsurers. We can write ES when we combine Equations 10.9 and 10.10 as

$$\text{ES}(\alpha, p_D, \rho) = \frac{1}{1 - \alpha} \int_\alpha^1 N \left(\frac{\sqrt{\rho} N^{-1}(x) + N^{-1}(p_D)}{\sqrt{1 - \rho}} \right) \text{x} \quad (10.14)$$

This integral can be evaluated numerically, using for example Mathematica.

Given that in the Solvency II framework VaR at the 99.5% quantile is proposed as the risk measure we would need to find a pragmatic solution for the case $n = 1$, for example, based on a simple interpolation.

RESULTS

The costs for taking credit risk for the insurer are in our current framework calculated as the sum of expected loss and unexpected loss. Note that this is actually a simplification, as other costs, eg, for administration, would need to be considered here as well. For the current purpose the following relation is sufficient

$$\text{costs} = p_D + \text{RoEC} \times EC(p_D, \rho, \alpha) \quad (10.15)$$

We have introduced a factor for the return on economic capital (RoEC) that may be demanded by the insurer for holding capital for credit risk. Thus the equation is the general case and can be used for pricing as well. For regulatory purposes we are interested in the total amount of capital, ie, the sum of expected and unexpected events, and hence RoEC is set to 1.

Table 10.2 contains numeric values for credit risk costs. We have evaluated the general solution in Equation 10.14 for specific rating categories, quantified by their default probability, using two

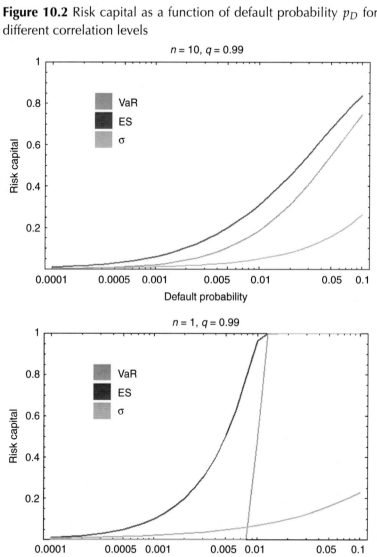

Figure 10.2 Risk capital as a function of default probability p_D for different correlation levels

Notes: This figure shows a well-diversified portfolio with $n = 10$ reinsurers (top) and a very concentrated with $n = 1$ reinsurer (bottom). The confidence level is $q = 99\%$ for all calculations in this figure.

Table 10.2 Risk costs and their components for different rating categories and number of reinsurers

q = 99%	Default probability	Number of reinsurers			
		1	2	5	10
Extremely strong	0.4	18	18	17	16
Very strong	1	51	50	45	42
Strong	5	247	227	183	166
Adequate	24	1,187	889	653	582
Speculative	114	5,000	2,562	1,863	1,666
Very speculative	549	5,000	4,492	3,766	3,505
Extremely speculative	2,639	5,000	4,995	4,922	4,862

q = 99.5%	Default probability	Number of reinsurers			
		1	2	5	10
Extremely strong	0.4	36	35	31	28
Very strong	1	103	97	79	71
Strong	5	494	407	299	264
Adequate	24	2,374	1,385	955	835
Speculative	114	5,000	3,264	2,373	2,115
Very speculative	549	5,000	4,756	4,152	3,901
Extremely speculative	2,639	5,000	4,999	4,963	4,925

Notes: The risk measure is ES at 99% (top) and 99.5% (bottom), LGD = 50%. All figures are given in basis points (1 bp = 0.01% = 0.0001).

confidence levels: 99% and 99.5%. The correlation coefficient is calculated using Equation 10.11 for the dependency on the number of reinsurers.

As expected, costs vary depending on the rating quality, as well as the number of different reinsurers in the portfolio. All figures are given in basis points. They are to be multiplied with the relevant exposure (Equation 10.2) to yield absolute amounts. For more than one reinsurer the weighted sum of respective risk cost and exposure has to be calculated

$$\text{total costs} = \sum_{i=1}^{n} w_i \, \text{costs}(p_{Di}, \rho(n))$$

The interesting and rather surprising result of this calculation is the following. The variation of costs within a particular row describes the diversification benefit to an insurer if he increases the number of reinsurers. Note that the variation in a particular

Figure 10.3 The difference in risk costs for one and five reinsurers is important only for lower quality reinsurers

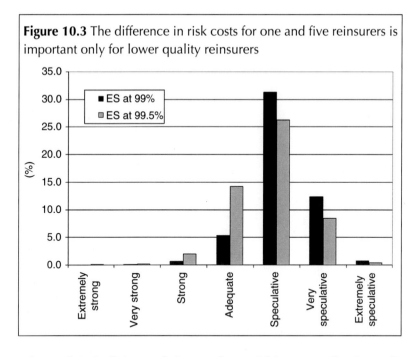

column (vertical) is much larger than within a row (horizontal). What is the interpretation of this result? See Figure 10.3 for an illustration. Apparently there is not much diversification benefit if the insurer goes from one to, say, five reinsurers, especially for very highly rated reinsurance companies. There is clearly a benefit of diversification, while it is much more important to choose a high-quality reinsurer. Rather than ceding business to a number of reinsurers, the superior strategy from a risk capital perspective is to look for the single best reinsurer around.

Also note that if the probability of default is larger than the confidence level, the entire portfolio is "at risk". In this mapping from p_D to rating categories, this is the case for the "speculative" classes and below. In Table 10.2 5,000bp correspond to the entire portfolio instead of the 10,000bp that is usually expected, because the figures have been multiplied by LGD = 50%.

This result makes sense and can be understood as follows: diversification benefit is material for the speculative class, and becomes less and less important for lower classes (see Figure 10.3). This is because risk costs are driven both by expected and unexpected loss, though only the unexpected loss component is sensitive to diversification. In very low rating classes the expected loss component dominates and unexpected loss becomes negligible.

CONCLUSION

We have analysed the credit risk relation between primary insurer and reinsurer. For quantitative treatment, as required in the Solvency II framework, we introduced and defined the relevant quantities. We proposed a framework for the calculation of probability of default and LGD in an economic setup. The probability of default and, hence, the credit risk can easily be related to the solvency capital position of the reinsurer. A strong capital position logically corresponds to a low credit risk.

We then developed a model for the calculation of risk costs that arise from expected and unexpected events in the reinsurance relation. The model is based on sound principles of credit risk modelling that are widely used by market practitioners. It captures the relevant effects of credit quality and concentration and contains the standard credit risk portfolio model in the limited case. The motivation of choice of all the model parameters has been explored. We arrived at a calibration of parameters, in particular the level of correlation in the portfolio as a function of numbers of reinsurers.

We were thus able to determine risk costs for the credit risk between primary insurer and reinsurer. The costs depend on the credit quality of the reinsurer as measured by its (economic) rating and the number of different reinsurers in the portfolio. The interesting result of the calculation was that while it is indeed better to use as many reinsurers as possible, it turned out that the effect of diversification is only for the second order of high-quality reinsurers. The number of reinsurers is not a critical parameter in the reinsurance strategy of an insurance company. Undoubtedly there exists some benefit in diversification, so distributing the portfolio to several reinsurers may make sense from a capital perspective. However, the better strategy is to look for the best reinsurer available and cede the entire portfolio to it, as the benefit of diversification is far outweighed by the impact of the credit quality of the reinsurer of choice. In this chapter we have given a comprehensive treatment of counterparty default risk. The model and its parameters are ready to be used in the counterparty default risk module of the Solvency II framework.

1   The views expressed in this paper are those of the author alone and do not necessarily reflect the position of Munich Re Group. The author would like to thank Matthias Almus and Stefan Jaschke from MunichRe and Charlie Shamieh from AIG for their valuable input and constructive discussions.

2   We use the term insurer to refer to companies who are involved in primary or direct insurance business as opposed to reinsurance business. Reinsurers obviously do the latter.

3   $1 \text{ bp} = 0.0001 = 0.01\%$.

4   We have seen this measure is used as well by other regulators, for example, Australian Prudential Regulation Authority (2006); Financial Services Authority (2005).

5   ASM is the available solvency margin, SCR denotes the required solvency capital.

6   The recovery rate is simply $1 - \text{LGD}$.

REFERENCES

Australian Prudential Regulation Authority, 2006, "GPS 110: Capital Adequacy", September, URL: http://www.apra.gov.au/General/upload/GPS-110-Capital-Adequacy-Sept-2006-2.pdf.

Basel Committee on Banking Supervision, 2006, "Basel II: International Convergence of Capital Measurement and Capital Standards: A Revised Framework – Comprehensive Version", Bank for International Settlements, June, URL: http://www.bis.org/publ/bcbs128.htm.

Bongers, O. and G. Stahl, 2006, "Economic Capital Use Test", Technical Report, BaFin.

CEIOPS, 2006, "Quantitative Impact Study II", URL: http://www.ceiops.eu//media/files/consultations/QIS/QIS2-SummaryReport.pdf.

Christian Redon, 2006, "Wrong Way risk modelling", *Risk*, 4, April, pp. 90–95.

Crosbie, P. and J. Bohn, 2003, "Modelling Default Risk", Research Paper, Moody's KMV.

Filipović, D. and M. Kupper, 2006, "Optimal capital and risk transfers for group diversification", CRO Forum Submission, January.

Financial Services Authority, 2005, "Insurance Sector Briefing: ICAS – one year on", November, URL: http://www.fsa.gov.uk/pubs/other/isb_icas.pdf.

Fitch Ratings, 2006, "Prism: Favorable Market Feedback and Clarifying Responses – Part 1", September.

Gesamtverband der Deutschen Versicherungswirtschaft, 2005, "Diskussionsbeitrag für einen Solvency II kompatiblen Standardansatz", December, URL: http://www.gdv.de/Themen/Querschnittsthemen/AufsichtBilanzierung/inhaltsseite15916.html.

Jaschke, S., 2006, Private Communication.

Xiao, J. Y., 2002, "Obligor R^2 in CreditMetrics", Technical Report, RiskMetrics Group, November.

Standard and Poor's, 2006, "Annual 2005 Global Corporate Default Study And Rating Transitions", January.

Vasicek, O., 1991, "Limiting Loan Loss Probability Distribution", Technical Report, KMV.

Zeng, B. and J. Zhang, 2001, "An Empirical Assessment of Asset Correlation Models", KMV, URL: http://www.moodyskmv.com/research/files/wp/emp_assesment.pdf.

Section III

Measuring and Managing Insurance Risk

Introduction

Marcelo Cruz

New York University

Solvency II changes completely the landscape for underwriting risks. Until now these risks were assessed and dealt with only by actuaries. The new framework brought in by Solvency II will require the separation of activities of the actuaries and risk managers following the principle of checks and balances. Actuaries are responsible for the business side – pricing risks correctly – and risk managers will have to make sure that this is the case. We can compare this relationship to what happens in an investment bank, where quant traders structure the deals (hopefully considering all the risks) and risk managers have to check these structured deals for risk purposes and for how they fit in the overall portfolio of risks for the firm. The impact of these proposed changes under Solvency II is tremendous. Risk departments in insurance companies, usually more qualitatively focussed, will have to start recruiting risk officers with a better understanding of underwriting risks to be able to discuss this at the same level as actuaries. This is a welcome outcome that will most certainly make insurance companies financially safer.

To organise this section, we informally separated it into two parts: the first few chapters cover non-life risks and the other part covers life risks. The section is opened with a chapter from Kathleen Ehrlich and Heinrich R. Schradin, providing an excellent overview of the impact of Solvency II on property-casualty insurers. They claim that the current solvency framework protects insurance companies only to a certain extent; by keeping an eye not just on financial market fluctuations but also on insurance-related risks, Solvency II brings welcome changes, according to the authors.

We have found a great contributor in Werner Hürlimann; he wrote the next couple of chapters on non-life risks. In his first chapter, "On the Non-Life Solvency II Model", he brings the value-at-risk (VaR) framework to calculate economic capital for a non-life insurer; he has been kind enough to provide an application of his models, so that users can verify how they are used. In his second chapter, Hürlimann deals with the issue of the optimisation of non-life risk diversification under Solvency II; again, this is a very technical subject, but the author has helped by including numerical examples.

We start the life risk sub-section with a chapter from two Italian academics: Annamaria Olivieri and Ermanno Pitacco. They assess the benefit of developing and using internal models versus standard formulas in solvency requirements for life annuities risks. They show that internally developed models are much more risk sensitive, and this is a great benefit from Solvency II. In the following chapter another two academics, Nadine Gatzert and Stefan Kassberger, tackle the subject "Risk Assessment of Life Contracts: A comparative Levy framework". The authors use an option-based framework to provide an innovative way to assess life policies risks. Another Italian academic, Francesco Menoncin covers the problem of asset allocation for pension funds considering "demographic assets". In the last chapter of this section, our friend Werner Hürlimann considers the optimal level of capital for a life contract based on the Swiss Solvency Test.

This is a rather technical section; I hope that readers appreciate that risk managers under Solvency II will have to be fluent in these subjects. We truly believe that this section provides enough coverage for a good start.

11

QIS4 for Property-Casualty Insurers' Total Balance Sheet Approach and its Impact on the Insurance Industry

Kathleen Ehrlich, Heinrich R. Schradin[1]

University of Cologne

Insurance companies are not only exposed to insurance-related fluctuations, but also to fluctuations in the capital markets. Both can be considered as triggers for solvency problems. By using regulatory instruments, policyholders should be sufficiently protected and insolvencies prevented (CEIOPS 2005, p. 85). The current solvency system only covers the financial situation of an insurance company to a limited extent. As early as the end of the 1990s, the system was increasingly criticised. The discussions over future solvency rules for insurance companies as part of the Solvency II project have not yet concluded. The project means a radical refocusing of the supervisory infrastructure with quantitative and qualitative elements. The principles involve setting risk-based capital requirements, which demonstrate the economic reality of the insurance business, and guaranteeing preservation of the company. Setting an adequate amount of risk capital as the basis and requirement for strengthening the policyholder's protection and improving competitiveness sees the insurance industry faced with enormous challenges, and this is discussed intensively in academic literature (eg, Nguyen 2008; Mummenhoff 2007; Hartung 2007; Ott 2005).

In April 2009, the European Parliament and the European Council agreed on the Framework Directive for supervising insurance companies and stipulated six sections for the quantitative requirements (see European Commission 2009). These are: evaluating the assets and liabilities, determining the technical provisions, calculating own funds, determining the solvency and minimum capital requirements and the capital investment requirements. The evaluation of assets and liabilities covers a series of individual issues, which includes the impact on capital requirements and own funds.

In light of this, the aim of this chapter is to analyse and evaluate the future requirements for evaluating an insurer's risk situation. The next section discusses the current status of the developments of the European standard approach, which has been tested as part of a fourth quantitative impact study (QIS4). The following section examines the own funds necessary for capital securisation. This is followed by an evaluation. The final section shows initial results from the impact study and finally deduces possible effects on the insurance industry.

THE EUROPEAN STANDARD APPROACH IN QIS4
Basic concept
The future quantitative regulations are based on a total balance sheet approach. Assets and liabilities must be consistently evaluated at market values. In doing so, the valuation standards for supervisory purposes should be in harmony with international accounting developments.[2] The use of local accounting regulations are in many cases not compatible with the aim of the Solvency II project, as they display a series of weaknesses (see Oletzky 1998, p. 36 and the references stated there).

Evaluating close to the market applies to a fair value inspection. If no market values are available, the balance sheet entries must be re-evaluated. The evaluation of the assets can be fundamentally based on the IFRS provisions. A best estimate plus a risk margin must be determined to assess the liabilities. The own funds are generated from the difference between assets and liabilities. Figure 11.1 shows the components of an economic balance sheet. If the own funds fall short of the required solvency capital, the supervisory

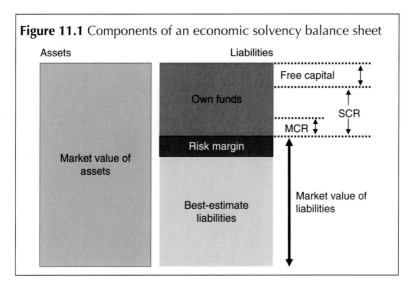

Figure 11.1 Components of an economic solvency balance sheet

authority will take measures to guarantee the insurer's solvency. The measures become stricter as the shortfall increases.

The coverage ratio produced from the ratio of eligible own funds and the solvency capital requirement (SCR), deemed to be necessary due to the insurance company's risk situation, acts as an indicator for evaluating the solvency capital resources. The SCR will be determined using either a given standard formula or a company-specific internal model, which is not, however, the object of this chapter. To ensure sufficient capitalisation from a solvency perspective, an insurance company must have eligible own funds totalling at least the same as the SCR.

Solvency capital requirement
The basis for the following plan for evaluating the SCR is the temporary standard formula that was tested as part of QIS4 (European Commission 2008). For the sake of simplicity, notation used in the original version of the QIS4 "technical specifications" is used here.

The underlying system for evaluating the SCR with the European standard formula has its origin in the modular approach of the US risk-based capital calculation for a property-casualty insurance company (Schradin and Telschow 1995, p. 363 ff):

1. definition of relevant risk categories;
2. establishment of a risk measure and confidence level;

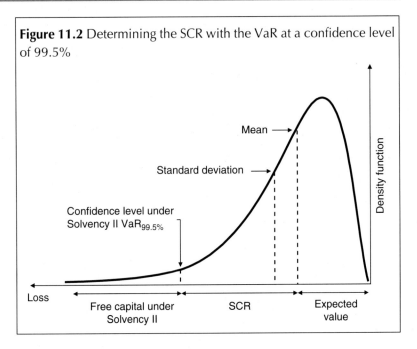

Figure 11.2 Determining the SCR with the VaR at a confidence level of 99.5%

3. identification of the capital requirements per risk category; and
4. aggregation of the individual capital requirements for a total capital requirement taking into account dependencies.

However, the currently discussed status for the standard formula to determine the SCR for European insurance companies, according to QIS4, is much more complex.[3] The approach will follow a principle-based policy and therefore grant companies room to move when selecting their evaluation methods.

The European standard approach aims to illustrate the entire risk spectrum of an insurance company.[4] The European Commission states in the Framework Directive (European Commission 2009, Article 101, Paragraphs 3 Clause 4) that, to cover the SCR, an insurance company must have eligible own funds of at least the same amount. The definitive risk measurement for this is value-at-risk (VaR) for one year with a confidence level of 99.5%.[5] Based on the aforementioned confidence level, the quantile/supervisory SCR can be determined as shown in Figure 11.2.

The European standard approach is bottom-up. The risk situation is initially evaluated for individual risks. According to the proposed design, a property-casualty insurer must quantify capital requirements for the three basic risk capital modules: underwriting risk, market and default risk, and also for operational risk. The approaches for determining the underwriting risk and default risk are predominantly factor-based;[6] and largely scenario-based for determining the market risk. For further specification, these risk modules are broken down into several sub-risk modules. For every sub-risk module, only the capital requirement is calculated. The capital requirements for the sub-modules of the three basic risks are aggregated into a capital requirement of the respective risk module, taking into account dependency structures.[7] Specific knowledge of existing dependencies between the individual risks is necessary for this. These must then be transferred to a total capital requirement for the basic SCR, taking into account dependency structures. Simply adding the sub-modules' capital requirements would mean that possible diversification effects from a balance within the portfolio would not be taken into account, and that the company's risk situation would, thus, not be illustrated properly in terms of risk. In this context, the total risk can be displayed in a modular way as shown in Figure 11.3.

The full quantification of all risks and aggregation for a total capital requirement, taking into account the interdependencies is, however, no mean feat. In doing so, the technical difficulties when forming the model are less of a focus than the problems of empirical validation and suitable parameter estimation.[8]

Dependencies identified between the individual sub-risk modules must initially be quantified. Thereafter, the dependencies between the three individual risk modules must be quantified. In general, various theoretical concepts exist to illustrate dependency structures. The most common, and so far most frequently used, concepts rely on linear dependency (for example Koryciorz 2004, p. 112 ff). The formula for determining the capital requirement is

$$\sqrt{\sum_j \sigma_j^2 + \sum_{i \neq j} \rho_{ij} \sigma_i \sigma_j} \tag{11.1}$$

with the correlation factor $\rho_{i;j} \in (-1; 1)$ between risks i and j allows dependency structures to be taken into account. If, for example, there is a strong dependency between two risks, the supervisory authority will set the correlation coefficient close to one to ensure

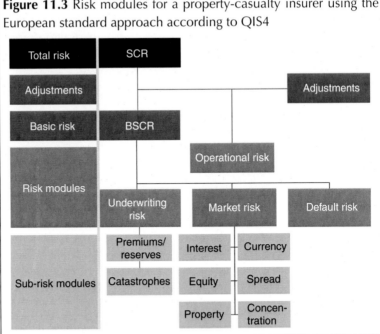

Figure 11.3 Risk modules for a property-casualty insurer using the European standard approach according to QIS4

the necessary conservativeness in the approach. If all lines of business are mutually independent from one another, the second term under the square root takes the zero value. Both cases can have a significant influence on the amount of risk capital to be set aside (IAA 2004, p. 6).

The capital requirement for the operational risk is determined separately. The total risk of a property-casualty insurer is finally generated from the sum of these two amounts. The Framework Directive stipulates adjusting the capital requirement for the loss absorbancy capacity of the technical provisions and deferred taxes.[9] Overall, the total SCR is formally generated from this as follows

$$SCR = BSCR + SCR_{op} - Adj \qquad (11.2)$$

with
SCR = total SCR
$BSCR$ = basic SCR
SCR_{op} = operational risk
Adj = adjustments

Dependencies are not taken into account in this step.

Description

Underwriting risk: the underwriting risk, as a risk unique to the insurance business, is of great significance for property-casualty insurers (QIS2 or QIS3 in CEIOPS 2006, 2007). It demonstrates the risk that an insurer's premiums and reserves will not be sufficient to cover the liabilities of a period as per the agreement. Thus it signifies the uncertainty regarding the obligations assumed along with the insurance policy, in light of their amount, their time of occurrence and their actual realisation (Schradin 1994, p. 37).

The sub-risks, premium and reserve risk, are typical of this risk module. Both modules take into account geographic diversification.[10] In addition catastrophe risk is taken into consideration. This sub-risk module shows claims expenses arising through extreme events, which are not yet shown in the premium and reserve risk. The SCR for the underwriting risk SCR_{nl} is finally calculated by aggregating the individual requirements for the premium and reserve risk NL_{pr} and the catastrophe risk NL_{CAT}. Uncorrelation between these two sub-risk modules is assumed. The capital requirement for this risk module is thus derived as follows

$$SCR_{nl} = \sqrt{NL_{pr}^2 + NL_{CAT}^2} \qquad (11.3)$$

Premium and reserve risk: premium risk describes the risk that the collected premiums are not sufficient to compensate for future losses. Reserve risk describes the risk that the absolute level of the claims provisions deviates from the estimated amount. The analysis of this risk module requires segmentation of the property-casualty insurance business into individual lines of business. The European standard approach stipulates performing the segmentation according to the division made to determine the technical provisions in homogeneous risk groups (European Commission 2008, p. 46). This segmentation by lines of business is, however, not directly compatible with the requirement for division into homogeneous risk groups. The aggregation of segments, which have been aggregated in one sector despite having varying clearing behaviour, is considered critical. Conversely, there are also lines of business with similar settlement periods that have nevertheless been allocated to different risk sectors. The aggregation of the first three sectors, which jointly take into account the two lines of business accident and health insurance, is not comprehensible.

A factor model is used as the basis for calculating the premium and reserve risk. The capital requirement is produced by multiplying a risk carrier by a risk factor.[11] The premium and reserve risks are initially calculated separately. This calculation is performed in several stages:

Step 1: For every line of business, the risk factor, the standard deviation σ of the loss ratio and the risk carrier, the volume measure of the underwriting risk must be determined separately for the premium and reserve risk.

Step 2: Analysis of the geographic diversification effect per line of business and determination of the total volume.

Step 3: An estimation of the total standard deviation for the premium and reserve risk is derived by aggregating the standard deviations and volume measures determined in step 1 per line of business, using linear correlation.

Step 4: The capital requirement for the premium and reserve risk is generated based on the total volume determined in step 2 and the total standard deviation determined in step 3.

Catastrophe risk: the standard approach stipulates that the premium and reserve risk only takes into account losses that occur at a regular frequency. Extreme events, which occur very rarely, have not been taken into account when calibrating the premium and reserve risk. Risks arising from extreme uncertainty regarding the price determination and inappropriate reserve prognoses for extreme and extraordinary events, are thus to be evaluated separately (European Commission 2009, Article 105 Para. 2a). These risks have a significant impact on the company earnings, as well as on the amount of capital required, for many lines of business.

Policies outlined for catastrophic events are often identified by national characteristics. In the test phase, even more options were observed. It was suggested by CEIOPS that the individual, national supervisory authorities should provide regional scenarios. However, companies also had the opportunity to determine the capital requirement using personalised scenarios. Furthermore,

QIS4 states that a standard approach was to be tested if the supervisory authorities did not provide regional scenarios or if companies did not have personalised scenarios.

Market risk: the insurer's market risk fundamentally consists of the risk of loss of regular capital maintenance, the failure of achieving profitability targets, as well as the risk of losing regular liquidity for asset values. The European standard approach initially covers the capital investment risk in the following sub-risk modules: interest-rate risk, equity risk, property risk, spread risk, currency risk and concentration risk.

There is no difference between directly or indirectly maintained investments. Instead, market values should be allocated to individual sub-risk modules.[12] The interest-rate, equity, property and currency risks are evaluated based on scenarios, while the evaluation of the spread and concentration risks are factor-based. Scenario-based approaches assess the risk capital required following a shock event. This loss is produced from the difference between the liabilities and assets. The approaches are principle-oriented so that companies have enough room to move when selecting their evaluation methods. These must only agree with the principles for calculating the SCR.

The capital requirements for these sub-risk modules are aggregated into the total risk capital for the capital investment module SCR_{mkt}, taking into account dependencies. Contracts in which the policyholder bears the investment risk are not taken into account in this risk module. The sub-risks in the European standard approach are specifically determined as follows.

Interest-rate risk: interest rate changes have an immediate impact on the market values of the assets and liabilities on an insurance balance sheet. Interest-rate risks usually arise when the duration for the capital investments differ from the due dates of insurance-related obligations. In the event of an interest-rate drop, a risk exists when the average duration of an investment on the assets side is shorter than on the liabilities side.[13] Capital investments that must be reinvested because the associated liability is not yet payable, can only be done so at a lower interest rate after an interest-rate decrease. The risk, thus, exists strictly when the company has not protected itself from interest-rate decreases through a hedging investment. In the event of an interest-rate increase, an interest-rate risk exists when the duration of the investment on the assets side is longer than the corresponding duration on the liabilities side. This risk frequently arises for property-casualty insurance companies.[14] The loss of market value on the assets side is usually greater than the profit on the liabilities side, which results from lower obligations.

To quantify the interest-rate risk for a property-casualty insurance company, the change in market value is observed for all assets and liabilities where the values react to changes in the interest curve or volatility in the event of an increase or decrease in interest as stated above. The structure of the interest-rate risk is demonstrated in Figure 11.4.

Interest rate changes in the net provisions on the liabilities side and for fixed-interest securities,[15] financing instruments and interest-rate derivatives on the liabilities side are important in the European standard approach. The capital requirement is produced by re-evaluating all interest-sensitive assets and liabilities from the more unfavourable interest-rate scenarios. The requirement for the interest decrease risk is generated by deducting the market value increase in the capital investments (gain) from the market value increase in the liabilities (loss). The European standard approach does not allow any risk relief through the interest decrease risk.[16] The requirement for the interest increase risk is generated by deducting the market value decrease in the liabilities (gain) from the market value decrease in the capital investments (loss). If the insurance company is exposed to several currencies, the re-evaluation must be determined with the help of the relevant interest curves. Both scenarios (interest-rate increase or decrease) are determined by the interest structure curve.

Equity risk: changes in capital market prices for equities and equity-like securities result in equity risk. To quantify the equity risk for a property-casualty insurance company, the change in market value is observed for all assets and liabilities where the values react to changes in equity prices. A distinction is made between systematic and unsystematic risks, whereby the standard approach only stipulates systematic risks for determining equity risk. Unsystematic

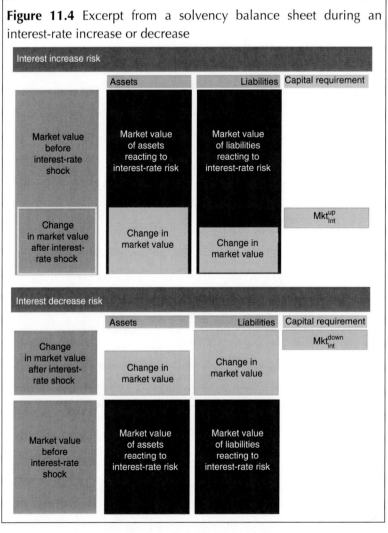

Figure 11.4 Excerpt from a solvency balance sheet during an interest-rate increase or decrease

risks must be taken into account when evaluating the concentration risk.

The standard approach identifies two types of capital investments:

- global: the equity of companies listed in EEA and OECD states and participation in companies based in EEA and OECD states;
- other: all the remaining equity of participation in companies.[17]

The capital necessary to cover the equity risk is generated in a two-step process.

Step 1: determination of the capital requirement per capital investment type.

Step 2: aggregation into a capital charge for equity risk.

Property risk: the property investment risk exists in the change in property prices in the capital market. The capital requirement is generated by analysing a stipulated scenario on the assets side. The market value loss must be stated under a relative property price decline of 20%. Financial instruments used to hedge property risks can be offset.

Spread risk: the spread risk covers the risk of a market value loss in capital investments through a change in the credit spread over the risk-free interest. The change occurs due to the difference in interest between risk-free and risk-bearing capital investments. The causes of such discrepancies include, for example, a change in the issuer's credit rating. To be able to determine the spread risk, the capital investments involving a credit risk must be analysed.

Currency risk: the currency risk is the risk that can arise due to incongruent coverage in the event the capital investment's currency depreciates compared with the currency of the insurance obligation. The capital requirement is generated by analysing scenarios. The market value change resulting from a 20% currency gain out of all currencies in which the insurance company has invested, compared with the euro, must be stated, as well as that resulting from a 20% currency loss. The capital requirement is generated from the more unfavourable scenario. Financial instruments that serve to hedge against currency losses can be offset.

Concentration risk: the concentration risk is the risk that losses can occur due to increased risk concentration in capital investments or assets under credit. Factors such as the concentration in geographic areas or industrial areas are not taken into account here. Also not taken into consideration are capital investments or guarantees from states of an OECD or EEA country, as well as bank deposits totalling up to €3 million, with a term of less than three months and a credit rating of at least AA.

The market value of the capital investments is used as a risk carrier. To be able to determine the concentration risk, the share allotted to one and the same counterparty, and which exceeds a set limit in the overall assets, is ascertained. The limits are specified based on the counterparty's rating. For equities or fixed-interest securities from issuers having a rating of at least A, the limit value is 5% of the entire assets.[18] The concentration risk for bonds from issuers where the rating is below A is measured from a risk exposure exceeding 3% of the total assets. The risk factor for the concentration risk allotted to a counterparty is also stipulated based on the rating (European Commission 2008, p. 152). The risk capital requirement per counterparty can thus be determined. The total risk capital requirement for the concentration risk is generated through aggregation.

Default risk: the credit or default risk is the risk that is generated from the unexpected loss or deterioration of the credit rating of counterparties and debtors of an insurance company.

The calculation of a counterparty's default risk is based on a factor approach, and can only be determined once the capital requirements of the individual risk modules SCR_{pr} and SCR_{mkt} are known. To do this, the volume measure, the loss given default (LGD),[19] and the probability of default (PD) must be determined for every single counterparty, i.[20] A probability of default PD_i depends on the respective degree of debtors and should be deduced based on external or internal ratings. The capital required to securitise the default risk[21] is generated in a three-step process:

Step 1: determination of the concentration risk.

Step 2: definition of the capital requirement per counterparty, Def_i.

Step 3: the total capital requirement for an insurer's credit risk is generated from the sum of the capital requirements of the individual counterparties

$$SCR_{def} = \sqrt{Def_i} \qquad (11.4)$$

Operational risk: an insurer's operational risk is the risk of losses resulting from inadequate or failed internal processes, or from personnel and system-related or external events (CEIOPS 2005, p. 100). The debates on this risk originate in the bank sector (Basel Committee on Banking Supervision 1989, 1998). Ever since the proposals made by the Basel Committee on Banking Supervision, operational risks have achieved fundamental importance in the finance sector (among many others see Albrecht *et al* 2007 and McNeil *et al* 2005, pp. 463–493). Operational risks also include legal risks. Reputational risks, as well as risks resulting from strategic decisions, are not taken into account. The evaluation of operational risks has proven to be extremely complex. The aforementioned factor approach is based on very simple assumptions, due to the insufficiency of statistical information on losses resulting from operational risks[22]

$$SCR_{op} = \min\{30\% \cdot BSCR; Op\} \tag{11.5}$$

where $Op = 2\% \cdot \max\{$gross earned premiums; gross technical provisions$\}$. The gross earned premiums or the gross technical provisions, depending on which value is higher, are used to determine the capital requirement for the operational risk. The higher of these two values is relevant for further calculation. Of this value, 2%, but no more than 30% of the basic SCR, must be set aside as risk capital. For the sake of simplicity, correlations with the risks within the basic risk are not taken into account.

Appraisal of the solvency capital calculations with the standard approach according to QIS4

The previously existing, pragmatic design of the insurance supervisory system becomes visibly more complex with Solvency II. The representation of an insurer's total risk situation is consistent with the theory of solvability (Farny 2006, p. 794). However, it remains difficult to conduct an economic evaluation. The proposal for the formulation of future solvency regulations to determine the capital requirement contains numerous, individual aspects, meaning an overall economic evaluation is difficult. Apart from the uncertainty regarding the specifications, the system gives insurance companies room to move when applying the Framework Directive. The approach developed by the European insurance industry, actuaries and supervisory authorities aims to create an economically, risk-oriented framework for the European insurance sector, and a balanced ratio between risk-sensitivity and practical applicability. The extensive test phases that facilitate the general acceptance of the approach are advantageous. The extent to which the approach actually reflects reality is still open to discussion. Various details of the regulations must, however, be viewed critically. Two criteria must be used to evaluate the standard approach.

- Evaluation using underlying characteristics stated in the Framework Directive: the central criteria are the going concern principle (going concern versus the run-off view), the risk orientation (risk measure, time horizon, completeness, bottom-up versus the top-down view, relevance) and the type of evaluation.
- Evaluation using underlying characteristics stated in the implementing measures: the appropriateness of the evaluation method, the practicability of the approach and the calibration of the risk modules must be evaluated.

Evaluation of the principles according to the Framework Directive
The going concern principle: the basic concept of the European standard approach aims to preserve the coverage interests of policyholders. The solvency system stipulates that an insurance company set aside a specific amount of capital so that it can, on average, go bankrupt no more than every 200 years. The SCR under Solvency II should be defined based on the assumption that a company performs its business activities according to the going concern principle (European Commission 2009, Article 101 Para. 2). Most insurers find themselves in such a situation at the time of the evaluation, as well as within the one-year evaluation period, which is why a going concern perspective appears suitable for supervisory purposes.[23] From an economic point of view, a supervisory solvability rule will not, however, completely prevent insolvencies. Instead, competition will be maintained (Schradin and Telschow 1995, p. 366, and references therein). This problem has been solved by basing the supervision on a prospective and risk-oriented approach, which stipulates the continuation of

business activities. An insurance company is thus stripped of its business licence, if the minimum capital requirement (MCR) cannot be covered by appropriate own funds. The supervisory authority must assume that the financial plan provided is inadequate, or that the affected company is not in a position to comply with the plan within a set time horizon for the MCR to be covered with sufficient capital.

Risk orientation: in the standard approach, the ruin probability is determined with VaR, although VaR is an insufficient risk measure from a theoretical point of view.[24] The risk measures alternatively proposed in risk management literature often cannot, however, sufficiently quantify actual risks. There have been questions about the robustness of tail VaR, as the data in the tails is often insufficient (Hartung 2007, p. 122; Zons 2005, p. 115). The selection of a suitable risk measure should only be made after the company-specific quality features have been established. Nevertheless, practical considerations argue in favour of using VaR: the main aim of the supervision is to protect the policyholder. The probability of ruin is limited to 0.5%. Companies must estimate the capital requirement from existing data. Sufficient quantities of data are necessary for a precise evaluation of the risk situation. The data in the tails is, however, generally insufficient, for instance, due to a lack of information on extreme events. Given the insurance supervision, insurance companies must be in a position to determine the SCR. Value-at-risk appears to be a suitable risk measure for this. The supervisory authority is, thus, more interested in VaR; the capital requirement, which should be measured in such a way that a company's default probability is not more than 0.5%, rather than in the average exaggeration of loss, which can be stated with the help of tail VaR. The ruin probability specification goes hand in hand with the definition over a set time horizon. There are studies that consider VaR to be effective at a confidence level of 99.5% during the course of one year (Ballwieser and Kuhner 2000, p. 373). Although higher confidence levels result in a lower capital requirement, as the loss amount is exceeded by a lower probability, they also lead to reduced accuracy when determining VaR (Johanning 1998, p. 122).

The Framework Directive stipulates using an observation period of one year as an adequate evaluation period for supervision.

The approach takes into account the current and future financial situation. This reorganisation must strictly be assessed as appropriate. By taking into account future time horizons, even unstable framework conditions can be accepted. The SCR will be set once a year, but this is not to be considered a problem, as companies will constantly monitor the amount of own funds available for the SCR. As the MCR must be calculated quarterly, it is easy to restrict the time horizon to a one-year period. A multi-year view would, in any case, have to be scrutinised critically. On the one hand, the reliability of statements on future developments within a company decreases as the number of periods increase, and on the other, it appears doubtful whether the existing own funds would be sufficient to cover the SCR for a multi-period time horizon (Hartung 2007, p. 285; Mummenhoff 2007, p. 139).

The use of a bottom-up approach to evaluate these categories must be classified as appropriate. However, it must be considered crucial that dependencies between sub-risk modules of various risk modules are not taken into account directly. This leads to unclear and unstable results (Groupe Consultatif 2005, p. 8). This is particularly disadvantageous, if intensifying dependencies lead to an accumulation of risks, and the own funds necessary for covering the capital requirement only apply to independently occurring risks (Hartung 2007, p. 196).

The basic SCR is a result of the aggregation of the capital requirements of the individual risk categories, which takes into account the dependency structures between risk modules. The process for measuring dependencies with the help of linear correlation does, however, display numerous weaknesses (Embrechts *et al* 1999; Koryciorz 2004, p. 115 ff). For example, non-linear dependencies are not taken into account: a correlation coefficient of zero implies the linear independent of two risk factors. However this cannot suggest independence of factors.[25] The total risk distribution cannot necessarily be clearly determined, if the distribution function of individual risks and their associated correlation coefficients are known (Koryciorz 2004, p. 116). The concept is, thus, not a suitable method for evaluating the capital requirement, taking into account stochastic dependencies between the risk categories. Risk management literature increasingly contains modern concepts with which dependency structures can be precisely identified. The copulas concept is one of these. Copulas attempt to completely record dependency structures (for example Embrechts *et al* 2001; McNeil *et al* 2005, p. 184 ff; IAA 2004, p. 171 ff; Hipp 2007). But this concept also has its weaknesses (Hartung 2007, p. 155). No statement on the orientation of the dependencies can be made, meaning cause–effect relationships cannot be examined sufficiently. Companies would also need to have adequate historic data to completely record dependency structures. The data in the tails is, however, usually insufficient.

Overall, the standard formula takes into account the important risk categories, meaning an insurer's risk situation can be estimated. In order to be able to evaluate the risks appropriately, the insurer must have the relevant data.

The future quantitative requirements stipulate a risk-based approach:

> in line with the latest developments in risk management, in the context of the International Association of Insurance Supervisors, the International Accounting Standards Board and the International Actuarial Association and with recent developments in other financial sectors

which encourages companies to develop their own internal models (European Commission 2009, p. 10). However, it is not explained how the right measurement and handling of risks could be encouraged. Reference is only made to the fact that the standard approach will lead to a higher capital requirement than is the case for an internal model, due to simplified assumptions and conservative parameterisation in the results. However, the QIS4 study results show the precise opposite for some risk modules. Although it is assumed that risk evaluation can illustrate a company's risk situation better using its own internal models compared with using a standardised method, the capital requirements for the market risk and operational risk from internal models tend to be higher.

Type of evaluation: in terms of the type of evaluation, the standard approach must be classified as principle-oriented. In future, insurers will not follow any rules, but rather uphold principles, which should be considered appropriate. Nevertheless, such approaches involve the risk of suggesting pseudo-accuracies. This primarily becomes a problem, if the know-how required for the evaluation is lacking or if the data is insufficient.

Evaluation of the principles for the implementing measures

The future solvency system, which only includes principles, is complemented by implementing measures. Among other things, these further specify the principles for measuring an insurer's risk situation using a standard approach, which will, however, be further developed over the years. Some individual points must be deemed particularly critical to business administration from a present-day perspective. Various criteria can be used as a basis for evaluating a solvency system. The practical feasibility of these principles was evaluated by QIS4, which had several aims, using the following aspects:

- appropriateness of the evaluation method;
- practicability of the approach; and
- calibration of the risk modules.

Appropriateness of the evaluation method: the approach sets an appointed date for part of its data (European Commission 2008, p. 8). However, this aids the influence of random effects. An insurer's risk situation is sometimes distorted, if extreme events take effect on the appointed date, such as a stock crash.

For property-casualty insurance companies, the underwriting risk is of great significance. The calculation of the premium and reserve risk must be viewed critically in the following points. Taking into account premium and reserve amounts involves the risk that insufficient pricing or reserving are recompensed with lower capital requirements. Sufficient pricing or reserving that aim to ensure the company's profitability are, on the other hand, penalised with higher requirements. Another problem results with fundamental changes, for example in the reinsurance structure or for company mergers that cause jumps in the existing time series. The standard approach renounces the differentiated observation of such factors here. The handling of risk-mitigating instruments must also be viewed critically. These directly influence the assessment of the premium and reserve risk, as they exercise a significant influence over the insurer's risk situation. Although the standard formula takes into account risk balancing effects to reduce the SCR by stating net values, the acceptance of risk-mitigating instruments is more pragmatic. For example, changes to the reinsurance structure are not dealt with appropriately.[26] According to the approach, if a reinsurance cover is not used, the volatility of the net loss expenses increases, and therefore so does the premium risk. This is the opposite of reality.

Market risks are also of enormous importance to property-casualty insurers.[27] The calculation of the concentration risk must be viewed as critical in the following points. Government loans are not taken into account. The risk factors are also stipulated on a flat-rate basis, resulting from the rating classification. A classification according to risk concentration is, however, not made here. Insurance companies that cannot produce a rating are treated very differently, regardless of whether they are subject to the Solvency II regulations or not.

Other critical points concern the flat-rate evaluation of operational risk. In doing so, the fundamental question of whether operational risks are quantifiable at all must be discussed (Young 1999, p. 10). This is due to the complexity and ignorance of this risk category. Some cases are thus never discovered, or only occur very rarely. There is also the view that, in contrast to market and default risks, there is no direct correlation between operational risk and the size and frequency of the losses arising. Great scepticism is appropriate insofar as an insurer's risk situation is expressed with the premium and reserve volume. The same points of criticism as those stated under Solvency I apply here: in the event of adequate pricing or reserving, a more dangerous risk situation is indicated compared with inadequate pricing or reserving. The lower limit for evaluating the capital requirement for operational risk is defined using a numerical process. This process does not appear to be appropriate in terms of risk. The capital investment side also remains completely ignored. Overall, the method does not provide the right incentives for appropriate risk management.

Lamfalussy's concept was created to ensure an efficient regulatory and supervisory structure for insurance companies in the European Union. However, this must be viewed critically: CEIOPS has founded several expert groups, comprised of representatives from different national supervisory authorities, to formulate the details.[28] These, once again, frequently draw on the work group results compiled by the insurance industry, as well as associated organisations. The reorganisation of the insurance supervision is thus significantly influenced by the interests of the insurance industry. The extent to which the aims required by the supervision are endangered by this cannot, however, be quantified.

Practicability of the approach: according to the Framework Directive, the standard approach will be distinguished by a balanced ratio between risk sensitivity and simple handling. The parameter to use VaR as a risk measure and the parameter for aggregating the risks through the linear dependency concept can be traced back to simple computer-based handling. The fact that the standard formula was implemented in an Excel-based environment is also considered to be advantageous. The evaluation of individual risk modules is, however, critical (CEIOPS 2008a, p. 192).

Inflation effects, such as those arising for market risks, are completely neglected for reasons of practical applicability.

The solvency capital required for the default risk totals on average 5% for property-casualty insurers, and thus also constitutes a relatively low share in the basic SCR. The risk measurement, however, is conducted using a very extensive process: insurers who distribute their business over several reinsurers must perform a series of calculations. They must determine the expected average loss per claim in the event the counterparty defaults. This is not, however, in proportion to the capital requirement. According to the policy of the proportionality principle, however, it is also possible to have simplifications that allow companies to treat counterparties of one rating category as one counterparty to limit the expense of the risk assessment.

Calibration of the risk modules: the development of a standardised method requires making suitable assumptions. The specifications for distributions in risk modules, for example the specifications of a log-normal distribution for the premium and reserve risk, can be irrelevant, taking into account risk-mitigating instruments. In the European standard approach, most risk parameters must be stated in a way that is consistent with the market, and must be examined every year. The estimation processes must be disclosed. However, the numerical specifications in the formulas for evaluating individual risk modules do not appear to be justifiable in the sub-areas in terms of risk, and can only be explained from the political decision-making process when developing the system.

The correlation matrices for determining the premium and reserve risk were not essentially calibrated based on data from the entire European insurance market, but rather based on individual markets (CEIOPS 2008b, p. 6). An analysis of parameter estimates shows that these reflect the situation of certain European insurance markets in many cases. This does not guarantee that current market factors are sufficiently taken into account. They thus only illustrate the company-specific risk situation appropriately in exceptional cases. Companies may, however, calibrate the factors according to their company-specific risk situation so that the SCR can be deemed as sufficient.

The 32% stress factor for the equity risk does not appear to adequately take into account the current market situation. The parameter selection is primarily based on the assumption that extreme share fluctuations must often only be viewed as critical temporarily, and that most are accompanied by direct recovery phases.

The stipulated parameters for determining the default risk also appear to contradict contemporary knowledge of current market factors. Even though no empirical research results so far exist regarding the concept of whether rating agencies can adequately estimate a company's risk situation, it appears that the assumption that "top" rated companies can be represented by low default probabilities can only be used to a limited extent in stress situations, such as those that can arise in capital market-related crisis situations. Parameter selection is also based on the assumption that such bad debts must often only be viewed critically temporarily, and that they are mostly accompanied by direct recovery phases.

Correlations between the operational risk and the risks within the basis risk are, for the sake of simplicity, not taken into account. However, a differentiation between these risks and the operational risk appears to be difficult. Although unfavourable developments in the loss event, in capital investments or at the counterparty's end must initially be taken into account within the relevant risk category of the individual risk modules, they can trigger financial losses due to a lack of controls, inadequate internal processes or staff- and system-based incidents (Hartung 2007, p. 82; GDV 2007b, p. 12). The extent to which these operational risks are already recorded in these basic risk categories can only be determined with great difficulty.

However, as the standard approach must be conservative, the double counting of parts of the operational risk can be accepted (GDV 2007b, p. 15). An insurance companies' database currently existing to quantify the operational risk is not sufficient for determining an appropriate capital requirement (see Nguyen 2008, p. 68 and the references stated there).

Minimum capital requirement

If the eligible own funds are not sufficient to cover the SCR, the supervisory authority will initiate measures depending on the extent of the shortfall. A going concern risk arises as soon as the insurance company does not have sufficient own funds of at least the required minimum capital. This irregularity leads to the supervisory authority taking ultimate supervisory measures and they may withdraw the authorisation to continue business activities (European Commission 2009, Article 142 Para. 1). According to the principle, the minimum level must be calculated clearly and simply. An adequate ladder of intervention demands that the SCR always be above the MCR. According to the Framework Directive, VaR at a confidence level of 85% over a one-year time horizon is definitive for determining the MCR (European Commission 2009, Article 127 Para. 1). The evaluation is based on a linear function, according to which the technical provisions, the written premiums, the capital-at-risk, deferred taxes and administrative expenses must be incorporated. The MCR totals at least 25%, but no more than 45%, of an insurance company's SCR. This must already contain any capital add-ons imposed. The linear formula relies on the rules of the current European solvency system. Although the approach is easy to calculate, due to its similarity to the current system, it must be viewed critically.

CAPITAL RESOURCES

Representation

Determining and classifying own funds

The amount of eligible own funds is generated by the basic own funds (European Commission 2009, Article 87), which form part of an insurance balance sheet, and the ancillary own funds, which are not included on the balance sheet. The basic own funds include the economic capital and subordinate liabilities.[29] Ancillary own funds are made up of capital components that do not belong to the basic own funds. They include liabilities that an insurance company can use to re-establish the level of eligible own funds and thus absorb losses.

Based on their ability to balance losses to a varying extent, own funds are divided into three quality categories, so-called tiers. The following criteria must be verified for this (European Commission 2008, p. 97):

1.   Subordination: in the case of winding-up, these funds are only refunded to its holders if the insurance company has complied with all other obligations to the policyholders and beneficiaries from insurance contracts.

2.   Full loss-absorbency on a going concern: such items, which can be called on and which are available if necessary, must be able to absorb losses on the premise of a going concern and in the case of winding-up.

3.   Permanence: these items are unlimited, or have a long enough duration to allow obligations to be absorbed, or these items are constantly available to the company, or are available on request, so as to permanently be able to absorb losses, including in the case of winding-up.

4.   The resources are not associated with any requirements:[30] there are also no incentives for refunding the nominal amount.

5.   No mandatory fixed charges: the items are not associated with any fixed costs.

6.   No other encumbrances: the items are free from any other encumbrances.[31]

Eligibility of own funds

Not all own funds can be completely drawn on to absorb losses. The eligibility of these items is therefore limited for covering the necessary SCR for supervisory purposes. The own funds are thus broken down into the three tier categories, based on the type of own funds and the degree of fulfilment of the described criteria, as shown in Table 11.1.

As a matter of principle, basic own funds, which can be completely drawn on to absorb losses and thus meet all six criteria, are included in tier 1. Basic own funds, which cannot be completely

Table 11.1 Classification of own funds into quality categories

Tier	Type of own funds	
	Basic own funds	**Ancillary own funds**
1	1–6	–
2	1, 3–6	1–6
3	other	other

drawn on to absorb losses but otherwise meet all other criteria, as well as additional own funds, which meet all six criteria, are included in tier 2. All other own funds are allocated to tier 3.

The amount of eligible own funds available on the solvency balance sheet, produced from the difference between the assets and liabilities, is made up of the three own funds categories. All own funds in these three quality categories can be drawn on to cover the solvency capital. It must technically be

$$\text{Tier1} + \text{Tier2} + \text{Tier3} \geq SCR$$

The proportion of tier 1 components in the eligible own funds must total at least one-third, and the proportion of tier 3 components no more than one-third. The proportion of available tier 2 components must be limited to half to cover the MCR. Ancillary own funds are not credited against the MCR, which results in

$$\text{Tier1} + \text{Tier2} \geq MCR$$

Appraisal
The total balance sheet approach developed by the European insurance industry, actuaries and supervisory authorities aims to create an economically risk-oriented framework for the European insurance sector. In doing so, the process for determining the available capital components for covering these capital requirements, the own funds, is fundamentally restructured. Various rules' details must, however, still be viewed critically.

• A uniform standard for determining regulatory own funds can only be set once the current problem of national differences regarding supervisory acknowledgement of various capital items has been resolved. However, the Solvency II project behaves rather conservatively with issues concerning accounting rules. In particular this must be viewed critically in terms of the risk of the harmonisation objective of ensuring a standard application of supervisory regulations in all member states.

- The specification of different criteria used to appropriately assess the breakdown into different quality categories, and therefore the degree of eligibility for covering the capital requirement justified by this, appears to be feasible. The description of the true risk from the individual capital instruments cannot, however, be directly derived from this. Furthermore, room for interpretation, different accounting rules, and local market factors lead to different definitions of capital items. Thus, for example, only a few member states consider subordinate liabilities as hybrid instruments.

- A few assumptions on the classification and eligibility of the own funds must be critically highlighted: it is presumed that not all own funds can be completely drawn on to absorb losses. This assumption should, in principle, be feasible. Given the aim of reflecting and methodically justifying a risk-oriented economic perspective, the eligibility of own funds through classification into tiers should be questioned. Furthermore, an evaluation of the quality of eligible own funds through double counting (to the basic own funds and ancillary own funds, as well as into three tiers) is not sufficient. The selected approach appears to have been established haphazardly. To illustrate the economic perspectives, an appropriate approach would be one that attaches importance to the two main risks for own funds: the default risk and the termination risk. For example, there is no indication that the default risk of subordinate liabilities is dependent on its amount (GDV 2007a, p. 17). For example, to evaluate the eligibility, the counterparty's default risk could be quantified and taken into account accordingly.

It appears that the approach for evaluating own funds can be implemented at no great expense. However, it is worth questioning whether it is necessary to limit the eligibility of own funds. In the interest of the protection of insured persons, it would be sufficient to assess adherence to the SCR by comparing it with the existing own funds. The process for determining eligible own funds, tested in QIS4, is one of the longest discussed topics in the insurance industry.

THE IMPACT OF THE TOTAL BALANCE SHEET APPROACH ON THE INSURANCE INDUSTRY

The Solvency II project aims to introduce new solvency rules based on economic risks. This will illustrate the insurer's true risk situation. The project also aims to increase transparency and the policyholder's protection, the former primarily through disclosure and reporting requirements.

Although it will not be converted to national law before 2012, many companies have already begun making initial arrangements. They must create internal requirements to be able to comply with the specifications from the time the Framework Directive is implemented. The implementation of the quantitative Solvency II requirements will undoubtedly set the insurance industry new, or sometimes unknown, tasks. Companies must use information provided by the financial markets. The future set of rules will set high standards for an insurer's data. Sufficient data histories, which may need to be established, are necessary to evaluate the technical provisions, as well as to measure risks. Companies can use their own data, as well as standardised data consistent with the market, to evaluate risks. In this context, it becomes clear why participation in the current QIS is of particular interest to companies.

The QIS must essentially demonstrate the impact of the future quantitative requirements on an insurance company's Solvency II balance sheet, based on the European standard approach. The studies primarily aim to display the impact on capitalisation. The standard approach is not comparable with present solvency rules. However, one of the study's aims was to compare the results of the two supervisory systems with one another, particularly each of the coverage ratios resulting from the ratio of the existing own funds and the SCR.

From the study results, it can be concluded that the property-casualty insurers must tend towards expecting an increasing capital requirement. The increase results from the fact that the standard approach takes into account all important risks, while the current system only applies to underwriting risks. The future capital requirement should reflect the company-specific risk profile of every insurer. Apart from the underwriting risks (premiums risk, reserves risk and catastrophe risk), market risks (interest, equity, currency, property, spread and concentration risks), default risks (bad debt risks to reinsurance companies and issuers of capital investment instruments) and operational risks are also examined. Risk-mitigating instruments are recognised. Diversification effects are also incorporated into the evaluation. However, the approach still has the disadvantage of an approximate, and sometimes of a flat-rate, evaluation. It is particularly worth questioning the economic feasibility of the parameters specified. Using the conventional, stipulated risk factors for the reserves risk leads to the capital requirement being estimated too high. Conversely, the stipulated stress factors for the equity risk do not appear to take into account the current market situation. The results imply that the calibration was defined less in an economic sense, and more in terms of not overstraining the companies compared with the existing ruling. Furthermore, the capital requirement resulting from using the European standard formula can, on average, only suffice to not exceed the stipulated ruin probability. The individual risk situation can only be displayed adequately once the company has adjusted the stipulated factors to the company-specific risk situation. If the insurer's capital requirement does not comply with the economically assumed risks, the validity and success of the project must, however, be questioned. The calculation of the SCR distinguished itself in QIS4 through a wide range of different options. This principle-oriented approach of testing several alternatives simultaneously without stating a minimum context prevents the results from being compared, due to the variety of possible forms.

Apart from increasing capital requirements, the companies can, however, also expect a rise in eligible own funds. This results from the market-oriented evaluation of the assets and liabilities. The value of the assets grows and the liabilities are reduced. The re-evaluation of the capital investments on the assets side at the market values of the Solvency II balance sheet was performed by most participants without any problem. The re-evaluation of the liabilities side, particularly the re-evaluation of the technical provisions, was somewhat more complex. The provisions could not yet be completely evaluated by all companies. However, a variety of property-casualty insurers have already used actuarial reserving methods. Many participants consider the projection of existing business until settlement of liabilities to be difficult from a practical point of view. A large number of participants also rated the risk margin evaluation, which is part of the technical provisions, as being too complex. Nevertheless, most difficulties were overcome using the simplification methods provided. The re-evaluation of liabilities is particularly important. On the one hand, their value has a direct impact on the amount of eligible own funds produced from the difference in assets and liabilities, and on the other, the capital requirement amount is dependent on this value. Fewer liabilities also lead to lower capital requirements. In comparison to Solvency I, property-casualty insurers display lower technical provisions in QIS4. The reduction can be justified as follows. While local balancing standards are frequently applied to separate valuation, the evaluation is based on a total portfolio for the economic approach. Assuming the same confidence level, the sum of the individually evaluated provisions is higher than the provision generated from the evaluation of the total portfolio, which must be assessed as a consequence of the group-balance concept. Equalisation funds and valuation reserves resulting from the economic evaluation of the technical provisions are not, however, shown as a liability on the Solvency II balance sheet, but rather as own funds. The rise in assets on the assets side and the reduction of liabilities on the liabilities side, thus, leads to an increase in eligible own funds on the Solvency II balance sheet compared with the previous solvency system. However, this was also expected and can be observed across Europe. The impact on the amount of own funds are all the greater, the sooner local evaluation standards, which revolve around the principle of prudence, form the present-day basis. At 193%, the average coverage ratio for European property-casualty insurers is much lower than under Solvency I with 277% (CEIOPS 2008a, p. 41). Whether the prudent evaluation methods led to companies forming excessive hidden reserves can only be examined through further analyses. The transition to a market-oriented approach will lead to more transparency. The hidden reserves within a company will be uncovered, allowing the risk situation to be better estimated (Kottke 2006, p. 231). The shift from creditor protection-oriented accounting, as is the basis for local accounting standards, will, however, also mean additional efforts for many companies.

Defining the eligible own funds appeared to be a problem for very few companies. What was interesting, however, was the finding that most companies exclusively show tier 1 own funds in their balance sheet. The breakdown into three quality categories appears to be done at random. There is no justification as to why exactly the six selected criteria are sufficient for dividing the classification into three tiers. The approach does not lead to any clear reduction in own funds for the entire European insurance market. The extent to which the classification of own funds is even necessary to assess the eligibility of own funds is thus questionable.

The study also showed that the total assets for property-casualty insurers tended to only increase slightly. On average, the ratio of the QIS4 balance sheet total assets to the current balance is 105% (CEIOPS 2008a, p. 60). The balance structures did, however, differ fundamentally. The differences are all the greater, the sooner the companies used local accounting principles instead of market-oriented accounting systems.

Companies are given incentives for capital relief, if they have suitable risk strategies. Insurers who have their own internal risk models for corporate management can also use these to determine the capital requirement for supervisory purposes. Prior approval from the supervisory authority is, however, necessary for this. To ensure comparability, the risk benchmark at a set confidence level, and the time horizon for evaluating the risk situation, must be used in the same way as for the standard approach. As internal models have frequently been developed for purposes other than supervisory purposes, these are not directly comparable with the European standard approach. Their modelling is often very complex. The extent to which an insurer must develop their own internal model, or can use the standard approach as a basis to create a complete and risk-oriented approach for purposes of value-based management, requires further examination.

However, Solvency II will not only take into account quantitative issues, but will also strengthen the development of a solid risk management system. The quantitative assessment of the solvency requirement must, in future, be a fixed component of an insurer's business strategy. The capital requirement calculation must include the internal evaluation of the risk situation and solvency. This evaluation must, on the one hand, be incorporated into a company's strategic decision-making process, and on the other, facilitate supervision for regulators. The examination is conducted in the supervisory review process as part of Pillar II. The results are provided to the supervisory authority as part of Pillar III from the information to be provided for supervisory purposes.

1   This chapter was originally published in German under the title QIS4 – Konzeption des europäischen Standardansatzes und Kapitalausstattung für Schaden-Unfallversicherer – Analyse und Beurteilung by Heinrich R. Schradin and Kathleen Ehrlich in Zeitschrift für die gesamte Versicherungswissenschaft and is published here by courtesy of Springer Science and Business Media.

2   Harmonisation of the supervisory system and accounting rules primarily aims to use the same figures for supervision and accounting purposes, a so-called "single set of accounts" (Waschbusch 2005, p. 20 f).

3   The calculation of the capital requirement for the reserve risk according to the US risk-based capital approach exclusively relates to historic data. The insurer's current risk situation is, thus, only shown to a limited extent. Dependencies within the sub-risks of the market risk risk category are not taken into account. Operational risks are also not taken into account. Other weakness in this approach can be found in Schradin and Telschow (1995, p. 382).

4   The selection of those risks relevant to a property-casualty insurance company according to QIS4 revolves closely around the risk categories described in the IAA Blue Book for 2004 (IAA 2004, p. 26).

5   According to this, insolvency occurs on average once every 200 years. The discussion on which risk measurement should be used for supervisory purposes is essentially limited to the two risk benchmarks VaR and tail VaR, CEIOPS (2005, p. 82).

6   Scenario-based approaches also apply for determining the capital requirement for catastrophe risk.

7   For underwriting risks, this also applies for the individual lines of business.

8   The International Actuary Association is responsible for modelling individual risk categories and for dealing with methods for aggregating capital requirements into a total capital requirement (IAA 2004; Sandström 2006).

9   It is particularly important for life insurers to take into account the loss absorbancy capacity of the technical provisions. Risk-absorbing effects result from future profit sharing from life insurance policies. Property-casualty insurers should incorporate deferred taxes when evaluating the asset values and liabilities. The risk-absorbing effect should be taken into account when determining the capital requirement.

10 According to the QIS4 standard approach, geographic diversification is only applied once an insurance company has no more than 95% of its insurance business in one geographic area.

11 In the standard approach, risk factors are mostly stipulated values that significantly influence the capital requirement amount. Company-specific data can be used to calculate this sub-risk module.

12 Mixed funds must thus, for example, be divided into individual investment categories according to fixed-interest securities, shares or property securities, and allocated to the sub-risk modules.

13 However, this risk only usually exists for life/health insurance companies. For a property-casualty insurance company, this risk generally only arises for liability insurance and accident insurance with a premium refund, for which the due date for paying the obligation can be well into the future.

14 Exceptions to this are, however, liability and accident insurance policies with a premium refund facility.

15 This includes, for example, bonds from national issuers.

16 If the effect of the interest-rate shock for the capital investments is greater than for the liabilities, the capital requirement is set to zero.

17 This includes those financial instruments based in an emerging or developing country or those not listed on the market, such as hedge funds, derivatives, management futures and investments in special purpose entities, which cannot be allocated to the spread risk or to the classic equity risk.

18 For these estimates, CEIOPS provides study results that show that the capital requirement for the concentration risk of capital investments from issuers with a rating of A or better is not substantial (CEIOPS 2008b, p. 10).

19 The loss given default LGD states the expected average loss per claim when a counterparty defaults.

20 Insofar as the LGD calculation per counterparty is too time-intensive, the calculation can also be performed per rating category according to the principle of proportionality. In this case, all counterparties of the same rating category are treated as one counterparty.

21 Assuming that a counterparty defaults on average once every 200 years.

22 In this chapter, the approach is only shown for a pure property-casualty insurer. The formula for insurance companies that also conduct life and health insurance business can be found in European Commission (2008, p. 126).

23 When using an internal model to evaluate an insurance company's risk situation, a run-off situation should, however, also not be completely neglected.

24 This risk measure, thus, generally breaches the axiom of subadditivity, see for example Koryciorz (2004, pp. 49, 278). Other weaknesses in VaR are described by Koryciorz (2004, p. 58) and Hartung (2007, p. 112).

25 For clarification, a standard normally distributed risk X and the risk $Y = X^2$ is observed. Both risks are obviously dependent on one another, but their correlation coefficient is zero.

26 A property-casualty insurance company requires historic data, and explicitly historic information on the premium income and loss ratios for this. This data is often not available if the reinsurance programme changes.

27 Taking into account diversification effects, around two-fifths of the basic capital requirement falls in this risk category. Of this, around half come under the equity risk and one-third under the interest-rate risk (CEIOPS 2008a, p. 177).

28 CEIOPS homepage http://www.ceiops.eu/content/view/67/120/.

29 The economic capital is produced from the excess of assets over the liabilities. In doing so, these amounts must be valued with the amount at which the asset values can be exchanged/liabilities transferred or settled between knowledgeable willing parties at an arm's length transaction (see European Commission 2009, Article 74, Paragraphs 1a and b).

30 Such requirements could, for example, be interest or dividend payments.

31 Such encumbrances could, for example, be payment guarantees, loans or other restrictions or costs that the insurance company cannot cancel, unless they are agreed on for the policyholder.

REFERENCES

Albrecht, P., E. Schwake and P. Winter, 2007, "Quantifizierung operationeller Risiken: Der Loss Distribution Approach", University of Mannheim, URL: http://www.risk-insurance.de/Invited_Papers/01_2007/Albrecht_Schwake_Winter.pdf.

Ballwieser, W. and C. Kuhner, 2000, "Risk Adjusted Return on Capital: Ein geeignetes Instrument zur Steuerung, Kontrolle und Kapitalmarktkommunikation?", in M. Riekeberg, and K. Stenke (eds) *Banking Perspektiven und Projekte, Hermann Meyer zu Selhausen zum 60* (Wiesbaden: Geburtstag, Gabler Verlag), pp. 367–381.

Basel Committee on Banking Supervision, 1989, "Risks in computer and telecommunication systems", URL: http://www.bis.org/publ/bcbsc136.pdf.

Basel Committee on Banking Supervision, 1998, "Operational Risk Management", URL: http://www.bis.org/publ/bcbs42.pdf.

CEIOPS, 2005, "Answers to the European Commission on the second wave of Calls for Advice in the framework of the Solvency II project", URL: http://www.ceiops.eu/media/files/publications/submissionstotheec/Doc07_05-AnswersEC2ndwaveSII.pdf.

CEIOPS, 2006, "QIS2 - Summary Report", URL: http://www.ceiops.eu/media/files/consultations/QIS/QIS2-SummaryReport.pdf.

CEIOPS, 2007, "CEIOPS' Report on its third Quantitative Impact Study (QIS3) for Solvency II", URL: http://www.ceiops.eu/media/docman/public_files/publications/submissionstotheec/CEIOPS-DOC-19-07%20QIS3%20Report.pdf.

CEIOPS, 2008a, "CEIOPS' Report on its fourth Quantitative Impact Study (QIS4) for Solvency II", URL: http://www.ceiops.eu/media/files/consultations/QIS/CEIOPS-SEC-82-08%20QIS4%20Report.pdf.

CEIOPS, 2008b, "QIS4 background document: Calibration of SCR, MCR and proxies", URL: http://www.ceiops.eu/media/docman/public_files/consultations/QIS/CEIOPS-DOC-02-08%20QIS4%20Background%20document%20on%20calibration%20cl.pdf.

Embrechts, P., F. Lindskog and A. J. McNeil, 2001, "Modelling Dependence with Copulas and Applications to Risk Management", Working Paper, ETH Zürich, URL: http://www.math.ethz.ch/~baltes/ftp/copchapter.pdf.

Embrechts, P., A. J. McNeil and A. Straumann, 1999, "Correlation and dependence in risk management: Properties and pitfalls", Working Paper, ETH Zürich, URL: http://www.ccfz.ch/files/Embrechtspitfalls.pdf.

European Commission, 2008, "QIS4 Technical Specifications". Annex to Call for Advice from CEIOPS on QIS4, 31 March 2008, URL: http://ec.europa.eu/internal_market/insurance/docs/solvency/qis4/technical_specifications_2008_en.pdf.

European Commission, 2009, "Amended Proposal for a Directive of the European Parliament and of the Council on the taking-up and pursuit of the business of Insurance and Reinsurance (Solvency II)", URL: http://register.consilium.europa.eu/pdf/en/09/st08/st08132.en09.pdf.

Farny, D., 2006, *Versicherungsbetriebslehre*, 4th edition (Karlsruhe: Verlag Versicherungswirtschaft).

Gesamtverband der Deutschen Versicherungswirtschaft, 2007a, "Kernpositionen zu Eigenmitteln unter Solvency II", URL: http://www.gdv.de/Downloads/Themen/SII_Eigenmittel_GDV_de.pdf.

Gesamtverband der Deutschen Versicherungswirtschaft, 2007b, "Operationale Risiken unter Solvency II aus Sicht der deutschen Versicherungswirtschaft und Versicherungsaufsicht", URL: http://www.gdv.de/Downloads/Themen/SII_OpRisk_de.pdf.

Groupe Consultatif Actuariel Européen, 2005, "Diversification", Technical Paper, URL: http://www.gcactuaries.org/documents/diversification_oct05.pdf.

Hartung, T., 2007, *Eigenkapitalregulierung bei Versicherungsunternehmen: Eine ökonomisch-risikotheoretische Analyse verschiedener Solvabilitätskonzeptionen* (Karlsruhe: Verlag Versicherungswirtschaft).

Hipp, C., 2007, "Dependence concepts in finance and insurance: Copulas", Working Paper, Karlsruhe University, URL: http://insurance.fbv.uni-karlsruhe.de/rd_download/Copulas.pdf.

International Actuary Association, 2004, "Report of the Insurer Solvency Assessment Working Party: A Global Framework for Insurer Solvency Assessment", URL: http://www.actuaries.org/LIBRARY/papers/global_framework_insurer_solvency_assessment-public.pdf.

Johanning, L., 1998, *Value at Risk zur Marktrisikosteuerung und Eigenkapitalallokation* (Bad Soden: Uhlenbruch Verlag).

Koryciorz, S., 2004, *Sicherheitskapitalbestimmung und -allokation in der Schadenversicherung. Eine risikotheoretische Analyse auf der Basis des Value-at-Risk und des Conditional Value-at-Risk* (Karlsruhe: Verlag Versicherungswirtschaft).

Kottke, T., 2006, "Fair Value Bilanzierung versicherungstechnischer Verpflichtungen vor dem Hintergrund der Entwicklung und der Implementierung eines einzuführenden IFRS für Versicherungsverträge", URL: http://deposit.ddb.de/cgi-bin/dokserv?idn=982438818&dok_var=d1&dok_ext=pdf&filename=982438818.pdf.

McNeil, A. J., R. Frey and P. Embrechts, 2005, *Quantitative Risk Management: Concepts, Techniques and Tools* (London: Princeton University Press).

Mummenhoff, A., 2007, "Analyse des deutschen Standardmodells für Lebensversicherer unter Solvency II", Institut für Finanz- und Aktuarwissenschaften, Ulm.

Nguyen, T., 2008, *Handbuch der wert- und risikoorientierten Steuerung von Versicherungsunternehmen* (Karlsruhe: Verlag Versicherungswirtschaft).

Oletzky, T., 1998, *Wertorientierte Steuerung von Versicherungsunternehmen, Ein Steuerungskonzept auf der Grundlage des Shareholder-Value-Ansatzes* (Karlsruhe: Verlag Versicherungswirtschaft).

Ott, P., 2005, *Solvabilitätsmessung bei Schaden-Unfall-Versicherungs-unternehmen, Anforderungen an stochastische interne Modelle und deren Prüfung* (Wiesbaden: Deutscher Universitäts-Verlag).

Rockel, W., 2004, *Fair Value-Bilanzierung versicherungstechnischer Verpflichtungen: Eine ökonomische Analyse* (Wiesbaden: Deutscher Universitätsverlag).

Sandström, A., 2006, *Solvency Models, Assessment and Regulation, Stockholm* (London: Chapman and Hall/CRC).

Schradin, H. R., 1994, *Erfolgsorientiertes Versicherungsmanagement: Betriebswirtschaftliche Steuerungskonzepte auf risikotheoretischer Grundlage* (Karlsruhe: Verlag Versicherungswirtschaft).

Schradin, H. R. and I. Telschow, 1995, "Solvabilitätskontrolle in der Schadenversicherung – eine betriebswirtschaftliche Analyse der Risk Based Capital (RBC)-Anforderungen in den Vereinigten Staaten", *ZVersWiss, Bd.* 84, pp. 363–406.

Waschbusch, G., 2005, "Fair Value - ein geeigneter Wertmaßstab in der Rechnungslegung von Versicherungsunternehmen?" in Universität des Saarlandes - magazin forschung, Heft 1, pp. 18–27.

Young, B., 1999, "Raising the standard", *in Operational Risk. A Risk Special Report, Risk*, pp. 10–12.

Zons M., 2006, *Value Based Management und IAS/IFRS im Schadenversicherungsunternehmen* (Köln: Josef Eul Verlag).

12

Optimisation of the Non-Life Insurance Risk Diversification in Solvency II

Werner Hürlimann

FRSGlobal Switzerland

Although it is an old idea, the measurement and allocation of diversification in portfolios of asset and/or liability risks is a difficult problem, which has so far found many answers. The diversification effect of a portfolio of risks is the difference between the sum of the risk measures of stand-alone risks in the portfolio and the risk measure of all risks in the portfolio taken together, which is typically non-negative, at least for positive dependent risks. The risk allocation problem consists of apportioning the diversification effect to the risks of a portfolio in a fair manner, to obtain new risk measures for the risks of a portfolio. The first mathematical approach to diversification is due to 1990 Nobel laureate Markowitz (1952, 1959, 1987, 1994), whose classic portfolio selection model applies to the efficient diversification of investments.

Within the unifying framework for insurer capital requirements, as initiated by the International Association of Insurance Supervisors (IAIS), this led to the fundamental IAA (2004) paper. From this the CRO Forum (2005, p. 20) has classified diversification benefits into four distinct categories:

- *Level 1 – within risk types*: the diversification in a homogeneous portfolio, for example, through aggregation of unrelated risks in a portfolio or by investing in an index of common shares rather than in a single company.
- *Level 2 – across risk types*: the diversification obtained by combining lines of insurance business or that obtained between insurance risk and market risk, providing claims results are unrelated to investment risks.

- *Level 3 – across entities, within a geographical location or country*: the diversification obtained by combining two or more insurance companies within a group.
- *Level 4 – across geographical locations or regulatory jurisdictions*: the diversification resulting from the consolidation of entities operating in different geographical locations or countries.

These four levels of classification help to understand the differences between diversification treatment within the many solvency frameworks applied around the world (eg, CRO Forum (2005, Table 2)). While Solvency I does not recognise any level of diversification, Australia's APRA solvency system already does so at all levels (with exceptions for geographical diversification).

The quantification of diversification effects usually follows two distinct roads:

- *The bottom-up method*: in order to obtain the total risk capital required at the highest level of a group, we start with calculations at the lowest level of sub-risks. The issue is then to design methods for combining these sub-risks to obtain the risk capital at various higher levels.
- *The top-down method*: exposures for each risk of an organisation are aggregated and then the overall required capital applied to risk modelling or scenario analysis is calculated. Then, to obtain the required capital at intermediate levels of the organisation, an appropriate capital allocation principle is applied.

The first method is discussed by the Groupe Consultatif Actuariel Européen (GCAE 2005) while Dhaene *et al* (2009) provide an advanced, comprehensive treatment of the second method. Hürlimann (2002) has developed a feasible, practical way for the top-down calculation of insurance risks, applying the classic risk theory. The latter proposal has been re-used in another context to construct a gamma distributed incurred but not reported claims reserving model with dependent development periods in Hürlimann (2007).

This chapter considers a new top-down method for calculating the level 4 diversification effect for a portfolio of non-life risks. According to the current Solvency II standard approach, which is specified in QIS4 (2008), non-life risk capital charges take into account geographical diversification by adjusting volume measures using a Herfindahl–Hirschman concentration index for premiums and reserves at the line of business level. The lower the Herfindahl–Hirschman index is, the less concentrated a portfolio is and the greater its diversification extent is. While from a theoretical point of view the link between diversification and concentration has been somewhat studied by Foldvary (2006), the present chapter's contribution focuses on the practical relevance of diversification in the Solvency II project.

The diversification factor for a portfolio of risks, with respect to some risk measure, is defined to be the quotient of the portfolio risk measure to the sum of the stand-alone risk measures over all risks in the portfolio. Maximum diversification is obtained by minimising the diversification factor. We observe that the greater the diversification reduction is, the less risk capital is needed and the more new business can be written. Therefore optimal diversification has an important practical relevance. According to the QIS4 proposal the minimum diversification factor is equal to 0.75. This value is not optimal. If the risk measure is proportional to the standard deviation of the risk, then the absolute minimum value of 0.707 allows for an additional diversification reduction of the maximum magnitude of 4.3%. The latter is true in the case of the value-at-risk (VaR) and the conditional value-at-risk (CVaR) measures for the class of multivariate elliptical risk distributions. However, the current Solvency II standard approach to non-life risk relies on lognormal distributions. Under this assumption, the minimum diversification factor, which depends on the volatility of the portfolio, is in the average equal to 0.667, which results in an absolute diversification reduction of magnitude 8.3% compared with QIS4. Extending the analysis to the class of multivariate log-elliptical risk distributions, further results on the minimum diversification factor can be obtained. For the class of multivariate log-Laplace distributions, which are able to model fat tails similarly to the class of generalised Pareto distributions in extreme value theory, this minimum value is in the average 0.68 resulting in an absolute reduction of the lower magnitude of 7%.

A more detailed account of the chapter follows. The next section reviews the Solvency II standard approach to non-life risks and presents a simple explanation for the proposed diversification factor, which is missing in QIS4 (2008). It is based on the intra-portfolio correlation coefficient. The subsequent section derives the minimum value of the diversification factor for risk measures proportional to the standard deviation of the risks. Typically, the obtained result applies to the class of multivariate elliptical distributions. A rigorous approach to the current standard Solvency II approach is found in the section "Diversification in a multivariate lognormal model", where minimum diversification factors are derived for the class of multivariate lognormal distributions. The section "Diversification in a multivariate log-elliptical model" extends the results to multivariate log-elliptical distributions, and exemplifies the results for the class of multivariate log-Laplace distributions. Finally, we illustrate the numerical impact of our findings on the current Solvency II standard approach.

SOLVENCY II NON-LIFE RISK DIVERSIFICATION ACCORDING TO QIS4

We recall the simple actuarial rationale for the non-life economic capital formula proposed for Solvency II in QIS3 (2007), which is presented by Hürlimann (2009).

Suppose that an insurance risk portfolio over a fixed time period, say over a one-year time period $[0, 1]$ between the times $t = 0$ and $t = 1$, is described by the following quantities:

P: the (net) risk premium of the portfolio for the time period; and
S: the random aggregate claims of the portfolio over the time period.

While the risk premium is supposed to be known at the beginning of the period, the random aggregate claims are not. The random loss of the portfolio at the beginning of the time period is described by the difference between aggregate claims and risk premium and defined by

$$L = S - P \tag{12.1}$$

In non-life insurance the aggregate claims over the time period are taken exclusive of the "run-off" and include the claims Y paid out during the time period and the change in claims reserves $\Delta R = R_1 - R_0$, where R_t denotes the claims reserves at time t, which consists of the total reserves for outstanding claims and for incurred but not reported claims. Therefore, we have the equality $S = Y + \Delta R$. At time $t = 0$ the claims reserve R_0 is known while R_1 is unknown. The volume $V = P + R_0$ of the portfolio, which is defined as the sum of the risk premium and the claims reserves at the beginning of the period, is known at time $t = 0$. Consider the ratio of the random loss to the volume, which can be written as

$$\frac{L}{V} = \frac{Y + R_1 - (P + R_0)}{P + R_0} = X - 1, \quad X = \frac{Y + R_1}{P + R_0} \tag{12.2}$$

where X represents a combined ratio of the portfolio (ratio of incurred claims inclusive of run-off to the premium and reserve volume). The actuarial equivalence principle or fair value principle $E[L] = 0$ implies that $E[X] = 1$. The Solvency II model assumes that X is lognormally distributed, say with parameters μ_X and σ_X. With $\sigma = \sqrt{\text{Var}[X]}$ we have

$$\mu_X = -\tfrac{1}{2}\sigma_X^2, \quad \sigma_X^2 = \ln(1 + \sigma^2) \tag{12.3}$$

The economic capital of the insurance risk portfolio to the confidence level α is supposed to depend only on the random loss and is denoted by $EC_\alpha[L]$. In the standard Solvency II approach, the economic capital is defined to be the VaR of the random loss taken at the confidence level $\alpha = 99.5\%$. Using Equation 12.2, the lognormal assumption on X and Equation 12.3 the non-life economic capital formula is derived as

$$EC_\alpha[L] = VaR_\alpha[L] = \rho_\alpha(\sigma) \cdot V \tag{12.4}$$

with

$$\rho_\alpha(\sigma) = \frac{\exp\{\Phi^{-1}(\alpha) \cdot \sqrt{\ln(1 + \sigma^2)}\}}{\sqrt{1 + \sigma^2}} - 1 \tag{12.5}$$

where $\Phi^{-1}(\alpha)$ denotes the α-quantile of the standard normal distribution $\Phi(x)$. Alternatively, and as first suggested in the CEIOPS consultation paper CP20 (2006, 5.309, p. 137), the economic capital can instead be defined as the tail value-at-risk (TVaR) or CVaR of the random loss taken at the confidence level $\alpha = 99\%$. With this choice of risk measure, the following economic capital formula is obtained

$$EC_\alpha[L] = CVaR_\alpha[L] = \rho_\alpha(\sigma) \cdot V \tag{12.6}$$

with

$$\rho_\alpha(\sigma) = \frac{\alpha - \Phi(\Phi^{-1}(\alpha) - \sqrt{\ln(1 + \sigma^2)})}{1 - \alpha} \tag{12.7}$$

As a novel feature QIS4 (2008) takes into account geographical diversification by adjusting volume measures using a Herfindahl–Hirschman index for premiums and reserves at a line of business level. However, a theoretical explanation for the proposed diversification factor is missing. For simplicity, let $V = \sum_{j=1}^n V_j$ be the geographical decomposition of the volume measure of a line of business into n geographical regions. Let us assume that diversification can be measured by the intra-portfolio correlation coefficient

$$Q = \sum_{i=1}^n \sum_{j=1}^n \rho_{ij} w_i w_j \in [-1, 1], \quad w_i = \frac{V_i}{V} \tag{12.8}$$

where ρ_{ij} represent the correlation coefficients and w_i the portfolio weights of the non-life risks in the geographical regions. Adjusting for diversification the QIS4 non-life risk capital can be represented as

$$\frac{1}{2}(1 + Q) \cdot EC_\alpha[L] \tag{12.9}$$

where $EC_\alpha[L]$ is the original non-life risk capital charge, which does not take diversification into account. If $Q = 1$ (perfect positive dependence between the regions) no reduction for diversification occurs, while if $Q = -1$ (perfect negative dependence) the non-life risk capital charge vanishes. If a linear dependence structure is assumed between perfect dependence and independence such that the correlation coefficients are given by

$$\rho_{ij} = \frac{1}{2} + \frac{1}{2}\delta_{ij}, \quad \delta_{ij} = \begin{cases} 1, & i = j \\ 0, & i \neq j \end{cases} \tag{12.10}$$

then we obtain

$$Q = \frac{1}{2}(1 + H), \quad H = \sum_{i=1}^n w_i^2 \tag{12.11}$$

where H denotes the Herfindahl–Hirschman index (see Hürlimann (2008) for motivating this choice). In this simple model the non-life risk capital charge reads (QIS4 2008, TS.XIII.B33, p. 222)

$$(0.75 + 0.25 \cdot H) \cdot EC_\alpha[L] \tag{12.12}$$

DIVERSIFICATION IN A MULTIVARIATE ELLIPTICAL MODEL

In general, an adjustment for diversification will be based on the theory of risk measures. Let X be the overall non-life risk per volume unit and let $X_j, j = 1, \ldots, n$, be the non-life risks per volume unit in the geographical regions. Then we have the equality $X \cdot V = \sum_{j=1}^{n} X_j \cdot V_j$. Using a positively homogeneous risk measure $\rho(\cdot)$, the non-life risk capital, which has been adjusted for diversification, has the representation

$$EC_\rho(X, V) = \rho(X) \cdot V = DF \cdot \sum_{j=1}^{n} \rho(X_j) \cdot V_j \qquad (12.13)$$

where

$$DF = \frac{\rho(X) \cdot V}{\sum_{j=1}^{n} \rho(X_j) \cdot V_j} \qquad (12.14)$$

is the diversification factor of the non-life portfolio with respect to the risk measure $\rho(\cdot)$ and $\sum_{j=1}^{n} \rho(X_j) \cdot V_j$ is the non-life risk capital before diversification (sum of the stand-alone non-life risk capitals over the geographical regions). Consider first a class of multivariate distributions of the risk vector $(X_1, \ldots, X_n)$ for which the risk measure $\rho(\cdot)$ is proportional to the standard deviation of the risk. For example, this is the case for the VaR and the CVaR measures for the class of multivariate elliptical distributions (Landsman and Valdez 2003; Dhaene *et al* 2008), which contains the ubiquitous multivariate normal distributions. In this situation we have

$$DF = \frac{\sigma \cdot V}{\sum_{j=1}^{n} \sigma_j \cdot V_j} \qquad (12.15)$$

with σ, σ_j, $j = 1, \ldots, n$, the standard deviations of X, X_j, $j = 1, \ldots, n$. Clearly we have

$$\sigma \cdot V = \sqrt{\sum_{i=1}^{n} \sum_{j=1}^{n} \rho_{ij}(\sigma_i V_i)(\sigma_j V_j)} \qquad (12.16)$$

with ρ_{ij} the correlation coefficients of the non-life risks in the geographical regions. For illustration and comparison purposes assume Equation 12.10. Then we obtain

$$DF = DF(H(\sigma)) = \sqrt{\tfrac{1}{2}(1 + H(\sigma))} \qquad (12.17)$$

with

$$H(\sigma) = \frac{\sum_j (w_j\sigma_j)^2}{(\sum_j w_j\sigma_j)^2} \tag{12.18}$$

a volatility weighted Herfindahl–Hirschman index. A maximum diversification effect is obtained for a minimum diversification factor or equivalently a minimum value of $H(\sigma)$ subject to the constraint $\sum_{j=1}^n w_j = 1$. Applying the Lagrange multiplier method we see that a solution of this optimisation problem solves the equations

$$\sigma_k \cdot \left(\frac{w_k\sigma_k}{\sum_j w_j\sigma_j} - H(\sigma) \right) = \frac{\lambda}{2}, \quad k = 1, \ldots, n, \quad \sum_{j=1}^n w_j = 1 \tag{12.19}$$

for some constant λ. The obvious solution with $\lambda = 0$ is

$$w_k = \sigma_k^{-1} \cdot \left(\sum_{j=1}^n \sigma_j^{-1} \right)^{-1}, \quad k = 1, \ldots, n \tag{12.20}$$

In this situation the minimum diversification factor for n regions equals

$$DF_{\min}^n = DF\left(H(\sigma) = \tfrac{1}{n}\right) = \sqrt{\tfrac{1}{2}\left(1 + \tfrac{1}{n}\right)} \tag{12.21}$$

Asymptotically the limiting minimum value is obtained

$$DF_{\min} = \lim_{n\to\infty} DF_{\min}^n = \tfrac{\sqrt{2}}{2} \tag{12.22}$$

Compared with the QIS4 limiting minimum value of 0.75 in Equation 12.12, the multivariate elliptical model allows for an additional diversification reduction of maximum magnitude 4.29%.

DIVERSIFICATION IN A MULTIVARIATE LOGNORMAL MODEL

Unfortunately, the simple results of the previous section do not apply directly to the current Solvency II approach to non-life risk because it relies on lognormal distributions of the risks as seen in the section "Solvency II non-life risk diversification according to QIS4". The portfolio non-life risk per unit of volume, given by $X = \sum_{j=1}^n w_j X_j$, is a sum of correlated lognormal random variables, whose distribution does not have an analytical closed-form expression, but can be approximated by means of several methods. In the context of Solvency II we assume that the random vector $(X_1, \ldots, X_n)$ is of the form $(e^{Z_1}, \ldots, e^{Z_n})$, where $(Z_1, \ldots, Z_n)$ has a multivariate normal distribution with mean vector $(E[Z_1], \ldots, E[Z_n]) = (-\frac{1}{2}\xi_1^2, \ldots, -\frac{1}{2}\xi_n^2)$, variance vector $(\mathrm{Var}[Z_1], \ldots, \mathrm{Var}[Z_n]) = (\xi_1^2, \ldots, \xi_n^2)$, and covariance matrix $(\mathrm{Cov}\lfloor Z_i, Z_j \rfloor) = (\theta_{ij}\xi_i\xi_j)$. This assumption is consistent with the requirement $(E[X_1], \ldots, E[X_n]) = (1, \ldots, 1)$, that is the expected targets of the combined ratios are one as explained in the section "Solvency II non-life risk diversification according to QIS4". Furthermore, with the variance notation $\sigma_i^2 = \mathrm{Var}[X_i]$, $i = 1, \ldots, n$, we have the relationship $\theta_{ij}\xi_i\xi_j = \ln\{1 + \rho_{ij}\sigma_i\sigma_j\}$. For illustration we assume that ρ_{ij} is again specified by Equation 12.10. We discuss two approximation methods.

Simple lognormal approximation

Firstly and most simply the portfolio combined ratio $X = \sum_{j=1}^n w_j X_j$ is approximated by a single lognormal random variable with mean and variance

$$E[X] = \sum_{j=1}^n w_j E[X_j] = \sum_{j=1}^n w_j = 1 \qquad (12.23)$$

$$\sigma^2 = \mathrm{Var}[X] = \sum_{j=1}^n (w_j \sigma_j)^2 + \sum_{i<j} w_i w_j \sigma_i \sigma_j$$

$$= \frac{1}{2}(1 + H(\sigma)) \cdot \left(\sum_{j=1}^n w_j \sigma_j\right)^2 \qquad (12.24)$$

where $H(\sigma)$ is the volatility weighted Herfindahl–Hirschman index defined in Equation 12.18. It is important to mention that this is only a rough lognormal approximation, which can be replaced by a more sophisticated single lognormal approximation if necessary (eg, Fenton 1960; Schwartz and Yeh 1982; Beaulieu and Xie 2004; Mehta et al 2007). A theoretical justification for the use of such approximations is found in Dufresne (2002). Now, for a minimum capital charge, Equation 12.5 or 12.7, under this approximation, Equation 12.24 has to be minimised subject to the constraint $\sum_{j=1}^n w_j = 1$. Applying the Lagrange multiplier method we see that a solution of this optimisation problem solves the equations

$$\sigma_k \cdot \left(\sum_{j=1}^n w_j \sigma_j\right) = \frac{\lambda}{2}, \quad k = 1, \ldots, n, \ \sum_{j=1}^n w_j = 1 \qquad (12.25)$$

for some constant λ. This is only possible, providing $\sigma_k = \sigma^*$, $k = 1, \ldots, n$, that is the volatilities are constant in each geographical region. In this situation $H(\sigma) = H$ coincides with the Herfindahl–Hirschman index Equation 12.11 and a calculation using the relationship in Equation 12.24 yields

$$\sigma_k = \frac{\sigma}{\sqrt{\frac{1}{2}(1 + H)}}, \quad k = 1, \ldots, n \tag{12.26}$$

The corresponding diversification factor Equation 12.14 reads

$$DF = DF(H) = \frac{\rho_\alpha(\sigma)}{\rho_\alpha\left(\sigma / \sqrt{\frac{1}{2}(1 + H)}\right)} \tag{12.27}$$

where $\rho_\alpha(\cdot)$ is either Equation 12.5 or 12.7. Its absolute minimum is attained when $H \to 0$ and given by

$$DF_{\min} = \lim_{H \to 0} DF(H) = \frac{\rho_\alpha(\sigma)}{\rho_\alpha(\sqrt{2} \cdot \sigma)} \tag{12.28}$$

In the current standard Solvency II approach we set $\alpha = 0.995$ for the VaR measure Equation 12.5 and $\alpha = 0.98675$ for the CVaR measure Equation 12.7 to obtain approximately $\rho_\alpha(\sigma) \approx 3 \cdot \sigma$ (see also Hürlimann 2009, Table 14.1). Under this approximation Equation 12.27 reads $DF \approx \sqrt{\frac{1}{2}(1 + H)}$ as in the previous section. An exact evaluation of Equation 12.28 yields the following results.

In this table the VaR and the CVaR columns represent the quotients $\rho_\alpha(\sigma)/\sigma$. Compared with the QIS4 limiting minimum value of 0.75 in Equation 12.12, the simple approximation of the multivariate lognormal model allows for an additional diversification reduction of the average magnitude of 8.3%. In case the volatilities in the geographical regions are not available or difficult to estimate, the assumption of constant volatilities is appropriate and justified by the above minimum property. Alternatively, by given volatility structure σ_k, $k = 1, \ldots, n$, $H(\sigma)$ in Equation 12.24 can be minimised subject to the constraint $\sum_{j=1}^{n} w_j = 1$ to again obtain the optimal weights (Equation 12.20). In this situation the diversification factor reads

$$DF_{\min}^n = \frac{\rho_\alpha\left(\sqrt{\frac{1}{2}\left(1 + \frac{1}{n}\right)} \cdot \bar{\sigma}\right)}{\frac{\bar{\sigma}}{n} \cdot \sum_{j=1}^{n} \frac{\rho_\alpha(\sigma_j)}{\sigma_j}}, \quad \frac{1}{\bar{\sigma}} = \frac{1}{n} \cdot \sum_{j=1}^{n} \frac{1}{\sigma_j} \tag{12.29}$$

In the special case of equal volatilities Equation 12.28 is recovered when $n \to \infty$.

Comonotonic maximum variance approximation

The second approximation of the sum of correlated lognormal random variables relies on the comonotonic approximation method considered originally in Kaas *et al* (2000) and Dhaene *et al* (2002). The developments by Vanduffel *et al* (2005, 2008) exactly suit these needs. Recall that $X = \sum_{j=1}^{n} w_j e^{Z_j}$, where $(Z_1, \ldots, Z_n)$ satisfies the assumptions at the beginning of this section. Consider the conditioning random variable Λ, which is defined by

$$\Lambda = \sum_{i=1}^{n} \gamma_i Z_i \tag{12.30}$$

for some constants γ_i. Following Kaas *et al* (2000) a random variable is defined as

$$X^\ell = E[X \mid \Lambda] = \sum_{j=1}^{n} w_j \exp\left\{-\frac{1}{2}(r_j \xi_j)^2 + r_j \xi_j \frac{\Lambda - E[\Lambda]}{\sigma_\Lambda}\right\} \tag{12.31}$$

where $r_j \xi_j \sigma_\Lambda = \text{Cov}[Z_j, \Lambda] = \sum_{k=1}^{n} \gamma_k \text{Cov}[Z_j, Z_k]$, $j = 1, \ldots, n$. We find the equality in distribution

$$X^\ell =_d \sum_{j=1}^{n} w_j \exp\{-\tfrac{1}{2}(r_j \xi_j)^2 + r_j \xi_j \Phi^{-1}(U)\} \tag{12.32}$$

with $\Phi(x)$ the standard normal distribution and U a uniform random variable on $(0, 1)$. If all of the correlation coefficients r_j defined in Equation 12.31 are non-negative, then X^ℓ is a comonotonic sum. In this situation it is well known that the VaR and CVaR risk measures are determined by (eg, Vanduffel *et al* 2005, Section 2.1)

$$VaR_\alpha[X^\ell] = \sum_{j=1}^{n} w_j \exp\{-\tfrac{1}{2}(r_j \xi_j)^2 + r_j \xi_j \Phi^{-1}(\alpha)\},$$

$$CVaR_\alpha[X^\ell] = \frac{1}{1-\alpha} \cdot \sum_{j=1}^{n} w_j \Phi(r_j \xi_j - \Phi^{-1}(\alpha)) \tag{12.33}$$

From the definitions in Equation 12.31 we see that a sufficient condition for $r_j \geq 0$ is that all $\gamma_j \geq 0$ and all $\text{Cov}\lfloor Z_j, Z_k \rfloor \geq 0$. Using Jensen's inequality it can be proved that X^ℓ is a convex lower bound of X, a fact written $X^\ell \leq_{cx} X$, which means that for any convex function $v(x)$ we have $E[v(X^\ell)] \leq E[v(X)]$. In Dhaene *et al* (2002) a comonotonic convex upper bound, denoted by X^u and such that $X \leq_{cx} X^u$, has also been proposed. In the lognormal context this random variable can be defined by imposing $r_j = 1$ in Equation 12.31. For this upper bound we have

$$X^u =_d \sum_{j=1}^{n} w_j \exp\{-\tfrac{1}{2}\zeta_j^2 + \zeta_j \Phi^{-1}(U)\} \qquad (12.34)$$

It is easy to see that the VaR and CVaR measures associated with Equation 12.34 correspond to the sum of the stand-alone measures in each geographical region, hence to the valuation before diversification. Since $X^\ell \leq_{cx} X \leq_{cx} X^u$ the following relationships hold

$$E[X^\ell] = E[X] = E[X^u] = \sum_{j=1}^{n} w_j = 1 \qquad (12.35)$$

$$\mathrm{Var}[X^\ell] = \sum_{i,j=1}^{n} w_i w_j (e^{r_i r_j \zeta_i \zeta_j} - 1)$$

$$\leq \mathrm{Var}[X] = \sum_{i,j=1}^{n} w_i w_j (e^{\theta_{ij} \zeta_i \zeta_j} - 1)$$

$$\leq \mathrm{Var}[X^u] = \sum_{i,j=1}^{n} w_i w_j (e^{\zeta_i \zeta_j} - 1) \qquad (12.36)$$

For more details on these results we refer to Kaas *et al* (2000) and Dhaene *et al* (2002). In view of the inequality Equation 12.36, it is clear that the best comonotonic lower bound approximations of X are those for which $\mathrm{Var}[X^\ell]$ is as close to $\mathrm{Var}[X]$ as possible. Vanduffel *et al* (2005) maximise the first-order approximation of $\mathrm{Var}[X^\ell]$ obtained by letting $e^{r_i r_j \zeta_i \zeta_j} - 1 \approx r_i r_j \zeta_i \zeta_j$ to obtain the following coefficients in Equation 12.30

$$\gamma_j = w_j, \quad j = 1, \dots, n \qquad (12.37)$$

This simple choice is retained here and defines the so-called comonotonic maximum variance approximation of X. For approximation purposes we assume that $\theta_{ij} \approx \rho_{ij}$, where the latter is again specified by Equation 12.10. Then the coefficients r_j in

Equation 12.33 are obtained from

$$\sigma_\Lambda^2 = \sum_{i=1}^{n} (w_i \xi_i)^2 + \sum_{i<j} (w_i \xi_i)(w_j \xi_j) = \frac{1}{2}(1 + H(\xi)) \cdot S^2$$

$$H(\xi) = \frac{\sum_{j=1}^{n} (w_j \xi_j)^2}{S^2}, \quad S = \sum_{j=1}^{n} w_j \xi_j \qquad (12.38)$$

$$r_j = \frac{w_j \xi_j + \frac{1}{2} \sum_{k \neq j} w_k \xi_k}{\sigma_\Lambda} = \frac{\sqrt{2}}{2} \cdot \frac{1 + \frac{w_j \xi_j}{S}}{\sqrt{1 + H(\xi)}}$$

It is useful to derive lower and upper bounds to Equation 12.33. For this set $\xi_{\min} = \min_{1 \leq j \leq n} \xi_j$, $\xi_{\max} = \max_{1 \leq j \leq n} \xi_j$, and let $\xi_0 = \xi_{\min}$ (lower bound) or $\xi_0 = \xi_{\max}$ (upper bound) in the following. Lower and upper bounds are then obtained from the formula

$$r_j \xi_j = \frac{\sqrt{2}}{2} \cdot \frac{1 + w_j}{\sqrt{1 + H}} \xi_0, \quad j = 1, \ldots, n, \; H = \sum_{j=1}^{n} w_j^2 \qquad (12.39)$$

In the special case of equal weights $w_j = \frac{1}{n}$ the corresponding diversification factors read

$$DF^n = \frac{\rho_\alpha\left(\sqrt{\frac{1}{2}(1 + \frac{1}{n})} \cdot \xi_0\right)}{\rho_\alpha(\xi_0)} \qquad (12.40)$$

where $\rho_\alpha(\cdot)$ is either Equation 12.5 or Equation 12.7. The absolute minimum of Equation 12.40 is attained when $n \to \infty$ and is given by

$$DF_{\min} = \lim_{n \to \infty} DF^n = \frac{\rho_\alpha\left(\frac{\sqrt{2}}{2} \cdot \xi_0\right)}{\rho_\alpha(\xi_0)} \qquad (12.41)$$

With $\xi_0 = \sigma^* = \sqrt{2} \cdot \sigma$ Equation 12.28 and the numerical results of Table 12.1 are recovered. We conclude that in the limiting case of minimum diversification the simple lognormal approximation and the comonotonic maximum variance approximation lead to parameter transformation of the same results.

DIVERSIFICATION IN A MULTIVARIATE LOG-ELLIPTICAL MODEL
A natural generalisation of the multivariate lognormal distribution is the class of multivariate log-elliptical distributions, which has been discussed recently in Dhaene *et al* (2008) and Valdez *et al* (2009).

Table 12.1 Minimum diversification factor for the simple lognormal approximation

	VaR	DF_{min}	CVaR	DF_{min}
Confidence level	0.995	0.995	0.98675	0.09675
Standard deviation (%)				
12.0	2.925	0.673	2.923	0.672
12.5	2.940	0.672	2.939	0.671
13.0	2.955	0.670	2.954	0.669
13.5	2.970	0.669	2.969	0.668
14.0	2.985	0.668	2.985	0.667
14.5	**3.000**	**0.667**	**3.000**	**0.666**
15.0	3.015	0.666	3.015	0.665
15.5	3.030	0.665	3.031	0.663
16.0	3.045	0.663	3.046	0.662
16.5	3.060	0.662	3.062	0.661
17.0	3.075	0.661	3.077	0.660

To extend the results of the previous section, we assume that the random vector $(X_1, \ldots, X_n)$ is of the form $(e^{Z_1}, \ldots, e^{Z_n})$, where $(Z_1, \ldots, Z_n)$ has a multivariate elliptical distribution with density generator $g(x)$, mean vector $(E[Z_1], \ldots, E[Z_n]) = (-\ln g(-\xi_1^2), \ldots, -\ln g(-\xi_n^2))$, variance vector $(\text{Var}[Z_1], \ldots, \text{Var}[Z_n]) = (-2g'(0)\xi_1^2, \ldots, -2g'(0)\xi_n^2)$, and covariance matrix $(\text{Cov}\lfloor Z_i, Z_j \rfloor) = (-2g'(0)\theta_{ij}\xi_i\xi_j)$. This assumption is again consistent with the requirement $(E[X_1], \ldots, E[X_n]) = (e^{E[Z_1]}g(-\xi_1^2), \ldots, e^{E[Z_n]}g(-\xi_n^2)) = (1, \ldots, 1)$ (see the section "Solvency II non-life risk diversification according to QIS4"). Furthermore, with the variance notation $\sigma_i^2 = \text{Var}[X_i]$, $i = 1, \ldots, n$, we have the relationship

$$1 + \rho_{ij}\sigma_i\sigma_j = \frac{g(-(\xi_i^2 + \xi_j^2 + 2\theta_{ij}\xi_i\xi_j))}{g(-\xi_i^2)g(-\xi_j^2)} \tag{12.42}$$

In the lognormal special case we have $g(x) = \exp(-\frac{1}{2}x)$ and Equation 12.42 is equivalent with the relationship $\theta_{ij}\xi_i\xi_j = \ln\{1 + \rho_{ij}\sigma_i\sigma_j\}$ of the previous section. In the illustrative examples we assume that $g'(0) = -\frac{1}{2}$, and that ρ_{ij} is again specified by Equation 12.10.

Simple log-elliptical approximation
In parallel to the "Simple lognormal approximation" section the portfolio combined ratio $X = \sum_{j=1}^{n} w_j X_j$ is approximated by a single

log-elliptical random variable with mean $E[X] = 1$ and variance

$$\sigma^2 = \mathrm{Var}[X] = \frac{1}{2}(1 + H(\sigma)) \cdot \left(\sum_{j=1}^{n} w_j \sigma_j\right)^2 \qquad (12.43)$$

where $H(\sigma)$ is defined in Equation 12.18. As in the "Simple log-normal approximation" section a minimum capital charge under this approximation is only possible, providing $\sigma_k = \sigma^*, k = 1, \ldots, n$. In this situation $H(\sigma) = H$ coincides with Equation 12.11. The corresponding diversification factor reads

$$DF = DF(H) = \frac{\rho_\alpha(\sigma)}{\rho_\alpha\left(\sigma / \sqrt{\frac{1}{2}(1 + H)}\right)} \qquad (12.44)$$

where $\rho_\alpha(\cdot)$ is either $\rho_\alpha(\sigma) = VaR_\alpha[X] - 1$ or $\rho_\alpha(\sigma) = CVaR_\alpha[X] - 1$. Its absolute minimum is attained when $H \to 0$ and given by

$$DF_{\min} = \lim_{H \to 0} DF(H) = \frac{\rho_\alpha(\sigma)}{\rho_\alpha(\sqrt{2} \cdot \sigma)} \qquad (12.45)$$

To illustrate consider a multivariate log-Laplace model with density generator $g(x) = (1 + \frac{1}{2}x)^{-1}$. Set $\alpha = 0.9877$ for the VaR measure and $\alpha = 0.96471$ for the CVaR measure to get approximately $\rho_\alpha(\sigma) \approx 3 \cdot \sigma$ (choice consistent with QIS4 calibration). An exact evaluation of Equation 12.45 is found in Table 12.2 and is based on the formulas

$$VaR_\alpha[X] = \left(1 - \frac{\sqrt{2}}{2}\xi\right) \cdot CVaR_\alpha[X]$$

$$CVaR_\alpha[X] = \left(1 + \frac{\sqrt{2}}{2}\xi\right) \cdot [2(1 - \alpha)]^{-\frac{\sqrt{2}}{2}\xi}$$

$$\xi = \sqrt{2\sqrt{1 + 5\sigma^2 + 4\sigma^4} - 2(1 + 2\sigma^2)} < \sqrt{2} \qquad (12.46)$$

where the latter expression follows from the general log-elliptical relationship

$$1 + \sigma^2 = \frac{g(-4\xi^2)}{g(-\xi^2)^2}, \quad -2g'(0) \cdot \xi^2 = \mathrm{Var}[\ln X] \qquad (12.47)$$

by noting that $g(x) = (1 + \frac{1}{2}x)^{-1}$ and solving Equation 12.47 for ξ.

Compared with the lognormal results of Table 12.1, the simple approximation of the multivariate log-Laplace model leads to similar capital charges for significantly lower confidence levels, which

Table 12.2 Minimum diversification factor for the simple log-Laplace approximation

	VaR	DF_{min}	CVaR	DF_{min}
Confidence level	**0.9877**	**0.9877**	**0.96471**	**0.96471**
Standard deviation (%)				
12.0	2.943	0.682	2.934	0.678
12.5	2.955	0.681	2.947	0.677
13.0	2.966	0.681	2.960	0.676
13.5	2.978	0.681	2.974	0.676
14.0	2.989	0.681	2.987	0.675
14.5	**3.000**	**0.680**	**3.000**	**0.675**
15.0	3.011	0.680	3.012	0.674
15.5	3.021	0.680	3.025	0.674
16.0	3.032	0.680	3.037	0.674
16.5	3.042	0.680	3.050	0.674
17.0	3.052	0.680	3.062	0.673

are due to the fat tails of this model. The diversification reduction of approximate magnitude 7% compared with QIS4 is a bit less than for the lognormal model. A formula similar to Equation 12.29 can also be derived.

A Taylor-based mean-preserving approximation

The second approximation of the sum of correlated log-elliptical random variables is based on Valdez et al (2008). Recall that $X = \sum_{j=1}^{n} w_j e^{Z_j}$, where $(Z_1, \ldots, Z_n)$ satisfies the assumptions at the beginning of this section. Consider the conditioning random variable Λ, which is defined by

$$\Lambda = \sum_{i=1}^{n} \gamma_i Z_i \tag{12.48}$$

for some constants γ_i. Following Valdez et al (2008), a random variable is defined as

$$X^{MP} = \sum_{j=1}^{n} w_j \cdot g\left(-(r_j \xi_j)^2\right)^{-1} \cdot \exp\left\{r_j \xi_j \frac{\Lambda - E[\Lambda]}{\sigma_\Lambda}\right\} \tag{12.49}$$

where $r_j \xi_j \sigma_\Lambda = \mathrm{Cov}[Z_j, \Lambda] = \sum_{k=1}^{n} \gamma_k \mathrm{Cov}[Z_j, Z_k]$, $j = 1, \ldots, n$. We find the equality in distribution

$$X^{MP} =_d \sum_{j=1}^{n} w_j \cdot g\left(-(r_j \xi_j)^2\right)^{-1} \cdot \exp\left(r_j \xi_j F_Z^{-1}(U)\right) \tag{12.50}$$

with $F_Z(x)$ the spherical distribution with density generator $g(x)$ and U a uniform random variable on $(0,1)$. Since $E[X^{MP}] = E[X]$ the approximation Equation 12.49 is a mean-preserving approximation. Moreover, if $g(x) = e^{-\frac{1}{2}x}$, then Equation 12.50 coincides with the comonotonic lognormal approximation Equation 12.31 (similar to Valdez *et al* 2008, Theorem 6.1). The VaR and CVaR risk measures of Equation 12.50 are determined by (eg, Valdez and Dhaene 2004)

$$VaR_\alpha[X^{MP}] = \sum_{j=1}^{n} w_j \cdot g\big(-(r_j\xi_j)^2\big)^{-1} \cdot \exp(r_j\xi_j F_Z^{-1}(\alpha))$$

$$CVaR_\alpha[X^{MP}] = \frac{1}{1-\alpha} \cdot \sum_{j=1}^{n} w_j \cdot g\big(-(r_j\xi_j)^2\big)^{-1} \cdot \overline{F}_{Z_j^*}(F_Z^{-1}(\alpha))$$

$$(12.51)$$

where Z_j^* is the Escher transform of Z with parameter $r_j\xi_j$, where the density is defined by

$$f_{Z_j^*}(x) = g\big(-(r_j\xi_j)^2\big)^{-1} \cdot \exp(r_j\xi_j x) \cdot f_Z(x) \qquad (12.52)$$

Valdez *et al* (2008) have suggested choosing the coefficients in Equation 12.48 such that Λ and X are "as alike as" possible, which results in the so-called Taylor-based mean-preserving approximation (see also Vanduffel *et al* 2008) with coefficients Equation 12.48 given by

$$\gamma_j = g(-\xi_j^2) \cdot w_j, \quad j = 1, \dots, n \qquad (12.53)$$

For approximation purposes we will as in the "Comonotonic maximum variance approximation" section assume that $\theta_{ij} \approx \rho_{ij}$, where the latter is specified by Equation 12.10. Then the coefficients r_j in Equation 12.51 are obtained from

$$\sigma_\Lambda^2 = \sum_{i=1}^{n} (w_i g(-\xi_j^2)\xi_i)^2 + \sum_{i<j} (w_i g(-\xi_j^2)\xi_i)(w_j g(-\xi_j^2)\xi_j)$$

$$= \frac{1}{2}(1 + H(\xi)) \cdot S^2$$

$$H(\xi) = \frac{\sum_{j=1}^{n} (w_j g(-\xi_j^2)\xi_j)^2}{S^2}, \quad S = \sum_{j=1}^{n} w_j g(-\xi_j^2)\xi_j$$

$$r_j = \frac{w_j g(-\xi_j^2)\xi_j + \frac{1}{2}\sum_{k \neq j} w_k g(-\xi_k^2)\xi_k}{\sigma_\Lambda} = \frac{\sqrt{2}}{2} \cdot \frac{1 + \frac{w_j g(-\xi_j^2)\xi_j}{S}}{\sqrt{1 + H(\xi)}}$$

$$(12.54)$$

It is useful to derive lower and upper bounds to Equation 12.51. For this set $\xi_{min} = \min_{1 \leq j \leq n} \xi_j$, $\xi_{max} = \max_{1 \leq j \leq n} \xi_j$, and let $\xi_0 = \xi_{min}$ (lower bound) or $\xi_0 = \xi_{max}$ (upper bound) in the following. Lower and upper bounds are then obtained from the formula

$$r_j \xi_j = \frac{\sqrt{2}}{2} \cdot \frac{1 + w_j}{\sqrt{1 + H}} g(-\xi_0^2)\xi_0, \quad j = 1, \ldots, n, \ H = \sum_{j=1}^{n} w_j^2 \quad (12.55)$$

In the special case of equal weights $w_j = 1/n$ the corresponding diversification factors read

$$DF^n = \frac{\rho_\alpha \left(\sqrt{\frac{1}{2}(1 + \frac{1}{n})} \cdot g(-\xi_0^2)\xi_0 \right)}{\rho_\alpha(g(-\xi_0^2)\xi_0)} \quad (12.56)$$

where $\rho_\alpha(\cdot)$ is either $\rho_\alpha(\sigma) = VaR_\alpha[X] - 1$ or $\rho_\alpha(\sigma) = CVaR_\alpha[X] - 1$. The absolute minimum of Equation 12.56 is attained when $n \to \infty$ and is given by

$$DF_{min} = \lim_{n \to \infty} DF^n = \frac{\rho_\alpha(\frac{\sqrt{2}}{2} \cdot g(-\xi_0^2)\xi_0)}{\rho_\alpha(g(-\xi_0^2)\xi_0)} \quad (12.57)$$

With $g(-\xi_0^2)\xi_0 = \sigma^*$ one recovers Equation 12.45 and the numerical results of Table 12.2 for the multivariate log-Laplace model. We conclude that in the limiting case of minimum diversification the simple log-elliptical approximation and the Taylor-based mean-preserving approximation lead to parameter transformation of the same results.

APPLICATION TO THE CURRENT SOLVENCY II STANDARD APPROACH

It appears instructive to consider the impact of our findings on the current Solvency II standard approach. We give a numerical example, which compares the current QIS4 specification with the new approach based on the common assumption of lognormally distributed non-life risks. For illustration purposes it suffices to restrict the analysis to the simple lognormal approximation of the section "Simple lognormal approximation". We suppose that the volatilities in the geographical regions of a line of business are unknown, and assume therefore that they are constant in each line of business (as motivated in "Simple lognormal approximation").

For the determination of the solvency capital requirement (SCR) for the combined premium and reserve risk the following data is required:

m: number of lines of business;

V_ℓ: volume measure of the line of business $\ell \in \{1, \ldots, m\}$;

σ_ℓ: volatility measure (standard deviation) of the line of business ℓ;

H_ℓ: Herfindahl–Hirschman index of the line of business ℓ; and

$C = (\rho_{k\ell})$: correlation matrix between the lines of business $k, \ell \in \{1, \ldots, m\}$.

Let $V = \sum_{\ell=1}^{m} V_\ell$ be the overall volume measure and consider the volume weights $w_\ell = V_\ell / V$, $\ell \in \{1, \ldots, m\}$, and the vector of weighted volatilities $\sigma_w = (w_1 \sigma_1, \ldots, w_m \sigma_m)$. Then, the overall standard deviation σ is obtained from the equation $\sigma^2 = \sigma_w^T \cdot C \cdot \sigma_w$. Without geographical diversification the capital requirement for premium and reserve risk at the confidence level $\alpha = 99.5\%$ is given by Equation 12.4, that is

$$SCR_{PR} = \rho_\alpha(\sigma) \cdot V \tag{12.58}$$

To take geographical diversification into account according to QIS4, we consider the geographically diversified volume measures

$$V_\ell^D = (0.75 + 0.25 \cdot H_\ell) \cdot V_\ell, \quad \ell \in \{1, \ldots, m\} \tag{12.59}$$

Let $V^D = \sum_{\ell=1}^{m} V_\ell^D$ be the overall diversified volume measure and consider the diversified volume weights $w_\ell^D = V_\ell^D / V^D$, $\ell \in \{1, \ldots, m\}$, and the vector of diversified weighted volatilities $\sigma_w^D = (w_1^D \sigma_1, \ldots, w_m^D \sigma_m)$. Then, the overall diversified standard deviation σ^D is obtained from the equation $(\sigma^D)^2 = (\sigma_w^D)^T \cdot C \cdot \sigma_w^D$. With geographical diversification the capital requirement for premium and reserve risk at the confidence level $\alpha = 99.5\%$ is now

$$SCR_{PR}^D = \rho_\alpha(\sigma^D) \cdot V^D \tag{12.60}$$

Alternatively, according to the simple lognormal approximation, we consider the geographically diversified volume measures, which are consistent with Equation 12.27 and defined by

$$\tilde{V}_\ell^D = \frac{\rho_\alpha(\sigma_\ell)}{\rho_\alpha\left(\sigma_\ell/\sqrt{\frac{1}{2}(1+H_\ell)}\right)} \cdot V_\ell, \quad \ell \in \{1, \ldots, m\} \quad (12.61)$$

Let $\tilde{V}^D = \sum_{\ell=1}^m \tilde{V}_\ell^D$ be the corresponding overall diversified volume measure and consider the diversified volume weights $\tilde{w}_\ell^D = \tilde{V}_\ell^D / \tilde{V}^D$, $\ell \in \{1, \ldots, m\}$, and the vector of diversified weighted volatilities $\tilde{\sigma}_w^D = (\tilde{w}_1^D \sigma_1, \ldots, \tilde{w}_m^D \sigma_m)$. The corresponding overall diversified standard deviation $\tilde{\sigma}^D$ is obtained from the equation $(\tilde{\sigma}^D)^2 = (\tilde{\sigma}_w^D)^T \cdot C \cdot \tilde{\sigma}_w^D$. With geographical diversification the alternative simple lognormal capital requirement for premium and reserve risk at the confidence level $\alpha = 99.5\%$ is given by

$$\widetilde{SCR}_{PR}^D = \rho_\alpha(\tilde{\sigma}^D) \cdot \tilde{V}^D \quad (12.62)$$

Table 12.3 illustrates at two single examples the numerical impact of the new approach under varying levels of geographical diversification as measured by the Herfindahl indexes. We suppose that there are $m = 5$ lines of business with the following correlation matrix

$$C = (\rho_{k\ell}) = \begin{pmatrix} 1 & 0.5 & 0.5 & 0.25 & 0.25 \\ 0.5 & 1 & 0.25 & 0.25 & 0.5 \\ 0.5 & 0.25 & 1 & 0.5 & 0.25 \\ 0.25 & 0.25 & 0.5 & 1 & 0.5 \\ 0.25 & 0.5 & 0.25 & 0.5 & 1 \end{pmatrix} \quad (12.63)$$

In example 1 the diversification effect equals 11% of the SCR without diversification under the QIS4 approach. Under the alternative approach this effect increases to 13.9%. In the more diversified example 2 the diversification effect increases from 18.4% to 24.4%. Since the line of business diversification factors satisfy the approximations $DF_\ell \approx \sqrt{\frac{1}{2}(1 + H_\ell)}$ and in virtue of the inequalities

$$\sqrt{\tfrac{1}{2}(1 + H_\ell)} \leq 0.75 + 0.25 \cdot H_\ell \quad (12.64)$$

we expect that the diversification effect always increases from the QIS4 approach to the alternative approach, which implies a release of required risk capital.

Table 12.3 QIS4 geographical diversification versus simple lognormal approximation

	Overall	Lines of business				
		400	250	200	100	50
Volumes	1,000	400	250	200	100	50
Standard deviations (std) (%)	14.5	12	20	25	30	50
SCR (without diversification)	**435.6**					
Example 1						
Herfindahl indexes		0.25	0.5	0.6	0.75	1
QIS4 diversified volumes	867.5	325	218.75	180	93.75	50
QIS4 diversified overall std	14.9%					
QIS4 SCR (with diversification)	**387.8**					
Alternative diversified volumes	832.7	306.26	210.29	174.21	91.90	50
Alternative diversified overall std	14.9%					
Alternative SCR (with diversification)	**375.1**					
Example 2						
Herfindahl indexes		0.1	0.2	0.3	0.4	0.5
QIS4 diversified volumes	803.75	310	200	165	85	43.75
QIS4 diversified overall std	14.7%					
QIS4 SCR (with diversification)	**355.6**					
Alternative diversified volumes	741.75	284.45	183.45	152.92	79.67	41.26
Alternative diversified overall std	14.8%					
Alternative SCR (with diversification)	**329.3**					

To conclude, let us mention that geographical diversification has been discussed previously in banking by Liang and Rhoades (1988) and Rose and Wolken (1990). A very recent paper on the copula approach to this topic is Larsen *et al* (2009), which studies geographical diversification in agriculture risk management.

REFERENCES

Beaulieu, N. C. and Q. Xie, 2004, "An Optimal Lognormal Approximation to Lognormal Sum Distributions", *IEEE Transactions on Vehicle Technology*, 53, pp. 479–89.

CEIOPS, 2007, "QIS3 Technical Specifications – Part I: Instructions", April, URL: http://www.pszaf.hu/data/cms1305277/pszafhu_szolvencia_QIS3techspec1.pdf.

CEIOPS, 2008, "QIS4 – Technical Specifications", March, URL: http://ec.europa.eu/internal_market/insurance/docs/solvency/qis4/technical_specifications_en.pdf.

CRO Forum, 2005, "A Framework for Incorporating Diversification in the Solvency Assessment of Insurers", URL: http://www.diversification_white_paper_200506101[1].pdf.

Dhaene, J., M. Denuit, M. J. Goovaerts, R. Kaas and D. Vyncke, 2002, "The Concept of Comonotonicity in Actuarial Science and Finance: Applications", *Insurance: Mathematics and Economics*, 31(2), pp. 133–61.

Dhaene, J., L. Henrard, Z. Landsman, A. Vandendorpe and S. Vanduffel, 2008, "Some Results on the CTE Based Capital Allocation Rule", *Insurance: Mathematics and Economics*, 42, pp. 855–63.

Dhaene, J., A. Tsanakas, E. A. Valdez and S. Vanduffel, 2009, "Optimal Capital Allocation Principles", Working Paper, URL: http://econ.kuleuven.be/tew/academic/actuawet/pdfs/OptimalAllocation-090123.pdf.

Dufresne, D., 2002, "The Log-Normal Approximation in Financial and Other Computations", *Advances in Applied Probability*, 36, pp. 747–73.

Fenton, L. F., 1960, "The Sum of Lognormal Probability Distributions in Scatter Transmission Systems", *IRE Transactions on Communication Systems*, CS-8, pp. 57–67.

Foldvary, F. E., 2006, "The Measurement of Inequality, Concentration and Diversification", *Indian Economic Journal*, 54(3).

GCAE, 2005, "Diversification", Technical Paper, Groupe Consultatif, URL: http://www.gcactuaries.org/documents/diversification_oct05.pdf.

Hürlimann, W., 2002, "Economic Risk Capital Allocation From Top Down", *Blätter der Deutschen Gesellschaft für Versicherungsmathematik*, XXV(4), pp. 885–91.

Hürlimann, W., 2007, "A Gamma IBNR Claims Reserving Model with Dependent Development Periods", 37th International ASTIN Colloquium and 50th Anniversary Celebration, URL: www.actuaries.org/ASTIN/Colloquia/Orlando/Papers/Hurlimann.pdf.

Hürlimann, W., 2008, "Solvency II Reinsurance Counterparty Default Risk", *Life and Pensions*, December, pp. 39–44.

Hürlimann, W., 2009, "On the Non-Life Solvency II Model", in M. Cruz (ed), *The Solvency II Handbook: Developing ERM Frameworks in Insurance and Reinsurance Companies* (London: Risk Books), pp. 349–370.

IAA, 2004, "A Global Framework for Insurer Solvency Assessment", Research Report of the Insurer Solvency Assessment Working Party, URL: http://www.actuaries.org/LIBRARY/Papers/Global_Framework_Insurer_Solvency_Assessment-public.pdf.

Kaas, R., J. Dhaene and M. J. Goovaerts, 2000, "Upper and Lower Bounds for Sums of Random Variables", *Insurance: Mathematics and Economics*, 27(2), pp. 151–68.

Landsman, Z. and E. A. Valdez, 2003, "Tail Conditional Expectations for Elliptical Distributions", *North American Actuarial Journal*, 7, pp. 55–71.

Larsen, R., D. Vedenov and D. Leatham, 2009, "Entreprise-Level Risk Assessment of Geographically Diversified Commercial Farms: A Copula Approach", Southern Agricultural Economics Association Annual Meeting, Atlanta, Jan 31–Feb 3.

Liang, N. and S. A. Rhoades, 1988, "Geographic Diversification and Risk in Banking", *Journal of Economics and Business*, 40, pp. 271–84.

Markowitz, H. M., 1952, "Portfolio Selection", *The Journal of Finance*, 7(1), pp. 77–91.

Markowitz, H. M., 1959, *Portfolio Selection – Efficient Diversification of Investments*. Second edn., 1991 (Oxford: Blackwell).

Markowitz, H. M., 1987, *Mean-Variance Analysis in Portfolio Choice and Capital Markets* (Oxford: Blackwell).

Markowitz, H. M., 1994, "The General Mean-Variance Portfolio Selection Problem", in S. D. Howison, F. P. Kelly and P. Wilmott (eds), *Mathematical Models in Finance*. Philosophical Transactions of the Royal Society of London, Series A, 347, pp. 543–49.

Mehta, N., J. Wu, A. Molisch and J. Zhang, 2007, "Approximating a Sum of Random Variables with a Lognormal", *IEEE Transactions on Wireless Communications*, 6(7), pp. 2,690–99.

Rose, J. T. and J. D. Wolken, 1990, "Geographic Diversification and Risk in Banking, Market Share Changes, and Viability of Small Independent Banks", *Journal of Financial Services Research*, 4, pp. 5–20.

Schwartz, S. and Y. Yeh, 1982, "On the Distribution Function and Moments of Power Sums with Lognormal Components", *Bell Systems Technical Journal*, 61, pp. 1,441–62.

Valdez, E. and J. Dhaene, 2004, "Convex Order Bounds for Sums of Dependent Log-Elliptical Random Variables", 7th International Congress of Insurance: Mathematics and Economics, Lyon.

Valdez, E. A., J. Dhaene, M. Maj and S. Vanduffel, 2009, "Bounds and Approximations for Sums of Dependent Log-Elliptical Random Variables", *Insurance: Mathematics and Economics*, 44(3), pp. 385–397.

Vanduffel, S., T. Hoedemakers and J. Dhaene, 2005, "Comparing Approximations for Sums of Non-Independent Lognormal Random Variables", *North American Actuarial Journal*, 9(4), pp. 71–82.

Vanduffel, S., X. Chen, J. Dhaene, M. J. Goovaerts, L. Henrard and R. Kaas, 2008, "Optimal Approximations for Risk Measures of Sums of Lognormals Based on Conditional Expectations", *Journal of Computational and Applied Mathematics*, 221(1), pp. 202–18.

13

On the Non-Life Solvency II Model

Werner Hürlimann

FRSGlobal Switzerland

This chapter fulfils a twofold modelling and statistical purpose. On the modelling side it offers a simple actuarial rationale for the economic capital formula proposed in QIS3 (2007). On the statistical side it improves on the methodology in QIS3 (2007) by defining company specific estimators for all quantities of interest including premium risk and reserve risk volatilities as well as correlation coefficients at the granularity level of lines of business. A more detailed account of the content follows.

The next section develops the non-life Solvency II economic capital formula, applying both the value-at-risk (VaR) and conditional value-at-risk (CVaR) risk measures under a lognormal distribution of the portfolio's combined ratio, which is defined as the ratio of incurred claims' inclusive "run-off" to the premium and reserve volume. We determine confidence levels under which both methods yield approximately identical practical results. Moreover, we point out that economic capital modelling should neither be restricted to a lognormal distribution assumption nor to the VaR and CVaR risk measures, and refer to the actuarial literature for various extensions on this. In the subsequent section the portfolio's combined ratio is decomposed in a weighted sum of the premium risk ratio and the reserve risk ratio as suggested in QIS3 (2007). Based on the basic portfolio risk ratio model summarised in the Appendix, we propose simple weighted estimators for all volatilities and correlation coefficients of interest. Finally, the section "Numerical illustration" illustrates the use of the proposed estimators.

THE NON-LIFE ECONOMIC CAPITAL FORMULA

Suppose that an insurance risk portfolio over a fixed time period, say over a one-year time period $[0, 1]$ between the times $t = 0$ and $t = 1$, is described by the following quantities:

P: the (net) risk premium of the portfolio for the time period; and
S: the random aggregate claims of the portfolio over the time period.

While the risk premium is supposed to be known at the beginning of the period, the random aggregate claims are not. The random loss of the portfolio at the beginning of the time period is described by the difference between the aggregate claims and the risk premium and defined by the random variable

$$L = S - P \qquad (13.1)$$

In non-life insurance the aggregate claims over the time period are taken exclusive of the run-off and include the claims Y paid out during the time period and the change in claims reserves $\Delta R = R_1 - R_0$, where R_t denotes the claims reserves at time t, which consists of the total reserves for outstanding claims or reported but not settled claims and the reserves for incurred but not reported claims. Therefore, one has the equality $S = Y + \Delta R$. At time $t = 0$ the claims reserve R_0 is known while R_1 is unknown. The volume $V = P + R_0$ of the portfolio, which is defined as the sum of the risk premium and the claims reserves at the beginning of the period, is known at time $t = 0$. Consider the ratio of the random loss to the volume, which can be written as

$$\frac{L}{V} = \frac{Y + R_1 - (P + R_0)}{P + R_0} = X - 1, \quad X = \frac{Y + R_1}{P + R_0} \qquad (13.2)$$

where X represents a combined ratio of the portfolio (ratio of incurred claims' inclusive run-off to the premium and reserve volume). By the actuarial equivalence principle or fair value principle, the random loss vanishes in the average, that is $E[L] = 0$. This implies that the expected target of the combined ratio is one or $E[X] = 1$. The Solvency II model assumes that the random combined ratio is lognormally distributed, say with parameters μ_X and σ_X (see QIS3 (2007, I.3.236, p. 81)). The portfolio volatility parameter $\sigma = \sqrt{\mathrm{Var}[X]}$ is defined to be the standard deviation of the combined ratio of the portfolio. By Equation 13.2 it identifies with the standard deviation of the ratio of the random loss to the volume, that is, alternatively, we have

$$\sigma^2 = \mathrm{Var}\left[\frac{L}{V}\right] \tag{13.3}$$

Since X is lognormally distributed with mean one, we have the equalities

$$E[X] = e^{\mu_X + \frac{1}{2}\sigma_X^2} = 1, \quad \sigma^2 = \mathrm{Var}[X] = e^{\sigma_X^2} - 1 \tag{13.4}$$

which imply the relationships

$$\mu_X = -\tfrac{1}{2}\sigma_X^2, \quad \sigma_X^2 = \ln(1 + \sigma^2) \tag{13.5}$$

The economic capital of the insurance risk portfolio to the confidence level α is supposed to depend only on the random loss and is denoted by $EC_\alpha[L]$. In the standard Solvency II approach, the economic capital is defined to be the VaR of the random loss taken at the confidence level $\alpha = 99.5\%$, that is $EC_\alpha[L] = VaR_\alpha[L]$. Using Equation 13.2, the lognormal assumption on X and Equation 13.5 the non-life economic capital formula is obtained (see QIS3 (2007, I.3.235, p. 81)) as follows

$$EC_\alpha[L] = VaR_\alpha[L] = VaR_\alpha\left[\frac{L}{V}\right] \cdot V = (VaR_\alpha[X] - 1) \cdot V$$
$$= \left(\exp\left\{\sigma_X \Phi^{-1}(\alpha) - \tfrac{1}{2}\sigma_X^2\right\} - 1\right) \cdot V = \rho_\alpha(\sigma) \cdot V \tag{13.6}$$

with the volatility-dependent function

$$\rho_\alpha(\sigma) = \frac{\exp\left\{\Phi^{-1}(\alpha) \cdot \sqrt{\ln(1 + \sigma^2)}\right\}}{\sqrt{1 + \sigma^2}} - 1 \tag{13.7}$$

where $\Phi^{-1}(\alpha)$ denotes the α-quantile of the standard normal distribution $\Phi(x)$. Alternatively, and as first suggested in the CEIOPS consultation paper CP20 (2006, 5.309, p. 137), the economic capital can instead be defined as the tail value-at-risk (TVaR) or CVaR of the random loss taken at the confidence level $\alpha = 99\%$. With this choice of risk measure, the following economic capital formula is obtained

$$EC_\alpha[L] = CVaR_\alpha[L] = CVaR_\alpha\left[\frac{L}{V}\right] \cdot V = (CVaR_\alpha[X] - 1) \cdot V$$

$$= \left(VaR_\alpha[X] + \frac{1}{1-\alpha}E[(X - VaR_\alpha[X])_+] - 1\right) \cdot V = \rho_\alpha(\sigma) \cdot V$$

(13.8)

with the volatility-dependent function

$$\rho_\alpha(\sigma) = \frac{\alpha - \Phi\left(\Phi^{-1}(\alpha) - \sqrt{\ln(1 + \sigma^2)}\right)}{1 - \alpha}$$

(13.9)

which is obtained by noting that for a lognormal distribution with the parameters from Equation 13.5 we have

$$E[(X - VaR_\alpha[X])_+]$$

$$= e^{\mu_X + \frac{1}{2}\sigma_X^2} \cdot \Phi\left(\frac{\mu_X - \ln(VaR_\alpha[X])}{\sigma_X} + \sigma_X\right)$$

$$- VaR_\alpha[X] \cdot \Phi\left(\frac{\mu_X - \ln(VaR_\alpha[X])}{\sigma_X}\right)$$

$$= \Phi(\sigma_X - \Phi^{-1}(\alpha)) - \Phi(-\Phi^{-1}(\alpha)) \cdot VaR_\alpha[X]$$

$$= 1 - \Phi\left(\Phi^{-1}(\alpha) - \sqrt{\ln(1 + \sigma^2)}\right) - (1 - \alpha) \cdot VaR_\alpha[X]$$

It is interesting to compare numerically the formulas in Equations 13.7 and 13.9. The QIS3 VaR proposal Equation 13.7 with $\alpha = 99.5\%$ is an implementation of the rule of thumb $\rho_\alpha(\sigma) \approx 3 \cdot \sigma$ (for another explanation see Hürlimann (2004, Example 7.1, p. 95)). For $\alpha = 99\%$ the CVaR method requires only slightly more economic capital. Table 13.1 provides a numerical comparison of the quotients $\rho_\alpha(\sigma)/\sigma$ and determines confidence levels under which both methods coincide approximately up to three decimal places.

At this stage, it must be pointed out that from an actuarial point of view, economic capital modelling should neither be restricted to a lognormal distribution assumption nor to the VaR and CVaR risk measures. In general, it is possible to consider gamma and elliptical-type distributions (eg, Hürlimann 2001; Landsman and Valdez 2003; Valdez 2005; Furman and Landsman 2005, 2007), compound Poisson distributions (eg, Hürlimann 2003) or even distribution-free methods (eg, Hürlimann 2002). On the other hand, different

Table 13.1 Comparison of the standard non-life Solvency II VaR and CVaR formulas

	VaR method				CVaR method		
Confidence level	0.99	0.995	0.99624	Confidence level	0.98675	0.99	0.995
Percentile	2.326	2.576	2.673	Percentile	2.219	2.326	2.576
Volatility (%)				Volatility (%)			
12.0	2.594	2.925	3.056	12.0	2.923	3.054	3.366
12.5	2.605	2.940	3.073	12.5	2.939	3.071	3.387
13.0	2.617	2.955	3.090	13.0	2.954	3.088	3.408
13.5	2.628	2.970	3.106	13.5	2.969	3.105	3.429
14.0	2.639	2.985	3.123	14.0	2.985	3.122	3.450
14.5	**2.650**	**3.000**	**3.139**	**14.5**	**3.000**	**3.139**	**3.471**
15.0	2.661	3.015	3.156	15.0	3.015	3.156	3.492
15.5	2.672	3.030	3.173	15.5	3.031	3.173	3.514
16.0	2.684	3.045	3.190	16.0	3.046	3.190	3.535
16.5	2.695	3.060	3.206	16.5	3.062	3.207	3.556
17.0	2.706	3.075	3.223	17.0	3.077	3.224	3.578

economic capital models can be designed and other risk measures can be considered (eg, Dhaene *et al* 2003; Hürlimann 2004). This opens the way for a wide variety of flexible internal models for Solvency II.

ESTIMATION OF THE VOLATILITY PARAMETER

To estimate the volatility parameter, historical data on the risk portfolio and insurance market information can be used. In contrast to the previous section, the time horizon for estimation is not restricted to the current one-year time horizon for economic capital evaluation, but it may include past observation periods or even simulated future periods. Let V_p denote the risk premium volume, V_r the claims reserve volume, and $V = V_p + V_r$ the portfolio volume of the current risk portfolio at time $t = 0$. The combined ratio Equation 13.2 can be rewritten as

$$ X = \left(\frac{V_p}{V} \right) \cdot X^p + \left(\frac{V_r}{V} \right) \cdot X^r \qquad (13.10) $$

where $X^p = Y/P$ represent the random ratio of paid claims to risk premiums and $X^r = R_1/R_0$ the random ratio of the end of year claims reserves to the beginning of year claims reserves, which in the Solvency II terminology are called the premium risk ratio and the reserve risk ratio, respectively (QIS3 (2007, I.3.226–I.3.229, p. 79)). The correlation coefficient between the premium risk and the reserve risk, denoted by ρ_{pr}, is defined by the covariance relationship

$$ \mathrm{Cov}[X^p, X^r] = \rho_{pr} \sigma_p \sigma_r, \quad \sigma_p = \sqrt{\mathrm{Var}[X^p]}, \quad \sigma_r = \sqrt{\mathrm{Var}[X^r]} \qquad (13.11) $$

Using Equations 13.10 and 13.11 one obtains the relationship

$$ \sigma = \frac{1}{V} \sqrt{(\sigma_p V_p)^2 + (\sigma_r V_r)^2 + 2 \rho_{pr} \sigma_p \sigma_r V_p V_r} \qquad (13.12) $$

According to Equation 13.12 the portfolio volatility depends on the premium volatility σ_p, the reserve volatility σ_r, the correlation coefficient ρ_{pr} and appropriate volumes. To estimate volatilities of random ratios, we apply the general method presented in the Appendix. For this, one has to modify the definition of the random ratios X, X^p, X^r by identifying them as (historical) weighted averages of variable annual random ratios X_k, X_k^p, X_k^r, $k = 1, \ldots, m$, and suppose that the following portfolio data over $m > 1$ (past) years is available:

P_k: (net) risk premiums for the time periods $(k - 1, k]$, $k = 1, \ldots, m$;

Y_k: paid claims (from all origin periods) during the time periods $(k - 1, k]$, $k = 1, \ldots, m$;

R_k: claims reserve (from all origin periods) at the end of the kth year, $k = 0, \ldots, m$; and

$\Delta R_k = R_k - R_{k-1}$: change in claims reserves during the time periods $(k - 1, k]$, $k = 1, \ldots, m$.

A portfolio-based estimator of the premium volatility is

$$\hat{\sigma}_p = \sqrt{\sum_{k=1}^{m} \frac{P_k}{P^\bullet} \cdot \left(\frac{Y_k}{P_k} - \hat{\mu}_p \right)^2}, \quad \hat{\mu}_p = \frac{\sum_{k=1}^{m} Y_k}{P^\bullet}, \quad P^\bullet = \sum_{k=1}^{m} P_k$$

$$(13.13)$$

A similar portfolio-based estimator of the reserve volatility is

$$\hat{\sigma}_r = \sqrt{\sum_{k=1}^{m} \frac{R_{k-1}}{R^\bullet} \cdot \left(\frac{\Delta R_k}{R_{k-1}} - \hat{\mu}_r \right)^2},$$

$$(13.14)$$

$$\hat{\mu}_r = \frac{\sum_{k=1}^{m} \Delta R_k}{R^\bullet} = \frac{R_m - R_0}{R^\bullet}, \quad R^\bullet = \sum_{k=1}^{m} R_{k-1}$$

which is obtained by noting that

$$\frac{\Delta R_k}{R_{k-1}} - \frac{R_m - R_0}{R^\bullet} = \frac{R_k}{R_{k-1}} - \frac{\sum_{j=1}^{m} R_j}{R^\bullet}$$

Applying the same technique, the following estimator of the portfolio volatility is obtained

$$\hat{\sigma} = \sqrt{\sum_{k=1}^{m} \frac{P_k + R_{k-1}}{P^\bullet + R^\bullet} \cdot \left(\frac{Y_k + R_k}{P_k + R_{k-1}} - \hat{\mu} \right)^2}$$

$$(13.15)$$

$$\hat{\mu} = \frac{\sum_{k=1}^{m} Y_k + \sum_{k=1}^{m} R_k}{P^\bullet + R^\bullet}, \quad P^\bullet + R^\bullet = \sum_{k=1}^{m} P_k + \sum_{k=1}^{m} R_{k-1}$$

Using these estimators, Equation 13.12 yields the following compatible estimator of the correlation coefficient between the premium risk and the reserve risk

$$\hat{\rho}_{pr} = \frac{1}{2} \cdot \frac{(\hat{\sigma}V)^2 - (\hat{\sigma}_p V_p)^2 - (\hat{\sigma}_r V_r)^2}{(\hat{\sigma}_p V_p) \cdot (\hat{\sigma}_r V_r)} \qquad (13.16)$$

In the current framework of the standard approach to Solvency II, the estimation of portfolio volatility should be done under the more refined granularity level of lines of business. Suppose that the portfolio consists of n lines of business (LoB), for which the following historical data over the $m > 1$ (past) years is available:

P_i^j: (net) risk premiums of LoB $i \in \{1, \ldots, n\}$ in year $j \in \{1, \ldots, m\}$;

Y_i^j: paid claims of LoB $i \in \{1, \ldots, n\}$ during year $[j-1, j]$, $j \in \{1, \ldots, m\}$;

R_i^j: claims reserve of LoB $i \in \{1, \ldots, n\}$ at beginning and end of year $j \in \{0, \ldots, m\}$; and

$\Delta R_i^j = R_i^j - R_i^{j-1}$: change in claims reserves of LoB $i \in \{1, \ldots, n\}$ during year $[j-1, j]$.

Again, let us apply the general method from the Appendix. For each LoB $i \in \{1, \ldots, n\}$, let $V_{p,i}$ denote its LoB risk premium volume, $V_{r,i}$ its LoB claims reserve volume, and $V_i = V_{p,i} + V_{r,i}$ its LoB volume at time $t = 0$. Then $V_p = \sum_{i=1}^{n} V_{p,i}$ represents the risk premium volume, $V_r = \sum_{i=1}^{n} V_{r,i}$ the claims reserve volume and $V = \sum_{i=1}^{n} V_i$ the portfolio volume of the current risk portfolio at time $t = 0$. Consider the premium risk ratio X_i^p and the reserve risk ratio X_i^r of the LoBs $i \in \{1, \ldots, n\}$. Let further $w_i^p = V_{p,i}/V_p$ be the risk premium weight and $w_i^r = V_{r,i}/V_r$ be the claims reserve weight associated with the LoB $i \in \{1, \ldots, n\}$, and let $w^p = (w_1^p, \ldots, w_n^p)$ and $w^r = (w_1^r, \ldots, w_n^r)$ be the corresponding weight vectors. The overall premium risk ratio and reserve risk ratio of the portfolio are defined by the linear combinations

$$X^p = \sum_{i=1}^{n} w_i^p X_i^p, \quad X^r = \sum_{i=1}^{n} w_i^r X_i^r \qquad (13.17)$$

The parameters of the premium risk ratio are described by the mean vector $v^p = (\mu_1^p, \ldots, \mu_n^p)$, where $\mu_i^p = E[X_i^p]$ is the mean premium risk ratio of the ith LoB, and the covariance matrix $\Sigma^p = (\rho_{ij}^p \sigma_i^p \sigma_j^p)$, where $\sigma_i^p = \sqrt{\text{Var}[X_i^p]}$ is the standard deviation of the premium risk ratio of the ith LoB and ρ_{ij}^p is the correlation coefficient between the premium risk ratios X_i^p and X_j^p, $i, j = 1, \ldots, n$. Similarly, the parameters of the reserve risk ratio are described by the mean vector $v^r = (\mu_1^r, \ldots, \mu_n^r)$, where $\mu_i^r = E[X_i^r]$ is the mean reserve risk ratio of the ith LoB, and the covariance matrix $\Sigma^r = (\rho_{ij}^r \sigma_i^r \sigma_j^r)$, where $\sigma_i^r = \sqrt{\mathrm{Var}[X_i^r]}$ is the standard deviation of the ith LoB reserve risk ratio and ρ_{ij}^r is the correlation coefficient between the reserve risk ratios X_i^r and X_j^r, $i, j = 1, \ldots, n$. According to Equation 13.17, estimators of the mean and variance of the portfolio premium risk ratio and reserve risk ratio necessarily satisfy relationships

$$\hat{\mu}_p = \hat{v}^p \cdot w^{p, T}, \quad \hat{\mu}_r = \hat{v}^r \cdot w^{r, T}$$
$$\hat{\sigma}_p^2 = w^r \cdot \hat{\Sigma}^p \cdot w^{r, T}, \quad \hat{\sigma}_r^2 = w^r \cdot \hat{\Sigma}^r \cdot w^{r, T} \tag{13.18}$$

where $\hat{v}^p$, $\hat{v}^r$, $\hat{\Sigma}^p$, $\hat{\Sigma}^r$ are estimators of the corresponding mean vectors and covariance matrices, which are obtained as follows. Let us begin with the premium risk ratio. Consider the premium risk ratios $X_i^{p, j} = Y_i^j / P_i^j$ with the weights $w_i^{p, j} = P_i^j / P_i^\bullet$, $P_i^\bullet = \sum_{j=1}^m P_i^j$, and the reserve risk ratios $X_i^{r, j} = R_i^j / R_i^{j-1}$ with the weights $w_i^{r, j} = R_i^{j-1} / R_i^\bullet$, $R_i^\bullet = \sum_{j=1}^m R_i^{j-1}$, $i = 1, \ldots, n$, $j = 1, \ldots, m$. Then one has the following mean and standard deviation estimators

$$\hat{\mu}_i^p = \sum_{j=1}^m w_i^{p, j} X_i^{p, j}, \quad \hat{\sigma}_i^p = \sqrt{\sum_{j=1}^m w_i^{p, j} \cdot (X_i^{p, j} - \hat{\mu}_i^p)^2}$$
$$\hat{\mu}_i^r = \sum_{j=1}^m w_i^{r, j} X_i^{r, j}, \quad \hat{\sigma}_i^r = \sqrt{\sum_{j=1}^m w_i^{r, j} \cdot (X_i^{r, j} - \hat{\mu}_i^r)^2} \tag{13.19}$$

To estimate the correlation coefficients ρ_{ij}^p, $i \neq j$ between a LoB's premium risk ratios, consider the subportfolios with premium risk ratios X_i^p and X_j^p, where the overall premium risk ratios are determined by the weighted mean

$$X_{ij}^p = \frac{P_i^\bullet}{P_i^\bullet + P_j^\bullet} X_i^p + \frac{P_j^\bullet}{P_i^\bullet + P_j^\bullet} X_j^p, \quad i \neq j, \, i, j = 1, \ldots, n \tag{13.20}$$

The historical data consists of premium risk ratios $X_{ij}^{p,k}$ and weights $w_{ij}^{p,k}$ defined by

$$X_{ij}^{p,k} = \frac{P_i^k}{P_i^k + P_j^k} X_i^{p,k} + \frac{P_j^k}{P_i^k + P_j^k} X_j^{p,k}$$

$$w_{ij}^{p,k} = \frac{P_i^k + P_j^k}{P_i^\bullet + P_j^\bullet}, \quad i \neq j, \ i,j = 1, \ldots, n, \ k = 1, \ldots, m$$

(13.21)

Interpreting the $X_{ij}^{p,k}$ as outcomes of X_{ij}^p with probability function $\Pr(X_{ij}^p = X_{ij}^{p,k}) = w_{ij}^{p,k}$, one obtains the following mean and standard deviation estimators of X_{ij}^p

$$\hat{\mu}_{ij}^p = \sum_{k=1}^m w_{ij}^{p,k} X_{ij}^{p,k} = \frac{P_i^\bullet}{P_i^\bullet + P_j^\bullet} \hat{\mu}_i^p + \frac{P_j^\bullet}{P_i^\bullet + P_j^\bullet} \hat{\mu}_j^p$$

$$\hat{\sigma}_{ij}^p = \sqrt{\sum_{k=1}^m w_{ij}^{p,k} (X_{ij}^{p,k} - \hat{\mu}_{ij}^p)^2}$$

(13.22)

A compatible estimator of the correlation coefficient ρ_{ij}^p is defined through the relationship

$$\hat{\rho}_{ij}^p = \frac{1}{2} \cdot \frac{[(P_i^\bullet + P_j^\bullet)\hat{\sigma}_{ij}^p]^2 - [P_i^\bullet \hat{\sigma}_i^p]^2 - [P_j^\bullet \hat{\sigma}_j^p]^2}{(P_i^\bullet \hat{\sigma}_i^p)(P_j^\bullet \hat{\sigma}_j^p)}$$

(13.23)

Similarly, to estimate the correlation coefficients ρ_{ij}^r, $i \neq j$ between a LoB's reserve risk ratios, consider the subportfolios with reserve risk ratios X_i^r and X_j^r, where the overall reserve risk ratios are determined by the weighted mean

$$X_{ij}^r = \frac{R_i^\bullet}{R_i^\bullet + R_j^\bullet} X_i^r + \frac{R_j^\bullet}{R_i^\bullet + R_j^\bullet} X_j^r, \quad i \neq j, \ i,j = 1, \ldots, n \quad (13.24)$$

The historical data consists of reserve risk ratios $X_{ij}^{r,k}$ and weights $w_{ij}^{r,k}$ defined by

$$X_{ij}^{r,k} = \frac{R_i^{k-1}}{R_i^{k-1} + R_j^{k-1}} X_i^{r,k} + \frac{R_j^{k-1}}{R_i^{k-1} + R_j^{k-1}} X_j^{r,k}$$

$$w_{ij}^{r,k} = \frac{R_i^{k-1} + R_j^{k-1}}{R_i^\bullet + R_j^\bullet}, \quad i \neq j, \ i,j = 1, \ldots, n, \ k = 1, \ldots, m$$

(13.25)

Interpreting the $X_{ij}^{r,k}$ as outcomes of X_{ij}^r with probability function $\Pr(X_{ij}^r = X_{ij}^{r,k}) = w_{ij}^{r,k}$, the following mean and standard deviation estimators of X_{ij}^r are obtained

$$\hat{\mu}_{ij}^r = \sum_{k=1}^{m} w_{ij}^{r,k} X_{ij}^{r,k} = \frac{R_i^{\bullet}}{R_i^{\bullet} + R_j^{\bullet}} \hat{\mu}_i^r + \frac{R_j^{\bullet}}{R_i^{\bullet} + R_j^{\bullet}} \hat{\mu}_j^r$$

$$\hat{\sigma}_{ij}^r = \sqrt{\sum_{k=1}^{m} w_{ij}^{r,k} (X_{ij}^{r,k} - \hat{\mu}_{ij}^r)^2}$$

(13.26)

A compatible estimator of the correlation coefficient ρ_{ij}^r is defined through the relationship

$$\hat{\rho}_{ij}^r = \frac{1}{2} \cdot \frac{\left[(R_i^{\bullet} + R_j^{\bullet}) \hat{\sigma}_{ij}^r \right]^2 - \left[R_i^{\bullet} \hat{\sigma}_i^r \right]^2 - \left[R_j^{\bullet} \hat{\sigma}_j^r \right]^2}{(R_i^{\bullet} \hat{\sigma}_i^r)(R_j^{\bullet} \hat{\sigma}_j^r)}$$

(13.27)

On the other hand, to estimate the portfolio's volatility a similar technique is applied. Let X_i be the combined ratio of the LoB $i \in \{1, \ldots, n\}$ with weight $w_i = V_i/V$. Then the combined ratio of the portfolio is defined by the linear combination of combined ratios

$$X = \sum_{i=1}^{n} w_i X_i$$

(13.28)

The parameters of the combined ratio are described by the mean vector $v = (\mu_1, \ldots, \mu_n)$, where $\mu_i = E[X_i]$ is the mean combined ratio of the ith LoB, and the covariance matrix $\Sigma = (\rho_{ij}\sigma_i\sigma_j)$, where $\sigma_i = \sqrt{\text{Var}[X_i]}$ is the standard deviation of the combined ratio of the ith LoB and ρ_{ij} is the correlation coefficient between the combined ratios X_i and X_j, $i, j = 1, \ldots, n$. According to Equation 13.28, estimators of the mean and variance of the portfolio combined ratio necessarily satisfy the relationships

$$\hat{\mu} = \hat{v} \cdot w^T, \quad \hat{\sigma}^2 = w \cdot \hat{\Sigma} \cdot w^T$$

(13.29)

where $\hat{v}, \hat{\Sigma}$ are estimators of the corresponding mean vectors and covariance matrices, which are obtained as follows. Consider the combined ratios $X_i^j = (Y_i^j + R_i^j)/(P_i^j + R_i^{j-1})$ with the weights $w_i^j = (P_i^j + R_i^{j-1})/(P_i^{\bullet} + R_i^{\bullet})$, $i = 1, \ldots, n$, $j = 1, \ldots, m$. Then one has the following mean and standard deviation estimators

$$\hat{\mu}_i = \sum_{j=1}^{m} w_i^j X_i^j, \quad \hat{\sigma}_i = \sqrt{\sum_{j=1}^{m} w_i^j \cdot (X_i^j - \hat{\mu}_i)^2}$$

(13.30)

To estimate the correlation coefficients ρ_{ij}, $i \neq j$ between the LoB combined ratios, consider the subportfolios with combined ratios X_i and X_j, whose overall combined ratios are determined by the weighted mean

$$X_{ij} = \frac{P_i^\bullet + R_i^\bullet}{P_i^\bullet + R_i^\bullet + P_j^\bullet + R_j^\bullet} X_i + \frac{P_j^\bullet + R_j^\bullet}{P_i^\bullet + R_i^\bullet + P_j^\bullet + R_j^\bullet} X_j,$$

$$i \neq j, \ i, j = 1, \ldots, n \quad (13.31)$$

The historical data consists of combined ratios X_{ij}^k and weights w_{ij}^k defined by

$$X_{ij}^k = \frac{P_i^k + R_i^{k-1}}{P_i^k + R_i^{k-1} + P_j^k + R_j^{k-1}} X_i^k + \frac{P_j^k + R_j^{k-1}}{P_i^k + R_i^{k-1} + P_j^k + R_j^{k-1}} X_j^k$$

$$w_{ij}^k = \frac{P_i^k + R_i^{k-1} + P_j^k + R_j^{k-1}}{P_i^\bullet + R_i^\bullet + P_j^\bullet + R_j^\bullet}, \quad i \neq j, \ i, j = 1, \ldots, n, \ k = 1, \ldots, m$$

Interpreting the X_{ij}^k as outcomes of X_{ij} with probability function $\Pr(X_{ij} = X_{ij}^k) = w_{ij}^k$, the mean and standard deviation estimators of X_{ij} is obtained

$$\hat{\mu}_{ij} = \sum_{k=1}^{m} w_{ij}^k X_{ij}^k = \frac{P_i^\bullet + R_i^\bullet}{P_i^\bullet + R_i^\bullet + P_j^\bullet + R_j^\bullet} \hat{\mu}_i + \frac{P_j^\bullet + R_j^\bullet}{P_i^\bullet + R_i^\bullet + P_j^\bullet + R_j^\bullet} \hat{\mu}_j$$

$$\hat{\sigma}_{ij} = \sqrt{\sum_{k=1}^{m} w_{ij}^k (X_{ij}^k - \hat{\mu}_{ij})^2}$$

$$(13.32)$$

A compatible estimator of the correlation coefficient ρ_{ij} is defined through the relationship

$$\hat{\rho}_{ij} = \frac{1}{2} \cdot \frac{[(P_i^\bullet + R_i^\bullet + P_j^\bullet + R_j^\bullet)\hat{\sigma}_{ij}]^2 - [(P_i^\bullet + R_i^\bullet)\hat{\sigma}_i]^2 - [(P_j^\bullet + R_j^\bullet)\hat{\sigma}_j]^2}{[(P_i^\bullet + R_i^\bullet)\hat{\sigma}_i][(P_j^\bullet + R_j^\bullet)\hat{\sigma}_j]}$$

$$(13.33)$$

Up to the correlation coefficient ρ_{pr} between the premium risk ratio and the reserve risk ratio, all parameters have now been estimated. A compatible estimator of ρ_{pr} is of the form in Equation 13.16 with the volatilities defined in Equations 13.18 and 13.29.

In fact, to estimate the economic capital formula, Equations 13.7 or 13.9, it suffices to determine Equation 13.15 providing overall portfolio information is used, or Equations 13.29, 13.30 and 13.33 if detailed information on the LoB is available. However, bear in mind that a desirable goal of any solvency model is also to measure all possible kinds of diversification effects, for example diversification between the premium risk and the reserve risk and diversification across the LoB (eg, CRO Forum 2005). To determine these diversification effects precisely, it is clear that all of the remaining estimators must be used.

Finally, it is important to note that the standard approach to Solvency II proposes quite different estimators for the above quantities. For the premium risk volatilities it uses a credibility mix between company-specific estimators and market-wide estimators; for the reserve risk volatilities it prescribes only line-of-business-dependent insurance-market-based fixed numerical values; and all required correlation coefficients are fixed numerical values (see QIS3 (2007, I.3.242, I.3.246, I.3.249–250)). The method proposes company-specific estimators for both the premium risk and the reserve risk as well as for the correlation coefficient between these risk factors at the granularity level of LoBs.

NUMERICAL ILLUSTRATION

We illustrate the use of the estimation method presented in the previous section to calculate the economic capital according to Solvency II, including various diversification effects. Table 13.2 lists the available information for a portfolio with $m = 5$ lines of business over $n = 5$ years. A short look at the statistics shows that LoB 1 and LoB 3 are relatively small and stable business segments, LoB 2 constantly loses its risk premium volume but still has important claims reserves, LoB 4 and LoB 5 contribute strongly to the overall slight growth of the portfolio's volume.

The economic capital is calculated according to the VaR method in Equation 13.7 at the confidence level $\alpha = 99.5\%$ as reported in Table 13.3. At the portfolio level the formulas in Equations 13.13–13.15 are applied and at the LoB level Equation 13.19 is used. The correlation coefficients between the premium risk and the reserve risk are evaluated with a formula of the type in Equation 13.16.

The economic capital of the portfolio's combined risk is 33,731 and compares with the sum of the stand-alone LoB economic capitals for the premium risk and the reserve risk of the total amount

Table 13.2 Risk premiums, paid claims and claims reserves for a non-life portfolio

Development year	0	1	2	3	4	5	Total years
Risk premiums/LoB							
1		1,000	800	1,200	1,000	1,000	5,000
2		8,000	7,000	6,000	5,000	4,000	30,000
3		2,100	1,700	2,700	2,100	2,400	11,000
4		6,000	6,000	7,500	8,000	8,500	36,000
5		1,000	2,000	3,500	5,000	6,500	18,000
Total LoB		18,100	17,500	20,900	21,100	22,400	100,000
Paid claims/LoB							
1		350	200	400	300	400	1,650
2		3,500	3,500	3,000	2,500	2,000	14,500
3		800	650	900	600	800	3,750
4		2,250	1,800	2,200	2,000	2,500	10,750
5		350	500	500	750	2,250	4,350
Total LoB		7,250	6,650	7,000	6,150	7,950	35,000
Claims reserve/LoB							
1	900	1,100	1,300	1,300	1,200	1,000	5,800
2	8,200	8,000	10,000	8,000	6,000	7,000	40,200
3	1,500	1,900	3,200	2,600	2,600	2,500	11,800
4	4,200	4,800	5,500	5,500	6,700	6,900	26,700
5	600	1,100	1,300	2,500	3,500	4,500	9,000
Total LoB	15,400	16,900	21,300	19,900	20,000	21,900	93,500
Δ Claims reserve/LoB							
1		200	200	0	−100	−200	100
2		−200	2,000	−2,000	−2,000	1,000	−1,200
3		400	1,300	−600	0	−100	1,000
4		600	700	0	1,200	200	2,700
5		500	200	1,200	1,000	1,000	3,900
Total LoB		1,500	4,400	−1,400	100	1,900	6,500

of 65,350. The total diversification effect of amount 31,619 is due to a diversification effect across the lines of business of amount 25,824 and a portfolio diversification effect between the premium risk and the reserve risk of amount 5,795. The correlation between the premium risk and the reserve risk is positive at the portfolio level and almost negative at the LoB level.

On the other hand it is also possible to evaluate the economic capital at the portfolio level using the formulas in Equations 13.18 and 13.29. In this situation it is necessary to calculate the correlation coefficients between the LoB for the premium risk, the reserve

Table 13.3 Economic capital and diversification effects using Equation 13.15 at the portfolio level

| Risk | Portfolio | Economic capital | | | | | | Diversification |
		LoB 1	LoB 2	LoB 3	LoB 4	LoB 5		LoB
Premium risk	10,021	646	2,201	1,010	3,756	4,818		2,410
Reserve risk	29,505	2,501	24,766	12,024	6,213	7,414		23,414
Combined risk	33,731	1,758	21,033	10,868	5,901	6,160		11,990
Diversification risks	5,795	1,389	5,934	2,166	4,069	6,072		13,834
		Correlation coefficient						
Premium risk versus reserve risk	0.415	−0.864	−0.691	0.207	−0.318	−0.405		

Table 13.4 Correlation matrices for the premium risk, the reserve risk and the combined risk

	Premium risk				
	1	2	3	4	5
1	1.000	−0.624	−0.107	0.289	0.579
2	−0.624	1.000	−0.434	0.084	0.243
3	−0.107	−0.434	1.000	0.912	0.818
4	0.289	0.084	0.912	1.000	0.730
5	0.579	0.243	0.818	0.730	1.000
	Reserve risk				
1	1.000	0.836	0.632	0.248	−0.650
2	0.836	1.000	0.633	−0.054	−0.545
3	0.632	0.633	1.000	0.490	−0.579
4	0.248	−0.054	0.490	1.000	−0.541
5	−0.650	−0.545	−0.579	−0.541	1.000
	Combined risk				
1	1.000	0.242	0.723	0.769	0.218
2	0.242	1.000	0.555	0.122	0.043
3	0.723	0.555	1.000	0.632	0.043
4	0.769	0.122	0.632	1.000	0.090
5	0.218	0.043	0.043	0.090	1.000

risk and the combined risk using the formulas in Equations 13.23, 13.27 and 13.33. Table 13.4 lists the obtained correlation matrices and Table 13.5 summarises the economic capital evaluation using this second estimation method. In Table 13.4 we observe positive correlation coefficients between the LoB for the combined risk and the mixed positive and negative correlation coefficients for the premium risk and the reserve risk.

The economic capitals of Tables 13.5 and 13.3 differ slightly: 9,330 compared with 10,021 for the premium risk, 29,553 compared with 29,505 for the reserve risk, and 31,371 compared with 33,731 for the combined risk. In this situation, the increased total diversification effect of amount 33,979 (compared with 31,619) is due to a diversification effect across the LoB of amount 26,467 (compared with 25,824) and a portfolio diversification effect between the premium risk and the reserve risk of amount 7,512 (compared with 5,795). The correlation between the premium risk and the reserve

Table 13.5 Economic capital and diversification effects using Equations 13.18 and 13.29

Risk	Portfolio	LoB 1	LoB 2	LoB 3	LoB 4	LoB 5	Diversification LoB
			Economic capital				Diversification
Premium risk	9,330	646	2,201	1,010	3,756	4,818	3,101
Reserve risk	29,553	2,501	24,766	12,024	6,213	7,414	23,366
Combined risk	31,371	1,758	21,033	10,868	5,901	6,160	14,349
Diversification risks	7,512	1,389	5,934	2,166	4,069	6,072	12,118
			Correlation coefficient				
Premium risk versus reserve risk	0.198	−0.864	−0.691	0.207	−0.318	−0.405	

risk is again positive but smaller, which explains the increased diversification.

APPENDIX: A BASIC PORTFOLIO RISK FACTOR RATIO MODEL

To evaluate the economic capital of portfolios of risks in practice, it is often judicious to express risk factors using random ratios. For example, insurance risk loss ratios are quotients from claims to risk premiums while financial risk loss ratios are just negative returns. In the general context of risk factors, it is possible to define the risk factor ratio of a portfolio as a weighted linear combination of the risk factor ratios of its components.

Consider a portfolio with random risk factors $S = (S_1, \ldots, S_n)$ and a deterministic vector of volumes $V = (V_1, \ldots, V_n)$ associated with these risk factors. The vector of the random risk factor ratios $X = (X_1, \ldots, X_n)$ is defined by $X_i = S_i/V_i$, $i = 1, \ldots, n$. Let $V = V_1 + \cdots + V_n$ be the total volume of the portfolio, and let $w = (w_1, \ldots, w_n)$ be the vector of portfolio weights with $w_i = V_i/V$ the weight associated with risk factor i, $i = 1, \ldots, n$. Then the overall risk factor ratio of the portfolio is defined by the linear combination

$$X = \sum_{i=1}^{n} w_i X_i \tag{13.A.1}$$

We assume the existence of the mean vector $v = (\mu_1, \ldots, \mu_n)$, where $\mu_i = E[X_i]$ is the mean, and the covariance matrix $\Sigma = (\rho_{ij}\sigma_i\sigma_j)$ such that $\sigma_i^2 = \mathrm{Var}[X_i]$ is the variance and ρ_{ij} is the correlation between the risk factor ratios X_i and X_j, $i, j = 1, \ldots, n$. Moreover, a joint multivariate distribution function $F_X(x_1, \ldots, x_n)$ with marginal distributions $F_i(x)$, $i = 1, \ldots, n$, has to be specified, which is compatible with the parameters v, Σ. In terms of the defined risk factor ratios, we are interested in the stand-alone (standard) risk factors $L_i = V_i \cdot (X_i - \mu_i)$, $i = 1, \ldots, n$, and in the portfolio (standard) risk factor $L = V \cdot (X - \mu)$. Using Equation 13.A.1 the mean and variance of the portfolio risk factor ratio are

$$\mu = v \cdot w^T, \quad \sigma^2 = w \cdot \Sigma \cdot w^T \tag{13.A.2}$$

For practical evaluation, there remains the modelling choice for the joint multivariate distribution function $F_X(x_1, \ldots, x_n)$, and the statistical estimation of the parameters v, Σ. Providing historical data is available, the latter task is solved as follows.

Let $S^j = (S^j_1, \ldots, S^j_n)$ and $P^j = (P^j_1, \ldots, P^j_n)$, $j = 1, \ldots, m$, represent the risk factors and volumes of the portfolio in m past periods. Consider the risk factor ratios $X^j_i = S^j_i / P^j_i$, and the weights $w^j_i = P^j_i / P^\bullet_i$, $P^\bullet_i = \sum^m_{j=1} P^j_i$, $i = 1, \ldots, n$, $j = 1, \ldots, m$. Interpreting the historical risk factor ratios X^j_i as outcomes of the ratio random variables X_i with probability function $\Pr(X_i = X^j_i) = w^j_i$, one obtains the mean and variance parameters

$$\mu_i = E[X_i] = \sum^m_{j=1} w^j_i X^j_i$$

$$\sigma^2_i = \mathrm{Var}[X_i] = \sum^m_{j=1} w^j_i \cdot (X^j_i - \mu_i)^2, \quad i = 1, \ldots, n \tag{13.A.3}$$

To estimate the correlation coefficients ρ_{ij}, $i \neq j$ between risk factors, consider the subportfolios with risk factor ratios X_i and X_j, where the overall risk factor ratios are determined by the weighted mean

$$X_{ij} = \frac{P^\bullet_i}{P^\bullet_i + P^\bullet_j} X_i + \frac{P^\bullet_j}{P^\bullet_i + P^\bullet_j} X_j, \quad i \neq j, \ i, j = 1, \ldots, n \tag{13.A.4}$$

The associated historical data consists of risk factor ratios X^k_{ij} and weights w^k_{ij} defined by

$$X^k_{ij} = \frac{P^k_i}{P^k_i + P^k_j} X^k_i + \frac{P^k_j}{P^k_i + P^k_j} X^k_j,$$

$$w^k_{ij} = \frac{P^k_i + P^k_j}{P^\bullet_i + P^\bullet_j}, \quad i \neq j, \ i, j = 1, \ldots, n, \ k = 1, \ldots, m \tag{13.A.5}$$

Interpreting the X^k_{ij} as outcomes of X_{ij} with probability function $\Pr(X_{ij} = X^k_{ij}) = w^k_{ij}$, one obtains the mean and variance parameters

$$\mu_{ij} = E[X_{ij}] = \sum^m_{k=1} w^k_{ij} X^k_{ij} = \frac{P^\bullet_i}{P^\bullet_i + P^\bullet_j} \mu_i + \frac{P^\bullet_j}{P^\bullet_i + P^\bullet_j} \mu_j \tag{13.A.6}$$

$$\sigma^2_{ij} = \mathrm{Var}[X_{ij}] = \sum^m_{k=1} w^k_{ij} (X^k_{ij} - \mu_{ij})^2 \tag{13.A.7}$$

Note that the formula in Equation 13.A.6 is compatible with the definitions in Equations 13.A.3 and 13.A.4. In order that Equation 13.A.7 is also compatible with Equations 13.A.3 and 13.A.4, the correlation coefficient ρ_{ij} must satisfy the relationship

$$\rho_{ij} = \frac{1}{2} \cdot \frac{[(P_i^\bullet + P_j^\bullet)\sigma_{ij}]^2 - [P_i^\bullet \sigma_i]^2 - [P_j^\bullet \sigma_j]^2}{(P_i^\bullet \sigma_i)(P_j^\bullet \sigma_j)} \quad (13.A.8)$$

and the probabilities $\Pr(X_{ij} = X_{ij}^k) = w_{ij}^k$ must be compatible with the probabilities $\Pr(X_i = X_i^k) = w_i^k$ and $\Pr(X_j = X_j^k) = w_j^k$. Using Equations 13.A.3 and 13.A.8 we see that the mean and the variance of the portfolio risk factor ratio are given by Equation 13.A.2.

Exhaustive conditions under which the estimator in Equation 13.A.8 defines a "true" correlation coefficient $\rho_{ij} \in [-1, 1]$ are not known to the author. Simulation examples show that $\rho_{ij} \notin [-1, 1]$ may occur, but with a very small probability.

In the following let us specify a simple practical method under which Equation 13.A.8 will define a "true" correlation coefficient $\rho_{ij} \in [-1, 1]$. Using regression analysis it is possible to fit for each $i \in \{1, \ldots, n\}$ the premium volumes to the following function

$$P_i^k = r^{k-1}\alpha_i, \quad k = 1, \ldots, m \quad (13.A.9)$$

where r is interpreted as a price index adjustment factor. Furthermore, set

$$P_i^\bullet = \sum_{k=1}^{m} P_i^k = \alpha_i \cdot S_r, \quad S_r = \sum_{k=1}^{m} r^{k-1} = \frac{r^m - 1}{r - 1} \quad i = 1, \ldots, n \quad (13.A.10)$$

Under Equations 13.A.9 and 13.A.10 the weights are simply given by

$$w_i^k = w_j^k = w_{ij}^k = \frac{r^{k-1}}{S_r}, \quad i \neq j, \ i, j = 1, \ldots, n, \ k = 1, \ldots, m \quad (13.A.11)$$

We see that Equations 13.A.3, 13.A.6 and 13.A.7 can be rewritten as

$$\mu_i = S_r^{-1} \cdot \sum_{k=1}^{m} r^{k-1} \cdot X_i^k$$

$$\sigma_i^2 = S_r^{-1} \cdot \sum_{k=1}^{m} r^{k-1} \cdot (X_i^k - \mu_i)^2, \quad i = 1, \ldots, n \qquad (13.A.3')$$

$$\mu_{ij} == \frac{\alpha_i}{\alpha_i + \alpha_j} \mu_i + \frac{\alpha_j}{\alpha_i + \alpha_j} \mu_j \qquad (13.A.6')$$

$$\sigma_{ij}^2 = S_r^{-1} \cdot \sum_{k=1}^{m} r^{k-1} \cdot \left[\frac{\alpha_i}{\alpha_i + \alpha_j}(X_i^k - \mu_i) + \frac{\alpha_j}{\alpha_i + \alpha_j}(X_j^k - \mu_j) \right]^2 \qquad (13.A.7')$$

Inserting into Equation 13.A.8 the correlation coefficient simplifies to the analytical expression

$$\rho_{ij} = \frac{\sum_{k=1}^{m} r^{k-1} \cdot (X_i^k - \mu_i) \cdot (X_j^k - \mu_j)}{\sqrt{\sum_{k=1}^{m} r^{k-1} \cdot (X_i^k - \mu_i)^2} \cdot \sqrt{\sum_{k=1}^{m} r^{k-1} \cdot (X_j^k - \mu_j)^2}} \qquad (13.A.12)$$

which reminds one in the special case $r = 1$ of the classic product moment estimator of the correlation coefficient, for which $\rho_{ij} \in [-1, 1]$ clearly holds.

REFERENCES

CEIOPS, 2007, "QIS3 Technical Specifications – Part I: Instructions", April, URL: http://www.pszaf.hu/data/cms1305277/pszafhu_szolvencia_QIS3techspec1.pdf.

CRO Forum, 2005, "A Framework for Incorporating Diversification in the Solvency Assessment of Insurers", URL: http://www.diversification_white_paper_200506101[1].pdf.

Dhaene, J., M. Goovaerts and R. Kaas, 2003, "Economic Capital Allocation Derived from Risk Measures", North American Actuarial Journal, 7(2), pp. 44–59.

Furman, E. and Z. Landsman, 2005, "Risk Capital Decomposition for a Multivariate Dependent Gamma Portfolio", Insurance: Mathematics and Economics, 37, pp. 635–49.

Furman, E. and Z. Landsman, 2007, "Economic Capital Allocations for Non-Negative Portfolios of Dependent Risks", Proceedings of the 37th International ASTIN Colloquium, Orlando, FL, URL: http://www.actuaries.org/ASTIN/Colloquia/Orlando/Papers/Furman.pdf.

Hürlimann, W., 2001, "Analytical Evaluation of Economic Risk Capital for Portfolios of Gamma Risks", ASTIN Bulletin, 31, pp. 107–22.

Hürlimann, W., 2002, "Analytical Bounds for Two Value-at-Risk Functionals", ASTIN Bulletin, 32(2), pp. 235–65.

Hürlimann, W., 2003, "Conditional Value-at-Risk Bounds for Compound Poisson Risks and a Normal Approximation", Journal of Applied Mathematics, 3(3), pp. 141–54.

Hürlimann, W., 2004, "Distortion Risk Measures and Economic Capital", *North American Actuarial Journal*, 8(1), pp. 86–95.

Landsman, Z. and E. A. Valdez, 2003, "Tail Conditional Expectations For Elliptical Distributions", *North American Actuarial Journal*, 7, pp. 55–71, URL: http://www.soa.org/library/journals/north-american-actuarial-journal/2003/october/naaj0310-5.pdf.

Valdez, E. A., 2005, "Tail Conditional Variance for Elliptically Contoured Distributions", *Belgian Actuarial Bulletin*, 5(1), pp. 26–36.

14

Solvency Requirements for Life Annuities Allowing for Mortality Risks: Internal Models versus Standard Formulas

Annamaria Olivieri; Ermanno Pitacco

University of Parma; University of Trieste

The advantages provided by "large" portfolio sizes with respect to the risk of random fluctuations justify somewhat the traditional deterministic approach to mortality in life insurance calculations. Actually, adopting a deterministic approach to actuarial valuations (namely using only expected values in calculating premiums and reserves) is, to some extent, underpinned by the nature of the insurance process, which consists of "transforming" individual risks through aggregation, so lowering the relevant impact.

However, this justification can only be accepted under the assumption that just the risk of random fluctuations in the mortality of insured lives is allowed for. Conversely, other sources of randomness should be recognised, hence the existence of risk components other than random fluctuations should be accounted for. When dealing with life annuities (and, in general, with long-term living products), special attention should be devoted to the risk of systematic deviations arising from the uncertainty in representing future mortality patterns.

Solvency targets and, consequently, the assessment of capital requirements according to a sound risk management approach, clearly witness the need for analysing all sources of risk and the relevant components. In this regard, it is interesting to note the progressive shift from simple (and, from a modern perspective rather simplistic) regulatory requirements based on compact short-cut formulas to more complex calculation structures. The use of internal models, which can capture the real risk profile of an insurance company, is a recent and, so far, probably the most important step in this process. An interesting review of the development of solvency requirements (also according to a historical perspective) is provided by Sandström (2006).

Great attention is currently devoted to the management of life annuity portfolios, both from a theoretical and a practical point of view, in particular because of the growing importance of annuity benefits paid by private pension plans. Among the risks that affect pension plans and life annuity portfolios, longevity risk, which arises from the unknown future trend in mortality at adult and old age, deserves a deep and detailed investigation, and requires the adoption of proper management solutions. From a risk management perspective, capital allocation constitutes an important tool for financing potential losses, clearly including those originating from unanticipated mortality improvements. For an extensive analysis of mortality dynamics and the impact of longevity risk on pensions and life annuities, the reader can refer to Pitacco *et al* (2009).

The European solvency regulation currently in progress (Solvency II) obviously accounts also for longevity risk; see CEIOPS (2007, 2008). On one hand, longevity risk is embraced by the so-called standard formula. On the other hand, the use of internal models, properly allowing for various sources of risk and the relevant components, is permitted.

Models for assessing the impact of longevity risk on life annuity portfolios and pension funds, and evaluating the consequent need for capital allocation, have already been proposed in actuarial literature. In particular, Olivieri and Pitacco (2003) focus on alternative approaches to solvency assessment over a multi-year time horizon. Approaches based on a deferral-and-matching or an asset-and-liability logic, therein proposed, are progressed further in this chapter. We discuss rules that could be adopted for internal models and the relevant results presented here are compared with the requirements described in the Solvency II project.

The chapter is organised as follows. In the next section, tools for the management of risks inherent in a life annuity portfolio (or pension plan) are briefly presented following the approach suggested by risk management principles. Then we focus on some aspects of longevity risk and the choice of a tractable modelling structure. Next, solvency targets, and related rules which can be adopted in internal models, are defined and discussed, while the Solvency II approach to longevity risk is described in the penultimate section. In the final section, some comparisons between internal rules and the regulatory requirements proposed in the Solvency II project are presented through numerical examples, together with some concluding remarks.

RISK MANAGEMENT OF LIFE ANNUITIES

Several tools can be developed for managing the risks of a life annuity portfolio, which can be analysed following the approach suggested by risk management principles.

The risk management process consists of three basic steps: namely the identification of risks (mortality risks, market risks and so on), the assessment (or measurement) of the relevant consequences and the choice of the most appropriate risk management solution (which is usually a combination of various actions). In what follows we refer to mortality risks only.

The identification of risks affecting an insurer can follow the guidelines provided by the supervisory authority, such as those underpinning the Solvency II project (see, for instance, CEIOPS 2007, 2008), or the recommendations suggested by some independent institution, such as the International Actuarial Association (IAA 2004). Mortality risks can be classified within underwriting risks; the relevant components are: random fluctuations, systematic deviations and catastrophe deviations (see the next section for details). The importance of mortality risks, and their components in particular, clearly depends on the specific composition of the insurer's portfolio. When life annuities are dealt with, random fluctuations and systematic deviations (the latter also named longevity risk, when they are originated by a downward mortality trend at adult and old ages) in particular are critical, as we discuss in the next section.

A rigorous assessment of the risks requires the use of stochastic models. The choice of the most appropriate model depends on the type of risks involved and the business we are dealing with. For the case of mortality risks, an example is provided in the next section. The stochastic model should lead to a risk measurement: such as a probability of default (or ruin probability), which is typically referred to in solvency investigations (see the later section on "Possible solvency rules in internal models"); a risk margin adjusting some expected quantity, which is typically adopted in pricing and reserving (again see the section on "Possible solvency rules in internal models"); or some other risk measures (not discussed in this chapter).

Risk management solutions for life annuities include a wide set of tools, which can be interpreted under an insurance perspective as portfolio strategies, aiming at risk mitigation. In this chapter we will consider in detail capital allocation only. However, in the remainder of this section we sketch a comprehensive framework of the several tools available; reference to mortality risks (only) is understood.

A portfolio strategy clearly affects portfolio results. Take, for example, the annual outflows relating to annuity payments only, which in any event constitute the starting point from which other portfolio results (eg, profits) may be derived. Reasonably, the insurer sets a threshold amount for the annual outgo, which represents a maintainable level of benefit payment. This amount is financed first by premiums via the portfolio technical provision, and then by shareholders' capital as the result of the allocation policy (consisting of specific capital allocations as well as accumulation of undistributed profits). If the annual outflow is above the threshold level, then a situation of default emerges. In order to keep the relevant probability at an acceptable level, the insurer can adopt various risk management actions. The target can be an increase in the maintainable annual outgo, and thus a higher threshold level, as well as a reduction (and smoothing) of annual outflows in the case of unanticipated improvements in portfolio mortality. Such targets may be reached through loss control and loss financing actions (according to the usual risk management terminology).

Loss control actions are mainly performed via the product design. The insurer should set policy conditions that will mitigate the loss frequency and lower the severity of the possible loss (ie, aiming, respectively, at loss prevention and loss reduction). Loss reduction requires taking control of the annuity amounts paid out, by adding some flexibility to the life annuity product. One action could be the reduction of the annual amount as a consequence of an unanticipated mortality improvement. However, in this case the product would be a non-guaranteed life annuity, although possibly with a reasonable minimum amount guaranteed. A more practicable tool, consistent with the features of a guaranteed life annuity, consists in reducing the level of investment profit participation when the mortality experience is adverse to the insurer. It is worth stressing that undistributed profits also increase the shareholders' capital within the portfolio, hence raising the maintainable threshold.

Loss financing actions include a wide range of techniques, in particular risk transfers obtained through reinsurance or alternative arrangements, namely securitisation. It is worthwhile mentioning that reinsurance is typically designed for random fluctuations, due to the stronger pooling effect that can be realised by a reinsurer in respect of what can be reached by an insurer. Conversely, reinsurers are not willing to take risks that are systematic for the overall insurance/reinsurance market, such as longevity risk. Alternative risk transfer solutions may help in this regard; for life annuities in particular the development of longevity bonds, where the performance is linked to some measure of longevity in a given population, are of interest. The availability of a longevity bond market, which is supposed to be more easily accessible for a reinsurer than an insurer (owing to the presumably large size of the deals), could support the development of a reinsurance market for longevity risk. Indeed, reinsurers could hedge the risks taken from insurers with capital market solutions: see Pitacco *et al* (2009) and references therein; we mention, in particular, Olivieri (2005) for reinsurance arrangements, Blake *et al* (2006) and Lin and Cox (2005) for alternative risk transfer solutions.

Among loss financing actions, we finally mention natural hedging. This term refers to the possibility of offsetting mortality risks emerging from living benefits with those emerging from death benefits. The diversification effect can be realised inside the life annuity portfolio, allowing for a death benefit combined with the life annuity; such a hedge is usually called "across time". Another possibility consists of offsetting risks in different business lines, namely life insurance providing death benefits with life annuities; this is the so-called hedging "across business lines". In both cases, the hedging is provided by the fact that if mortality is lower than anticipated, the value of life annuity liabilities is higher than expected, but meanwhile the value of life insurance liabilities (namely, those with a positive sum at risk) is lower than expected. While diversification across time can easily be achieved (providing that the policyholder is willing to pay for both living and death benefits), diversification across business lines can hardly produce a satisfactory effect, due to the different range of ages, and hence the different mortality profile, involved in the life annuity and the life insurance business (for references see Pitacco *et al* 2009).

To the extent that mortality/longevity risks are retained by an insurer, the impact of a poor experience falls on the insurer itself. In order to meet an unexpected amount of obligations, an appropriate level of advance funding may provide a substantial help. To this purpose, shareholders' capital must be allocated to the life annuity portfolio, and the relevant amount should be determined to achieve the insurer's solvency.

MORTALITY RISKS

Mortality risks emerge as deviations in the experienced mortality frequency in respect of the (forecasted) mortality rates. Such deviations may in particular involve individual or aggregate mortality. In the former case, deviations are simply due to the fact that one individual may outlive or underlive the average lifetime in the population. The relevant risk is the well-known process risk (also named insurance risk or risk of random fluctuations), where the severity reduces as the individual position becomes negligible in respect of the overall portfolio. The process risk can be hedged by achieving an adequate pooling effect, as well as through traditional risk transfer arrangements, as it reduces as soon as the portfolio is made of similar policies and its size is large enough. We note further that actuaries are familiar with the relevant modelling issues.

Deviations involving aggregate mortality may be permanent or temporary. The latter case usually consists of a sudden jump in mortality rates due to epidemics, severe climatic conditions, natural disasters and so on. A catastrophe risk emerges, which is short in time and produces a profit for a provider of living benefits. Therefore, we do not address this aspect in this chapter.

In the case of random fluctuations only, the average lifetime experienced in the population typically turns out to be close to what is expected. Conversely, when mortality frequencies are experienced permanently below or above the expected levels, the average lifetime of the population deviates from what is expected. Such a systematic deviation, which we refer to as a permanent deviation in aggregate mortality, may be the result of either a mis-specification of the relevant mortality model or a biased assessment of the relevant parameters. The former aspect is referred to as the model risk, the latter as the parameter risk. The term uncertainty risk is often used to refer to model and parameter risk jointly, meaning uncertainty in the representation of a phenomenon, such as future mortality. When adult or old age is concerned, the uncertainty risk may emerge in particular because of an unanticipated reduction in mortality rates. In this case, the term longevity risk is used instead of uncertainty risk. Pooling arguments do not apply for its hedging, due to its systematic nature. We note further that modelling issues still constitute an open problem.

It must be pointed out that the terminology used above is common in actuarial literature, as it is based on a detailed analysis of the possible causes of deviations in mortality rates. In practice, some shortened terminology may be preferred, as it is the case within the Solvency II project. Indeed, within Solvency II both the terms mortality and longevity risk denote a situation of uncertainty risk. While the term mortality risk is used to refer to situations of extra mortality when death benefits are dealt with, the term longevity risk addresses the possible realisation of extra survivorship when living benefits are involved (CEIOPS 2007, 2008). Unless otherwise stated, in the following we prefer to adopt the detailed terminology, as it makes clearer the discussion about modelling issues.

In order to represent mortality risks, a stochastic model is required. Since the scope of this chapter is solvency for living benefits, we disregard catastrophe risk. The stochastic mortality model should then allow for random fluctuations (process risk), deviations due to the shape of the time-pattern implied by the mortality model, in respect of both age and calendar year (model risk), as well as deviations due to the level of the parameters of the mortality model (parameter risk). Clearly, when dealing with living benefits at adult ages, appropriate mortality projections should be adopted.

Let $T_{x\tau}$ be the remaining lifetime of an individual current age x, born in calendar year τ. We denote by $F_{x\tau}(t \mid H(\tau))$ the relevant cumulative distribution function (CDF), conditional on assumption $H(\tau)$ about the future behaviour of mortality for cohort τ; namely $F_{x\tau}(t \mid H(\tau)) = \mathbb{P}[T_{x\tau} \leq t \mid H(\tau)]$. The CDF $F_{x\tau}(t \mid H(\tau))$ allows for random fluctuations, given that $H(\tau)$ describes the aggregate mortality trend forecasted for cohort τ.

A naive, but practical, way to account also for systematic deviations consists of assigning alternative hypotheses about the future aggregate mortality trend of cohort τ. An example can be found in projections developed by CMI, addressing the cohort effect and assuming three hypotheses about the persistence in the future of such an effect (CMI 2002, 2006). We denote by $\mathcal{H}(\tau)$ the set of alternative mortality assumptions for cohort τ. These assumptions may originate from different sets of relevant parameters of the underlying projection model; in this way, parameter risk is addressed. Otherwise, the alternative assumptions may be given by mortality projections obtained under different procedures; in this case, model risk would also be addressed. However, it is intrinsically difficult to perform an explanatory comparison of different models, so henceforth reference is understood to the parameter risk only.

If, following Olivieri (2001), we further define a (non-negative and normalised) weighting structure on $\mathcal{H}(\tau)$, then the family $\{F_{x\tau}(t \mid H(\tau)) \mid H(\tau) \in \mathcal{H}(\tau)\}$ allows for both random fluctuations and systematic deviations. Experience providing data for estimating the weighting structure is lacking and so expert judgement is often required in this respect. We let $\mathcal{H}(\tau) = \{H_1(\tau), H_2(\tau), \ldots, H_m(\tau)\}$; the weight assigned to assumption $H_h(\tau)$ is denoted by ρ_h, with $0 \leq \rho_h \leq 1$ for $h = 1, 2, \ldots, m$ and $\sum_{h=1}^{m} \rho_h = 1$.

It is worthwhile noting that the structure introduced above can, to some extent, be classified as a static representation of stochastic mortality. Indeed, the notation expresses that the set $\mathcal{H}(\tau)$ and the weights ρ_h are assigned at the valuation time (when the individual is aged x, so in calendar year $x + \tau$); an update based on experience or new information is not embedded in the model. A Bayesian inferential procedure could be set in order to update the weights to the observed number of deaths (Olivieri and Pitacco 2002). In order to deal within a dynamic stochastic setting of mortality, either the probability of death or the force of mortality (or some other mortality index) could be modelled as a path of a random process. In the literature some proposals have focused on this approach, mainly aiming at the pricing of longevity securities. Most investigations move from assumed similarities between the force of mortality and interest rates or simply from the assumption that the market for longevity securities should behave like other aspects of the capital market. The application to mortality of some stochastic models developed originally for financial purposes is then tested. In particular, interest rate and credit risk models have been considered; the theory of incomplete markets is also explored: see, among others, Biffis (2005), Biffis and Millossovich (2006), Cairns *et al* (2006) and, for further references, Pitacco *et al* (2009). The basic building blocks of the new theory still require careful discussion and investigation; indeed, financial models are not necessarily suitable for describing mortality. Given that we are not dealing with a pricing problem, we prefer to keep the simpler structure previously introduced, which can anyhow be useful for internal valuations.

Extending the prevailing notation, we let $_tq_{x\tau}^{[H(\tau)]} = F_{x\tau}(t \mid H(\tau))$; in particular, for $t = 1$ we let $_1q_{x\tau}^{[H(\tau)]} = q_{x\tau}^{[H(\tau)]}$. We then assume

$$\frac{q_{x\tau}^{[H(\tau)]}}{1 - q_{x\tau}^{[H(\tau)]}} = G^{[H(\tau)]} (K^{[H(\tau)]})^x \qquad (14.1)$$

Hence, the third term of the first Heligman–Pollard law, that is the one describing the old-age pattern of mortality, is adopted in order to express the mortality profile involved in our calculations. Note in particular that the relevant parameters are cohort-specific and, further, their value is specific to the adopted mortality assumption for the cohort. Uncertainty then concerns the level of parameters $G^{[H(\tau)]}$, $K^{[H(\tau)]}$.

We define the seven alternative sets of parameters quoted in Table 14.1. We refer to the cohort of the Italian male (annuitants born in 1955). Parameters under scenario $H_4(1955)$ have been obtained by fitting Equation 14.1 to the projected table IPS55. Assumptions $H_h(1955)$ for $h = 1, 2, 3$ embed some hypotheses of higher mortality

Table 14.1 Parameters for the Heligman–Pollard law

	$G^{[H_h(1955)]}$	$K^{[H_h(1955)]}$	$\mathbb{E}[T_{65,1955} \mid H_h(1955)]$
$H_1(1955)$	5.561×10^7	1.153	19.874
$H_2(1955)$	9.542×10^7	1.144	20.442
$H_3(1955)$	1.414×10^6	1.137	21.099
$H_4(1955)$	2.005×10^6	1.130	21.849
$H_5(1955)$	2.533×10^6	1.125	22.711
$H_6(1955)$	2.972×10^6	1.121	23.676
$H_7(1955)$	3.294×10^6	1.118	24.706

(as it is witnessed by the expected lifetime $\mathbb{E}[T_{65,1955} \mid H_h(1955)]$, which is quoted in Table 14.1); conversely, assumptions $H_h(1955)$ for $h = 5, 6, 7$ embed some hypotheses of lower mortality (see $\mathbb{E}[T_{65,1955} \mid H_h(1955)]$ in Table 14.1). Figures 14.1 and 14.2 show, respectively, the relevant survival functions and curves of deaths (namely the probability density functions of the remaining lifetime). Assumption $H_4(1955)$ will be referred to as the best-estimate description of the mortality trend for cohort 1955.

POSSIBLE SOLVENCY RULES FOR INTERNAL MODELS

When dealing with life annuities, capital allocation rules should carefully account for all the risks retained by the insurer. With reference to mortality risks, to which this chapter is devoted, longevity risk is in particular critical; however, proper care should be devoted also to other risk components. In this section we investigate rules suitable for an internal model. Conversely, in the next section standard regulatory requirements will be addressed. Consistently with the aim of the chapter, we disregard all but mortality risks. We refer to conventional immediate life annuities, so that there is no allowance for participation in financial or other profits. In order to make the main findings easier to understand, we further assume that no risk transfer has been undertaken. We focus on benefit outflows; therefore, expenses and related expense loadings are not accounted for.

The portfolio we refer to consists of one cohort of immediate life annuities. We assume that all the annuitants are aged x_0 at the time t_0 of issue, and are all entitled to receive the annual amount b at each time t, $t = 1, 2, \ldots$ until death. The lifetimes of annuitants

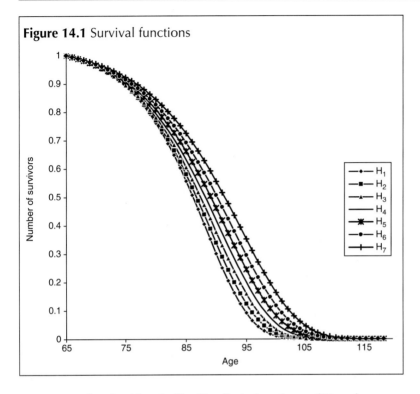

Figure 14.1 Survival functions

are assumed to be identically distributed and, conditional on any given mortality assumption, independent of each other.

We let N_t denote the random number of annuitants at the duration time t, $t = 0, 1, \ldots, \omega - x_0$ (and hence at the beginning of the calendar year $t_0 + t$), with $N_0 = n_0$ a specified number representing the initial size of the portfolio and ω the maximum attainable age. We note then that $N_{\omega - x_0 + 1} = 0$. The in-force portfolio at time t is defined as $\Pi_t = \{j \mid T^{(j)}_{x_0 \, \tau} > t\}$, where $T^{(j)}_{x_0 \, \tau}$ represents the remaining lifetime for annuitant j at age x_0.

Annual outflows for the portfolio are defined, for $t = 1, 2, \ldots, \omega - x_0$, as

$$B_t^{(\Pi)} = b \, N_t$$

The present value of future portfolio outflows can be defined as

$$Y_t^{(\Pi)} = \sum_{h=t+1}^{\omega - x_0} B_h^{(\Pi)} \, (1 + i)^{-(h-t)} = \sum_{h=t+1}^{\omega - x_0} b \, N_h \, (1 + i)^{-(h-t)}$$

where, for brevity, we have considered a flat term structure of interest rates (hence, i is the annual interest rate).

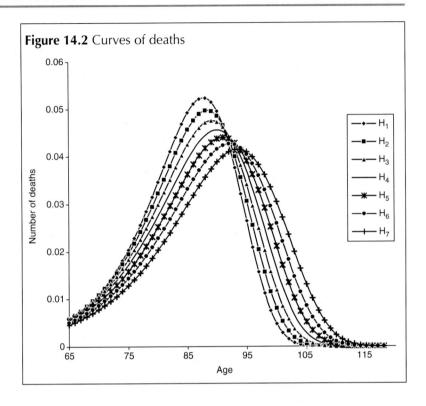

Figure 14.2 Curves of deaths

We let A_t be the amount of portfolio assets at time t and $V_t^{(\Pi)}$ the portfolio reserve (or technical provision) at the same time. These quantities are random at the valuation time, because of the risks, mortality in particular, borne by the portfolio. Let z be the valuation time ($z = 0, 1, \ldots$). The random path of portfolio assets is recursively described for $t = z + 1, z + 2, \ldots$ as follows

$$A_t = A_{t-1}(1 + i) - b\, N_t \tag{14.2}$$

with A_z given (including both the reserve and capital in the amount required according to a chosen solvency rule).

According to current legislation, the portfolio reserve $V_t^{(\Pi)}$ should include a risk margin in order to face adverse future scenarios. In traditional practice, such a risk margin is implicitly assessed by calculating directly the reserve $V_t^{(\Pi)}$ as the expected present value of future benefits net of future premiums, according to a prudential description of the future scenario. In explicit terms, the portfolio reserve can be expressed as

$$V_t^{(\Pi)} = V_t^{(\Pi)[BE]} + RM_t$$

where $V_t^{(\Pi)[BE]}$ is the portfolio reserve calculated according to best-estimate assumptions about the future scenario, and RM_t is the risk margin. Reserving formulas leading to an explicit risk margin have been widely discussed under various Solvency II projects, as well as under the fair value project for international financial reporting standards. See the next section for the Solvency II proposal.

The quantity M_t, defined as

$$M_t = A_t - V_t^{(\Pi)[BE]}$$

represents the assets available to meet the risks. Thus M_t should back both the risk margin, to be then included into the portfolio reserve, and the required capital. We note that if the risk margin is funded by premiums paid by policyholders (as should occur for a going-concern sound management of liabilities), then it also consists of expected profit to the insurer.

Capital requirements suitable for internal models assume that the insurer can be considered to be solvent in respect of portfolio obligations if, with an assigned (high) probability, assets meet liabilities within a chosen time horizon, according to a realistic probabilistic structure. Several details need to be specified for a practical implementation of such a definition.

- As far as assets are concerned, reference can be to assets available to meet risks, M_t, which are required to be non-negative, or to the total amount of assets, A_t, which are required to be non-lower than the present value of future payments, $Y_t^{[\Pi]}$.
- The time horizon T may range from a short–medium term (one to five years, say), to the residual duration of the portfolio, $w + 1 - x_0 - z$ (at time z, $z = 0, 1, \dots$).
- When a time horizon longer than one year is adopted, the overall trajectory of assets within the time horizon can be addressed, or just their final value at time T.
- The portfolio needs to be defined in a run-off or a going-concern perspective. When dealing with life insurance, a run-off approach is more reasonable.

Let z be the time at which solvency is ascertained ($z = 0, 1, \ldots$). According to the possible choices listed above, the following (alternative) rules are available for assessing the capital required at time z

$$[R1]: \quad \mathbb{P}[(M_{z+1} \geq 0) \wedge (M_{z+2} \geq 0)$$
$$\wedge \cdots \wedge (M_{z+T} \geq 0)] = 1 - \varepsilon_1 \tag{14.3}$$

$$[R2]: \quad \mathbb{P}[M_{z+T} \geq 0] = 1 - \varepsilon_2 \tag{14.4}$$

$$[R3]: \quad \mathbb{P}[(A_{z+1} - Y_{z+1}^{(\Pi)} \geq 0) \wedge (A_{z+2} - Y_{z+2}^{(\Pi)} \geq 0)$$
$$\wedge \cdots \wedge (A_{z+T} - Y_{z+T}^{(\Pi)} \geq 0)] = 1 - \varepsilon_3 \tag{14.5}$$

where ε_i, $i = 1, 2, 3$, is the accepted default probability under the chosen rule. Clearly, in all of the solvency models above, the relevant probability is assessed conditional on the current information at time z.

The difference between rules $[R1]$ and $[R2]$ is apparent. We first note that the quantity M_t originates from the initial capital allocation at time z, where the amount must be assessed through a solvency rule, and from the surplus (possibly negative) emerging year by year. Under rule $[R2]$, only the total surplus in the time interval $[z, z + T]$ is addressed, while under rule $[R1]$ its yearly emergence is also checked. When addressing permanent systematic deviations in the mortality of immediate life annuitants, it is likely that a loss in a year is followed by further losses, so that a negative total surplus then emerges. Disregarding further profit sources, as we are doing, outputs from rule $[R2]$ can then be supposed to be similar to those of rule $[R1]$, so that one of the two can be disregarded. Rule $[R2]$ is more straightforward to implement; conversely, rule $[R1]$ is more accurate, as a possible lack of funds is detected sooner. So in the following we will not consider rule $[R2]$.

With reference to rule $[R3]$, it is worthwhile to rearrange the relevant expression. The recursion Equation 14.2 leads to

$$A_t = A_z (1 + i)^{t-z} - \sum_{h=z+1}^{t} b N_h (1 + i)^{t-h}$$

The probability in Equation 14.5 can then be rewritten as

$$\mathbb{P}\left[\bigwedge_{t=z+1}^{z+T} A_z \, (1+i)^{t-z} - \sum_{h=z+1}^{\omega-x_0} b \, N_h \, (1+i)^{t-h} \geq 0\right]$$

$$= \mathbb{P}\left[\bigwedge_{t=z+1}^{z+T} (1+i)^{t-(\omega+1-x_0)} \left(A_z \, (1+i)^{\omega+1-x_0-z} \right. \right.$$

$$\left. \left. - \sum_{h=z+1}^{\omega-x_0} b \, N_h \, (1+i)^{\omega+1-x_0-h} \right) \geq 0 \right] \qquad (14.6)$$

If we note that the quantity

$$A_z \, (1+i)^{\omega+1-x_0-z} - \sum_{h=z+1}^{\omega-x_0} b \, N_h \, (1+i)^{\omega+1-x_0-h} = A_{\omega+1-x_0}$$

represents the amount of portfolio assets available when the cohort is exhausted, the probability in Equation 14.6 reduces to

$$\mathbb{P}\left[\bigwedge_{t=z+1}^{z+T} (1+i)^{t-(\omega+1-x_0)} A_{\omega+1-x_0} \geq 0\right]$$

$$= \mathbb{P}\left[\bigwedge_{t=z+1}^{z+T} A_{\omega+1-x_0} \geq 0\right] = \mathbb{P}\left[A_{\omega+1-x_0} \geq 0\right]$$

We can note further that

$$A_{\omega+1-x_0} = M_{\omega+1-x_0}$$

as all obligations have been fulfilled at time $\omega + 1 - x_0$. So, finally, rule [R3] can be rewritten as

$$\mathbb{P}\left[M_{\omega+1-x_0} \geq 0\right] = 1 - \varepsilon_3 \qquad (14.7)$$

It is useful to note that such results hold in particular because: (a) the portfolio is closed to new entrants; (b) the probability in Equation 14.5 (as well as in Equations 14.3 and 14.4) is assessed according to the real-world probability distribution of assets and liabilities (so that no risk-adjustment is applied, for example in a risk-neutral fashion); (c) such probability is implicitly conditional on the information available at time z on the relevant variables (current number of survivors, investment yields, and so on). A similar simplification can however be obtained when more than one cohort is addressed, as well as when the term structure of interest rates is not flat.

Comparing rules [R1] and [R3], the apparent difference consists of the way liabilities are summarised, in terms of portfolio reserve in rule [R1] and the present value of future payments in rule [R3]. A deeper comparison emerges when we consider Equation 14.7. Assume that in Equation 14.3 the time horizon $T = \omega + 1 - x_0 - z$ is set. In both cases, the total amount of the surplus would be considered. However, under rule [R1] its emergence is driven by the reserve (which may smooth annual losses), while under [R3] the initial income and the annual outgoings are simply accounted for. According to valuation terminology, rule [R1] is based on a "deferral and matching" logic, while [R3] is based on an "asset and liability" approach. Further, rule [R1] allows for a preferred time horizon, whilst under [R3] the maximum possible time horizon is necessarily adopted.

Solving Equation 14.3 with respect to M_z, through stochastic simulation, the amount of assets to meet risks required at time z is found; we will denote such an amount by $M_z^{[R1]}(T)$. Then, $A_z^{[R1]}(T) = V_z^{(\Pi)[BE]} + M_z^{[R1]}(T)$ is the total amount of assets required at time z. Solving Equation 14.7, again through stochastic simulation, one finds the total amount of assets required at time z, denoted as $A_z^{[R3]}$; the required amount of assets to meet risks at time z is then: $M_z^{[R3]} = A_z^{[R3]} - V_z^{(\Pi)[BE]}$. A numerical investigation is presented and the related findings are discussed in the concluding section.

THE SOLVENCY II APPROACH TO MORTALITY RISKS

In defining the new regulatory capital requirement, the Solvency II project adopts a disaggregated approach. First risks are focused, then a capital charge for each risk is defined, and finally the capital required is determined by merging the several charges and considering reasonable correlation assumptions among the risks. The parameters of the relevant formulas are set so that the amount of the required capital is consistent with value-at-risk at a 99.5% confidence level with a one-year time horizon.

As far as mortality risks are concerned, the uncertainty and the catastrophe components are considered. In relation to the uncertainty risk, the possible permanent situation of extra-mortality for life insurance covers with a positive sum at risk is named mortality risk. In contrast, longevity risk is the term used to define a permanent situation of under-mortality for insurance products with a negative sum at risk (eg, life annuities). A charge for catastrophe mortality is required for those insurance products bearing a positive sum at risk.

Given the scope of this chapter, and the assumptions adopted about risks other than those linked to the lifetime, we address only the charge for longevity risk (with the meaning just specified).

The capital charge for longevity risk at time z, $\text{Life}_{\text{long}, z}$, is defined as follows

$$\text{Life}_{\text{long}, z} = \Delta\text{NAV} \mid \text{longevity shock} \qquad (14.8)$$

where, with reference to the in-force portfolio, ΔNAV is the change in the net asset value (NAV), namely the value of assets minus liabilities, in the face of a longevity shock defined as a (permanent) 25% decrease in the mortality rate at each age (in respect of the best-estimate assumption). An explicit reduction of the capital charge is admitted in case the insurer has the possibility to reduce profit participation in adverse scenarios; we will not consider such possibility, as we are referring to fixed benefits.

We note that in defining $\text{Life}_{\text{long}, z}$ a deterministic setting is considered in respect of systematic deviations, as only one level for the possible shock is considered. In order to avoid a double charge for risks, the value of liabilities involved in Equation 14.8 is not risk-adjusted. So in Equation 14.8, we can define the NAV as follows

$$\text{NAV}_z = A_z - V_z^{(\Pi)[\text{BE}]}$$

Since we are addressing immediate life annuities, ΔNAV_z and the capital charge for longevity risk then reduces to

$$\Delta\text{NAV}_z = \text{Life}_{\text{long}, z} = V_z^{(\Pi)[-25\%]} - V_z^{(\Pi)[\text{BE}]}$$

where $V_z^{(\Pi)[-25\%]}$ is the expected value of future payments, calculated with a life table where the mortality rates are 25% lower than those in the best estimate table. Indeed, current assets are not affected by the shock scenario, while the value of liabilities must be updated.

The risk margin RM_z to be embedded into the portfolio reserve is defined in the Solvency II framework according to a cost-of-capital logic. More specifically, RM_z is the amount of money rewarding the capital to be allocated to the business of the insurance company in the current and future years, until exhaustion. The cost-of-capital factor is set to 6% above the risk-free interest rate, r_f, and the capital to be allocated is stated in terms of the solvency capital required (SCR), which under our assumptions reduces to the capital charge for longevity risk. The risk margin is then calculated as follows

$$RM_z = \sum_{h=0}^{m} 0.06 \cdot \text{SCR}_{z+h} \left(1 + r_f\right)^{-h}$$

where m is the time to exhaustion of the in-force portfolio and $\text{SCR}_{z+h} = \text{Life}_{\text{long},\,z+h}$ in our case. The quantities SCR_{z+h} are estimated through the current best-estimate assumptions. We note that the size of the risk margin is consistent with the risks accounted for in the SCR, that is, the longevity risk in our case. However, RM_z clearly provides assets for facing all the residual risks in respect of those met by the SCR.

The calculation of $\text{Life}_{\text{long},\,z}$ and RM_z is clearly based on two different logics. Further, $\text{Life}_{\text{long},\,z}$ should be backed by shareholders' capital, while RM_z should be mainly funded with premiums. In any case, assets backing $\text{Life}_{\text{long},\,z}$ joint to those backing RM_z represent, in total, the amount of money facing risks. Just in order to compare results obtained with internal models and within the Solvency II framework, we define

$$M_z^{[\text{Solv2}]} = \text{Life}_{\text{long},\,z} + RM_z$$

as the total amount of money required, under Solvency II, to face mortality risks.

COMPARISONS AND CONCLUDING REMARKS

In this section, some comparisons among internal rules and the regulatory requirement proposed in the Solvency II project are performed through numerical implementation.

We refer to a portfolio with the features described in the section "Possible solvency rules in internal models". The entry age is $x_0 = 65$; the annual interest rate is $i = 0.03$. Internal rules are adopted with an accepted default probability consistent with the relevant assumption underlying the Solvency II proposal; thus,

Table 14.2 Individual reserve

Time z	Reserve $V_z^{(1)[BE]}$	Reserve $V_z^{(1)}$
0	15.259	16.342
5	12.956	13.887
10	10.599	11.357
15	8.294	8.874
20	6.167	6.581
25	4.336	4.611
30	2.877	3.050
35	1.807	1.913

we have set $\varepsilon_1 = \varepsilon_3 = 0.005$. For the internal rules, the mortality assumptions are those described earlier, see Table 14.1, with weights: $\rho_1 = \rho_7 = 0.05$; $\rho_2 = \rho_3 = \rho_5 = \rho_6 = 0.1$; $\rho_4 = 0.5$. We note that the best-estimate assumption has been assigned the highest weight, while the lowest weight has been given to the extreme assumptions (among those considered, ie, $H_1(1955)$ and $H_7(1955)$).

Table 14.2 quotes the individual reserve net and inclusive of the risk margin required by Solvency II, denoted respectively as $V_z^{(1)[BE]}$ and $V_z^{(1)}$. Note that such quantities are defined as (or based on) expected values. Thus, if n_z is the number of annuitants observed at time z, then $V_z^{(\Pi)[BE]} = n_z \, V_z^{(1)[BE]}$ and $V_z^{(\Pi)} = n_z \, V_z^{(1)}$.

Table 14.3 displays the amount of capital (per unit of portfolio reserve net of the risk margin, $V_z^{(\Pi)[BE]}$) required according to the solvency rules $[R1]$ and $[R3]$ for several portfolio sizes. For rule $[R1]$, the maximum possible time horizon has been chosen, ie, the time to the portfolio exhaustion, $T = \omega + 1 - x_0 - z$. As we would expect from the previous discussion, the two requirements lead to similar outputs, at least when only mortality is addressed. In this case, at least, the output suggests that rule $[R1]$ is to some extent independent of the reserve when T takes the maximum possible value for the time horizon. Indeed, between random fluctuations and systematic deviations in mortality, the latter have the most severe impact. Furthermore, due to the fact that longevity risk is long-term, to some extent the total relevant loss is more important than the timing of its emergence. When interpreting the size of the required capital quoted in Table 14.3, we finally recall that $M_z^{[R1]}(T)$ and $M_z^{[R3]}$ represent the assets required to meet the risks. Such amount

Table 14.3 Required assets to meet risks based on rules [R1] and [R3], facing longevity risk and mortality random fluctuations

Time z	Rule [R1], with $T = \omega + 1 - x_0 - z$, $\dfrac{M_z^{[R1]}(\omega+1-x_0-z)}{V_z^{(II)|BE}}$			Rule [R3], $\dfrac{M_z^{[R3]}}{V_z^{(II)|BE}}$		
	$n_0 = 100$ (%)	$n_0 = 1\,000$ (%)	$n_0 = 10\,000$ (%)	$n_0 = 100$ (%)	$n_0 = 1\,000$ (%)	$n_0 = 10\,000$ (%)
0	13.647	10.730	9.819	13.647	10.730	9.819
5	17.588	13.870	12.757	17.573	13.868	12.757
10	22.915	18.240	16.813	22.880	18.240	16.813
15	29.927	23.757	22.125	29.759	23.753	22.125
20	41.014	31.319	29.205	40.742	31.308	29.205
25	56.901	42.052	38.545	56.472	42.025	38.545
30	86.748	57.285	50.622	84.647	57.210	50.605
35	180.337	86.445	66.553	170.443	85.749	66.450

must partially back the risk margin, to be included into the technical provision, and the required capital.

In Table 14.4, outputs from rule $[R1]$ are investigated for shorter time horizons. Comparing Table 14.3 with 14.4, the long-term nature of longevity risk clearly emerges. We note that, both in Table 14.3 and 14.4, at each valuation time and for each rule, the amount of required assets decreases when a larger portfolio is considered. This is obviously due to the pooling nature of random fluctuations.

Results displayed in Table 14.5 address random fluctuations only. In particular, the required amount of assets has been calculated adopting only the best-estimate mortality assumption $H_4(1955)$. In Table 14.6, in contrast, only longevity risk has been accounted for, by assuming that whatever is the realised mortality trend, the actual number of deaths in each year is the same as what we expect under the relevant trend assumption. We note that in the latter case the required amount of assets per unit of portfolio reserve (net of the risk margin) is independent of the size of the portfolio; this is due to the systematic nature of longevity risk. Regarding Table 14.5, we point out that the random fluctuations accounted for in such a table are not fully comparable with those emerging in Tables 14.3 and 14.4. Indeed, in these latter tables a mixture of the random fluctuations which can be appraised under several mortality assumptions in $\mathcal{H}(1955)$ is addressed. When comparing Table 14.5 (lower panels) with Table 14.4, we can see that, if rule $[R1]$ is implemented with a short time horizon, in practice we are mainly accounting for random fluctuations, rather than systematic deviations; again, this is due to the long-term nature of longevity risk. Tables 14.5 and 14.6 do provide us with some useful information. However, it must be pointed out that implementing an internal model allowing for a component only of a risk represents an improper use of the model itself. Just to sketch the idea, we note that on summing up the results in Tables 14.5 and 14.6, for a given rule and portfolio size, we do not find results corresponding to those in Table 14.3 or 14.4. Thus, some aspects are missed when only working with marginal distributions (as is the case when we only address random fluctuations or systematic deviations).

Table 14.7 quotes the amount of assets required under Solvency II to meet risks; we also split it into risk margin (to be included into the

Table 14.4 Required assets to meet risks based on rule [R1], per unit of portfolio reserve (net of the risk margin): $M_z^{[R1](T)}/V_z^{(II)[BE]}$, facing longevity risk and mortality random fluctuations

Time z	Time horizon $T = 1$			Time horizon $T = 3$		
	$n_0 = 100$ (%)	$n_0 = 1\,000$ (%)	$n_0 = 10\,000$ (%)	$n_0 = 100$ (%)	$n_0 = 1\,000$ (%)	$n_0 = 10\,000$ (%)
0	0.574	0.473	0.212	1.834	1.063	0.525
5	1.058	0.743	0.376	3.358	1.688	1.006
10	1.951	1.159	0.694	5.162	2.659	1.941
15	3.600	2.034	1.343	8.689	4.679	3.812
20	6.639	3.602	2.559	14.046	8.532	7.301
25	12.246	6.338	4.954	23.787	15.426	13.449
30	22.588	12.168	9.449	46.170	28.301	24.099
35	41.664	26.210	18.265	124.167	54.361	41.379

Table 14.5 Required assets to meet risks based on rules [R1] and [R3], facing mortality random fluctuations only; mortality assumption $H_{4((1955)}$

| Time z | Rule [R1], with $T = \omega + 1 - x_0 - z$ $\frac{M_z^{[R1]}(\omega+1-x_0-z)}{V_z^{(II)[BE]}}$ | | | Rule [R3] $\frac{M_z^{[R3]}}{V_z^{(II)[BE]}}$ | | |
	$n_0 = 100$ (%)	$n_0 = 1\,000$ (%)	$n_0 = 10\,000$ (%)	$n_0 = 100$ (%)	$n_0 = 1\,000$ (%)	$n_0 = 10\,000$ (%)
0	7.813	2.832	0.879	7.031	2.698	0.800
5	9.983	3.071	1.067	9.436	2.949	1.040
10	12.144	4.040	1.217	11.543	3.759	1.193
15	16.153	5.202	1.544	14.982	4.921	1.462
20	22.343	6.938	2.091	21.292	6.554	1.936
25	29.728	10.388	3.072	28.546	9.642	2.983
30	54.183	16.871	5.547	51.253	16.807	5.152
35	155.859	36.795	11.715	144.058	34.809	11.207

| Time z | Rule [R1], with $T = 1$ $\frac{M_z^{[R1]}(1)}{V_z^{(II)[BE]}}$ | | | Rule [R1], with $T = 3$ $\frac{M_z^{[R1]}(3)}{V_z^{(II)[BE]}}$ | | |
	$n_0 = 100$ (%)	$n_0 = 1\,000$ (%)	$n_0 = 10\,000$ (%)	$n_0 = 100$ (%)	$n_0 = 1\,000$ (%)	$n_0 = 10\,000$ (%)
0	0.574	0.473	0.171	1.834	0.983	0.378
5	1.058	0.743	0.271	3.358	1.443	0.479
10	1.951	0.932	0.388	5.162	1.957	0.657
15	3.600	1.642	0.583	8.604	2.630	0.932
20	6.639	2.458	0.806	13.304	3.775	1.329
25	12.246	4.633	1.379	19.609	7.129	2.166
30	22.588	7.878	2.804	41.023	13.181	4.168
35	41.664	21.058	7.321	124.167	32.954	10.176

Table 14.6 Required assets to meet risks based on rules [R1] and [R3], facing longevity risk only

	Required assets to meet risks			
Time z	$\dfrac{M_z^{[R1]}(1)}{V_z^{(\text{II})[\text{BE}]}}$ (%)	$\dfrac{M_z^{[R1]}(3)}{V_z^{(\text{II})[\text{BE}]}}$ (%)	$\dfrac{M_z^{[R1]}(\omega+1-x_0-z)}{V_z^{(\text{II})[\text{BE}]}}$ (%)	$\dfrac{M_z^{[R3]}}{V_z^{(\text{II})[\text{BE}]}}$ (%)
0	0.110	0.366	9.402	9.402
5	0.247	0.805	12.270	12.270
10	0.531	1.691	16.134	16.134
15	1.105	3.423	21.301	21.301
20	2.233	6.681	28.102	28.102
25	4.389	12.511	36.826	36.826
30	8.346	22.240	47.599	47.599
35	15.214	36.932	60.269	60.269

Table 14.7 Required assets to meet risks according to Solvency II

Time z	$\dfrac{M_z^{[\text{Solv2}]}}{V_z^{(\text{II})[\text{BE}]}}$ (%)	$\dfrac{RM_z}{V_z^{(\text{II})[\text{BE}]}}$ (%)	$\dfrac{\text{Life}_{\text{long},z}}{V_z^{(\text{II})[\text{BE}]}}$ (%)
0	14.369	7.095	7.274
5	16.266	7.186	9.080
10	18.533	7.156	11.377
15	21.288	6.995	14.293
20	24.713	6.712	18.000
25	29.123	6.356	22.767
30	35.123	6.020	29.102
35	43.922	5.856	38.067

technical provision) and required capital. It is clear that, in relative terms such an amount is independent of the portfolio size. We further recall that, under Solvency II, no specific capital allocation is required for the risk of random fluctuations, since they are treated as hedgeable risks.

In Tables 14.6 and 14.7, at any valuation time the required capital is flat in respect of the portfolio size. This may suggest a deterministic approach for allocating capital to deal with longevity risk. In particular, the assessment of the required capital could be based on a comparison between the actual reserve (net of the risk margin) and a reserve (again net of the risk margin) calculated under a more severe mortality trend assumption (as turns out to be the case under Solvency II).

Let $V_z^{(\Pi)[B]}$ be the expected present value of future payments for the portfolio, based on a mortality assumption worse than the best-estimate assumption, ie, on a lower mortality hypothesis; thus

$$V_z^{(\Pi)[BE]} \leq V_z^{(\Pi)[B]}$$

We note that $V_z^{(\Pi)[B]}$ represents the technical provision, net of the risk margin, based on assumption B. The required amount of assets to meet risks would then be

$$[R4]: \quad M_z^{[R4]} = V_z^{(\Pi)[B]} - V_z^{(\Pi)[BE]}$$

We note that rule $[R4]$ would account for longevity risk only. Further, no default probability is explicitly mentioned; however, the mortality assumption adopted in $V_z^{(\Pi)[B]}$ clearly implies some value for the default probability. The time horizon implicitly considered is the maximum residual duration of the portfolio, given that this is the time horizon referred to in the calculation of the reserve. Further, given that $M_z^{[R4]}$ is a difference between expected values, it turns out to be linear in respect of the portfolio size.

In order to compare rules $[R1]$, $[R3]$ and $[R4]$, we define the following ratios

$$QM_z^{[R1]}(T; n_z) = \frac{M_z^{[R1]}(T)}{V_z^{(\Pi)[BE]}}$$

$$QM_z^{[R3]}(n_z) = \frac{M_z^{[R3]}}{V_z^{(\Pi)[BE]}}$$

$$QV_z = \frac{M_z^{[R4]}}{V_z^{(\Pi)[BE]}}$$

The ratios $QM_z^{[R1]}(T; n_z)$ and $QM_z^{[R3]}(n_z)$ depend on the size of the portfolio, n_z, as they also account for the risk of random fluctuations, while the ratio QV_z, which addresses just the longevity risk, is independent of the portfolio size. On the other hand, rules $[R1]$ and $[R3]$ could be implemented considering only the risk of random fluctuations or longevity risk, as we have illustrated in the calculations in Tables 14.5 and 14.6, respectively. As can be seen from Table 14.6, when addressing longevity risk only, the ratios $QM_z^{[R1]}(T; n_z)$ and $QM_z^{[R3]}(n_z)$ are independent of the size of the portfolio; this situation could suggest a deterministic approach instead of a simulation-based procedure. However, we have already commented that addressing just a component of the mortality risks represents an improper use of rules $[R1]$ and $[R3]$. A further difference between ratios $QM_z^{[R1]}(T; n_z)$ and QV_z stands in the possibility to set a preferred time horizon; indeed, time horizons other than the maximum one may be chosen only when rule $[R1]$ is adopted.

It is not possible to derive general conclusions regarding the comparison between the outcoming levels of ratios $QM_z^{[R1]}(T; n_z)$ and $QM_z^{[R3]}(n_z)$, on one hand, and QV_z, on the other. We just consider the results previously illustrated, first noting that the quantity $\text{Life}_{\text{long}, z} / V_z^{(\Pi)[BE]}$ provides us with an example of ratio QV_z. We can comment on the fact that a simplified rule, such as $[R4]$ and that implicit in Solvency II, while more direct to implement may result in an amount of required assets that is too high or too low in relation to the portfolio size and the duration of the portfolio. This is due to neglecting the pooling component, where the impact depends on portfolio size (and age as well). We further note that under Solvency II the risk margin, where the amount depends on the capital required for longevity risk, may stress this aspect.

Undoubtedly, the advantage of rule $[R4]$ is its simplicity. Of course, it is possible to find the reserving basis avoiding unsatisfactory situations (but to be sure, one should first perform the valuation through an internal model, at least for some typical compositions of the portfolio). The possibility to adopt different solvency time horizons for the different mortality risk components supports the separate treatment of the components themselves. So we could choose the maximum possible value for T when accounting for longevity risk only (adopting the simplified rule $[R4]$) and a short–medium time horizon when accounting for random fluctuations only (if rule $[R1]$ is adopted, with say $T = 1$–5 years). For practical purposes, this approach could represent a good compromise, provided that the relevant assumptions are properly disclosed. If valuation tools other than an internal model are available, or are required for the risk of random fluctuations (as should be the case for Solvency II), then rule $[R4]$ is certainly able to capture properly the feature of longevity risk (only).

REFERENCES

Biffis, E., 2005, "Affine Processes for Dynamic Mortality and Actuarial Valuations", *Insurance: Mathematics & Economics*, 37(3), pp. 443–468.

Biffis, E. and P. Millossovich, 2006, "A Bidimensional Approach to Mortality Risk", *Decision in Economics and Finance*, 29, pp. 71–94.

Blake, D., A. J. G. Cairns and K. Dowd, 2006, "Living with Mortality: Longevity Bonds and Other Mortality-Linked Securities", *British Actuarial Journal*, 12, pp. 153–228.

Cairns, A. J. G., D. Blake and K. Dowd, 2006, "A Two-Factor Model for Stochastic Mortality with Parameter Uncertainty: Theory and Calibration", *The Journal of Risk and Insurance*, 73(4), pp. 687–718.

CEIOPS, 2007, "QIS3. Technical Specifications, Part I: Instructions", April, URL: http://www.pszaf.hu/data/cms1305277/pszafhu_szolvencia_QIS3techspec1.pdf.

CEIOPS, 2008, "QIS4. Technical Specifications", December, URL: http://ec.europa.eu/internal_market/insurance/docs/solvency/qis4/technical_specifications_en.pdf.

CMI, 2002, "An Interim Basis for Adjusting the "92" Series Mortality Projections for Cohort Effects", Working Paper 1, The Faculty of Actuaries and Institute of Actuaries.

CMI, 2006, "Stochastic Projection Methodologies: Further Progress and P-Spline Model Features, Example Results and Implications", Working Paper 20, The Faculty of Actuaries and Institute of Actuaries.

IAA, 2004, "A Global Framework for Insurer Solvency Assessment", Research Report of the Insurer Solvency Assessment Working Party, International Actuarial Association. URL: http://www.actuaries.org/LIBRARY/Papers/Global_Framework_Insurer_Solvency_Assessment-public.pdf.

Lin, Y. and S. H. Cox, 2005, "Securitization of Mortality Risks in Life Annuities", *The Journal of Risk and Insurance*, 72(2), pp. 227–252.

Olivieri, A., 2001, "Uncertainty in Mortality Projections: An Actuarial Perspective", *Insurance: Mathematics & Economics*, 29(2), pp. 231–245.

Olivieri, A., 2005, "Designing Longevity Risk Transfers: The Point of View of the Cedant", *Giornale dell'Istituto Italiano degli Attuari*, 68, pp. 1–35. Reprinted in: *ICFAI Journal of Financial Risk Management*, 4, 2007, pp. 55–83.

Olivieri, A. and E. Pitacco, 2002, "Inference About Mortality Improvements in Life Annuity Portfolios", *Transactions of the 27th International Congress of Actuaries* Cancun (Mexico).

Olivieri, A. and E. Pitacco, 2003, "Solvency Requirements for Pension Annuities", *Journal of Pension Economics & Finance*, 2, pp. 127–157.

Pitacco, E., M. Denuit, S. Haberman and A. Olivieri, 2009, *Modelling Longevity Dynamics for Pensions and Annuity Business* (Oxford University Press).

Sandström, A., 2006, *Solvency: Models, Assessment and Regulation* (New York: Chapman and Hall).

15

Risk Assessment of Life Insurance Contracts: A Comparative Study in a Lévy Framework

Nadine Gatzert; Stefan Kassberger

University of Erlangen-Nuremberg; Ulm University

In recent years implicit options in life insurance contracts have attracted substantial attention, especially after British Equitable Life had to close to new business in 2000 due to an improper hedging of provided options. Participating life insurance contracts feature embedded options in the form of an interest rate guarantee and participation in the return generated by the insurer's reference portfolio. Requirements concerning proper valuation of these options have been implemented in the context of international accounting standards (eg, International Financial Reporting Standards) and play a substantial role within regulatory frameworks (eg, Solvency II in the European Union). Since insurance companies normally cannot or do not follow perfect hedging strategies, they remain at risk. Failure to quantify and handle this risk adequately can endanger an insurer's ability to meet financial obligations. In this respect, modelling assets and liabilities is of central importance in practice, say, for determining solvency capital. Generally, the most relevant source of model risk is the process specification of the reference portfolio, which has a significant impact on the price and risk of participating contracts and, in particular, the options embedded in them. It can thus imply substantial solvency risk for insurance companies. The aim of this chapter is to analyse the impact of the asset model specification on pricing and risk measurement by comparing the risk of fair contracts in the standard Black–Scholes framework with a Lévy-type model. The investigation uses a three-step procedure, which allows a very clear and detailed identification of the effect of asset process characteristics.

The fair pricing of various types of participating life insurance contracts have been studied by several authors, including Briys and de Varenne (1994), Grosen and Jørgensen (2000, 2002), Hansen and Miltersen (2002) and Ballotta et al (2006). All of the cited literature builds on the assumption of a geometric Brownian motion model for the dynamics of the asset base. Recently, models based on Lévy processes as the driving noise of the underlying reference portfolio have been applied in the literature to evaluate participating life insurance contracts. These models allow for jumps in asset price paths and skewness (asymmetry) and excess kurtosis (fat tails) in asset price returns, all of which are commonly observed features across almost all financial asset classes.

Ballotta (2006) employs a variance gamma process to model the dynamics of the reference portfolio, whereas Le Courtois and Quittard-Pinon (2008) use a double exponential jump diffusion, also known as a Kou process, for the same purpose. Ballotta (2005) employs a Merton-style jump diffusion model to evaluate a participating contract commonly used in the UK. Kassberger et al (2008) generalise the latter approach by comparing the impact of different Lévy process specifications on pricing and fair contract parameters for various popular designs of participating life insurance policies. Their analysis reveals significant model risk, as reflected in differing contract prices. The consideration of real-world risk measurement is an important aspect that is usually omitted in the pricing process, as demonstrated by the above-mentioned articles, even though fair contracts do not necessarily bear the same risk. Gatzert and Kling (2007), for instance, address this problem and compare the risk of fair contracts for different types of participating life insurance policies within a Black–Scholes framework, thus identifying key risk drivers. Consideration of risk will be of particular interest and relevance when the dynamics of the insurer's reference portfolio are based on a Lévy process that makes it possible to even better capture the properties of real-world return distributions.

In this chapter we investigate the impact of the asset process specification on pricing and risk assessment of a participating life insurance contract. In the analysis, we contrast results from the Black–Scholes framework, based on a geometric Brownian motion, with outcomes from an asset return process using a Lévy process with jumps, specifically, a normal inverse Gaussian process. Where previous literature has focused on either risk-neutral pricing or risk measurement, we take the analysis further by integrating these two approaches. This has not been done so far, even though a comprehensive analysis of the effect of asset dynamics on shortfall risk requires comparable ("fair") initial conditions. To achieve this, we first calibrate fair contract parameter combinations of guaranteed interest rates, annual surplus participation rates and terminal bonus participation rates for both asset models and then calculate the corresponding shortfall risk. If contracts (with guaranteed interest rate, annual and terminal surplus participation rate) under the Brownian model and under Lévy specifications are calibrated separately to be fair and thus to have the same market value, it is not clear in the first place whether a Lévy process with jumps still implies a higher shortfall risk than a geometric Brownian motion without jumps. To capture the downside risk, we use lower partial moments as the relevant risk measures, comparing shortfall probability and expected shortfall.

We employ a three-step approach, which is described as follows. First, we assume that the insurance company invests in a reference portfolio that evolves according to a geometric Brownian motion. In this setting we identify contract parameters that lead to the same market value and measure the corresponding risk under the real-world measure. In a second step, the risk of the contracts found in the first step in the Brownian motion setting is recalculated, this time assuming that the reference portfolio follows an exponential normal inverse Gaussian process. This results in the contracts no longer being fair. Hence, in a third step we recalibrate the contract parameters to obtain fair contracts under the normal inverse Gaussian model and then, again, calculate the associated risk. By proceeding in this way, we can consecutively and comprehensively identify the effects of the asset model on pricing and risk assessment in comparable situations.

The remainder of the chapter is organised as follows. In the next section, the basic model framework for the participating life insurance contract is described based on the contract design in Ballotta *et al* (2006) and fair valuation and risk measurement are presented. The subsequent section introduces the two considered asset models and the measure transform to relate risk neutral and real-world measure. Numerical simulation results are then given, including a comparison of fair contracts under Brownian motion with those found employing a Lévy model and an analysis of the corresponding risk of fair contracts. The penultimate section contains a sensitivity analysis to assess the parameter risk in both models and the final section concludes.

BASIC MODEL FRAMEWORK
The life insurance contract
To initiate the contract, policyholders pay a single premium P_0. The company's initial equity capital is denoted by E_0. The sum of the initial contributions $A_0 = E_0 + P_0$ is invested in the reference portfolio. Hence, for $0 < k \leq 1$, it holds that $P_0 = k \cdot A_0$ and $E_0 = (1 - k) \cdot A_0$, where k represents the leverage of the company. The dynamics of the reference portfolio will be discussed in the next section.

Let P denote the policyholders' account, which is the book value of the policy reserves. The policy reserve P is a year-to-year, or cliquet-style, guarantee: that is, it annually earns the greater of the guaranteed interest rate or a fraction α of the annual surplus generated by the insurer's investment portfolio. For $t = 1, 2, \ldots, T$, the development of the policy reserve is given by

$$P(t) = P(t - 1) \cdot \left(1 + \max\left[g, \alpha\left(\frac{A(t)}{A(t-1)} - 1 \right) \right] \right)$$

with $P(0) = P_0$ and $A(0) = A_0$. At maturity, a fraction $\delta \in [0, 1]$ of the terminal surplus $B(T) = [kA(T) - P(T)]^+$ is distributed to the policyholders according to the parameter k. If the company is insolvent at the time of maturity, it will not be able to pay the policyholders' claims $P(T)$ in full. In this case, policyholders receive the total value of the reference portfolio at maturity.[1] The value of liabilities $L(T)$ can be summarised as

$$
\begin{aligned}
L(T) &= P(T) + \delta[kA(T) - P(T)]^+ - [P(T) - A(T)]^+ \\
&= P(T) + \delta B(T) - D(T)
\end{aligned}
\tag{15.1}
$$

where $D(T)$ denotes the default put option. The residual claim of the equityholders $E(T)$ is determined as the difference between market value of the reference portfolio $A(T)$ and the policyholders' claim $L(T)$, that is

$$E(T) = A(T) - L(T) = \max(A(T) - P(T), 0) - \delta B(T) \geq 0$$

Fair valuation

Valuation of the claims given in Equation 15.1 can be conducted using risk-neutral valuation ("risk pricing"). Hence, the market value, which is calculated under the risk-neutral measure Q is

$$
\begin{aligned}
\Pi^* &= E_Q(e^{-r \cdot T} L(T)) \\
&= E_Q(e^{-r \cdot T} P(T)) + E_Q(e^{-r \cdot T} \delta B(T)) - E_Q(e^{-r \cdot T} D(T)) \\
&= \Pi^P + \Pi^B - \Pi^{\text{DPO}} \quad\quad\quad\quad\quad\quad (15.2)
\end{aligned}
$$

Equation 15.2 shows that the value of the policyholder payout is composed of three parts. The first two terms sum up to the value of the insurance liabilities, ie, the payout promised to the policyholders in terms of the policy reserves Π^P and the terminal bonus participation Π^B. The third term is the value of the default put option Π^{DPO}, which reduces the insurance liabilities ($\Pi^P + \Pi^B$) to Π^*. This leads to the implication that companies with higher default risk should *ceteris paribus* charge a lower competitive premium, whereas insurers with lower default risk can charge higher rates. Hence, in the valuation of liabilities, possible insolvency of the company is explicitly taken into account by the default put option.

Several parameters have an impact on the value of the default put option. For instance, with increasing leverage coefficient k less initial equity is available, which raises the risk of default, see Equation 15.1. In contrast, distribution of terminal surplus participation is optional and thus does not cause additional shortfall risk for the insurer. Insolvency risk is induced only by the guaranteed interest rate and the annual surplus participation.

In a no-arbitrage setting, an up-front premium is regarded as fair if it is equal to the market value of the liabilities at time $t = 0$, which can be expressed by the following equilibrium condition

$$\Pi^* = P_0 \quad\quad\quad\quad\quad\quad (15.3)$$

This requirement is equivalent to the condition that the value of the equity holders' payout be equal to their initial contribution. We use Equation 15.3 to identify parameters of fair contracts by calibrating the guaranteed interest rate g, the annual surplus participation rate α, and the terminal surplus participation rate δ.

From the contract components, the default-value-to-liability ratio d^* can directly be derived from the value of the claims in Equation 15.2, which is a common measure of insurance company solvency (see, for example, Butsic 1994 and Barth 2000). The default-value-to-liability ratio is defined as the default put option value divided by the expected value of the liabilities under Q and thus permits a comparison of insurance companies of different sizes

$$d^* = \frac{\Pi^{DPO}}{\Pi^P + \Pi^B}$$

Risk measurement

In the following we consider shortfall only possible at maturity and, hence, only European-style contracts, see Grosen and Jørgensen (2000). A shortfall is defined as occurring when the value of the assets at maturity does not cover the book value of the policy reserves, ie, $A(T) < P(T)$.

Under the objective measure $\mathbb{P}$, the shortfall probability SP is given by

$$SP = \mathbb{P}(A(T) < P(T))$$

and the (unconditional) expected shortfall ES is defined by

$$ES = E^{\mathbb{P}}([P(T) - A(T)]^+)$$

BLACK–SCHOLES AND LÉVY MODELS FOR ASSET PRICES

This section compares two models for the asset prices, namely the traditional Brownian motion based Black–Scholes setting and the normal inverse Gaussian (NIG) model.

The Black–Scholes model for asset prices

Let $(W^{\mathbb{P}}(t))$, $0 \leq t \leq T$, be a standard Brownian motion on a probability space $(\Omega, \mathcal{F}, \mathbb{P})$ and $(\mathcal{F}_t)$, $0 \leq t \leq T$, be the filtration generated by the Brownian motion. In the standard Black–Scholes framework, the total market value of assets A evolves according to a geometric

Brownian motion (under the objective measure $\mathbb{P}$)

$$dA(t) = mA(t)\,dt + \sigma A(t)\,dW^{\mathbb{P}}(t)$$

with constant asset drift m, volatility σ and a $\mathbb{P}$-Brownian motion $W^{\mathbb{P}}$, assuming a complete, perfect and frictionless market. The solution of the stochastic differential equation is given by (see, eg, Björk (2004) for details)

$$
\begin{aligned}
A(t) &= A(0) \cdot \exp((m - \sigma^2/2)t + \sigma \cdot W^{\mathbb{P}}(t)) \\
&= A(t-1) \cdot \exp(m - \sigma^2/2 + \sigma \cdot (W^{\mathbb{P}}(t) - W^{\mathbb{P}}(t-1)))
\end{aligned}
$$

Under the unique equivalent martingale measure Q, the drift changes to the risk-free interest rate r, and the solution of the stochastic differential equation under Q is then obtained analogously

$$A(t) = A(t-1) \cdot \exp(r - \sigma^2/2 + \sigma \cdot (W^Q(t) - W^Q(t-1)))$$

where W^Q is a Q-Brownian motion.

A Lévy model for asset prices

We next consider the case where annual log returns $X(t) - X(t-1)$ under the empirical measure $\mathbb{P}$ follow an $NIG(\alpha, \beta, \delta, \mu)$ distribution (see Barndorff-Nielsen 1997).[2] The parameter α relates to steepness, β to asymmetry, δ to scale and μ to the location of the density. The class of Lévy models encompasses the Brownian model as a special case but, in contrast to the Brownian model, allows for jumps in the price paths, and skewness and excess kurtosis in asset return distributions, and thus takes into account features often observed in real-world asset prices. The asset price follows an exponential Lévy process with

$$A(t) = A(t-1) \cdot \exp(X(t) - X(t-1))$$

where $(X(t))$ is an NIG process with $X(t) \sim NIG(\alpha, \beta, \delta t, \mu t)$. In order for the exponential moment $E(\exp(X(t)))$ to exist, which becomes necessary when pricing options involving $A(t)$, we need the additional condition $\alpha \geq \beta + 1$.

The characteristic function of a $NIG(\alpha, \beta, \delta, \mu)$ random variable has the form

$$\phi_{NIG}(u) = \exp\left(\delta\sqrt{\alpha^2 - \beta^2} - \delta\sqrt{\alpha^2 - (\beta + iu)^2} + iu\mu\right) \quad (15.4)$$

The characteristic function can be used for efficient pricing of standard European options using the fast Fourier transform algorithm; see Carr and Madan (1999).

Option pricing in general Lévy models

While the risk involved in an insurance contract must be calculated under the real-world measure $\mathbb{P}$, pricing needs to be carried out under a risk-neutral measure Q. Normally, Lévy models lead to incomplete markets with an infinite number of equivalent martingale measures Q. In principle, there are two ways to determine the martingale measure. We can start from the statistical measure $\mathbb{P}$ and determine the martingale measure (also called the risk-neutral measure) Q by transforming $\mathbb{P}$. In this case, the measure Q and – thus also option prices – will depend on the type of transform used. Alternatively, we can directly model under Q without any explicit reference to the statistical measure $\mathbb{P}$. This can be done by calibrating the parameters of the driving process to the prices of options in the reference portfolio, if such prices are observable.

In our analysis, we use the Esscher transform for changing a measure $\mathbb{P}$ to an equivalent measure Q (Gerber and Shiu 1994, 1996; Bühlmann *et al* 1996; Kassberger *et al* 2008). In this case, the measures are related by

$$\left. \frac{dQ}{d\mathbb{P}} \right|_{\mathcal{F}_t} = Z_t^\theta = \frac{\exp(\theta X_t)}{E_{\mathbb{P}}(\exp(\theta X_t))}$$

with θ a real number and $(\mathcal{F}_t)$ the natural filtration. θ will be chosen such that the discounted asset price process satisfies a given drift restriction.

If, under the martingale measure Q, the log-return process $(X(t))$ follows an NIG process with $X(t) \sim NIG(\alpha, \beta, \delta t, \mu t)$ where $\alpha \geq 1/2$ and $(r - \mu)^2 \leq \delta^2(2\alpha - 1)$, then under a measure $\mathbb{P}$ arising from Q through an Esscher transform with parameter θ, $(X(t))$ remains an NIG process, but the distribution of the marginal log-returns changes to $X(t) \sim NIG(\alpha, \beta + \theta, \delta t, \mu t)$. Thus, the NIG class is closed under the Esscher transform. If $(X(t))$ is a Brownian motion, the Esscher transform simply amounts to a change of drift.

Apart from the Esscher transform, there are other ways to relate risk-neutral and empirical measures, for instance the mean-correcting transform (eg, Schoutens 2003). This is based on the idea

Table 15.1 Risk-neutral parameters according to Schoutens (2003) and corresponding risk-neutral moments for the S&P 500 index

	NIG	BM
$\alpha_{S\&P}$	6.1882	-
$\beta_{S\&P}$	-3.8941	-
$\delta_{S\&P}$	0.1622	-
$\mu_{S\&P}$	0.1421	-
Standard deviation	0.2363	0.1812
Skewness	-2.1374	0
Kurtosis	12.9374	3

of adjusting the location parameter of a distribution such that a certain drift condition is met.

NUMERICAL ANALYSIS
Input parameters
We use the following parameter set as the basis for all simulation analyses, unless otherwise stated

$$m = 5\%, r = 3.5\%, T = 10, E_0 = 10, P_0 = 100$$

We further assume that an insurer invests in a realistic reference portfolio with a 25% portion in risky investments, which is modelled based on the S&P 500 index.

The NIG-parameters $\alpha_{S\&P}, \beta_{S\&P}, \delta_{S\&P}$ for the evolution of the S&P 500 index under Q are taken from Schoutens (2003), who obtains these parameters by calibrating a NIG distribution to match market prices of traded options.[3] Furthermore, the latter author also calibrates a standard Black–Scholes model to the same dataset. These option-implied risk-neutral parameters and the corresponding moments for annual log-returns of the S&P 500 index in the NIG and Brownian models are reported in Table 15.1. $\mu_{S\&P}$ was obtained using the fact that for a riskless interest rate r of 3.5% and Y following a NIG distribution with parameters as in Table 15.1, $E_Q(\exp(Y)) = \exp(r)$ has to hold. $\mu_{S\&P}$ was calculated by solving $\phi_{NIG}(-i) = \exp(r)$ for $\mu_{S\&P}$ (see Equation 15.4).

As we want to model a more realistic reference portfolio, that is, one for an insurer that has investments other than and in addition to those represented in the S&P 500 index, we reduce the standard

Table 15.2 Risk-neutral and real-world parameters and moments for the reference portfolio

	Q		$\mathbb{P}$	
	NIG	**BM**	**NIG**	**BM**
α	24.7496	-	24.7496	-
β	−15.5734	-	−9.6571	-
δ	0.04055	-	0.04055	-
μ	0.06615	-	0.06615	-
Drift	-	0.035	-	0.05
Standard deviation	0.0591	0.0453	0.0458	0.0453
Skewness	−2.1374	0	−1.2177	0
Kurtosis	12.9374	3	8.2238	3

deviation of the reference portfolio to one fourth of the index volatility, while leaving skewness and kurtosis unchanged. This procedure preserves the essential features of most financial return distributions, namely negative skewness and excess kurtosis. The parameters $(\alpha, \beta, \delta, \mu)$ of the reference portfolio can be inferred from the moments[4] and the martingale condition, and are exhibited in the left column of Table 15.2.

For risk measurement purposes, the asset portfolio dynamics under the real-world measure $\mathbb{P}$ are needed. By the discussion on the Esscher measure, $E_{\mathbb{P}}(\exp(Y)) = \exp(m)$ needs to be solved for θ^*, where $Y \sim \text{NIG}(\alpha, \beta + \theta^*, \delta, \mu)$. For a real-world drift of $m = 5\%$, β then changes to $\beta^* = \beta + \theta^* = -9.6571$. Numerical results are obtained using Monte Carlo simulation with 200,000 runs (Glasserman 2004).

The impact of the asset process specification on risk pricing

In a first step, we compare fair contracts derived from the Black–Scholes and Lévy models. The guaranteed interest rate g and annual surplus participation rate α are calibrated to satisfy the equilibrium set out in Equation 15.3 using the Newton method for numerical root finding. Fair parameter combinations (g, α) are displayed in Figure 15.1 for different choices of terminal surplus participation rate ($\delta = 0\%$, 40% and 80%) under a Brownian motion ("BM", dashed line in Figure 15.1) and an NIG process ("Lévy", solid line).[5]

To ensure the fairness condition in both models, the annual surplus participation rate decreases as the guaranteed interest

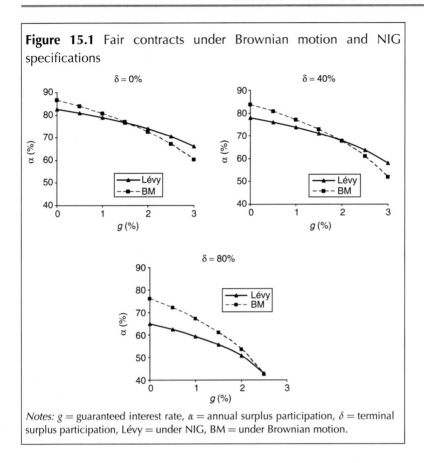

Figure 15.1 Fair contracts under Brownian motion and NIG specifications

Notes: g = guaranteed interest rate, *α* = annual surplus participation, *δ* = terminal surplus participation, Lévy = under NIG, BM = under Brownian motion.

rate increases. When no terminal surplus participation is offered ($\delta = 0\%$), the isoquant obtained in the NIG model is above the Brownian motion isoquant if $g \geq 1.5\%$, ie, the insurance company can offer higher annual surplus participation in this case. The isoquants calculated in the two models run near each other and intersect in the range considered. With increasing terminal surplus participation δ, the intersection point is shifted to the right. For example, when $\delta = 80\%$ and $g < 2.5\%$, pricing the contract under the Black–Scholes model leads to higher fair annual participation rates than under the NIG model.

Decomposition of policyholders' claims into contract components

To investigate the sources of the differences observed in Figure 15.1, we decompose policyholders' claims into their contract

Table 15.3 Decomposition of fair contract value in contract components under Brownian motion and NIG specifications for $\delta = 40\%$

	g (%)	α (%)	Π^*	Π^P	Π^B	Π^{DPO}	d^* (%)
BM	0.50	80.58	100.00	99.03	1.25	0.28	0.28
Lévy not fair		80.58	101.18	102.47	1.33	2.62	2.52
Lévy		76.04	100.00	100.42	1.81	2.23	2.18
BM	1.50	72.67	100.00	99.05	1.52	0.57	0.57
Lévy not fair		72.67	100.40	101.42	1.79	2.81	2.73
Lévy		71.06	100.00	100.71	1.96	2.67	2.60
BM	2.50	60.93	100.00	99.26	1.85	1.11	1.09
Lévy not fair		60.93	99.40	100.05	2.38	3.03	2.95
Lévy		63.69	100.00	101.13	2.13	3.26	3.14

Notes: g = guaranteed interest rate, α = annual surplus participation, δ = terminal surplus participation, Π^* = value of policyholders' claims in US dollars, Π^P = value of policy reserves in US dollars, Π^B = value of terminal bonus payment in US dollars, Π^{DPO} = value of default put option in US dollars, d^* = default-value-to-liability ratio = $\Pi^{DPO}/(\Pi^P + \Pi^B)$, BM = under Brownian motion, Lévy = under NIG, Lévy not fair = NIG for fair parameter combinations under Brownian motion.

components. Table 15.3 shows the total value of the contract Π^* and its components as given in Equation 15.2: the value of the policy reserve Π^P, the value of the terminal bonus Π^B, and the value of the default put option Π^{DPO}. Furthermore, the default-value-to-liability ratio d^* is given.

To analyse how asset model specifications affect the contract components, we proceed in three steps. First, we calculate the component values for fair contracts under the Black–Scholes model as displayed in Figure 15.1. In the second step, the values of the contracts found in the first step and characterised by parameter combinations that are fair under Black–Scholes are calculated, now assuming that the reference portfolio follows an exponential NIG process instead of a geometric Brownian motion, resulting in the contracts no longer being fair. Hence, in the third step, the annual surplus participation rate α is recalibrated to obtain a fair contract under the Lévy model, as shown in Figure 15.1, and then, again, the corresponding component values are calculated. Table 15.3 shows selected results for a guaranteed interest rate of 0.50%, 1.50% and 2.50% in the case where $\delta = 40\%$.[6]

We look first at the Black–Scholes model where fair contracts are calibrated in the Brownian motion setting, but the market exhibits

Lévy characteristics ("BM" and "Lévy not fair"). Since the contracts are no longer fair in this case, the market value of the policyholders' payout Π^* differs from the policyholders' initial payment of US\$100. For $g = 0.50\%$, the market value increases to US\$101.18. As the guaranteed interest rate increases, the market value decreases, for example, for $g = 2.50\%$, Π^* decreases from US\$100 to US\$99.40, which is less than the initial up-front premium. The difference in the market value of the claims under the Lévy specification may appear minor, but this is an inaccurate observation as the individual contract components are significantly shifted when the driving process is changed. It is the counterbalancing effects of Π^P, Π^B, and Π^{DPO} that make the change in the total market value appear negligible. This effect was also observed by Ballotta (2005) in a similar context for a different type of contract. In particular, the overall decrease under the NIG model for $g = 2.50\%$ is mainly caused by a higher default put option value, which even dominates the increase in the terminal bonus component. In the Black–Scholes setting, the values of all contract components are clearly lower compared with the Lévy model.

The increase in the default put option also affects the default-value-to-liability ratio. Even though the market value of the claims Π^* is lower for $g = 2.50\%$ under the NIG model, the insurer's insolvency risk increases significantly ($d^* = 1.09\%$ versus $d^* = 2.95\%$), illustrating that the Black–Scholes model underestimates the insurer's default risk in the considered example. Note that the value of the default put option corresponds to the lower partial moment of degree one (termed unconditional expected shortfall); see Wirch and Hardy (1999). The use of the risk-neutral measure $\mathbb{Q}$ is appropriate for risk pricing, ie, for premium calculation; however, measuring the real-world risk of future insolvency in scenario analyses should be conducted under the real-world measure $\mathbb{P}$, which will be done in the next section.

We now turn to the third situation in Table 15.3, where fair pricing is completely conducted under Lévy specifications ("Lévy"). For fixed g, the annual surplus participation rate α is adjusted so as to obtain fair contracts. Now, the values of all components Π^P, Π^B and Π^{DPO} are higher than in the Black–Scholes scenario, but still result in the same contract value Π^*. The share of the default

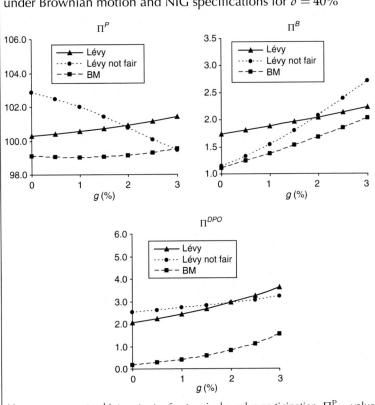

Figure 15.2 Decomposition of fair contract value in building blocks under Brownian motion and NIG specifications for $\delta = 40\%$

Notes: g = guaranteed interest rate, δ = terminal surplus participation, Π^P = value of policy reserves in US dollars, Π^B = value of terminal bonus payment in US dollars, Π^{DPO} = value of default put option in US dollars, BM = under Brownian motion, Lévy = under NIG, Lévy not fair = NIG for fair parameter combinations under BM.

put option in the value of the policyholder's payout is significantly higher (eg, for $g = 2.50\%$: $d^* = 1.09\%$ versus $d^* = 3.14\%$).

To provide further insight and a broader view, Π^P, Π^B and Π^{DPO} are graphically displayed in Figure 15.2 as functions of the guaranteed interest rate for the three situations described in Table 15.3 ("BM", "Lévy not fair" and "Lévy") for $\delta = 40\%$. For every g, different annual surplus participation is provided as given in Figure 15.1. In particular, the participation rate is reduced as the guaranteed interest rate increases.

It can be seen that even though the isoquants in Figure 15.1 run near each other and even intersect, the values of the individual components shown in Figure 15.2 can differ tremendously. In particular, the Black–Scholes model leads to an underpricing of all components Π^P, Π^B and Π^{DPO} of fair insurance contracts given in Figure 15.1 compared to the fair Lévy model.

Further, Figure 15.2 shows that the two curves "BM" and "Lévy not fair" seem to behave oppositely for Π^P and Π^B. In the first graph Π^P, the curves converge as g increases, whereas in the second graph Π^B, they diverge. Moreover, the trend of the curves "BM" and "Lévy" is noticeable. The distance between the curves of the bonus option value Π^B for fair parameters under both Lévy and Black–Scholes is lessened when the guaranteed interest rate increases. In contrast, the distance between the three default put option curves remains fairly stable across changes in contract design.

In summary, decomposition into individual contract components revealed that considerable model risk is involved in pricing the contract components, even though fair contracts have the same market value under both models and even though the isoquants of fair contracts appear to run near to each other. The value of the default put option is generally underestimated in the Black–Scholes model, which implies that the insurer's insolvency risk might not be adequately reflected when that model is employed, a topic given more detailed treatment in the next section, where the empirical risk of fair contracts is measured and compared for Brownian motion and Lévy settings.

The impact of the asset process specification on risk measurement

We next calculate the shortfall risk that corresponds to the contracts with parameter combinations (g, α, δ) from Figure 15.1 measured with lower partial moments. Figure 15.3 depicts the risk of these contracts and shows a comparison of results under Brownian motion and NIG process specifications.

From left to right, the graphs in Figure 15.3 display shortfall probability and expected shortfall. Shortfall risk is given for the three situations described in Table 15.3: "BM", "Lévy not fair" and "Lévy". Every point on the curve "BM" depicts the risk of a fair

Figure 15.3 Shortfall probability and expected shortfall of fair contracts in Figure 15.1

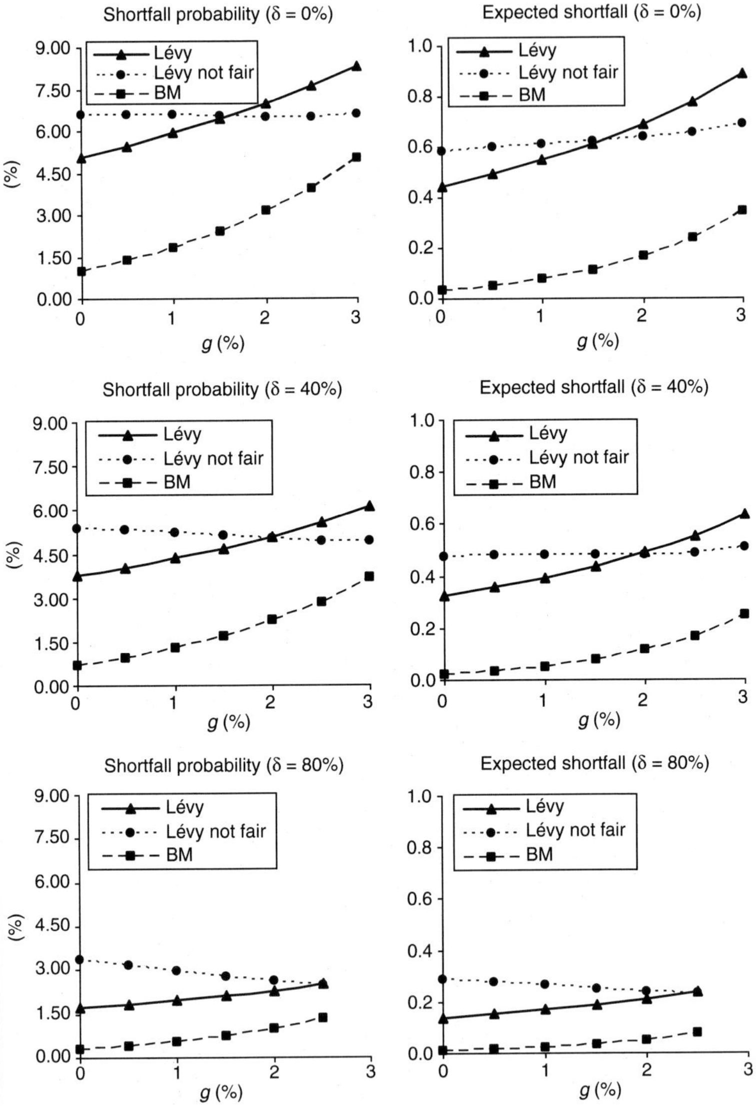

Shortfall probability ($\delta = 0\%$)

Expected shortfall ($\delta = 0\%$)

Shortfall probability ($\delta = 40\%$)

Expected shortfall ($\delta = 40\%$)

Shortfall probability ($\delta = 80\%$)

Expected shortfall ($\delta = 80\%$)

Notes: g = guaranteed interest rate, δ = terminal surplus participation, BM = under Brownian motion, Lévy = under NIG, Lévy not fair = NIG for fair parameter combinations under BM.

contract as displayed in Figure 15.1 under the standard Black–Scholes model. Hence, for different levels of g, different annual surplus participation α is provided according to Equation 15.3. For example, if $\delta = 40\%$, Figure 15.1 shows that $g = 1.5\%$ implies $\alpha = 72.67\%$ in the Brownian motion case. The corresponding shortfall probability in the middle graph of Figure 15.3 ("BM") is 1.71%. Under NIG specifications, however, these contracts are no longer fair, as illustrated in Table 15.3. Hence, every point on the curve "Lévy not fair" corresponds to the risk of the same contract that underlies the "BM" curve. When the asset process actually follows NIG specifications, the risk of a contract with $g = 1.5\%$ and $\alpha = 72.67\%$ is 5.11%. To make the contract fair under the NIG model, the annual surplus participation rate α is lowered to 71.06%, which leads to a corresponding shortfall probability of 4.68% ("Lévy").

The graphs demonstrate how the risk of fair contracts varies: both shortfall probability and expected shortfall increase in contracts with a guaranteed interest rate, despite the simultaneous decrease in the annual surplus participation. This tendency is independent of both the underlying asset process (Brownian motion and NIG process) and the choice of risk measure (shortfall probability and expected shortfall). However, the insurer's risk level differs tremendously depending on the choice of the underlying asset process, a fact that could lead to serious misestimation in the context of, for example, solvency capital.

Increasing δ allows the annual surplus participation coefficient to be lowered, which leads to a considerable reduction in risk. This occurs because risk does not depend on δ, only on α. Thus, terminal bonus participation is a key feature in reducing shortfall risk. In the standard Black–Scholes (Lévy) case, for $g = 1.50\%$, shortfall probability is reduced from 1.22% (3.39%) to 0.53% (1.51%) when terminal bonus participation is raised from 40% to 80% – the corresponding fair annual surplus participation rates are given by 72.67% (71.06%) for $\delta = 40\%$ and 61.19% (55.61%) for $\delta = 80\%$ in the Brownian (Lévy) case.

In general, the distributional characteristics of the underlying asset process will have a stronger impact on the value of the policyholders' claims for higher participation rates. For high participation rates, the guaranteed policy reserves at maturity mainly consist of the annual surplus participation, which thus induces a larger

Table 15.4 Risk-neutral and real-world parameters and moments for a portfolio with 50% stocks and 50% bonds

	$\mathbb{Q}$		$\mathbb{P}$	
	NIG	**BM**	**NIG**	**BM**
α	12.3763	-	12.3763	-
β	−7.7881	-	−5.8551	-
δ	0.0811	-	0.0811	-
μ	0.0942	-	0.0942	-
Drift	-	0.035	-	0.065
Standard deviation	0.1182	0.0906	0.0979	0.0906
Skewness	−2.1375	0	−1.5092	0
Kurtosis	12.9374	3	9.4296	3

influence of the asset process on pricing and risk assessment. With increasing guarantees and decreasing surplus participation, this effect is weakened.

Figure 15.3 illustrates that the model risk involved in the asset process may be misleading with respect to contract prices and the insurer's actual risk level. Both curves that represent the risk of contracts under the Lévy model ("Lévy" and "Lévy not fair") run above the Brownian-motion-based risk curve, which indicates that insurers may need to account for substantially higher risk.

SENSITIVITY ANALYSIS

In this section we analyse the robustness of the previous results with respect to changes in input parameters. Starting with the parameters given in the previous sections, we only vary the volatility of the insurer's portfolio and initial equity and investigate the effect on fair values and risk figures. In each case, fair contracts and shortfall probabilities are provided under Brownian motion and an NIG process for $\delta = 40\%$.

Volatility

To see the effect of increasing the asset volatility, we now assume the reference portfolio to have half of the volatility as the S&P 500 index, and leave skewness and kurtosis unchanged. For an adjusted real-world drift $m = 6.5\%$, the risk-neutral and real-world parameters for the new portfolio are obtained (see Table 15.4).

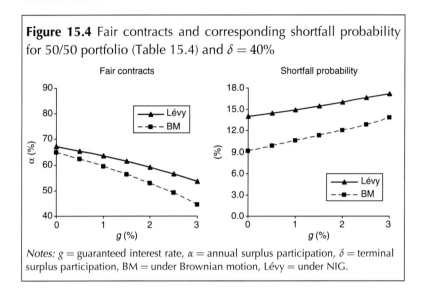

Figure 15.4 Fair contracts and corresponding shortfall probability for 50/50 portfolio (Table 15.4) and $\delta = 40\%$

Notes: g = guaranteed interest rate, α = annual surplus participation, δ = terminal surplus participation, BM = under Brownian motion, Lévy = under NIG.

Figure 15.4 displays parameter combinations (g, α) of fair contracts and the corresponding shortfall probabilities for the 50/50 portfolio. Compared to the original portfolio in Figure 15.1, the annual surplus participation rate α is substantially lower for a fixed guaranteed interest rate under both the Lévy and the Brownian model.

The more volatile the market, the lower the annual surplus participation offered to the policyholders in the case of a fixed guaranteed interest rate. Despite the much lower participation rates, Figure 15.4 shows that shortfall probability levels change enormously as g increases by approximately eight percentage points. The general tendencies are similar to the original case: shortfall probability increases when the guaranteed interest rate increases, despite decreasing participation rates.

Equity capital

The effect of variations in equity capital is shown in Figure 15.5. Here, we raise the initial contribution of the equity holders from $E_0 = 10$ to $E_0 = 15$, keeping everything else constant. This implies a decrease in the leverage coefficient from $k = 91\%$ to 87%.

As illustrated in Figure 15.5, an increase in equity capital leads to a lower annual surplus participation rate and to a substantial reduction in the shortfall probability. For example, when increasing

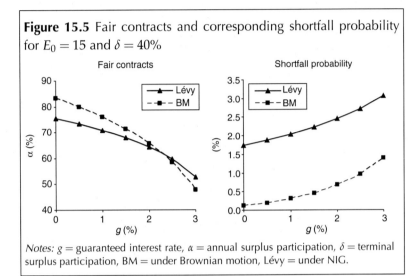

Figure 15.5 Fair contracts and corresponding shortfall probability for $E_0 = 15$ and $\delta = 40\%$

Notes: g = guaranteed interest rate, α = annual surplus participation, δ = terminal surplus participation, BM = under Brownian motion, Lévy = under NIG.

E_0 to 15 under the Lévy process for $g = 2.5\%$, α decreases from 63.69% to 59.54%, and the shortfall probability decreases from 5.56% to 2.72%. Overall, the sensitivity analysis showed that the central results remain robust with respect to changes in volatility and equity capital, even though the level of shortfall risk differs.

SUMMARY

In this chapter we have analysed the effect of the asset process specification of a participating life insurance contract on pricing and risk assessment by comparing the Brownian and NIG settings for the asset model. We contribute to the literature by combining risk pricing and risk measurement. This is achieved by calculating the real-world risk associated with contracts under the Brownian and NIG settings, if both models are each (separately) calibrated to be fair. This risk pricing procedure implies that fair parameter combinations (guaranteed interest rate, annual and terminal surplus participation rates) under both asset models differ, but still lead to the same market value. Using these contract configurations as a starting point allows a more comprehensive analysis of asset dynamics' impact on risk measurement. The numerical results showed that shortfall probability and expected shortfall of fair contracts were still several times higher under the Lévy process than in the Brownian case, even though contract parameters were calibrated to ensure the same value under the risk-neutral measure Q, a result that may not have been expected in the first place.

A decomposition of the market value of liabilities into individual contract components (guaranteed maturity payment including annual bonus, terminal bonus and default put option value) provided additional insight into the insurer's actual risk and pricing situation. Even though fair contracts have the same market value under both models and their isoquants appear to run very near to each other, the components' values differ substantially and are generally lower in the Brownian setting. This finding is of particular importance in the context of the default put option, the value of which was several times higher under the NIG process than for Brownian motion.

We further showed that even if contracts have the same (fair) market value, they can pose substantially different risks to insurers. This result is significant because in the Lévy setting, higher risk needs to be taken into account in pricing fair contracts. The finding is true for both shortfall probability and expected shortfall and implies that the insurer's insolvency risk might not be sufficiently reflected when a Brownian motion is used as the driving noise for the asset return process. We found that the guaranteed interest rate is the key risk driver for both models. Additionally, terminal bonus participation is a key feature in reducing risk: promising a higher share in the terminal bonus lowers the guaranteed interest rate and the annual surplus participation, thus reducing risk.

The outcomes also depend on the choice of input parameters, and further research on estimating input parameters is vital. Overall, the impact of the asset process specifications should not be neglected, since it can have a considerable impact on pricing and risk assessment of fair participating life insurance contracts. This result is of relevance for all main sectors in insurance companies, including internal risk models, solvency capital calculations and management decisions. The findings indicate that insurers should use alternative models instead of, or in addition to, Brownian motion-based ones for valuation and risk assessment when attempting to determine company-specific economic key figures.

1 As in Ballotta *et al* (2006), early surrenders or deaths are ignored in this setting.

2 Kassberger *et al* (2008) conduct a study on the impact of the type of Lévy process on fair valuation by comparing fair contract values for the NIG process with those derived from the Meixner-process. They find that the actual type of Lévy process used is not of central importance for pricing, as long as it is able to accurately replicate higher moments of empirical log returns (in particular, skewness and kurtosis). For this reason, we limit our considerations to the NIG process.

3 Even if the data needed to estimate the real-world distribution of the annual return are available, these data reflect the past and may not accurately capture the market's opinion on the future. Therefore, it may be more appropriate to try to extract the market's opinion on the pricing measure from option prices, which reflect market participants' expectations of future prices of the underlying.

4 The moments are given by $E(X) = \mu + \delta\beta/\sqrt{\alpha^2 - \beta^2}$, $\text{Var}(X) = \alpha^2\delta/(\alpha^2 - \beta^2)^{3/2}$, $\text{Skew}(X) = 3\beta/(\alpha\sqrt{\delta\sqrt{\alpha^2 - \beta^2}})$ and $\text{Kurt}(X) = 3 + 3(\alpha^2 + 4\beta^2)/(\delta\alpha^2\sqrt{\alpha^2 - \beta^2})$.

5 A detailed analysis of feasible sets of individual contract parameters when employing fair valuation within a Black–Scholes framework only can be found in Ballotta *et al* (2006).

6 Similar results are obtained for $\delta = 0\%$ and 80%.

REFERENCES

Ballotta, L., 2005, "A Lévy Process-Based Framework for the Fair Valuation of Participating Life Insurance Contracts", *Insurance: Mathematics and Economics*, 37(2), pp. 173–96.

Ballotta, L., 2006, "Pricing and Capital Requirements for With-Profit Contracts: Modelling Considerations", Actuarial Research Paper No. 175, Cass Business School.

Ballotta, L., S. Haberman and N. Wang, 2006, "Guarantees in With-Profit and Unitized With-Profit Life Insurance Contracts: Fair Valuation Problem in Presence of the Default Option", *Journal of Risk and Insurance*, 73(1), pp. 97–121.

Barndorff-Nielsen, O. E., 1997, "Normal Inverse Gaussian Distributions and the Modelling of Stock Returns", *Scandinavian Journal of Statistics*, 24, pp. 1–13.

Barth, M. M., 2000, "A Comparison of Risk-Based Capital Standards Under the Expected Policyholder Deficit and the Probability of Ruin Approaches", *Journal of Risk and Insurance*, 67(3), pp. 397–414.

Björk, T., 2004, *Arbitrage Theory in Continuous Time* (New York: Oxford University Press).

Briys, E. and F. de Varenne, 1994, "Life Insurance in a Contingent Claim Framework: Pricing and Regulatory Implications", *Geneva Papers on Risk and Insurance – Theory*, 19(1), pp. 53–72.

Bühlmann, H., F. Delbaen, P. Embrechts and A. N. Shiryaev, 1996, "No-arbitrage, Change of Measure and Conditional Esscher Transforms", URL: citeseer.ist.psu.edu/69629.html.

Butsic, R. P., 1994, "Solvency Measurement for Property-Liability Risk-Based Capital Applications", *Journal of Risk and Insurance*, 61(4), pp. 656–90.

Carr, P. and D. B. Madan, 1999, "Option Valuation Using the Fast Fourier Transform", *The Journal of Computational Finance*, 2(4), pp. 61–73.

Gatzert, N. and A. Kling, 2007, "Analysis of Participating Life Insurance Contracts: A Unification Approach", *Journal of Risk and Insurance*, 74(3), pp. 547–70.

Gerber, H. U. and E. S. W. Shiu, 1994, "Option Pricing by Esscher Transforms", *Transactions of the Society of Actuaries*, 46, pp. 99–191.

Gerber, H. U. and E. S. W. Shiu, 1996, "Actuarial Bridges to Dynamic Hedging and Option Pricing", *Insurance: Mathematics and Economics*, 18(3), pp. 183–218.

Glasserman, P. 2004, *Monte Carlo Methods in Financial Engineering* (New York: Springer).

Grosen, A. and P. L. Jørgensen, 2000, "Fair Valuation of Life Insurance Liabilities: The Impact of Interest Rate Guarantees, Surrender Options, and Bonus Policies", *Insurance: Mathematics and Economics*, 26(1), pp. 37–57.

Grosen, A. and P. L. Jørgensen, 2002, "Life Insurance Liabilities at Market Value: An Analysis of Insolvency Risk, Bonus Policy, and Regulatory Intervention Rules in a Barrier Option Framework", *Journal of Risk and Insurance*, 69(1), pp. 63–91.

Hansen, M. and K. R. Miltersen, 2002, "Minimum Rate of Return Guarantees: The Danish Case", *Scandinavian Actuarial Journal*, 2002(4), pp. 280–318.

Kassberger, S., R. Kiesel and T. Liebmann, 2008, "Fair Valuation of Insurance Contracts under Lévy Process Specifications", *Insurance: Mathematics and Economics*, 42(1), pp. 419–33.

Le Courtois, O. and F. Quittard-Pinon, 2008, "Fair Valuation of Participating Life Insurance Contracts with Jump Risk", *The Geneva Risk and Insurance Review*, 33(2), pp. 106–36.

Schoutens, W., 2003, *Lévy Processes in Finance* (Chicester: Wiley).

Wirch, J. L. and M. R. Hardy, 1999, "A Synthesis of Risk Measures", *Insurance: Mathematics and Economics*, 25(3), pp. 337–47.

16

Demographic Assets and the Asset Allocation Problem for Pension Funds

Francesco Menoncin

Brescia University

The major risk sources for any institutional investor are market risk and credit risk. Pension funds also bear a very particular risk: demographic risk. If there are no assets correlated with demographic risk in the financial market, then such a risk is not hedgeable and it can be classified as a background risk.

Nevertheless, there are some types of demographic assets that can be thought of as derivatives on the stochastic force of mortality. Thanks to these assets the financial market becomes complete, even with respect to the demographic risk (for the so-called longevity bonds see Azzoppardi (2005) and Menoncin (2006b, 2008)).

When a pension fund and a sponsor settle on a pension scheme (either defined contributions or defined benefits), the sponsor agrees to pay contributions during the accumulation phase (until they retire), while the fund agrees to pay pensions during the distribution phase (until the sponsor dies). In this framework, it is evident that longevity risk plays a crucial role. In fact, it translates into the risk that the fund would have to pay a pension for a length of time that is longer than was foreseen. For managing the risks in a pension fund see, for instance, Menoncin (2006a), Battocchio *et al* (2007) or Hainaut and Devolder (2007).

Risk management can be done in three different ways: (i) increasing capital in order to face the potential losses due to an increase in risk; (ii) sharing or transferring the risk; or (iii) hedging the risk.

Increasing capital is the most expensive solution since the return on capital is higher than that of other funds. The idea of sharing or transferring risk leads to the issue of the so-called asset-backed securities. Finally, a risk can be hedged if an asset correlated with such a risk can be found in the financial market. This is rightly the case of demographic assets.

Furthermore, sharing and hedging risk has other advantages, for example there is a reduction in the capital that must be kept for meeting capital requirements.

In this chapter we compute, in a closed form, the optimal asset allocation for a pension fund that is subject to both interest-rate risk and demographic risk. We take into account a continuous time framework and we solve the optimisation problem using the so-called martingale approach shown in Cox and Huang (1991).

In the optimal portfolio, the only asset playing a role in hedging against the demographic risk is, of course, the demographic asset, and the amount of money that must be invested in it is taken from the money invested in the ordinary bond. Furthermore, we show that the amount of money invested in the demographic asset must increase during the accumulation phase while it must decrease during the distribution phase.

The next section describes the financial market where there exists: (i) a riskless asset; (ii) a risky asset; and (iii) a zero-coupon bond as a derivative on the stochastic interest rate. The section following on introduces the demographic risk, presents the structure of a demographic asset and discusses the problem of market completeness. We then present a suitable framework for a pension fund and its objective function. Subsequently we show the optimal asset allocation and present a numerical simulation. Some technicalities are left to the Appendix.

THE FINANCIAL MARKET

We take into account a simple framework where market risk coincides with price risk and interest-rate risk.

The interest-rate risk is modelled by taking into account the stochastic evolution of the instantaneously risk-free interest rate that solves the following equation

$$dr(t) = \mu_r(t, r)\, dt + \sigma_r(t, r)\, dW_r(t)$$
$$r(t_0) = r_0 \tag{16.1}$$

where r_0 is known at time t_0 (ie, it is deterministic) and $W_r(t)$ is a Wiener process ($dW_r(t)$ is its differential representation). The functions μ_r and σ_r are such that Equation 16.1 has a unique solution. Two of the most used stochastic models for the spot risk-free interest rate belonging to the family 16.1 are those of Vasiček (1977) and Cox *et al* (1985).

The interest rate $r(t)$ is the return on a risk-free asset where the price $G(t)$ solves the differential equation

$$\frac{dG(t)}{G(t)} = r(t)\,dt$$

$$G(t_0) = 1 \tag{16.2}$$

We call $B(t)$ the value of a zero coupon. By using both the non-arbitrage condition and Itô's lemma we can conclude that $B(t)$ evolves according to the following differential equation

$$\frac{dB(t)}{B(t)} = (r(t) + \nabla_r^B \sigma_r(t,r)\xi_r(t))\,dt + \nabla_r^B \sigma_r(t,r)\,dW_r(t) \tag{16.3}$$

where

$$\nabla_r^B \equiv \frac{\partial B(t)}{\partial r(t)}\frac{1}{B(t)}$$

is the semi-elasticity of $B(t)$ with respect to the interest rate. When the interest rate follows a Merton process (ie, μ_r and σ_r are constant) the semi-elasticity coincides with the duration.

In Equation 16.3 we show that ξ_r is the so-called market price of the interest-rate risk where the value is unique if, and only if, the market is complete. We return to this point later.

The price risk is modelled by assuming that the price of a risky asset follows a diffusion process such as

$$\frac{dS(t)}{S(t)} = (r(t) + \sigma_{Sr}(t,S)\xi_r(t) + \sigma_S(t,S)\xi_S(t))\,dt$$

$$+ \sigma_{Sr}(t,S)\,dW_r(t) + \sigma_S(t,S)\,dW_S(t) \tag{16.4}$$

$$S(t_0) = S_0$$

where $W_S(t)$ is a Wiener process independent of $W_r(t)$. Here, σ_{Sr} accounts for the correlation between the risky asset return and the zero-coupon return (if $\sigma_{Sr} = 0$, then the correlation between dS/S and dB/B is zero). Here, ξ_S is the market price of the risky asset's own risk.

THE DEMOGRAPHIC RISK AND THE DEMOGRAPHIC ASSETS

Three main demographic variables can be taken into account:

1. the mortality density function $f(t)$ of the death time τ;
2. the survival probability between t_0 and t; this can be computed as the complement of the probability of death between t_0 and t as

$$p(t_0, t) = 1 - \int_{t_0}^{t} f(s) \, ds$$

3. the (instantaneous) force of mortality $\lambda(t)$ measured as the hazard rate of $f(t)$, ie, the ratio between $\pi(t)$ and the survival probability until t

$$\lambda(t) = \frac{f(t)}{1 - \int_{t_0}^{t} f(s) \, ds}$$

Differentiating the value of $p(t_0, t)$ with respect to t and taking into account the value of $\lambda(t)$ gives

$$\frac{dp(t_0, t)}{p(t_0, t)} = -\lambda(t) \, dt$$

$$p(t_0, t_0) = 1$$

which is akin to the differential equation for the risk-free asset $G(t)$.

When taking into account a so-called double stochasticity for the death time τ, not only do we assume that τ is stochastic but also that either $\pi(t)$, $\lambda(t)$ or $p(t_0, t)$ are stochastic themselves. In order to draw a parallel between the financial risk and the demographic risk, we continue the analogy between $p(t_0, t)$ and $G(t)$ by assuming that $\lambda(t)$ is stochastic (as $r(t)$ is) and its value solves the differential equation

$$d\lambda(t) = \mu_\lambda(t, \lambda) \, dt + \sigma_\lambda(t, \lambda) \, dW_\lambda(t)$$

Here, we assume that $W_\lambda(t)$ is independent of the other stochastic processes, which means that the demographic risk is not correlated with other risks on the financial market (price risk and interest-rate risk) and, accordingly, the demographic risk cannot be hedged with the financial assets. In other words, no portfolio exists that is able to replicate the demographic risk.

Here, we do not specify any particular functional form either for μ_λ or for σ_λ and we only ask for the value of $\lambda(t)$ to be positive (a force of mortality is positive by definition). The same structure is presented by Dahl (2004) and Biffis (2005) where the authors use affine mortality structures (akin to the interest rate specification of Cox *et al* (1985)).

A demographic asset $D(t)$ is a derivative on $\lambda(t)$ in the same way as the zero coupon $B(t)$ is a derivative on $r(t)$. Accordingly, the no-arbitrage condition and Itô's lemma allow us to write

$$\frac{dD(t)}{D(t)} = \left(r(t) + \nabla_r^D \sigma_r(t,r)\xi_r(t) + \nabla_\lambda^D \sigma_\lambda(t,\lambda)\xi_\lambda(t)\right) dt$$
$$+ \nabla_r^B \sigma_r(t,r) \, dW_r + \nabla_\lambda^D \sigma_\lambda(t,\lambda) \, dW_\lambda$$

where ∇_λ^D and ∇_r^D are the semi-elasticities of the demographic asset with respect to the force of mortality and the interest rate, respectively.

The market where there is a zero coupon B, a risky asset S and a demographic asset D is complete since there exists one, and only one, vector of market price of risk. The relationship between the drift, the diffusions and the market price of risk is given by (for the sake of simplicity we neglect the functional dependences)

$$\underbrace{\begin{bmatrix} \nabla_r^B \sigma_r & 0 & 0 \\ \sigma_{Sr} & \sigma_S & 0 \\ \nabla_r^B \sigma_r & 0 & \nabla_\lambda^D \sigma_\lambda \end{bmatrix}}_{\text{diffusion matrix }(\Sigma')} \underbrace{\begin{bmatrix} \xi_r \\ \xi_S \\ \xi_\lambda \end{bmatrix}}_{\text{market price of risk }(\xi)} = \underbrace{\begin{bmatrix} \nabla_r^B \sigma_r \xi_r \\ \sigma_{Sr}\xi_r + \sigma_S\xi_S \\ \nabla_r^D \sigma_r \xi_r + \nabla_\lambda^D \sigma_\lambda \xi_\lambda \end{bmatrix}}_{\text{risk premia}}$$

(16.5)

If there exists one market price of risk ξ in the financial market and this value satisfies a finiteness condition, then there exists a so-called risk-neutral probability (or martingale equivalent measure) Q such that

$$dW^Q = \xi \, dt + dW$$

Furthermore, we can conclude that in the financial market the value of any asset equates to the expected present value of the asset payouts discounted by the risk-free interest rate and computed under probability Q.

Hereafter, we define $g(t,T) \equiv G(t)/G(T)$ as the discount factor between time t and time $T > t$. If the financial market is arbitrage free, then the value of a zero coupon coincides with the expected value (under Q) of the discount factor

$$B(t) = \mathbb{E}_t^Q[g(t,T)]$$

THE MANAGEMENT OF A PENSION FUND

In a so-called fully funded system, the management of a pension fund can be suitably divided into two phases:

1. during the accumulation phase the sponsors pay contributions (u) to the fund, which are invested in the financial market;
2. during the distribution phase the sponsors receive their pensions (v) from the fund, which uses its accumulated wealth for these payments.

Either contributions or pensions (or both) may be stochastic. The sponsor generally agrees to contribute a fixed percentage of their wage. Nevertheless, since the dynamics of this wage is stochastic, then contributions are also stochastic. During the distribution phase pensions may be stochastic, if they are linked to the fund's performance in the financial market (as happens in a defined contributions setup).

Although we might separately model contributions and pensions using two different stochastic processes, we prefer to model them together. In particular, we call $L(t)$ the total amount of contributions received until time t reduced by the amount of pensions paid until time t. Accordingly, $dL(t)$ measures the marginal increase (or decrease) in $L(t)$, ie, the contribution $u(t)$ during the accumulation phase or the pension $v(t)$ during the distribution phase. Then, we can write

$$dL(t) = \underset{1\times 3}{\mu_L(t, L)}\, dt + \underset{3\times 1}{\sigma_L(t, L)'}\, dW(t)$$

where the prime denotes transposition and dW is the vector containing dW_r, dW_S and dW_λ. Furthermore, we set

$$\mu_L(t, L) \equiv u(t, L)\mathbb{I}_{t<T} - v(t, L)(1 - \mathbb{I}_{t<T})$$
$$\sigma_L(t, L) \equiv \sigma_u(t, L)\mathbb{I}_{t<T} - \sigma_v(t, L)(1 - \mathbb{I}_{t<T})$$

where $\mathbb{I}_{t<T}$ is the indicator function where the value is one if $t < T$ and zero otherwise.

By using the new variable $L(t)$, we can measure at any time t the expected present value of all of the contributions and pensions that still have to be received and paid, respectively. This measure coincides with the so-called "prospective mathematical reserve"

$$A(t) = \mathbb{E}_t^{Q,\tau}\left[\int_t^{\tau} g(t,s)\,dL(s) + g(t,\tau)A(\tau)\right]$$

$$= \mathbb{E}_t^{Q,\tau}\left[\int_t^{\infty} \mathbb{I}_{s<\tau}g(t,s)\,dL(s) + \int_t^{\infty} f(s)g(t,s)A(s)\,ds\right]$$

where all of the cashflows are discounted under the risk-neutral probability. If τ is independent of the other stochastic variables, then the expected value $\mathbb{E}_t^{Q,\tau}[\bullet]$ can be disentangled as the composite expected value $\mathbb{E}_t^Q[\mathbb{E}_t^{\tau}[\bullet]]$. Furthermore, since we know that the expected value of an indicator function of an event coincides with the probability of such an event, then we can write the prospective mathematical reserve as

$$A(t) = \mathbb{E}_t^Q\left[\int_t^{\infty} (_sp_t)g(t,s)\,dL(s) + \int_t^{\infty} \lambda(s)(_sp_t)g(t,s)A(s)\,ds\right]$$

$$= \mathbb{E}_t^Q\left[\int_t^{\infty} (_sp_t)g(t,s)(dL(s) + \lambda(s)A(s))\right]$$

In actuarial mathematics the so-called "retrospective mathematical reserve" is also sometimes used. The retrospective mathematical reserve at time t is the total compounded amount of contributions and pensions that have been received and paid until time t. Accordingly, the value in t of the retrospective mathematical reserve can be computed as

$$K(t) = \int_{t_0}^{t} g(t,s)\,dL(s)$$

where there is no need to take into account the expected value since at time t all of the contributions and pensions received and paid from t_0 up to t are perfectly known.

The relevance of either the prospective mathematical reserve or the retrospective mathematical reserve depends on the way the pension fund is managed. In fact, there are two main ways to manage a pension fund.

1. Defined contributions: contributions are fixed in advance and pensions are suitably computed in order to keep the fund in balance, and also according to the performance of the fund in the financial market. In this case the pensioner receives higher pensions, if the fund performs better in the financial market

and vice versa. In this framework, the fund is not asked to guarantee any pension level and it can optimise its portfolio by taking into account the increase in the managed wealth, net of the retrospective mathematical reserve.

2. Defined benefits: pensions are fixed in advance, when the pension agreement is signed, while the contributions are suitably adjusted, during the accumulation phase, in order to keep the fund in balance. In this case, higher performance of the fund in the financial market translates into lower contributions paid by workers. In this framework, the fund is obliged to meet the agreed pension level and its optimisation problem must take into account this constraint. Accordingly, the fund's wealth must always be sufficiently high to cover the prospective mathematical reserve.

In both cases, contributions and pensions must meet a so-called fairness condition asking for their expected present values to be equal. In other words, the contributions and pensions (ie, the values of u and v) must be such that the prospective mathematical reserve is initially set to zero

$$\Delta(t_0) = 0$$

Under this condition it is evident that the prospective mathematical reserve is constantly negative for any $t > t_0$.

While the management of a pension fund in the defined contributions case is not very different from the management of other investment funds, we concentrate on the defined benefits case.

THE OBJECTIVE FUNCTION
In a defined benefits scheme, the pension fund must manage its wealth in such a way that its optimal level never goes below the amount of the prospective mathematical reserve. In other words, the fund must constantly be able to meet the discounted expected value of all future payments (pensions). If the fund's preferences belong to the constant relative risk aversion family, then this condition can easily be met by modelling these preferences as follows

$$U(R(t)) = \frac{1}{1-\gamma}(R(t) + \Delta(t))^{1-\gamma}$$

where γ is the constant relative risk aversion index. This form of the utility function guarantees that the optimal wealth never falls below the value of $-\Delta(t)$, which is the expected present value of the pensions (net of the contributions) that still have to be paid (we stress that $-\Delta(t)$ is always positive).

In order to model risk-averse behaviour, the parameter γ must be positive. Furthermore, we assume that γ is also greater than one (this will allow us to avoid convergence problems). When $\gamma = 1$ we obtain the same results as for a log utility function.

If we assume that the fund optimises its wealth (net of the prospective mathematical reserve) at the date of the sponsor's death, then the problem can be written as

$$\max_{R(\tau)} \mathbb{E}^{\tau}_{t_0} \left[\frac{1}{1-\gamma} \rho(t_0, \tau)(R(\tau) + \Delta(\tau))^{1-\gamma} \right]$$

where $\rho(t_0, t)$ is the subjective discount factor.

Since we have assumed that τ is independent of the other (financial) stochastic variables, this problem can then be reformulated as

$$\max_{R(t)} \mathbb{E}_{t_0} \left[\int_{t_0}^{\infty} \frac{1}{1-\gamma} \rho(t_0, t) p(t_0, t) \lambda(t)(R(t) + \Delta(t))^{1-\gamma} \, dt \right] \quad (16.6)$$

and it becomes an intertemporal optimisation problem (see Richard (1975) for a seminal study of this), where the initial amount of wealth must equate the sum between the discounted present value of all of the future pensions' net of the contributions and the discounted final wealth

$$R(t_0) = \mathbb{E}^{Q, \tau}_{t_0} \left[\int_{t_0}^{\tau} -g(t_0, t) \, dL(t) \, dt + g(t_0, \tau)R(\tau) \right]$$

where the wealth present value is computed under the martingale equivalent measure.

We can simplify this constraint by separately computing the expected value with respect to the death time τ

$$R(t_0) = \mathbb{E}^{Q}_{t_0} \left[\int_{t_0}^{\infty} g(t_0, t) p(t_0, t)(-dL(t) + \lambda(t)R(t) \, dt) \right] \quad (16.7)$$

THE OPTIMAL PORTFOLIO

Now, we call w_B, w_S and w_D the amounts of money invested in the zero coupon, in the risky asset and in the demographic asset, respectively.

Proposition 1 *The optimal portfolio solving Problem 16.6 under the constraint 16.7 is*

$$
\begin{bmatrix} w_B \\ w_S \\ w_D \end{bmatrix} = \begin{bmatrix} \frac{1}{\nabla_r^B \sigma_r} \sigma_{Lr} - \frac{\sigma_{Sr}}{\nabla_r^B \sigma_r \sigma_S} \sigma_{LS} \\ \frac{1}{\sigma_S} \sigma_{LS} \\ \frac{1}{\nabla_\lambda^D \sigma_\lambda} \sigma_{L\lambda} \end{bmatrix} + \frac{R(t) + \Delta(t)}{\gamma} \begin{bmatrix} \frac{1}{\nabla_r^B} \left(\frac{\xi_r}{\sigma_r} - \frac{\sigma_{Sr}}{\sigma_r} \frac{\xi_S}{\sigma_S} \right) \\ \frac{\xi_S}{\sigma_S} \\ \frac{1}{\nabla_\lambda^D} \frac{\xi_\lambda}{\sigma_\lambda} \end{bmatrix}
$$

$$
+ \frac{R(t) + \Delta(t)}{F(t)} \begin{bmatrix} \frac{1}{\nabla_r^B} \frac{\partial F(t)}{\partial r} \\ 0 \\ \frac{1}{\nabla_\lambda^D} \frac{\partial F(t)}{\partial \lambda} \end{bmatrix} + \begin{bmatrix} -\frac{1}{\nabla_r^B} \frac{\partial \Delta(t)}{\partial r} - \frac{\nabla_r^D}{\nabla_r^B} w_D \\ 0 \\ -\frac{1}{\nabla_\lambda^D} \frac{\partial \Delta(t)}{\partial \lambda} \end{bmatrix}
$$

where the function $F(t)$ is defined in Equation 16.A.1, as the value of a life insurance.

Proof See the Appendix. ☐

We can accordingly conclude that the optimal portfolio is formed by four components: three of them can be thought of as hedging components, while one takes the role of a speculative component. Let us study these components more closely.

1. A hedging component due to the stochasticity of contributions and/or pensions (ie, σ_L). This component is the opposite of the ratio between the contribution/pension diffusion (σ_L) and the risky asset diffusion (Σ). This term can also be written as

    $$
    -\Sigma^{-1}\sigma_L = -\Sigma^{-1}\Sigma'^{-1}\Sigma'\sigma_L = -(\Sigma'\Sigma)^{-1}\Sigma'\sigma_L
    $$

    where we see the variance–covariance matrix $\Sigma'\Sigma$ and the vector $\Sigma'\sigma_L$ containing the covariances between the risky asset returns and the contributions/pensions. This portfolio component minimises the portfolio variance. In fact, the (sufficient) first-order condition on the problem

    $$
    \min_{w}(w'\Sigma' + \sigma_L')(\Sigma w + \sigma_L)
    $$

    is

    $$
    2\Sigma'\Sigma w + 2\Sigma'\sigma_L = 0
    $$

    from which we obtain the first portfolio component. The value of w that minimises the variance also makes it zero.

2. The second portfolio component can be seen as a purely speculative component since it is proportional to both the wealth, net of the absolute value of the prospective mathematical reserve (we recall that $\Delta(t)$ is negative for any $t > t_0$), and the market price of risk (ξ), while it negatively depends on both the risky asset diffusion (Σ) and the risk aversion parameter (γ).

3. The third portfolio component hedges against the (relative) changes in the life insurance contract $F(t)$ due to the changes in the state variables $((1/F(t))(\partial F(t)/\partial r)$ and $(1/F(t))(\partial F(t)/\partial \lambda))$. This portfolio component is proportional to the fund's wealth, net of the absolute value of the prospective mathematical reserve, and is weighted by the correlation between the state variables and the risky assets. In fact, the term $\Sigma^{-1}\Omega$ can be decomposed as

$$\Sigma^{-1}\Omega = \Sigma^{-1}\Sigma'^{-1}\Sigma'\Omega = (\Sigma'\Sigma)^{-1}\Sigma'\Omega$$

where $\Sigma'\Omega$ contains the covariances between the state variables and the asset returns, while $\Sigma'\Sigma$ is the variance–covariance matrix of the risky assets.

4. The fourth portfolio component hedges against the changes in the prospective mathematical reserve due to the changes in the state variables (r and λ). As in the previous case, the derivatives of $\Delta(t)$ with respect to r and λ are weighted by the opposite of the ratio between the covariances between the state variables and the asset returns (in vector $\Sigma'\Omega$) and the variance–covariance matrix of the risky assets ($\Sigma'\Sigma$).

5. Even if the stock S is correlated with the interest rate, it does not play any hedging role and it is just used for speculative purposes.

6. Even if the demographic asset D is correlated with the interest rate, it does not play any role in hedging against the changes in the interest rate.

7. The amount of money that must be invested in D is taken from the wealth invested in the bond B (by the ratio ∇_r^D/∇_r^B) and in the risk-free asset (by the ratio $1 - \nabla_r^D/\nabla_r^B$); if the demographic asset and the bond have the same duration (ie, $\nabla_r^D = \nabla_r^B$) then the money invested in D is just taken from the wealth invested in B without altering the other portfolio weights.

8. The zero coupon B is the only asset used for hedging against the changes in the interest rate.

A NUMERICAL SIMULATION

In this section we want to show the optimal amount of money that must be invested in a demographic asset when all of the other risks except the demographic are neglected. Such a framework is very simple indeed but it can be very useful too in order to understand the behaviour through time of the demographic asset hedging role.

If the interest rate is assumed to be deterministic, there is then no room for a zero-coupon bond where the behaviour is not different from that of the risk-free asset. Accordingly, we just need the stock $S(t)$ and the demographic asset $D(t)$ in the financial market.

We assume that both the contributions and pensions are deterministic (as in Battocchio *et al* (2007)), ie

$$\mu_L(t) = u\mathbb{I}_{t<T} - v(1 - \mathbb{I}_{t<T})$$

The optimal portfolio can accordingly be written as

$$w_S = \frac{1}{\gamma}(R(t) + \Delta(t))\frac{\xi_S}{\sigma_S}$$

$$w_D = \frac{1}{\gamma}(R(t) + \Delta(t))\frac{1}{\nabla_\lambda^D}\frac{\xi_\lambda}{\sigma_\lambda}$$

$$+ \frac{R(t) + \Delta(t)}{F(t)}\frac{1}{\nabla_\lambda^D}\frac{\partial F(t)}{\partial \lambda} - \frac{1}{\nabla_\lambda^D}\frac{\partial \Delta(t)}{\partial \lambda}$$

If we assume that the subjective discount factor $\rho(t, T)$ and the market prices of risk are all constant, then $\lambda(t)$ is the only stochastic variable, and the functions $F(t)$ and $\Delta(t)$ can then be written as

$$F(t) = \int_t^\infty \mathbb{E}_t^{Q_\gamma}[\lambda(s)e^{-\int_t^s \lambda(u)\,du}]$$
$$\times e^{-((1/\gamma)\ln\rho+(1-1/\gamma)(r+(1/2)(1/\gamma)(\xi_S^2+\xi_\lambda^2)))(s-t)}\,ds$$

$$\Delta(t) = \int_t^\infty \mu_L(s)\mathbb{E}_t^Q[e^{-\int_t^s \lambda(u)\,du}]e^{-r(s-t)}\,ds$$

In order to simplify the computations, we present now the deterministic parallel of these two functions by assuming that the

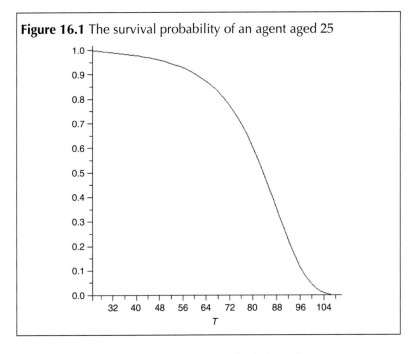

Figure 16.1 The survival probability of an agent aged 25

force of mortality follows a Gomperz–Makeham law

$$\lambda(t) = \phi + \frac{1}{b}e^{(t-m)/b}$$

where all of the parameters are positive constants and have the following meaning: (i) ϕ captures the age-independent component of mortality rate (such as accidents); (ii) m measures the modal value of life; and (iii) b is the dispersion parameter of life. Typical value for these parameters (consistently chosen from Milevsky (2006)) are

$$\phi = 0.001, \quad m = 82.3, \quad b = 11.4 \tag{16.8}$$

In this case the survival probability can be represented as in Figure 16.1. We can see that after the age of about 104, the survival probability is not significantly different from zero.

If we furthermore assume (consistently with Menoncin (2008))

$$r = 0.05, \quad \gamma = 2.5, \quad \ln\rho = 0.05$$
$$\xi_S = 0.4, \quad \xi_\lambda = 0, \quad u = 1$$

and $t_0 = 25$ as the starting age of the pension fund sponsor, while $T = 65$ is the retirement age, then the pension v that the fund is able

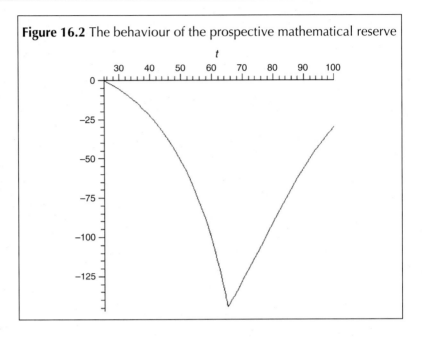

Figure 16.2 The behaviour of the prospective mathematical reserve

to pay to its sponsors must satisfy the condition $\Delta(t_0) = 0$, from which we have

$$
v = \frac{\int_{t_0}^{T} e^{-\int_{t_0}^{s} \lambda(u)\,du} e^{-r(s-t_0)}\,ds}{\int_{T}^{\infty} e^{-\int_{t_0}^{s} \lambda(u)\,du} e^{-r(s-t_0)}\,ds} = 12.2
$$

This means that paying €1 during the accumulation phase (40 year length) allows the recipient to receive a pension of €12.2 until the time of death (ie, more or less for a length of 10 or 15 years).

In Figure 16.2 we see the behaviour of the prospective mathematical reserve. This starts from zero ($\Delta(t_0) = 0$), is always negative, reaches its lowest level for the retirement age, and tends towards zero while time goes on.

For computing the optimal portfolio, the derivative of $\Delta(t)$ with respect to $\lambda(t)$ must be computed. The numerical simulation allows us to obtain the values of $\partial\Delta(t)/\partial\lambda(t)$ as shown in Figure 16.3.

From this last figure, we can conclude that the demographic risk can be hedged by investing higher and higher amounts of money in the demographic asset during the accumulation phase,

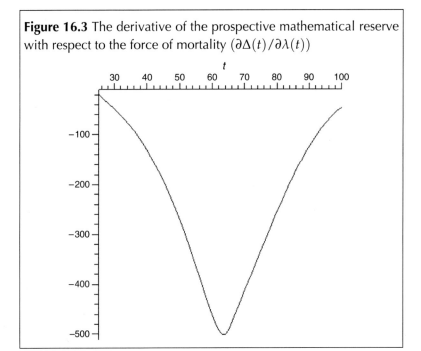

Figure 16.3 The derivative of the prospective mathematical reserve with respect to the force of mortality $(\partial \Delta(t)/\partial \lambda(t))$

while reducing this investment during the distribution phase. The amount of money invested in the risky asset, instead, must be kept constant as a proportion of the fund's wealth (reduced by the amount of the prospective mathematical reserve).

APPENDIX   THE OPTIMAL ASSET ALLOCATION

Once the market price of risk has been defined, then we can also write the so-called kernel price

$$m(t_0, t) = e^{-(1/2) \int_{t_0}^{t} \xi(s)' \xi(s) \, ds - \int_{t_0}^{t} \xi(s) \, dW(s)}$$

which is the solution to the following stochastic differential equation

$$\frac{dm(t_0, t)}{m(t_0, t)} = -\xi(t)' \, dW(t)$$

$$m(t_0, t_0) = 1$$

This discount factor $m(t_0, t)$ is always positive and (under the Novikov condition) its expected value is

$$\mathbb{E}_{t_0}[m(t_0, t)] = 1$$

The kernel price allows us to switch from the historical to the risk-neutral probability and vice versa. For instance, the value of a zero coupon can be written as

$$B(t_0, t) = \mathbb{E}^Q_{t_0}[g(t_0, t)] = \mathbb{E}_{t_0}[m(t_0, t)g(t_0, t)]$$

We recall that the product $g(t_0, t)m(t_0, t)$ is the so-called stochastic discount factor.

The constraint 16.7, can accordingly be written as

$$R(t_0) = \mathbb{E}^Q_{t_0}\left[\int_{t_0}^{\infty} g(t_0, t)p(t_0, t)(-dL(t) + \lambda(t)R(t)\, dt)\right]$$

$$= \mathbb{E}_{t_0}\left[\int_{t_0}^{\infty} m(t_0, t)g(t_0, t)p(t_0, t)(-dL(t) + \lambda(t)R(t)\, dt)\right]$$

If the pension fund maximises the objective function 16.6 under this constraint, the Lagrangian is

$$\mathcal{L} = \mathbb{E}_{t_0}\left[\int_{t_0}^{\infty} \frac{1}{1-\gamma}p(t_0, t)\rho(t_0, t)\lambda(t)(R(t) + \Delta(t))^{1-\gamma}\, dt\right]$$
$$- \phi(t_0)\mathbb{E}_{t_0}\left[\int_{t_0}^{\infty} m(t_0, t)g(t_0, t)p(t_0, t)(-dL(t) + \lambda(t)R(t)\, dt)\right]$$
$$+ \phi(t_0)R(t_0)$$

where $\phi(t_0)$ is the Lagrangian multiplier. The first derivative of $\mathcal{L}$ with respect to $R(t)$ is

$$\frac{\partial L}{\partial R(t)} = \mathbb{E}_{t_0}\left[\int_{t_0}^{\infty} p(t_0, t)\rho(t_0, t)\lambda(t)(R(t) + \Delta(t))^{-\gamma}\, dt\right]$$
$$- \phi(t_0)\mathbb{E}_{t_0}\left[\int_{t_0}^{\infty} m(t_0, t)g(t_0, t)p(t_0, t)\lambda(t)\, dt\right]$$

Since this derivative must be identically zero for any time and any state of the world, it is then sufficient to set the argument of the integral equal to zero. Accordingly, we obtain an implicit form for the optimal wealth as

$$R^*(t) = \left(\phi(t_0)\frac{m(t_0, t)g(t_0, t)}{\rho(t_0, t)}\right)^{-1/\gamma} - \Delta(t)$$

where we still have to compute the value of the multiplier $\phi(t_0)$.

Here, we clearly see that the optimal wealth level never goes below $-\Delta(t)$ since all of the functions ϕ, m, g and ρ take only positive values.

Since the constraint must be satisfied at any instant in time (let us say u), then we can write

$$R^*(u) = \mathbb{E}_u\left[\int_u^\infty m(u,t)g(u,t)p(u,t)(-\mu_L(t) + \lambda(t)R^*(t))\,dt\right]$$

After substituting for the optimal value $R^*(t)$ and rearranging the terms, we obtain

$$R^*(u) = \left(\phi(t_0)\frac{m(t_0,u)g(t_0,u)}{\rho(t_0,u)}\right)^{-1/\gamma}$$

$$\times \mathbb{E}_u\left[\int_u^\infty m(u,t)g(u,t)p(u,t)\lambda(t)\left(\frac{m(u,t)g(u,t)}{\rho(u,t)}\right)^{-1/\gamma}dt\right]$$

$$- \mathbb{E}_u\left[\int_u^\infty m(u,t)g(u,t)p(u,t)(\mu_L(t) + \lambda(t)\Delta(t))\,dt\right]$$

The role of the two expected values is definitely fundamental and now we show how to simplify them. Since the kernel price $m(u,t)$ makes it possible to switch from the historical to the risk-neutral probability (and vice versa), then the second expected value can be rewritten as

$$\mathbb{E}_u\left[\int_u^\infty m(u,t)g(u,t)p(u,t)(\mu_L(t) + \lambda(t)\Delta(t))\,dt\right]$$

$$= \mathbb{E}_u^Q\left[\int_u^\infty g(u,t)p(u,t)(\mu_L(t) + \lambda(t)\Delta(t))\,dt\right]$$

$$= \Delta(u)$$

Thus, we have shown that the second expected value exactly coincides with the prospective mathematical reserve.

Now, let us take into account the other expected value. In this case, computation is less easy because the kernel price $m(t_0,t)$ appears raised to the power $1 - 1/\gamma$. Through Itô's lemma we obtain

$$\frac{d(m(t_0,t)^{1-1/\gamma})}{m(t_0,t)^{1-1/\gamma}} = -\frac{1}{2}\left(1 - \frac{1}{\gamma}\right)\frac{1}{\gamma}\xi'\xi\,dt + \left(1 - \frac{1}{\gamma}\right)\xi'\,dW$$

from which we see that $m(t_0, t)^{1-1/\gamma}$ cannot be considered as a Radon–Nykodym derivative because it is not a martingale (its drift is different from zero). Nevertheless, we can decompose this stochastic process into the product of two processes: (i) one deterministic process measuring a discount factor

$$\frac{dY(t_0, t)}{Y(t_0, t)} = -\frac{1}{2}\left(1 - \frac{1}{\gamma}\right)\frac{1}{\gamma}\xi(t)'\xi(t)\,dt$$

$$Y(t_0, t) = 1$$

and (ii) the other stochastic process measuring a Radon–Nykodym derivative

$$\frac{dZ(t_0, t)}{Z(t_0, t)} = \left(1 - \frac{1}{\gamma}\right)\xi(t)'\,dW(t)$$

$$Z(t_0, t_0) = 1$$

where the new subjective probability measure Q_γ is such that

$$dW^{Q_\gamma}(t) = \left(1 - \frac{1}{\gamma}\right)\xi(t)\,dt + dW(t)$$

It is worth noting that when $\gamma = 1$ (ie, for a log utility function) the subjective probability coincides with the historical probability. Instead, when the risk aversion tends towards infinity, the subjective probability coincides with the risk-neutral probability, in fact

$$\lim_{\gamma \to 1} dW^{Q_\gamma}(t) = dW(t) \Leftrightarrow Q_\gamma = \mathbb{P}$$

$$\lim_{\gamma \to +\infty} dW^{Q_\gamma}(t) = \xi(t)\,dt + dW(t) \Leftrightarrow Q_\gamma = Q$$

Finally, we can write

$$\mathbb{E}_u\left[\int_u^\infty m(u, t)g(u, t)p(u, t)\lambda(t)\left(\frac{m(u, t)g(u, t)}{\rho(u, t)}\right)^{-1/\gamma}dt\right]$$

$$= \mathbb{E}_u\left[\int_u^\infty Y(u, t)Z(u, t)g(u, t)p(u, t)\lambda(t)\left(\frac{g(u, t)}{\rho(u, t)}\right)^{-1/\gamma}dt\right]$$

$$= \mathbb{E}_u^{Q_\gamma, \tau}\left[\rho(u, \tau)^{1/\gamma}g(u, \tau)^{1-1/\gamma}e^{-(1-1/\gamma)\int_u^\tau (1/2)(1/\gamma)\xi'\xi\,ds}\right]$$

Thus, the value of the function $F(u)$ is

$$F(u) \equiv \mathbb{E}_u^{Q_\gamma, \tau}\left[e^{-\int_u^\tau ((1/\gamma)\ln\rho(u, s) + (1-1/\gamma)(r(s) + (1/2)(1/\gamma)\xi(s)'\xi(s)))\,ds}\right]$$

$$(16.A.1)$$

The interpretation of this term is less clear than that of the previous expected value. In fact, here, the risk aversion parameter γ plays a crucial role and makes the function $F(u)$ coincide with the expected present value of a monetary unit available at death time τ, discounted by a subjective discount rate. Accordingly, we can conclude that $F(u)$ is a kind of life insurance evaluated subjectively.

It is interesting to compute the value of $F(u)$ in the two limit cases with $\gamma = 1$ and $\gamma \to \infty$

$$\lim_{\gamma=1} F(u) = \mathbb{E}_u^\tau \left[e^{-\int_u^\tau \ln \rho(u,s)\, ds} \right]$$

$$\lim_{\gamma\to\infty} F(u) = \mathbb{E}_u^{Q,\tau} \left[e^{-\int_u^\tau r(s)\, ds} \right]$$

In the first case $F(u)$ is the value of the life insurance, under the historical probability, and discounted by the subjective discount factor ρ. In the second case, $F(u)$ is the value of a zero coupon that pays one monetary unit at the time of death of an agent. As a zero coupon, it is obviously computed under the risk-neutral probability and discounted by the risk-free interest rate.

Now, the optimal wealth can be written as

$$R^*(u) = \left(\phi(t_0) \frac{m(t_0,u)g(t_0,u)}{\rho(t_0,u)} \right)^{-1/\gamma} F(u) - \Delta(u) \qquad (16.A.2)$$

Here, R^* is a function of both the state variables: the interest rate $r(t)$ and the force of mortality $\lambda(t)$. If we call $z \in \mathbb{R}^3$ the vectors of these state variables and we define

$$dW = \begin{bmatrix} dW_r \\ dW_S \\ dW_\lambda \end{bmatrix}, \quad \Omega' = \begin{bmatrix} \sigma_r & 0 & 0 \\ 0 & 0 & \sigma_\lambda \end{bmatrix}$$

then the differential of R^* can be computed through Itô's lemma as

$$dR^*(t) = (\ldots)\, dt + \frac{1}{\gamma} \left(\phi(t_0) \frac{m(t_0,t)g(t_0,t)}{\rho(t_0,t)} \right)^{-1/\gamma} F(t)\xi'\, dW$$
$$+ \left(\phi(t_0) \frac{m(t_0,t)g(t_0,t)}{\rho(t_0,t)} \right)^{-1/\gamma} \left(\frac{\partial F(t)}{\partial z} \right)' \Omega'\, dW$$
$$- \left(\frac{\partial \Delta(t)}{\partial z} \right)' \Omega'\, dW$$

and, since from Equation 16.A.2 we have

$$\frac{R^*(t) + \Delta(t)}{F(t)} = \left(\phi(t_0)\frac{m(t_0, t)g(t_0, t)}{\rho(t_0, t)}\right)^{-1/\gamma}$$

we finally obtain

$$dR^*(t) = (\dots) \, dt + \frac{1}{\gamma}(R^*(t) + \Delta(t))\xi' \, dW$$

$$+ \frac{R^*(t) + \Delta(t)}{F(t)}\left(\frac{\partial F(t)}{\partial z}\right)' \Omega' \, dW$$

$$- \left(\frac{\partial \Delta(t)}{\partial z}\right)' \Omega' \, dW \qquad (16.A.3)$$

We have neglected the drift term since it will not play any relevant role in computing the optimal portfolio.

If $w \in \mathbb{R}^n$ contains the amount of money invested in any risky asset, then the fund's wealth given by both the contributions/pensions and this portfolio evolves according to the following stochastic differential equation

$$dR = (\dots) \, dt + (w'\Sigma' + \sigma'_L) \, dW(t) \qquad (16.A.4)$$

where Σ has been defined in Equation 16.5.

In an arbitrage-free market, the portfolio w replicates the optimal wealth R^* if and only if the diffusion terms in Equations 16.A.3 and 16.A.4 are equal. Then, we must set

$$w'\Sigma' + \sigma'_L = \frac{1}{\gamma}(R(t) + \Delta(t))\xi'$$

$$+ \frac{R(t) + \Delta(t)}{F(t)}\left(\frac{\partial F(t)}{\partial z}\right)' \Omega' - \left(\frac{\partial \Delta(t)}{\partial z}\right)' \Omega'$$

from which we finally obtain

$$w^* = -\Sigma^{-1}\sigma_L + \frac{1}{\gamma}(R(t) + \Delta(t))\Sigma^{-1}\xi$$

$$+ \frac{R(t) + \Delta(t)}{F(t)}\Sigma^{-1}\Omega\frac{\partial F(t)}{\partial z} - \Sigma^{-1}\Omega\frac{\partial \Delta(t)}{\partial z}$$

After substituting for the matrices Σ, Ω and ξ we obtain what was presented in Proposition 1.

REFERENCES

Azzoppardi, M., 2005, "The Longevity Bond", in *First International Conference on Longevity Risk and Capital Markets Solutions.*

Battocchio, P., F. Menoncin and O. Scaillet, 2007, "Optimal Asset Allocation for Pension Funds Under Mortality Risk During the Accumulation and Decumulation Phases", *Annals of Operations Research*, 152, pp. 141–65.

Biffis, E., 2005, "Affine Processes for Dynamic Mortality and Actuarial Valuations", *Insurance: Mathematics and Economics*, 37, pp. 443–68.

Cox, J. C. and C. F. Huang, 1991, "A Variational Problem Arising in Financial Economics", *Journal of Mathematical Economics*, 20, pp. 465–87.

Cox, J. C., J. E. Ingersoll, Jr and S. A. Ross, 1985, "A Theory of the Term Structure of Interest Rates", *Econometrica*, 53, pp. 385–407.

Dahl, M., 2004, "Stochastic Mortality in Life Insurance: Market Reserves and Mortality-Linked Insurance Contracts", *Insurance: Mathematics and Economics*, 35, pp. 113–36.

Hainaut, D. and P. Devolder, 2007, "Management of a Pension Fund Under Mortality and Financial Risks", *Insurance: Mathematics and Economics*, 41, pp. 134–55.

Menoncin, F., 2006a, "Optimal Asset Management for Pension Funds", *Managerial Finance*, 32, pp. 347–74.

Menoncin, F., 2006b, "Understanding Longevity Bonds", *Life & Pensions*, November.

Menoncin, F., 2008, "The Role of Longevity Bonds in Optimal Portfolios", *Insurance: Mathematics and Economics*, 42, pp. 343–58.

Milevsky, M., 2006, *The Calculus of Retirement Income* (Cambridge University Press).

Richard, S., 1975, "Optimal Consumption, Portfolio and Life Insurance Rules for an Uncertain Lived Individual in a Continuous Time Model", *Journal of Financial Economics*, 2, pp. 187–203.

Vasiček, O., 1977, "An Equilibrium Characterization of the Term Structure", *Journal of Financial Economics*, 5, pp. 177–88.

17

On the Optimal SST Initial Capital of a Life Contract

Werner Hürlimann

FRSGlobal Switzerland

An insurance company needs capital in order to be able to take risks from its policyholders. The appropriate amount of capital is determined according to some solvency regulator's rules. For example, the Swiss Solvency Test (SST) is a system to determine the amount of

- available capital ("risk bearing capital"); and
- required capital according to the risks ("target capital").

This system has an economic point of view, which means that all portfolios are not evaluated on a statutory accounting but on an economic basis using a market-consistent valuation of assets and liabilities (for a recent introduction see Wüthrich *et al* (2008)).

Apart from determining the target capital and the risk bearing capital, the SST aims to increase the insurer's quantitative awareness of the risks. To this end the SST does not consist of a defined model but is based on a set of first principles. These principles define a boundary in which insurance companies can develop and run their own risk models (the so-called internal models) to quantitatively evaluate risks in a manner that is useful to them. In addition, a publicly available standard risk model is provided by the supervisor. An excellent introduction to the SST can be found in a white paper available from the homepage of the Swiss Federal Office of Private Insurance (FOPI 2004). Technical guidelines to the SST can be found in FOPI (2006).

In this chapter, we present a new perspective on the SST for a life insurance contract under the assumption that the insurance company is risk neutral with respect to mortality. This means that mortality risk is assumed to be diversifiable. In fact, if the portfolio of an insurance company is not too small, the law of large numbers for mortality risks can be applied and mortality dependent random cashflows can be replaced by their expected cashflows with respect to some life tables. In this setting, the SST driver is the random assets in the insurance portfolio, which depend on the realised future investment returns on the capital market. The corresponding SST target capital can be viewed as an approximate value of the market risk of a life insurance contract. The chapter is organised as follows.

In the next section we recall the definition of the SST target capital in terms of a multi-period SST risk measure in the mathematical sense. From a methodological point of view, capital risk measures should be coherent risk measures. However, Filipovic and Vogelpoth (2008) have shown through a counterexample that the SST risk measure does not satisfy the axiom of monotonicity for coherent multi-period risk measures. These authors have determined the largest coherent risk measure among those dominated by the SST risk measure, here called the SST coherent risk measure. The latter risk measure, if appropriate, might be used as a valuable alternative to the SST risk measure. The section entitled "Mean and variance of the random assets" contains the core of this approach. Under the assumption that the accumulated rates of return on investment in discrete time periods are independent and lognormally distributed, and are independent of the random premium income and stochastic insurance costs, we determine in Theorem 17.1 the mean and variance of the random assets of an arbitrary insurance portfolio at each future valuation time. In order to apply the result to a life insurance contract, we examine the technical values of a life insurance contract that are required in a concrete evaluation. Then we show how the SST risk measure is determined and conclude with a numerical example for a typical endowment contract. We observe that in all of the examples presented, which depend on the choice of the expected rate of return and the volatility of return, the expected shortfall of the first year risk-bearing capital is negative. If we assume that at the entry date of the endowment contract there is no liability and set the SST target capital equal to its initial capital, then the defined implicit equation offers a unique initial capital as the solution. Moreover, the obtained unique solutions correspond to either a vanishing SST risk measure or to a vanishing SST coherent risk measure. A unique solution is either called the optimal SST initial capital or the optimal SST coherent initial capital. An immediate reinterpretation yields the following rule of thumb. Under the made assumptions, the risk margin or market value margin (MvM) of an endowment contract coincides in absolute value with the expected shortfall of the first year risk-bearing capital.

THE SST RISK MEASURE

Risk-bearing capital is defined as the difference between the market-consistent values of the assets and the best estimate of the liabilities (see FOPI 2004, Section 2.5):

Market-consistent values of assets	Best estimate of liabilities
	Risk-bearing capital

The target capital relates the risks incurred by an insurer to the solvency capital requirement. It is defined as the sum of the required economic capital and the risk margin (or MvM):

Target capital	Economic capital = risk measure of the change of the risk-bearing capital over a given time horizon
	Risk margin = appropriate amount of capital besides the best estimate of liabilities allocated to cover future liabilities

The SST has adopted the following recommendations made by the International Actuarial Association (2004):

- the total balance sheet approach;
- the expected shortfall (ES) – also called conditional value-at-risk (CVaR), tail value-at-risk (TVaR) or conditional tail expectation (CTE) – as a risk measure used to calculate economic capital;

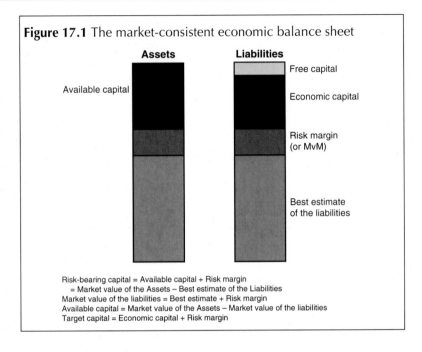

Figure 17.1 The market-consistent economic balance sheet

the time horizon of one year for calculating economic capital; and
the explicit definition of the risk margin.

Let us illustrate the previous concepts within the economic balance sheet for the SST (eg, Keller 2006), see Figure 17.1. Modelling the risk margin, we are concerned by the question of what portion of the available funds a company should allocate to cover the future liabilities (reserves), and hence is not available to fulfil the standard capital requirements. In this context future liabilities are defined as the sum of the best estimate of the future liabilities (= net present value of the future liabilities). Within the Committee of European Insurance and Occupational Pensions Supervisors (CEIOPS), the European Union and various groups working on Solvency II development, the basic issue is the actual aim of a risk margin for future liabilities covering a period of several years (Solvency II 2005, Newsletter no. 5).

There have been two proposals for defining the risk margin: the quantile approach and the cost of capital approach.

The quantile approach

The risk margin is primarily considered as security, providing policyholders with a certain probability that they will receive payment pending a final settlement. This view, which is officially adopted in Australia and Singapore, was initially favoured by the European Commission. In this situation the risk margin is calculated on the basis of the probability distribution of the future liabilities until they are settled. It is the difference between the best estimate of the liabilities and a selected quantile of the probability distribution. By December 2005, the European Commission had selected this approach as a working assumption and set the quantile provisionally at 75%. However, the current QIS specifications tend towards the next approach.

The cost of capital approach (incorporated in the SST)

This approach reflects the wish to get closer to the market value approach. In the attempt to define a market value for future liabilities, the distinction must be made between tradable risks in the financial markets and those for which there is no market. Non-tradable risks include, for example, the mortality risk in life insurance and underwriting risks in property and casualty insurance. For these risks, a substitute for market value is used as an approximation.

The risk margin is defined as the cost of capital for the future regulatory capital needed for the run-off of the portfolio, following any financial distress experienced by the company. For the regulator it is imperative that in the case of insolvency, the rightful claimants be protected. Policyholders are best served if a third party can take over the assets and liabilities of their initial insurer. A third party will only be prepared to do this if the cost of setting up the regulatory capital that would be required, is covered by the portfolio. As the regulatory capital depends on both the assets and liabilities, risks emanating from the asset portfolio enter the calculation of the risk margin. The risk margin is set so that one part of it can be used to pay for the necessary regulatory capital for the current year, while the other part is sufficient enough to set up the risk margin at the end of the current year.

The risk margin is calculated as being the discounted value of the future costs of maintaining the SST target capital level, if the insurance portfolio was being run-off by a third party. For the SST, the cost of capital rate has been set at 6%.

For theoretical and practical reasons it is useful to define the SST target capital in a formal mathematical way as follows.

Notations
We use the following notations here:

T: finite time horizon;

(Ω, F, P): probability space endowed with a filtration $(F_t)_{t=0}^T$ such that $F_0 = \{\Omega, \emptyset\}$ and $F_T = F$ (think of F_t as the information available up to time t);

$L^\infty(F_t)$: the space of essentially bounded random variables on (Ω, F, P); and

R^∞: the space of essentially bounded stochastic processes on (Ω, F, P) that are adapted to the filtration $(F_t)_{t=0}^T$.

Expected shortfall
The ES to the confidence level $\alpha \in (0,1)$ of a loss $X \in L^\infty(F_t)$ is defined by

$$ES_\alpha[X] := \frac{1}{\varepsilon} \cdot \int_\alpha^1 Q_X(u)\, du \tag{17.1}$$

where $Q_X(u)$ is a quantile function of X. It represents the average of the $100\varepsilon\%$ worst losses, where $\varepsilon = 1 - \alpha$ denotes the loss probability. The ES is known to coincide with the notion of CVaR (=conditional expected loss, given the loss strictly exceeds its value-at-risk (VaR)) and satisfies a lot of equivalent formulas of common use in the fields of reliability, actuarial science, finance and economics (Hürlimann 2003).

The SST target capital
Let $C \in R^\infty$ be the stochastic process of the risk-bearing capital and consider the stochastic process $SC = -C \in R^\infty$, which represents the shortfall risk-bearing capital (= negative of the risk-bearing capital). The determination of target capital (denoted as TC) according to the SST approach follows two steps.

Step 1: Determination of the economic capital
The economic capital is the one-year risk capital required to cover the risk of the asset–liability portfolio within a one-year

time horizon and is given by the ES of the change in shortfall risk-bearing capital

$$EC := ES_\alpha[SC_1 - SC_0] = C_0 + ES_\alpha[SC_1] \qquad (17.2)$$

Step 2: Determination of the risk margin

The risk margin (denoted as RM) assigns a capital requirement to the run-off of the in force asset–liability portfolio and is defined by

$$RM := i_{CoC} \cdot \sum_{t=2}^{T} ES_\alpha[SC_t - SC_{t-1}] \qquad (17.3)$$

where the cost of capital rate i_{CoC} represents the spread between interest rates at which money can be borrowed and reinvested risk free.

Summarising the two steps, we write

$$TC = EC + RM$$

$$= C_0 + ES_\alpha[SC_1] + i_{CoC} \cdot \sum_{t=2}^{T} ES_\alpha[SC_t - SC_{t-1}]$$

$$= C_0 + R_\alpha^{SST}[SC] \qquad (17.4)$$

where

$$R_\alpha^{SST}[SC] := ES_\alpha[SC_1] + i_{CoC} \cdot \sum_{t=2}^{T} ES_\alpha[SC_t - SC_{t-1}] \qquad (17.5)$$

The functional $R_\alpha^{SST} : R^\infty \to R$ defines the SST risk measure.

The SST risk measure is a prototype of a multi-period risk measure used in risk assessment within a multi-period framework. The design and properties of multi-period risk measures is not yet well understood. From a methodological point of view capital risk measures should be coherent risk measures. However, Filipovic and Vogelpoth (2008) have shown by counterexample that the SST risk measure does not satisfy the axiom of monotonicity for coherent multi-period risk measures. If for $X, Y \in R^\infty$ one has $X \geq Y$ with probability one, then $R_\alpha^{SST}[X] \geq R_\alpha^{SST}[Y]$ does not necessarily hold, that is a higher risk does not necessarily lead to a higher target capital, which is unsatisfactory. The largest coherent risk measure among those dominated by the SST risk measure, is given by

$$R_\alpha^{SST,\,c}[SC] := (1 - i_{CoC}) \cdot ES_\alpha[SC_1] + i_{CoC} \cdot ES_\alpha[SC_T] \qquad (17.6)$$

and (if appropriate) could be used as a valuable alternative to the SST risk measure. The risk measure Equation 17.6 will be called the SST coherent risk measure. For a discussion of problems encountered with the application of "coherent risk measures" in a solvency framework, Dhaene *et al* (2003) should be consulted. However, the task of consistent capital assessments over time within Solvency II has scarcely been discussed. Dynamic time-consistent aspects in the context of the SST are studied by Vogelpoth (2006).

THE MEAN AND VARIANCE OF THE RANDOM ASSETS

Consider the stochastic dynamic evolution of the random asset values of an insurance portfolio in a discrete time setting over a time horizon $[0, T]$. Let A_t be the random value of the assets at time $t \in \{1, \ldots, T\}$. In the time period $(t - 1, t]$ the cash inflow consists of random premiums of amount P_t at time $t - 1$, and the cash outflow consists of random insurance costs of amount X_t at time t. The latter amount includes insurance claims, expenses and bonus payments to the insured. The assets at time t satisfy the recursive equation

$$A_t = (A_{t-1} + P_t) \cdot (1 + I_t) - X_t, \quad t \in \{1, \ldots, T\} \qquad (17.7)$$

where I_t denotes the random rate of return on investment in the time period $(t - 1, t]$ and A_0 denotes the initial capital of the insurance portfolio. It follows that the asset value at time T is given by

$$A_T = A_0 \cdot \prod_{t=1}^{T} (1 + I_t) + \sum_{t=1}^{T} \{P_t \cdot (1 + I_t) - X_t\} \cdot \prod_{j=t+1}^{T} (1 + I_j)$$

$$(17.8)$$

The goal is the determination of the mean and variance of the assets under the following model assumptions:

(M1) The random premiums P_t and insurance costs X_t are independent rom the returns $I_1, \ldots, I_T$ and their means andvariances are given by $\mu_{P_t} = E[P_t]$, $\sigma_{P_t}^2 = \mathrm{Var}[P_t]$ and $\mu_{X_t} = E[X_t]$, $\sigma_{X_t}^2 = \mathrm{Var}[X_t]$, respectively.

(M2) The random accumulated rates of return in time period $(t-1, t]$ are independent and lognormally distributed such that

$$Z_t = \ln\{1 + I_t\}, \quad t \in \{1, \ldots, T\} \qquad (17.9)$$

is normally distributed with mean μ and standard deviation σ.

To simplify calculations, we consider the random variables $Z_{t,T}$ defined by

$$\exp(Z_{t,T}) = \prod_{j=t}^{T} (1 + I_j), \quad t \in \{1, \ldots, T\} \qquad (17.10)$$

which represent the random accumulated rates of return over the time period $(t-1, T]$. Clearly, the random sum $Z_{t,T} = \sum_{j=t}^{T} Z_j$ is normally distributed with mean and standard deviation

$$\mu_{t,T} = E[Z_{t,T}] = (T - t + 1) \cdot \mu$$
$$\sigma_{t,T} = \sqrt{\mathrm{Var}[Z_{t,T}]} = \sqrt{T - t + 1} \cdot \sigma \qquad (17.11)$$

The constant one-period expected accumulated rate of return over the time horizon $(t-1, t]$ is denoted and given by

$$r = E[\exp(Z_t)] = \exp(\mu + \tfrac{1}{2}\sigma^2), \quad t \in \{1, \ldots, T\}. \qquad (17.12)$$

We are ready for the following result.

Theorem 17.1 *Under the model assumptions* (M1) *and* (M2), *the mean and variance of the random assets of an insurance portfolio are given by the expressions*

$$E[A_T] = r^T \cdot \left\{ A_0 + \sum_{t=1}^{T} r^{-t} \cdot (\mu_{P_t} \cdot r - \mu_{X_t}) \right\} \qquad (17.13)$$

$$\mathrm{Var}[A_T]$$

$$= r^{2T} \cdot \left\{ \begin{array}{l} A_0^2 \cdot \left(e^{T\sigma^2} - 1 \right) \\[2mm] + A_0 \cdot \sum_{t=1}^{T} r^{-t} \cdot \left\{ \left(\mu_{P_t} r - \mu_{X_t} \right) \left(e^{(T-t)\sigma^2} - 1 \right) + \mu_{P_t} r e^{(T-t)\sigma^2} \left(e^{\sigma^2} - 1 \right) \right\} \\[2mm] + \sum_{t=1}^{T} r^{-t} \cdot \left\{ \begin{array}{l} \left(\mu_{P_t} r - \mu_{X_t} \right)^2 \left(e^{(T-t)\sigma^2} - 1 \right) + \left(\mu_{P_t} r \right)^2 e^{(T-t)\sigma^2} \left(e^{\sigma^2} - 1 \right) \\[1mm] + \sigma_{P_t}^2 r^2 e^{(T-t+1)\sigma^2} + \sigma_{X_t}^2 r^2 e^{(T-t)\sigma^2} - 2\mathrm{Cov}[P_t, X_t] \cdot r e^{(T-t)\sigma^2} \end{array} \right\} \\[4mm] + 2 \cdot \sum_{1 \le s < t \le T} r^{-(s+t)} \cdot \left\{ \begin{array}{l} \left(\mu_{P_s} r - \mu_{X_s} \right) \left(\mu_{P_t} r - \mu_{X_t} \right) \left(e^{(T-t)\sigma^2} - 1 \right) \\[1mm] + \left(\mu_{P_s} r - \mu_{X_s} \right) \mu_{P_t} r e^{(T-t)\sigma^2} \left(e^{\sigma^2} - 1 \right) \\[1mm] + \mathrm{Cov}\left[P_s r - X_s, P_t r e^{\sigma^2} - X_t \right] \cdot e^{(T-t)\sigma^2} \end{array} \right\} \end{array} \right.$$

$$(17.14)$$

Proof With the notation of Equation 17.10 the expression 17.8 can be rewritten as

$$A_T = A_0 \cdot \exp(Z_{1,T}) + \sum_{t=1}^{T} \{ P_t \cdot \exp(Z_{t,T}) - X_t \cdot \exp(Z_{t+1,T}) \},$$

$$(17.15)$$

from which Equation 17.13 is obtained without difficulty. To obtain the expression for the variance, several terms must be calculated. We have

$$\mathrm{Var}[A_0 \cdot \exp(Z_{1,T})] = A_0^2 \cdot \left(e^{2T(\mu+\sigma^2)} - e^{T(2\mu+\sigma^2)} \right)$$
$$= A_0^2 \cdot r^{2T} \cdot \left(e^{T\sigma^2} - 1 \right)$$

For $1 \le t \le T$ we have using assumption (M1) that

$$\mathrm{Var}[P_t \cdot \exp(Z_{t,T}) - X_t \cdot \exp(Z_{t+1,T})]$$
$$= \mathrm{Var}[E[P_t \cdot \exp(Z_{t,T}) - X_t \cdot \exp(Z_{t+1,T}) \mid Z_{t,T}, Z_{t+1,T}]]$$
$$\quad + E[\mathrm{Var}[P_t \cdot \exp(Z_{t,T}) - X_t \cdot \exp(Z_{t+1,T}) \mid Z_{t,T}, Z_{t+1,T}]]$$
$$= \mathrm{Var}[\mu_{P_t} \cdot \exp(Z_{t,T}) - \mu_{X_t} \cdot \exp(Z_{t+1,T})]$$
$$\quad + E[\sigma_{P_t}^2 \cdot \exp(2Z_{t,T}) + \sigma_{X_t}^2 \cdot \exp(2Z_{t,T})$$
$$\quad - 2\mathrm{Cov}[P_t, X_t] \cdot \exp(Z_{t,T} + Z_{t+1,T})]$$
$$= \mu_{P_t}^2 \cdot \mathrm{Var}[\exp(Z_{t,T})] + \mu_{X_t}^2 \cdot \mathrm{Var}[\exp(Z_{t+1,T})]$$
$$\quad - 2\mu_{P_t}\mu_{X_t} \cdot \mathrm{Cov}[\exp(Z_{t,T}), \exp(Z_{t+1,T})]$$
$$\quad + \sigma_{P_t}^2 \cdot E[\exp(2Z_{t,T})] + \sigma_{X_t}^2 \cdot E[\exp(2Z_{t+1,T})]$$
$$\quad - 2\mathrm{Cov}[P_t, X_t] \cdot (E[\exp(Z_{t,T})] \cdot E[\exp(Z_{t+1,T})]$$
$$\quad + \mathrm{Cov}[\exp(Z_{t,T}), \exp(Z_{t+1,T})])$$

By assumption (M2) Z_t is independent from $Z_{t+1,T}$ and we have

$$
\begin{aligned}
\mathrm{Cov}&[\exp(Z_{t,T}), \exp(Z_{t+1,T})] \\
&= \mathrm{Cov}[\exp(Z_t) \cdot \exp(Z_{t+1,T}), \exp(Z_{t+1,T})] \\
&= E[\exp(Z_t)] \cdot \mathrm{Var}[\exp(Z_{t+1,T})] \\
&= r^{2(T-t)+1} \cdot (e^{(T-t)\sigma^2} - 1)
\end{aligned}
$$

Inserting that into the preceding expression we obtain

$$
\begin{aligned}
\mathrm{Var}&[P_t \cdot \exp(Z_{t,T}) - X_t \cdot \exp(Z_{t+1,T})] \\
&= \mu_{P_t}^2 \cdot r^{2(T-t+1)} (e^{(T-t+1)\sigma^2} - 1) + \mu_{X_t}^2 \cdot r^{2(T-t)} (e^{(T-t)\sigma^2} - 1) \\
&\quad - 2\mu_{P_t}\mu_{X_t} \cdot r^{2(T-t)+1} (e^{(T-t)\sigma^2} - 1) \\
&\quad + \sigma_{P_t}^2 \cdot r^{2(T-t+1)} e^{(T-t+1)\sigma^2} + \sigma_{X_t}^2 \cdot r^{2(T-t)} e^{(T-t)\sigma^2} \\
&\quad - 2\mathrm{Cov}[P_t, X_t] \cdot r^{2(T-t)+1} e^{(T-t)\sigma^2}
\end{aligned}
$$

On the other hand, for $1 \le s < t \le T$ we have

$$
\begin{aligned}
\mathrm{Cov}&[P_s \exp(Z_{s,T}) - X_s \exp(Z_{s+1,T}), P_t \exp(Z_{t,T}) - X_t \exp(Z_{t+1,T})] \\
&= E[P_s P_t] \cdot \mathrm{Cov}[\exp(Z_{s,T}), \exp(Z_{t,T})] \\
&\quad + \mathrm{Cov}[P_s, P_t] \cdot E[\exp(Z_{s,T})] \cdot E[\exp(Z_{t,T})] \\
&\quad - E[X_s P_t] \cdot \mathrm{Cov}[\exp(Z_{s+1,T}), \exp(Z_{t,T})] \\
&\quad + \mathrm{Cov}[X_s, P_t] \cdot E[\exp(Z_{s+1,T})] \cdot E[\exp(Z_{t,T})] \\
&\quad - E[P_s X_t] \cdot \mathrm{Cov}[\exp(Z_{s,T}), \exp(Z_{t+1,T})] \\
&\quad + \mathrm{Cov}[P_s, X_t] \cdot E[\exp(Z_{s,T})] \cdot E[\exp(Z_{t+1,T})] \\
&\quad + E[X_s X_t] \cdot \mathrm{Cov}[\exp(Z_{s+1,T}), \exp(Z_{t+1,T})] \\
&\quad + \mathrm{Cov}[X_s, X_t] \cdot E[\exp(Z_{s+1,T})] \cdot E[\exp(Z_{t+1,T})] \\
&= r^{2T-(s+t)+2} \cdot (\mu_{P_s}\mu_{P_t} \cdot (e^{(T-t+1)\sigma^2} - 1) + \mathrm{Cov}[P_s, P_t] \cdot e^{(T-t+1)\sigma^2}) \\
&\quad - r^{2T-(s+t)+1} \cdot (\mu_{X_s}\mu_{P_t} \cdot (e^{(T-t+1)\sigma^2} - 1) \\
&\qquad\qquad\qquad + \mathrm{Cov}[X_s, P_t] \cdot e^{(T-t+1)\sigma^2}) \\
&\quad - r^{2T-(s+t)+1} \cdot (\mu_{P_s}\mu_{X_t} \cdot (e^{(T-t)\sigma^2} - 1) + \mathrm{Cov}[P_s, X_t] \cdot e^{(T-t)\sigma^2}) \\
&\quad + r^{2T-(s+t)} \cdot (\mu_{X_s}\mu_{X_t} \cdot (e^{(T-t)\sigma^2} - 1) + \mathrm{Cov}[X_s, X_t] \cdot e^{(T-t)\sigma^2})
\end{aligned}
$$

where the covariance terms are obtained as follows. Since $Z_{s,T} = Z_{s,t-1} + Z_{t,T}$ and $Z_{s,t-1}$ is independent from $Z_{t,T}$, we obtain

$$\mathrm{Cov}[\exp(Z_{s,T}),\exp(Z_{t,T})]$$
$$= \mathrm{Cov}[\exp(Z_{s,t-1})\cdot\exp(Z_{t,T}),\exp(Z_{t,T})]$$
$$= E[\exp(Z_{s,t-1})]\cdot\mathrm{Var}[\exp(Z_{t,T})]$$
$$= r^{2T-(s+t)+2}\cdot(e^{(T-t+1)\sigma^2}-1)$$

In a similar way, for $1 \le t \le T$ we have

$$\mathrm{Cov}[A_0\exp(Z_{1,T}), P_t\exp(Z_{t,T}) - X_t\exp(Z_{t+1,T})]$$
$$= A_0\mu_{P_t}\cdot\mathrm{Cov}[\exp(Z_{1,T}),\exp(Z_{t,T})]$$
$$- A_0\mu_{P_t}\cdot\mathrm{Cov}[\exp(Z_{1,T}),\exp(Z_{t+1,T})]$$
$$= A_0 r^{2T-t}\cdot(\mu_{P_t}r\cdot(e^{(T-t+1)\sigma^2}-1) - \mu_{X_t}\cdot(e^{(T-t)\sigma^2}-1))$$

Gathering all terms together appropriately we finally obtain Equation 17.14. □

TECHNICAL VALUES OF A LIFE INSURANCE CONTRACT

We consider a life insurance contract with level premium payments subject to the single mortality cause of decrement over the time horizon $[0, n]$ in a discrete time setting. At the time points $t \in \{1, 2, \ldots, n\}$ the contract offers to a policyholder the following benefits:

D_t: death benefit paid end of period in case the policyholder dies in time period $(t-1, t]$; and
E_n: survival benefit paid in case the policyholder survives the whole period at time n.

To be able to describe the random underwriting gain within the classic model of life insurance (Wolff 1970; Bowers *et al* 1986; Gerber 1986; Wolfsdorf 1986; Hürlimann 1988; Gerber 1995), we consider the following deterministic basic actuarial quantities:

π_t^R: risk premium for the time period $(t-1, t]$ due at time $t-1$;
π_t^S: saving premium for the time period $(t-1, t]$ due at time $t-1$;
$\pi^N = \pi_t^R + \pi_t^S$: net premium for the time period $(t-1, t]$ due at time $t-1$;

$\pi_t^{E,R}$: expense risk premium for the time period $(t-1, t]$ due at time $t-1$;

$\pi_t^{E,S}$: expense saving premium for the time period $(t-1, t]$ due at time $t-1$;

$\pi^E = \pi_t^{E,R} + \pi_t^{E,S}$: expense premium for the time period $(t-1, t]$ due at time $t-1$;

$\pi = \pi^N + \pi^E$: gross premium for the time period $(t-1, t]$ due at time $t-1$;

$_tV^N$: the net actuarial reserve required at time t such that $_nV^N = E_n$;

$_tV^E$: the expense reserve required at time t such that $_nV^E = 0$;

$_tV = {_tV^N} + {_tV^E}$: the gross actuarial reserve required at time t; and

c_t: the operating cost charge for the time period $(t-1, t]$ due at time t.

The precise model description and mathematical definitions of these quantities can be found in the references. For example, the net actuarial reserve represents the actuarial present value of future net cashflows (the difference between insurance benefits and net premiums). The idea of including the expense reserve into the gross actuarial reserve is due to Zillmer (1831–93) (eg, Gerber 1986, p. 103). In this traditional setting, pricing is based on a single decrement mortality table with the entries:

q_x: probability a life aged x will die within one year; and
$p_x = 1 - q_x$: probability a life aged x will survive to age $x + 1$;

and some fixed technical interest rate i. The technical discount factor is denoted by $v = (1+i)^{-1}$. The technical values satisfy the following relationships:

$$\pi_t^R = v \cdot q_{x+t-1} \cdot (D_t - {_tV^N}), \quad t = 1, \ldots, n-1, \; \pi_n^R = 0 \tag{17.16}$$

$$_tV^N = ({_{t-1}V^N} + \pi_t^S) \cdot (1+i) \tag{17.17}$$

$$\pi_t^{E,R} = -v \cdot q_{x+t-1} \cdot {_tV^E}, \quad t = 1, \ldots, n-1, \; \pi_n^{E,R} = 0 \tag{17.18}$$

$$c_t = ({_{t-1}V^E} + \pi_t^{E,S}) \cdot (1+i) - {_tV^E}, \quad t = 1, \ldots, n \tag{17.19}$$

The derivation of the formulas in Equations 17.16 and 17.17 is well known and found in any classic text on life insurance. The formulas in Equations 17.18 and 17.19 are derived similarly in Hürlimann (1988, p. 184).

Example 5 For the classic endowment contract such that $D_1 = D_2 = \cdots = D_n = E_n = 1$ and for an acquisition cost rate α, the closed form formula is obtained

$$c_t = (\pi^E - \alpha \cdot \pi^N) \cdot (1+i) - \alpha \cdot i, \quad t = 1, \ldots, n \qquad (17.20)$$

Indeed, inserting the expression $_tV^E = -\alpha \cdot (1 - _tV^N)$ (eg, Gerber 1986, p. 102) for the expense reserve into the formula in Equation 17.19 for the operating cost charge, we obtain with the expressions in Equations 17.16 and 17.18 for the expense risk premiums and the risk premiums

$$c_t = (-\alpha + \alpha \cdot {_{t-1}}V^N + \pi^E - \pi_t^{E,R})(1+i) + \alpha - \alpha \cdot {_t}V^N$$
$$= -\alpha \cdot i + \alpha \cdot ({_{t-1}}V^N \cdot (1+i) - {_t}V^N)$$
$$\quad + \pi^E \cdot (1+i) - \alpha \cdot q_{x+t-1} \cdot (1 - {_t}V^N)$$
$$= \pi^E \cdot (1+i) - \alpha \cdot i + \alpha \cdot ({_{t-1}}V^N \cdot (1+i) - {_t}V^N - \pi_k^R \cdot (1+i))$$
$$= \pi^E \cdot (1+i) - \alpha \cdot i - \alpha \cdot (\pi_t^S \cdot (1+i) + \pi_t^R \cdot (1+i))$$
$$= (\pi^E - \alpha \cdot \pi^N) \cdot (1+i) - \alpha \cdot i$$

Owing to regulatory laws, insurance companies are usually allowed to only guarantee relatively low technical interest rates to their policyholders. To compensate for this, policyholders are typically entitled to participate in the gross surplus of an insurance company. Additional variable bonus payments are periodically credited to the policyholder's account or bonus fund. Specification of the bonus fund depends upon the bonus policy of a life insurance company. Usually, the bonus depends highly upon the realised investment return I_t in period $(t - 1, t]$. For simplicity and illustration we will assume a bonus rate of the type $I_t^b = \max(I_t - \delta, i)$, where δ is some interest spread. In general, the bonus rate is at least equal to the guaranteed technical interest rate. A possible specification of the size of the bonus fund of an n-year life insurance, which is viewed as a deterministic saving account and denoted by B_t, may be the following one. The bonus fund at the end of a period consists of the bonus fund at the beginning of a period accumulated with the bonus interest on the bonus fund and the excess bonus interest above the technical interest on the net actuarial reserves and net premiums. Expressed in a formula we have

$$B_t = B_{t-1} \cdot (1 + I_t^b) + ({_{t-1}}V^N + \pi^N) \cdot (I_t^b - i) \qquad (17.21)$$

The bonus fund of a policyholder is paid out by death or by survival at expiration date. We are interested in the expected value of the bonus fund at time t. Consider the bonus' relevant capital in time period $(t-1, t]$, which is denoted and given by

$$c_t^b = ({}_{t-1}V^N + \pi^N), \quad t \in \{1, \ldots, n\}. \tag{17.22}$$

We rewrite Equation 17.21 in the form

$$B_t = (B_{t-1} + {}_{t-1}V^N + \pi^N) \cdot (1 + I_t^b) - ({}_{t-1}V^N + \pi^N) \cdot (1 + i) \tag{17.23}$$

Then, similarly to Equation 17.8 we have

$$B_t = \sum_{j=1}^{t} \{c_j^b \cdot (1 + I_j^b) - c_j^b \cdot (1 + i)\} \cdot \prod_{k=j+1}^{t} (1 + I_k^b) \tag{17.24}$$

In general, the valuation of guaranteed stochastic funds of the type in Equation 17.24 is rather complex because it involves implicit or embedded options. Two simple models to handle this problem have been proposed by Hürlimann (2006). As a simple approximation, we assume here that the stochastic bonus rate exceeds the sum of the technical interest and the interest spread with almost certainty, that is we assume that $I_t^b \geq \delta + i$ with probability one. Then the formula Equation 17.13 of Theorem 17.1 can be applied with I_t replaced by $I_t - \delta$ to obtain the expected bonus fund

$$b_t = E[B_t] = \sum_{j=1}^{t} \{c_j^b \cdot (r - \delta) - c_j^b \cdot (1 + i)\} \cdot (r - \delta)^{t-j} \tag{17.25}$$

THE SST RISK MEASURE FOR A LIFE INSURANCE CONTRACT

Consider the stochastic process $E_t = A_t - L_t$, $t \in \{0, 1, \ldots, T\}$, of the equity at time t of a life insurance contract, where the assets A_t satisfy a recursive relationship of the type in Equation 17.7 and the liabilities L_t include the net actuarial reserves, the expense reserves and the bonus fund.

For simplicity, we assume that the insurance company is risk neutral with respect to mortality. This means that mortality risk is assumed to be diversifiable. In fact, if the portfolio of an insurance company is not too small, the law of large numbers for mortality risks can be applied and random cashflows can be replaced by expected cashflows. The evaluation is illustrated for an endowment contract with technical values as considered in the previous section.

To determine the mean and variance of the assets according to the assumptions in the section "Mean and variance of the random assets", we therefore need the expected cash inflow of premiums given by

$$p_t = E[P_t] = {}_{t-1}p_x \cdot \pi \qquad (17.26)$$

and the expected cash outflow of insurance costs, which includes, besides the expected insurance benefits, the expected cost charges and the expected bonus payments, given by

$$x_t = E[X_t] = {}_{t-1}p_x \cdot q_{x+t-1} \cdot (1 + b_t) + \delta_t^n \cdot {}_n p_x \cdot (1 + b_n) + {}_t p_x \cdot c_t \qquad (17.27)$$

where $\delta_t^n = 1$ if $t = n$ and $\delta_t^n = 0$ otherwise. From Theorem 17.1 with time horizon $[0, t]$ and deterministic cashflows, the following formulas are obtained

$$E[A_t] = r^t \cdot \left\{ A_0 + \sum_{j=1}^{t} r^{-j} \cdot (p_j \cdot r - x_j) \right\} \qquad (17.28)$$

$\text{Var}[A_t]$

$$= r^{2t} \cdot \left\{ \begin{array}{l} A_0^2 \cdot (e^{t\sigma^2} - 1) + A_0 \cdot \sum_{j=1}^{t} r^{-j} \\ \qquad \cdot \{(p_j r - x_j)(e^{(t-j)\sigma^2} - 1) + p_j r e^{(t-j)\sigma^2}(e^{\sigma^2} - 1)\} \\ + \sum_{j=1}^{t} r^{-j} \cdot \{(p_j r - x_j)^2 (e^{(t-j)\sigma^2} - 1) \\ \qquad + (p_j r)^2 e^{(t-j)\sigma^2}(e^{\sigma^2} - 1)\} \\ + 2 \cdot \sum_{1 \le i < j \le t} r^{-(i+j)} \cdot (p_i r - x_i) \\ \qquad \cdot \{(p_j r - x_j)(e^{(t-j)\sigma^2} - 1) + p_j r e^{(t-j)\sigma^2}(e^{\sigma^2} - 1)\} \end{array} \right. \qquad (17.29)$$

By the risk-neutral assumption on the mortality risk, the liabilities are viewed as a deterministic quantity with expected value

$$E[L_t] = (1 - \delta_t^n) \cdot {}_t p_x \cdot ({}_t V^N + {}_t V^E + b_t) \qquad (17.30)$$

To evaluate the SST target capital according to the section "The SST risk measure", we consider the stochastic process of the shortfall risk-bearing capital at time t, which is defined as market-consistent discounted value at time $t = 0$ of the negative equity at time t, that is

$$SC_t = D_t \cdot (L_t - A_t) \tag{17.31}$$

where D_t is the market-consistent discount factor, that is the actual price at time $t = 0$ of a unit zero coupon bond, which pays one unit at time t. To evaluate the SST risk measure, it is necessary to specify the distribution of Equation 17.31. In general, it is possible to consider gamma or elliptical type distributions (eg, Hürlimann 2001; Landsman and Valdez 2003; Valdez 2005; Furman and Landsman 2005, 2007). However, by the made simplified assumptions, the standard normal distribution assumption will suffice for our purpose. Therefore, we assume that $SC_t, t \in \{1, \dots, T\}$, is normally distributed with mean and variance

$$E[SC_t] = D_t \cdot (E[L_t] - E[A_t]), \quad \mathrm{Var}[SC_t] = D_t^2 \cdot \mathrm{Var}[A_t] \tag{17.32}$$

Similarly, the difference in shortfall risk-bearing capital $\Delta SC_t = SC_t - SC_{t-1}$ (required in the formula in Equation 17.5 for the SST risk measure) is also normally distributed with mean $E[\Delta SC_t] = E[SC_t] - E[SC_{t-1}]$ and variance determined by

$$\mathrm{Var}[\Delta SC_t] = D_t^2 \cdot \mathrm{Var}[A_t] - D_{t-1} \cdot (2rD_t - D_{t-1}) \cdot \mathrm{Var}[A_{t-1}] \tag{17.33}$$

where use has been made of the following covariance expression

$$\mathrm{Cov}[A_{t-1}, A_t] = \mathrm{Cov}[A_{t-1}, A_{t-1} \cdot \exp(Z_t) + p_t \cdot \exp(Z_t) - x_t]$$
$$= E[\exp(Z_t)] \cdot \mathrm{Var}[A_{t-1}] = r \cdot \mathrm{Var}[A_{t-1}] \tag{17.34}$$

The previous section and the section "The SST risk measure of a life insurance contract" contain all of the specifications required to now evaluate the SST target capital of an endowment contract using both the SST risk measure Equation 17.5 and the SST coherent risk measure Equation 17.6. The next section provides concrete numerical calculations.

A NUMERICAL EXAMPLE

We illustrate the numerical evaluation of the SST target capital with a 10-year endowment contract for a life aged $x = 40$ with 1,000 units as the level insured sum. The technical interest rate is chosen at

Table 17.1 Life table

Year	Probability of death q_{x+t-1}	Probability of survival $_{t-1}p_x$
1	0.0027812	1.00000
2	0.0029818	0.99722
3	0.0032017	0.99425
4	0.0034427	0.99106
5	0.0037070	0.98765
6	0.0039966	0.98399
7	0.0043141	0.98006
8	0.0046621	0.97583
9	0.0050436	0.97128
10	0.0054617	0.96638

$i = 2.5\%$, the acquisition cost rate at $\alpha = 4\%$ and the operating cost rate (in percent of the gross premium) at $\beta = 5\%$. The probabilities of death and survival in Table 17.1 are taken from the illustrative life table in Bowers *et al* (1986, p. 560). Table 17.2 provides the technical values of the endowment contract and Table 17.3 lists expected values needed in the formulas of the section "The SST risk measure of a life insurance contract".

The confidence level in the SST risk measure is set at $\alpha = 99\%$, the cost of capital rate at $i_{CoC} = 6\%$ and the market discount factor corresponds for simplicity to a risk-free rate of 3%. The bonus spread is taken as constant and equal to $\delta = 0.25\%$. We observe that in all of the examples, which depend on the choice of the expected rate of return and the volatility of return, the ES of the first year shortfall risk-bearing capital is negative, that is $ES_\alpha[SC_1] < 0$. We assume that at the entry date of the endowment contract there is no liability, that is $L_0 = 0$, hence $E_0 = A_0$. This implies that the implicit equation $TC = A_0$ obtained by setting the SST target capital to its initial capital has a unique solution A_0. By Equations 17.4–17.6 the unique solutions obtained correspond either to a vanishing SST risk measure $R_\alpha^{SST}[SC] = 0$ or to a vanishing SST coherent risk measure $R_\alpha^{SST,\,c}[SC] = 0$. A unique solution is either called optimal SST initial capital or optimal SST coherent initial capital. An immediate reinterpretation yields the following rule of thumb. Under the made assumptions, the risk margin or MvM of an endowment contract coincides in absolute value with the ES of the first year shortfall risk-bearing capital.

Table 17.2 Technical values of an endowment contract

Year	Net premium 88.719		Expense premium 8.406			Gross premium 97.125		
	$_tV^N$	$_tV^E$	π_t^S	π_t^R	$\pi_t^{E,S}$	$\pi_t^{E,R}$	c_t	b_t
1	88.402	−36.464	86.246	2.473	8.307	0.099	4.978	1.996
2	179.101	−32.836	86.331	2.388	8.310	0.096	4.978	6.076
3	272.185	−29.113	86.446	2.273	8.315	0.091	4.978	12.391
4	367.750	−25.290	86.595	2.124	8.321	0.085	4.978	21.100
5	465.901	−21.364	86.787	1.932	8.329	0.077	4.978	32.372
6	566.754	−17.330	87.030	1.689	8.338	0.068	4.978	46.389
7	670.438	−13.182	87.332	1.387	8.351	0.055	4.978	63.341
8	777.097	−8.916	87.705	1.014	8.365	0.041	4.978	83.430
9	886.891	−4.524	88.162	0.557	8.384	0.022	4.978	106.874
10	1,000	0	88.719	0	8.406	0	4.978	133.902

Table 17.3 Expected values of various quantities

Year	Cash in or gross premium	Benefits	Cost charge	Expected values				
				Bonus benefits	Cash out without bonus	Cash out with bonus	Gross actuarial reserve	Bonus fund
1	97.125	2.781	4.964	0.006	7.745	7.751	51.793	1.991
2	96.855	2.974	4.949	0.018	7.923	7.941	145.423	6.041
3	96.566	3.183	4.933	0.039	8.116	8.156	240.900	12.280
4	96.257	3.412	4.916	0.072	8.328	8.400	338.231	20.839
5	95.926	3.661	4.898	0.119	8.559	8.678	437.419	31.854
6	95.570	3.933	4.878	0.182	8.811	8.993	538.467	45.464
7	95.188	4.228	4.857	0.268	9.085	9.353	641.369	61.810
8	94.777	4.549	4.835	0.380	9.384	9.764	746.118	81.034
9	94.335	4.899	4.810	0.524	9.709	10.233	852.701	103.281
10	93.860	966.380	4.784	129.400	971.164	1,100.564	0	0

Table 17.4 Optimal SST initial capitals

	Optimal SST initial capital					
	Without bonus			With bonus		
	Volatilities			Volatilities		
Return (%)	8%	10%	12%	8%	10%	12%
4	45.331	77.600	118.712	50.637	83.584	125.635
5	43.417	76.167	118.075	53.076	87.084	130.751
6	41.477	74.724	117.463	55.588	90.713	136.101
	Optimal SST coherent initial capital					
4	−2.345	9.915	23.740	2.309	14.864	29.074
5	−4.580	7.877	21.931	3.868	16.871	31.639
6	−6.824	5.844	20.143	5.486	18.964	34.325

Table 17.4 summarises various values of the optimal SST (not coherent and coherent) initial capital without or with bonus. We note a dramatic decrease of the optimal SST coherent initial capital compared with the original optimal SST initial capital. The obtained values are very sensitive to the volatility parameter. The dependence upon the expected rate of return is less sensitive but opposite in behaviour for an endowment without or with bonus participation.

As a conclusion we would like to point out that the very different results obtained constitute a challenge rather than an answer to what should be appropriate. Unfortunately, a more detailed analysis could not yet be undertaken. Understanding differences, not only between the SST risk measure and its coherent version, but also with respect to a standard regulatory approach, remains a main modelling task within any solvency system.

REFERENCES

Bowers, N. L., H. U. Gerber, J. C. Hickman, D. A. Jones and C. J. Nesbitt, 1986, *Actuarial Mathematics* (Itasca, IL: Society of Actuaries).

Dhaene, J., M. Goovaerts and R. Kaas, 2003, "Economic Capital Allocation Derived from Risk Measures", *North American Actuarial Journal*, 7(2), pp. 44–59.

Filipovic, D. and N. Vogelpoth, 2008, "A Note on the Swiss Solvency Test Risk Measure", *Insurance: Mathematics and Economics*, 42, pp. 897–902.

FOPI, 2004, "White Paper of the Swiss Solvency Test", URL: http://www.finma.ch/archiv/bpv/download/e/WhitePaperSST_en.pdf.

FOPI, 2006, "Technisches Dokument zum Swiss Solvency Test", October, URL: http://www.finma.ch/archiv/bpv/download/d/SST_technischesDokument_061002.pdf.

Furman, E. and Z. Landsman, 2005, "Risk Capital Decomposition for a Multivariate Dependent Gamma Portfolio", *Insurance: Mathematics and Economics*, 37, pp. 635–49.

Furman, E. and Z. Landsman, 2007, "Economic capital Allocations for Non-Negative Portfolios of Dependent Risks", *Proceedings of the 37th International ASTIN Colloquium*, Orlando, FL, URL: http://www.actuaries.org/ASTIN/Colloquia/Orlando/Papers/Furman.pdf.

Gerber, H. U., 1986, *Lebensversicherungsmathematik* (Berlin: Springer).

Gerber, H. U., 1995, *Life Insurance Mathematics*, 2nd edn (Berlin: Springer).

Hürlimann, W., 1988, "Allgemeine Lebensversicherungen: Überschuss und Rentabilität", Mitteilungen der Vereinigung schweizerischer. Versicherungsmathematiker, Heft 2, pp. 179–209.

Hürlimann, W., 2001, "Analytical Evaluation of Economic Risk Capital for Portfolios of Gamma Risks", *ASTIN Bulletin*, 31, pp. 107–22.

Hürlimann, W., 2003, "Conditional Value-at-Risk Bounds for Compound Poisson Risks and a Normal Approximation", *Journal of Applied Mathematics*, 3(3), pp. 141–54.

Hürlimann, W., 2006, "Economic Risk Capital of Guaranteed Cash-Flows Under Fréchet-Markov Return Models", *Proceedings of the 28th International Congress of Actuaries*, Paris, URL: http://www.ica2006.com/Papiers/384/384.pdf.

IAA, 2004, "A Global Framework for Insurer Solvency Assessment", Research Report of the Insurer Solvency Assessment Working Party, URL: http://www.actuaries.org/LIBRARY/Papers/Global_Framework_Insurer_Solvency_Assessment-public.pdf.

Keller, P., 2006, "SST presentation at the University of Zürich", Jan 10, 2006, URL: http://www.finma.ch/archiv/bpv/download/e/SST_Pres_20060110_UniZurich.pdf.

Landsman, Z. and E. A. Valdez, 2003, "Tail Conditional Expectations for Elliptical Distributions", *North American Actuarial Journal*, 7, pp. 55–71.

Solvency II, 2005, "Newsletter No. 5", Dec 2005, URL: http://www.gcactuaries.org/documents/sol_news_5.pdf.

Valdez, E. A., 2005, "Tail Conditional Variance for Elliptically Contoured Distributions", *Belgian Actuarial Bulletin*, 5(1), pp. 26–36.

Vogelpoth, N., 2006, "Some Results on Dynamic Risk Measures", Diploma Thesis, University of Munich.

Wolff, K. H., 1970, *Versicherungsmathematik* (Berlin Heidelberg: Springer-Verlag).

Wolfsdorf, K., 1986, *Versicherungsmathematik, Teil 1: Personenversicherung* (Leipzig: Teubner).

Wüthrich, M. V., H. Bühlmann and H. Furrer, 2008, *Market-Consistent Actuarial Valuation*, EAA Lecture Notes, 1 (Berlin Heidelberg: Springer-Verlag).

Zillmer, A., 1831–1893, "Wikipedia entry", URL: http://de.wikipedia.org/wiki/August_Zillmer.

Section IV

Measuring and Managing Operational Risk

Introduction

Marcelo Cruz

New York University

It was not a surprise for me when, researching areas that needed to be included in this book, I did not find anything meaningful on the subject of operational risk. I have been working within the insurance industry for quite a while; usually insurers, despite agreeing that operational risk is a key risk, do not invest many resources in the area to identify and manage the risks that make up operational risk.

It is estimated that operational risk represents 15%–25% of the total risk an insurance company runs, comparable with their actuarial risks. Having browsed an external database from one of the largest vendors of this material, I found that the following few items make clear the importance of the subject:

- There have been 55 reported operational risk events with losses in excess of US$50 million since 1990; the average loss from these high-impact events is approximately US$220 million.
- The frequency and severity of operational risk loss events has continuously increased over the past two decades.
- Events related to clients, products and business practices account for two thirds of operational risk losses.
- Life and P&C insurers are almost evenly affected by operational risk loss events in terms of frequency and severity.
- Whereas in life insurance suitability, disclosure and fiduciary issues are predominant, event types in P&C are more diverse, with significant numbers of internal fraud cases.
- Operational risk losses may eat up a considerable amount (up to 5%) of the premium received.

Insurers have a lot to catch up on in this area. In the lonely chapter constituting this section, I provide a step-by-step guide to how one can kick off an operational risk program inside an insurance company, also providing a numerical example to make the application and importance very clear.

18

Modelling and Measuring Operational Risk in Insurance Companies: A Step-by-Step Guide to a Quick Start

Marcelo Cruz

New York University

Modelling operational risk is a relatively new challenge for the insurance industry after it was decided to include this risk in the Solvency II scope, following what Basel II has done for the banking industry. Developing a complete framework for a "new" risk inside an insurance company is a long and complex process that would take many years to achieve, as it also needs to influence and change several cultural aspects within the organisation. Bearing this in mind, we try to provide a step-by-step quick-start guide on how to measure operational risk in this chapter. We also provide a numerical example with a fraud database to try and make it as clear as possible.

As the Solvency II deadline approaches insurance companies are being forced to pay more attention to operational risk. Although most firms are used to investing time and resources in measuring and managing financial risks this has not been the case for operational risk. This was the same in the banking industry, which only paid more attention to this (very important) area when it was pushed by the regulators through Basel II. We assume that the same story will happen in the insurance industry.

The first task of the risk manager, as usually performed for market and credit risks, is to define what operational risk is and what its sources are. In service industries in general, there are typically four main sources of operational failures, namely:

(i)   people;
(ii) technology;
(iii) process or procedural; and
(iv) external.

All four sources of risk can play a role in virtually every service organisation; the probabilities of certain operational errors occurring may also depend on exogenous factors or environmental conditions. These factors and conditions may be caused by human decision-making, by acts of nature or by threats from the outside world (say, criminals, terrorists).

People risks are due to incompetence, fatigue or fraud committed by an employee or manager of a firm. Technology risk events may be due to system failures, telecommunication failures, programming errors and information risk. Process or procedural risk relates to the standard procedures that are in place for each activity and how closely they are being followed and monitored. In financial services, process risk may be divided into three subcategories: namely model risk, transaction risk and operational control risk. The model risk may be due to a methodology error or a mark-to-model error. The transaction risk may be due to product complexity, an execution error, a booking error or a settlement error. The operational control risk can be due to volume risk, security risks, etc. Even if these three internal sources work well, a firm can still have external problems in the form of legal suits, environmental problems and class actions, for example. The occurrence of accidents may be influenced by a number of things, including weather conditions, operator fatigue and trading volume.

An efficient mitigation framework can only succeed by addressing all sources of risk. People risk can be reduced through better training, improved oversight and proper staffing. Technology risk can be reduced through improved system design, optimal redundancy, backup strategies and so on. Process risk can be mitigated through the implementation and enforcement of proper procedures with independent oversight (neutral reporting of errors), etc.

Many types of events that occur in the service industries cause only minor material or economic damage. For example, a customer who feels that they have not been treated well may never return, resulting in an economic loss for a firm. The frequency of such events occurring may be relatively high, but the expected loss incurred each time will be small. In any case, the sum of the costs of these minor events can still be significant over a certain period of time. However, the total cost is often quite predictable (in the sense of expectation) and may have a relatively small variance (eg, auto insurance losses due to fraud each month). On the other hand, different types of events may occur with a very low frequency in the service industries, but may cause a huge amount of damage. These events are typically referred to as catastrophic events. The damage may be measured either in economic (monetary) terms or in loss of life (although this is unlikely in financial services, particularly compared with other industries like health care and transportation where operational errors usually result in deaths).

In the finance industry a failure typically only results in monetary damage. On the other hand, operational risk in finance has an additional dimension that is not present in aviation or health care that increases the risk. A person involved in any transaction may have a personal incentive (ie, for personal gain) to perform transactions in an inappropriate manner. (In the aviation industry, a pilot has a clear incentive to follow regulations, since his own life is at stake as well.)

Operational risk failures in financial services may typically result in:

(i)   transaction errors;
(ii) loss of or damage to assets;
(iii) theft, fraud and unauthorised activities;
(iv) regulatory, compliance and taxation penalties; or
(v)   legal liabilities.

Transaction errors may include execution errors, booking errors or settlement errors. Loss of or damage to assets may be due to acts of nature or acts of terrorism. Because of such potential losses, a certain amount of redundancy may have to be built into the system. Fraud and unauthorised activities are fairly common[1] in the finance world. There are studies that say that such activities are caused by fatigue and overworked employees. Therefore, the Securities and Exchange Commission in the US imposes mandatory rules with regard to vacations and days that employees have to stay away from the office. (In Europe, such rules may not be as strictly enforced, like at Société Générale for example.) Regulatory penalties may be incurred if insider information is used improperly, which may ultimately lead to legal liabilities as well.

Developing any risk management programme is a long-term commitment. It needs to be borne in mind that there are not only quantitative issues involved, but there is also a strong cultural component that cannot be resolved in a few months. Different to market and credit risks, any employee in a firm can be a source of operational risk and, therefore, the challenge of the operational risk manager is much more complex and involves dealing with many different areas of a firm, such as compliance, legal, internal audit, operations, etc. This chapter can be used as a short-cut to quickly get into measuring and managing operational risk in a more quantitative way than most insurance companies do today. It is just an appetiser to a much more complex dinner. Rolling out such a programme across a firm will take a much longer time and quite a lot of effort, but it completely changes the way you manage a firm in the end.

After this short disclaimer, I will go on and introduce you to this "operational risk quick start" in three steps. The first step describes the importance of risk mapping and to identify operational risks embedded in the processes of a firm (internal and external – ie, involving clients directly or indirectly). The second step oversees the models for measuring operational risk and a quick examination of step 3 highlights the importance of using what you achieve in the two initial steps to report operational risk internally and also to manage risk more proactively.

STEP 1: MAPPING OPERATIONAL RISK AND DATABASE MODELLING

An operational risk loss can be defined as a negative impact on the earnings or equity value of a firm due to an operational risk event. An operational risk event is an incident that happened due to inadequate or failed processes, people or systems or due to external facts and circumstances: basically any procedural error in processing transactions or any external events (legal suit, terrorism, etc).

The tracking of internal operational loss data is essential to the entire operational risk management and measuring process. This data must be collected and organised in time series. The internal loss database will be fundamental in the estimation of economic capital to cover against operational risk.

In terms of operational loss data gathering, the data should preferably be collected straight from the profit and loss (P&L) system and related systems whenever it is possible and economically feasible. The basis for this logic lies in the fact that when an operational risk loss affects assets or accounts maintained on a mark-to-market basis, the economic impact of the event is usually the same as the accounting impact. In such cases, the basis for measurement is the loss adjustment as recognised in the P&L.

Due to the industry-wide lack of concern for collecting operational loss information until a few years ago, banking regulators demanded that financial institutions use four types of data for measuring operational risk instead of only an organisation's own loss experience. We would expect Solvency II to follow the same standards. The first type is the aforementioned historical losses (internal loss data), as a time series that happened inside the organisation. The second type of data is external losses, ie, losses that took place in other firms, usually very large losses that are available in public databases. The third type is key risk indicators (KRIs) that would help to assess the quality of the control environment at a certain point in time. The last type of data is scenario analysis. The argument for this type of information is that many times only the first three types of data are used and this is not enough to assess the real level of operational risk in financial institutions.

The first type of data: internal loss data

In order to model operational risk an insurance company first needs to establish a database with internal historical losses. There are a number of regulatory and technical prerequisites that a firm must follow in order to achieve minimum supervisory and modelling requirements. An insurance company's internal loss data must be thorough so that it captures all material activities and exposures from all the appropriate subsystems and geographic locations; therefore the internal loss data collection will cover firm-wide operational losses with the participation of every business unit in all the banks' locations throughout the world. A minimum threshold for data collection could also be established for the collection of internal loss data.

Definition of gross loss amount

The gross operational loss should include:

- Charges to the P&L and write-downs due to operational risk events.
- Market losses due to operational risk events.
- Payments made to third parties for lost use of funds, net amounts earned on funds held pending a late payment.
- In cases where a single event causes both positive and negative impacts, the two should be netted together. If the net amount is negative and exceeds the reporting threshold, it should be submitted.
- Loss is determined at the time of the event, without regard to any eventual remediation. Thus, for example, if a security is bought when a sale was intended, the market value of the day of the transaction is utilised for the purpose of calculating the losses, even if the security is held for periods of time afterwards until a more favourable market environment develops.
- It is understood that certain losses happen in core functions that are not directly involved with the P&L, like the IT department for example. Losses happening at such departments should also be reported as long as they meet the conditions mentioned above.
- Operational risk losses that are related to market risk are to be treated as operational risk for the purposes of calculating minimum regulatory capital (eg, misrepresentation of market positions or P&L due to operational errors, stop loss violations, losses produced by market valuation models that fail to work properly for any reason, losses taken from market positions taken in excess of limits, etc).
- Legal risk is considered to be an operational risk and should be reported as such. Events related to legal risk usually are disputes that may include litigation in court, arbitration, claims negotiation, etc.

- Some operational risks embedded in credit risk should be reported, such as:
  - procedure failures: where processing errors prevent recovery on a loan or actually enable a loss, as where a cash advance is made on a credit facility that was earlier cancelled by a credit officer;
  - legal issues: loan documents that may contain legal errors (invalid clauses or terms, etc); or
  - scoring models: errors in scoring models might result in the approval of transactions that would otherwise not be admitted.

Exclusions from the definition of gross loss amounts

The following events should not be included in the gross loss:

- Internal reworks (cost of repair and/or replacement), overtime, investments, etc;
- Near misses (potential losses that have not materialised);
- Costs of general maintenance contracts on equipment, etc, even if used for repairs or replacements in connection with an operational risk event;
- Events causing only reputational damage. Reputational risk is not considered to be an operational risk. Reputational risk is the risk of any damage to a firm's reputation caused by internal or external factors; and
- Losses arising from flawed strategic or discretionary processes are not recordable, as such losses are considered to be the result of business or strategic risks. This type of risk is often associated with senior management decision making (eg, merger and acquisition decisions, regional or global strategy etc).

The second type of data: external losses

Large operational risk losses are so rare that they have only happened once in several years. As this is the case, firms should also collect external loss data, which can be used either by mixing it with the internally collected data points or used to develop scenario analysis and/or stress tests. This data follows the same specification as the internal data but refers to losses that happened in other insurance companies or financial institutions. These databases can usually be bought at a fee from a vendor, like Fitch, SAS or ORX.

The third type of data: business control environment factors (key risk indicators)

Firms should also establish and collect business and control environment factors. These so-called KRIs are very important to the overall process as operational risk is actually a function of the control environment of a firm. If this control were loose, this would be reflected in large error rates, large volumes of processes by employees, and large numbers of minutes that a system is offline, for example. Of course, in such an environment more economic capital is needed to support operational risk.

The fourth type of data: scenario analysis

Due to the fact that large catastrophic events, owing to their exceptionality, should not happen frequently, historical loss data alone might not be a good indicator of the operational risk level of a firm, at least in the early stages of the measurement process. Considering these facts, the operational value-at-risk (VaR) model, using only internal data, might also have some limitations when performing robust estimations of large/infrequent events. By including scenario analysis, decisions on both capital and operational risk management can be based on more information than the initially scarce data collected internally. Scenario analysis can provide useful information about a firm's risk exposure that VaR methods can easily miss, particularly if VaR models focus on the "regular" risk rather than the risks associated with rare or extreme events. Such information can then be fed into strategic planning, capital allocation, hedging and other major decisions.

To start the scenario analysis modelling process, it is necessary to develop a clear procedure for generating a representative set of scenarios, which takes into account all the relevant risk drivers that might influence its control environment and will ultimately determine the operational risk level. Understanding the relationship of these risk drivers with the frequency, severity or aggregated operational losses is important in the development of these scenarios, as they make it easier to incorporate expert opinions into the model. The risk drivers can then be categorised and give rise to scenario classes (eg, system crashes).

There are quite a few ways to generate these scenarios. Some of them include stressing the parameters or results of the VaR and causal models. In accordance with the operational risk measure, the scenario analysis process must lead to an evaluation of the potential frequency and severity of the financial impact of particular scenarios. The scenario analysis would consider every input available, such as expert opinion, KRIs, historical internal losses and any relevant external events. The weighting attributed to each would depend on the quality of the information available.

The envisaged scenario analysis model would deal with the different ways to generate scenarios from the different inputs and models and help in the validation process.

The scenario analysis process is a complex one and involves more than just quantitative analysis. It also implicates the analysis of shocks and how they would affect a particular business unit or the entire firm. The scenario analysis process starts by defining the risk profile of a certain business unit and then proceeds by investigating how the business would behave given a series of hypotheses, which might be arbitrary, historical (based on events that happened in the past with this firm or another firm) or sensitivity tests. A summary of the hypothesis tests can be seen in the Table 18.1.

The scenario analysis for operational risk will involve all data sources in addition to sensitivity tests, which will aim at estimating extreme losses that might arise from negative situations. These hypotheses, defined by the shocks and the sensitivity tests, will also be further tested and benchmarked during a second stage.

STEP 2: MEASURING OPERATIONAL RISK
Introduction to the measurement framework
According to Solvency II, insurance companies will have to start allocating capital against operational risk. One option would be to develop a model to estimate capital against this risk. In order to establish some ground rules for such models, there are a series of standards that insurance companies must follow to be able to use these models, as determined by the regulators.

In order to meet the regulatory requirements of using different types of data, it is possible that a number of models would have to be developed to cope with the different types of data, which need to be used for the regulatory requirements: the risk measurement (VaR model), the causal and the scenario analysis model. Each model will cover a different aspect of operational risk, supplementing each

Table 18.1 Hypothesis tests for scenario analysis and sources of data

Hypothesis test	Data source	Note
Historical shocks	Internal experience, external data	The external data available in the database can be analysed to estimate its eventual impact on a firm considering a specific firm's control environment. In addition to that, in the case that a firm experienced large events in a particular type of situation that can also be used.
Arbitrary shocks	Expert opinions, internal data, KRIs	The arbitrary shocks might be designed based on the expert opinions collected from the BSA or even from internal workshops with business units experts and leaders.
Sensitivity tests	All available	Aim at understanding the changing variance in the correlation between several KRIs and the loss data and the eventual extreme losses arising from that. These relationships can be "stressed" to verify their impact on the P&L.

other. The overall risk measurement outline might be thought of in terms of capital estimation, in which there are three layers of coverage usually considered by firms: expected losses, unexpected losses and catastrophic losses. Expected losses are not considered to be a risk as this is the amount a firm presumes to lose in a given period and, therefore, would not demand capital, however this will be covered through provisions or it will be embedded in the product's pricing. Unexpected losses are considered to be a risk and will demand capital. There are also the very high infrequent losses ("catastrophic") that will not necessarily demand capital as they have a very low probability but need to be fully understood to be avoided.

Regarding the models to assess these three levels of estimation, the expected losses can be seen as simply the expected average of the losses for a certain period. The unexpected losses can be estimated by VaR-type models and the "catastrophic" (or extreme) losses can be estimated by scenario analysis or by performing stress tests. The causal model will include KRIs in the analysis and try to find relationships and correlations between these and the losses. This type of analytical framework will help to identify which indicators play an influential role in determining the losses.

Operational VaR model

The VaR-type model, whose development began in the financial industry in the early 1990s, is currently considered to be the standard measure for market risk and was even extended to credit risk measurement. From a market risk viewpoint, VaR measures the estimated losses within a certain confidence interval in the market value of a portfolio, which can be expected to be incurred until the position can be neutralised. Putting it another way, VaR estimates losses resulting from holding a portfolio for a determined period using a measure of the volatility of the asset prices over the last n days.

A similar logic can be applied in operational risk. However, as the underlying stochastic processes in market and operational risks are different, changes will have to be made to the framework developed for market VaR. In operational risk two separate stochastic processes will be investigated: the frequency and the severity of the losses. The operational VaR will be the aggregation of these processes, ie, the aggregated loss distribution. Putting it simply, VaR = frequency $\times$ severity.

In more formal terms, the aggregated losses at time t given by $X(t) = \sum_{i=1}^{N(t)} U_i$ have the distribution function (where U represents the individual operational losses)

$$F_{X(t)}(x) = \Pr(X(t) \leq x) = \Pr\left(\sum_{i=1}^{N(t)} U_i \leq x \right)$$

The derivation of an explicit formula for $F_{X(t)}(x)$ is, in most cases, impossible. It is usually assumed that the processes $\{N(t)\}$ and $\{U_n\}$ are stochastically independent. Deriving the formula above, we see the following fundamental relationship

$$VaR_{OR} = F_{X(t)}(x) = \Pr(X(t) \leq x) = \Pr\left(\sum_{i,k=0,1}^{n} p_k(t) F_U^{*k}(x) \right)$$

where F_U^{*k} refers to the kth convolution of U with itself, ie, $F_U^{*k}(x) = \Pr(U_1 + \cdots + U_k \leq x)$, the distribution function of the sum of k independent random variables with the same distribution as U.

More practically, the operational VaR model will take as its input a time series of internal loss data and try to use this dataset to estimate losses, at several confidence intervals, for different periods ahead.

Extreme value theory

A typical operational loss database will present a distribution that is not Gaussian. In general an operational risk database is composed of a few large events and several smaller ones. For risk management purposes, the interest is to understand the behaviour of the tail of the curve (or the most significant losses). One way of dealing with this type of situation is to use a certain type of distribution that fits very well with this pattern of events. These distributions are consolidated under the extreme value theory (EVT). The application of EVT will be used for severity distributions and will only work with the largest events of a database (above a certain threshold). For more details please refer to Cruz (2002).

Causal model (multi-factor model)

Although the operational VaR model estimates the risk level, it still misses a feature that explains the influence that internal factors play in determining these estimates. This is an important feature in risk management models. Just as a comparison, for market risk VaR risk analysts can easily verify the impact of any changing factor (eg, increasing interest rates) in the VaR figures by stress testing the model. Considering the structural differences between market and operational VaR models, this would not be possible in the operational one because factors are not embedded in the model as they are in market risk. In order to overcome this limitation, an additional model would have to be developed incorporating the use of internal factors (KRIs) as inputs to explain which manageable factors are important in determining the operational losses.

One way of dealing with causal models is to consider the relationship between the dependent and independent variables as linear and apply multifactor models to explain the losses. Basically, such models will try to relate losses to a series of KRIs suggesting the following relationship

$$Y_t = \alpha_t + \beta_1 X_1 + \cdots + \beta_n X_n + \varepsilon_t$$

where Y represents the operational losses in a particular business in a particular period and X represents the KRIs. The α and β are the estimated parameters.

There are several approaches to estimate the parameters of the model, but one of the most popular is the ordinary least squares (OLS) method. In summary, this method basically solves the equation above for ε_t and minimises

$$\hat{\varepsilon}_t = Y_i - \hat{\alpha}_1 - \hat{\alpha}_2 X_i \quad \text{or} \quad \hat{\varepsilon} = Y_i - \widehat{Y}_i$$

The OLS method squares the residuals and minimises their sum by solving the problem

$$\min \sum \hat{\varepsilon}_i = \sum (Y_i - \hat{\alpha}_1 - \hat{\alpha}_2 X_i)^2$$

The parameters that solve the above equation for the minimum value of the residuals are picked.

STEP 3: REPORT AND MANAGE OPERATIONAL RISK

The overall framework should be composed of three key elements: the database, the models and the outcomes. The database, as described in step 1 of this chapter, will be composed of time series of the internal losses and KRIs, but will also include expert opinion collected from the business self-assessment process and external data. The input from these will feed the three models, the operational VaR, the causal and the scenario analysis models. Interfaces between the database and the models will have to be developed, allowing the model's users to load data from different databases. These models will allow the estimation of economic and regulatory capital; to perform sensitivity and cost/benefit analysis, and to perform more proactive operational risk management. Among the outcomes of the models are also the official periodic reports to be submitted to the regulators.

NUMERICAL EXAMPLE

In order to try to crystallise some of the key concepts developed during the chapter, we present a short example demonstrating the application of the measuring techniques in a database. Suppose that a certain large insurance company started to collect an operational database of frauds against their policies. This database (Table 18.2) is for the month of March 2007 and should be seen just as an example of how losses can impact an insurer.

Notice that this company is facing a terrible fraud situation and losses can reach millions on a single day and the frequency of losses can be up to 12 in a single day. This situation by itself should worry management and this is a typical situation during an economic recession. Anecdotally, the number of car frauds increased 230% in 2009 in the US mostly due to customers trying to illegally cash in their policies as the used car market depreciated tremendously, making it more financially advantageous to burn the car and claim insurance (which is of course a crime) than to sell it in the secondary market. Similar situations are occurring in the housing market, mortgage insurance, etc.

Following the presented framework we will need to fit severity and frequency distributions separately and then aggregate them to get to the operational VaR. In this case we will not perform any scenario analysis as we have plenty of data. Therefore, the first step is to model the severity distribution. In this case we will pick three simple distributions: normal, lognormal and exponential. Using the method of moments we find that the parameters are:

Distribution	Parameters	
Normal	$\mu = 323{,}765.45$	$\sigma = 345{,}681.08$
Lognormal	$\mu = 11.59$	$\sigma = 2.41$
Exponential	$\lambda = 3.08865569213126\mathrm{E}{-06}$	

Please refer to Cruz (2002) to see how to estimate parameters for these distributions.

In order to pick the best fit distribution we apply a graphical technique called probability–probability plot (PP-plot) in which we match these distributions against an empirical one. The distribution that stays closer to the empirical one would be considered the best fit (very similar to a Kolmogorov–Smirnov test). Figure 18.1 shows the results.

In this case, considering Figure 18.1 we would pick the exponential distribution as the best fit.

Table 18.2 Example of a fraud database for an insurance company

Date	Total daily losses (US$)	Individual losses											
		1	2	3	4	5	6	7	8	9	10	11	12
3/1/2007	922,789.55	212,451.87	98,539.42	169,463.89	96,957.83	338,639.33	6,000.00	737.21					
3/2/2007	67,158.89	61,457.87	3,134.81	2,566.21									
3/5/2007	341,741.13	1,007.32	61,765.25	133,100.61	145,867.96								
3/6/2007	871,618.93	52,333.44	270,932.30	197,264.44	351,088.75								
3/7/2007	5,002,319.77	438,113.91	1,151,733.99	364,249.70	884,937.55	267,283.09	1,895,473.32	499.99	15.00	13.22			
3/8/2007	845,706.21	521.11	269,902.43	450,368.05	48,493.59	76,421.03							
3/9/2007	651,008.53	128,826.96	84,913.89	381,839.81	55,427.87								
3/12/2007	1,220,947.97	175,312.67	351,970.46	55,057.61	363,285.21	275,322.02							
3/13/2007	1,174,227.57	80,551.52	458,309.19	265,220.90	187,890.48	182,255.47							
3/14/2007	2,349,576.25	405,159.62	788,171.10	557,058.42	115,625.21	460,022.25	11,441.22	7,651.34	334.11	4,112.98	55.42	312.34	91
3/15/2007	2,139,660.10	382,762.47	874,691.60	646,149.80	85,353.18	149,979.62	723.43						
3/16/2007	838,912.59	28,431.29	259,387.81	350,042.47	78,371.09	122,679.93							
3/19/2007	699,384.69	445,646.78	91,918.41	8,144.65	153,674.85								
3/20/2007	1,679,930.97	124,601.44	111,946.35	601,256.86	295,378.56	546,747.75							
3/21/2007	967,647.49	470,283.76	453,137.12	44,226.60									
3/22/2007	2,446,791.18	717,230.60	335,086.19	1,091,276.30	293,660.48	9,537.60							
3/23/2007	2,440,100.55	552,620.65	134,835.35	670,419.45	751,948.83	360,276.26							
3/26/2007	978,103.83	467,368.79	53,031.67	115,707.84	341,995.53								
3/27/2007	78,239.69	78,239.69											
3/28/2007	336,633.95	301,144.19	28,639.84	6,849.93									
3/29/2007	778,106.47	3,746.40	143,371.22	416,848.81	214,140.04								
3/30/2007	569,948.56	255,908.72	151,492.54	143,926.89	18,620.42								

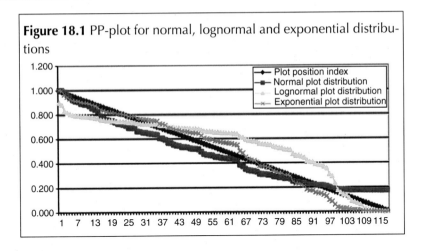

Figure 18.1 PP-plot for normal, lognormal and exponential distributions

For the frequency distribution, just for simplification purposes, we went with a Poisson parameter. Considering our database, we used the Poisson parameter $\lambda = 5.04$.

Now that we fit distributions for frequency (Poisson) and severity (exponential), we need to run a simulation to find the aggregate distribution and the operational VaR.

This simulation is technically very simple to do but can consume a significant amount of computing time. This work can be done as a one-off in an Excel spreadsheet by using the uniform random number (0 to 1) as a proxy for the random distributional quantiles. Please see Table 18.3 for a lognormal/Poisson combination.

In the case of our example, this combination would give us a 99% VaR at around US$4.6 m a day. Annualising this will shoot the yearly 99% fraud capital to around US$1 billion. Clearly, for firms moving to Solvency II, this level of fraud is a big issue that needs to be tackled immediately, otherwise significant capital will have to be deployed to cover against these risks.

CONCLUSION

Operational risk modelling has evolved significantly since the term was first mentioned in the mid-1990s. Virtually every financial institution of a reasonable size in the world should have a team or at least someone responsible for the management of operational risk. The models presented here are just a blueprint of what can really be done to measure and manage this type of risk. Many other

Table 18.3 Example of a Monte Carlo simulation to combine frequency and severity distributions

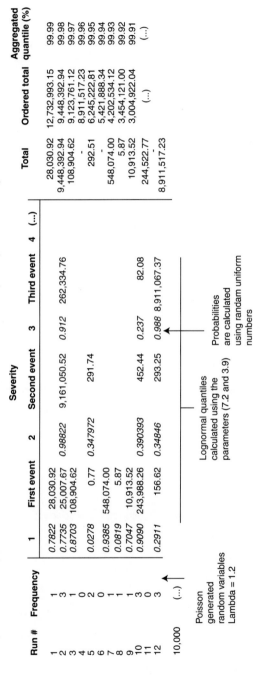

| Run # | Frequency | | | | Severity | | | | | | Total | Ordered total | Aggregated quantile (%) |
		1	First event	2	Second event	3	Third event	4	(...)				
1	1	0.7822	28,030.92								28,030.92	12,732,993.15	99.99
2	3	0.7735	25,007.67	0.98822	9,161,050.52	0.912	262,334.76				9,448,392.94	9,448,392.94	99.98
3	1	0.8703	108,904.62								108,904.62	9,123,761.12	99.97
4	0	0.0278									-	8,911,517.23	99.96
5	2		0.77	0.347972	291.74						292.51	6,245,222.81	99.95
6	0	0.9385	548,074.00								-	5,421,888.34	99.94
7	1	0.0819	5.87								548,074.00	4,202,534.12	99.93
8	1	0.7047	10,913.52								5.87	3,454,121.00	99.92
9	1	0.9090	243,988.26	0.390393	452.44	0.237	82.08				10,913.52	3,004,922.04	99.91
10	3										244,522.77	(...)	(...)
11	0										-		
12	3	0.2911	156.62	0.34846	293.25	0.988	8,911,067.37				8,911,517.23		
10,000	(...)												

Poisson generated random variables Lambda = 1.2

Lognormal quantiles calculated using the parameters (7.2 and 3.9)

Probabilities are calculated using random uniform numbers

aspects should be taken into consideration like the use of a hedge, correlations/dependence, etc. This is still a young area with quite a way to go to mature. Books like Cruz (2004) bring a number of approaches and techniques that can be used in operational risk.

1   As can unfortunately be seen in recent cases such as Bernard Madoff's Ponzi scheme and many others in the US.

REFERENCES

Cruz, M., 2002, *Modeling, Measuring and Hedging Operational Risk* (Chichester: Wiley).

Cruz. M., 2004, *Operational Risk Modeling and Analysis: Theory and Practice* (London: Risk Publications).

Section V

Economic Capital and Hedging Under Solvency II

Introduction

Marcelo Cruz

New York University

In the previous sections we provided chapters that illustrate how to measure individual risks under Solvency II. At the start of this book we also provided introductory chapters on how other concurrent initiatives like MCEV and IFRS 4 are related to Solvency II and how they impact insurers' efforts. Facing all these challenges is obviously very difficult, but from practical experience, having worked as a chief risk officer for a very large insurance company, I know that one way to approach these challenges is to develop an analytical framework and another one is to embed them into the firm's culture. In this section we try to provide a more consolidated perspective on how to aggregate these measures into a single number, considering the correlation of the different risks and, more particularly, how to insert this framework into the decision-making process.

In this section there are four excellent chapters included to close the book. In the first chapter, Susan Witcraft discusses the important topic of economic capital and how insurers can use this to manage their companies. This is an important topic as Solvency II also demands that insurers embed risk management into the day-to-day running of the companies and decision making; this involves quite a bit of cultural change. In the second chapter, Tamas Mayer, Andreas Kull, Philipp Keller and Helga Portman develop a solvency model for the group level. This is an important topic as many insurance firms are either part or fully lead by very large financial groups with many subsidiaries and the issue on how to calculate solvency and capital in these circumstances is never an easy task. In the following chapter Andrew D. Smith gives us a very good overview of the issue of dependency in the calculation of the final aggregate capital numbers. Given the sophistication of the financial products and the risk measurement techniques used by insurance companies, it is unlikely that simple linear correlation techniques would work. The author presents numerical examples of the benefit of using copulas to assess correlation in economic capital measurement. In the last chapter of this section, and of this book, Mark Schouten, Albert Mentink and Roy Kouwenberg give us a perspective on how Solvency II changes the game for hedging inflation-linked liabilities.

19

Corporate Decision Making Using Economic Capital Models

Susan E. Witcraft

Guy Carpenter & Company, LLC

In the 1980s many large general insurance companies investigated the use of dynamic financial analysis for corporate decision making. Only a small number of insurers and reinsurers,[1] many of which were European, were able to develop dynamic financial models that were adequate for use in decision making. The primary obstacles to implementation were actuarial knowledge and computer technology. By the early 2000s, technology had improved, actuaries had developed techniques that allowed better quantification of insurance risks and dynamic financial analysis had evolved into enterprise risk management (ERM) supported by economic capital models. With these improvements, regulators began to develop solvency rules that create incentives for insurers to implement economic capital models. Although the current impetus for economic capital models is regulatory, the original purpose of enhanced strategic decision making is still valid and companies that use their economic capital models for ERM will be industry leaders.

Economic capital models can be used to inform many aspects of corporate decision making, including:

- quantifying corporate risk;
- identifying capital needs as viewed from different perspectives;
- understanding of the sources of risk that drive capital needs;

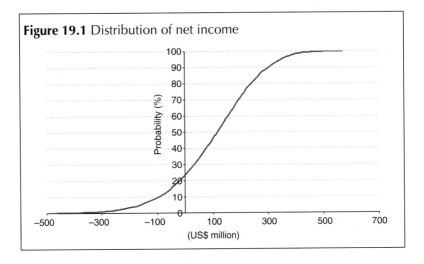

Figure 19.1 Distribution of net income

- cost allocation;
- risk-adjusted measurement of returns; and
- strategic decision making.

Each of these uses is discussed in this chapter.

QUANTIFYING CORPORATE RISK

Traditional models have focused on the individual risks of an insurance company in isolation or point estimates: such as reserve levels, the range of reasonableness around the reserve estimate, rates to be charged, the corporate plan and the riskiness of the current accident year result in light of the selected reinsurance structure.

With an economic capital model, an insurer can understand the threats to its overall financial position from the aggregation of the risks it assumes. For example, an insurer might be interested in understanding the probability of an underwriting loss, the probability that its operating ratio will exceed 100%, the probability that its net worth[2] will decrease by a stated percentage, the probability that its solvency ratio will fall below a certain minimum, or the probability that a rating agency metric will fall below that required for a particular rating. An economic capital model provides probabilistic financial projections from which all of these probabilities can be estimated.

Figures 19.1 and 19.2 illustrate probability distributions of net income and Best's capital adequacy ratio (BCAR) for a hypothetical

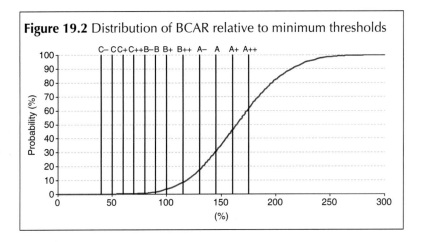

Figure 19.2 Distribution of BCAR relative to minimum thresholds

general insurance company. As can be seen, this company has a slightly more than 20% chance of a net loss and median net income of approximately US$150 million.

In an ERM framework, companies define their risk appetites, risk profiles and risk tolerances.

- Risk appetite represents the risks that a company is willing to accept in order to earn its target rate of return. Some insurers are willing to write very large risks or highly concentrated catastrophe risks to earn a very high return on average. Other insurers prefer to write lower-risk business in exchange for a lower return.
- Risk profile describes the characteristics of the business written, for example, lines of business, geographic spread and limits written.
- Risk tolerance puts boundaries on the risk that a company is willing to assume in the aggregate, such as the maximum amount that a company is willing to lose at certain return periods for a specific event or on a per annum basis or the probability that its capital adequacy ratio will fall below a certain threshold.

The distribution in Figure 19.1, along with key metrics such as the mean, can be used to evaluate whether the business written by the company is consistent with its stated risk appetite and risk tolerances. The model, of course, reflects the company's risk profile. If there are inconsistencies in either the average net income or the probabilities of adverse events, the company can use its economic capital model to test changes in its risk profile to bring consistency with its risk appetite and risk tolerance.

When using an economic capital model, it is critical to understand its limitations because there are many risks for which insufficient information is available for specifying distributions of results. A scenario approach can be used for some of these risks. For example, scenarios could be selected for emerging risks or for specific high-severity low-frequency risks. The model can also be tested with some specific scenarios for risks that are included in the model but for which the historical data and therefore the modelled distributions may not include extreme events.

IDENTIFYING CAPITAL NEEDS

Capital needs can be defined from a number of different perspectives:

- regulatory: which focuses on the probability of insolvency;
- rating agency: which focuses on both the probability of insolvency and the ability to continue with the current rating; and
- going concern: which focuses on the ability to continue to implement current plans.

The perspective determines the types of metrics that will be used to establish the level of capital required.

Many regulators require or plan to require insurers to have a 1-in-200 probability of becoming insolvent in a calendar year. In those situations, the negative of value-at-risk (VaR) at the 99.5% probability level for one calendar year of change in net worth will determine the capital requirement.

Rating agencies similarly look at the probability of becoming insolvent, though the threshold used varies among agencies. Many such agencies are interested in not only the probability of insolvency but also the amount. As such, their focus is on the tail value-at-risk (TVaR), which is the average amount of loss across a stated set of scenarios, or the expected policyholder deficit (EPD), which is the average amount of insolvency given that there is one.

Value-at-risk, TVaR and EPD can be estimated from an economic capital model. Figure 19.3 shows the economic capital needed to

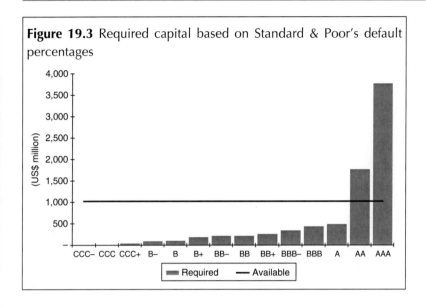

Figure 19.3 Required capital based on Standard & Poor's default percentages

meet the probabilities of default associated with various Standard & Poor's ratings.

The probability distribution of the change in net worth is used to determine the amount of capital needed to ensure that the probability of insolvency is less than that corresponding to each Standard & Poor's rating. For example, at a Standard & Poor's rating of A, the approximate probability of default is 0.15%. For this insurer, the change in net worth at the 0.15th percentile is US$−480 million, so the capital needed to limit the probability of default to less than that of an A-rated instrument is US$480 million. The chart shows that this company has a net worth of about US$1 billion, so it has much more capital than is needed by this metric. If this metric is the only one used for evaluating capital adequacy, the company might consider stockholder or policyholder dividends, taking on more risk in its investment portfolio, reducing its use of reinsurance or writing more business through indigenous growth or acquisition.

For ongoing business management, many companies look at metrics that reflect their abilities to continue with business as planned. For example, companies might want at least a 70% chance that their BCAR will stay above the minimum threshold for an A rating or a 90% chance that the loss of net worth over some stated time period will be no more than 5%. Again, with the results of an economic capital model, the amount of net worth needed to meet these objectives can be estimated.

Figure 19.4 shows the capital needed to ensure that impairments of different levels happen less frequently than selected return times. To determine the amount of capital needed for a 90% chance that the change in net worth will be worse than a 20% loss, the change in net worth at the 90th percentile (US$−80 million) is determined. For this amount to be no more than 5% of net worth, the insurer must have five times that amount in net worth or US$400 million.

Figure 19.5 uses BCAR and selected return times to determine required capital. Figure 19.5 shows the net worth needed to keep BCAR above the minimum threshold for each rating at selected return times. The shades of black and gray correspond to return times, as shown in the figure's key.

The capital needed to support an A− rating exceeds the company's net worth about once every 10 years, whereas the capital needed to support an A++ almost always exceeds the company's net worth. As such, this company is unlikely to attain an A++ rating, but will generally have enough capital to meet the minimum requirement for an A− rating from AM Best.

If, for example, the company stated one of its risk tolerance requirements to be no more than a 50% chance that its BCAR would fall below the minimum requirement for an A rating, it would either need to increase its net worth or reduce its risk. The economic capital model can be used to identify the best choice among options such as a capital contribution, a reduction in writings, purchase of more reinsurance, a move towards greater diversification in the business written or a move to less risky assets.

Another important use of analysis of capital requirements is capitalisation of groups in totality and by company. An economic capital analysis can be instrumental in understanding and quantifying the impact of diversification effects across companies within a group. The capital allocation techniques discussed later in this chapter can also provide indications as to whether specific companies within the group are over- or under-capitalised and whether capital contributions or dividend distributions may be appropriate.

Figure 19.4 Capital requirements (in US$ thousand) by percentage loss and return period

Return period	% of net worth									
	10%	20%	30%	40%	50%	60%	70%	80%	90%	100%
10	797,070	398,535	265,690	199,267	159,414	132,845	113,867	99,634	88,563	79,707
20	1,542,938	771,469	514,313	385,734	308,588	257,156	220,420	192,867	171,438	154,294
25	1,797,963	898,981	599,321	449,491	359,593	299,660	256,852	224,745	199,774	179,796
50	2,490,542	1,245,271	830,181	622,636	498,108	415,090	355,792	311,318	276,727	249,054
100	3,097,910	1,548,955	1,032,637	774,478	619,582	516,318	442,559	387,239	344,212	309,791
200	3,594,813	1,797,406	1,198,271	898,703	718,963	599,135	513,545	449,352	399,424	359,481
250	3,832,343	1,916,172	1,277,448	958,086	766,469	638,724	547,478	479,043	425,816	383,234
500	4,641,367	2,320,683	1,547,122	1,160,342	928,273	773,561	663,052	580,171	515,707	464,137
1000	5,664,665	2,832,333	1,888,222	1,416,166	1,132,933	944,111	809,238	708,083	629,407	566,467

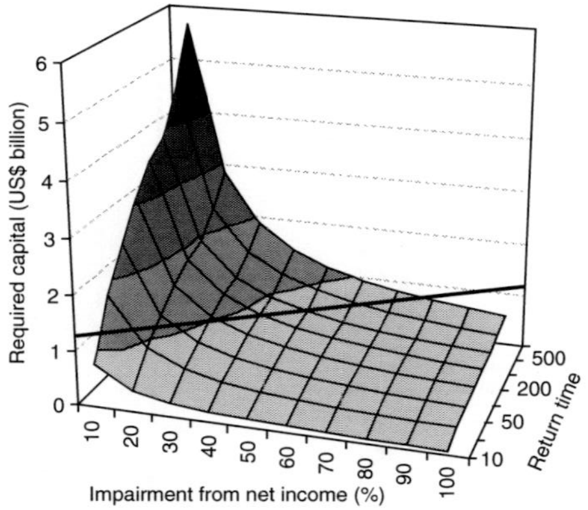

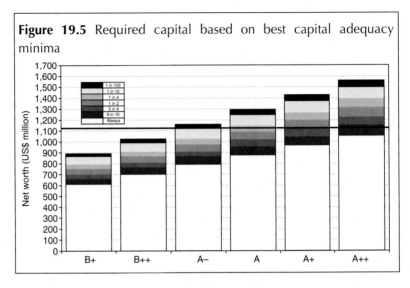

Figure 19.5 Required capital based on best capital adequacy minima

UNDERSTANDING THE SOURCES OF RISK

Although the advantage of an economic capital model over many traditional risk models is its ability to evaluate risk on an enterprise basis, it can also be used to understand the sources of risk within an organisation. There are many hierarchies used for identifying the sources of risk of an insurance company. Figure 19.6 shows the hierarchy proposed by the Financial Supervisory Authority in the UK, along with probability distributions for each source of risk for the hypothetical insurer.

By putting all of these distributions on a single chart and showing the differences from the respective means, as in Figure 19.7, the relative magnitude of the risks can be compared.

In this illustration, reserve development is the largest contributor to downside risk, with non-catastrophe losses having similar downside risk. This information is critical for identifying which risks need to be evaluated for mitigation, management or transfer, especially if the company's net worth is less than is required by its risk tolerance.

RISK-ADJUSTED RETURN MEASUREMENT

Once an insurer has evaluated its capital position relative to its risk profile, it may need to adjust the balance between the two. In the situation in which the insurer has too much capital, it may want to expand its existing business, enter new markets or return

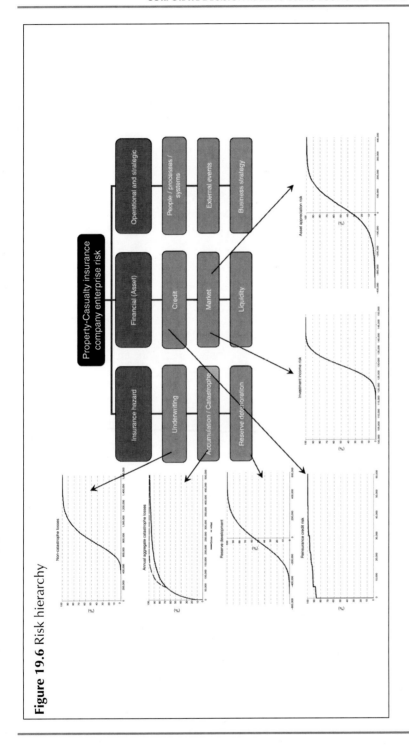

Figure 19.6 Risk hierarchy

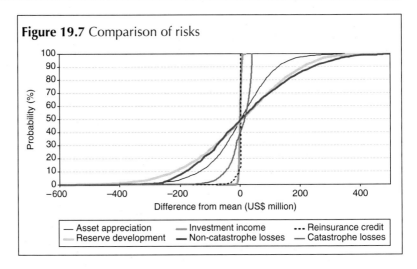

Figure 19.7 Comparison of risks

some of its capital. If the insurer has too little capital, on the other hand, it may want to reduce risk through a change in invested asset mix, increased purchase of reinsurance or reduction in its gross underwriting portfolio.

Traditionally, these decisions were evaluated using different measurement metrics for different sources of risk, making comparisons among options difficult. With an economic capital model, the returns gained or lost from each option can be compared with the amount of capital expended or saved, with the quantification of the capital being made on a risk-adjusted basis.

In this chapter capital allocation will be used as the tool by which risk-adjusted capital is measured. There are many pros and cons of capital allocation that have been discussed elsewhere at great length (see, for example, Mango 2003).

As this is the case for the evaluation of capital adequacy, there are several risk metrics that can be used to allocate capital, many of which are the same as, or are related to, those used for evaluating capital adequacy. Metrics that have been used to allocate capital include standard deviation, VaR, TVAR, marginal impact on any of those measures and others (see Witcraft 2004). For this discussion, co-xTVaR will be used, which is the average excess over the mean of a particular statistic conditional upon some criterion being met. For example, co-xTVaR might be calculated using underwriting profit by line conditional on the total underwriting profit being less than some threshold.

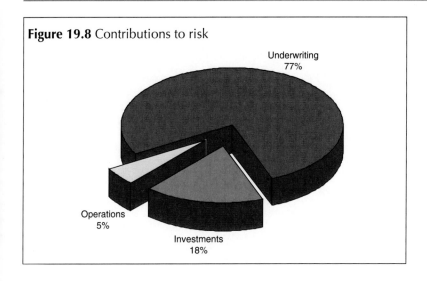

Figure 19.8 Contributions to risk

While the choice of metric can have a significant impact on the allocation of capital, it is important to recognise that any of these metrics can be calculated from the output of an economic capital model. Once a metric has been selected, preferably a co-measure (a measure calculated for each segment conditional on the same criterion for all segments) so allocation is consistent across varying degrees of granularity, capital can be allocated to any combination of business segments. At the highest level, capital can be allocated among the investment function, the underwriting function and operational risk and strategic risk.[3]

Figure 19.8 shows the allocation of capital to these risks for the hypothetical insurer.[4] Consistent with Figure 19.7, underwriting risk is much larger than investment or operational risks.

Within underwriting, capital use can be allocated in a number of different ways. One choice of allocation is by source: credit risk on reinsurance recoverables, reserve risk and current accident year risk, with the latter often separated between catastrophe and non-catastrophe losses. Figure 19.9 shows an example of such an allocation. For many insurers, credit risk on reinsurance recoverables is the smallest of these risks, but can become quite large if reinsurance usage is heavy.

A different perspective for capital allocation within underwriting risk is by line of business. In this allocation, each of the risks in

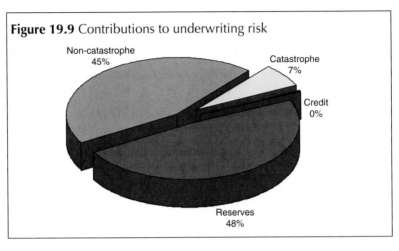

Figure 19.9 Contributions to underwriting risk

Non-catastrophe 45%
Catastrophe 7%
Credit 0%
Reserves 48%

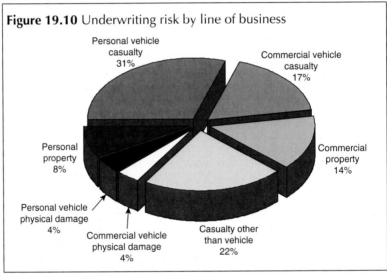

Figure 19.10 Underwriting risk by line of business

Personal vehicle casualty 31%
Commercial vehicle casualty 17%
Personal property 8%
Commercial property 14%
Personal vehicle physical damage 4%
Commercial vehicle physical damage 4%
Casualty other than vehicle 22%

Figure 19.9 is separated into its contribution by line resulting in an allocation such as is shown in Figure 19.10.

REINSURANCE COST ALLOCATION

In the process of evaluating profitability and contribution to risk, insurers need to allocate costs to segments. Allocations might be between personal and commercial lines, among lines or among states, such as might be needed for pricing. One of the important costs to be allocated is reinsurance. When allocating reinsurance premium to segment, there are three components to be considered: losses, reinsurer expenses (including ceding commissions and brokerage) and the profit or risk margin. The provision for losses is often allocated in proportion to the present value of expected losses; the provision for expenses, in proportion to the sum of the loss and profit allocations. An economic capital model can be quite valuable in deriving the expected losses by line, especially in the presence of aggregate features, such as limited reinstatements, aggregate limits or deductibles or loss corridors.

The profit margin can be allocated using the techniques described above for allocating the total capital of an organisation. Specifically, the risk metric (eg, co-TVaR or co-XTVaR) is calculated using the losses ceded to the contract to determine the allocation of the profit margin component of the reinsurance premium. Figure 19.11 shows an illustration of the allocation of two different contracts among lines.

The allocations vary significantly depending on the type of contract, as shown in Figure 19.11. For low-layer catastrophe and excess of loss contracts (such as the one on the top), most of the premium is allocated in proportion to the present value of expected losses, whereas most of the premium for higher layer contracts (such as that on the bottom) is allocated in proportion to the risk metric used to allocate the profit or risk margin. Proper allocation of costs is critical to the evaluation of profitability.

USES OF RISK-ADJUSTED CAPITAL

Once capital has been allocated in a risk-adjusted manner, it can be used to determine target returns by segment or compared with historical or expected returns by segment to evaluate profitability. The premium-to-net worth leverage ratios are among the key assumptions in many pricing analyses. They can be calculated directly (as shown in Figure 19.12) after capital has been allocated to line in a risk-consistent manner.

In this example, the net worth previously allocated to underwriting was loaded for operating risk and then allocated to line. Using this approach, the remaining net worth would need to be allocated to investments.

With the corporate target return on net worth and the segment-specific expense ratios, target loss ratios can be calculated for use

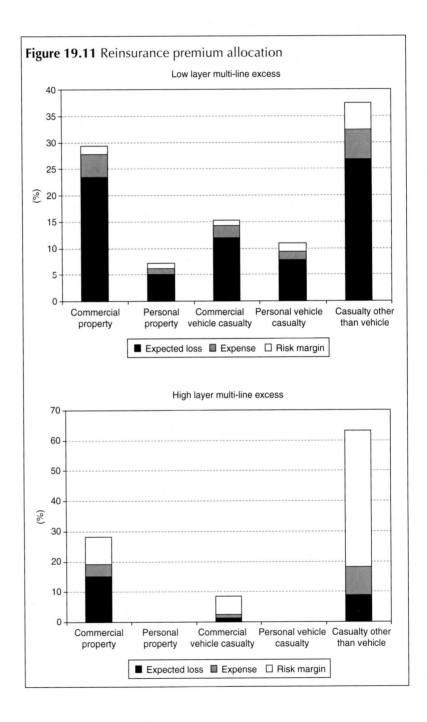

Figure 19.11 Reinsurance premium allocation

Figure 19.12 Target premium leverage ratios (in US$ thousand)

Line of business	Capital	Net earned premium	Leverage Calculated	Leverage Selected
Personal property	65,116	198,566	3.05	**3.05**
Personal vehicle casualty	236,582	303,655	1.28	**1.28**
Commercial vehicle casualty	137,024	156,370	1.14	**1.14**
Commercial property	113,084	229,584	2.03	**2.03**
Casualty other than vehicle	171,969	174,798	1.02	**1.02**
Commercial vehicle physical damage	29,328	85,680	2.92	**2.92**
Personal vehicle physical damage	31,838	139,523	4.38	**4.38**
Total	784,942	1,288,175	1.64	**1.64**

Figure 19.13 Target and expected loss ratios

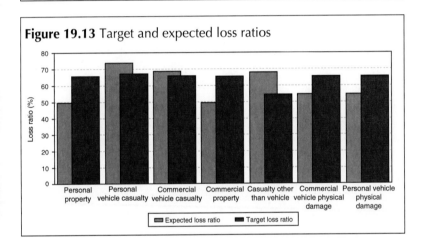

in pricing. The target loss ratios that will produce risk-equivalent profits are shown in Figure 19.13.

The bars on the left in Figure 19.13 reflect the expected loss ratio (based on analysis of trended, developed, on-level historical experience) and the bars on the right reflect the target loss ratios that will produce the desired return on capital. As such, any segment for which the left bar is significantly higher than the right bar is one that is not expected to generate its risk-adjusted profit target. For example, the projected loss ratios for personal vehicle casualty, commercial vehicle casualty and casualty other than vehicle are all higher than those needed to achieve the company target return on capital, as defined by its risk tolerance. In this situation, the company would need to evaluate whether it is willing to raise rates, change its underwriting practices, find savings in claim costs, write

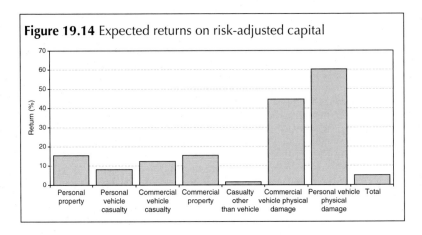

Figure 19.14 Expected returns on risk-adjusted capital

less of this business to eliminate any drag on earnings or transfer some of this risk. It also will need to consider the extent to which policies are written on a package basis. For example, both personal and commercial vehicle physical damage have expected loss ratios that are significantly less than their targets. The economic capital model can help the company evaluate whether the high profitability from the vehicle physical damage business is sufficient to offset the lower than expected profits from the vehicle casualty business.

The expected profit or loss for each segment can be compared to the allocated capital to derive a risk-adjusted return on capital by segment, as shown in Figure 19.14.

Consistent with Figure 19.13, vehicle casualty and casualty other than vehicle have returns that are below the company's 15% target. Figure 19.14 shows that the total return is also lower than the 15% target.

Figure 19.15 provides a bit more information than Figure 19.14, in that both the amount of allocated capital and the risk-adjusted return on capital are shown.

The height of the solid black line corresponding to each segment represents the risk-adjusted return. The length of the each segment represents the amount of capital used. In Figure 19.15, it is easy to identify those business segments that are consuming a lot of capital at a lower than required return, in this case personal vehicle casualty and casualty other than vehicle.

With this information, the company can focus on modifying its mix of business to reduce the riskiness, transfer some of the

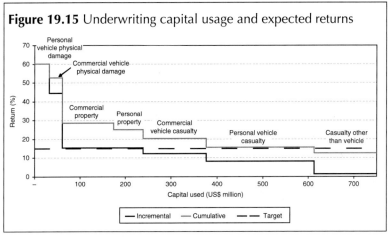

Figure 19.15 Underwriting capital usage and expected returns

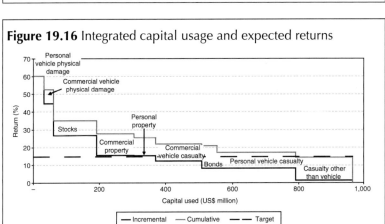

Figure 19.16 Integrated capital usage and expected returns

risk, increase the profitability or decrease the volume for lines of business on the right end of this chart. Concurrently, it may want to take on more risk, reduce rates or increase the volume for line of business on the left end of Figure 19.15.

Similar comparisons can be made for other types of risk, such as comparing the returns in relation to riskiness of different invested asset classes, as shown in Figure 19.16.

This chart shows that stocks are consuming about the same amount of capital as commercial vehicle casualty, but are earning a return on that capital that is higher than the company's 15% target. By comparison, bonds are using very little capital, but are still earning less than the target. If the company has determined that

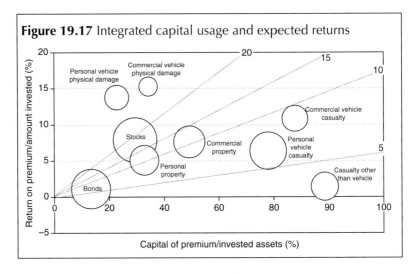

Figure 19.17 Integrated capital usage and expected returns

it has more net worth than is required to meet its risk appetite and risk tolerance metrics, it might want to shift some of its investments from bonds to stocks. If the net worth is similar to its minimum capital requirement, it might want to shift some of the risk it is taking in underwriting in the less profitable business (any of the casualty lines) into its investment portfolio by owning more stocks to increase its return to closer to its target.

Figure 19.17 expands even further by including the returns on premium and the relative amounts of premium (or invested assets or other risk source).

In this figure, the y-axis shows the return on premium, while the x-axis shows allocated capital as a percentage of the premium. With this layout, business segments with equivalent returns on capital fall on the same diagonal line, as shown by the light gray lines. Further, the size of each segment is represented by the size of the bubble. As can be seen, of the poor performing lines and investments, bonds are the largest, followed by personal vehicle casualty. The profitable vehicle physical damage lines are much smaller than the corresponding casualty business.

COMPARISON OF STRATEGIC ALTERNATIVES

Once this framework of quantifying and evaluating risk-adjusted returns has been established, it can be easily extended to evaluating alternate strategies. Such comparison can include capital

Figure 19.18 Cost of capital (in US$ thousand) for strategy change

	Current	Proposed	Change
Average total return	156,338	161,055	4,717
Required capital	962,186	1,158,354	196,167
Return on capital used			2.4%

management and choice of investment, reinsurance, growth or other strategies.

If a company determines that it has too little or too much capital, opportunities for increasing or reducing capital can be compared with opportunities for growth or reduction in risk in a structured framework. For a company with more capital than required, opportunities for assuming more risk, such as riskier assets, increase in reinsurance retention, growth or acquisition, can be compared with the cost of keeping capital. If the returns on these opportunities are higher than the target return on equity, the company will take advantage of these opportunities. If the returns are lower, the company might consider returning some or all of the excess capital in the form of a dividend, depending on its expectations about opportunities in the future and the cost of acquiring additional capital if needed in the future. Figure 19.18 shows an illustration of such a comparison.

The marginal impact on net income is compared to the change in required capital by retaining or assuming more risk. The implicit return on capital is 2.4%. The insurer can compare this return with those of other opportunities or with its cost of capital to determine whether this strategy is preferable to returning capital or other risk-increasing strategies. This calculation can be made for any risk taken or transferred by the company, be it underwriting, investment, credit (eg, different qualities of reinsurers), hedging or reinsurance.

Economic capital models are also of tremendous value in increasing the transparency of strategic decisions. Evaluation of a company's overall risk profile was discussed earlier in this chapter. Comparisons of the risk profile can be made under different strategies, as illustrated in Figure 19.19 which shows the impact on the entire distribution of net income and Figure 19.20 which focuses on the portion of the distribution that might be used in determining required capital.

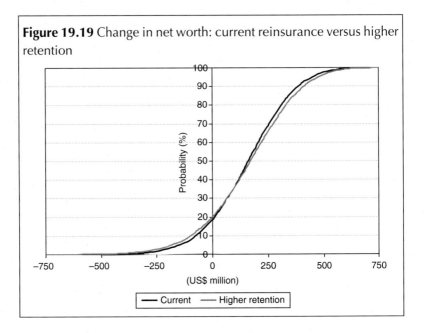

Figure 19.19 Change in net worth: current reinsurance versus higher retention

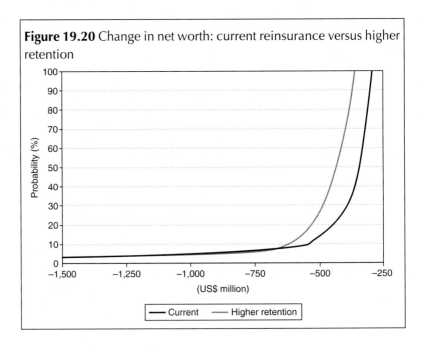

Figure 19.20 Change in net worth: current reinsurance versus higher retention

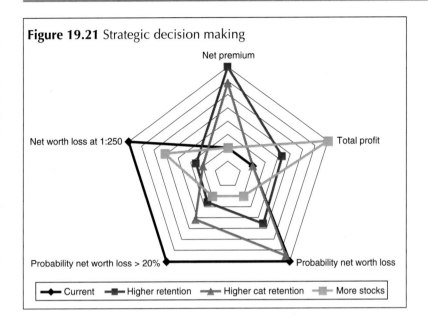

Figure 19.21 Strategic decision making

These risk profiles can be compared with the company's risk tolerance and risk appetite to determine which strategy is more closely aligned with the corporate strategy.

Many insurers use a number of different metrics for evaluating strategic decision making. The numerical metrics can all be calculated from an economic capital model and compared in a structure format, such as is shown in Figure 19.21.

In this figure, the lines represent different strategies and the corners represent different metrics. The metrics are scaled so that better values are towards the outside of the chart and worse values are towards the inside of the chart. Thus, strategies with the greatest area within the boundaries of their lines are generally preferred to those that have a smaller area. The relative importance of each metric can be incorporated by weighting the relative value of each metric such as is shown in Figure 19.22.

In this illustration, the current approach ranks most favourably given the weights assigned to each metric by the company. If the company re-evaluates its priorities, the new weights can be applied and the relative ranks of the strategies recalculated. The flexibility to use strategies from different parts of the organisation makes this use of economic capital output powerful.

Figure 19.22 Strategy selection

	Current	Higher retention	Higher catastrophe retention	More stocks	Weights (%)
Net premium	1.0	4.0	3.4	1.0	10
Total profit	1.0	2.2	1.0	4.0	30
Probability net worth loss	4.0	2.3	3.7	1.0	30
Probability net worth loss > 20%	4.0	1.3	2.1	1.0	20
Net worth loss at 1:250	4.0	1.3	1.0	2.5	10
Total score	2.8	2.1	2.3	2.1	

CONCLUSION

The framework of risk and reward measurement created by the use of economic capital models mandated by regulators, when applied consistently, can provide valuable information to insurers in their strategic decision making. Uses identified include evaluation of the overall level of capital, understanding of the sources of risk facing the insurer, allocation of capital to form the basis of risk-adjusted return measurement, allocation of reinsurance costs and comparison of strategic alternatives.

1 For ease of reading, "insurers" will be used throughout this chapter and will be assumed to include reinsurers as all concepts discussed apply to both types of entity.

2 Throughout this chapter, net worth will be used to represent capital as measured under an accounting paradigm. Depending on the context and jurisdiction, it is sometimes referred to as economic capital, policyholder surplus, net assets or net worth, among others.

3 Presently, it is common practice to incorporate operational and strategic risks as percentage loads on the total capital required, ranging from 5% for a low-risk entity to 15% or 20% for a high risk-entity. Significant research is in progress in these areas.

4 When evaluating investment risk, it is important to understand the basis on which investment risk is measured. Under many accounting paradigms, bonds, at least those expected to be held to maturity, are carried at an amortised cost. If invested asset risk measurement is performed on an accounting basis using one of these paradigms, invested asset risk will appear relatively small. On an economic basis, under which invested assets are all modelled at their market values, invested asset risk will appear much larger. The purpose of the risk-adjusted return measurement and the likelihood that invested assets will need to be liquidated will determine the choice of measurement basis for bonds. In Figure 19.8, bonds are shown at their market value. Also, the risk-free rate is credited to underwriting and deducted from investments in determining results.

REFERENCES

Mango, D. F., 2003, "Capital Consumption: An Alternative Methodology for Pricing Reinsurance", *2003 Winter Casualty Actuarial Society Forum* (Washington DC: Casualty Actuarial Society), pp. 351–379.

Witcraft, S. E., 2004, "Risk Statistics", in J. L. Teugels and B. Sundt (eds), *Encyclopedia of Actuarial Science* (Chichester: John Wiley & Sons, Ltd).

20

Risk Sharing in Insurance Groups

Tamas Mayer[1]; Andreas Kull; Philipp Keller; Helga Portmann

Ernst & Young Ltd; AXA Winterthur; Deloitte LLP;
Federal Office of Public Health

Insurance deregulation introduced during the 1990s, together with the stock market turmoil of 2002, clearly demonstrated the limitations of factor-based solvency frameworks like Solvency I. As a consequence, the European Union began working on a fundamental revision of its existing solvency supervision system. Currently a supervisory framework, Solvency II, is being developed that will define risk-based solvency capital requirements (SCR) and adopt a three-pillar approach similar to the Basel II Accord. The Solvency II draft directive was released in June 2007 and revised in February 2008. The latest version of the directive was adopted by the European Parliament's plenary session on 22 April 2009 (Commission of the European Communities 2009), and Solvency II is to be fully implemented by October 31, 2012. For an overview of the Solvency II process see Eling *et al* (2007).

In Switzerland, the Federal Office of Private Insurance (FOPI) initiated the "Swiss Solvency Test" (SST) project in 2003. The SST is a risk-based supervisory framework designed to reflect the solvency of insurance companies according to economic principles. While there is a standard SST model (Bundesamt für Privatversicherungen 2004, 2006a), the SST is principle based and insurance companies, for which the standard model is inappropriate, as well as reinsurance companies and insurance groups are required to develop internal models.

One of the key remaining issues concerns the solvency requirements for insurance groups. Final guidance on the requirements for assessing the solvency of insurance groups is still pending. Draft guidelines require, at least in the case of the SST, an explicit modelling of both the value and risk dimensions inherent in the ownership structure and to capital and risk transfer between entities of the group.

Starting from this key requirement, this chapter investigates capital optimisation problems at the insurance group level and proposes a model for optimising intra-group capital and risk transfers with the objective of minimising the regulatory capital requirement for the group as a whole. We will take key concepts for the model into account, such as modelling the credit risk associated with guarantees of parent companies and the limited liability of a parent company towards its subsidiaries.

The chapter is organised as follows. In the first section we describe the group level solvency concepts. Based on these concepts we then develop a group level solvency model. Following this we construct and numerically study a simplified version of the model. The final section contains the conclusions.

GROUP LEVEL SOLVENCY CONCEPTS
General aspects of the SST and Solvency II
Both the SST and Solvency II frameworks are based on an economic balance sheet that indicate a market-consistent valuation of all asset and liability positions. This is straightforward for positions with observable market prices. The market-consistent valuation of non-traded instruments, however, is more difficult. For insurance groups this includes the valuation of subsidiaries, guarantees and other group internal capital and risk transfer instruments.

In the context of the SST, the market-consistent value of liabilities corresponds to the best estimate (discounted at the risk-free interest rate) and a market value margin. The market value margin is identified by the cost of holding the regulatory capital necessary for the run-off of the liabilities. The risk-bearing capital for the SST is defined as the market value of assets less the discounted best estimate of the liabilities. The market value margin is defined as a part of the target capital requirement. For our purposes, however, we focus on the market-consistent value of liabilities and define the risk-bearing capital (ie, available capital) as the difference between the market value of assets less the market-consistent value of the liabilities. In turn, the SCR does not include the market value margin.

Following the SST and Solvency II, we link risks to the possible adverse changes in the balance sheet of the company over a one year horizon. The balance sheet at $t = 0$ is known and can be determined exactly. The balance sheet in one year is unknown and has to be modelled probabilistically.

Let us denote the available capital at time t by $AC(t)$. The SCR model for the SST with a one-year horizon can then be written as

$$
\begin{aligned}
SCR &= ES_\alpha(AC(0) - AC(1)) \\
&= ES_\alpha(-AC(1)) + AC(0)
\end{aligned}
\tag{20.1}
$$

where $AC(0) - AC(1)$ is the change of the risk-bearing capital within a year; losses correspond to positive values. Furthermore ES_α denotes the coherent risk measure expected shortfall. The confidence level prescribed by the SST is $\alpha = 99\%$. Equation 20.1 can also be understood in the following way: the number $ES_\alpha(-AC(1))$, if positive, represents the capital that has to be added so that the SCR becomes acceptable to meet the solvency requirement. If it is negative, it represents the capital above the solvency requirement.

Group level SST and Solvency II concepts

The group level solvency requirements for the SST and Solvency II are still in development. As of May 2008, FOPI is working on an SST directive that will contain an appendix on requirements for insurance groups. The current Solvency II directive, which is to be implemented by 2012 (Commission of the European Communities 2009) abandons the concept of group support after intensive negotiations between the Commission, the European Parliament and the European Council. The topic, however, will be addressed again by the Commission in 2015. In this chapter we will concentrate on the draft guidance available for the SST (Bundesamt für Privatversicherungen 2006b) and will investigate solvency requirements at the group level.

Definitions of an insurance group can be found in the "Supervisory Standard on Group Coordination" published by the International Association of Insurance Supervisors (IAIS 2002) and in the Swiss Federal Law on the Supervision of Insurance Companies (Schweizerische Rechtssammlung SR 961.01 2004). The IAIS defines an insurance group as a financial group consisting of two or more insurers (and possibly other non-licensed entities). The following definition can be found under Swiss Federal Law and is also used for the SST.

Two or more companies form an insurance group, if

1. at least one of them is an insurance undertaking;
2. as a whole, they operate primarily in the insurance sector; and
3. they form an economic unit or are linked in some other way by influence or control.

Next, we discuss the group level solvency guidelines of the SST. These principles are also studied comprehensively by Luder (2007).

A natural idea that comes to mind when defining group level solvency requirements is the use of a fully consolidated group balance sheet, containing all of the assets and liabilities of the group. All the assets are grouped together and can be used to cover the aggregate of all the liabilities. The SCR for the whole group is then calculated according to Equation 20.1 by taking the consolidated balance sheet to define the available capital. The consolidated approach is also the starting point of one of the methods under Solvency I. The main advantage of such a method is that it is straightforward and avoids the problem of double-counting capital. Furthermore, the model naturally eliminates group internal risk transfers. There are, however, some serious drawbacks that need to be considered. Most importantly, the legal entity structure of the group is completely ignored in this model, which implies that assets are available to cover losses independent of their origin. Suppose that one entity in the group suffers a severe loss. In such a case, the parent company frequently transfers capital to help the troubled subsidiary. There could, however, be limitations on the fungibility of capital, for example, the parent company might not be legally obligated to help out a subsidiary. For this reason, on the group level, the SST assigns high importance to the so-called capital and risk transfer instruments.

Capital and risk transfer instruments are legally binding and clearly formalised financial instruments that facilitate the transfer of capital and risk between the legal entities in a group. Examples include intra-group retrocession or guarantees. A group consists of different legal entities, a parent company and its subsidiaries, which are potentially supervised by different regulators in different jurisdictions and a web of legally binding capital and risk transfer instruments between the members in the group.

If a legal entity is a parent company, then its subsidiaries are considered to be assets of that parent company. Since future asset values are random, holding them constitutes risk for the parent company.

If there are no legally enforceable capital and risk transfer instruments between the entities of the group, the parent cannot provide reinsurance or guarantees to the subsidiaries. Group diversification cannot be allocated to the subsidiaries, which means that the members of the group cannot benefit from being a part of the group in this case. It is the parent company that benefits from the diversification effect because it owns the portfolio of subsidiaries. Figure 20.1 shows an exemplary group structure, the capital and risk transfer instruments are represented by the arrows. Subsidiaries benefit from being members of the group through internal (legally binding) capital and risk transfer agreements.

Considering that the subsidiaries are assets of the parent company we could argue that only the top holding of the group has to be solvent. Although this definition is interesting there is a big disadvantage. If we assume that the top holding is a pure holding company without any capital and risk transfer instruments in place, the group would always be solvent because of the option to let the subsidiaries go into run-off.

We use the following definition for group-wide solvency.

Definition 1 (Group-wide SCR) The group-wide SCR is given as the sum of SCRs of all the legal entities in the group.

In general, the objective of the group is to minimise the group-wide SCR. In practice, the legal entity level SCRs for the subsidiaries should be treated as constraints to this minimisation. Optimisation can be accomplished through a web of legally binding capital

Figure 20.1 Schematic group balance sheet structure for the legal entity approach

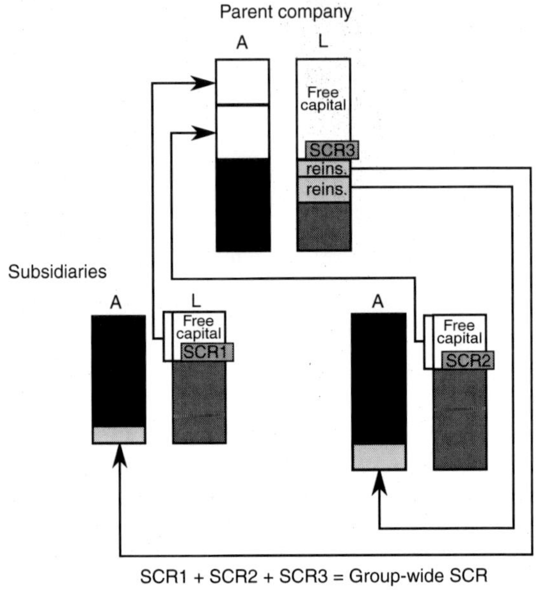

Parent company

Subsidiaries

SCR1 + SCR2 + SCR3 = Group-wide SCR

Note: The capital and risk transfer instruments are represented by arrows. The group-wide SCR is the sum of SCRs of all of the legal entities.

and risk transfer instruments (typically some form of reinsurance agreement).

Since the subsidiaries and the parent company can reside in different jurisdictions, they could be subject to different regulations concerning a minimal capital requirement. In addition, the subsidiaries are also subject to legal entity level SCR. If their capital level falls below this value, a "yellow flag" is then raised. Moreover, even if it falls below the minimal capital requirement, a "red flag" is then raised and the subsidiary is considered insolvent.

The prerequisite for implementing the group solvency approach discussed in this section is either the uniform application of solvency concepts throughout the world or the home-state supervisor having the power to set solvency standards for all subsidiaries of the groups with headquarters within that country. The solutions to these problems are still under discussion by the regulatory authorities.

A GROUP LEVEL SOLVENCY MODEL

The general setting

In this section we develop a group level solvency model following the principles as outlined by Bundesamt für Privatversicherungen (2006b). Group level solvency models were discussed previously by Filipović and Kupper (2007, 2008). In their group optimisation model the authors accounted for a key group level concept: the limited liability of the parent with respect to its subsidiaries. Recently, Filipović and Kunz (2008) also studied the effect of parental default in a new bottom-up modelling setting. In our approach we extend their analysis and develop a group level optimisation model that takes the relevant regulatory requirements into account.

The concepts of the model can be summarised as follows:

- The model should take the credit risk associated with the parent company explicitly into account. This is very important; if the parent itself is considered insolvent, the reinsurance contracts may then not be paid.
- The model should also account for the limited liability of the parent with respect to its subsidiaries.
- The legal entity level SCRs of the subsidiaries and their dependencies on the capital and risk transfer should be taken explicitly into account within the model.
- According to the industry best practice, there often exists an ordination between the subsidiaries. This means that in the case of financial distress the reinsurance contracts will be paid according to the ordination: for example, subsidiary 1 will be paid first, then subsidiary 2 and so on. The model should take this issue into account.
- The parent is to be considered solvent as long as its surplus exceeds a minimal capital requirement.
- The premium that the subsidiary pays to the parent for the reinsurance contract is to be taken into account in the form of a well-defined premium principle. The premium has to be valued consistently with the market.

We model an insurance group that is made up of a parent company (legal entity 0) and its directly owned $i = 1, \ldots, m$ subsidiaries. We denote the current available capital of the ith entity by

$$v_i = a_i - l_i, \quad i = 0, \ldots, m \tag{20.2}$$

where a_i and l_i represent the assets and the best estimate of the market value of liabilities, respectively. These values are assumed to be deterministic at $t = 0$. Furthermore, the liability of each legal entity consists of $j = 1, \ldots, n$ liability classes

$$l_i = \sum_{j=1}^{n} l_i^j, \quad i = 0, \ldots, m$$

The terminal value of the asset–liability portfolio is given by

$$V_i = A_i - L_i, \quad i = 0, \ldots, m \qquad (20.3)$$

where A_i, L_i are the (discounted) values of the assets and liabilities. These values are random variables as seen from $t = 0$. Furthermore, for simplicity we use the valuation principle

$$\mathbb{E}(V_i) = v_i \qquad (20.4)$$

Modelling subsidiaries

We consider modelling the subsidiaries balance sheet. The net liability classes (lines of businesses) $j = 1, \ldots, n$ of subsidiaries $i = 1, \ldots, m$ are given by $L_i^j(r_i^j)$, with the interpretation that $L_i^j - L_i^j(r_i^j)$ is the amount reinsured by the parent (or recovered by the subsidiary). Examples include proportional reinsurance (quota share) for which $L_i^j(r_i^j) = r_i^j L_i^j$ holds or non-proportional reinsurance (eg, stop-loss) $L_i^j(r_i^j) = \min(L_i^j, r_i^j)$.

In general, for each liability class the parameter r_i^j describes the amount that was reinsured by the parent company. Let us denote by $R = (r_i^j)$ the matrix that characterises the reinsurance contracts and by r_i the ith column of R.

The net liability of subsidiary i can be written as $\sum_{j=1}^{n} L_i^j(r_i^j)$. The surplus $V_i(R)$ of subsidiary i is of course affected by the fact that a portion of its liabilities is now reinsured by the parent. Further it also depends on the premium that the subsidiary pays the parent for the reinsurance contracts. In particular we may write

$$V_i(R) = A_i + A_{\text{recovery}, i}(R) - \sum_{j=1}^{n} \left(L_i^j + P_i^j(r_i^j) \right),$$

$$i = 1, \ldots, m \qquad (20.5)$$

where $A_{\text{recovery},\,i}(R)$ is the amount that subsidiary i recovers in the case that the reinsurance contracts are realised and $P_i^j(r_i^j)$ denotes the premium that the subsidiary pays for the reinsurance contracts at $t = 0$. The premium is calculated according to the premium principle

$$P_i^j(r_i^j) = (1 - \delta)\mathbb{E}\left[(L_i^j - L_i^j(r_i^j))\right] + \delta\text{ES}_\alpha\left((L_i^j - L_i^j(r_i^j))\right),$$
$$i = 1, \ldots, m, \; j = 1, \ldots, n \quad (20.6)$$

with a loading factor $\delta = 10\,\%$ (which we use for capital costs).

The recovered amount is affected by the fact that the parent may not be able to pay, ie, the credit risk of the parent. The recovered amount, including the credit risk, may be calculated as

$$A_{\text{recovery},\,i}(R) = \left[\min\left\{\sum_{j=1}^n [L_i^j - L_i^j(r_i^j)], \left(\frac{\tilde{V}_0(R) - mcr_0}{m}\right)\right\}\right]^+,$$
$$i = 1, \ldots, m \quad (20.7)$$

where we have denoted the minimal capital requirement of the parent company by mcr_0. Here we assume that the parent only fulfils its obligations in a solvent situation. Further we denoted by $\tilde{V}_0(R)$ the surplus of the parent as seen by the subsidiaries when recovering reinsurance. This surplus does not include the credit risk, ie, the parent company does not consider its own credit standing when valuing its payment obligations towards the subsidiary. It is given by

$$\tilde{V}_0(R) = A_0 - \sum_{j=1}^n L_0^j + \sum_{i=1}^m \left[\tilde{A}_{\text{sub},\,i}(r_i)\right.$$
$$\left. - \sum_{j=1}^n [(L_i^j - L_i^j(r_i^j)) - P_i^j(r_i^j))]\right] \quad (20.8)$$

where we have assumed that the parent has its own assets A_0 and liabilities $\sum_{j=1}^n L_0^j$. Furthermore, since the subsidiaries are considered to be assets of the parent company, the surplus also contains

$$\tilde{A}_{\text{sub},\,i}(r_i) = A_i - \sum_{j=1}^n (L_i^j(r_i^j) + P_i^j(r_i^j)), \quad i = 1, \ldots, m \quad (20.9)$$

Note that Equation 20.9 does not reflect the limited liability of the parent with respect to its subsidiaries – that is the subsidiaries do not take into account the limited liability (the improved solvency ratio due to limited liability) when determining their recoveries. We will, however, consider the limited liability on the parent level, see Equation 20.11.

Equation 20.7 can be understood in the following way: as long as the reinsured amount $\sum_{j=1}^{n}[L_i^j - L_i^j(r_i^j)]$ exceeds the surplus of the parent minus some minimal capital requirement the full amount is paid, if however, $(\widetilde{V}_0(R) - mcr_0)/m$ is smaller than $\sum_{j=1}^{n}[L_i^j - L_i^j(r_i^j)]$ only a portion will be recovered. Finally, if the surplus $\widetilde{V}_0(R)$ falls below the minimal capital requirement mcr_0 then the parent itself is considered insolvent and the subsidiary does not recover anything (in the case of group-wide insolvency there are usually legal settlements, which we do not explicitly model here).

Furthermore, we notice that the premium $P_i^j(r_i^j)$ that the subsidiary pays appears in both $\widetilde{V}_0(R)$ and $\tilde{A}_{\text{sub},i}(r_i)$. Moreover it cancels out in $\widetilde{V}_0(R)$ and therefore the recovered amount $A_{\text{recovery},i}(R)$ (and consequently the credit risk) does not depend on the reinsurance premium.

In practice, there often exists an ordination of the subsidiaries due to legal considerations. This means that in the case of financial distress the reinsurance contracts will be paid according to the ordination, for example, subsidiary 1 will be paid first, then subsidiary 2 and so on. Assuming an ordering on the subsidiary level, where index i reflects this ordering, we may write for the subsidiaries $i = 1, \ldots, m$

$$A_{\text{recovery},i}(R) = \left[\min \left\{ \sum_{j=1}^{n} [L_i^j - L_i^j(r_i^j)], \right. \right.$$
$$\left. \left. \left(\widetilde{V}_0(R) - mcr_0 - \sum_{k=1}^{i-1} \sum_{j=1}^{n} [L_k^j - L_k^j(r_k^j)] \right) \right\} \right]^{+},$$
$$i = 1, \ldots, m \quad (20.10)$$

meaning that the recovery of subsidiary i is also affected by the fact that the higher ordered subsidiaries will be paid first. An ordering on the liability class level could also be constructed in a similar fashion.

Modelling the parent company

We consider modelling the parent company's balance sheet. We pre-viously assumed that the parent has its own assets and liabilities, which we denoted by A_0 and $\sum_{j=1}^{n} L_0^j$. Furthermore, the subsidiaries are considered to be assets of the parent company, thus we write

$$A_{\text{sub},\,i}(r_i) = \left[A_i - \sum_{j=1}^{n}(L_i^j(r_i^j) + P_i^j(r_i^j))\right]^{+}, \quad i = 1, \ldots, m \quad (20.11)$$

Equation 20.11 represents the value of the subsidiaries, reflecting the limited liability of the parent towards them. Notice that we set the minimal capital requirements (values at default) of the sub-sidiaries to zero when modelling the limited liability. Furthermore the difference

$$\Delta_i^{\text{put}} = A_{\text{sub},\,i}(r_i) - \tilde{A}_{\text{sub},\,i}(r_i), \quad i = 1, \ldots, m \quad (20.12)$$

can be understood as a put option to let subsidiary i go into run-off, owned by the parent company.

The surplus of the parent, which includes its limited liability with respect to its subsidiaries, is given by

$$V_0(R) = A_0 - \sum_{j=1}^{n} L_0^j + \sum_{i=1}^{m}\left[A_{\text{sub},\,i}(r_i)\right.$$
$$\left. - \sum_{j=1}^{n}\left[(L_i^j - L_i^j(r_i^j) - P_i^j(r_i^j))\right]\right] \quad (20.13)$$

We notice that the premium $P_i^j(r_i^j)$ that the subsidiary pays does not cancel out in $V_0(R)$ due to the limited liability of the parent. Therefore the SCR of the parent depends on the premium that the subsidiary pays for the reinsurance contracts.

The group solvency model

The group would like to minimise the group-wide SCR. This means that the optimisation problem

$$\min_{R} \sum_{i=0}^{m}[\text{ES}_\alpha(-V_i(R)) - \mathbb{E}[-V_i(R)]] \quad (20.14)$$

should be solved. Here the expected shortfall is taken at the $\alpha = 99\%$ level. The decision variables for the optimisation are the risk transfer control parameters r_i^j, which describe the reinsurance agreements. Even though the expected shortfall is a convex function, the minimisation is non-convex in general. Non-convexity is introduced through group level effects, such as the parent's credit risk. Furthermore non-convexity may also be introduced through non-proportional reinsurance.

The legal entity level SCRs for the subsidiaries should be treated as constraints to minimisation. In practice this corresponds to the situation in which the management of the insurance group has to decide where the capital is actually going to be localised. In order to calculate the group capital requirement in this case, we should solve the problem

$$\left.\begin{array}{ll} \min_R & \sum_{i=0}^{m} [\text{ES}_\alpha(-V_i(R)) - \mathbb{E}[-V_i(R)]] \\[2em] \text{subject to} & \text{ES}_\alpha(-V_i(R)) - \mathbb{E}[-V_i(R)] \geq \beta_i, \quad i = 1, \ldots, m \end{array}\right\}$$

(20.15)

Here β_i represents the legal entity level SCR of subsidiary i. Even if the minimisation problem Equation 20.14 is convex, the constraints in Equation 20.15 introduce non-convexity and the problem would belong to the class of global optimisation problems with a reverse convex constraint. In general, however, the problem Equation 20.15 is a non-convex optimisation problem with $m \times n$ variables, which is difficult to solve in practice if m or n is large.

Given an optimal solution, the SCR for the group is calculated as

$$\text{SCR}_{\text{CRT}} = \sum_{i=0}^{m} [\text{ES}_\alpha(-V_i^{\text{opt}}) - \mathbb{E}[-V_i^{\text{opt}}]]$$

(20.16)

In the next section we consider a simplified version of the model, where the dimensionality of the optimisation problem is reduced.

A SIMPLIFIED EXAMPLE

The simplified model

In this section we describe a simplified version of the model we have developed in the previous section. Let the net liability of subsidiaries $i = 1, \ldots, m$ given by $L_i(r_i)$, with the interpretation that $L_i - L_i(r_i)$ is the amount reinsured by the parent (or recovered by the subsidiary). Examples include proportional reinsurance (quota share) for which $L_i(r_i) = r_i L_i$ holds or non-proportional reinsurance (eg, stop-loss) $L_i(r_i) = \min(L_i, r_i)$. Here we made the simplification that all of the liabilities of subsidiary i are aggregated into L_i, ie, the reinsurance contract is written on the aggregated liability portfolio of subsidiary i. Let us denote by $R = (r_i)$ the vector that characterises the reinsurance contracts.

For the surplus $V_i(R)$ of subsidiary i we write

$$V_i(R) = A_i + A_{\text{recovery}, i}(R) - P_i(r_i) - L_i, \quad i = 1, \dots, m \quad (20.17)$$

where $A_{\text{recovery}, i}(R)$ is the amount that subsidiary i recovers and $P_i(r_i)$ denotes the premium, determined by

$$P_i(r_i) = (1 - \delta)\mathbb{E}[(L_i - L_i(r_i))] + \delta\text{ES}_\alpha((L_i - L_i(r_i))),$$
$$i = 1, \dots, m \quad (20.18)$$

with a loading factor $\delta = 10\,\%$.

The recovered amount is affected by the credit risk of the parent. It is calculated as

$$A_{\text{recovery}, i}(R) = \left[\min\left\{ (L_i - L_i(r_i)), \left(\frac{\tilde{V}_0(R) - mcr_0}{m} \right) \right\} \right]^+,$$
$$i = 1, \dots, m \quad (20.19)$$

where mcr_0 is the minimal capital requirement of the parent. Here the surplus of the parent is calculated as

$$\tilde{V}_0(R) = A_0 + \sum_{i=1}^{m}[\tilde{A}_{\text{sub}, i}(r_i) - (L_i - L_i(r_i)) + P_i(r_i)] - L_0 \quad (20.20)$$

where we have introduced

$$\tilde{A}_{\text{sub}, i}(r_i) = (A_i - L_i(r_i) - P_i(r_i)), \quad i = 1, \dots, m \quad (20.21)$$

which reflects that the subsidiaries are assets of the parent, but it does not take into account the limited liability of the parent. Moreover we assumed that the parent company also has its own assets and liabilities, which we denoted by A_0 and L_0.

Now let us consider the parent company. Taking into account the limited liability of the parent towards the subsidiaries we write

$$A_{\text{sub}, i}(r_i) = \max(A_i - L_i(r_i) - P_i(r_i), 0), \quad i = 1, \dots, m \quad (20.22)$$

The surplus of the parent without its own credit standing considered is given by

$$V_0(R) = A_0 + \sum_{i=1}^{m} [A_{\text{sub}, i}(r_i) - (L_i - L_i(r_i)) + P_i(r_i)] - L_0 \quad (20.23)$$

The group would like to minimise the group-wide SCR. This means that we must solve the problem

$$\left. \begin{array}{c} \min_{R} \quad \sum_{i=0}^{m} [\text{ES}_\alpha(-V_i(R)) - \mathbb{E}[-V_i(R)]] \\[2ex] \text{subject to} \quad \text{ES}_\alpha(-V_i(R)) - \mathbb{E}[-V_i(R)] \geq \beta_i, \quad i = 1, \ldots, m \end{array} \right\}$$

$$(20.24)$$

The decision variables for the optimisation are the risk transfer control parameters r_i, $i = 1, \ldots, m$. The model Equation 20.24 is a non-convex programming problem with m variables. We note that its dimensionality is reduced in comparison with the model in Equation 20.15. The reason is that we considered only reinsurance contracts written on the aggregated liabilities of the subsidiaries. If we had taken into account all the different liability classes separately, the dimensionality of the problem Equation 20.24 would increase to $m \times n$.

The SCR for the group is calculated as

$$\text{SCR}_{\text{CRT}} = \sum_{i=0}^{m} [\text{ES}_\alpha(-V_i^{\text{opt}}) - \mathbb{E}[-V_i^{\text{opt}}]] \quad (20.25)$$

Calculating the group level solvency capital for a group with one representative subsidiary

In this first example we calculate the group level solvency capital for a parent company (entity 0) and one representative subsidiary. The liabilities of the representative subsidiary are aggregated into one liability class L_1. Furthermore the capital and risk transfer instrument is assumed to be quota share retrocession, thus $(1 - r_1)L_1$ is the amount reinsured by the parent. It is important to keep in mind that all subsequent discussions will be specific to proportional (quota share) reinsurance and the results may be different for stop-loss contracts.

The stylised group capital structure at $t = 0$ is given in Table 20.1. This example is constructed to illustrate the effects of the credit risk

Table 20.1 Group capital structure at $t = 0$

Parent company		Subsidiary	
Assets (a_0)	Liabilities (l_0)	Assets (a_1)	Liabilities (l_1)
US$8	US$6	US$4	US$3

and limited liability on the group-wide SCR. Because of these effects we will observe that the risk transfer that minimises the group-wide SCR lies below 100%. Later we will also consider a fully solvent situation, for which 100% risk transfer will be ideal (see Figure 20.5).

We model the future random values of the assets and liabilities following Filipović and Kupper (2007). The assets of the parent and subsidiary are assumed to be perfectly correlated, while their liabilities are independent. Hence the values of assets at $t = 1$ are given as

$$A_{0,1} = a_{0,1}(1 + \mu + \sigma_A W_A)$$

where $\mu = 0.01$ represents the expected return on assets and $\sigma_A = 0.02$ is the volatility. The source of randomness is $W_A \sim N(0, 1)$. The future values of the liabilities are assumed to be independent, lognormally distributed. They are modelled by

$$L_{0,1} = l_{0,1} \exp\left(\sigma_{L_{0,1}} W_{L_{0,1}} - \frac{\sigma_{L_{0,1}}^2}{2}\right)$$

where the volatilities are chosen as $\sigma_{L_0} = 0.08$ and $\sigma_{L_1} = 0.1$. Furthermore, the sources of randomness $W_{L_{0,1}} \sim N(0, 1)$ are independent. Consequently, we obtain for the consolidated group SCR

$$SCR_{cons} \simeq \$1.74 \tag{20.26}$$

The minimal capital requirement (value at default) of the subsidiary in the model is assumed to be zero. For the parent company it is given by

$$mcr_0 = 0.2 \times (v_0 + ES_\alpha(-V_0))$$

in other words the minimal capital requirement depends on both the initial capitalisation of the parent as well as on possible future changes of the asset–liability portfolio.

In Figure 20.2 (top) we show the calculated group SCR (objective function value of the problem in Equation 20.24) as a function of the

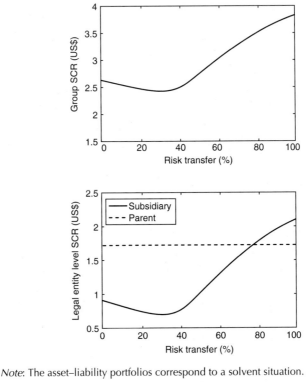

Figure 20.2 Group-wide (top) and individual (bottom) SCR as a function of the risk transfer in the regulatory (capital and risk transfer) approach

Note: The asset–liability portfolios correspond to a solvent situation.

risk transfer $(1 - r_1)$. The values are calculated with 10^5 scenarios for the asset–liability portfolios. We observe that there is a global minimum group-wide SCR.

We should not forget that in the model the group SCR also depends on the legal entity level SCR of the subsidiary (the constraint of the problem Equation 20.24). For this reason we show in Figure 20.2 (bottom) the individual capital requirements of the parent and subsidiary. In this particular case the legal entity level SCR of the subsidiary is a non-convex function. Depending on the legal entity level SCR of the subsidiary there may be several feasible solutions. Furthermore, as the legal entity level SCR appears in both the objective and constraint of the problem in Equation 20.24, we conclude that the problem in Equation 20.24 is a non-convex optimisation problem. The reason for this particular curvature of the SCR of the subsidiary can be explained as follows: for low risk transfers the parent can always pay the full amount, which means that the credit risk of the parent is low; as the risk transfer increases, the parent will only be able to pay a portion of the reinsured amount after a certain point. This portion will be paid from the parent's surplus, which is not perfectly correlated with the reinsured liabilities hence the SCR of the subsidiary increases. If the risk transfer is very high, the parent will not be able to pay anything back, it defaults.

Let us now take a look at the parent company in Figure 20.2 (bottom). We notice that the SCR of the parent is almost constant, thus the put option in Equation 20.12 has a negligible value. In other words, the option to let the subsidiary go into run-off has practically no value for the parent. This situation therefore describes a group where both the parent and the subsidiary are currently in a solvent situation.

In Figure 20.3 we also show the group-wide and individual solvency ratios, defined as

$$SR_{0,1} = \frac{-\mathbb{E}[-V_{0,1}]}{SCR_{CRT_{0,1}}}$$

As expected, the solvency ratios closely resemble the SCR, $SCR_{CRT_{0,1}}$, reflected on the diagonal.

Let us now consider the case where the group (parent and subsidiary) is in financial distress. We modify the asset–liability portfolio of Table 20.1 by setting $a_1 = US\$4$ and $l_1 = US\$3.5$, and $a_0 = US\$8$ and $l_0 = US\$7.5$.

In Figure 20.4 (top) we show the calculated group SCR (objective function value of the problem in Equation 20.24) as a function of the risk transfer. We see that in the case of a group-wide financial distress it is not worth it to enter into any reinsurance contract (the credit risk of the parent is very high). The group-wide SCR increases when the risk transfer increases.

In Figure 20.4 (bottom) we also show the individual SCR. We observe that the SCR of the parent is not constant like before, now its value reflects the option to let the troubled subsidiary go into run-off. In general, the effect of the limited liability of the parent company on the SCR is small and only appears when the subsidiary

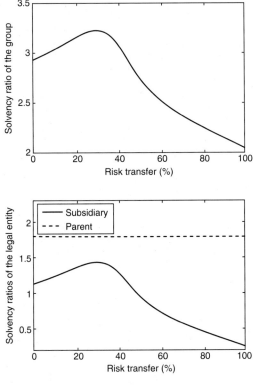

Figure 20.3 Group-wide (top) and individual (bottom) solvency ratios as a function of the risk transfer in the regulatory (capital and risk transfer) approach

Note: The asset–liability portfolios correspond to a solvent situation.

is in financial distress. This can mainly be attributed to the premium that the subsidiary pays for the reinsurance contracts. In this case of financial distress the SCR of the parent attains its minimum at the same risk transfer (zero) as the SCR of the subsidiary. Therefore in this situation risk transfer is not preferred. We conclude that the limited liability of the parent has only a small effect on the SCR.

As a last example we consider a group that is in a particularly good financial situation. This corresponds to the typical situation, where the pooling of risk is advantageous. We set $a_1 = \text{US\$4}$ and $l_1 = \text{US\$2}$, and $a_0 = \text{US\$8}$ and $l_0 = \text{US\$4}$. The group-wide and individual SCR are shown in Figure 20.5. We observe that the SCR

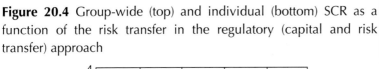

Figure 20.4 Group-wide (top) and individual (bottom) SCR as a function of the risk transfer in the regulatory (capital and risk transfer) approach

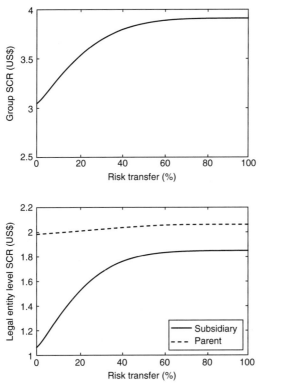

Note: The asset–liability portfolios correspond to a financially troubled situation.

of the parent is constant thus the put option in Equation 20.12 has a negligible value. The group-wide SCR is minimal for maximum risk transfer, ie, in this case the subsidiary should reinsure all of its liabilities as they will always be paid due to the parent company's good financial situation.

Calculating group level solvency capital for a group with two subsidiaries and the effect of ordination

In this example we calculate the group level solvency capital for a parent company (entity 0) and two subsidiaries. We assume that the subsidiaries' liabilities are each aggregated into one liability class: L_1 and L_2. As a capital and risk transfer instrument we again use

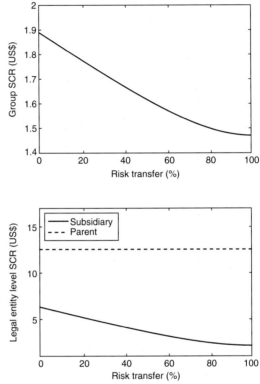

Figure 20.5 Group-wide (top) and individual (bottom) SCR as a function of the risk transfer in the regulatory (capital and risk transfer) approach

Note: The asset–liability portfolios correspond to a particularly good financial situation.

quota share retrocession: that is $(1 - r_1)L_1$ and $(1 - r_2)L_2$ are the amounts reinsured by the parent. We stress that all subsequent discussions will be specific for proportional (quota share) reinsurance and the results may be different for stop-loss contracts.

The stylised group capital structure is given in Table 20.2. This example is constructed to study the effects of the credit risk and limited liability on the group-wide SCR. Furthermore, we would like to illustrate the combined effects of the credit risk and an ordination between the subsidiaries. The available capital of the parent company at $t = 0$ is given as $v_0 = $ US\$2 and for the subsidiaries $v_1 = v_2 = $ US\$1.3. The future values of assets and liabilities

Table 20.2 Group capital structure at $t = 0$

Parent company	
Assets (a_0)	Liabilities (l_0)
US$8	US$6

Subsidiary 1		Subsidiary 2	
Assets (a_1)	Liabilities (l_1)	Assets (a_2)	Liabilities (l_2)
US$4	US$2.7	US$4	US$2.7

are modelled the same way as in the previous section. The assets of the group are perfectly correlated and normally distributed. The liabilities are independent and lognormally distributed. Further, the minimal capital requirement of the parent is assumed to be given as

$$mcr_0 = 0.4 \times (v_0 + ES_\alpha(-V_0))$$

The consolidated capital requirement for this group is calculated as

$$SCR_{cons} \simeq 1.94\ \$ \tag{20.27}$$

In Figure 20.6 (top and bottom) we show the calculated group SCR (objective function value of the problem in Equation 20.24) as a function of the risk transfers $(1 - r_1)$ and $(1 - r_2)$. We observe that the objective function is quite symmetrical, due to the fact that the asset–liability portfolios of the two subsidiaries are the same. Unfortunately, the optimisation problem in Equation 20.24 is non-convex, see the contour lines of the objective function in Figure 20.6. Furthermore, an additional non-convexity is introduced via the constraints.

In Figure 20.7 (top and bottom) we show the objective function in the situation where there exists an ordination between the subsidiaries, ie, the reinsurance contract of subsidiary 1 will be paid first and then that of subsidiary 2. In this case if the risk transfer of subsidiary 1 is large, it is not then optimal for subsidiary 2 to transfer any risk to the parent. We see that in this situation the objective function changes drastically. We observe that the optimisation problem remains non-convex, see Figure 20.7.

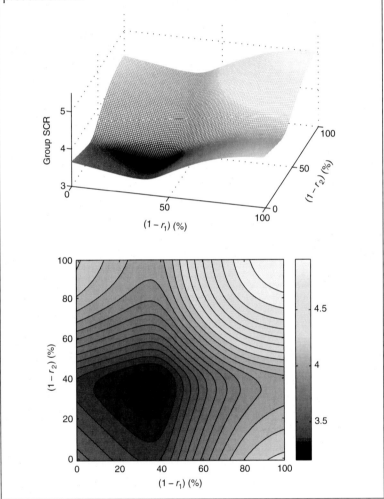

Figure 20.6 Group-wide SCR as a function of the risk transfers in the regulatory (capital and risk transfer) approach for a group with two subsidiaries and no ordination; a 3D (top) and a contour (bottom) plot are shown

Figure 20.7 Group-wide SCR as a function of the risk transfers in the regulatory (capital and risk transfer) approach for a group with two subsidiaries and an ordination between the subsidiaries (subsidiary 1 is preferred); a 3D (top) and a contour (bottom) plot are shown

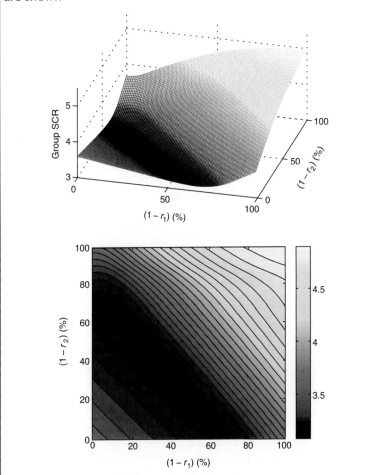

CONCLUSIONS

We have studied solvency modelling on the insurance group level. We have developed a toy model that takes into account relevant regulatory requirements. In practice the model is difficult to apply, because of the non-convex nature of the group level minimisation problem. In particular for large insurance groups with numerous subsidiaries and many liability classes the group level capital and risk transfer optimisation problem is difficult to solve exactly. In practice we should therefore perform a sub-consolidation on the liability class and/or subsidiary level before optimising group capital and risk transfer transfers. An exact solution of the optimisation problem would only be possible if we neglect key concepts, such as modelling the credit risk associated with the parent company.

We have studied several concepts of group level solvency within an example of a small hypothetical insurance group. In particular we have seen that the default of the parent has a large effect on the group level SCR. If the group is in a solvent situation it is optimal for the subsidiaries to transfer all risk to the parent. If, however, the group is in financial distress, transferring risks becomes unattractive. We have also demonstrated that the put option of the parent to let the subsidiaries go into run-off has only a small value. This is mainly due to the premium that the subsidiary pays for the reinsurance contracts. Finally, we demonstrated on a simple example that a possible ordination of the subsidiaries has a considerable effect on the SCR of the group through the impact of the credit risk of the parent.

The approach of sharing risk in insurance groups has applications not only for regulatory purposes, but also for the group's own capital and risk management. Using clearly defined capital and risk transfer instruments allows for a rational way of allocating capital and downstreaming diversification from the parent to its subsidiaries.

In addition, the approach presented allows for a consistent capital calculation for both the group and its legal entities. A model that captures the group with all its ownership relations and the web of capital and risk transfer instruments between the legal entities can be used not only on a group level (as for example a model using a consolidated approach), but also for the calculation of the economic state of all legal entities. Therefore there is no need to have several, potentially inconsistent, models that capture the legal entity level SCR of the subsidiaries of the group.

1   The author would like to thank Professor Hans-Jakob Lüthi (Institute for Operations Research, ETH Zürich), Professor Erich Walter Farkas (Swiss Banking Institute, University of Zürich) and Dr Jörg Behrens (Ernst & Young AG, Zürich) for their support. This work is based in part on the thesis of the author at the Master of Advanced Studies in Finance UZH/ETH Zürich programme.

REFERENCES

Commission of the European Communities, 2009, "European Parliament legislative resolution of 22 April 2009 on the amended proposal for a directive of the European Parliament and of the Council on the taking-up and pursuit of the business of Insurance and Reinsurance (Recast)", URL: http://ec.europa.eu/internal_market/insurance/solvency/index_en.htm [accessed 22 July 2009].

Bundesamt für Privatversicherungen, 2004, "White Paper of the Swiss Solvency Test", URL: http://www.bpv.admin.ch/themen/00506/00552/ [accessed 17 June 2008].

Bundesamt für Privatversicherungen, 2006a, "Technical document on the Swiss Solvency Test", URL: http://www.bpv.admin.ch/themen/00506/00552/ [accessed 17 June 2008].

Bundesamt für Privatversicherungen, 2006b, "Draft: Modelling of Groups and Group Effects", URL: http://www.bpv.admin.ch/themen/00506/00530/ [accessed 17 June 2008].

Eling, M., H. Schmeiser and J. T. Schmidt, 2007, "The Solvency II Process: Overview and Critical Analysis", *Risk Management and Insurance Review*, 10(1), pp. 69–85.

Filipović, D. and M. Kupper, 2007, "On the Group Level Swiss Solvency Test", Research Paper 188, University of Technology Sydney.

Filipović, D. and M. Kupper, 2008, "Optimal Capital and Risk Transfers for Group Diversification", *Mathematical Finance* 18, pp. 55–76.

Filipović, D. and A. Kunz, 2008, "Realizable Group Diversification Effects", *Life & Pensions*, May, pp. 33–40.

IAIS, 2002, "Supervisory Standard on Group Coordination", URL: http://www. iaisweb.org/index.cfm?pageID=40 [accessed 17 June 2008].

Luder, T., 2007, "Modelling of Risks in Insurance Groups for the Swiss Solvency Test", SAV Bulletin Heft 1 (Bern: Stmpfli), pp. 85–96.

Schweizerische Rechtssammlung SR 961.01, 2004, "Bundesgesetz vom 17. Dezember 2004 betreffend die Aufsicht über Versicherungsunternehmen (Versicherungsaufsichtsgesetz, VAG)", URL: http://www.admin.ch/ch/d/sr/c961_01.html [accessed 17 June 2008].

21

Dependency and Copulas

Andrew D. Smith[1]

Deloitte LLP

DIVERSIFIERS AND HEDGERS

The primary tool of insurance risk management is the careful selection of risks to be accepted. Insurers also use secondary risk management techniques, diversification and hedging, that exploit the ways that different risks interact with each other.

Diversification means spreading risks across many different categories, for example, an insurer might spread their life insurance risks by trying to attract a large number of policyholders and setting a maximum sum assured. To spread risks further, an insurer might extend into other lines of business, home insurance or pensions for example. Insurers may also take market risks, that is, exposure to interest rate or share price moves, in the interest of diversification. This works because a profit on one risk might offset a loss on another. Diversification fails if the risks are dependent. If, for example, stock market crashes were inevitably associated with flood events and lethal epidemics, then there would be little benefit to spreading risks. Diversifiers want to avoid high correlations between risks.

Hedging means passing a risk on to capital markets, for example, an insurer might offer investment funds with a capital guarantee if the investments do poorly. Investment guarantees are also available from banks in wholesale markets, but these are not exactly the guarantees that policyholders have been promised. Available bank guarantees, for example, might be on a standard index portfolio and available only for terms shorter than the underlying insurance policy. To hedge, the insurer buys the guarantees that are available, hoping for a sufficiently high correlation between risks.

To sum up, insurers who hedge rely on high correlations and insurers who diversify rely on low correlations. In this chapter, we investigate ways to measure these correlations in order to quantify the risks faced by hedgers and diversifiers.

The remainder of the chapter

Using an example of US and UK equity markets, we use historical simulation to quantify the risks faced by hedgers and by diversifiers. We then seek to capture the historical simulation results using three techniques. We start with the bivariate Gaussian model (that is, a Gaussian distribution in two variables connected by a correlation parameter), and demonstrate the correspondence to standard formulas in Solvency II. We show how the correlation parameter affects different types of market participants, with high correlations good for hedgers and low correlations good for diversifiers, but the data also illustrates the potential errors in the Gaussian approach.

Two possible enhancements to the Gaussian approach are the use of copula and eggbox techniques. We examine each of these in turn, using the UK and US equity data for numerical illustration. We conclude with a comparison of the different techniques.

HISTORICAL SIMULATION
What is historical simulation?

Historical simulation is the practice of testing current strategies directly against past events. In the example, we will look at various equity investment strategies and use historical simulation to investigate what would have happened to those strategies if the past were to repeat itself.

The past in question is the history of UK and US stock markets, from December 1969 through to June 2009, measured in US dollars. We measure monthly returns from month end to month end. Figure 21.1 shows the source data set in a chart.

UK investor perspective

An investor exposed only to UK assets is concerned about the returns on those assets. Many possible statistics could summarise

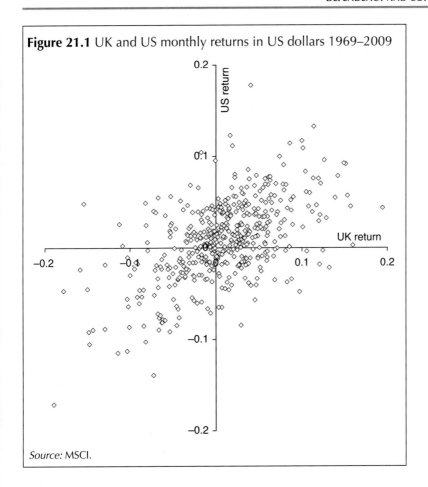

Figure 21.1 UK and US monthly returns in US dollars 1969–2009

Source: MSCI.

the data. We choose to examine sample deciles. The sample deciles for UK returns can be illustrated as a series of parallel vertical lines, partitioning the data into 10 subsets, each of which contains one tenth of the points. Figure 21.2 shows the relevant lines.

For solvency purposes, we are particularly interested in extreme percentiles. An insurer might, for example, hold UK shares against fixed US dollar liabilities, in which case large negative UK equity returns are the chief concern from the perspective of financial strength. Under the Solvency II regime, insurers are expected to be resilient to a 1-in-200 year event; that is, the probability of surviving the next year should be at least 99.5%. This is difficult to measure from 40 years of data; some form of distribution extrapolation is needed in order to investigate events beyond what has occurred in

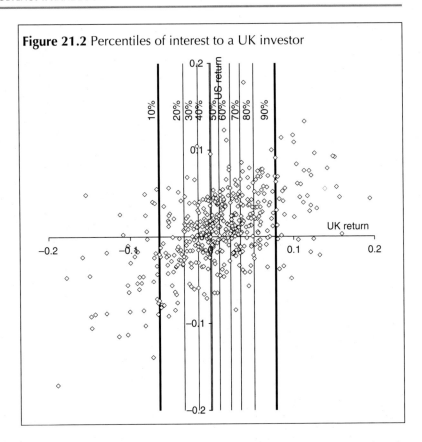

Figure 21.2 Percentiles of interest to a UK investor

the relatively short history reliably available to us. For more details on how this extrapolation is approached in practice, see Frankland *et al* (2008). In this chapter, we are concerned with dependencies so to avoid the complexities of extrapolation we focus instead on the worst 1-in-10 month event, that is, points to the left of the left-most bar in Figure 21.2. We use the term "half space" to describe this and any other region of the plane bounded by a straight line.

Most insurance firms exposed to equity markets have long positions, which means that free assets increase when equities rise and free assets fall when equity markets fall. It is possible, however, for short positions to arise. For example, an insurer might have promised to policyholders benefits linked to an equity index and then failed to invest in those equities. In that case, the insurer is concerned about a rise, and not a fall, in equity markets. The 90th percentile, and not the 10th percentile, then becomes more relevant because it is the highest returns in excess of the 90th percentile

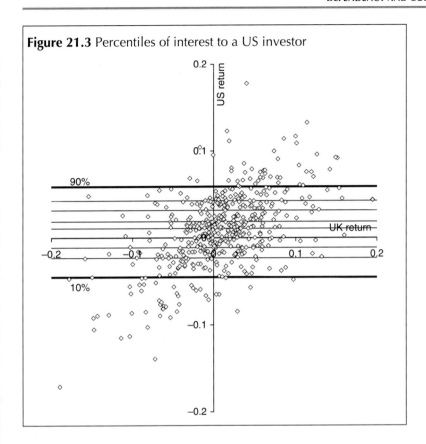

Figure 21.3 Percentiles of interest to a US investor

that pose the biggest threat to the short investor. To highlight the importance of the extreme percentiles, we have marked these in Figures 21.2–21.5 with bold lines.

US investor perspective

The US investor is interested in percentiles of US equity returns. In Figure 21.3, percentiles of US equity returns are illustrated as horizontal lines, partitioning the data set into 10 subsets, each of which contains one tenth of the data.

Diversifier perspective

Let us now consider a diversifier with 50% of a portfolio in UK shares and the remaining 50% in US shares. The diversifier hopes that a fall in one market is offset by a rise in the other. They are most worried about a simultaneous fall in both share markets.

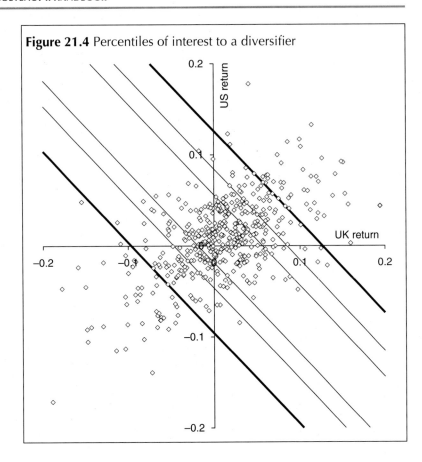

Figure 21.4 Percentiles of interest to a diversifier

We can also show percentiles for the diversifier on the chart, in Figure 21.4. Pick any line and the diversifier is indifferent between outcomes on that line because all give rise to the same portfolio return. In other words, each line corresponds to a contour of equal portfolio value for a diversifier with the lines to the bottom left representing the worst outcomes. As before, these parallel lines partition the data into 10 subsets, with the same number of observations in each. To avoid congestion, we have omitted the 40th, 50th and 60th percentiles.

In this case, it is not easy to read off from the chart the portfolio return that corresponds to a particular percentile. To identify the portfolio return at a particular percentile, choose a point on the corresponding percentile line and take the average of the two coordinates, reflecting the assumed 50%/50% portfolio composition.

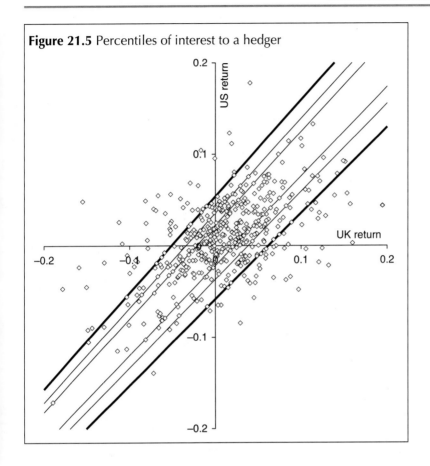

Figure 21.5 Percentiles of interest to a hedger

Just as long and short positions can arise with single markets so we can imagine a diversified short position, in which a firm had written liabilities linked to both UK and US markets, against fixed US dollar assets. In that case, the lines to the top right represent the most painful events because these are where the liabilities show the greatest increase.

Although we have illustrated the situation of a 50%/50% hedger, other portfolio mixes can be reflected in a similar way. The resulting lines of equal wealth are still parallel, but with a common slope greater or less than the −45° in our example.

Hedger perspective
We now consider the perspective of a hedger who takes long positions in one asset and short positions in another, for example,

a hedger might have liabilities linked to the UK stock market and assets in the US. From a risk perspective, the hedger is relying on a strong correlation between the two markets, although the underlying rationale for the trade is likely to be a belief that in the short term the US will perform better than the UK.

Figure 21.5 shows the lines of equal value for a hedger. As before, these lines partition the data into 10 equally sized subsets. To avoid congestion, the 40th, 50th and 60th percentile lines are omitted. However, unlike in previous cases the lines are no longer parallel. The reason is that the hedger worries most about the performance of one asset relative to the other, specifically, the quantity of US assets required to provide sufficient confidence of exceeding UK liabilities. The key statistic for determining the required assets is then $(1 + \text{UK equity return})/(1 + \text{US equity return})$. Rather than being parallel, the lines in the chart all pass through $(-1, -1)$.

Calculating capital requirements

Under Solvency I, the predecessor of Solvency II, the capital calculations called for were straightforward. Liabilities are valued and assets equal in value to the liabilities are allocated as technical reserves. Any remaining assets are available capital. The required capital is expressed (for life assurance, at least) as a percentage of the liabilities, usually 4% but sometimes 1%, depending on the nature of the liabilities. The entity is permitted to write new business provided that the available capital is at least equal to the required capital. This approach had many drawbacks, including a failure to capture asset risk, but it had the practical advantage of being clear as to both how much capital was required, and the quantum of additional assets needed in the case of insufficient capital.

Solvency II uses a different methodology. It adopts the "total balance sheet" approach in which all of a firm's assets and liabilities are taken into the capital calculation. The result of the capital calculation is the solvency capital requirement (SCR), which is intended to estimate current assets minus liabilities compared with the 0.5 percentile of assets minus liabilities after one year. The test of sufficient capital is then that the initial assets exceed the initial liability by at least the SCR. This is equivalent to saying that the 0.5 percentile of assets minus liabilities after one year must not be negative.

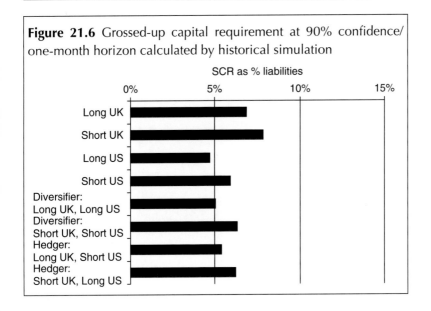

Figure 21.6 Grossed-up capital requirement at 90% confidence/ one-month horizon calculated by historical simulation

The practical problem here is that the SCR depends on the value of assets, creating a circular reference. If we have insufficient assets, then the SCR tells us how much is needed. However, if we make up the shortfall with some additional assets, there is still insufficient capital to meet the SCR because the SCR itself increased when the extra assets were added. This calculation is economically logical but practically exasperating.

To work around this problem, we can measure the SCR as the proportion of liabilities at which the SCR calculation stabilises. In other words, this is the amount of assets for which the SCR exactly equals the capital available. Where assets themselves are risky, the SCR calculation requires grossing up the future liability value, using the asset return in a bad outcome.

Figure 21.6 shows the requirements for the eight strategies we have so far considered. This chart reveals a number of interesting features. Firstly, short positions require more capital than long positions. This effect is largely artificial and reflects the fact that the simplified example allows for no interest credited on fixed US dollar assets, nor discounting of US dollar liabilities. More significant is the observation that diversification does not seem to work, in that the capital required for a 50/50 UK/US portfolio is greater (whether in a long or short position) than for 100% in the US market.

Table 21.1 Fitted mean and standard deviation based on UK and US data

	UK monthly returns		US monthly returns	
	Fit to moments (%)	Fit to percentiles (%)	Fit to moments (%)	Fit to percentiles (%)
Mean	1.01	0.71	0.83	0.70
1.28 * standard deviation	8.35	7.13	5.77	5.21

Adding the UK to the portfolio brings more in higher volatility than is gained by diversification. Viewed the other way around, the strategy works brilliantly, in that adding US assets to an existing UK portfolio reduces volatility both because the US assets are less volatile and because of diversification.

ANALYTICAL AGGREGATION – THE CORRELATION METHOD
Percentile estimates for single risks

An alternative to historical simulation for capital calculation is the use of analytical distributions. Before modelling dependencies, the usual starting point is to describe the marginal distribution of each risk individually. For example, we might assume that the returns on UK and US equity markets over a particular time horizon are Gaussian (also known as "normal"), with means m_{uk}, m_{us} and standard deviations σ_{uk}, σ_{us}, respectively. In this case, the 10th and 90th percentiles are given by expressions of the form $m \pm q\sigma$, where $q = 1.28$ is taken from the Gaussian distribution. More precisely, q is chosen such that $\Phi(q) = \alpha$ or equivalently $\Phi(-q) = 1 - \alpha$, where Φ is the standard Gaussian cumulative distribution function and $\alpha = 0.9$ is the required confidence level. To implement other percentiles α, use a different value of q, for example, for $\alpha = 99.5\%$ confidence as Solvency II requires use $q = 2.58$ because $\Phi(2.58) = 0.995$.

There are different ways to calibrate the m, σ parameters. One way is to examine the sample mean and standard deviation (that is, the sample moments) of the historical data. Another possibility is to calibrate the parameters from the observed 10th and 90th percentiles. Because the historical data is not exactly Gaussian, these two approaches give slightly different fitted parameters, as Table 21.1 shows.

Table 21.2 Quantile and SCR calculations

	Assets minus liabilities
Current values	$A - L$
$(1 - \alpha)$ quantile	$A - (1 + m + q\sigma)L$
SCR = current less $(1 - \alpha)$ quantile	$(m + q\sigma)L$

Table 21.3 Quantile and SCR calculations with grossing up

	Assets minus liabilities
Current value	$A - L$
$(1 - \alpha)$ quantile	$(1 + m - s)A - L$
SCR = current value $- (1 - \alpha)$ quantile	$(s - m)A$

We see that, in this example, the standard deviation fitted to percentiles is a smaller value than the conventional historical standard deviation. In addition, the centre of the distribution estimated via percentiles lies below the sample mean. These could both be evidence of non-normality in the investment return distribution.

Total balance sheet and grossing up

We consider the situation of an insurer with liabilities L linked to the equity market and fixed assets A. Suppose the assets earn no interest, but the equity market returns are Gaussian with mean m and standard deviation σ. As the liabilities are linked to the equity market, the bad scenario is one where the equity market rises. The $1 - \alpha$ quantile assets in one year's time, and the SCR, are calculated in Table 21.2.

Here the Solvency II calculation is restated in Solvency I form. It is necessary only to replace the flat 4% capital requirement by $m + q\sigma$. In what follows, we will write the stress test $s = q\sigma$, so that the capital requirement is $m + s$.

Some grossing up (that is, restatement in units of initial assets) is required if the assets, rather than the liabilities, are risky. Let us take the long equity example, with liabilities of L and assets of A invested in equities. Now the relevant stress event is a downward equity move. The SCR calculation appears in Table 21.3.

In the example, grossing up requires solution of the equation

$$A - L = (s - m)A$$

The solution is

$$\frac{\text{required capital}}{\text{liabilities}} = \frac{A - L}{L} = \frac{s - m}{1 + m - s}$$

If the parameters m and s are calibrated to the historical $1 - \alpha$ and α quantiles, then these analytical expressions give the same capital requirements as historical simulation.

Aggregation: big bang approach

We have calculated capital requirements for UK and US investors. We now consider the main purpose of this chapter, which is the treatment of exposures to two risks simultaneously in the hands of hedgers or diversifiers.

As we have already seen, one approach to this sort of question is historical simulation. However, this requires sequential calculations from a stored database of historical returns. It would be more convenient to store parameters instead of the entire history because this is less data. It would therefore be helpful to find a way of aggregating the capital requirements for single-economy strategies, in order to calculate the capital requirements for diversifiers and hedgers.

A simple approach is to assume for capital purposes that each market simultaneously moves to its α or $1 - \alpha$ level. The direction of the movement is whatever is worst for the particular entity. For example, a diversifier with a long equity position would assume that both markets fall simultaneously. A hedger with a short US and long UK position would assume that the US market rises while the UK market falls.

The practical effect of the big bang approach is simply to add up the capital requirements for each component of a strategy. For example, the capital requirement for a diversified portfolio is an average of the capital requirements for each component. A hedger adds together the capital requirements for the long and short positions.

The big bang approach to capital requirements is implicit in how insurers often measure their performance. Insurers make money by bearing risks so it is natural for insurers to measure their profit according to the risks they take, with this risk being measured in terms of a capital requirement. The big bang method provides a capital calculation that clearly breaks down into constituent terms for each risk. This means that the return achieved per unit of risk can also be broken down by risk type, giving important insights into the relative rewards available for different risks.

In the calculations underlying Figure 21.6, the required capital is close to the sums under the big bang, but (except for the short diversifier) they are not exactly equal because of grossing-up effects. In each case, especially for hedgers, the big bang approach gives a more onerous requirement than historical regression.

Aggregation: sum of squares approach

It is clear from historical simulation that the big bang approach overstates the risk of both hedging and diversifying strategies. The reason is intuitively clear: if each risk is stressed to its 0.5 percentile level, to assume that all risks suffer these stresses simultaneously is adding stresses on top of stresses. It is more realistic to assume some benefit of risk spreading.

This motivated the search for an aggregation method that produces a number less than the sum of capital for each risk, but is still larger than each component. One approach that achieves this is to take the required capital in respect of each individual risk factor (in the example UK and US equity risk), square it, add up the total and then take the square root. We call this the sum of squares (SSQ) approach. The difference between this capital requirement and that under big bang, called the diversification benefit, is large if several types of risk attract similar capital requirements, but is small if risks are dominated by a few risk types.

The effect of the diversification benefit is a reduction in the required capital for all risks combined. For management purposes, it is helpful to attribute that reduction back to individual risks and business units. Because the risk aggregation is no longer linear, there is room for debate regarding the best method of attribution.

Aggregation: correlation method

A further alternative to the big bang approach is an explicit calculation using correlations. For example, we might assume that the returns on the two markets are bivariate Gaussian, with means m_{UK} and m_{US}, standard deviations σ_{UK} and σ_{US}, linked with a correlation ρ.

We consider first the position of a diversifier, with 50% invested in the UK and 50% in the US. The mean and standard deviation of the average return are given by the following standard statistical formulas

$$m_{DIV} = \tfrac{1}{2}m_{UK} + \tfrac{1}{2}m_{US}$$

$$\sigma_{DIV} = \sqrt{\tfrac{1}{4}\sigma_{UK}^2 + \tfrac{1}{2}\rho\sigma_{UK}\sigma_{US} + \tfrac{1}{4}\sigma_{US}^2}$$

Suppose that the desired percentile is set at q standard deviations. As before, we write $s = q\sigma$. We can now calculate capital for long and short positions, as shown in Table 21.4.

For the last two cases the formula is more complex. This is because both assets and liabilities are risky. Under these circumstances, grossing up involves a circular reference where the SCR depends on the quantity of assets held, but in a non-linear function. An analytical solution to the equation is still possible.

These are the formulas underlying the capital requirements in Figure 21.7, which compares the three approaches discussed in the previous subsections with this one, using $\rho = 60\%$. The calculations reveal a close correspondence between the correlation method and historical simulation. The correlation removes some of the double-counting of risk that is inherent in the big bang approach.

Multivariate models

The correlation method extends easily to three or more dimensions. For an n-dimensional random vector X, suppose that the ith component has mean m_i with α and $1 - \alpha$ percentiles of $m_i \pm s_i$. In the example, the first component is the UK equity return and the second is the US equity return. Let u be an arbitrary vector. Then the α and $1 - \alpha$ quantile of $u.X$ are given by the following formulas

$$\text{Prob}\left\{ u.X \le u.m - \sqrt{\sum_i s_i^2 u_i^2 + 2\sum_{i<j} \rho_{ij}s_i s_j u_i u_j} \right\} = 1 - \alpha$$

$$\text{Prob}\left\{ u.X \le u.m + \sqrt{\sum_i s_i^2 u_i^2 + 2\sum_{i<j} \rho_{ij}s_i s_j u_i u_j} \right\} = \alpha$$

Table 21.4 SCR calculations for different investment strategies

Strategy	SCR per unit liability
Short equity	$s + m$
Long equity	$\dfrac{s - m}{1 + m - s}$
Short diversified portfolio	$\sqrt{\tfrac{1}{4}s_{UK}^2 + \tfrac{1}{2}\rho s_{UK}s_{US} + \tfrac{1}{4}s_{US}^2} + \tfrac{1}{2}m_{UK} + \tfrac{1}{2}m_{US}$
Long diversified portfolio	$\dfrac{\sqrt{\tfrac{1}{4}s_{UK}^2 + \tfrac{1}{2}\rho s_{UK}s_{US} + \tfrac{1}{4}s_{US}^2} - \sqrt{\tfrac{1}{4}s_{UK}^2 + \tfrac{1}{2}\rho s_{UK}s_{US} + \tfrac{1}{4}s_{US}^2}}{1 + \tfrac{1}{2}m_{UK} + \tfrac{1}{2}m_{US}}$
Hedger: long UK/short US	$\dfrac{(1 + m_{UK})(1 + m_{US}) - \rho s_{UK}s_{US} + \sqrt{\begin{array}{c}[(1 + m_{UK})(1 + m_{US}) - \rho s_{UK}s_{US}]^2 \\ -[(1 + m_{UK})^2 - s_{UK}^2][(1 + m_{US})^2 - s_{US}^2]\end{array}}}{(1 + m_{UK})^2 - s_{UK}^2} - 1$
Hedger: short UK/long US	$\dfrac{(1 + m_{UK})(1 + m_{US}) - \rho s_{UK}s_{US} + \sqrt{\begin{array}{c}[(1 + m_{UK})(1 + m_{US}) - \rho s_{UK}s_{US}]^2 \\ -[(1 + m_{UK})^2 - s_{UK}^2][(1 + m_{US})^2 - s_{US}^2]\end{array}}}{(1 + m_{US})^2 - s_{US}^2} - 1$

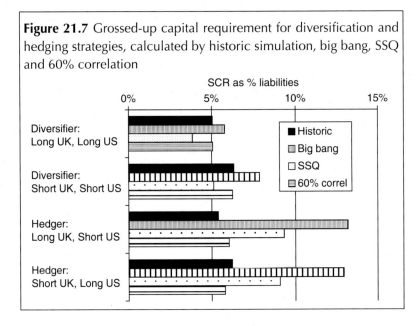

Figure 21.7 Grossed-up capital requirement for diversification and hedging strategies, calculated by historic simulation, big bang, SSQ and 60% correlation

Here, ρ_{ij} is the correlation between the ith and jth components of X. This formula is valid for multivariate Gaussian distributions, but also for any family of distributions where the α and $1 - \alpha$ quantiles are a fixed number of standard deviations from the mean. Such distributions are known as elliptically contoured; this is a criterion that also includes the multivariate Student t distribution.

We can see from Figure 21.7 that the correlation method gives a close approximation to the results of historical simulation. There are still deviations but they are small and could be caused by randomness in the data set just as plausibly as by a failure of the elliptically contoured hypothesis. Similar conclusions typically arise from examination of other asset pairs: the evidence to reject elliptically contoured distributions is generally weak.

Nevertheless, some still believe it is important to capture those deviations within a model. To do so involves a leap in model complexity, and experts still debate whether the additional effort is merited by any more accurate descriptions of the world or ability to better manage risks. Here we outline the techniques, with their strengths and limitations, to allow the reader to make up her own mind.

USING QUADRANT PROBABILITIES TO CAPTURE DEPENDENCIES

Quadrant probabilities

The classical measure of dependency between two random variables is the correlation, a measure that takes into account the whole distribution. In solvency problems, we are often interested only in a part of the distribution. This motivates a search for local measures of dependency that focus on that part of a distribution of most interest for solvency purposes.

In the case of a continuous bivariate distribution (X, Y), let us suppose we are particularly interested in the dependency around the ath quantile x_a of X and the bth quantile y_b of Y. Then, by definition

$$\text{Prob}\{X \leq x_a\} = a$$
$$\text{Prob}\{Y \leq y_b\} = b$$

Figure 21.8 shows a quadrant example for our data set.

To measure dependency, we could look at probabilities of quadrants, that is, probabilities for events of the form

$$c(a, b) = \text{Prob}\{X \leq x_a \text{ and } Y \leq y_b\}$$

Given the probability of this lower left quadrant, we can compute the probabilities of the other quadrant as well (see Table 21.5). If $c(a, b)$ is large, this says that combined low values (and combined high values) occur frequently, which is good news for hedgers and bad news for diversifiers; on the other hand, small values of $c(a, b)$ represent good news for diversifiers and bad news for hedgers.

Copulas

The function $c(a, b)$ is called a copula function. Figure 21.9 shows the empirical copula function for the UK and US data set.

As probabilities in all four quadrants have to be positive, there are upper and lower limits on the copula function $c(a, b)$, known as the upper and lower copulas, respectively. If X and Y are independent, then $c = ab$. This gives three standard copula functions. Table 21.6 lists these copula functions together with three parameterised families (the Gaussian, Clayton and Student t).

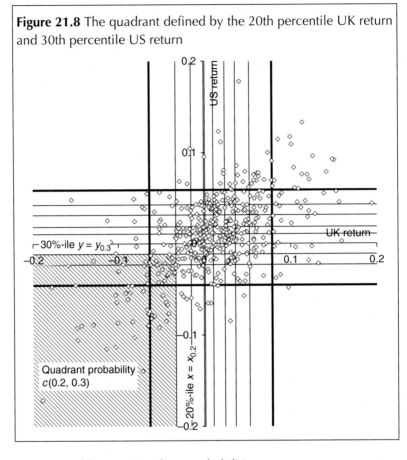

Figure 21.8 The quadrant defined by the 20th percentile UK return and 30th percentile US return

Table 21.5 Quadrant probabilities

	$X \leq x_a$	$X > x_a$	Total
$Y > y_b$	$a - c$	$1 + c - a - b$	$1 - b$
$Y \leq y_b$	c	$b - c$	b
Total	a	$1 - a$	1

For further possible families, see Dorey *et al* (2005), Nelsen (1999) or Embrechts *et al* (2001). To specify the Gaussian copula, we need to introduce the standard functions Φ and Φ_2, defined by integrating the bivariate Gaussian density. In the numerical examples we have used an algorithm from West (2009). A similar issue arises with the Student t copula, resulting in complicated formulas we will not reproduce here.

Figure 21.9 Empirical copula for UK and US returns

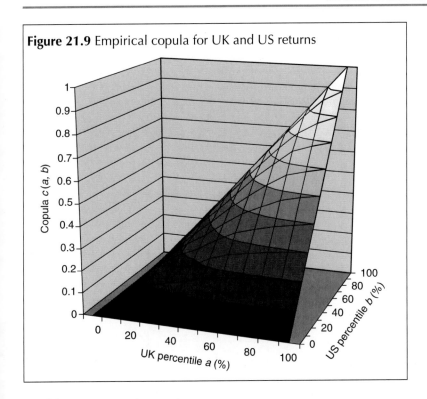

Table 21.6 Example copulas

Copula name	Formula
Lower	$\mathrm{Max}\{0, a + b - 1\}$
Independent	ab
Upper	$\mathrm{Min}\{a, b\}$
Gaussian $(-1 < \rho < 1)$	$\Phi_2[\Phi^{-1}(a), \Phi^{-1}(b), \rho]$
Clayton $(-1 < \theta)$	$\begin{cases} (a^{-\theta} + b^{-\theta} - 1)^{-1/\theta} & a^{-\theta} + b^{-\theta} > 1 \\ 0 & a^{-\theta} + b^{-\theta} \leq 1 \end{cases}$
Student t	Omitted here

The Gaussian copula reduces to the lower copula when $\rho = -1$, the independent copula when $\rho = 0$ and the upper copula when $\rho = 1$. The Clayton copula has an advantage over the Gaussian copula of an analytical formula. It also has the lower, independent and upper copulas as limiting cases for $\theta = -1, 0$ and $+\infty$, respectively.

The Student t copula also reduces to the upper and lower copulas for $\rho = -1$ and $+1$ respectively. However, when $\rho = 0$ this no longer reduces to the independent copula.

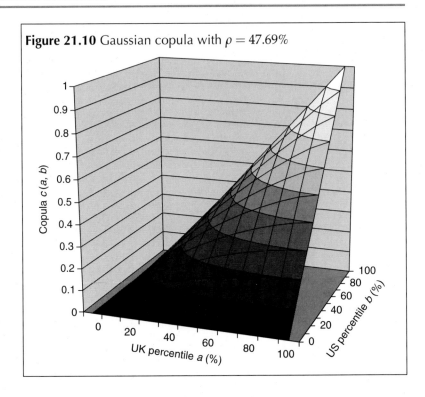

Figure 21.10 Gaussian copula with $\rho = 47.69\%$

We can fit copulas by equating one of the quadrant probabilities. For example, to fit the Gaussian copula, we might find the value of the parameter ρ that replicates the empirically observed $c(0.5, 0.5)$, that is, the empirical probability that both returns simultaneously lie below their respective medians. Figure 21.10 shows the fitted Gaussian copula using this method.

To the unaided eye this looks remarkably similar to the empirical copula. The differences are most easily understood when we show the difference between the empirical and Gaussian copulas. By construction, the errors must be zero at the boundaries and at the combined median return $(a = 0.5, b = 0.5)$. The observed error structure shows that the Gaussian assumption understates the empirical copula for combined low quantiles but more spectacularly for combined high quantiles.

We can also fit other copula families, for example the Clayton copula. This, too, looks visually very much like the empirical copula. However, a plot of the differences in Figure 21.12 shows systematic differences. A comparison with Figure 21.11, the vertical

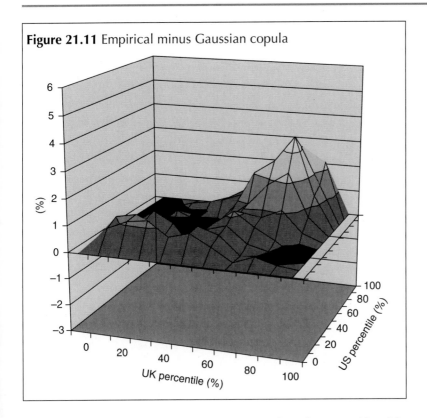

Figure 21.11 Empirical minus Gaussian copula

axes are the same, shows the Gaussian copula to be a considerably better fit to the data overall. However, the shape of the errors is different, with the Clayton copula overstating the copula for combined low percentiles and understating it for combined high percentiles.

Figure 21.12 shows the error in fitting the empirical copula using Clayton's formula. As with the fitted Gaussian copula, we can see that the error is zero around the perimeter and, by construction, at the joint 50th percentile point. What we can also see is that the error is worse in absolute terms than with the Gaussian copula. Whereas the Gaussian copula understates the frequency of adverse combined events, the Clayton copula, at least calibrated in this way, overstates how often low percentile joint events occur.

We have fitted these copulas by the simple method of equating the value $c(0.5, 0.5)$. Other methods are possible, such as maximum likelihood or equating rank correlations. However, in the example, none of these devises would dramatically improve the fit to the

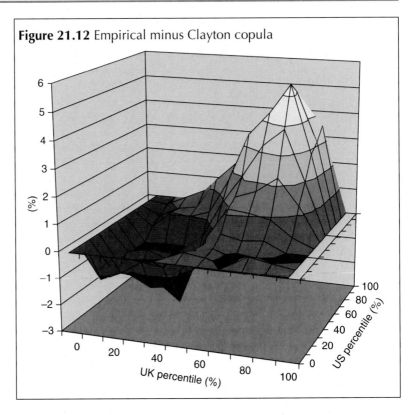

Figure 21.12 Empirical minus Clayton copula

historical data, as the most significant constraint is the use of copula families in which only a single parameter can be varied.

This example has taught us some useful lessons about copulas. In theory, a copula exists for any pair of distributions. But there are infinitely many possible copulas and it is necessary for practical reasons to cut down the search in some way.

The practical solution is to explore copulas already documented in statistical literature. There are boundary and monotonicity conditions on what functions can constitute a valid copula. It is not easy to dream up analytical functions to satisfy these conditions, and those mathematicians with the imagination to do so are rewarded by having copulas named after them.

Unfortunately, empirically good fit to financial data has not been a criterion in the development of standard copula formulas until now. For most copula families it is possible to back-solve for a parameter that will replicate an empirical copula at one or two points, as we have seen in the Gaussian and Clayton examples.

Smith (2002) and Tsanakas and Smith (2007) offer a wider class of copulas based on mixed Gaussian distributions, but with the greater theoretical flexibility of more parameters comes the greater practical difficulty in estimating them. Experience shows the search for an appropriate copula to be therefore something of a hit and miss affair – usually more of the miss than of the hit.

Copula aggregation

We have described the use of copulas to link two risks. We now consider the extension to three or more risks.

Mathematics offers three-dimensional copulas, four-dimensional copulas and so on, but these are difficult to construct and so seldom used. Instead, several popular software packages allow risks to be linked pairwise using bivariate copulas. The book by Bedford and Cooke (2001) describes this technique, sometimes called "vine copulas", in more detail.

Let us take the example of seven risks. This gives rise to 21 pairs of risks. However, it is not usually possible to specify copulas for all 21 risks. Instead, each risk is linked to its neighbours by a copula. Other risk pairs are connected only through a chain involving those neighbours. This means that only six copulas are specified independently with the others being described indirectly. The seven risk factors need not be connected in a linear chain, marked (a) in Figure 21.13. Another possibility is that six of the seven all link to one central risk, marked (b) in Figure 21.13. There are 10 possible topologies; in each case the risks must be assigned one to each node.

Figure 21.13 illustrates the copula model calibration. The driver distributions and pairwise copulas are selected from families named after mathematicians. The parameters are then set. In a final step, a topology is chosen to join the risks together.

Implied correlation surfaces

We can apply the Gaussian, Clayton or Student t copulas in reverse. Given a value of a and b, we can observe $c(a, b)$ from a data sample and back-solve to find the copula parameter that replicates the observed quadrant probability. In the case of a Gaussian copula, this can be interpreted as an implied correlation at the point (a, b).

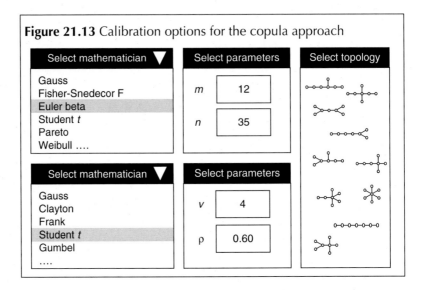

Figure 21.13 Calibration options for the copula approach

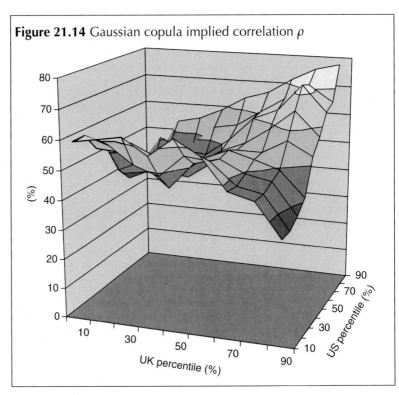

Figure 21.14 Gaussian copula implied correlation ρ

Having defined these quantities, we now investigate their empirical properties. Solvency II calculations should be concerned with 0.5 percentiles and 99.5 percentiles over a one-year time horizon. In the absence of thousands of years of data, these percentiles are not directly observable. Analysts have developed a number of ways to overcome this problem, most involving some prior view of a suitable distribution family that is fitted to the limited available data and then extrapolated. To avoid the significant additional complexity of extrapolation, we choose to work with more frequent data and less extreme confidence intervals. Ranking the data and partitioning into 10 buckets allows us to focus on the 10th, 20th, 30th, . . . , 90th percentiles.

We can compute implied correlations at points (a, b), where a and b are integer multiples of 0.1. This gives 81 (ie, 9×9) implied correlations. Figure 21.14 shows the implied correlations as a function of a and b. In this example, the implied correlation rises slightly for small values of a and b (and also for large values). This, a phenomenon typical for investment series, is sometimes expressed by saying that correlations become higher in tail events.

The localisation method
The localisation method is an important intuitive tool in finance. The idea is that not all regions of a probability distribution are equally important. If, for example, we are interested in the region where US and UK markets both fall, we can construct a correlation assumption that works well in that region, and then use that local correlation in an aggregation formula. The fact that the same correlation would be inappropriate in other regions is irrelevant because we have already established that the relevant region consists of joint low returns.

In this context, we can see the implied Gaussian copula correlation as a measure of local correlation in a particular region, with the overall correlation being in some sense an average of the local correlations. Might we then be able to approximate well the required capital using the standard correlation formula with local correlations substituted? Unfortunately, the answer to this question is "no"; one reason is that the unadjusted correlation method is considerably more robust than is often credited so there is often simply no need for a local version.

We have derived the analytical approach on the assumption of bivariate Gaussian distributions, but the approach is valid for a broader class of processes than that. In particular, any elliptically contoured distribution still supports the correlation approach exactly, even though the copula may be far from Gaussian. In this case, for elliptically contoured distributions, no adjustments are required for local correlation. See the monograph by Fang *et al* (1990) for more details.

The reason that local methods are so confusing is that copula methods are inherently concerned with quadrant probabilities. However, the regions of interest for insurers are typically half-spaces. Either the quadrant or the half space approach can characterise a distribution, but translating from one format to another is far from straightforward.

Monte Carlo approaches

Copula approaches often suffer from a lack of analytical tractability, leaving Monte Carlo simulation as the most practical approach for implementation. Firms may be unable to replicate calculations, even approximately, by simple arithmetic. Surprising results are common. Reasons include these:

- mistakes in coding;
- copula calibration process producing a copula that poorly represents the underlying risks;
- inappropriate input parameters that, due to the complexity of the model, remain undetected;
- other short cuts, such as simplified liability approximations – required for acceptable runtime but introducing further errors; or
- answers that are in fact correct but unexpected.

Therefore, in addition to the technical tools for simulating from copulas, it is helpful to develop systems and controls around those models, as a check on the copula models and to provide intuition in relation to the results.

In the final section we examine how half-space probabilities are useful for validating copula results. Actually, under some circumstances, these half-space models can entirely replace the copula approach.

USING HALF-SPACE PROBABILITIES TO CAPTURE DEPENDENCIES

The relevance of half-space probabilities

The ruin region of a financial firm means the set of driver values for which that firm would fail. In the equity examples, such a region is a half-plane, a subset of the plane bounded by a straight line, as shown in Figures 21.2–21.5.

More generally, in higher dimensions, the ruin region is typically a half-space, that is, a subset of n-dimensional space bounded by an $(n - 1)$-dimensional sub-space, or at least approximately of that form. This observation suggests that approaches to modelling dependency in the context of insurance solvency might more profitably focus on half-space probabilities, rather than on quadrant probabilities.

The bagplot

In this section, we return to the initial example of hedgers and diversifiers, but this time show simultaneously all of the 10th and 90th percentile lines. These eight lines are a subset of all possible lines separating 10% probability from 90% probability. Together, they are tangents to a blob, which we refer as the "likely set". Conversely, given the likely set, we can reconstruct the 10th and 90th percentile lines as the tangents. Figure 21.15 shows the likely set for the data.

The same construction can be used at other levels of confidence. We thus obtain what Rousseuw *et al* (1999) call a bagplot, proposed in an insurance context by Sheldon and Smith (2005). This is shown in Figure 21.16.

The bagplot provides an easy way to visualise a data set. If the underlying distribution is elliptically contoured, then the bagplot is a set of concentric ellipses. This is a sufficient condition for the correlation method of aggregation to be appropriate. If, on the other hand, the likely sets are not elliptical, then there is an argument for adjusting the correlation method to take account of the departure from ellipticity.

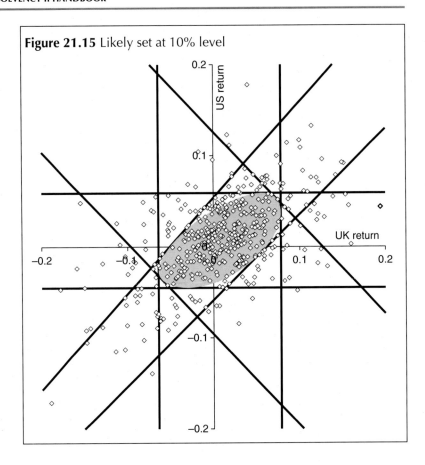

Figure 21.15 Likely set at 10% level

Graduation and quadrant correlation

Half-space probabilities are an alternative to quadrant probabilities for capturing dependency patterns. Once again, we consider bivariate distribution (X, Y). Focussing on the α-quantile, we define m and s with the following equations

$$\text{Prob}\{X < m_x - s_x\} = \text{Prob}\{Y < m_y - s_y\} = 1 - \alpha$$
$$\text{Prob}\{X \leq m_x + s_x\} = \text{Prob}\{Y \leq m_y + s_y\} = \alpha$$

If X and Y are jointly elliptically contoured with parameter ρ, then we can use the correlation formula to determine half-space probabilities. Particularly simple expressions arise when X and Y

Figure 21.16 Bagplot for UK and US data

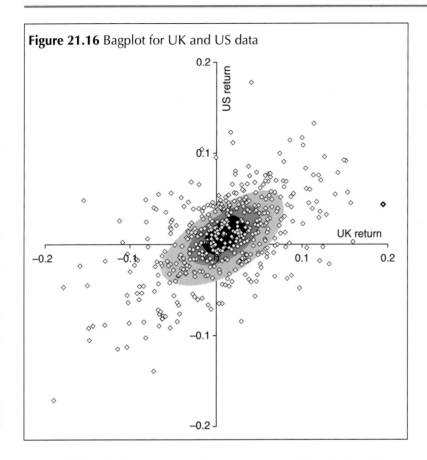

are scaled by their inter-quantile ranges m, resulting in the following formulas

$$\alpha = \text{Prob}\left\{\frac{X - m_x}{s_x} + \frac{Y - m_y}{s_y} \le \sqrt{2 + 2\rho}\right\}$$

$$= \text{Prob}\left\{\frac{m_x - X_i}{s_x} + \frac{Y - m_y}{s_y} \le \sqrt{2 - 2\rho}\right\}$$

$$= \text{Prob}\left\{\frac{m_x - X_i}{s_x} + \frac{m_y - Y}{s_y} \le \sqrt{2 + 2\rho}\right\}$$

$$= \text{Prob}\left\{\frac{X_i - m_x}{s_x} + \frac{m_y - Y}{s_y} \le \sqrt{2 - 2\rho}\right\}$$

If the joint distribution is not elliptically contoured, then we may not be able to find a single value of ρ that satisfies all four of these equations.

Table 21.7 Evaluation of quadrant correlations

Quadrant correlation	Implicit definition	Value of ρ from UK/US data set, 10/90 %-iles/ (%)
ρ^{NE}	$\alpha = \text{Prob}\left\{ \dfrac{X - m_x}{s_x} + \dfrac{Y - m_y}{s_y} \leq \sqrt{2 + 2\rho^{NE}} \right\}$	65
ρ^{NW}	$\alpha = \text{Prob}\left\{ \dfrac{m_x - X}{s_x} + \dfrac{Y - m_y}{s_y} \leq \sqrt{2 - 2\rho^{NW}} \right\}$	60
ρ^{SW}	$\alpha = \text{Prob}\left\{ \dfrac{m_x - X}{s_x} + \dfrac{m_y - Y}{s_y} \leq \sqrt{2 + 2\rho^{SW}} \right\}$	44
ρ^{SE}	$\alpha = \text{Prob}\left\{ \dfrac{X - m_x}{s_x} + \dfrac{m_y - Y}{s_y} \leq \sqrt{2 - 2\rho^{SE}} \right\}$	54

What we can do is define the quadrant correlations by making ρ the subject of these equations. We label the implied correlations according to the quadrant that defines them. For example, the critical region for the first equation arises when X and Y are large, which is the upper right-hand side, or north-east. Thus we use the corresponding quantile to define an implied quadrant correlation ρ^{NE}.

Putting these together, we have the implicit definitions for the four quadrant correlations in Table 21.7. These are easy to evaluate numerically from the data sample quantiles, so we have done this for the UK/US data.

Using quadrant correlations: local approach

The beauty of quadrant correlations is that this is exactly the number that has to be put into the correlation formula to obtain the "right" answer, at least when two risks of equal magnitude are to be combined. Where one risk dominates, the correlation is irrelevant and so the correlation formula still stands.

Provided, then, that the relevant quadrant can be readily identified, the use of quadrant correlations provides a transparent and practical approach to capital aggregation, avoiding the need for simulations. In this case, the north-east quadrant is most relevant for the short diversifier, the north-west for the long UK and short US hedger, the south-west for the long diversifier and the south-east for the short UK and long US hedger.

More advanced approaches are needed if the relevant quadrant cannot be easily identified. In all of the examples, the financial exposures were unambiguously long or short in each equity market. But sometimes real situations are not so clear, for example, an insurer writing endowments may choose to invest in a bond port-folio to immunise interest-rate risk, based on a certain assumption about lapses. However, if actual lapses deviate from the stated assumption, then the insurer may be exposed to rises or falls in interest rates without being able to say in advance which of these causes the greater loss.

In such cases, a single model is needed that captures quadrant correlations in all four quadrants. We consider this now.

Fitting the likely set

Figure 21.15 showed how the likely set is defined by a set of tangents, where each tangent defines two half-planes, with prob-abilities $1 - \alpha$ and α. Conversely, given a likely set we can construct the tangents.

In two variables, we have the parameters m_x, s_x, m_y, s_y, ρ^{NE}, ρ^{NW}, ρ^{SW} and ρ^{SE}. These parameters define eight tangents to the likely set. These tangents do not fully define the likely set, but they do significantly constrain it. We can imagine two distinct likely sets sharing these eight tangents, but the two sets could not differ substantially. This suggests an approach to likely set construction: to find a smooth analytical formula consistent with the eight given tangents.

Let us define the "quantile function" $a(u, v)$ to be the α-quantile of $uX + vY$. This means that

$$\text{Prob}\{uX + vY \le a(u, v)\} = \alpha$$

The parameter definitions already imply eight constraints on a. We can arrange these geographically, as in Table 21.8.

We now seek an appropriate smooth function $a(u, v)$ to satisfy these constraints. In addition, it must be positive homogeneous, in that for $\lambda > 0$, we have

$$a(\lambda u, \lambda v) = \lambda a(u, v)$$

Table 21.8 Constraints on quantile functions

$a\left(-\dfrac{1}{s_x},\dfrac{1}{s_y}\right)$ $= -\dfrac{m_x}{s_x} + \dfrac{m_y}{s_y} + \sqrt{2 - 2\rho^{NW}}$	$a(0,1)$ $= m_y + s_y$	$a\left(\dfrac{1}{s_x},\dfrac{1}{s_y}\right)$ $= \dfrac{m_x}{s_x} + \dfrac{m_y}{s_y} + \sqrt{2 + 2\rho^{NE}}$
$a(-1,0) = -m_x + s_x$		$a(1,0) = m_x + s_x$
$a\left(-\dfrac{1}{s_x},-\dfrac{1}{s_y}\right)$ $= -\dfrac{m_x}{s_x} - \dfrac{m_y}{s_y} + \sqrt{2 + 2\rho^{SW}}$	$a(0,-1)$ $= -m_y + s_y$	$a\left(\dfrac{1}{s_x},-\dfrac{1}{s_y}\right)$ $= \dfrac{m_x}{s_x} - \dfrac{m_y}{s_y} + \sqrt{2 - 2\rho^{SE}}$

By trial and error, I created several formulas passing through the given constraints, of which the following was the simplest

$$a(u,v) = m_x u + m_y v$$
$$+ \sqrt{\begin{aligned} & s_x^2 u^2 + s_y^2 v^2 \\ & + (\rho^{NE} + \rho^{NW} + \rho^{SW} + \rho^{SE})\frac{s_x s_y u v}{2} \\ & + (\rho^{NE} - \rho^{NW} - \rho^{SW} + \rho^{SE})\frac{s_x^2 s_y u^2 v}{\sqrt{2 s_x^2 u^2 + 2 s_y^2 v^2}} \\ & + (\rho^{NE} + \rho^{NW} - \rho^{SW} - \rho^{SE})\frac{s_x s_y^2 u v^2}{\sqrt{2 s_x^2 u^2 + 2 s_y^2 v^2}} \\ & + (\rho^{NE} - \rho^{NW} + \rho^{SW} - \rho^{SE})\frac{s_x^2 s_y^2 u^2 v^2}{s_x^2 u^2 + s_y^2 v^2} \end{aligned}}$$

For reasons that will later become clear, we call this the bivariate eggbox formula. The enthusiastic reader may wish to verify that this does, indeed, fit the eight constraints.

Boxness

Figure 21.17 shows some likely sets based on this formula with different quadrant correlations. We focus first on the cases where $\rho^{NE} = \rho^{SW}$ and $\rho^{NW} = \rho^{SE}$. The central row corresponds to the classical case of elliptical likely sets. The likely sets in the central column possesses four lines of symmetry, as $\rho^{NE} = \rho^{SW} = -\rho^{NW} = -\rho^{SE}$.

In the classical case of elliptical contours, any increase in correlations is good for hedgers and bad for diversifiers. On the

Figure 21.17 Likely sets with different choices of quadrant correlations

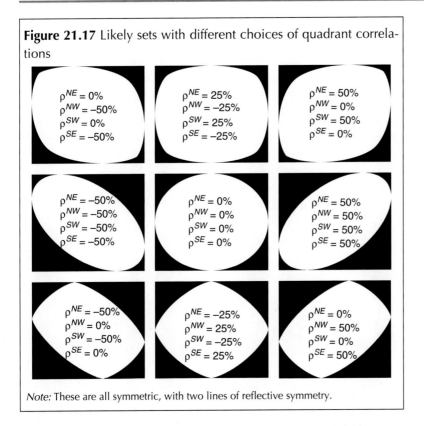

Note: These are all symmetric, with two lines of reflective symmetry.

other hand, falling correlations are bad for hedgers and good for diversifiers.

Within the eggbox framework, we recall that ρ^{NE} and ρ^{SW} are of most interest to diversifiers, while ρ^{NW} and ρ^{SE} are of most interest to hedgers. In contrast to the situation with the classical correlation method, these quadrant correlations are now free to move in opposite directions. A bad outcome for everyone occurs in the case when $\rho^{NE} = \rho^{SW} > \rho^{NW} = \rho^{SE}$ because then correlations are large for diversifiers and small for hedgers. Visually, this results in a likely set that is more box-shaped than elliptical, as the top row of Figure 21.17 shows. Sheldon and Smith (2005) refer to this as "boxness". Positive boxness corresponds to a positive coefficient in the last (quartic) term of the eggbox formula.

Negative boxness is also possible, in which case both hedgers and diversifiers benefit, relative to elliptically contoured distributions. This corresponds to the bottom row of Figure 21.17

Figure 21.18 Egg-shaped likely sets

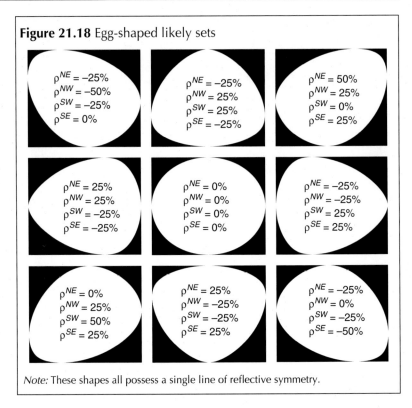

Note: These shapes all possess a single line of reflective symmetry.

and a negative coefficient in the last term of the eggbox formula. The data for UK and US equity returns exhibits slightly negative boxness at the 90% confidence level.

Eggness

For other choices of quadrant correlations, the likely set may be egg-shaped. This happens in the asymmetric cases when $\rho^{NE} \neq \rho^{SW}$ or $\rho^{NW} \neq \rho^{SE}$ or both. The asymmetry arises from the middle two (cubic) terms in the eggbox formula. Figure 21.18 shows some examples of how eggness can arise.

Multivariate aggregation

Multivariate aggregation using eggboxes is considerably easier than aggregation using copulas. There is no need to select a topology, or to pick the pairs whose dependency will be fully modelled. Instead, given a random vector X in n dimensions, the four quadrant correlations must be specified for each pair (i, j) with

$i < j$. Quadrant correlations for $i > j$ then follow by symmetry

$$\rho_{ji}^{NE} = \rho_{ij}^{NE}; \quad \rho_{ji}^{NW} = \rho_{ij}^{SE}; \quad \rho_{ji}^{SW} = \rho_{ij}^{SW}; \quad \rho_{ji}^{SE} = \rho_{ij}^{NW}$$

As before, we define m_i and s_i such that the $(1 - \alpha)$ quantile of X_i is $m_i - s_i$ and the α-quantile of X_i is $m_i + s_i$.

We proceed to seek a formula for the quantile function $a(u)$, defined for arbitrary vectors $u \neq 0$ by

$$\text{Prob}\{u.X \leq a(u)\} = \alpha$$

In the case of n dimensions, the specified quantiles and quadrant correlations impose $2n^2$ constraints on the function $a(u)$; for example, in two dimensions we had eight constraints. We must in addition preserve first order homogeneity.

There are infinitely many smooth functions that can satisfy a given set of constraints. One of the simpler ones is an extension of the bivariate eggbox formula. We therefore propose the multivariate eggbox formula, which takes the following form

$$r(u) = \sqrt{\sum_i s_i^2 u_i^2}$$

$$a(u) = u.m + \sqrt{\begin{aligned} &r(u)^2 + \frac{1}{2} \sum_{i<j} (\rho_{ij}^{NE} + \rho_{ij}^{NW} + \rho_{ij}^{SW} + \rho_{ij}^{SE}) s_i s_j u_i u_j \\ &+ \frac{1}{\sqrt{2}r(u)} \sum_{i<j} (\rho_{ij}^{NE} - \rho_{ij}^{NW} - \rho_{ij}^{SW} + \rho_{ij}^{SE}) s_i^2 s_j u_i^2 u_j \\ &+ \frac{1}{\sqrt{2}r(u)} \sum_{i<j} (\rho_{ij}^{NE} + \rho_{ij}^{NW} - \rho_{ij}^{SW} - \rho_{ij}^{SE}) s_i s_j^2 u_i u_j^2 \\ &+ \frac{1}{r(u)^2} \sum_{i<j} (\rho_{ij}^{NE} - \rho_{ij}^{NW} + \rho_{ij}^{SW} - \rho_{ij}^{SE}) s_i^2 s_j^2 u_i^2 u_j^2 \end{aligned}}$$

This formula provides an aggregation approach in multiple dimensions, calibrating to an observed dependency structure for each pair of risks. Calibration to historical data is simple and intuitive. Aggregation proceeds with a closed-form analytical expression in a natural extension of the existing popular correlation method.

CONCLUSIONS

Solvency II has seen a dramatic escalation in the modelling technology applied to risk and capital measurement. Building on simple stress tests, firms used first sum-of-squares algorithms and then correlation matrices to aggregate capital requirements across risk classes.

The correlation method is sufficient to account for most of the patterns seen in historical data, but some players have taken the methodology further, using copula or eggbox methods to give greater flexibility in the modelling of dependencies. For any pair of risks, correlation gives an indication of whether they tend to move together or in opposite directions over all of their range.

In theory, quadrant or half-space methods allow the capture of more subtlety in these relationships, such as

- two variables that most of the time act in an uncorrelated fashion but which in a minority of cases both take extreme low values;
- two variables that are not correlated but such that extreme (high or low) values of one variable are more likely associated with extreme values in the other; and
- two variables linked by a U-shaped relation: large positive or negative values of X produce high values of Y, whereas X close to zero produces low Y.

However, the use of more sophisticated methods adds significant complication to the calculation of capital.

Firstly, calibration becomes more troublesome. If correlations are difficult, it is even more difficult to estimate higher order dependency attributes with any confidence, even in high-frequency financial data.

Secondly, there is some uncertainty over the best way to stitch dependencies together when three or more variables are involved. One common practice to work around this problem is the use of tree structures, where each variable depends directly on its immediate neighbours. However, the increased flexibility in specifying dependency between adjacent nodes is spoiled by the lack of flexibility for non-adjacent nodes. The eggbox method provides a simpler, formula-based approach, calibrating to all the bivariate dependency patterns without adjacency constraints.

Thirdly, there is runtime and systems overhead. Dependencies seldom give rise to tractable models that can be computed analytically. Monte Carlo is usually required for the copula approach, although the eggbox method provides some more economical algorithms.

Fourthly, there is a substantial loss of transparency. This arises from the complex nature of the assumptions, restrictions enforced via tree topology and the black-box nature of some computational approaches. The lack of transparency increases the difficulty of communicating model results; it also exacerbates the risk of undetected mistakes in model implementation.

Technology for computing the result of dependencies has now got some way ahead of many insurers' ability to calibrate, understand and use those models. Visualisation tools such as an eggbox have a valuable role to play in validating, communicating and using the results of complex models.

1   The author is grateful to Gabriela Baumgartner, Neil Cox, Paul Coulthard, Oliver Lockwood and Alex McNeil for comments on earlier drafts of this chapter. He is also indebted to participants at the 2009 Actual Teachers and Lecturers Conference at Queens University, Belfast, for useful suggestions. All views expressed and any remaining errors are those of the author alone.

REFERENCES

Bedford, T. and R. Cooke, 2001, *Probabilistic Risk Analysis: Foundations and Methods* (Cambridge University Press).

Committee of European Insurance and Occupational Pension Supervisors, 2009, "Draft CEIOPS' Advice for Level 2 Implementing Measures on Solvency II: Articles 118 to 124 – Tests and Standards for Internal Model Approval", Consultation Paper No. 56, July, URL: http://www.ceiops.eu/media/files/consultations/consultationpapers/CP56/CEIOPS-CP-56-09-L2-Advice-Tests-and-Standards-for-internal-model-approval.pdf.

Dorey, M. and P. Joubert, 2005, "Modelling Copulas – An Overview", Working Paper, Staple Inn Actuarial Society, URL: http://www.sias.org.uk/data/papers/ Dependencies/DownloadPDF.

Embrechts, P., A. McNeil and D. Straumann, 2001, "Correlation and Dependence in Risk Management", in Dempster, M. A. H. (ed), *Risk Management: Value at Risk and Beyond* (Cambridge University Press).

Fang, K.-T., S. Kots and K.-W. Ng, 1990, *Symmetric Multivariate and Related Distributions* (London: Chapman & Hall).

Frankland, R., A. D. Smith, T. Wilkins, E. Varnell, A. Holtham, E. Biffis, S. Eshun and D. Dullaway, 2008, "Modelling Extreme Market Events: A Report of the Benchmarking Stochastic Models Working Party", *British Actuarial Journal*, presented to the Institute of Actuaries, November 3. URL: http://www.actuaries.org.uk/ __data/assets/pdf_file/0007/140110/sm20081103.pdf.

Joe, H., 1997, *Multivariate Models and Dependence Concepts* (Chapman & Hall).

Nelsen, R., 1999, *An Introduction to Copulas* (New York: Springer).

Rousseeuw, P. J. and I. Ruts, 1999, "The Depth Function of a Population Distribution", *Metrika*, 49, pp. 213–244.

Rousseeuw, P. J., I. Ruts and J. W. Tukey, 1999, "The Bagplot: A Bivariate Boxplot", *The American Statistician* 53(4), pp. 382–387.

Schmidt, R., 2005, "Tail Dependence", in Cizek, P., W. Härdle and R. Weron (eds), *Statistical Tools for Finance and Insurance* (Berlin: Springer).

Shaw, R. and G. Spivak, 2009, "Correlations and dependencies in economic capital models", presented to the 2009 Risk and Investment Conference, Institute of Actuaries. URL: http://www.actuaries.org.uk/?a=158967.

Sheldon, T. J. and A. D. Smith, 2005, "Do I Really Need All Those Sims?" Presentation to the 2005 Life Convention, Cardiff, Institute & Faculty of Actuaries, http://www.actuaries.org.uk/__data/assets/pdf_file/0007/156571/SheldonSmith.pdf.

Smith, A. D., 2002, "Dependent Tails", Paper to the 2002 General Insurance Convention, Institute and Faculty of Actuaries, http://www.actuaries.org.uk/__data/assets/pdf_file/0019/18730/Smith_tails.pdf.

Tsanakas, A. and A. D. Smith, 2007, "High Dimensional Modelling and Simulation with Asymmetric Normal Mixtures", Working Paper, Cass Business School and Deloitte & Touche, LLP, http://ssrn.com/abstract=1005894.

West, G., 2009, "Better Approximations to Cumulative Normal Functions", *Wilmott Magazine*, July, http://www.wilmott.com/pdfs/090721_west.pdf.

22

Hedging Inflation-Linked Pension Liabilities under Solvency II

Mark Schouten, Albert Mentink; Roy Kouwenberg[1]

AEGON Netherlands; Madihol University,
Erasmus University Rotterdam

Insurers often guarantee defined benefit pension liabilities for corporate pension funds, taking over the responsibility for both asset allocation and risk management in return for an annual fee and premium payments. Many pension funds would prefer to offer the plan's participants full inflation indexation of their pension rights to protect the participants' wealth against real depreciation.[2] An insurer that can guarantee not only the nominal value of the liabilities, but also the real value, by promising full indexation of pension rights can therefore be an attractive proposition for corporate pension funds and their participants.

Guaranteed inflation indexation of pension benefits introduces several problems for the insurer, however, since inflation is uncertain and imperfectly correlated with the returns on typical institutional portfolios consisting of stocks and bonds. Further, under the new Solvency II regulatory framework an inflation indexation guarantee leads to a higher economic capital requirement for the insurer. The cost of this increased capital requirement will eventually be passed on to pension customers and might make a fully inflation-indexed guarantee too expensive in practice. In this chapter we construct hedge portfolios for an insurer offering full inflation indexation linked to Eurozone inflation. We show that the best hedge portfolios eliminate inflation risk and nominal interest-rate risk very effectively, reducing the additional capital requirements for the insurer drastically (to nearly zero).

Insurers can decrease their exposure to inflation risk by constructing a hedge portfolio that increases in market price in response to increasing inflation. Moreover, an insurer would also like to have a portfolio that increases in market price with decreasing nominal interest rates, as a decrease of the nominal interest rate reduces the present value of the liabilities. In this chapter we design such a hedge portfolio using four types of instruments: namely inflation-linked bonds, interest rate swaps, inflation swaps and swaptions. These instruments respond to changes in inflation and nominal interest rates, and consequently changes in real interest rates, so they can be used to design an effective hedge portfolio. The main research question we would like to answer is which instruments are most suited to creating a hedge portfolio that can mitigate both inflation risk and nominal interest-rate risk? Further, we would like to demonstrate the impact of various hedging strategies on the required economic capital for an insurer under Solvency II.

This research extends the current literature; here we explicitly design a hedge portfolio that is able to cope with both shocks in inflation and nominal interest rates, whereas traditionally the focus is placed on nominal interest-rate risk only (Carcano and Foresi 1997; Gong and He 2005). This chapter addresses the inflation hedging qualities of instruments explicitly linked to inflation, whereas other literature focuses on hedging qualities of traditional asset classes, such as equity (eg, Bodie 1975; Fama and Schwert 1977; Fama 1981; Ely and Robinson 1996; Schotman and Schweitzer 2000) and real estate (for a broad overview of the literature, see Benjamin *et al* 2001).

The chapter also goes one step further than simply comparing correlations between the market value developments of the real liabilities and the hedge portfolio. Here, we explicitly design a hedge portfolio by carefully matching the real modified duration and convexity of the hedge portfolio and the value of the real liabilities. Further, we evaluate the hedge portfolios within the new Solvency II framework that demands an insurer holds sufficient economic capital to cope with extreme shocks in inflation and the nominal interest rate; this is exactly the research topic that Gajek

(2005) claims to be absent from the current literature. We find that hedge portfolios consisting of inflation-linked bonds and swaps can result in a dramatic reduction of the required economic capital.

INFLATION AND NOMINAL INTEREST-RATE RISK FOR AN INSURER

In this chapter we study the hedging problem of a European insurer that guarantees defined benefit pension liabilities, including full indexation linked to the Eurozone Harmonised Index of Consumer Prices excluding Tobacco (HICPxT). We focus on Eurozone HICPxT inflation, as various European inflation-linked financial instruments based on HICPxT are available in the markets, as discussed next. We assume that the insurer is located in the Netherlands to illustrate the implementation of the new Solvency II regulatory regime by the Dutch Central Bank. Solvency II has been implemented by the Dutch Central Bank since 2007, as explained in the "Solvency II" section of this chapter, including detailed guidelines on economic capital requirements for insurers based on extreme interest rate and inflation shock scenarios that provide a very rigid test for the hedge portfolios.

Inflation-linked pension liabilities

Suppose that the insurer guarantees the expected annual real cash-flows of a defined benefit pension fund in the period 2007–80. The real cashflow equals €2 million in 2007 and then declines by 10% every consecutive year as we can see in Figure 22.1.

The insurer guarantees full indexation of these cashflows based on the Eurozone HICPxT. As part of the insurance contract, the insurer also takes over the responsibility for the investment strategy of the pension asset portfolio. Under the Dutch Solvency II framework the insurer is considered as the party carrying all the risks stemming from the pension's liabilities and therefore needs to hold sufficient economic capital to cover unforeseen losses. The pension fund, on the other hand, no longer faces much risk after signing the full insurance contract and is only required to set aside a small amount of capital for potential downgrades of the insurer's credit rating.

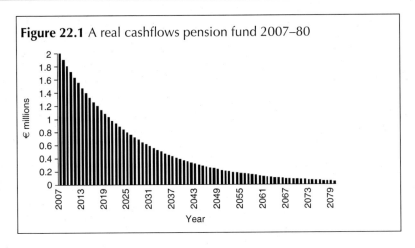

Figure 22.1 A real cashflows pension fund 2007–80

Before going into detail on calculating the present value of the real liabilities, we first give a brief preview of the final result to illustrate the relevance of hedging nominal interest rate and inflation risk for the insurer. Suppose that the insurer invests the plan's assets in a typical institutional portfolio consisting of 40% stocks and 60% nominal bonds (with a modified duration of five). Under the Solvency II framework specified by the Dutch Central Bank, given this investment portfolio the minimum required economic capital for nominal interest rate and inflation risk is equal to 14% of the present value of the real liabilities.[3] However, given the carefully constructed hedge portfolio, we will later see that the amount of required capital can be reduced to only 0.342%.

Solvency II

The Solvency II framework demands that a financial institution must maintain a buffer so that it can remain solvent over a one-year horizon with a probability of 99.5%. This buffer, which is referred to as economic capital, must be at least such that in 99.5% of cases the insurer can cover losses due to adverse investment returns, as well as changes in nominal interest rates and inflation rates. The Dutch central bank has formulated a standardised solvency test,[4] which can be used by insurers to determine their required economic capital. In short, the standardised solvency test formulates scenarios with extreme shocks to nominal interest rates and the inflation rate. The required economic capital is equal to the maximal mismatch between the market value development of the assets and the liabilities among all scenarios (given that the development is unfavourable for the insurer). This scenario approach of the Dutch financial supervisor should be seen as a special case of future regulations in the Solvency II framework. Therefore, the required economic capital is also relevant to insurers in other European countries. The Dutch approach is only different in its specification of a small number of "standardised" interest rate and inflation scenarios to facilitate the computation of economic capital.[5] A more advanced approach would probably apply similar shock scenarios, but they would follow from an economic or statistical model that described the future evolution of the term-structure of interest rates and inflation. However, the particular choice of interest and inflation scenarios does not affect the hedging methodology and qualitative outcomes presented in this chapter.

INFLATION

This section provides a more detailed overview of the various inflation types relevant to this research. First, each Eurozone country publishes the Harmonised Index of Consumer Prices (HICP). This measures each country's general price developments. This inflation index was introduced to compare inflation across Eurozone countries based on the same methodology. Second, Eurostat uses the weighted average of the Eurozone countries' HICP to calculate the overall Eurozone HICP (based on gross domestic product (GDP)). This overall index is used to assess general price level developments in the Eurozone. The third inflation index is HICPxT. This index is relevant for the inflation hedging analysis as most European inflation-linked financial instruments are based on HICPxT.[6]

Liquid markets for financial instruments linked to country-specific inflation rates in Europe do not exist yet, except for France. Instead most instruments are linked to HICPxT to be attractive to the larger European market. In order to use the HICPxT-linked instruments for hedging payments linked to a country-specific inflation rate, a high correlation with the country-specific HICP is desired. We examine whether this is true by calculating the yearly correlation for the 13 Eurozone countries with the Eurozone HICPxT. Table 22.1 shows the resulting correlations. As expected, the largest countries in the Eurozone, in terms of GDP, exhibit the

Table 22.1 Correlation Eurozone HICPxT and national HICP: January 1997–July 2006

Country	Correlation
France	0.87
Austria	0.85
Spain	0.82
Germany	0.81
Belgium	0.76
Luxembourg	0.75
Italy	0.69
Portugal	0.60
Ireland	0.54
Netherlands	0.45
Finland	0.38
Greece	0.01
Slovenia	−0.03

Source: Eurostat.

highest correlation with Eurozone HICPxT, but the correlation is rather low for smaller countries such as Ireland, Finland, Greece and the Netherlands.

In this chapter we assume that the insurer tries to avoid potential basis risk and the lack of liquid hedge instruments by not offering guarantees linked to country-specific inflation rates, but rather linked to the Eurozone HICPxT inflation. Given the trend of steadily increasing integration among Eurozone economies, this choice of indexation is not without rationale. Further, using over-the-counter derivatives contracts, it is certainly feasible to swap the hedge portfolios linked to Eurozone HICPxT inflation into hedge portfolios linked to any country-specific inflation in the Eurozone.[7]

HEDGING

In this section we first explain the general hedging strategy used, which is a combination of duration and convexity matching, with a bucket approach to safeguard against non-parallel changes in the interest rate term structure. We then review the fixed income instruments available in the markets for implementing the general strategy. Finally, we present the approach for assessing the effectiveness of a hedge portfolio.

Hedge principles

A perfect hedge implies that both the hedge instrument's market price and the liabilities' present value must move in the same direction and with the same amount in response to a change in the inflation rate and nominal interest rates. In order to find such a hedge portfolio we first need to determine the present value, the real modified duration and the convexity of the real liabilities. First, the present value of the real liabilities $Liabilities_{real}$ is equal to the sum of the present value of the expected real cashflows, $CashFlow_{real,\,t}$, for the coming T years discounted with the zero-coupon real interest rate for year t, $r_{real,\,t}$.[8] The first element of the hedge is to construct a hedge portfolio that has the same market value as the present value of real pension liabilities.

The second important characteristic of the real liabilities is its sensitivity with respect to a change in the real interest rate, summarised by the real modified duration measure. We calculate the real duration of the liabilities as the weighted time to maturity of the real cashflows from period 1 to T. After dividing by the real yield to maturity y_r we find the real modified duration: $Duration_{real,\,mod} = Duration_{real}/(1 + y_r)$. In a similar fashion we also define the nominal modified duration and the breakeven inflation modified duration, which are measures of the sensitivity of the value of the real liabilities to a change in the nominal interest rate and the breakeven inflation (this is the realised inflation that is necessary to be indifferent between a nominal and a real investment[9]) respectively. In addition to the first-order approximation duration, we also aim to match the second-order effect, ie, the convexity of the real liabilities.

As the hedge portfolio should be able to cope with non-parallel shifts of the term structure as well, we can divide the present value of the real liabilities into several different buckets based on maturity. By matching the duration and convexity of the liabilities in each of the maturity buckets, we make sure that the hedge portfolio is more immune to non-parallel changes in the yield curve. An alternative approach for defining the buckets that we apply here uses cut-off points based on the cumulative real interest exposure, precisely defined as the cumulative real liabilities multiplied by its real modified duration, using information about both the timing and the size of the discounted real cashflows.

Hedge instruments

This general hedging strategy, consisting of duration and convexity matching with a bucket approach, can be implemented with several fixed income instruments. We now discuss the potential usefulness of several classes of these instruments from a hedging perspective, focusing both on inflation risk and nominal interest-rate risk (which are both part of the insurer's risk exposure).

Inflation-linked bonds

The vast majority of traded inflation-linked bonds are capital indexed bonds, where the coupon payment consists of a real coupon multiplied by the compounded HICPxT inflation rate starting from the issue date of the bond. The principal payment consists of the original face value multiplied by the compounded inflation from the date of issue. Typically, the principal payment is protected against deflation. This means that in all cases the face value is guaranteed. For valuation techniques for this type of inflation-linked bond see, for example, Jarrow and Yildirim (2003), as well as Desclée *et al* (2003) for pricing details about inflation-linked bonds in the Eurozone area. Since inflation-linked bonds provide a certain risk-free real return, they are very well suited to hedge real interest-rate risk.

Interest rate swaps

In a plain vanilla interest rate swap one party pays a fixed interest rate on a notional principal and gets in return a floating interest (eg, Euribor[10]) for a number of years: see, for example, Hull (2002) for more details about valuing interest rate swaps. Interest rate swaps can be used to hedge against nominal interest-rate risk, because decreasing nominal interest rates lead to an increase in both the market price of interest rate swaps and the present value of the nominal liabilities. Interest rate swaps are less suitable for hedging real interest-rate risk, since typically changes in nominal interest rates and inflation shocks are imperfectly correlated. This may lead to a situation where the present value of the real liabilities does not change much in response to a shock in the nominal interest rate, whereas the value of the interest rate swaps changes dramatically in response to a shock in the nominal interest rate, thereby harming the hedge quality.

Inflation swaps

An inflation swap is an agreement between two parties to exchange a floating (ie, uncertain) inflation rate for a fixed rate of inflation. The fixed inflation rate is chosen so that at the inception date the market price of the swap is equal to zero. The standard contract is the so-called zero-coupon inflation swap, with only one payment exchange at maturity. For more details about valuing inflation swaps see, for example, Mercurio (2005) and Kerkhof (2005). Inflation swaps are very useful for hedging inflation risk, as they provide a higher return in times of increased inflation.

Swaptions

A swaption is an agreement that gives the buyer the right, but not the obligation, to enter the underlying swap contract as the receiver of fixed interest rate payments. In contrast to interest rate swaps, the market value of a swaption cannot become negative. However, when the contract is initiated the buyer of the swaption must pay a premium. The standard in the market are European swaptions, which can only be exercised at the maturity date of the swaption. Valuation of European swaptions is normally based on the Black model (Black 1976). To protect against decreasing nominal interest rates it may be attractive to buy a receiver swaption, which increases in market value when nominal interest rates decrease. However, the upside potential stays intact as the market value cannot decrease below zero when interest rates increase.

Evaluating the effectiveness of hedge portfolios

To test the quality of the hedge portfolios we administer extreme shocks to the initial zero-coupon nominal term structure and the initial breakeven inflation term structure, using the eight different scenarios defined in Table 22.2. Please note that scenarios 2 and 5 have a similar impact on the real interest rate. However, as the hedge portfolios (particularly swaptions) may react in a different way to shocks in the nominal interest rate and breakeven inflation, the distinction between the two scenarios is relevant and this is also the reason why we incorporate scenarios that cause changes in the real interest rate by either shocking the nominal interest rate or inflation.

Table 22.2 Overview of the eight breakeven inflation and nominal interest shock scenarios

Scenario	Breakeven inflation shock	Nominal interest shock
1	Parallel 1% point up	Parallel 1% point up
2	Parallel 1% point up	Equal
3	Parallel 1% point up	Gradual up
4	Equal	Parallel 1% point up
5	Equal	Parallel 1% point down
6	Parallel 1% point down	Parallel 1% point down
7	Parallel 1% point down	Equal
8	Parallel 1% point down	Gradual 1% point down

Figure 22.2 Zero-coupon nominal term structure in five scenarios

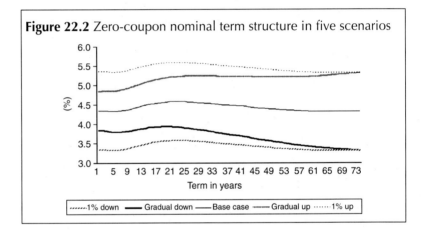

As an illustration, Figure 22.2 shows the initial nominal term structure, as well as the term structures resulting after applying the various interest rate shock scenarios defined in Table 22.2. We note that apart from parallel shocks, the scenarios also include non-linear interest rate shocks that are relatively stronger at longer maturities.

After shocking the nominal and real term structures with one of the eight scenarios in Table 22.2, we recalculate the value of the real liabilities and the value of the hedge portfolio to assess the hedging error. This difference between assets and liabilities (when non-zero) is defined as the hedging error, also referred to as the hedging mismatch, and is expressed as a percentage of the value of the real liabilities.

As we only consider hedge portfolios consisting of fixed income instruments, the market value of the hedge portfolio can be determined exactly after administering the shocks in a particular scenario. The same holds for the value of the real liabilities. Rather than replicating, or simulating, historical term structure movements (which tend to be rather small), we prefer to put the hedge portfolio trough a stress test using a small number of extreme scenarios. This approach is in line with the Solvency II framework, as well as its current implementation by the Dutch regulator.

DATA

In order to conduct stress tests for various hedge portfolios in a realistic setting, we use market data of the term structure of nominal and real interest rates, as well as the market prices of various fixed income instruments such as inflation swaps and swaptions. The data are all from May 8, 2007, unless explicitly specified otherwise. As explained previously, the stress test approach does not require time series data. The available time series of pricing data for inflation swaps and swaptions are relatively short,[11] which limits their usefulness for evaluating hedge portfolios.

The term structure of nominal and real interest rates

The value of the real pension liabilities can be calculated by discounting the expected real cashflows with the appropriate rates from the zero-coupon real interest rate term structure. To construct this curve we combine information about the breakeven HICPxT inflation swap curve and the zero-coupon nominal interest term structure. We use the breakeven inflation curve as a measure of the expected inflation plus the inflation-risk premium.[12] We use the Eurozone nominal zero-coupon term structure published by the Dutch central bank. The original source of information for this nominal term structure data is Eurozone zero-coupon swap curve data from Bloomberg. The nominal rates are available up to a maturity of 60 years. For longer maturities we assume that the curve remains constant at the 60-year rate.

The real interest rate can then be calculated using the extended Fisher equation. This method gives the zero-coupon real term structure, which was relatively flat around 2.3% on May 8, 2007.

Four hedge instruments[13]

Barclays provides data on Eurozone sovereign inflation-linked bonds indexed with HICPxT, including the coupon size, the maturity date, the number of coupon payments per year and the dirty price. The following countries issue inflation-linked bonds indexed against HICPxT: France (OAT€i, 5), Italy (BTP€i, 6), Greece (GGB€i, 2) and Germany (DBRI, 1), where the symbol between brackets indicates the bond name, followed by the number of bonds available in the market.

We collect data of the Euribor par swap curve to value plain vanilla interest rate swaps. The swap curve was relatively flat on May 8, 2007, around 4.4–4.6% for maturities ranging from one to 50 years.

To value receiver zero-coupon inflation swaps we collect inflation swap rates for the following maturities: 2–10, 12, 15, 20, 25 and 30 years, together with their fixed breakeven inflation percentage.

We further collect prices of European at-the-money swaptions with a time-to-maturity of one year, in line with the horizon of the solvency requirement. The underlying interest rate swap contracts pay two floating payments per year and have a maturity of 1–9, 10, 15, 20, 25 and 30 years. The forward rate of the underlying swap is equal to the strike rate of the swaption, because the swaptions are at-the-money.

RESULTS

In this section we present the main results of our analysis, namely the mismatch between the assets and the liabilities of the insurer in the eight stress test scenarios for the various hedge portfolios. Before we proceed, we first provide information about the risk profile of the liabilities and the liability buckets used for constructing the hedge portfolios.

Risk profile of the liabilities

To immunise the insurer against non-parallel shifts in the term structure, we divide the total present value of the real pension liabilities (equal to €27.89 million) in 10 buckets with similar real interest exposure. The aim is to construct hedge portfolios that match the market value, the modified duration and convexity of the real liabilities in each of these 10 buckets. Table 22.3 shows these

Table 22.3 Pension liability buckets: final cashflow year, real interest exposure and fraction of the real liabilities per bucket

Bucket	Final cashflow year	Fraction real interest exposure	Fraction real liabilities
1	2013	0.11	0.46
2	2017	0.08	0.15
3	2021	0.11	0.10
4	2025	0.11	0.06
5	2029	0.10	0.05
6	2034	0.11	0.05
7	2039	0.09	0.04
8	2046	0.10	0.03
9	2057	0.10	0.03
10	2080	0.10	0.03

Table 22.4 Pension liability buckets: real, breakeven inflation and nominal modified duration and convexity per bucket

Bucket	Real modified duration	Breakeven inflation modified duration	Nominal modified duration	Convexity
1	3.19	3.20	3.13	15.79
2	9.33	9.36	9.14	92.46
3	13.24	13.27	12.96	184.87
4	16.70	16.74	16.35	292.91
5	19.63	19.67	19.22	404.53
6	23.01	23.05	22.52	556.07
7	26.94	26.96	26.36	760.59
8	30.86	30.88	30.19	997.06
9	35.64	35.65	34.88	1,330.67
10	49.43	49.40	48.37	2,622.60

buckets for the real liabilities, while the duration and convexity corresponding to each bucket are depicted in Table 22.4.

Hedge portfolios
Hedging with inflation-linked bonds
Short selling allowed: we match the real modified duration and convexity of the 10 buckets using inflation-linked bonds.[14] A hedge portfolio should consist of at least three inflation-linked bonds for each bucket, because the portfolio is chosen to satisfy three equations: the first two equations match the real modified duration

Table 22.5 Real modified duration and convexity of the inflation-linked bonds used for constructing the hedge portfolio

Bond description	Real modified duration	Convexity
BTP€i 1.65% 15-Sep-08	1.81	3.39
BTP€i 0.95% 15-Sep-10	3.70	14.34
OAT€i 3% 25-Jul-12	4.80	24.98
OAT€i 1.6% 25-Jul-15	7.57	62.23
DBRI 1.5% 15-Apr-16	8.21	73.37
OAT€i 2.25% 25-Jul-20	11.29	145.23
GGB€i 2.9% 25-Jul-25	14.21	243.05
GGB€i 2.3% 25-Jul-30	17.79	385.47
OAT€i 3.15% 25-Jul-32	17.92	407.58
OAT€i 1.8% 25-Jul-40	24.22	737.62

Note: The bond description consists of the name of the bond, coupon percentage and maturity date.

Table 22.6 Mismatch (%) for a hedge portfolio of inflation-linked bonds using real modified duration and convexity matching

Scenario	1	2	3	4	5	6	7	8
Total mismatch	0.001	0.036	−0.012	−0.018	0.035	−0.001	−0.021	−0.012

and convexity; furthermore, the sum of the portfolio weights must equal one. For each bucket we select the three inflation-linked bonds with durations closest to the real modified duration of the liability bucket.[15] Table 22.5 shows the real modified duration and convexity of the inflation-linked bonds used in the analyses.

Now we turn to the hedge effectiveness. Table 22.6 shows the total mismatches in the eight scenarios compared with the base scenario.

The mismatch is very small in all scenarios. This indicates that both the value of the real liabilities and the hedge portfolio move in the same direction in response to shocks in the breakeven inflation and the nominal interest rate. To check whether convexity matching adds value we also set up a hedge portfolio using only real modified duration matching. In this case we match a liability bucket with only two inflation-linked bonds because we have one restriction less on the hedge portfolio. This gives a maximal total mismatch of 0.097%, which is relatively large compared with the largest total mismatch of 0.036% with duration and convexity matching. Finally,

Table 22.7 Mismatch (%) in eight scenarios using inflation-linked bonds for a hedge portfolio with a short selling restriction

Scenario	1	2	3	4	5	6	7	8
Total mismatch	0.000	0.145	−0.138	0.055	0.142	0.000	0.057	0.114

using no bucket division and convexity and duration matching gives a maximal total mismatch of 0.074%.

Short selling not allowed: when short selling inflation-linked bonds is not allowed we have to create a new set of larger, clustered buckets, as the real modified duration of buckets 6 through 10 is too large to match with the inflation-linked bonds available in the market. To match these durations we cluster buckets 3 to 10 into one large bucket with a real modified duration of 23.92. The disadvantage of this approach is the large bucket size, which makes the hedge more vulnerable to non-parallel shocks in the real interest rate. Furthermore, we cannot match the convexity of any bucket, as this would result in negative portfolio weights.[16] With this approach we obtain the mismatch results shown in Table 22.7.

Despite the limited number of buckets and the lack of convexity matching, the resulting hedging errors are not very large. The largest total mismatch is in scenario 5, namely 0.142% of the value of the real liabilities. Without using bucket division the maximal hedging error increases to −0.960%.

Hedging with swaptions
The second type of hedge instrument we apply is the swaption. Swaptions differ from the other hedge instruments considered: they require an upfront option premium payment and are only exercised when in-the-money (after a decrease of the nominal interest rate). The hedge results of the swaption portfolio must therefore be interpreted in a slightly different way. In the previous section a hedge is considered poor when the mismatch deviates strongly from zero. However, in this case we do not exercise the swaption portfolio during times of increasing nominal interest rates. This follows from the fact that the real liabilities decrease strongly in present value, but the hedge portfolio only loses the market price of the swaptions. This leads to a large mismatch, but in this case

Table 22.8 Maturity in years, nominal modified duration and convexity interest rate swaps

Maturity (years)	Nominal modified duration	Convexity
1	0.46	0.75
2	1.38	3.62
3	2.26	8.21
4	3.10	14.37
5	3.91	21.95
6	4.68	30.82
7	5.42	40.85
8	6.12	51.90
9	6.79	63.86
10	7.43	76.60
15	10.20	148.88
20	12.39	229.37
25	14.18	312.95
30	15.66	396.59

the mismatch is desired since it indicates a positive market value development for the insurer.

We construct a hedge portfolio of swaptions that matches the nominal modified duration and convexity of the 10 liability buckets with the nominal modified duration and convexity of the interest rate swaps underlying the swaptions. Table 22.8 shows the available underlying interest rate swap maturities together with their nominal modified duration and convexity.

Note that the swaption contracts in the hedge portfolio all have a time-to-maturity of one year. Hence, given the one-year risk management horizon, we assume that the swaptions can be exercised exactly at the time the various scenario shocks take place. Now we have all the information we need to compare the present value developments of the real liabilities and the market value of the hedge portfolio for the different scenarios.

Table 22.9 displays the results. The largest mismatch is 16.849% and occurs in scenario 2. In scenario 2 the real interest rate decreases and the breakeven inflation goes up, while the nominal interest rate remains unchanged. Hence, the value of the real liabilities increases strongly but the hedge portfolio of swaption contracts does not respond (as nominal interest rates remain unchanged), leading to a large hedging error. Overall, the results show that swaptions on nominal interest rate swaps are not well suited for an

Table 22.9 Mismatch (%) per bucket in eight scenarios using a swaption hedge portfolio

Scenario	1	2	3	4	5	6	7	8
Total mismatch	2.631	16.849	6.766	−8.694	2.383	−12.195	−9.015	−11.144

insurer that has guaranteed real payments (ie, with inflation-linked liability cashflows). The main reason for the poor hedging results is that nominal interest rates and real interest rates do not always move in lockstep, hampering the effectiveness of a hedging strategy that focuses on nominal interest-rate risk only. Similar poor results prevail when we construct a hedge portfolio of nominal interest rate swaps.

Hedging with real interest swaps

A hedge portfolio consisting of interest rate swaps only, or inflation swaps only, performs well with changes in the nominal interest rate or breakeven inflation, but does not hedge all risks properly. Therefore, as an alternative, we now construct a hedge portfolio of synthetic "real interest rate swaps" as proposed by Van Capelleveen (2006). We do this by matching the nominal modified duration and convexity of the 10 buckets with plain-vanilla interest rate swaps and using inflation swaps to match the breakeven inflation modified duration and convexity of the buckets. To construct the hedge portfolio we use nominal interest rate swaps with a maturity of 1–10, 15, 20, 25 and 30 years (see Table 22.8) and the 14 available inflation swaps with maturity ranging from two to 30 years shown in Table 22.10.

The real interest rate hedge portfolio, effectively a portfolio combining both interest swaps and inflation swaps, leads to the hedge results shown in Table 22.11. The largest mismatch is only 0.072%, demonstrating the effectiveness of this hedging strategy. The bucket division adds value, as the maximal mismatch increases to 0.188% when we apply duration and convexity matching without buckets. Finally, using no bucket division and only duration matching, the largest mismatch increases further to 0.955%.

From a hedging perspective, the real interest rate swaps portfolio has one important advantage compared to the inflation-linked bond

Table 22.10 Breakeven inflation modified duration and convexity of 14 available inflation swaps

Maturity (years)	Breakeven inflation modified duration	Convexity
2	1.96	4.00
3	2.94	9.00
4	3.91	16.00
5	4.89	25.00
6	5.87	36.00
7	6.85	49.00
8	7.83	64.00
9	8.80	81.00
10	9.78	100.00
12	11.74	144.00
15	14.67	225.00
20	19.55	400.00
25	24.43	625.00
30	29.31	900.00

Table 22.11 Mismatch (%) in eight scenarios using a hedge portfolio of interest rate swaps and inflation swaps

Scenario	1	2	3	4	5	6	7	8
Total mismatch	0.003	0.032	0.056	−0.010	0.033	0.008	−0.009	0.072

portfolio. A hedge portfolio of inflation-linked bonds provides a certain (risk-free) real return, which matches the implicit real return on the future real cashflows. As the risk-free real return will in practice be rather low, there is limited scope for the pension fund and the insurer to earn excess returns. In contrast, the synthetic real interest rate swap portfolio can be applied as an "overlay" strategy, leaving the original strategic investment portfolio largely intact, as swaps do not need a large initial investment.

Solvency requirements for interest-rate risk and inflation risk

The standardised Solvency II test imposed by the Dutch central bank formulates extreme shocks in the term structure of nominal interest rates and inflation. The economic capital that the insurer is required to hold by the regulator is equal to the largest difference between the value of the liabilities and the value of the asset port-folio that occurs in these extreme scenarios. The economic capital definition therefore is equal to the mismatch definition, except that only unfavourable outcomes for the insurer are considered.

Nominal interest-rate risk

The Dutch central bank's standardised solvency test defines nom-inal interest rate shocks that can be used to calculate the required economic capital. The extreme shocks in the zero-coupon nominal term structure are either upwards or downwards compared with the current zero-coupon nominal term structure. The shock scenar-ios are far from parallel, ranging from +3.2% for short maturities to +1.4% for long maturities in the positive shock scenario, and ranging from −1.9% for short maturities to −1.1% for longer matu-rities in the negative shock scenario. Further, both scenarios con-tain some very unusual kinks. Overall, the solvency test probably leads to relatively large mismatches compared to the nine scenarios in Table 22.2, which are less extreme and relatively smooth in comparison.

When we hedge with the best hedge portfolio of inflation-linked bonds, the upward shock scenario for the nominal term structure of interest rates leads to a situation where the hedge portfolio decreases 0.304% more than the value of the real liabilities. In the negative shock scenario the value of the real liabilities increases 0.342% more than the market value of the hedge portfolio. Con-sequently, the total economic capital required by the regulator for nominal interest-rate risk equals 0.342% of the value of the real liabilities.

Inflation risk

The insurer is also explicitly exposed to inflation risk, as it guaran-tees full indexation of the real cashflows. The supervisor demands only an increased amount of economic capital for both inflation and nominal interest-rate risk, when the economic capital required for inflation risk is larger than the economic capital required for nominal interest-rate risk. Since changes in expected inflation are strongly related to changes in the nominal interest rates, the stan-dardised solvency test formulates a shock in the inflation rate that must be combined with a shock in the nominal interest rates. This shock in inflation is an increase (or decrease) in the breakeven inflation term structure with 50% compared to the initial situation. The economic capital required for inflation risk is the worst outcome for the insurer in all combinations of the two inflation shock scenarios and the two previously discussed nominal interest rate shock scenarios.

We find that a combined upward shock in inflation and the nominal interest rate term structure leads to a situation where the hedge portfolio decreases 0.392% less than the present value of the real liabilities. Under the reverse shock, the value of the real liabilities increases 0.339% more than the market value of the hedge portfolio. Consequently, the economic capital required for inflation risk equals 0.339% of the value of the real liabilities.

Overall, the total required economic capital for nominal interest rate and inflation risk is equal to 0.342% with a hedge portfolio consisting of inflation-linked bonds. The use of buckets as part of the hedging process adds value, as the required economic capital without bucket division equals 1.148%. The alternative hedge portfolio of real interest rate swaps results in a required economic capital for inflation and nominal interest-rate risk of 0.859% (and 0.957% without bucket division). Hence, when more extreme shock scenarios are administered, the real swap hedge portfolio is less effective than the inflation-linked bond portfolio. The required economic capital for a typical unhedged institutional portfolio consisting of 40% stocks and 60% nominal bonds (with a modified duration of five) equals about 14%.

SENSITIVITY ANALYSIS

This section evaluates whether our best performing hedge portfolio of inflation-linked bonds gives similar good results under various adjusted conditions, while applying the shock scenarios from the "Evaluating the effectiveness of hedge portfolios" section.

Different types of pension liabilities

We first evaluate whether the mismatch results are similar for different types of (hypothetical) real pension liabilities. The alternative liability scenarios are derived by dividing the original real cashflows into three groups of equal size, namely the cashflows in the periods 2007–14, 2015–27 and 2028–80. We construct three new types of pension liabilities (young, middle and old) by increasing the cashflows of one of the groups by 50% and decreasing the other two by 25%. The results show that the maximal total mismatches for the young, middle and old pension liabilities are equal to 0.025%, 0.027% and 0.060%, respectively. This gives an indication that it is more difficult to hedge long-term liabilities with the currently available inflation-linked bonds. Overall the mismatches are still relatively small, demonstrating the effectiveness of the hedging approach.

Construction of buckets
In the main analyses we use 10 buckets based on real interest exposure. We now construct the buckets by dividing the value of the real liabilities into 10 equal buckets, such that each bucket is (almost) equal to 10% of the total present value of the real cashflows. The hedging results are slightly worse than in the original situation, with a maximal total mismatch of 0.050%, but overall still rather small. The slight decrease in hedge effectiveness can be explained by the relatively large size of the last bucket, which now contains all cashflows from 2037 to 2080. Hence, it is probably better to take both the size and the timing of the cashflows into account when defining the buckets, ie, to use real interest exposure.

CONCLUSIONS
This chapter has evaluated the nominal interest rate and inflation hedging qualities of four financial instruments. The aim is to reduce the exposure to inflation and nominal interest-rate risk of an insurer that guarantees full inflation indexation of pension benefits with the Eurozone HICPxT inflation rate. The hedge portfolios evaluated consist of inflation-linked bonds, inflation swaps, interest rate swaps and swaptions.

We construct the hedge portfolios by matching the real modified duration of the real liabilities with the real modified duration of the portfolio, a relatively simple method. We improve this basic approach by adding two factors, namely convexity matching and the use of buckets based on real interest exposure. Convexity matching improves the hedge effectiveness since it also takes into account the second order effect of small changes in the zero-coupon real term structure. Further, we divide the value of the real liabilities in 10 different buckets and construct a separate hedge portfolio that matches the duration and convexity of each of these buckets. The bucket approach increases the effectiveness of the hedge in case of non-parallel shocks in the term-structure of nominal interest rates and the term-structure of breakeven inflation rates.

A portfolio of inflation-linked bonds has the best hedge qualities (maximal mismatch 0.036%) followed by a hedge portfolio of inflation swaps and interest rate swaps (maximal mismatch 0.072%). Swaptions are less suitable for hedging purposes, because of the initial premium payments and the incomplete protection against shocks in the term structure of real interest rates. Swaptions probably have more value for institutions that are fully exposed to nominal interest-rate risk, but only partially to real interest-rate risk (for example, a pension fund offering only conditional indexation of pension benefits).

We find that matching the convexity is useful since a hedge portfolio of inflation-linked bonds without convexity matching has a maximal mismatch of 0.145%, compared with a maximal mismatch of 0.036% with convexity matching. Adding buckets to the hedging procedure is especially useful when we consider extreme shocks such as prescribed in the Solvency II framework incorporated by the Dutch central bank: the mismatch is only 0.342% when using 10 buckets, versus 1.148% without bucket division.

The Dutch financial supervisor has formulated a standardised, Solvency II compliant, solvency test for insurers to determine the required amount of economic capital for nominal interest-rate risk and inflation risk. This test formulates extreme shocks to the term-structures of nominal interest rates and breakeven inflation rates that an insurer must be able to withstand. Since the framework is Solvency II compliant our results are also relevant for European insurers in general. The required economic capital for our insurer equals 14% of the value of the liabilities when the insurer holds a typical unhedged portfolio consisting of 40% stocks and 60% nominal bonds. Using our best hedge portfolio of inflation-linked bonds, the required economic capital is only 0.342% of the value of the real liabilities. An alternative hedge portfolio consisting of nominal interest rate swaps and inflation swaps results in a required economic capital of 0.859%. Further, the swap portfolio can be implemented as an overlay strategy, leaving the opportunity for the insurer to pursue higher expected returns with the bulk of the asset portfolio.

This research focuses on the Eurozone inflation hedging qualities of different financial instruments. A direction for further research is to construct portfolios hedging the inflation in individual Eurozone countries (ie, the inflation rate in Germany, France and the Netherlands). Currently, with the exception of France, this extension of the research is very hard to execute as only Eurozone inflation linked instruments are available with a wide range of maturities and traded in liquid markets. For example, for many individual Eurozone countries the zero-coupon term structure of real interest rates cannot be estimated reliably due to a lack of traded instruments and up-to-date market prices.

1 The views expressed in this chapter are those of the authors and do not necessarily reflect those of the employers or colleagues.

2 In practice, indexation is mostly conditional on the nominal funding ratio of the pension fund, which is defined as the market value of assets divided by the present value of nominal liabilities.

3 The present value of real liabilities increases about 18%, whereas the asset portfolio only increases about 4% in market value in response to the extreme shock scenario.

4 For more information please consult http://www.dnb.nl/dnb/home/supervision/en/47-150691-64.html.

5 Another country that is relatively advanced in implementing Solvency II is the UK. Their framework (internal capital assessments) also allows the use of stress tests to evaluate the interest-rate risk in hedging liabilities, which is similar to the Dutch standardised scenarios (Association of British Insurers 2007).

6 The reason that tobacco prices are not included in this index is for legal and constitutional reasons in France.

7 However, such a conversion will carry a price, which will eventually result in higher pension premiums.

8 Given the assumption of the existence of an inflation-risk premium the nominal interest rate consists of three parts, namely the real interest rate $r_{\text{real}, t}$, the expected inflation $E(\pi_t)$ and the inflation-risk premium ψ_t (Shen 1998). This is also called the extended Fisher equation: $(1 + r_{\text{real}, t}) = (1 + r_{\text{nom}, t})/((1 + E(\pi_t))(1 + \psi_t))$, where π_t is defined as the mean inflation from period 1 to t.

9 In loose terms the breakeven inflation can be seen as the expected inflation. Although the largest part of the breakeven inflation is the expected inflation other factors also play a role, namely the compounding effect, inflation lag, taxes, liquidity and the inflation-risk premium. However, besides the last factor the total size is quantified at only 0.11–0.14% (Alonso et al 2001). An unquantified, but important factor (especially for this research) that also influences the breakeven inflation is the inflation-risk premium.

10 Euribor (Euro Interbank Offered Rate) is the rate at which euro interbank term deposits within the Eurozone are offered by one prime bank to another prime bank (source: www.EURIBORG.org).

11 Historical time series for swaptions are available from 1999 onwards and for inflation swaps from 2003 onwards (with a limited time to maturity of 10 years, because of the thin inflation swap market at that time).

12 Alonso *et al* (2001) show that, apart from the expected inflation and the inflation-risk premium, the breakeven inflation rate consists of more parts, with a total size ranging 0.11%–0.14%. Therefore, we correct the breakeven inflation with the average amount of 0.12% to find a value for the expected inflation plus inflation-risk premium.

13 Data comes from Lehman Brothers unless otherwise specified.

14 As the goal of the hedge portfolio is to hedge real interest-rate risk of the liabilities the appropriate measure is real modified duration. When inflation-linked bonds are part of a nominal investment portfolio, with a focus on hedging the nominal modified duration we encounter a different problem. In this case we have to assign a modified duration to inflation-linked bonds, which incorporate simultaneous movements in the nominal interest rate and inflation. This in turn affects the real interest rate and the valuation of inflation-linked bonds. The problem with this approach is the unstable relationship between nominal and real interest rates, which makes it difficult to assign a reliable modified duration to inflation-linked bonds in a nominal world. For a further discussion see Rudolph-Shabinsky and Trainer (1999).

15 We use a similar approach for the buckets that require short selling of inflation-linked bonds, because short selling a short duration inflation-linked bond to obtain the desired (long) real modified duration is often a poor strategy, because short- and long-term real interest rates do not have a high correlation.

16 The real modified duration of the bucket lies between the real modified duration of two inflation-linked bonds, therefore, the weights are positive. When we also try to match convexity we add an extra restriction, which leads to negative weights and thereby short selling, which is not allowed.

REFERENCES

Association of British Insurers, 2007, "Individual Capital Assessment (ICA) – A Guide to the ICA Process for Insurers", Working Paper, Association of British Insurers.

Alonso, F., R. Blanco and A. del Rio, 2001, "Estimating Inflation Expectations using French Government Inflation Indexed Bonds", Working Paper, Bank of Spain.

Benjamin, J. D., G. S. Sirmans and E. N. Zietz, 2001, "Return and Risk on Real Estate and Other Investments: More Evidence", *Journal of Real Estate Portfolio Management*, 7, pp. 183–214.

Black, F., 1976, "The Pricing of Commodity Contracts", *Journal of Financial Economics*, 3, pp. 167–79.

Bodie, Z., 1975, "Common Stocks as a Hedge Against Inflation", *Journal of Finance*, 31, pp. 459–70.

Carcano, N. and S. Foresi, 1997, "Hedging Against Interest Rate Risk: Reconsidering Volatility-adjusted Immunization", *Journal of Banking & Finance*, 21, pp. 127–41.

Desclée, A., M. Klaeffling and D. Menzed-Vives, 2003, "A guide to Inflation-linked Government Bonds in the Euro Area", Lehman Brothers – Fixed Income Liquid Market Research.

Ely, D. and K. Robinson, 1996, "Are Stocks a Hedge Against Inflation? International Evidence Using a Long-run Approach", *Journal of International Money and Finance*, 16, pp. 141–67.

Fama, E. F., 1981, "Stock Returns, Real Activity, Inflation, and Money", *American Economic Review*, 71, pp. 545–65.

Fama, E. F. and G. W. Schwert, 1977, "Asset Returns and Inflation", *Journal of Financial Economics*, 5, pp. 115–46.

Gajek, L., 2005, "Axiom of Solvency and Portfolio Immunization under Random Interest Rates", *Insurance: Mathematics and Economics*, 36, pp. 317–28.

Gong, P. and X. He, 2005, "A Risk Hedging Strategy Under the Nonparallel-shift Yield Curve", *Physica A: Statistical Mechanics and its Applications*, 354, pp. 450–62.

Hull, J., 2002, *Options, Futures and Other Derivatives*, 5th edn (Englewood Cliffs, NJ: Prentice-Hall).

Jarrow, R. and Y. Yildirim, 2003, "Pricing Treasury Inflation Protected Securities and Related Derivatives using an HJM Model", *Journal of Financial and Quantitative Analysis*, 38, pp. 337–58.

Kerkhof, J., 2005, "Inflation Derivatives Explained: Markets, Products and Pricing", Lehman Brothers, Fixed Income Quantitative Research.

Mercurio, F., 2005, "Pricing Inflation-indexed Derivatives", *Quantitative Finance*, 5, pp. 289–302.

Rudolph-Shabinsky, I. and F. H. Trainer, Jr., 1999, "Assigning a Duration to Inflation-protected Bonds", *Financial Analysts Journal*, 55(5), pp. 53–9.

Schotman, P. C. and M. Schweitzer, 2000, "Horizon Sensitivity of the Inflation Hedge of Stocks", *Journal of Empirical Finance*, 7, pp. 301–15.

Shen, P. 1998, "How Important is the Inflation Risk Premium?", *Economic Review*, 83, pp. 35–47.

Van Capelleveen, H., 2006, "Hedgen met Swaptions: Een Reëel Voordeel?", *The Financial Analyst*, (August/September), pp. 41–4.

Index